LOOKING FOR
PRINCE CHARLES'S DOG

A personal voyage through paranoid schizophrenia

DR CLIVE HATHAWAY TRAVIS

LOOKING FOR
PRINCE CHARLES'S DOG

A personal voyage through paranoid schizophrenia

DR CLIVE HATHAWAY TRAVIS

Bedford, England

First published in Great Britain, North America and Australia in 2013
by Wymer Publishing, England
www.wymerpublishing.co.uk

First edition. Copyright © 2013 Clive Travis / Wymer Publishing.

Softback: **ISBN 978-1-908724-20-5**
eBook: **ISBN 978-1-908724-49-6**

Draft editing by Emily Barker, Alison Bass, Caroline Lavelle, Alistair Sladdin, Christopher Thatcher, Edward Travis, Tom Travis, Luke Tuchscherer and Michael Wallis.
Final editing by Jeremy Francis-Broom, Clive Travis and Jessica Victor.

Typeset by Wymer UK.
Printed and bound by Lightning Source.

A catalogue record for this book is available from the British Library.

Cover paintings by Brent Nokes.
Cover design by Skinny Dog and Queen Eye Graphics.

This book is dedicated to the memory
of those who did not make it

Contents

Glossary

CCF: Combined Cadet Force.

DOAE: Defence Operational Analysis Executive.

DISC: Defence Intelligence and Security Centre.

DRA: Defence Research Agency.

EAH: Electronically-Augmented Hearing.

EAI: Electronically-Augmented Imagination.

EAT: Electronically-Augmented Thinking.

EAV: Electronically-Augmented Vision.

FRU: Force Research Unit – the secretive unit of the British Army known for sabotage and break-ins.

FSB: The Russian Secret Service, though I largely refer to them as the KGB herein.

GCHQ:General Communications Headquarters, the secretive government communications agency involved in electronic warfare and cryptography.

Ground-MTRUTHing: Ground-truthing is intelligence-speak for verifying spy satellite observations by sending in an agent on, or close to, the ground. In the latter case this would be a drone. Hence ground-MTRUTHing takes place when the agent is an MTRU with full MTRUTH capability.

KGB: The Soviet Secret Service.

Lodestone chip: A key component of MTRUTH. Lodestone is a stone consisting of a magnetic oxide of iron – magnetite – and when dangled on a piece of twine, aligns with north/south. The devices I refer to would be unlikely to contain lodestone as such. They work by using the earth's magnetic field to stimulate an electric current in three directions, the currents continually recording the chip's movement and therefore position and orientation (It's positively simple: sea animals navigate with magnetic maps, *The Sunday Times*, 30th November 2008). The same effect can be obtained using three axis accelerometers, such as microscopic "nano" versions of the ADXL330, which can continuously monitor their position. This is the technique used in the Nintendo Wii remote. The iPhone uses the LIS302DL.

MI4: Joint Air Reconnaissance Intelligence Centre (JARIC). The department of military intelligence concerned with aerial reconnaissance.

MI5: The department of military intelligence concerned with state security. The official term for MI5 is the Security Service.

MI6: The department of military intelligence concerned with espionage. The official term for MI6 is the Secret Intelligence Service.

MTRU: Mobile Tactical Reconnaissance Unit.

MTRUTH: Mobile Tactical Reconnaissance Unit Telecommunications Harness (see below for full definition).

Psychic-ether: Before the formulation of Einstein's Special Theory of Relativity, it was proposed that light travelled through an 'ether'. By "psychic-ether" I simply mean the inside of the virtual model of reality into which my MTRUTH is connected – this I refer to as *Colchester*. I am not proposing the existence of some psychic medium beyond this.

RARDE: Royal Armaments Research and Development Establishment.

RATS: Rebroadcast Army Telecommunications System. This picks up the weak MTRUTH radio signals broadcast from electronic devices inside the human body and relays them.

RFID: Radio Frequency Identification Tags – talk of civilians walking about in military-style virtual worlds may sound a bit futuristic but, using RFID tags, it may well become the norm. In fact members of the public will likely end up walking around in a whole swarm of multifarious parallel universes consisting of RFIDs attached to products in their possession while, for example, shopping. "Could we be constantly tracked through our clothes, shoes or even our cash in the future? I'm not talking about having a microchip surgically implanted beneath your skin, which is what Applied Digital Systems of Palm Beach, Florida, would like to do." (Big Brother in small packages, www.news.com.com, 13th January 2003). With these devices it is now possible to track the purchasers of their goods everywhere they go. These tags contain devices capable of drawing radio energy as small as half a grain of sand.

RSRE: Royal Signals and Radar Establishment.

SenseCam: "Downloading your life into a computer, once the stuff of science fiction, has become reality. Microsoft's British engineers are to unveil a miniature camera, SenseCam, that records a person's entire day and stores it in a computerised diary", (Human black box to log your daily life, *The Sunday Times*, 9th May 2004).

SOE: Special Operations Executive. A British World War II organisation. Following Cabinet approval, it was officially formed by Minister of Economic Warfare Hugh Dalton on 22 July 1940, to conduct espionage, sabotage and reconnaissance in occupied Europe against the Axis powers, and to aid local resistance movements.

Special Intelligence Service: An ultra-elite and wholly imaginary body born in 1926 numbering less than 10 people at any one time, spanning MI5, MI6 (the *Secret* Intelligence Service), the KGB and its successor the FSB, with no documentary evidence it exists except within the minds of those who were and are members of it.[1] Since much of this book is born of the imagination, I have referred to the Special Intelligence Service rather than the Secret Intelligence Service.

MTRUTH

A dvances in technology mean that human beings are becoming more and more computerised. MTRUTH is the logical ultimate mobile phone both for a combat soldier, secret service agent, tourist, shopper or psychiatric patient. It features:

Subcutaneous Lodestone RFID chips to record all the movements of the subject and his or her limbs in the earth's magnetic field or using 3 axis accelerometry. These enable, for example, what he writes and what he is looking at in the latest virtual version of the real world to be remotely monitored.

Ocular cameras as well as aural and dental microphones enabling the subject's MTRUTH operator to 'be' him at a remote location and the subject's life to be totally recorded SenseCam-style (Bionic video eyes help blind people see again, *The Times*, 9th May 2003. Bionic eye restores sight to the blind, *The Times*, 17th February 2007).

In-vision drop-down screens enabling the MTRUTH subject to receive intelligence on what he is looking at from supercomputer-facilitated databases/web search engines. "Computer images superimposed onto the field of vision could give soldiers and doctors real-time information about their environment" (And next – the contact lens that lets email really get in your face, *The Times*, 2nd February 2008).

Brain implants enabling the subject to move a cursor in his field of view. "Scientists say they have developed a technology that enables a monkey to move a cursor on a computer screen simply by thinking about it" (Soldiers to become robots, *The Times*, 12th April 2005, Through the mind's eye, *New Scientist*, 6th May 2006)).

Cochlea implants enabling remote acoustic realities to be superimposed on that of the MTRUTH subject. Digital extraction of sounds, such as those masked by loud music in venues, is enabled. Likewise remotely-sited agents can experience the same acoustic reality as the subject, or MTRU.

Ability to remotely smell, taste and feel things by the firing of ultrasound pulses directly into targeted parts of the brain (Sony patent takes first step to real-life Matrix, *New Scientist*, 9th April 2005).

Real-time biomedical monitoring. "Doctors are to implant computerised sensors into patients to enable them to monitor their medical condition minute-by-minute from miles away." (Patients get 999 chip implants, *The Sunday Times*, 12th June, 2005; How computer spy in the office will monitor everything you do, *The Times* 16th January 2008).

Ability to monitor thoughts. "Scientists are now able to read your mind." (They know what you're thinking, *The Sunday Times*, 3rd May 2009; "Psychic computer shows your thoughts on screen", *The Sunday Times*, 1st November 2009).

Nano motion sensors inside the eyes enabling remote monitoring of the eyes' movements.

Acknowledgements

My heartfelt thanks go to the following friends, relations and others for their assiduous help in the correction and editing of this book: Emily Barker, Alison Bass CPN, Caroline Lavelle, Alistair Sladdin, Christopher Thatcher, Tom Travis, Luke Tuchscherer, Jessica Victor, Michael Wallis, and most of all my father: Edward Travis; Karen Sime, who suggested I write it; the musical artists after whose songs I have named the chapters; Michele Atkinson and Ravi Kang at Castle Print and the Colourshop, for their help with preparation of the drafts; the British Establishment for its despicable attempts to drive me to suicide[2]; the kind lady in Liskeard who gave me a packet of ginger nuts; all the other kind people who helped me through; and finally the unknown ship on the horizon in Newquay whose light saved my life.

The Disappearance of Prince Charles's Dog

Prince Charles's dog, Pooh, named like her mother Tigga, after an A.A. Milne character, came to national prominence on a wintry April day back in 1994 when she mysteriously disappeared at Balmoral, leading to the most-publicised dog-hunt in British history. Pooh was walking with the Prince and her mother Tigga in Ballochbuie Forest, near Brig of Dee on the expansive 50,000 acre Balmoral estate. Pooh ran off into trees and was never seen again, despite bailiffs, gillies and estate workers scouring the estate, and psychic intuition being offered. News of the Prince's loss erupted when His Royal Highness placed a small advertisement in a local paper offering a reward. There were several sightings – the least likely being in Maida Vale, north-west London – and the search party was swollen as Fleet Street's finest dashed to the scene, offering their own generous rewards. But to no avail...
(Source: angelfire.com).

70 Lost & Found

TERRIER LOST!!!

On Sunday in the Ballochbule/Brig O' Dee area in the afternoon a tan and white terrier with long tail went missing. Any information or assistance that would lead to the return of this dog would be gratefully received.

Please ring either 03397 42334 or Ballater Police Station.

A reward is being offered.

Small ad from *The Aberdeen Press and Journal*, April 19th 1994, placed by HRH Prince Charles

Foreword

This very interesting book makes a unique contribution to our understanding of serious mental illness. It is a first person account by an articulate young man of the severe psychotic illness, which both tormented and entertained him intermittently for nearly a decade. For long periods, his illness was dominated by delusions of alien influence and hallucinations. A plethora of incidental everyday events assumed extraordinary personal significance. These are the symptoms characteristic of schizophrenia. In addition, he experienced episodes of depression and episodes of manic excitement. He provides a graphic description not only of schizophrenic psychosis but also of depression and of mania. At one point he reports "My brain chemistry felt about as stable as a glass jug of water which was on the point of falling off the edge of the table." But perhaps the key message of the book is that an individual who suffers from a schizophrenic illness is not defined by that illness, but rather by the range of interests, hopes and personal characteristics that shape him. Dr Travis obtained a PhD in physics; rowed for his college and ran a marathon; embarked on a hair-raising journey across Africa; organised boat trips on the Thames to raise money for charity; founded a record company that released two CDs, and was devastated by the breakdown of his relationship with the girlfriend he loved dearly. Indeed the announcement by his girlfriend, Amanda, that she did not wish to marry him, was one of the factors precipitating his slide into illness. He describes schizophrenia as "partly an experience-derived illness". Later, he proposes "My main problem was that of heartbreak, which had gone undiagnosed by the NHS." Many chapters describe his chaotic travels though the length and breadth of Britain, Ireland and parts of Europe. At times his express purpose was to escape from psychiatric treatment, but this does not keep him from his spiritual goal of finding Prince Charles's dog in this odyssey of self-discovery and healing.

He is critical of the treatment he received from the psychiatric services. With some justification, he attributes two of his episodes of manic excitement to treatment with antidepressant medication. He is scathing about the effects of medication, especially the depression induced by these drugs. In fact the relationship between psychosis, depression and antipsychotic treatment is very complex. Depression is an integral part of schizophrenia. It can occur at any phase of the illness, and is especially prominent in the resolving phase of a psychotic episode. Under some circumstances, antipsychotic medication can help alleviate depression, but it can also contribute to depression. Stultifying sluggishness induced by blocking the natural energising effects of the brain chemical, dopamine, leaves the individual feeling like a zombie. More paradoxically, blockade of dopamine by antipsychotic medication can also produce extremely distressing restlessness. The complexity of the relationship between psychosis, depression and antipsychotic treatment can lead to apparent conflict between the subjective evidence based on the experience of an individual patient, and the purportedly objective scientific evidence derived from the careful observation of many patients. Dr Travis's account brings home the importance of listening carefully to the individual's own reports of the effects of medication, and of adjusting medication to minimise the distressing side effects. However, in predicting the future consequences of treatment, it is equally important to take account of the evidence derived from careful observation of large numbers of patients. There is very strong evidence that continued use of antipsychotic medication reduces the risk of relapse over a time scale of several years. While antidepressant medication probably precipitated the acute manic agitation that led to his first two admissions to psychiatric hospitals, it is equally likely that discontinuation of antipsychotic medication predisposed him to his third relapse in the summer of 1997.

But this speculation brings us to a crucial issue raised by Dr Travis. He reports that none of his doctors suggested the possibility that antipsychotic medication might ever be safely discontinued. The prospect of indefinite treatment with medication having such distressing side effects was intolerable to him. Unfortunately, on this issue there is a gaping hole in the scientific evidence. While an abundance of evidence demonstrates that antipsychotic medication reduces the risk of psychotic relapse over a time scale of several years, there is a paucity of good evidence regarding treatment in the longer term. Virtually all of the available evidence indicates that over a time scale of decades, between a third and a half of individuals suffering severe schizophrenia recover to the point where they no longer require antipsychotic medication[3]. The mind and its brain have an amazing capacity to adapt to changing circumstances. It might be argued that the primary goal of psychiatry is to promote the circumstances that will maximise the likelihood that mind and brain adapt constructively rather than destructively. In individual cases, the prediction of the course of adaptive processes over a time scale of decades is fraught with difficulty. However, Dr Travis exhibits several characteristics, which bode well. While the intensity of his emotional responses is a source of torment in the short term, it also augurs well for a better outcome in the longer term. In addition, the intelligent way in which he grapples with the illness increases the likelihood of recovery. At one point he attempts to wrest back a sense of personal autonomy from the alien forces that appear to control him by a technique involving a random number generator. He is intelligent enough to realise that this provides only an illusion of autonomy, but this illusion is perhaps the crucial requirement. After all, what is free will? More pragmatically, his battle with the psychiatric services is an expression of his continuing determination to re-establish his autonomy. Perhaps the greatest tragedy in the delivery of psychiatric services to patients with psychotic illnesses is the failure to establish that collaboration might offer the best prospect for recovery of autonomy. In the face of the turmoil of psychosis, there is no easy prescription for achieving collaboration, but this book eloquently makes the point that the first step is engagement in dialogue.

Professor Peter Liddle BSc, BMBCh, PhD, MRCPsych,
Professor of Psychiatry, Queen's Medical Centre, Nottingham, August 2007

Part I

Some fake travel expenses

Introduction
It's All Too Much

This book is about events pertaining in my mind, and one or two other places, to the disappearance of Prince Charles's dog on April 16th 1994. In these pages you can find details of my subsequent search for the dog, a dog you will see I found extremely hard to handle but equally determined to find. A number of newshounds descended on Balmoral to help with the pursuit in the days after its disappearance (unless that is you believe the whole escapade was an imagined operation, and they donated their various travel expenses to the very charity funds this book supports). Either way, by the time they were alleged to have called off the search, I was only really beginning to get going in mine, perhaps as you will see, exactly as was intended.

The search details a voyage through, at times, severe mental illness at the interface of the Mental Health Act (1983) with the most sensitive British Intelligence telecommunications system: MTRUTH (Mobile Tactical Reconnaissance Unit Telecommunications Harness). This is a complete virtual reality system entirely embedded within the soldier, patient or subject's body and incorporates an encrypted radio link to, for example, Military High Command, for ingoing and outgoing information. The system is similar to that which Arnold Schwarzenegger had in the film *The Terminator,* though in addition it embeds the subject in a virtual version of the real world. The reader can decide whether I had actually had such a system, a powerful EAI (Electronically Augmented Imagination) – which MTRUTH partly consists of, and the person with it likewise, or that I simply had either a good visual and aural imagination. No matter that I had no certain knowledge of any invasive surgery being performed for the installation of such gadgetry. Hence you will see I will refer to EAH (Hearing), EAV (Vision) and EAT (Thinking) at this interface of mental illness and defence technology. EAH consists of devices fitted in the ears which pick up sounds entering them transmitting them as radio signals whilst receiving incoming signals in authentic 3D surround sound, a key feature of MTRUTH.

A thin film behind the cornea using Fourier imaging, or even using optic nerve implants, could both superimpose information on what the patient sees and act as a camera to enable the controller of the patient not only to see and hear what his charge is but to actually 'be' them. Hence MTRUTH enables the patient to be coached remotely in everything they do. Of course I was well aware that if cameras in the eyes were possible, but weren't fitted, it would be a relatively simple matter to trick somebody into thinking they indeed had ocular cameras. This awareness did not, 'unfortunately', extend to realising I was simply suffering from paranoid schizophrenia.

It is clear that a system such as MTRUTH is capable of either successfully treating, mimicking, or actually causing schizophrenia. Indeed I might even say you could not treat it properly without MTRUTH. In fact, in the absence of a robust existential self, MTRUTH is capable of subsuming and controlling the free will of the person to whom it is fitted using subliminal broadcasts. Furthermore, as I demonstrate herein, MTRUTH can be of great use in all manner of tasks from species identification to divining.

As for whether it really does exist, that is total virtual reality subsumed entirely in the body, is up to you to imagine. You might decide I know it does and cannot confirm or deny it for reasons of official secrecy.

There is plenty of intuition in this story, intuition that something big was going on. As they say, life is not a practice – it's the actual thing. Hence it seems worth saying before I tell the story that "it is not an exercise" but a real war – on mental illness and, from very early in the story, on poor treatment of it. This is the case whatever I might say during the telling of my experiences, as it often seemed as if I were well away from the scent, the scent of success and the actual goal I set out to achieve.

One night in the pub, when I described my illness, this brought the response "Let me get my head round that. You say you had schizophrenia? Surely that means you never did?" This reply shows the general lack of understanding of the illness by the public. People can recover from the illness in a variety of ways even to the point of requiring no medication, recovery, and indeed relapse, depending on a variety of factors. Interestingly if you have an identical twin with the illness your chance of getting it can be less than 50 per cent, suggesting the illness to be experience-based, as well as having the known genetic component.

However severe the schizophrenia I suffered, either through a biochemical disturbance in my brain or through an invisible virtual reality headset, is again up to the reader to decide. Suffice it to say, whilst there is no doubt I have suffered schizophrenia, I have lived to tell the tale, sadly unlike a number I met during this time. As you will see, I was nearly one of them.

The whole perspective of the book leads back to the loss of His Royal Highness's dog, its disappearance being so overwhelmingly fascinating to my mind that I could not regain my sanity without writing this account of events which, from my perspective both led to, and followed its sad loss. Indeed during these events there were times when I began to think *I* was Prince Charles's dog myself so, whilst this story is really about me, the course of events, though not the illness itself, leads back to that strange time of the Royal dog's disappearance – in these pages I hope you will agree I made a thorough search for the missing Royal pet. You could well say that I was looking for it before it disappeared only the announcement that it had been lost really kicked me into gear.

Therefore the book will be of great interest to anyone involved in the field of psychiatry, be they a professional psychiatrist, a patient, a friend or relative of a sufferer, or anyone simply interested to know what it is like to suffer from schizophrenia and all that goes with it.

I also hope the book will be of help to anyone who chooses to maintain that Diana, Princess of Wales, did not die in a car crash in Paris in 1997. Because of schizophrenia, I found no real grounds to enable me to believe that her death in a car crash was not faked in a white magic Comic Relief stunt. For much of this story that was what I was actually thinking; it was just too alluring a thought to do otherwise. I say schizophrenia though it is known that disbelief is common in grief. I thought that she was alive and well, living on *the island of Mystique*, if not Princess Margaret's old holiday destination. This delusion determined my plan of action, as you will see, with the result that she really was not dead, at least to the extent that I proceeded as though she were still alive.[4]

Severe schizophrenia, the most common reason in this country for hospitalisation of younger persons for more than six months, can be a terrible illness; so this book is no Mills and Boon. If it is it's a bloody funny one. But the illness can also be rather interesting and enjoyable if it is more of the manic variety and, in any case it is a highly variable condition. But, if severe, it can also be very dangerous for the sufferer. In writing this account I hope to eradicate the common misconception that there are paranoid schizophrenics on one hand and normal people on the other – with nothing in between and no hope of recovery. For between the two, lies the hope of good mental health where, rather than descending into full-blown mental illness, the patient maintains an objective uncertainty in place of deluded certainty.

Initial drafts of this book were produced with the intention that nowhere was there evidence the writer had lost insight during its actual writing. However this would have resulted in overuse of words such as "believed", "thought", "felt", "seemed", "imagined", "knew", "guessed" and "was convinced". Placing unqualified baldly insane statements (with these words left out) in Italics to indicate such made the text look too messy and jarring to the eye, *as did sentences half of which were in Italics*. I got over the vain issue of writing the book so that nobody could say I was ill when I wrote it. So now the reader will sometimes just have to wonder exactly how insane I was during the book's writing. I am sure, however, they won't have to wonder too hard at numerous points in the story. Furthermore, for the sake of readability, words like "believed", "thought", "felt", ... where I do use them are often interchangeable; in any case they are not always an accurate indication of the extent of my delusions at the time – as it is sometimes difficult to recall very precisely what the extent was. These delusions principally concerned the existence of an ultra-elite intelligence body, the Special Intelligence Service and their deployment of MTRUTH using those organisations, like MI5, which are known to exist. Therefore I have been rather free with my use of the names of these bodies. To an extent the reader can regard MI5, MI6, the Security Services and even the KGB and its successor the FSB as interchangeable – as they were all totally penetrated by the Special Intelligence Service operating darkly in the background throughout this story.

I hope that by telling this story, I will demonstrate the possibility of complete recovery. For some sufferers the reading of my adventures may even aid their recovery, thereby saving them from the stress and danger of making the same voyage I have made. This voyage was at times terrible though not, by and large, when I was actually suffering schizophrenia. I was very lucky, as that was exciting – when it was not utterly horrible because of the treatment for it.

Here is my story. Read of how I went from an Able-Bodied Seaman in the Naval Section of the School Combined Cadet Force to situations where, time and time again, the only sensible way to approach what I was facing was to believe I was actually serving in the Special Forces, in my own Admiralty-selected Special Boat Service (SBS) Reserve unit. To believe that what I was facing was a privilege, and that I was involved in a Special Forces psychological warfare exercise would prove a powerful weapon to protect me, time and time again, from certain death. I had to assume I was in the 25 per cent[5] who had made this dangerous journey but did not survive it and had to extricate myself from that statistic. I had to assume that I was under orders not to surrender in this war of the mind. I had to keep my secret as the secret put me in great danger of being effectively eliminated by side effects I could not tolerate.

So prepare to enter the bizarre, dangerous, harrowing, hilariously deluded, pitiable, and yet very often exciting world of paranoid schizophrenia, of which this is a painful account by one who has enjoyed, suffered and survived.

Part II

A Trip to NATO, a Long Walk, and Some Memories

Chapter One

Seashell

I was lying in the field listening to my younger brother Tom's band, The Flashapjacks, playing live at the mini-festival. It was dark. I had seen the Lion on its way to Cassiopeia's throne. In reality it was just a light aircraft I had spotted flying over the village of Bletsoe, the birthplace of the mother of the Tudor dynasty and King Henry VII. It was flying from Leo the Lion to Cassiopeia. It seemed there was a purpose in the flight which pertained to me – and that I was meant to see it. I felt I *was* that lion, at least at that moment. For much of the summer I had kept thinking I was a dog. In truth my brain chemistry was looking more and more like the Redox reaction, the most energetic experiment permitted in the explosion-cabinet during chemistry lessons at school. I got up and approached the band. I believed I'd had cameras put in my eyes by MI5, or if not, MI6. I knelt down and looked at the band like a cameraman composing the shots. The band was playing *Seashell* and I pulled a fossilised one I had found, millions of years old, from my pocket. All seemed historic and revelational. All was connected.

That night, as usual, I slept well. Next morning, by a reasonably quick route, I set off by car to NATO HQ Northwood, as I now had enough information to justify going there.

As I arrived at Northwood I saw a man let his dog off its lead and thought this meant I was off mine too.

****

I believed he had done it deliberately on orders, that I had a state-of-the-art British Intelligence MTRUTH fitted. I thought, therefore, that as far as the armed forces were concerned, I was merely an MTRU – that is, an electronically-augmented human being whose thoughts could be controlled as surely as a dog's lead stops it wandering off. MTRUTH had been invented as a concept at a meeting of some MI5 officers in a pub near the old MI5 HQ one Friday afternoon in 1926. In that very pub, somewhere through the second, or maybe third pint of Courage bitter, I could only guess, *The Question* had been asked: what does it mean to build Jerusalem in England's green and pleasant land? The question was not merely rhetorical, but one of exhortation. In my euphoric mania *The Question* and Blake's statement had come together to inspirational ends. Now, like a boomerang, the MTRUTH idea was returning in the direction of its most sedulous of creators. After 68 years MTRUTH had reached a crucial stage.

> *I will not cease from mental fight,*
> *Nor shall my sword sleep in my hand,*
> *Till we have built Jerusalem*
> *In England's green and pleasant land.*

I knew such a thing as MTRUTH existed because somebody had deliberately left out the file, marked "Absolute Secret", and detailing such a thing, on top of the filing cabinet at work one day at the Royal Armaments Research and Development Establishment (RARDE), Fort Halstead. It seemed it had been left out so that I would see it – which I did. I had read it avidly thinking I was unobserved, and left it as I had found it. I wondered if I was really supposed to be reading it. It was no longer there the next day. Why would they allow me to read it? Because I'd had an MTRUTH fitted without my knowledge, and with the subliminality level correctly set, it is impossible to tell whether one is experiencing electronic augmentation of the visual and aural imagination, or actual schizophrenia. I felt that fair play dictated I at least must know of such a thing.

****

As I approached the gates, their location known to me from the time I worked there, a large dumper truck appeared and turned through them, right in front of me. Whoever the driver was, I thought it must be a pretty large contract he had. I had met him before. I had his full support in this. I really did think he was in the Special Air Service (SAS) Regiment of the British Army – if not the Special Boat Service of the Royal Navy. My mind measured the power as well as a pretty accurate meter would.

I parked my car behind the lorry and approached the gatehouse. Happily I was not faced with a phalanx of armoury, at least not this time.

I demanded to see an officer of rank no lower than lieutenant colonel. I was invited through into the office where the Captain interviewed me. I wondered if the guard with him had been told to sit there rolling his foot over the football, which did not go unnoticed by me. I was hardly expecting a gin and tonic after what had happened, at least not yet. But perhaps something more like a showing of the *Monty Python* Funniest Joke Ever Told sketch video would have been appropriate. Mindful of the extent I had considered myself to be a dog; his rolling of the ball under his foot certainly did not exclude the possibility of there being play-related activities. The song *Anything Goes* was coming from the radio, which was on in the office. I was beginning to think *anything did go*. The song was playing so I would hear it. Therefore the possibility of an order having been made to roll a football back and forth seemed quite unsurprising.

I informed the Captain that the Lieutenant Colonel and a whole list of defence contractors I had been working with at my firm were Russian Agents and members of the Unification Church. I claimed my car was bugged and Radio 1 knew its location from moment to moment. George Orwell would have choked: the day's newspaper contained an article describing how rule-breaking motorists could soon be prosecuted by computer using personalised microchips in their cars.

****

How had I come to such a paranoid conclusion? Well, to start with, my grandmother's house, 89 Cornwall Road, Ruislip, Middlesex, was only a couple of minutes walk from the bungalow in which the Kroger Portland spies lived during the Cold War – before their arrest for espionage and repatriation to the Soviet Union. My grandmother had United States Air Force lodgers in her house and she would sing at their base. But why, during the '50s, did my grandmother ask one of these helpful Americans to concrete over the foot of her garden? And why had the American told me? Why would an eight-year-old need to know that? These events were all playing on my mind – inviting and beguiling me into paranoiac, if not alluringly fantastic, thoughts about myself and the situation I was in.

The garden stopped peculiarly, short of the fence, and it was the remainder, which he mysteriously claimed to have been the one to concrete over. Concreted over it certainly was and an alleyway separated by a small fence from the concreted-over garden foot led through to the Krogers' house: 45 Cranley Drive. As an eight-year-old I sensed a level of mystery and intrigue, which went way beyond my own personal scale. I remembered how, having been told this story by my grandmother's US airman lodger I had myself wandered through to take a look at the bungalow in question as well as the mysteriously concreted-over garden foot, partly concealed in the years' overgrowth since it was put down.

From then on I always thought of the unspeakability of a full-scale nuclear war as well as filthy treachery whenever I saw a bungalow. On at least one occasion I had dreamt, whether unaided or through my MTRUTH in dream-machine mode, that I was in a 1948 Chevrolet pick-up arriving at ground zero in a Nevada desert ghost town, a nuclear test being imminent. No matter how hard I drove to get away I kept coming back to the bomb, its detonation perpetually more imminent on every occasion.

My mind told me that the KGB[6], and one sole MI5 double agent, possibly Prince Charles, had been leaking concept documents to chosen agents in the music industry. I had always wondered why Prince Charles appeared on television feeling his shirtsleeve as though he had something up it. This mannerism had been coached into him from an early age by his Special Intelligence Service advisors. His doing so was traceable through Special Intelligence Service history back to that very quietly celebrated Friday afternoon in 1926. And so it had been that a few beers all those years earlier had given birth to this ultra-secret organisation, the Special Intelligence Service, spanning a small section of specially chosen individuals in MI5, MI6, and the KGB. This was an organisation so secret no documentary evidence existed in which it was named. The alternative to such a state of affairs, the unacceptable consequences of a nuclear war, had soon become apparent – in Japan, after the plan was put in place. It was I, and the others in my unit, all our KGB files now being in the hands of the Special Intelligence Service[7], who were up his sleeve. The only written material produced by the group was a technical document outlining the principle of MTRUTH and how, at a later date, it would come to fruition, the technology not existing in 1926 to bring it to reality.

In Joy Division's song *The Eternal*, Ian Curtis sang of his view stretching out from the fence to the wall at the foot of his garden. This wall now became the Berlin Wall and I was overwhelmingly sucked into the notion that Ian Curtis had been a Special Intelligence Service double agent himself. But this was without his having the knowledge that the source of his information was actually the KGB. This information, which had been presented to him as a series of paper concept documents, all went into his lyrics. One of these documents revealed what lay beneath the concrete. Like Ian Curtis, I would receive concept documents, images and orders, but on my MTRUTH, and these I would have to make existential sense of. That is, where these orders were concerned, it seemed sensible to assume that I was to decide myself whether or not to carry them out.

The danger I was sensing prevented me from believing, by virtue of a healthy level of paranoia, that Ian Curtis had taken his own life. I remembered a story I had once been made party to, as to how Joy Division got a flat tyre on the M1 on the way to a gig. Whilst parked on the hard shoulder they had narrowly escaped death from a rolling lorry wheel. I came upon the conviction that the tyre had been shot out by an extremist Mossad splinter group who then had a go at them with the rolling wheel. How could I possibly discount the possibility that Ian Curtis had been driven to his death with drugs? Certainly there were drugs available capable of driving a man to suicide – as I was to find to my cost, again and again, at the hands of a murderous[8] but well-meaning NHS, which made a nonsense of prevailing health and safety regulations.

Why might an extremist Jewish group want to get rid of Joy Division? The band had been controversially named after groups of women selected into forced prostitution in Nazi concentration camps, and had not kept their heads down. Rumours about the band had abounded and were hardly dispelled when, after Ian Curtis's death, they became New Order – suggestive of a military revolution.

Right now, all I could imagine was gold bullion, the bodies of traitors, or both, buried there with the original 1926 designs for MTRUTH at the foot of the garden in Cornwall Road. It had been desired that I should remember this later, the reason being that from the cradle, or even, by predestination, before I was born, I had been a KGB subject unknown to all but one person in British Intelligence – one double agent in MI5. A KGB file had shots of me as an eight-year-old looking at the Krogers' house and examining the foot of my grandmother's garden that day back in the '60s. But they would not have pinned all their hopes solely on me; they had kept a close eye on quite a few other English primary school pupils from the class of '68.

A Royal Signals chap I had worked with told me one day how a number of executions had taken place subsequent to the last publicised in 1965 – on Good Friday 1968. What possible reason could there be for his telling me this, if it was not real, other than to test my imagination? Perhaps these executions were not literal; perhaps those 'executed' had merely become party to something, the MTRUTH Absolute Secret, of which I was only to learn 26 years later. Surely there had not really been any executions? And why would he have told me this unless he was winding me up? I then had to address the meaning of 'wind up'. It seemed this meant the level of security I was designated to be at was being progressively increased. In such a situation, imagination was the only limit.

My own parents' marriage had been made the subject of a KGB operation too. In fact it had been arranged, from before their first meeting on the grass in Hyde Park where my mother was sitting before a prom in the adjacent Royal Albert Hall. My father asked my mother-to-be if he could look at her paper to read of the prom that evening, for which they were both waiting, and which they then attended together. And what was happening now was 'merely' the latest development in the 1926 MTRUTH file and that Friday afternoon chat over drinks. The fact that my father had served in all three armed services did nothing to dispel this line of thought. He would also do the shopping sometimes, meaning I could joke he had also been in the Royal Fleet Auxiliary (the fourth Service). It had of course been realised at the meeting in 1926 exactly what consequences there would be if it were one day possible not just to spy on someone but to actually experience being them as well as control their behaviour using subliminal and supra-subliminal inputs of information. It must have been realised that the extent to which somebody's free will was subsumed would depend, to an extent, on the level of awareness the agent had about the operation of his, or her, MTRUTH. For example they might hear, through their EAH, quiet voices in their ears, which left them thinking in the second person. These second person voices would be their only clue to what was really going on.

This strange new sense of power seemed so unlikely that only an equally unlikely explanation made what I was thinking possible: every single thing I had ever done had been documented in detail by the KGB. Given that possibility, nothing in my mind could now be discounted. Of course there is rather a large difference between clearly thinking in the second, or even third person, and actually hearing a voice which is not there. But in schizophrenia you can have both and somewhere they have to meet: subliminal auditory and visual hallucinations or clever MTRUTH incoming signals?

For example I had found myself thinking such apparently preposterous thoughts as the KGB having had a camera hidden inside the television when I was a child, to monitor everything I did, for example on the day of the assassination of President Kennedy in November 1963, when, aged 2 and a half I announced his death to my mother. Joy Division's *No Love Lost* only aided this delusion – if it were a delusion, Ian Curtis singing:

> *Two-way mirror in the hall,*
> *They like to watch everything you do,*
> *Transmitters hidden in the walls,*
> *So they know everything you say is true,*
> *Turn it on.*[9]

The old children's television programme *Why Don't You Just Switch Off Your Television Set and Go Out and Do Something Less Boring Instead?* now became something which had been aimed at me alone. But I was not upset by this possibility. Instead I liked the idea as it confirmed my feelings of enormous power and potential.

So how long did I think my imagination had been augmented? The fact that every night for some years I had dreamt, totally convincingly, I could fly, seemed relevant. It could have been years since my MTRUTH had been fitted, operating to begin with only in dream-machine mode. I had released a record on my own label, having read *Jonathan Livingston Seagull*, which I quoted on the sleeve of the CD, with a photo of seagulls flying. Then, one evening I had watched a natural history programme with shots taken from seagulls on the wing. I felt I was actually looking through the gulls' eyes and from then on I believed there was something pretty unusual going on in mine, the programme giving me the clue to what was happening to me. And it was not lost on me that "gull" can also mean a person who is easy to trick or deceive. I felt threatened by this fact.

****

The Captain at NATO HQ seemed healthily unlike the average psychiatrist and asked to have a look at my car.

****

A few months earlier I had been driving down the Embankment in Bedford when I had to slow for a couple of ducks crossing the road in front of me. MI5, at the behest of the Special Intelligence Service, had fitted cameras not only to my eyes but also to my car near the headlights. East/West relations had reached a stage cooperative enough that the one MI5/KGB double agent who knew of me had compromised my status to them, a copy of my KGB file coming into the hands of British Intelligence. The agent, my controller, had noted the ducks crossing and, as a result, had a Ducks Crossing sign intriguingly erected at that exact point in the road in order to influence me. The Defence Intelligence and Security Centre (DISC) had a virtual version of reality through which my car was travelling. By the cameras in the front of my car, if not in my own eyes, seeing the ducks, I had effected a change not only in reality but also in the DISC virtual world I was travelling through. That is, I was potentially in a powerful position. Or else the erection of the Ducks Crossing sign could have been entirely coincidental which, nevertheless, might look rather amusing in my CV: "Not sure if I was part of the team responsible for the erection of two Ducks Crossing signs on the Embankment, Bedford." One would have to think rather hard to name a job requiring such experience, but one definition of a person is a list of all they are unsure of. They were just playing with me.

In fact there was only one such sign on the whole Embankment, visible to eastbound traffic. I had been driving west. Normally this would have helped me realise the sign had nothing to do with me. Instead it just reinforced my delusion by making me think MI5 wished to keep me wondering. Such an idea was far more appealing than the more mundane explanation that a simple mistake had been made, or that the other sign had gone missing. I considered raising this with the Department of Transport and asking if they thought ducks only crossed when eastbound traffic was approaching, and in the direction indicated on the sign, one duck at a time. By similarly Irish humour, many cars might collide with trains on unprotected level crossings because the sign showed the train coming from only one direction.

On another occasion I had been in the car when my mind made the connection between the laughter of some people on the radio and something quite insignificant, which had happened in the car's vicinity. I knew that virtual realities existed as I had worked *with* them though not quite *in* them – at least not until now. But now I was actually in one and through this appendage to reality, my car's every movement was being followed. In the radio studio, or in some respect near it, they knew where I was and what had happened, hence the laughter. It was not difficult to then go a stage further and imagine I'd had a sub-millimetric lodestone microchip placed inside or on me. This chip would orient and position in this virtual world not just my car, but my own body and MTRUTH, to an accuracy of less than a millimetre. Whether this was just my imagination or not, I again felt massively empowered by the thought. Such a chip would enable MI5, subject out of courtesy to KGB approval, to see what I was looking at in their latest version of the real world. As for whether they could actually see what I was looking at was another thing. But there was certainly a whole range of possibilities in between an agent with actual cameras in his eyes (which did not impede his vision) and, say, an agent with a passer-by on the pavement, the passer-by simply having a good idea what the agent was looking at.

At the very least I could say I was the eyes, ears and mouth of the Security

Services. Thoughts of my having an MTRUTH with EAI fitted along with lodestone microchips in my limbs, as well as my head, were then a mere state of mind. This was made more real by any written intelligence material I, or someone watching me, came up with. I believed I would be ill if I ruled out the possibility that I was a state-of-the-art hybrid human/Robocop – not if I ruled it in – such a belief, it seemed, turning schizophrenia on its head.

I remembered the pioneer British Telecom information system project set up in Colchester during the early days of the Internet. The significance of this now became wildly exaggerated in my mind. It now seemed I was walking about in the latest military-reserved version of it. Whatever basis in reality this thought had, Colchester was simply home of the Royalist Lucas family during the English Civil War. What was really being referred to by *Colchester* was a select number of the group of citizens who had MTRUTH capability. As well as having MTRUTH this ultra-elite group had been *told* they had MTRUTH and also that their EAI input level could be set well above the subliminal, in the EAV mode. They could just click their fingers to make the GUI (Graphical User Interface) come up in their eyes. I was a Royalist, and not only did I have cameras in my eyes but also the ability to receive incoming information on screens behind the cornea. This information would be in the form of Fourier transforms of the images required at the retinae, as that is the way the eye works. But nobody had told me and I sensed I was unique in this. Likewise I had microphones and radio receivers inside my ears with a microphone in my teeth fitted secretly by my dentist. But this was all invisible, and who was going to tell me rather than let me work it out for myself? But I recalled how the dentist had screwed as he capped my tooth; so I suspected he had installed a device in it enabling everything I said to be heard where it was required, whatever that might mean. It was about now I began wondering how much this premium rate number cost and what my bill was. Later it became clear I had got the first blue tooth.

Whatever it was that had happened to my mind, it certainly seemed that somebody was looking at exactly what I was looking at, in all of the ways that was possible. But the information coming into my eyes on my MTRUTH was limited, at this stage, to black streaks across my vision. One day during that summer of 1994, a filling had fallen out of my mouth. The filling looked rather more like a watch battery than a piece of dentist's amalgam and I found myself thinking it was radioactive and had been the cause of the streaks.

A colleague at work at the former Royal Signals and Radar Establishment (RSRE) had once shown me a classified document entitled *Intuition on the Battlefield*. If it was possible for another person to 'be me' then that would be a rather good test of the theory presented there. As for the Establishment, I can report the portrait of Her Majesty the Queen was still proudly displayed.

I had begun thinking that Kim Philby, who fled to the Soviet Union, was not such a big traitor after all: he had sacrificed himself in the noblest manner possible. He loved his country, his reputation being more a side effect of the war against fascism than any truth based purely in espionage. Suddenly I realised there to be a close connection between us, the connection being his knowledge, before I was born, of my future status as a Soviet MI5 agent. Thus, the connection had been there all my life but only now could I appreciate it. My later reading of his autobiography, *My Silent War*, did nothing to dispel this feeling; after all, it was written in Moscow under the eye of his controllers. And, as

Graham Greene said, "In Philby's own eyes he was working for a shape of things to come from which his country would benefit."

One sunny morning, in the churchyard at Barnes, I had read the SAS story *The One That Got Away*. The sun was glinting through the trees as the soft summer breeze blew hundreds of years of military tradition through my psyche. Philby came along to MI6 a while after the 1926 meeting. There was no doubting he knew about it though, and had himself one or two question marks about *Jerusalem*. I was firmly convinced that whenever he had done so he had asked the same questions. Everything now seemed to have boiled down to that. Whether you called him a traitor or not, my imagination told me I was now the star in a classic British film which included, in the first scene, morning assembly back at school: a scene where *Jerusalem* was being sung. This would be followed by my famous solo try against the Haberdashers Aske's school in 1978, when I ran the length of the pitch to score, and "Bomber" Jeffrey converted from the touchline.

Whatever it was that was going off in and around my head it was as dangerous and alluring as the sirens calling Ulysses. At the same time I felt extraordinarily powerful, as though I had just been switched on in some way. All my thoughts had become ludicrously grandiloquent and no possibility was too farfetched. Again, turning schizophrenia on its head, it would be insane not to have such thoughts, as that would render me guilty of negativity. Therefore, everything now seemed possible: there was no point in negative thinking. I had been stripped of any privacy by a lifetime of minute-by-minute intelligence on me, and an international psychological warfare experiment was going on in my head.

I remembered another classified piece of work for the Ministry of Defence in which my University tutor had been involved. This enabled a remotely-sited agent to hear, in authentic 3D surround sound, exactly what somebody else was hearing rather than what a mere microphone would. It involved a model head with microphones in its ears, the head manufactured with the same internal acoustics as a human one. You will understand what this is about if you remember how, the first time you heard a recording of your voice, you did not recognise it as your own[10]. At this moment a magnificent wave of deluded inspiration told me the plastercast head the police had made of the unknown victim of the King's Cross fire was no more than a humorous reference to this piece of work. It also seemed the Security Services were, for some reason, fond of slipping non-existent people into lists of casualties in accidents. Why they would do that was only a question of how good my imagination was. And after all I knew of MI5's famous Man Who Never Was in World War II as well of course as the British Naval Commander (Sean Connery) who had his death faked by British Intelligence in *You Only Live Twice*.

My thoughts were flying: I even considered it possible that nobody had really died in the King's Cross fire at all. Instead, it seemed, an officer in the Special Intelligence Service had spotted the dangerous state of the escalators there, and the entrance hall had been filled with the recently deceased bodies of former servants to Her Majesty the Queen. It was just a mass MI5 funeral. I had heard the reports of the burnt bodies arriving at University College Hospital from my friend Amanda Black – a junior doctor working in casualty that night. So at least I had some grounds to believe there were bodies. It only seemed natural that they should donate their bodies to such ludicrous ends: like having them dumped outside the office of the psychiatrist voted the most incompetent that week.

I now wondered for what purpose my body might best be used after my death, and imagined it being flung back and forth between two mediaeval ballistae until the point where it was not clear what constituted the majority of my body. I was to plan more efficacious obsequies, though not for another five years of this psychiatric assault course that was being inflicted on me. As unlikely as it sounds, I was not going to have to wait until I was dead to find out what exactly the ballistae obsequies might feel like; such was the power of the mental/virtual illness I would be subject to. But if my MTRUTH had previously been limited by wooden bars with padlocks securing the controller's keyboard at some unknown military establishment, either in Great Britain, the former Soviet Union, the USA or even the Republic of Ireland, I would not have to wait long before they had all been unlocked – of that I was sure. Then I could have information clearly superimposed by MI5 through my MTRUTH on what I saw and heard normally.

Then I recalled the night I left The Red Lion pub in Barnes, London, and, on the pavement, found I was overcome with the most extraordinary dizziness. I was so dizzy, in a way I had never been before, that I had to go down on one knee. But it passed in seconds and I just walked home, a little shocked. The next day, driving down Church Road, the same thing happened again, but only for a few seconds. That night I had called home and spoke to my mother, who told me she had fallen over and cut her head. She told me the doctor had said her dizziness was labyrinthitis caused by a virus. I had not seen her for a month and was suspicious about the delay in onset. We had both been given the virus deliberately – if that is, my mother was not lying through her teeth on the instructions of her KGB controller, now an MI5 employee.

✱✱✱✱✱✱✱✱✱✱✱✱✱✱✱✱✱

So there I was, at NATO HQ, with this tremendous and sudden realisation upon me. But I was frustrated with my lack of certainty. I could almost have said to the Captain, with a hopelessly resigned anger, "Now look at my car. As you can well see there are no bugs, BBC Radio 1 has no idea where my car is, they have not got a nationwide street map in the studio showing my moment-to-moment position, and I am the biggest arsehole you ever met! Okay?" Funnily, I think that was pretty much what I did say, in a rather frustrated manner, as I did not believe in what I was saying. So I got in and drove off. Whether I was right or wrong, somebody now knew something of what I was thinking. They knew I was bonkers.

I was now on the way to my flat, and somewhere in North London I passed a procession of Orthodox Jews. I felt very unwell, but perhaps they were all builders – building Jerusalem. Soon I was in my flat: it did not seem to be mine anymore.

Looking around the living room, perhaps you would not have thought there was anything particularly wrong; it could have done with a new carpet, and certainly a new settee. But you would have had to look very closely at the goings-on in the room over the previous months in order to determine that things were not quite right. Though let me assure you of one thing: there was a very unusual tension there – a sense of danger all around. I had seriously considered seeing the vicar in Barnes about exorcising the flat which, bugged to the back of beyond or not, seemed as though it had something seriously wrong with it.

Intriguingly, whilst my own passport containing details of my voyages in Africa had disappeared, another passport had taken its place. It was a passport produced by Fuller, Smith and Turners' Brewery in Chiswick. I had originally obtained the passport in my local: The Red Lion, Barnes. This passport, which contained the full list of Fullers' pubs, had to be carried around and stamped in each pub to prove the holder had drunk there. Ultimately he could then obtain his reward – not a VC or George Cross, but a polypin of Extra Strong Bitter (ESB) and a T-shirt.

I had visited only one of the pubs, and therefore had only one stamp. However one day I found the passport and, upon examining it, found that a number of pubs I had never been to, or even heard of, had been stamped. The names of these pubs seemed to stick out as though whoever had got them stamped had chosen them deliberately. They included: The Volunteer, The Vulcan, The Buckingham and other pubs whose names seemed to convey a mysterious message to me. I was quite certain they had not been stamped in my presence previously. It seemed therefore that somebody was trying to influence my mind.

The one explanation I came up with was that a friend, to whom I had given one of these passports, had made the effort to get these well-scattered pubs stamped to play a trick on me, swapping my passport with his. Later I would imagine that if it was not him it could only be the KGB, MI5, MI6 or some elite Army unit like the FRU (Force Research Unit) who had done it. And if so there seemed no doubt they had also been responsible for the mysterious disappearance of the copy of *The Eagle* magazine in 1979 reporting my try in a rugby match against the Haberdashers. But for now I just felt a tremendous wave of paranoia. This paranoia was only added to by remembering the regular wrong number calls to my flat for an "Avro Travel". Avro being, coincidentally, the manufacturer of the famous wartime Lancaster bomber. All these people calling for Avro Travel were just 617 Squadron, the "Dambusters", who flew Avro Lancasters, calling at the behest of MI5 and the Special Intelligence Service. Then I remembered the phone message on my answering machine one evening from some well-spoken chap who said he was flying in from Moscow the same night, and I felt a mysterious and alluring paranoia about that too. Someone was attempting to affect the way I was thinking. No doubt they would argue they were continuing as normal – whether it was MI5 or the Special Intelligence Service.

And there was another mystery playing on my mind: the crashing of the fractured parts of a comet into Jupiter. This led me to the belief I did, in fact, have an MTRUTH. One evening, a couple of years earlier, I had met an old friend, Joss, from my days at the Royal Greenwich Observatory, Joss now being a professor of astronomy. At the meeting I had suggested such a thing, I believed from my own imagination. Now the comet strike actually appeared to happen, leading me to imagine I did have a microphone in my mouth through which the Special Intelligence Service had learnt of my idea. The CIA had gone ahead and hoaxed the comet splash to see how I responded – to test my intuition. Of course, I was incorrect in this belief; nevertheless I did imagine the incident was merely a virtual event. Or should I have said of course?

The flat had been broken into. Amongst things taken was my ghetto blaster. At the time it was taken it had a CD in it entitled *Happiness* by The Beloved. No criminal offence had taken place – somebody, if not God himself, was just getting his own back on me for some minor misdemeanour. Some sort of instant justice had come into play. An identical ghetto blaster appeared for sale second-hand a while later in Bedford. It was mine – they wanted me to pay to get it back.

****

I was caught up in a big game. Herman Hesse's *The Glass Bead Game* came to mind – an amazing story of how the intellectual elite was creamed off into some fantastically learned environment to pursue aesthetic excellence. I was being creamed off. It had been decided, back in 1926, to actually try and play the game. The game was determined to finish only when the Ministers of the Glass Bead Game in the German section of MI6 had universally agreed that I "had got out of it" – whatever "get out," meant. This might not have been decided yet, though what I had read about the exploits of an SAS rookie in a second file marked "Absolute Secret" at RARDE might be relevant. How *would* somebody with MTRUTH fitted against their will "get out of it"? The clock was ticking in the Masonic lodge – and the bill being run up whilst the game went on was truly astronomical.

I was a one and only. I had even met Chesney Hawkes, singer of *I Am the One and Only*, in the pub in Barnes. As a physicist, my thoughts turned to another one and only – Uri Geller. His trick of bending cutlery was a device to which security services in both the West and East were party to – a bridge-building manoeuvre to help keep the peace. Only special cutlery and the above could account for his success. This was a very long-term manoeuvre I was involved in – a manoeuvre that did not allow Geller's secret to be revealed in his lifetime.

In this manoeuvre I was to receive a particular concept image on my MTRUTH, of my colleague in this ludicrously inverted inside-out war, the SAS rookie. He had built himself an electromagnetically-shielded lair in a remote place. From time to time he would open the trapdoor to his lair to see if the rather unwanted incoming radio transmissions to his own MTRUTH had ceased. Amusingly, he always made a laughable dismissive gesture when it was clear to him the broadcasts had not stopped. He remained down his lair for another four years – but I would see him again.

I would like to be able to say I did not necessarily believe this associate of mine existed and had really built that lair, because it is not possible for an individual to distinguish between his own imagination and his electronically-augmented imagination, if, as already described, the EAI input level is correctly set. But I did believe he was there. Years later into this experiment I would receive further intelligence via my EAI, or if not, my own imagination, on the other members of my imagined *Dirty Dozen*-style Special Forces Unit – including the chap mentioned. All of them were having quite ferociously designed and targeted virtual wars being waged against them by their own nation – British Intelligence in fact. This was being done just out of curiosity to see how they responded. It wouldn't be long before I wished I had a lead-lined crash helmet to put on at bedtime to give me a break from it.

I was receiving orders via my MTRUTH. But you can only carry out orders for so long before, as an existentially well-founded Soviet/MI5 double agent, you find yourself being ordered to jump off Beachy Head – in which case you have to be determined not to do so. I found myself going round in all sorts of circles trying to please whoever was controlling me silently using my MTRUTH.

Who do you tell if you think you have been fitted up with an invisible virtual reality headset? Logic dictated to me that to go into a police station and complain of this condition announcing one's status in the Special Forces, a quite permissible tactic, would without any doubt result in forced hospitalisation under the Mental Health Act. An unpublished series of security levels were secretly attached to the Act so that in this circumstance, for fairness in this Glass Bead Game, not just the 'member of the Special Forces' making the complaint but those who sectioned him were also, unknown to them, sectioned too. Also sectioned with them would be all their staff right down to the cleaners. They would become more actively recognised, as well as involved, in the patient's treatment; though perhaps not quite to the extent of carrying out a full lobotomy in between cleaning the toilets and mopping down the smoking room. They would all be ground-MTRUTHed.

The only other avenue of reality that was made known to me on my MTRUTH was that of a colleague at my firm who had once told me that he too had been, at one stage, party to top secret intelligence. I would see him in my MTRUTH making a quiet trip to the High Court on my behalf. Hence there seemed no need for me to go to Law (for having had invasive surgery performed on my body without my permission) – at least for now.

****

Still in my flat, I took the record from its sleeve; it was *Power, Corruption and Lies* by New Order. I placed it on the turntable so that it looked like I had just listened to the side with *Your Silent Face* on it. That song is alchemy worth a sackful of the best chocolate money, and is a beautiful funereal march based on Kraftwerk's *Europe Endless* – hence its prototype name *KW1*. It was a nonchalant and timeless goodbye at that, just the way I wanted it. Leaving another few clues around the room as to my state of mind at my final departure, I forget what they were, I left the room for the 'last time'. As I left I noticed that, rather than that having been the last piece of music I ever listened to, Peter Gabriel's *Modern Love* could equally have been the next – a more positive view of the future. That was the next song on the tape in the Hitachi cassette tape recorder, which I had bought many years before with my newspaper-round money.

Intriguingly, I now found a letter in my flat, which I had received from my father in RAF Sharjah in the Trucial States (now the United Arab Emirates) back in the '60s. I had not seen it since then. In the letter he said "I am sure you will do your best." Purportedly, he had only been talking about me mowing the lawn in the old orchard behind the house where we lived back in 1970. For some reason I thought the address of New Scotland Yard was "Old Orchard" and a magical layer of schizophrenia descended upon me in relation to the old orchard where I played in my childhood. My father was working for the Special Intelligence Service. The letter had been written only recently and placed there to encourage me. I was now on a very dangerous psychological warfare assault course. The truth is, I was right – it *was* dangerous. Then I recalled the occasion when, aged 10, a car had overtaken and flagged down my father's. We were just leaving RAF Brampton, home to MI4, where my father worked at the time. I had been under surveillance even then. This was not just some random incident in which another driver had noticed my car door was dangerously open – I was a vital asset to those spying on me to be protected at all costs and I was being followed 24/7. I wondered where my sew-on Blue Peter badge must be. I left the flat.

****

If anyone had asked me what I was then doing I would have said that I had no intention whatsoever of taking my life. Yet here I was performing this ceremony, or at least trying to give the impression that there had been one. But probably, forgetting for the moment my belief I had an MTRUTH fitted, it would never really be noticed that I had held such a ceremony. Either way it is now plain to see that I was in danger because, whatever the effect of my MTRUTH, I no longer appeared to be in control of my environment: it was controlling me. That is, I was reacting to the presence of whatever stimuli were around me in a manner, which meant my safety was not guaranteed. It was a bit like driving on a road on which all the signs had been swapped around randomly, so the speed limit was 70 down a narrow side road in town, and a sign saying "All Traffic" pointed up someone's driveway. If you could think of the brain as a rather sophisticated computer on the Internet, then it felt very much like someone had hacked into mine and taken control of the operating system – this suggesting I had indeed had an MTRUTH fitted. In the flat I had performed what had really been a bizarre ritual – one I might once have been burnt alive for. But I now had a new and rather unusual ambition – to see my own obituary. Such an ambition would have certain consequences.

****

Outside it was getting dark. I turned right and began walking up towards the old overgrown cemetery. I was not going to it for my own funeral, at least not directly, and hardly expected to find my own epitaph, let alone obituary – though I admit I did not look terribly closely into the undergrowth. If I had done and found it that would have hardly have surprised me as nothing seemed out of the question. The cemetery just happened to be the way I was going; the footpath to Putney went through it and I was often to be found going that way, perhaps for a drink at The Duke's Head or to see some friends.

****

I said I was not going to my funeral directly, but I had once walked past a funeral parlour that had 999 in its telephone number. At that precise moment the ghost of a hearse with a flashing police-style light and siren shot past at some speed. I presumed, not that it was just my own bizarre imagination, but that it was Prince Charles poking fun at me on my MTRUTH (on this rare occasion in supra-subliminal mode). In his position as Grandmaster of the Masons, I saw him as a source of such harmless trickery and tomfoolery. But you see something had happened to my mind, which now allowed it the full scope of my imagination.

However far that imagination stretched, there would always be some truth in what it thought. For example, a person might claim they were being spied on. Well even the least spied on person in the country would have some government statistic pertaining to them, like a National Insurance number or even just some figure estimating the number of illegal immigrants, the figure including them. Either way, my imagination was now in overdrive and the Ducks Crossing sign, amongst other things, was pushing it to the limit.

I certainly had no desire to tell anyone about my MTRUTH at this stage – I could not quite believe it myself. To that extent I was suffering some sort of obsessive secrecy syndrome and this would last several years, though I do not regret having suffered from it. Most of this story might never have happened if I had been the sort of person inclined to tell someone what I was thinking, rather than maintain a deluded investigative secrecy about such thoughts. For now it would just be a very powerful secret born out of the work I had been engaged in for the Ministry of Defence. I was not running experiments. I *was* the experiment. No wonder, it seemed, certain pieces of software were noticeable by their absence, at work at the Defence Operational Analysis Executive (DOAE), West Byfleet. Here I was running the computer studies for the two-and-a-half-billion pound procurement of the Army's new Apache anti-tank helicopter. The study was to demonstrate the helicopter's effectiveness. The apparently deliberate absence of certain pieces of software and tools led me to the obvious conclusion that even if my imaginations were too farfetched and I had not been designated a future MI5 Soviet agent before my birth, I was one now. Now *my* view stretched out from the fence at the foot of the garden in Cornwall Road, Ruislip, to the Berlin Wall, which had fallen four years earlier. I was a strange hangover from the Soviet Union – and the hedge at the bottom needed trimming back. It seemed the Apache helicopter was merely incidental to what was happening here – and that is saying something, for such a fearsome piece of weaponry. Moreover it was as if I wasn't really even involved with its procurement – that had all been decided elsewhere beforehand. The project was a front.

My whole environment, 24 hours a day, had been determined following the handover of my KGB file to MI6, or MI6 obtaining it by some other less straightforward means, shortly after the fall of the wall. But I could see the humour in this situation – and could not imagine anybody would simply come up and tell me in the office one day that I was an agent, and a very unusual one at that.

Everything that had happened to me over the previous four years was scripted in *particular* detail. This would happen, in more or less exactly the same way, to either later MI6 Soviet section or KGB British section recruits. For what was now happening was more to do with nuclear arms talks than procurement of the Apache – or the Soviets' own attack helicopter for that matter. What was discussed openly in the Club Rich UK late-drinking bar back in Bedford was now a tool for this international Glass Bead Game version of BBC's *It's a Knockout*. Conversations in that bar had been designated as extremely sensitive, including any making reference to Peter Gabriel's song, inspired by the European stage of that old programme: *Games Without Frontiers*.

So what was really going on here? My imagination was being driven to a terrifyingly farfetched reality – or was it farfetched? I knew that such a thing as a reality war existed and virtual ones had been waged. These were waged, to my personal belief, from a secret nuclear bombproof reality generation centre under the old boardroom of Charrington's brewers, West Byfleet, which was where DOAE was in those days.

A religious cult, operating almost unspotted, was creating drones so badly brainwashed that their souls had been stripped right back to the most elementary levels ready for reprogramming. At this stage I was not sure where they actually were doing this. But I intended to find out. *And I would.* I had learnt to see people, not as individuals but software entities, all living a more or less deterministic existence. This existence was not the product of their own existentially well-founded behaviour but controlled by the environment they were subject to.

My suspicions about the model I was running at work for the effectiveness study were largely more alluring than paranoiac. It was almost as if the real purpose of the model was to assess *my* effectiveness, as though I was part of a machine to train a few carefully chosen agents. The model was what they call discrete and deterministic, that is, limited by the nature of the computer software and by the law of determinism, a bit like some military careers. It felt like I had become part of the software, as though I was deterministically controlled by it, and was myself part of the military manoeuvre the model described. In truth I had begun an unofficial military investigation of schizophrenia, though had not realised this yet as the nature of that illness is the lack of awareness that you have it. But I realised one thing: something strange was going on.

****

Traffic was busy as usual in the early evening, and in the distance, on the horizon some six miles away, I could see the Post Office Tower and my thoughts turned to my days at University College London (UCL) in Bloomsbury, some 11 to 14 years earlier.

****

These were happy memories. I had worked hard some of the time, socialised plenty and spent a not inconsiderable amount of time exercising myself sportingly, mostly at the boathouse or the rugby ground. I split my time between the three in a not particularly effective way, certainly as to the class of the degree I was to obtain.

But I had got through and that was the main thing, along with making my interview for the Royal Marines at The Admiralty Arch on time despite the trains being delayed by snow – this obviously being a notable day in Soviet history. I had hired a smart suit, a trilby and some shiny shoes from Moss Bros for the interview at which, a little dangerously, I carried a copy of *An Phoblacht*, the Irish Republican newspaper. The marine who interviewed me was a computer expert. He asked me to sign the Official Secrets Act and offered me a glass of 25-year-old Talisker single malt Scotch. He insisted I add some water. I kindly refused, as I always did, even with cask strength whiskies: I'm quite a religious person.

But I was to take a rather unusual route towards the Royal Marines following my interview – as you will see. In fact technically speaking I was AWOL from the Royal Marines' Commando Training Centre, Lympstone, and had been since the summer holiday of 1975, when I did not turn up for Combined Cadet Force

(CCF) summer training. Not the most auspicious way to pursue an affiliation with the SBS. The route, whilst difficult, was not too difficult to choose however. I had been in the Naval Section of the CCF at school and had done plenty of arduous training – particularly if you put that alongside my rowing training. I failed to get into the University of London rowing club twice, though on one occasion the Head Coach told me I was the most technically proficient bow-side oarsman he had ever seen. I just did not have the cardiovascular physiology to reach the highest standard in rowing. I was probably rather better at running, completing a half-marathon in one hour 27 minutes. But I did get into the Imperial College squad, eventually reaching, in the Imperial College 2nd VIII, 40th in the Head of the River Race out of over four hundred and fifty crews. The crew was said to be the best 2nd VIII they had ever had. That really was my proud peak and getting appendicitis shortly after, sadly saw me out of the Henley crew.

One evening, when I knew my first degree was in the bag, I had decided that at nine o'clock I would go for a drink in my favourite bar at St. Pancras Station: The Shires Bar. I could hear the bells of St. Pancras Church strike a quarter to. Before I left to get my well-earned beer I wrote the following:

St. Pancras Bells

Fifteen minutes more to concentrate the mind,
St. Pancras bells do me remind,
That goading sound, the time is near,
Quantum mechanics, electromagnets, now give me beer!

A visitor once saw, by the door: Clive Travis: three rings,
But rang four for disappointment.
No such random wave of hope and heat do your bells bring,
Inanimate yes, but sensible in insentience!

And when at last you call (I knew you would),
Unending time reflects my aimless love,
As when beneath St. Pancras terminus arches where I stood,
Imaged in a puddle, I saw your namesake's face above.

Dry and at home, beneath this Godly canopy,
Two-score travellers and many more,
Each alone anticipates...

I had always had a bit of a romantic outlook on the subject of future relationships and had gone through most of my university days firmly of the belief that somewhere there was a girl whom I was going to meet who would really make my life complete. Destiny, I believed, determined this would happen and that we could happily lie on my bed listening to my Joy Division records. Sure enough, towards the end of my final year, a good friend by the name of Robert Wickham asked me if he could send along a friend of his to my party, as he could not make it, having to go to a wedding. The friend was Amanda, of whom you have already heard. He told me that, apparently, she was very fond of me. At the time I did not know her name came from the Latin: "One to be loved."

He also sent another person, a certain William Easton. As part of his degree William pretended to be a dog for two weeks. Despite my own experiences, I am not quite sure what that meant for him. I do know that he was said to have gone into his viva voce at UCL's Slade Art School barking, and had eaten some dog food during the interview. Another stunt he pulled was swapping lives with somebody for two weeks. The two rendezvoused in the gents toilets at Euston Station and, passing all their belongings under the partition, proceeded to attempt to live each other's lives for the next 14 days, meaning, as we shared a house with this chap, we were all drawn into the pretence for the duration. Imagine swapping lives with somebody to discover he or she is actually a dog!

Robert was a reliable drinking partner throughout my university days – so I could only assume his sending Amanda was a reliable indication of her romantic intentions. But the party went ahead without her turning up. Still, it was a great party at which the first two people to arrive, a couple of school friends, were also the last to leave. One of them, whose father was an expert on the occult and had the largest collection of books on the subject outside the British Library, drove a Hillman Avenger, which had, painted on its bonnet, the sleeve design from Joy Division's first classic album, *Unknown Pleasures*. The design had been lifted from a copy of *The Cambridge Encyclopaedia of Astronomy* and showed what, for a few brief days back in the '60s, was believed to be the first contact with extraterrestrial life. But it turned out to be a new astronomical phenomenon, which was then named a pulsar.

The party was to start at The Frog and Firkin pub down in Ladbroke Grove. But as there were too many of us, one person had to go in the boot, and it turned out to be me, which was a bit silly as I was the only one who knew the route there. This meant I had to navigate blind, an interesting test of one's "Knowledge". At the pub others arrived and one person in particular was of note: he was a chap called Chris George, not a bad bloke, who was notable for two reasons. Firstly, a few years later he gave me a right telling-off for turning up at a fancy dress party dressed as a member of the Afrikaner Weerstandsbeweging, the Afrikaner White resistance movement – who were campaigning for the establishment of a Boer-only homeland in part of South Africa. Chris died shortly after of a heroin overdose making him one of a disturbing number of friends and acquaintances I have had that have died prematurely from either drugs or suicide. Shortly before he died, another mutual friend, also a heroin addict, rather ineptly telephoned through a warning of a bomb at McDonald's from Chris's mother's house, completely forgetting as he did so that they would simply trace the call back to them. I believe he escaped prison on psychiatric grounds though how he has escaped death I'll never know – no one else in his group survived.

Returning to the party, I soon received a visit from the Vice-Warden who insisted I turn the music down. Well, I was not really going to let her put the dampers on my party, and so a pattern set in for the evening whereupon she would regularly turn up making vague threats and demands.

Earlier that day, I had come across a fire extinguisher engineer sitting in his van and persuaded him to sell me one. A feature of life at the halls of residence had been regular fights with fire extinguishers, which I can honestly say I had never been involved in. However I would certainly admit to having been responsible for large quantities of water being jettisoned from my window on various occasions. Once I dropped a four-ply black bin liner full of water. The explosion was rather impressive. Having the extinguisher meant I could let it off whilst, mysteriously, no empty official extinguishers could then be found in the building; so it seemed a laugh to have one at the party... purely for safety reasons of course!

At one point in the first year things had developed into a veritable $H2O$ war, much of which involved my roommate. He would often send, and receive; more than one letter a day to and from his girlfriend and checked his pigeonhole obsessively. The result of this was that I knew exactly how many seconds it took him from appearing around the corner from the Law School and checking his pigeonhole, to being right under the window. At the end of his last examination I hid at the back of the room so, having got wise to it, he could not see me, started the clock ticking, and at the precise moment I knew he would be at the door below the window I emptied a large bucket of water through it. As it happened the Vice-Warden that year was standing there and he took the entire contents of this freak rainstorm right on his head. He tried to blame it on my roommate, who was more or less dry, but dying laughing. Sometime later I happened to see this chap coming towards me down Southampton Row. Recognising me, he gestured amusingly with his overcoat and glanced upwards as though he was now expecting a sudden downpour.

The party was hotting up, and so was my temper because this year's Vice-Warden had appeared again. Downstairs the two-piece band Seona Dancing had started playing their single *More to Lose*. They were called Seona Dancing because their singer, Ricky Gervais, later to become the well-known comedian, had seen a girl called Seona dancing at the Union disco, and liked the way she did so. I decided to change my approach and go on the attack, hoping to make sure this was the Vice-Warden's last visit. After all, the term had hardly begun yet. So I reached under the bed, got the carbon dioxide fire extinguisher out and pointed the nozzle right at her crotch, squeezing the trigger. A powerful jet of freezing carbon dioxide shot out of the nozzle covering the area around her upper thighs with an icy white layer. She seemed absolutely stunned by this, turning her head slowly to look; as though she simply could not believe either what was happening or that I had the temerity to do such a thing. This raised the level of hilarity at the party to unforeseen levels. She left and was not seen again, allowing the party to follow its natural course. At this time I could not possibly foresee how a simple fire extinguisher would later feature so prominently in my life – albeit in a somewhat deluded manner.

A few weeks later I did meet Amanda. There she was standing in front of me in the Student Union bar, with her back to the pillar. She had lived down the corridor from me, although I had not seen her recently. Robert Wickham was having a party over near Marble Arch; so I did not hesitate and asked her along, arranging to meet her there.

I cycled to the party, carrying a plastic bagful of booze, and soon reached the end of Oxford Street, feeling a little wary, as I had no lights on my bike. I now heard sirens and turned into the street where the hall of residence was. At the door the police were arriving and I found myself standing in the lift with two policemen and Amanda, who looked like a very nice mixture of Joan Bakewell and Diane Keaton standing there. It transpired that the police were going to the same party and I mentioned my brother Howard's number and force. Into the party we all walked and one of the policemen switched off the television as it announced "Conservatives hold Beaconsfield with a majority of 26,000" or something, it being election night. Some people at the party had decided, because it was the end of the year, that they no longer had any need of any furniture and had begun throwing it out of the window. Somebody spotting this had called the police, *or at least that was what I was told.* Everyone was severely admonished, and the police left.

Later we went to Robert's room where an Etonian friend of his joined us for drinks, and finally, as we both lived back in Bloomsbury, I asked Amanda if we should now go and she agreed. I took her hand, not realising that the reason I had not seen her recently was that she now lived down the corridor from Robert. So there we went and I did not come out until most of the election results were out the next afternoon, after a night of the most passionate lovemaking possible without taking one's clothes off.

My manner of departing was amusing, as immediately before my departure I descended into a fearful panic because my throat began swelling alarmingly to the point where I was worried that soon I would not be able to breathe. Looking in the mirror my uvula was also impressively swollen and I headed for the doctor at the UCL Medical Centre – a Dr. Lancaster. He seemed a little amused and asked me what I had been doing in the last 12 hours. I seemed to be suffering some kind of allergic reaction.

****

Reaching the footpath across Barnes Common I passed by the curious concrete and brick marker. I never knew what the purpose of this was. If it had been the top of a wall, possibly around the old cemetery, then what had happened to the wall? And if the wall was elsewhere, then why had someone brought the marker here? All I knew was that this strange marker was there, a few short feet from the spot where, one evening I had spotted what I thought was a dead body. Stepping off the path to take a closer look I was shocked to see that there was movement of a rapid nature coming from underneath the coat covering the 'body'. This, it now became apparent, was two homosexuals, one tossing the other off. Without interrupting them I walked off, a little amused and also a little shocked. I had read that the old graveyard was a place for what is known as cruising, which is just turning up in the hope of taking part in homosexual activities. I was reminded of a lift I once got in America. The moment I got in the superbly customised van I knew the driver was extraordinarily homosexual. I sat down and he asked me where I was from and what I was doing. Well within a minute of getting in his van he said "Tell me, in the course of your travels, have many people have given you a blow-job?" I was so stunned with this I could only reply "Well no, actually." To this he replied, "Well, I'd love to give you one!" I spent the next few minutes gently declining his kind offer, explaining that my girlfriend would not be very happy (though I did not have one at the time) and thinking amusedly what my friends from school would have thought of this. The back of his van was lined with fur the whole way round, including the walls, back door and ceiling and he suggested, when I explained I was not physically capable of participating, that I could just lie back and think of my girlfriend. He even began offering me money, asked me how much I wanted (to be given the blow-job) and suggested I could make a lot of money engaging in such activities around there. He was such a nice guy it was almost a shame I was not at least bisexual.

****

I had been to a public school. Someone once told me it was the cheapest available though I certainly never observed that in terms of the quality of the teaching, which I have to say, was very good. Contrary to popular belief, I saw little true homosexuality there, though I do recall the older boys holding wanking races in the dormitory of the school boarding house. I also remember well an incident when somebody in my rowing crew appeared out of the blue on his bike and told me that he loved me. He told me it was not a sexual thing but not being gay, or even a little bisexual, I did not receive this advance easily. I might even say I was not particularly impressed by his remark, though whatever homophobia I was then suffering it did not prevent me from later happily attending Gay Soc discos when I went up to University. Along the road, we happened on a girl at the telephone box on whom I had a massive teenage crush. Unfortunately she professed to have a thing about his legs, and mine were then too skinny. It was a bizarre love triangle. But I did not embarrass him by telling anyone.

Somebody else in the crew was keeping something secret too. One day 27 years later he walked into the Rowing Club dressed as a woman and announced he had known he was trapped in the wrong body since the age of nine and wished to be known as Rachel and not Richard. Nobody believed him but he was absolutely serious and proved it by, amongst other things, having his testicles removed.

So maybe I was not the only one having difficult teenage years. I found myself tortured with a crippling self-consciousness. It was this that enabled my later fantasy that I had been AWOL from the Royal Marines for 25 years, and the last thing I needed was some adolescent poof fancying me. I became terrified of the hairdresser and really was a bloody pathetic specimen who should have been dragged in and given a skinhead – and I wish I had been. I remember thinking that I was under so much pressure that surely my mind must be in danger of sustaining some sort of severe damage, though I had no idea what that might be. It was hardly as if I was in danger of arrest but I recalled how my CO, who was my form master, had made a big song and dance about it when I returned to school for the autumn term, not having turned up at the Commando Training Centre. I told him I'd had a cold, although I was not sure he believed me.

If the truth be told I did not turn up because I was suffering body dysmorphic syndrome. This is a condition where the sufferer finds part of their body insufferably ugly. For example one of their limbs, and there are examples where the sufferer has had the limb amputated by a surgeon. That was not an option because it was with my head I had the problem. This possibly accounts for some people laying their neck on the railway track looking for free cosmetic surgery care of a railway company. In my case it meant I could not get to Lympstone because I could not bear to be away from the bathroom mirror. It must be hard to understand if such an illness has not befallen you. Anyway it gradually faded away over the next year or two. Apparently the illness is often closely associated with anorexia nervosa and bulimia. I can vouch for that. I recall when I was about 14 or 15 I developed a delusion I had a fat arse and actually fasted secretly for a week or so at one point. It seems laughable now. Years later I would go into a book shop and pick up a copy of *The SAS Survival Guide*. I read the section on smoking. It said that in order to give up you had to want to. I eventually did. Interestingly, while I noticed sections on bulimia and anorexia nervosa, I could not seem to find one on schizophrenia and developed a delusional theory it had been removed by the MoD as it compromised the positions of too many ex-Special Forces personnel operating undercover in the NHS.

****

In the dark, I continued past the old cemetery across the Common; not the sort of place a person previously mugged would venture in at night. But I held no fears of that kind, nor of the graveyard. However, that is not to say there were things in my life of which I was not absolutely terrified, and if being terrified of something constitutes a weakness, then I have to say I had some pretty weak areas, the biggest being the schizophrenia.

Soon I was over the Common and walking down the Lower Richmond Road. A Mini sped past heading up Queen's Ride. I thought of Marc Bolan from T Rex doing just that some 17 years earlier. He was only seconds from death and unable to do anything about it because someone else was driving. Already there was some evidence I had about as much control over myself as he'd had in the sense that I was being driven along in a completely invisible and challengingly driven car – my MTRUTH.

In The Duke's Head I ordered a drink, unhampered by my MTRUTH but at this stage I was not extended a *Good Beer Guide* drop-down assessment on the television screens to help me choose which beer. I sat down. I was looking at the pint of bitter as though it were my last. Again, if anyone had known this, and asked me why this was, I would probably have ridiculed the suggestion and yet that was the way I was thinking. It was an avenue of thought which was simply too alluring to resist – the possibility of my demise had something seemingly romantic about it, though only really to the extent of how good this 'last' beer was. But they say heroin has velvet claws and a sting in the tail. I suppose you could say the same about the state of mind I was in; you cannot jump off a cliff without thinking of doing so, unless your reality has been completely replaced by your MTRUTH, and you cannot see you are by a precipice. On one occasion I did think something rather like this had happened.

****

I was driving and pulled out, believing nothing was coming. Having pulled out I looked in my rear-view mirror and suddenly a car had appeared from nowhere. Rather than having appeared from nowhere it was not even there now – except on my MTRUTH. I had a great secret, a secret that I had obtained over the previous few months. Even the air around me seemed special. I was the one who had hacked into the world's most secure computer system and nobody had spotted me. But now possession of the secret had turned very sour and I really did feel quite literally sick in the head. I had not hacked into it; it had hacked into me – on an operating theatre bed.

This was not what I had been thinking of when, a few years earlier, I had asked a friend of mine to consider a personal scale of secrecy from one to 10.

The level of secrecy was so great that I could only tell him I had reached the first and lowest level, level one, but could not tell him what I had done to award myself that level of secrecy. What I actually did was lie down in the middle of some bushes in the park on the way back from the pub one summer night. Not such a tremendously secret thing to do. But something interesting had happened when I did. As I lay there a car stopped nearby and a chap got out and came and pissed into the bushes a few feet from where I was lying. He got back into the car and drove off. The coincidence seemed a little too much. I was being watched so closely that my presence in the bush had been spotted. I wondered: was the bloke pissing just to make me think? Perhaps the same person was responsible for the placing of the stamped passport in my flat. Or perhaps it was mere coincidence.

It was as though Jean-Paul Sartre's existential work *Nausea* had been distilled into a highly-concentrated intellectual essence and placed slap-bang in the centre of my mind, the effect being that of an emotional emetic. This had made me wander aimlessly around Barnes Common that afternoon leaving regular pools of emotional vomit in the MTRUTH psychic-ether all over it, plus quite a few tears; but on a happier note, I noticed an immature sparrow hawk sitting on the lamp-post.

Part of the Common is heavily cratered and I imagined were caused by a German bomber who fancied a pint in The Sun pub when the War was over, and so deliberately missed the houses. I was certainly very ill, though maybe not for imagining that.

****

Enjoying the beer I looked around at the other drinkers. The clientele were a healthy mixture of up-and-coming yuppie types (the females wearing the usual blue uniform, including the pearl necklace) and the odd male working-class Londoner, in the latter case usually drinking, as I was, a pint of Young's bitter. The pub was one of the few in the country where the beer was still delivered by dray horse, which could only make it taste better. I had once written to the Director of the brewery to congratulate him on the new Oatmeal Stout. I received a handwritten response from Sir John Young and when I read it I could almost hear the clock ticking in the boardroom and smell the furniture polish on the wooden-panelled walls. I ordered another beer and as I supped into it again felt that it was to be my last, at least in some sense, feeling a little resigned to this.

Soon I had left The Duke's Head and was heading over Putney Bridge. Behind me was The White Lion.

****

I had been in The White Lion on my own one fateful night back in 1987. That morning the BBC Radio 1 DJ, Simon Mayo, had broadcast a warning of severe weather for the coming night. So the BBC television weather forecaster Michael Fish, who famously informed a worried viewer who had called in that there was no hurricane coming, must have seen another synopsis. As I left the pub that night in 1987, I remember the wind had noticeably got up in the time I'd had two or three pints. I was now at the same spot I had been on that occasion, seven years earlier. Here the wind had caught me, making me stationary for a moment.

It was a shame, I have since thought, and I had not stayed up to experience the full brunt of the hurricane; though I was certainly awoken in the middle of the night by the fan in the window going around at a tremendous rate. I had got up to take a look outside and saw the trees swaying like palm trees in a tropical cyclone, and then went back to bed. The following morning the power had gone. I got up and went outside to survey the scene, which was one of utter devastation, the wind now having subsided to a very stiff breeze. I could not but help see this in an emotional context when I found one particular tree by the Thames, which really did look like it was bleeding from its snapped trunk.

A Wish Granted

The roots of this tree bled blood,
Whilst my sap-sucked heart lay bleeding
In another bedsit room,
For each and every year I put down roots.
Your unconsidered remark, it blew me down,
And now I lie here listening to the breeze,
Motionless, like so much dead wood.

****

I thought of the strange old lady who would drink in The White Lion, whom I would often meet in Putney High Street. Invariably she would ask me what the time was, although she had a watch on. I never told her, as I didn't wear a watch, but this didn't stop her. I presume she was suffering some unusual obsessive disorder, or maybe just senile dementia. As she asked she would pull back her sleeve to check, asking me again promptly. There was something a bit Alice in Wonderland about this. At some point the landlord banned her, telling me she put off the young drinkers and wet the chair, though if she did, I would have been surprised. What proof did he have? I continued my strange hypermanic walk by the river, still reminiscing. I saw a party-boat go by, the sound of the disco and the noisy joyous chatter reaching me across the water.

Chapter Two

Part of the Fire

I had often seen the party-boats going by Putney pier and on the night of the hurricane, it being some five years after the fire extinguisher party, my thoughts had turned to having another. The possibility of a boat party appealed. I had asked a couple of bar staff in Putney how much the party boats cost to hire and they both supposed about two hundred quid. I was a little disappointed when I later found out the price was more than a thousand, but soon became convinced I could persuade two hundred people to part with a fiver, the only question being how to do that. On the night of the hurricane, sitting in the same pub I had just left, I had suddenly got the urge to write some things down although I had no idea as to what the purpose of doing so might be. I finished my beer, which had greatly contributed to this notable venture, and hurried around to my bedsit. I got down what I had to say and within a couple of days was sending out my first newsletter.

I felt driven and completely taken over by my new idea within a short space of time. I telephoned Amanda to see if she had got her copy but she said she hadn't. Quite possibly because she thought it was just junk mail and had thrown it away. But I had written it wishing to impress her and did not want it to be overlooked. So I sent another and the effect was dramatic. I will never forget her giggling down the phone as she held the newsletter in one hand and the phone in the other. By now I was deeply in love with her and just sitting next to her would give me a lovely warm romantic feeling, which I have never experienced with anyone else. On one occasion I took her to see New Order at the Michael Sobel Sports Centre. Standing on the Tube platform afterwards I said to her "We're young." She replied "And?" It was a memorable moment in my life, which I'll never forget. Every time I was with her was better than being given a block of gold bullion by a million times.

Party day arrived and it was clear I had broken even, after settling to pay all the promotion costs myself, which meant I could give a fair sum to charity. As planned, the hardcore partygoers met at The Monument (to the Great Fire of London – the theme of the party), where I had The House of Love's first CD playing on my ghettoblaster. We wandered around to Saint Lawrence Pountney Hill and in the graveyard there witnessed what must have been an extremely unusual event. I had worked as a security guard next to it years earlier and had been fascinated by the key to the graveyard, which had no church as it had been destroyed in the Great Fire. I had to open the graveyard every morning using the key and this had been done since the records had begun at the office where I worked, the office of an old City stockbroker. I wrote a poem about it.

Thoughts upon opening the gate to Saint Lawrence Pountney Graveyard

Three hundred years ago today, at one minute to eight, the key slipped in,
Great skinny clinking thing,
And with a clockwise turn that brought the time to eight,
The lock undid and open did the graveyard gate.

Then, one sunny summer's day, at noon, upon a
tomb, I saw a young man lie to rest.
He said "Like this the view's the best."
I knew he'd opened up my eyes to only happy places
(For only friendly, joyful spirits play here today)
And wondered what he had looked forward to, that fateful autumn day.

As the key rejoined its bunch of mates,
Rarely did he spare a thought for me,
But oh! for a summer's day in Kent, that's how he wished his life away.

Again upon the grave I saw the young man's figure,
And then again I saw him fade away.
But only on the dimmest, dullest English winter's day
Will fallen gravestones say they fell in sympathy
With falling, burning buildings, three hundred years ago today.

A black Mercedes with blacked out windows pulled up. Out got The Electra Strings, a group of musicians more or less ubiquitous on modern pop recordings of the more intellectually accessible variety. Complaining it was a little cold for their fingers, they began playing Bach in the graveyard. Perhaps the graveyard was mysteriously cooler than the surrounding streets. The reason they were playing several feet above the pavement was that they were on top of a plague-pit into which so many bodies had been dumped that the level of the ground rose.

Just beyond the western extremity of the Fire, the party-force was now beginning to show up at a pub, The George, opposite the High Court and once frequented by George Bernard Shaw.

Soon we were on the boat, where not everything was to go as planned, leading me to later imagine sabotage, or rather "low intensity warfare" as a cause of the subsequent events. Perhaps this was not such a schizophrenic thought, as it might seem, if one believes in the inadvisability of meddling with dormant powerful forces, especially as I was being watched anyway. I held the party as a celebration of the life of Robert Hubert, a Huguenot watchmaker of the City of London. One side of the ticket showed a contemporary engraving of London ablaze, the Great Fire of London of 1666 in fact, for the starting of which Monsieur Hubert went to the gallows. Wonderful isn't it? You do everyone a favour by burning down a city that is rotten and plague-ridden to the core, and what do they do – string you up. With unimaginable folly I described Monsieur Hubert, on the ticket, as a complete lunatic. I received a cheque for £16.66 from a friend with the following *jeu d'esprit*:

Dear Clive,
My watch has been in the family for nigh on four hundred years and always
kept perfect time. I have long known the timepiece to be of French extraction
for, delicately engraved on its silver exterior are the words "resistance de l'eau,
resistance de feu" and sure enough the heavy char on the original leather strap
is proof of the latter quality. But only recently did I discover that the maker of
the watch was one Robert Hubert in whose honour your party is being thrown.
The name, by now barely legible, was pointed out to me by my jeweller when,
last week, I had cause to take the watch in to have its battery replaced.
With Regards,
Neil

It was a fine evening as we embarked, leaving behind Angus McChesney and
his girlfriend, who were late, the Captain refusing to pick them up, and we
headed up towards Putney. Somebody said "Don't worry – he's in the Special
Boat Service." Well, when we got to Putney, Mac had got there first, by Tube,
and came alongside with his girlfriend in a motor-launch demanding that the
Captain put in at Putney Pier, which he did, allowing them to embark. Real or
imagined, the presence of the Special Forces at the party was welcome and not
quite as surprising as it might otherwise have been, as I had invited the Prime
Minister, Margaret Thatcher – an invitation which was politely refused. I had
not yet realised I was, if only by virtue of my imagination, a Soviet agent, and
had also quite forgotten about how I had been interviewed in The Admiralty
Arch that snowy day six years earlier. But I had not considered the possibility
that my invitation to the Prime Minister alone might encourage Forces of
Darkness to be present on the voyage – if they were not coming anyway because
the price of the boat hire, £1,035, eerily contained the flight number of the
Lockerbie plane: 103. One of the partygoers would later take that flight. Nor had
I imagined the French Secret Service being present (the party being held in
honour of Monsieur Hubert).

Things *seemed* fine on board, and the buffet, which I had bought at
Sainsbury's in Burpham was being enjoyed. Which reminds me of my first
meeting with a certain French girl present at the party. I had asked her where
she was from and she said "Burr Firm", meaning Burpham, a village outside
Guildford where I once saw Phil Collins at the Sainsbury's fishmonger's counter.
I said "Oh, in France?" and she said "Non – near Sens Burries."

But the generator was playing up so the power to the disco kept failing, the
boat later being plunged into darkness a number of times. Eventually, at around
10pm, the power went for the last time, mysteriously halfway through Joy
Division's *Love Will Tear Us Apart*. Perhaps this was a good thing as, so caught
up in the party spirit was I that I did not spend a minute to learn how to DJ
properly which, in respect, was quite embarrassing. Either way the premature
end to the music reminded me of the singer Ian Curtis's death, whether it was
by suicide or a secret extremist Israeli cell using drugs and mind control. The
Captain came and told me that was it for the disco, and I could apply for a
reduction on another cruise.

Next day I telephoned the boat company requesting that, in the 'light' of the
generator's failure, they make a donation to charity. I was rather miffed,

considering the hire fee of £1035 that they should offer only £25. I felt I had little choice but to take legal action. The whole matter became mysteriously troublesome making me wonder why I had called Mr Hubert a "complete lunatic".

I submitted a small claim to the County Court, which was returned because I had made a mistake in its submission. I corrected the mistake and resubmitted it. Again it was returned. I resubmitted it quite a number of times, I think as many as seven, before the court eventually returned it one more time and told me I had come to the wrong court.

So I resubmitted it to the correct court and it was returned because, they said, the fee I had submitted was incorrect for the sum I was claiming. By coincidence, the sum I was claiming, £300 just happened to be at the cut-off point between two fee levels. I hit the roof and wrote back to point out that £300 was not "more than £300". The whole episode seemed never-endingly perplexing.

It almost seemed something must be seriously wrong when they actually served the summons on the boat company, so used to all this had I become. I was left feeling as though I was being personally abused in a deliberate manner. I felt a certain fear at the thought that the summons was actually being served.

I was beginning to gather evidence, which would make me feel a little threatened, and that the party had been jinxed. This included the suicide of a friend, Andrew Woods; meaning two partygoers were dead before the year was out. When I was planning the party and thinking of whom I was to invite, it became apparent that there were not enough females on my list. So I began getting the names and addresses of any very attractive or otherwise pleasant women I encountered. One such woman was the blonde, Jo Hudson, who came into The White Horse, Parson's Green, where I worked, one night. Having very quickly established she had an amenable personality, she went on my list.

After the party I had been flying back from San Diego after my visit there to give a lecture useful to the United States Navy on submarine detection, at the International Conference on Quantitative Non Destructive Evaluation. I later wished I had invited Amanda. On the flight to Newark, New Jersey I had an empty seat next to me, which implied I was meant to have taken someone with me: I even imagined it deliberate. After refuelling, I was waiting for takeoff when a familiar face appeared in the cabin. The combination of her deep suntan and the unfamiliar environment made me think I did not know her, but in fact it was her – Jo Hudson. Later in the flight she came up and whispered "Hi Clive" in my ear. We spoke and I said goodbye when she met her mother at London. I even phoned her to get a date but she was not in and I actually never saw her again.

A few months later, it was eerie to see her face on the front page of a newspaper, a tragic victim of the Lockerbie bombing. This became a strong feature in my later mental illness, in that I began to imagine that she was not dead, and even that the plane, and Lockerbie, had been empty and the plane crashed in a stunt, if at all.

It could have been me dying too as the plane both of us were on crashed, instead of flight 103 (The Clipper Maid of the Seas). I am told that many people who suffer mental illness appear not to remember what happened, or what they did. The truth may be just that they only appear to. They only appear to for a variety of reasons – one being embarrassment. But, like anyone else, they tell fibs too – in doing so possibly appearing to remember things that did not happen. I would once tell somebody the following happened. Jo called me back a few days before the flight, we met and I ended up with a standby ticket in another part of the plane, to fly out to stay at her sister's with her for Christmas in America. Having boarded I asked the person sitting next to her if she would mind swapping with me, so we could sit together. Shortly before the flight departed an argument broke out close to me as I came back from the toilet, an argument in which I was foolish enough to intervene. I got hit during my intervention and ended up being thrown off the plane, saving my life.

Jo may have died because the person I had voted for, Margaret Thatcher, had allowed the Americans to try and bomb Colonel Qadaffi's tent. In that sense Margaret Thatcher killed a friend of mine and missed killing me by one flight – some payback for voting for someone.[11]

****

As I walked onto Putney Bridge all seemed clear. Jo was a CIA agent whose cover was terminated simply by her insertion into the passenger list – she was safe back in the States. I had got the only copy of the newspaper in which her death was announced. The Special Intelligence Service had printed it.

Possibility was to become liquid in my mind, and reality I would no longer have a handle on. Such a thought was alluring, not just because it meant Jo, or whoever she really was, was not dead, but also because it made me more powerful than I really was. My paranoia in relation to my near death at Lockerbie, and Jo's actual demise, had another paranoid effect on me. I thought back to the May bank holiday of 1980.

****

I had been on the houseboat of one Neil O'Connor, the singer in a not very famous, but very good band called The Flys who released an album *Flys Own* on EMI in 1979. As we sat watching Cliff Thorburn winning the Embassy World Snooker Championship there was a newsflash as the SAS successfully raided the Iranian embassy. Neil had been telling me about one of the songs on the album, *16 Down*, having been inspired by a dream he'd had in which he was on an airliner which was crashing into a town. This would set off a paranoia in my head the CIA would have been proud of: some terrorist organisation knew of this dream and that I knew of it too, the organisation blowing up the plane at the exact moment required for it to crash into Lockerbie. The very word "Lockerbie" took on farfetched hidden meanings involving locks and, through the letters "er", the Queen. I thought they wanted to get at me – tragically improbable of course, but that's schizophrenia for you.

The boat party claim was paid straight away and I sent the money to the charities, The Woodland Trust and Childline, which gave me a satisfied virtuous feeling – assuaging my feelings I had got caught up in black magic. The Woodland Trust spent the sum in memory of Josephine Hudson and Andrew Woods at Bramingham Wood near Luton. One day I visited the wood where I found a small pond on which were some water boatmen. I remembered how I had once dead-heated with Andrew's crew at Bedford Regatta. He maintained he'd had a hangover and won the re-row. I had always suspected we won the first race by two feet but the umpire, Michael Maltby, was an MI5 employee (he was actually), and knew I was a Soviet Agent. Quite possibly he was a member of the Special Intelligence Service. This might explain why I felt a slight tug on my oar blade as we went under the town bridge.

My developing talent in being unable to consider items of news to be in any way accurate would later lead me to suspect I had been personally responsible for the Mull of Kintyre helicopter crash. I suspected all that actually happened was that an empty Chinook was deliberately crashed there. That same umpire, who had judged our race, was an MI5 Northern Ireland specialist and was one of the people who died in the accident. The responsibility for negotiations with the IRA seemed to have been handed over to me. But I had little idea what to do other than go to Ireland. All those supposed to be aboard had scattered themselves, undead, around the country, fake funerals having been held, funerals which they had attended in disguise as mourners. To me this, and later events, would become something of a key to the problem of the six counties of Northern Ireland. A fake helicopter crash killing all the British military Northern Ireland top brass was the only thing that would do it justice. Why? Because they knew I was being brainwashed using a state-of-the-art virtual reality headset, my MTRUTH. These funerals would be a little like the one described in the book *Dare to be Free* about a Kiwi escaping a Nazi prison hospital in wartime Crete to Turkey via Greece. In the story, one escape attempt failed because the escapee was heard laughing inside the coffin. I imagined them all lodged in their scattered B&Bs ready for some later massive national denouement and street party when my negotiations with the IRA succeeded. They had all fallen out so badly with their families because of the secrecy of their work that the whole exercise was a great relief to them. Those who had 'died' had each done me the courtesy of walking past me in the street after their 'deaths' as depicted on the sleeve of the following year's Oasis album *(What's the Story?) Morning Glory*. One in particular grabbed my attention – he looked like one of the lecturers during my undergraduate course but *in fact* was from Military High Command. They had decided to the man to remain 'dead' until negotiations conducted by me were successful. In other words the Mull of Kintyre helicopter crash was a military joke told purely in response to my actions – and the historic technological achievement of electronic subliminal mind control, which demanded some pretty extraordinary side effects. Unfortunately I have not seen that umpire recently – not even a double. And perhaps those who walked past me were simply MI5 agents on the run from the Troubles.

So Andrew came back as a water boatman. But that was not the only message I received from Andrew Woods in his afterlife. He was to provide me with evidence that I had indeed been spied on every minute of the day throughout my life. What the umpire came back as was never an issue – it would take me several bouts of full-blown mental illness to consider he was probably really dead.

I was already sending out further communiqués and planning another boat party the next year. For this I booked a slightly larger boat from the same company. This, sad to say, was perhaps a little naïve, for I did not think that they might have somehow got it in for me for having taken them to court. That is certainly what it came to look like – if, that is, my boat parties were not simply jinxed from start to finish.

Party night number two came around and on board I began to receive complaints from the partygoers. They were extremely apologetic they should have to complain to me, but the general gist of what they all said was that they were quite astonished at the treatment they were getting from the crew. Paula had baked a cake and raffled it, enabling her to pay the most of anyone for her ticket. For this, as promised, I was to personally buy her a bottle of champagne. Approaching the bar, already aware of the complaints, I found the attitude of the barmaids most insidious. They now refused to serve me and called the Captain down from the bridge. He demanded that *I apologise to them*.

The Captain gave me an ultimatum, then called the river police. They boarded the boat, before the official end of the hire, though I have no idea why as the partygoers were all very well behaved. I think he wanted to go home early, if it wasn't just to spoil our party. Some might say I asked for this – yet a refund of little more than a quarter of the hire fee had seemed only reasonable, especially as it all went to charity.

Afterwards I went with Amanda, her sisters and Robert for an Indian meal in the restaurant run by a chap from *It Ain't Half Hot Mum* and I determined to sue the boat company again. At the dinner I handed Amanda a Holt's Bank cheque on the back of which I had written part of Robert Frost's *The Road Not Taken*. On the front of the cheque I had filled in the payee section: "Everything I have, only" and where the figures went: "The Lot." I signed the cheque without filling in the date. It was probably one of the more unusual uses of a Holt's cheque. The bank was an elite and unusual organisation and had been the original banker to the Army and Navy. In fact the bank had been the originator of the expression "keeping a tally". This involved making nicks on a stick of wood to show that soldiers or sailors had been paid, the stick on which the nicks were made being called a tally-stick, and the making of the nicks "keeping a tally". Holt's was used by MI6 during the Falklands War when a secret account had been set up from which any available Exocet missiles were bought to prevent them falling into the hands of the Argentinians. When at university I would visit the bank and be greeted by a doorman wearing white gloves who would escort me over to the cashiers. They had a record of how my signature had gradually decayed from something more or less legible to something approaching a straight line. I would later make the comparison between my signature and a read-out of a heartbeat. When my signature became a purely straight line perhaps I would be dead.

A few weeks after my second boat party *The Marchioness* disaster happened, which did not come as a surprise, not with people like that lot in charge of river-going vessels. I collected 28 letters of complaint from my partygoers all eager to have their complaints heard. Some of the complaints were matters of purely personal insult, including one from a person who complained he was told by a member of the crew that he looked like Scooby Doo. I attempted another court action but became busy elsewhere and the delay in the court procedure stopped me seeing it through to victory. It seemed the partygoers had been conspired against that night – and when I looked at all the letters of complaint I had procured it did not seem I had imagined this. And the conspiracy seemed evidently more than one simply caused by my being a disgruntled litigant. What Robert Hubert might have thought one can only imagine.

****

Now, on the bridge, it was clear: *The Marchioness* disaster was simply an

SBS/Comic Relief stunt in which there were no fatalities. If only – Laurence Dallaglio the England rugby player, whose sister drowned that night, would say.

****

The next year I got one of my helpers to book the party, and on the night that same Captain refused to embark with me on board. He walked up and down the gangplank suggesting to people he thought he recognised them and asking whether they knew me. Eventually somebody said "Yes, he's over there." I moped off to *The Tattershall Castle* boat-pub with Robert whilst the Captain took the party out into the North Sea – away from all the pretty sights, the bemused Railroad Earth entertaining the partygoers. Railroad Earth was sailing away from me in more ways than one. For after they released a track on my record label's first CD they would leave to record their album and two singles with REM's manager, Jefferson Holt, on his own label: Dog Gone Records. I could not compete with their millions. As for dogs departing you can be the judge of that.

Years later, and quite ill, I felt sure these strange events were down to my inviting the Prime Minister and the resultant presence of the Special Forces. If British Intelligence really did have my KGB file it was hardly surprising, in paranormal terms, that something pretty funny would happen – and that was quite apart from the Robert Hubert faux pas. Reading back through the letters years later, and wondering if it is too late to take action for the second party, it seems most unfortunate that the crew had gone to the lengths they had to spoil our evening. I wondered how much Intelligence paid Comic Relief to get the Captain to play those dirty tricks. There was some evidence the company had targeted certain people whilst others claimed not to notice anything was wrong. Most people would say that's an appalling claim to make but in the world of my developing delusional mindset and the Absolute Secret files I read, it looked rather conspiratorial. Where military intelligence is concerned, nothing, including dirty tricks, is out of the question provided it produces the desired outcome.

****

I continued my walk across the bridge under which the boat party would preferred to have gone, for the view and the lights, instead of out to sea. I turned left past St. Mary's church where Patrick Troughton was speared by a stake flying from the steeple in *The Omen*. Next I walked past Fulham Football Ground. Close by I noticed the spot where Suzie Lamplugh's car had been found after she was abducted and murdered by Mr Kipper. A boat party went past and all seemed fine. I thought back to the highlights of my three boat parties, although I had only been at two.

Soon I was at Hammersmith Bridge. This I crossed, passing an old plaque on the handrail announcing: *Lieutenant Charles Campbell Wood RAF. of Bloemfontein South Africa dived from this spot into the Thames at midnight 27th December 1919 and saved a woman's life. He died from the injuries received during the rescue.* He should have jumped. Then I took the towpath to Chiswick Bridge having made the decision to jump off it. Perhaps if I had actually read the plaque at the time, and not later, I would have decided otherwise. As I crept down the towpath in the dark I felt an air of secrecy and mystery about what I was doing – I was almost enjoying myself. Why was I doing this? That is an easy question to answer – I was in a hypermanic state. This was made far worse by a mistaken prescription of antidepressants – and now some alcohol too. I had no intention to kill myself, or even make a demonstration. In fact I had been vividly minded to crash my car off the bridge on an earlier occasion; somebody was testing me with that thought – and the idea came via my MTRUTH. I even reasoned that if, upon approaching the bridge in my car, I found there to be a diversion, this would mean I was not to do so. I also decided I must check to see that no masonry could come through the windscreen as I crashed through the balustrade, and that being the case, I thought I would be quite capable of pulling off the stunt.

Now I was at the bridge – it was late and dark, and I climbed over the balustrade. This now concentrated my mind and I had to consider the likely outcome of my decision to jump – should I do so. The possibilities included: landing on a floating railway sleeper and being crippled and drowned; surfacing and swimming away to the brewery; being drowned under water by the Special Boat Service; or disappearing under water because the Service had a miniature submarine ready to smuggle me away to Buckingham Palace. What did not occur to me was that I was not near the middle of the stream and the water may not have been deep enough for a safe jump.

Even if I just swam away, there was a powerful feeling that I was being watched in everything I did. This was an intuitive feeling due not merely to my belief I had an MTRUTH fitted, but also because I believed I was thinking along the same lines as MI5 – who knew all about me.

I was unable to decide whether to jump or not and found myself in a crouched position hidden from the traffic. Two days previously I had telephoned Amanda's father under the pretext that I was having a party. He asked me if I knew she was now married, and I feigned indifference, took down her phone number, said goodbye, put the phone down and broke down completely. I could not accept, and was not capable of believing, that what I had been told was the truth. She had never said goodbye to me. As I hung off the edge of the bridge, I formulated in my mind the possibility that the person I had been speaking to on the phone, ostensibly her father, was actually a GCHQ officer mimicking him by speaking through a voice-morphing box.

So there I was, at approaching midnight on 6th September 1994, deciding whether to jump or not, and, as they say, your whole life flashes before your eyes. I had already proved that to be true during the nostalgic walk from my flat. But at this moment the sound of a dog barking urgently in Mortlake cemetery distracted me from jumping. Why might there be a dog in the locked Mortlake cemetery at midnight? Whose dog was it? I was intrigued. Let me now take you back to April/May of that year – and in particular a most peculiar event on 29th May.

Part III

A Request for Some Scrumpy, and a Strange Event

Chapter Three

Solsbury Hill

I have called this chapter Solsbury Hill for two reasons. Firstly, because *Solsbury Hill* is the title of one of the most classic of all pieces of modern music, whose lyrics could easily serve as an anthem for this story, and secondly because next to the hill in question is a lesser known hill – Bannerdown Hill. This was the scene of the most profound, extraordinary and supernatural experience in my life. What I saw on Bannerdown Hill felt like a revelation. If it had not been for Solsbury Hill, I'd probably never have known of Bannerdown Hill.

But the song was only ultimately responsible for leading me to Bannerdown Hill. Other things had drawn me to Wiltshire – like, as I came to believe during that summer, my MTRUTH. As I was drawn there I had a completely inexplicable feeling, which seemed beyond mystical. So profound was the experience that it really shocked me with the most deep-seated intuitive dread I have ever encountered. Real terror was yet to be experienced. Imagine you accidentally discovered a truth so terrible you wished you had never discovered it. That was how it felt. However amusing events of that day now seem, it was a frighteningly profound experience at the time. What happened at Bannerdown Hill? Let me tell you.

One lunchtime during early April of that year, 1994, I was at work at DOAE where I had been brought in, according to the Lieutenant Colonel, to "sort out the problem once and for all". I went to get my sandwiches in the local Waitrose supermarket. I recall standing at the fishmonger's counter and having a strange feeling that perhaps somebody was playing a joke on me or that I was being watched. It was only much later that I perceived the significance of it, but at the time it just seemed spooky and I had no idea why – I did not think of MTRUTH, at least not quite yet. The significance was that this was the moment in my life when I first experienced schizophrenia – aged nearly 33.

Now that was certainly a key moment – but it was not the only one. I was sitting in my Austin A35 in the slow-moving traffic going west along Mortlake High Street. As I sat there in the traffic I glanced to my right and saw a poster showing James Hunt promoting a motoring event. The fact that James Hunt, like me, drove an Austin A35 only made this feel more peculiar. I arrived at work to learn that James Hunt had died that morning, and that he had died very close to the time I saw his face on the poster. Some magical force, like MTRUTH, had given me foreknowledge of the announcement of Mr Hunt's death. The Security Services had arranged this.

This reminded me of the occasion when the engine of my A35 blew up – a quite frightening event. My old friend Ario, half Iranian, half Iraqi, had grabbed a lift from me for the one and only time, and the explosion made a loud crunching smashing sound as a con rod blasted a hole in the side of the engine casing. Now it was clear; this was all the work of the Special Intelligence Service. Even the most innocent parking of a Lebanese girl's pink Austin A30 next to mine years earlier during my PhD days in Surrey now set my most farfetched paranoid thoughts going about interference from one or another intelligence organisation. But what if I knew of Mr Hunt's death before the event? The implications were very disturbing, and I was disturbed.

My brother Tom had bought a new car; its number plate contained the letters UTM. To me this meant Universal Transverse Mercator, a kind of map projection I was using at work. I felt utterly paranoid in an almost pleasant way about it. This type of projection, UTM, was the one used in the computer model for the Apache anti-tank helicopter effectiveness study. MI5 had chosen that number plate and manipulated him into buying this particular car. I later said something to him that was indicative of my paranoia, and he just shook his head dismissively.

I had somehow become addicted to BBC Radio 1. The explanation for this was quite straightforward. I had been trying to launch my record label and had approached the DJ Mark Goodier, of BBC Radio 1. This I did in order to have something interesting to put in my newsletter and to provide a vehicle to give him a copy of the album I had released by the band Crystal Trip. It transpired that he brought the road show to Bedford, and perhaps I missed an opportunity. But by then I was becoming very unwell in that I was beginning to have unrealistic thoughts about the situation, and that really was the end of the label. I began to experience powerful feelings that I was receiving messages from the radio and that pieces of music put on were somehow aimed at me. I did not fight these feelings, as I liked them in one respect since they gave me an enormous sense of power. Perhaps my record label was going to be a great success after all! This made the feelings very dangerous to the point where I have little doubt that the Radio 1 controller would be easily able, should the need arise, to quite literally drive somebody in that state of mind over Beachy Head, again. My feelings of power were confused by contrary feelings that I was also under attack, which certainly affected my brain chemistry in some way.

During the Apache study, at my request, I had an Army Major sitting next to me. He told me he was getting married and somehow I did not quite believe him; it was as though he was saying *I* should be getting married. There was someone called Amanda Cadwallader working at DOAE, and I felt rather uncomfortable with her name seeming to recall it being the name of a villain in the 1960s *Batman* series. I was not really appreciating the power I had, being unaware that Cadwaladr was a 7th century Welsh king, instead resorting to wildly pertinent thoughts that the Amanda I had known was with somebody of profound disrepute. Cadwallader wasn't the girl's real name, and perhaps even more so, if it was, instead of grasping this source of power, I was cowered by it.

I filled in an employee satisfaction form with very low scores and left it on the table. The next day the Major marched into the room and straight over to where the form was, deliberately making me think he somehow knew it was there and I was under his surveillance. Then he came over and asked me *The Question* to which I replied enigmatically. To my mind *The Question* related to the singing of *Jerusalem* that day in morning assembly back at my old school, as recorded accurately in my KGB file, a copy of which was now in the hands of MI6. It seemed *The Question* was one and the same *Question* that had been asked at the 1926 meeting.

The situation was so profound we each knew what the other was thinking but discussed the matter no more. For myself, his remark, which I felt had been directed by Military Intelligence, or MI6 itself, also seemed to be a question about how long it would take to write a book entitled *The Question*. This went back to the 1926 meeting, the SALT talks in 1972 and the concreted-over foot of the garden in Ruislip – quite an impressive conspiracy. He had asked the question of me in my role as an MI6 Soviet double agent – though at the time I had not quite developed the delusion, belief, or actual knowledge I was one. And if I had I had forgotten for the time being. Nevertheless my mind wished to construct some immense scheme, which I myself was the subject of. This would involve anything from a conversation with Adolf Hitler in the Berghof to the disappearance of the World Cup in 1966, the cup being found by a dog named Pickles out on a walk. I wished to be the hero in all of this.

But I felt I was in terminal decay, rather like the former Soviet Union. My shoes were leaking and somehow I seemed incapable of rectifying the decline. I felt like I was sitting in a pool of piss left by some dossers in the corner of a room in the empty, abandoned Libyan Embassy, the window partly open, the worn curtains flapping spookily in the draught, pigeons cooing on the windowsill, and inches of their droppings all over the floor.

One day, as I left my flat in Barnes, I had the most convincing feeling that I was being spied on from the observation deck atop the distant Empress State Building, and from the van parked outside the house. Certainly the roof of that distant building would provide an excellent vantage point from which to spy on my front door, without risk of detection, using optical equipment. I heard a voice in my head saying "I am associating my own physical and mental health with that of the nation." *It did not seem to come from me.* Over the summer of 1994 I would come to believe it came through my MTRUTH.

These feelings of terminal decline were then interspersed with feelings of awesome power, like the afternoon when the phone rang but no one was there when I answered it. The strange call seemed to say "I'm waiting for you" and I believed it and left work early. I got in my car and at the moment I passed the security gate, Phil Collins' song about 'terrorism', *We Wait and We Wonder,* came on the radio and I felt that it had all been co-ordinated. It was clear the song was also about me and what a hero I was going to be. In fact I already was. *I was the most powerful person on the planet.* I could make the *QE II* hover I was so powerful. My whole life started here.

Another afternoon, as I drove back towards London, a song was playing which had the line, "He's coming in my direction", or something similar, and I felt the creeps like never before. It was some kind of intuitive fear. The line referred to me! Now wait a minute, there's something going on here, I thought, and became convinced that my flat was bugged. I drove straight back to it, even though it was Friday when I would normally go to Bedford, to see friends and family.

When I got to my flat I rushed in and tore the covering off my mattress, looking for a bug. If it was there, it was there because of *The Question*, I believed. I had certainly been bitten a number of times but was looking for something electronic. I was beginning to think if there really was a bug in the bed, I would have difficulty finding it unless I shredded the mattress into tiny pieces. As for my own body, I was certainly not prepared at this stage to conduct any internal examination, though I was aware of others who had taken to looking for bugs in their wrist by cutting into it. I remembered the call on my answering machine from the chap saying he was coming in from Moscow, as well as those for Avro Travel. I retaliated by calling international directory inquiries and asking for the number of the Texas School Book Depository (from which President Kennedy was shot). That'll get GCHQ thinking, I thought, imagining a personal computer at Menwith Hill (the Government's eavesdropping station), which had a blue flashing light and siren attached, both of which went off whenever I made a call. My flat seemed to be enveloped in a nauseous cloud, and so was I.

Then there were the dogs – almost as if I was being readied for what was to happen. I think it started with the story of Ollie, a German Shepherd dog reported by *The Daily Telegraph* to have found his way home all the way from Staffordshire to Derbyshire. Something fascinated me about the story, which amused me in some way. It seemed a little unlikely to start with. I also seemed to be hearing a lot of dog noises and references to them on BBC Radio 1 and I was certain there was some reason for this. In particular one record then in the chart by Crystal Waters called *100% Pure Love* appeared to have a dog sampled on it and I could not but help make the connection with Ollie. I told Tom I could hear dogs on the radio and once again he shook his head like a fatigued psychiatrist. He then said, quite laughably, "No Clive, there are no dogs." I began looking for and expecting dog references in the media and feeling pleased when I spotted one, or thought I had. A record by the group It Bites was playing. I was bitten. Next one by Eighth Wonder with the line "Tonight the streets are full of actors, I don't know why" came on. I would think to myself: there you are, I'm not imagining it, because as well as the dogs I had begun to feel some sort of actors were following me. But again there were horrendously sinister feelings associated with these 'actors'. It was somehow as though they were empty shells of humanity who had been released from a factory after reprogramming – a factory I would later find in the psychiatric ward of an NHS hospital. The only record the NHS would have of these poor people was a file lost down the back of a filing cabinet within the dark and dusty recesses of the Department of Health. They were all robots and I could see no soul in them.

Feeling I was being watched I began to do some things in a manner designed to make those spying on me, using my MTRUTH or otherwise, ask, "Why has he done that?" I did these things even though I knew it was possible nobody was watching me – *it just felt like they were*. Some of the things I did were obviously bizarre, but I did not see it that way; it just seemed a reasonably logical response to the situation – like seeking the number of the Book Depository at international directory inquiries. I called Uttoxeter racecourse from work, told them I had a friend flying in from America and asked them for details of the aerodrome. Laughably or tragically, probably both, I did this because the racecourse had been near where Ollie had disappeared. The person on the other end did not seem in the least surprised by this request and gave me the conning tower frequencies. Of course it was a fiction; I only did it for the same reason I tried to get the number of the Book Depository. And, at least at the time, it did not seem such a ridiculous thought that my calls might have been monitored because I was working on the Apache anti-tank helicopter procurement programme.

One morning, for no apparent reason, Steve Wright, the Radio 1 DJ, asked, "Are there aliens in the Ministry of Defence?" Certainly there were now aliens in my mind, and he had put them there with demonstrable consequences, as I will explain. He also played the well-known song which goes "Every time you go away, you take a piece of me with you" but then said "Every time you go away, you take a piece of *meat* with you", this doing nothing to allay my dog obsession or stop me cracking up laughing: Quite insane. I thought of the pulsar story and the Joy Division album sleeve. My state of mind led me to question its veracity.

I sent some faxes to Radio 1, and on one or two occasions received a definite response. One of these was when I sent a mad fax about the Book Depository and cod and asparagus bake (seriously), which amused the DJ Anne Nightingale enough to read it out on the air. But I was not quite able to disengage from the radio to which my head seemed locked, and began to feel strange hypnotic effects from it. I even started believing there were subliminal messages superimposed at some stage in the broadcasting process, whether through the radio or on my MTRUTH. I thought it might be possible that everyone was physically receiving the acoustic energy, but only I was sensitive to it, or perhaps it was being superimposed in my near vicinity. This led me to have suspicions about those in the adjacent flats. I seemed to be able to hear sinister dripping, scraping and knocking sounds from the one on the south side. It seemed to be a disturbing mixture of Chinese water torture and hypnosis.

In addition, the person in that flat had spent months knocking and banging and I began to believe it was some kind of psychological attack I was under. He was a Canadian with the suspicious name of Oscar Aarts – which only increased my suspicions that actors surrounded me. One day I found his address book in the street and felt it might have been put there deliberately for some reason. I posted it back through his door.

The bank holiday weekend was approaching, and I had an overwhelming feeling of expectation. I was totally convinced that something fantastic was going to happen to me. I began to imagine things like an Army helicopter landing in the playing field opposite and taking me off to somewhere nothing less than mythical. *(What's The Story?) Morning Glory* later captured this daydream. I thought of the Major banging on my front door at 0800 hours. As in the song, probably being written at that very moment, I needed a little time to wake up. Funnily, the name of the operation I was imagining was Operation "Wake Up"[12], at least that was what I would soon believe. This was a real military operation in which I took a leading role – not just some bizarre concoction of my mind – in which I was such a complete hero the Army would indeed send a helicopter for me one morning.

Radio 1 was really tightening the pressure on me. I paced up and down my flat. *Tubular Bells* was being played. It was the early '70s; I was Richard Branson and was about to make it big. A helicopter buzzed the flat, shaking the whole building. I had been picked out and nurtured by the Special Intelligence Service – and now it was all coming to fruition. The Radio 1 DJ, Steve Lamacq, kept announcing "Keep calm, heavy interference in this area." What area? I had no idea but could only take the message literally. I looked out of the rear window and, mysteriously, a Japanese woman was sitting at a window opposite. It felt like I was temporarily trapped in a scene from Hitchcock's *Rear Window*.

To and fro I walked expectantly, looking out of the rear window each time I got to it. Again, I had a strange experience. Suddenly, out of nowhere, a cat appeared standing on the top of the tree, where the original top had been lopped off. I could not believe that it had simply run up it. But I could reason it was some elaborate illusion. Then, overhead, some eight hundred to a thousand feet up, I saw a hovering helicopter and thought the cat had been lowered there from it. The pub cat, Pepper, had disappeared, as a notice above the bar in The Red Lion pub announced. The sign said "It Bites", the name of the band I mentioned. This seemed most mysterious. The cat atop the tree, which strongly resembled the pub cat, now disappeared too, making me wonder if it had ever been there to start with. I was in a most odd frame of mind and even thought its presence was an optical illusion put on by Professor Dainty (who had overseen my MSc in Applied Optics at Imperial College of Science and Technology). I went next door and asked the lady if I could look in her garden. She said she had guests but I was welcome to go around the back. I thought she might be under instructions from these guests. They were MI5 agents.

Around the back of the flat, I found a pile of For Sale signs, which seemed odd. The previous occupants of my flat had all met some horrible fate, and the house had never really been for sale, this accounting in some way for the pile of signs.[13] I had been deceived into believing the flat had been in my ownership. It was just a Soviet/MI6 training department safe house left over from the Cold War. I remembered how the deeds said the previous owner had the same name as a murdered homosexual butcher by the name of Spiteri whom I had read about in the paper.

I looked in the garden but could see no sign of the cat. Being that the cat was called Pepper, I thought of Pepper's Ghost, a famous optical illusion, and a chill went through me. It all seemed so mysterious and perplexing.

I did what the radio had said and laid low in my flat. No doubt something big was going to happen. I thought the plan was that soon I would be dead, with another For Sale sign outside the flat and this too would be dumped around the back. But I felt I was too clever not to avoid that fate. I remembered a Woolwich "Sold" postcard I had spotted on the lawn. It was a display of power and control by the Security Services running this operation. Later I got its meaning: it was a leaked message to me about the forthcoming float of the Woolwich Building Society. Once the float was announced the memory of the card on the lawn came with a heavy paranoia weighing the same as several million such cards.

Then one night, heavily intoxicated by unsuspected mental illness associated with listening to the radio, I was going off to sleep and heard, *or thought I heard*, the oddest piece of news on BBC Radio 1. It was that a dog had been spotted flying low in a light aircraft near Uttoxeter racecourse. I could only laugh. I went to sleep. Upon waking the next morning, at 7am, on came my radio and, within seconds, I broke the world record for waking up and being reduced to paralytic laughter. The news was *"Prince Charles's dog, Pooh, has gone missing."* A massive burst of energy entered my body.

Suddenly I had become some sort of sociological singularity. This was all just a gigantic joke, presaged by the previous night's news bulletin. So why did I not, even for a moment, consider this was anything other than joke? I did not think about it until later, so convulsed with laughter was I. I finally thought it through 'logically' and then I knew that there was only one proper way to proceed: by going back to the Vale of Glamorgan by-election result. I had written a jocular article about it in which a politician's house burnt down, he and his entire family had been murdered, but his dog was still out campaigning for him and, as losing election candidates always say, he (the dog) was "building for the future". My campaign was only just beginning. I felt I had just discovered an enormous source of power. And therefore I *had* discovered an enormous source of power. There was no doubt about it. *This was massive.* I did not even think of Dog Gone Records.

That morning on the way to work I heard Steve Wright announce that there was going to be a wild-goose chase. How right he was. At work, for whatever reason, I said to the Major that Richard Branson and MI5 were following me. He replied "...and pigs might fly". I was not to see the Major again. Well, not quite, as you will later see.

I went to get my lunch as usual at the local supermarket. On the way back I noticed a van parked outside the entrance gates on the other side of the road, and facing towards London. The driver appeared to be looking at a map or something on the passenger seat, but I gained the impression that he was merely pretending to look at it, and in fact he had just been told to do so. The van said on the side "Tigga Hygiene" and had little trouble making me think of Prince Charles's dog, Pooh. I had a feeling I should report the van to security. It seemed the Special Intelligence Service, *or somebody,* had parked the van there for me to see. It was most eerie. My later discovery that actually it was the local council's dog-waste bin contractor hardly lessened this eeriness. What seemed more eerie was that three times I had found my car offside rearview mirror had been broken during the night. Then on the way to work one day a sort of gunge had hit my windscreen: a gunge which, upon inspection, looked like it might be some kind of alien matter whose presence on earth was quite inexplicable. I almost gave up having the mirror mended. On another day the cam belt went and in a laughable situation with an RAC man my engine got written off. I suspected the belt had been cut and moreover that I was being deliberately interfered with.

I left work, and it was as though the very helicopters in the model I had been working on were now swarming around me. I imagined that Prince Charles's dog and I had miraculously appeared on the computer-generated battlefield but, unlike the units in the battlefield, I still had some free will. I took cover in the woods near the village of Ripley and felt a great sense of security as a helicopter flew overhead above the trees. I could feel something. I could almost touch it – it was this feeling I had MTRUTH and that it was switched on.

To seek reassurance I made a phone call to my old tutor, another Soviet agent who I thought had not been on the electoral register since the '60s, and expressed my suspicions about the announcement that Camelot had been awarded the lottery, suspecting that Camelot was really Richard Branson's company. There seemed something intangibly conspiratorial and elusive about the award – which fascinated me as though I was close to some magnificent truth. I got back in the car and saw a helicopter flying towards Gatwick and the urge to follow it was overwhelming. To Gatwick I went. There I found myself hanging around in the departure hall, not quite sure what I was doing and expecting something to happen. My presence had been required there for security reasons, my MTRUTH being used in passive mode.

From Gatwick I drove off down firstly to Brighton, heavily confused and somehow in search of, if not a Jack Russell, I knew not what. I got to Brighton and remembered being on the seafront there with Amanda and felt sad and nostalgic. I still loved her but had no idea what had happened to her. I remembered a poem I had written for her.

Autumn

Realised rarely are our lovely dreams,
But in a dream it was conceived,
So in hope I stepped out today.
Exulting now, I remember luck and love,
As such as they were first perceived.
And so such weather moves me more,
Kicking leaves beneath the trees,
Through which autumn beams,
Crisp, cold happiness,
As summer's green forsakes the sunlight,
Which we accept,
As did then the opaque sky,
It wrapped us in as time went by.
And time went by for no man,
Who savoured as did I,
As night drew nigh,
Your longing face;
How I wish it longed for I.

I now made for Eastbourne, and then to The Six Bells pub at Chiddingly, where my friend Caroline Lavelle, the cellist singer/songwriter, was living at the time. Her landlord next to the pub, Ken, was ex-SAS (he really was) and had an impressive collection of vintage motorbikes, including an old Wilkinson, made by the same company who produce razorblades.

For whatever reason I did not make my presence known to her, even though she was my friend and only next door, but instead went into the pub alone. Sitting at the bar were two people having a conversation. They were talking about dogs and at some point in the conversation one of them said that they, whoever "they" were, had "shot the dog through another one." I did not really know what they meant. It would seem the two dogs were fighting ferociously and there was no time to get an aim on the target dog so the other dog had to be sacrificed. Very odd I felt, and what with my newfound obsession with dogs, it only added to the mystery. "They" knew I was there somehow and the words were meant for me. "They" could only be the Special Intelligence Service. I bought a drink and the bargirl apologised for giving me eight one pound coins saying she had no five pound notes. I found myself examining the pound coins in my change and noticed they were all 1983 ones. It did not occur to me that most pound coins are 1983 ones because that was the year the pound coin was first minted. Instead I decided, and believed, the coins had been deliberately sorted to remind me of my good times in 1983 with Amanda. They were manipulating me and there was no doubt about it.

I headed off again through Kent, eventually arriving back at the flat quite late, and drained further psychologically. I wondered: had the conversation been spontaneous or was it somehow aimed at me? I also wondered if they were not talking of firearms when they said, "shoot" but of filming. The dogs had MTRUTHs and, like with mine, the Special Intelligence Service could film through their eyes.

The next morning was the Saturday of the bank holiday weekend and there seemed to be a lot of very flash high-powered motorbikes around. I did not think they were simply out to enjoy the weather. They seemed to have been put there, and were somehow inviting me, guiding me, encouraging me, but I did not know what to do. And perhaps it was only once or twice that somebody went past me, jogging a few steps in my immediate vicinity – but it felt like many more. It somehow disturbed me: there seemed something cultish and dangerous about it. Their behaviour seemed designed to affect me psychologically.

I went into the pub intrigued and having precisely no idea how to respond or proceed. There were some glamorous people in there about to go to a wedding. The landlady came around putting lucky heather in the small vases on the tables, wishing me good day as she did so. This was auspicious and only confirmed my feeling all were behind me, that is I had plenty of support in this venture – whatever it was. I returned to my flat ready to depart. I played *It's History* by The Comsat Angels, doing so because I believed it *was* history. That was the power of Prince Charles's dog in my mind.

At some point I decided to drive down to Wiltshire. I knew aliens were said to have landed at Warminster earlier in the twentieth century, and I was thinking about what Steve Wright had said about "aliens in the MoD". Perhaps I was also thinking about things I had not even noticed. But I wanted to know what was going on and I felt that by going there I might find out.

But first of all I was feeling lonely and had developed a hypnotically induced attachment to the Radio 1 DJ, Lynn Parsons. Perhaps it was some sort of Stockholm syndrome – where you become attached to your tormentor. I believed she lived in New Malden and I made a ludicrous token visit there as if she was going to come to Wiltshire with me. Here I have no doubt I was suffering acute erotomania otherwise known as de Clerambault's syndrome, a condition in which the sufferer becomes convinced that he, or more usually she, is loved by someone who does not know they exist. I drove into a garage to fill up.

On the radio the DJ, Danny Baker, said "Where is Prince Charles's dog? Perhaps we will find it today." I thought back to Ollie, as well as the various other dogs I had heard of whose exploits brought them fame. There was Bobbie, a collie from Silverton, Oregon, who was said to have followed his master's car three thousand miles home, taking over six months, making Ollie's feat almost everyday. I had heard of a dog that delivered *The Daily Telegraph* to subscribers in Yarmouth in 1869 and, given the military nature of events as I saw them, I could not possibly forget to mention the equally unlikely story, given the presence of the English Channel, of Prince, an Irish terrier and mascot of the Staffordshire Regiment in 1914. Prince was owned by Private James Brown of the 1st Battalion, North Staffordshire Regiment. When the battalion went to France on 12th September 1914, Prince was left behind. On 27th September Mrs Brown wrote to her husband that the dog had gone missing. In fact, it is said, Prince had travelled over 200 miles through southern England, crossed the

Channel and then, after another 60 miles, rejoined his master in the trenches. But dogs were not just good at finding their way home over long journeys. There was a collie in Germany called Rico. It was able to correctly pick any of two hundred different toys from its collection when given the toy's name. It seemed to me the whole nation was in danger of missing a trick. If ordinary dogs such as these could perform such amazing feats what could Prince Charles's dog do? The newshounds who had descended on Balmoral to look for it when the small ad had been spotted were surely on the right lines but even they did not see the full potential of the animal. But for Danny Baker's remark, the news of the dog's mysterious disappearance had already died down. Only one person in this whole nation had seen the full and glorious potential that was now there. Prince Charles's dog would rise from its unknown grave (if any) to historical glory and I was the one to see that it did. Can you imagine how excited I felt at this?

I filled up with petrol, went through the car wash, and the Frankie Valli and the Four Seasons number *You're Ready Now* started playing on the radio – ready for what? Obviously to go and look for Prince Charles's dog. This entailed a lot. After all it was not just any old dog but the future King of Great Britain's dog. And it was about much more than even the corporeal substance of the Royal hound. The message was aimed at me. Several motorbikes went by. They were outriders providing me with an escort, gently guiding me in the right direction.

After a while I arrived at Aldershot, home of the British Army. I wanted to test the defences, as I was damn sure the Security Services were after me. I wanted to see if I could provoke some sort of response, possibly through the radio. Mark Goodier was on the air now and as I came through the security gate he said "You know he makes sense." I believed he was talking to me.

Soon I was driving past Middle Wallop, headquarters of the Army Air Corps, for whom I was working on the attack helicopter contract. An Army helicopter was now flying alongside me going in the same direction, though I still had no idea where I was going or what I was to do, other than head for Warminster. It had flown next to me on orders. Soon I was in Salisbury and I picked up two hitch-hikers, a young man and a woman. We chatted and, for whatever reason, I now said to the girl sitting in the front that I had Prince Charles's dog behind me. It seemed a reasonably logical thing to say at the time. Not surprisingly she looked around at her boyfriend as though to say, "What's he on?" But to me there was some kind of indisputable truth in what I had said; it was almost my duty to tell her.

I do not know if, when I said this, I had already decided to go to Warminster Police Station, and cannot remember what, if anything I had decided I might say, but I now asked the girl if she knew where Solsbury Hill was. I was not sure what to do. I was not too sure how I had got where I was, but whether or not I was going to do anything, I had to go to the hill first. Perhaps I did not need to do anything, I thought. But at the very least, now I was down there, I could not miss going to the hill if only out of a sense of curiosity. But I would not be going to the police station – I had bigger plans.

Australia is criss-crossed with the ancient aboriginal ley lines or songlines on which the aborigines go walkabout to the sacred places of the dreamtime – the time of the creation. It was as though I was on my own aboriginal walkabout and I was in search of my own dreamtime. I wondered whether what I was about to do would make perfect sense to an aborigine. I am sure it would to a poor

African child.

I was driving a red Rover 414Sli, made in England with a British engine; that was important too, for what I was about to do was a very British thing, if not Irish. Soon my car would become the Irish Rover.

As I drove from Warminster towards Solsbury Hill my radio reception began to deteriorate markedly and I felt surrounded by extraordinarily magical and mystical powers. Perhaps I *was* on a ley line. My reception was actively and steadily being jammed by GCHQ – this was the area Steve Lamacq had been talking about when his trailer kept announcing "Keep calm, heavy interference in this area." It seemed so natural and yet so strange. It never, even once, occurred to me that I might simply need to retune. I was now making my approach to the hill and, though I had never been there before, I believed I was on the correct course.

Then I saw the sign. It shocked me. It was a blue RAC notice directing traffic to the left – up Bannerdown Hill. It said "RAC Dog Show". If, because of Prince Charles's dog, that was not a revelation, then what would happen next certainly was. I was staggered and amazed, so drawn in was I. All seemed apocalyptic and revelational. I was caught up in a combined NATO/ex-Warsaw pact military manoeuvre. I had been brought there by some divine and supreme power. The military had made me go there using "all means available", including my MTRUTH. It certainly was an occasion when one is led to wonder what free will actually is, though if this was not existential behaviour I don't know what is[14].

I automatically turned left and with the change in direction my radio reception collapsed to almost nothing. The car was driving itself! Up the hill I went and, there by the road, was the biggest group of dogs I had ever seen. A whole field was totally full of dogs with a radio transmitter in the middle of it! There were literally thousands of dogs in the field.[15] The feeling of dread when I saw the dogs was overwhelming. Okay, it was just a field of dogs, and not one of angels, but in my state of mind I was totally staggered. Thinking I had been lured there, it seemed that if I stopped and got out to look for the Prince's dog (he had offered a reward for its return, as you saw in the small ad), I might be shot. I was so paranoid I thought I might nearly have been shot anyway as I drove past. Two SAS soldiers had disobeyed orders and decided not to shoot me at the last moment. Now they were with me.

Still I was imagining a well-defined series of events, which linked me with the alleged meeting in 1926, the first of the Special Intelligence Service. There was nothing in the least bit funny about it. I was frightened beyond belief. I drove straight past the dogs and turning right, went down a road I hoped would lead to Peter Gabriel's house and his recording studio, Real World.

I was back on the main road and saw a shop. It was called Hobby Horse. I stopped, got out and stared in through the window with my hand held like a visor to help me see what was in there. "Don't look a gift horse in the mouth" I said to myself, and I felt as though I were on some ultra-dangerous treasure trail. Now I headed for Solsbury Hill and, visiting the anti-road camp, I entered my name in the book before ascending the hill. Near the top I met some strange creatures standing like country fairies, almost in a bush as though they lived in it. Their hair was in dreadlocks and I imagine they indeed lived in a grotto under it, inside Solsbury Hill.

One of them, who looked a little like Lizzie Dripping[16], asked me if I was the farmer, doing so in such an inoffensive way it was almost as though, if you were in their company, you would never have a care in the world. I spoke to a cow, and all the other cows stared back at me. I got to the top. Looking up, I saw an Army Hercules transport plane eerily flying over quite high up, heading west. Needless to say, I thought this had something to do with me, no doubt involving surveillance.

I descended the hill and as I came down, having already signed the visitors' book in the anti-road camp at the bottom before the ascent, I formulated my plan of attack. During my descent I passed the anti-road pixies again and returned to the anti-road campaign book. In it, I wrote a demand I was to repeat later that day. But I had not yet decided to whom or where. After the demand I wrote "...and I want some scrumpy and my car serviced." I was to get both. Having done this, there was really only one possible correct and logical response to this set of circumstances. As I had driven through Salisbury I had noticed the sign: "Her Majesty's Land Forces UK Headquarters". I headed off to find it.

I was still hypnotised into believing that my radio was being jammed, but as I moved away from what I risibly deduced had been the landing site for the alien dogs, reception improved a little. Where the transmitter was, reception had been poor because, I thought, of jamming and not the more obvious explanation of blind spots near it. All the battlefield simulations I had been working on now seemed to have unfolded on the countryside around me. I was part of the software and, as in the line from *Solsbury Hill*, I had "walked right out of the machinery". What truth was there in this? Well, if I had now got an MTRUTH fitted, the truth was that the software was part of me. Now I was wargaming for real with 'alien' dogs. Of course I did not really believe they were aliens, it was just a military war game I had to play. In the mindset of the Security Services, mere members of the public and of dog clubs practically *were* aliens. I was trapped in an edition of *Doctor Who*, and if I did not do something dramatic pretty quickly I would be swept away and drowned in the stream of consciousness. Basically I wanted somebody, the right person, to know I believed something was going on, and I wasn't going down without a fight.

On the way back to Wilton, where the HQ was, I felt a force trying to make me go back to Bannerdown Hill and at a Y junction there were some motorcyclists, again on high-powered machines. They were turning around and it seemed they were trying, pretty desperately, to make me do so too and return to the hill. But whereas on Solsbury Hill in the company of those pixies I had not a care in the world, now I felt in mortal danger. My mind was almost being torn apart, whether by my MTRUTH, the motorcyclists, or just my own tortured thoughts, making me think I had to do what they wanted. But I did not, and the nearer I got to Wilton the less this force pulled me.

As I approached the turning to HQ a Toyota MR2 overtook me going even faster and the person driving reminded me of Adrian Gibson, an old friend in the music industry, although I hardly got a good look at him. Moving at some speed he turned left and so, somehow, I had to also. By the time I had turned, he was well off down the road but I kept close enough to see him turn into the entrance of HQ. He came straight out again. The meaning seemed obvious: if I did not go in through that gate I was in serious trouble.

Still I did not know what exactly was going to happen and when I got to HQ I decided there was something else I needed to do first. This of course was to drive to Stonehenge. I say "of course" because there was no reason other than what I suppose was just natural politeness, which I did not even think about, it being an historical situation to me. I travelled there at some speed and soon was parked, with the engine running, directly facing the stones only a few yards away. This seemed almost ceremonious, exactly as I had intended and it seemed the whole of the history of these isles was egging me on. I wondered what the henge's builders would think of an MTRUTH.

Now I was ready. I had been fully trained, in spirit, for the manoeuvre I was about to carry out, by Lieutenant Commander D.G. "Digger"" Roberts when in the school Combined Cadet Force on camp in Ampthill Park. Then, on a route march, we had got points for bringing a police officer back to our camp. Evening was upon the stones and, again at some speed, I headed off back to Wilton. I drove past the gate and turned round. "My heart was going boom, boom" as in *Solsbury Hill*. I was facing a horrendous mixture of both danger and possible complete humiliation, whatever I did. If I drove in the gate, my career could be over as my security clearance would be withdrawn. I knew I had MTRUTH. Moreover I wanted it to be known I knew – that I had worked it out. But I wanted to be *told* I had MTRUTH. So this seemed a required career move. If I did not drive in through the gate I would regret it forever.

I drove back and forth. This time. No, once more up the road and back and then I'll do it, I thought. I will drive in through the gate. I had my Ministry of Defence Security identity card. I parked and tried to think of what I would say. The sun sank lower. Again I had an excuse to put it off. When the sun goes down then I'll do it, I thought, and remembered the song *Sun Goes Down* by Killing Joke. It seemed most fitting. It must be when the sun goes down. If I do not do this I will be right, with nothing. On the other hand, if I do it I will be wrong with everything and left with nothing, I thought, peculiarly. It seemed to me that everyone else was facing the same dilemma, a disturbing piece of knowledge to have depending on which way you looked at it. I had to drive in through the gate. My whole life had become a bomb and, again in the words of the song that is the title of this chapter, I did not know "which connection I should cut". I was in a quandary.

I drove off again. I must have driven up and down past the entrance maybe twenty times, not having the courage to do it. I was almost a salesman proffering a rather odd piece of reality: I was a door-to-door MTRUTH sales executive – but nobody had told me what I was selling. I just had to use my skill and judgment in matters of intuition on the battlefield to close the sale. In reality I might as well have gone in and shown them my record collection, though I did not have much of it with me, *just* my Peter Gabriel tape to my recollection.

I watched the last rays of sunlight beam through the trees. Now was the time. In through the gate I went and parked. Guards approached the car. I was ordered to get out. I imagined smoke grenades begin to go off, the sound of machine gun fire nearby and the drone of a hovering helicopter overhead. I showed my pass with my hands up and was ordered to the ground, imagined guns pointing at me from every direction. "So you were expecting me gentlemen?" I said, rather like James Bond – I was so cool. MI5 knew I was there and had informed HM Land Forces HQ before I arrived – this accounting for the impressive and polite welcome I received. But this also raised the possibility that my presence there was not down to my behaviour that day being existentially well founded after all. My presence there was down to no one but MI5 and the Special Intelligence Service. They were responsible for this uncommon situation. I had been brought here using my MTRUTH.

I felt the muzzle of a gun in the back of my neck - but this one was real. I was searched and ordered to stand up. I was marched into the guardhouse at gunpoint – no free will evident there – I was just doing what I was told. I had believed I was expected and now it seemed obvious I was. They sat me down at the desk and I asked to make a statement. I made the statement, which involved Prince Charles's dog, an alien space ship crewed by intelligent dogs from Sirius the Dog Star, Bannerdown Hill, the BBC, an operation to place electronic implants in my body and a payment of £10 million to Comic Relief which had to be paid by the opening of business after the bank holiday "or the dog would die". The guard wrote it all down, the words being open to interpretation. He asked me if there were any other reasons the sum should be paid and I said, *"Because I'm worth it."* Now I was going to have to somehow prove it.

I was a long way from saying that the Army Intelligence Corps, on the instructions of the Special Intelligence Service, had turned me into an MTRU – that was too secret to mention even there. It seemed that if I really had an MTRUTH fitted, my presence here could well have been the result of my free will having been totally subsumed into this manoeuvre on Salisbury Plain. This involved the builders of the henge, the manufacturers of my car and the Red Army – let alone my record collection. As for whether *I* was worth it, I certainly found out, through the advertising media, that quite a few other people thought *they* were: the expression "Because I'm worth it" becoming rather popular in television make-up advertisements.

I then complained that my radio had been jammed whereupon one of the guards said theirs was fine, told me to listen, and turned it on again so I could hear. I was mystified and felt a bit like I was back at the hedge with the pixies. I was escorted back to my car after a short wait. All was now quiet in my mind: the imagined firing and smoke grenading had stopped and the helicopter had gone. I was ordered to leave and drove off again now feeling even more mystified. At the end of the road past HQ I noticed a police car was parked at an angle and I wondered if the road was about to be sealed off, or maybe it just had been.

"What the fuck have I done?" I asked myself. But I knew that in the theory of catastrophes in sociological mathematics, one is either a genius or a lunatic depending on the route one had travelled to reach the current position.[17] This seemed particularly true if an invasive procedure had been carried out on my eyes, ears and mouth – and this was the truth I was trying to sell by claiming my body had been invaded by aliens. Perhaps it *had* been the KGB who had fitted my MTRUTH. I believed I must appear to be a lunatic – though I did not get treated like one. But there was much more to it. I believed I was a genius and now I had to prove it. In the words of George Harrison "If you don't know where you're going, any road will take you there."

If I had hoped my tactic would end the messages from the radio, I was to be disappointed. I could still just hear Radio 1 and, as I made my way back to London, I heard a song telling me someone was going to be knocking on my door. I drove back towards Bannerdown Hill as though I had to see it again. I could not quite believe what I had done, but at least I had done it and I was glad

I had done it too. It was dark now and I sped past the field where the dogs had been earlier, too frightened to get out of the car, but inquisitive enough to go there. This had been a profound experience.

Late that night I got back to my flat. I felt like a man who had seen a ghost. At some time I formed the belief that all this had been done to teach me a lesson. But then perhaps the opposite was the case and the Security Services, all now aware I believed I had MTRUTH, were sitting there saying "good move" I thought.

I really believed I had been especially chosen many years before my birth, at the 1926 meeting. They probably had control of me years ago, I believed, and felt totally naked. I went to bed, my heart still beating hard, my skin sweating hot and cold. There was little doubt in my mind that Oliver North, the controversial United States Army officer once involved in a dubious arms deal, would have done the same. If he could not have done this himself, then I was happy for it to be considered I did it for him. I was a strange diplomat. In the words of Peter Gabriel's song once more "To keeping silence I resigned – my friends would think I was a nut." I was to utter not a single word of the secret of Prince Charles's dog, I decided, until it became a legend. But to my mind, it already had. Then I imagined a gay hairdresser finding himself on Solsbury Hill and a little confused about life. *I was* that gay hairdresser.

Although I was seriously deluded, and my behaviour utterly bizarre, if I had been asked if I really believed in what I had told the guard, I may have said that I did not. Only it seemed to be the logical thing to say, given the circumstances I found myself in. Perhaps my body *had* been invaded, perhaps I did have an MTRUTH – how could I safely rule that out? I do not suppose the BBC's Anneka Rice ever heard about my challenge but I was later to surmise that the Security Services did – as one would expect with a potentially hostile canine alien spacecraft landing on sovereign territory. Only the next day, I obtained what I thought was proof they and the BBC had taken action.

So profound was the experience that I am minded to leave my strange story of Wiltshire, and travel thousands of miles away to Central Africa. There I will now go in search of a meaningful literary explanation for my presence at the gate to Her Majesty's Land Forces HQ that Saturday afternoon of the Whitsun bank holiday 1994, an explanation that, aside from mere insanity, makes full sense of it.

Part IV

Africa, a Witch Doctor's Spell, and a Grain of Sand

Chapter Four

I'll Find My Way Home

After graduation I did not really feel like getting stuck into a career, and certainly not getting married, it just was not the right time in my life. Although I was extremely fond of Amanda, and loved her as much as I did, something held me back. I could not see her just as somebody simply for sex with because I had deep romantic feelings for her. Part of me did not believe in sex before marriage. Anyway, the commitment seemed too much, and I preferred to stay free for the time being.

So I took a job as a security guard with Centuryan Security in London and was posted to the Metropolitan Police Administration Building in Pimlico, an unusual building that looked like a Martello tower. Here I met a chap who had been in the Palestine Police, and an ex-mercenary who had just returned from Africa. They told me with whom I was to work, a West Indian by the name of Rashford Lyttle. I was warned he would play reggae music all night, which did not particularly disturb me, and sure enough, there we were the very next night listening to the Bob Marley song *Buffalo Soldier*. Rashford began calling me "Buffalo Soldier" and eventually "Buff". This resulted in everyone calling each other Buffalo and Buff, and by the time my PhD days arrived, despite Rashford not being around, everyone continued with the name, this at times becoming laughably confusing camaraderie. As well as the eyebrow-raising use of the appellation "Buffalo" more eyebrows were raised by the interesting dialectal use of the word "homosexual" as a mildly complimentary or derogatory noun and adjective. For example when at the Students' Union snooker table, if one of us played a good shot, he would immediately face accusations of homosexuality both in the noun and adjectival form of the word. Similarly he would be 'praised' for a fluke shot, the shot or himself being described as homosexual. "You homosexual" said in a slightly derogatory manner. We hardly thought about it at the time but I rather miss being called a homosexual.

So there I was that next night with Rashford and another chap, Ray, who had been a Tube train driver. He told me that somebody had tried to commit suicide in front of his train but had only succeeded in losing their legs. The person later came back in a wheelchair, which seems a little unlikely, and this time succeeded in killing himself in front of the train ahead of Ray's.

We would block up the pool table pockets with tissues so we did not have to pay for each game, and play for a while after the cleaners had gone. Soon I was working in all sorts of places around London – 136 hours one week, having the goal of saving enough for my trip either to India or Africa. Ray and Rashford knew what I was at, and on occasions I turned up at 6pm having been at work elsewhere since the previous evening at least. They sent me straight off to get some kip.

During this happy summer of hard work I gained experience as a dog handler, working with two German Shepherds the renowned Centuryan dogs Duke and Prince, experience that would obviously put me in good stead to tell this tale.

My choice of destination was partly decided by my having to deliver my brother Rupert's post to the offices of the South African shipping company, Safmarine, in St. Mary Axe, a street near the heart of the city. Behind the receptionist's desk was a large panorama of Table Mountain, which was very inviting. A few days later I woke up in the middle of the night, and decided there and then: I was to go to Cape Town overland. Through a friend I met a heroin addict, Jerry, who was going to do his cold turkey by making the African trip. I got details and signed up for the voyage.

And so, in early December 1983, I tearfully said goodbye to Amanda at St. Pancras Station and was soon travelling down through Europe. Looking around at those on the truck in the cold it never occurred to me what powerful connections many of them had – not least a number of whom were Australian vets. It was a bright sunny and cold morning as we arrived in Paris. Parked up and taking in the crisp morning Paris air we found ourselves talking to a British woman with a French accent who said she had met Churchill in the desert during the War – when she must have been quite a cracker. Thoughts of her having been sent by the French resistance or the Special Operations Executive (SOE) and of legendary missing dogs were then more than a decade away. So were any deluded inferences about the presence of any of my travelling companions – not one of whom I had met before.

We had to camp out in the Bois de Boulogne for a week or so whilst our visas came through (some of the countries were Francophile former colonies and did not have embassies in England). It was a bit chilly but at least it was dry. During the days I wandered around Paris and on one day happened on a World War II memorial with a burning gas flame. Here I warmed my hands on the light that never went out, before heading back to camp for supper.

The visas arrived and next morning we were off to Rome. Here somebody did me the courtesy of showing me where people committed suicide inside St. Peter's basilica. I had a bad hangover - the previous night being the only occasion in my life I have drunk any quantity of vodka. I had a hammering headache and, as we drove through Rome, I suddenly knew my moment had come. I made my way hurriedly to the back of the Bedford truck, which I then designated as an open-air vomitarium, took hold of the rope and announced "Friends, Romans, and countrymen, when in Rome do as the Romans!" Then I chundered spectacularly out of the back in full view of the car behind. The passenger pointed at me, laughing. We were coming around what seemed to be Rome's equivalent of Hyde Park Corner where, funnily enough, I had once done pretty much the same thing. This was also from a moving vehicle after a heavy night and equally heavy rowing training the following morning. Appropriately Pompeii was our next call, a whole town once full of 'bulimics'. For in case you did not know, the Romans were fond of eating a meal and then making themselves sick before gorging themselves again. They even had rooms in their homes called vomitariums in which to do this.

The weather was as cold, wet and miserable as in Roman England, but by the time we reached Sicily, the weather was really more than spring-like although it was December. Arriving in Messina I went to a café and ordered a cappuccino. I was astonished when it arrived in a British standard dimpled imperial pint glass beer jug full to the brim, certainly the largest cup of coffee I had ever seen. It was a mystery even then.

Soon we were crossing the Mediterranean, and the prospect of the entire continent of Africa ahead was now a truly awesome thought. During the crossing, for the first time in my life, I ate a banana, as I suspected that from now on I would have to eat whatever came along. It did not seem too bad, and more to the point it did not make me retch, which some foods certainly did. Bread and butter pudding being a good example which I had been forced to eat at my school boarding house: Absolutely disgusting. There we had rock cakes, which were said to retain their shape if thrown into the road and left overnight.

The beach party in Tunis certainly was not disgusting though, and I lay pensively on the sand at the top of Africa listening to the sound of Vangelis, one of the pioneers of electronic music, drifting up the beach from the stereo installed in the back of the truck. Everyone was there. But only I seemed to notice, in my mind, the presence of Jon, the former singer from Yes, and Vangelis, who wrote the music for the film *Chariots of Fire*, playing personally for me on the beach. All these years later, I can still recall my intense feelings at this moment. I was going to *Find My Way Home*, the song they were singing, to my tribal roots in Africa, which my ancestors had left maybe hundreds of thousands of years ago.

As I sat on the beach soaking up the beautiful North African evening I wrote a short cartoon story depicting the idea that the trip was not quite what it seemed. The story illustrated the trip as a theatre performance in which rolls of scenery were being unfurled on either side of the lorry. This aroused much hilarity with my fellow travellers.

Tunis seemed mysterious and magical despite the high proportion of women wearing western clothes. Of much amusement was the blood donor caravan from which was blaring, out of a loudhailer, the ardour of what sounded a bit like John Peel's North African World Service. It just seemed a little comical, and I would normally laugh at anything, given half an excuse.

I turned down the offer to smoke through one of the popular shisha pipes – these being large glass pipes containing water through which tobacco is smoked along a tube, such pipes being popular in Northern Africa and Islamic countries. However I was not to leave Africa without an infusion, in fact I was almost not to leave at all.

It did not take long though before I made the acquaintance of a Frenchman who engendered in me a certain level of fear. There was something politically active about him, something worrying. My first thought was that I certainly did not feel comfortable in his presence. On the other hand, I also met a Tunisian for whom I felt no enmity. This was unlike the strange bitterness I had somehow sensed in that Frenchman. From him a political unease exuded towards me.

The Tunisian's name was Hassam Regufz and he invited me to his house, quaintly apologising for the "roadworks". In fact there were no roadworks since there was no proper road, which seemed extraordinary in a capital city. I was introduced to his mother and given tea before heading back to camp.

Next day we drove off into the desert and, after sitting on the circular communal toilet in one of the old Roman towns, we made for Khairoun, where we spent Christmas day. We were awoken before dawn by the sound of the muezzin making the call to prayer through a loudspeaker atop the minaret – a most holy experience as his voice seemed to emanate from the heavens. Though we were not in a Christian country it certainly had a biblical feel about it, what with all the goats wandering around. But to everyone there, of course, Christmas morning was just another day. I went to the baths, an experience never to be forgotten. Each bath was hotter than the previous one, and the steam room was inhabited by strange shadowy figures of men giving off long steamy beams. Fathers and sons made their monthly progress through the rooms and, without any formality whatsoever, a bathhouse worker would set to work on them with some tool to remove the dead skin. The final bath was really so hot that I saw little prospect of ever getting in but eventually succeeded.

New Year's Eve, and we were at a town where an American oil company had a strong presence. Somebody happened to meet one of them and they were happy to invite us to their camp for the celebrations. There was a surfeit of meat of every variety on which I gorged myself in a totally carnivorous manner. It was rather like being the honoured guest of some unseen ancient eastern king with a harem, only we were the ones who had brought the women.

Reaching the Algerian border I was alarmed to discover I now had to cough up £300 to buy Algerian dinar, only having about this much for the rest of the trip. Forms were handed out at the border-post concerning this. At the bank one of the chaps on my truck, named Veggy John, decided to reach over the counter and steal the bank's stamp in order to forge everyone's papers, which he then proceeded to do.

We continued on through the desert by the less-travelled eastern route, which was most desolate. The only vehicles I remember seeing were an Algerian Army vehicle and a most bizarre lorry load of Germans who were travelling in what looked like a cross between a mobile pigeon loft and one of those cheap Japanese micro-hotels, each having their own coffin-shaped compartment in the side of the lorry into which they retired to sleep.

High up in the Tassili N'Ajjer it was unexpectedly cold and we drank leek soup in driving cold sleet, the surroundings looking more like the surface of Mars than Africa. I was happy to have my Harris tweed cap. And somewhere out there were the buried chariots of a long-gone and hardly-known civilisation, though the conversation on the truck was more concerned with talk of beer in Agadez. I was just hanging on for the warmer weather – which I knew would come soon.

As we descended into the sandy desert the moon rose very high overhead and the desert was as bright as a winter day with a clear sky following a fall of snow back in England. The sand here was like crisp snow. I got up at dawn to have a piss. Minutes later it had frozen.

There was no describing the desolation of this place. I wanted to savour every minute of it, as I knew I would never be in such isolation again. I wandered out over the desert away from the truck and, dangerously, beyond the horizon as far as I dared, certain death being the outcome if I made one fatal mistake in navigation. I lay there and stared up at the completely unpolluted sky, counting the stars in Orion's sword. I filled my hand with sand and let it drain away between my fingers until, with the help of a finger, one solitary grain was left in the palm of my hand – one solitary grain from trillions in the whole desert. The place was as mystical as the constellations themselves. Many tragic stories told of the terrible deaths of travellers lost, and to be lost, in this beautiful isolation.

Next day we continued on our way to Tamanrasset, but not before we met some desert tribesmen, who invited us to join them over small cups of hot, sweet tea. They told me of how one can tell the future from looking at the grains of sand in the palms of one's hand – like I had done the previous night.

A medical emergency now occurred, making my indisposition (I had a cold) seem rather trivial. As I said, there happened to be a number of Australian vets on the lorry. Of course, vets are not trained to ask their patients if they are allergic to anything. Pam Ayres, as I called her (being as she was from the same part of the country as the rustic poetess of that name), had some infection. One of the Aussie vets, out of Estonia, gave her some penicillin, to which she happened to be allergic. She then suffered what presumably could have been a fatal reaction. She looked in a pretty bad way; so did the vet when he realised his mistake. Still, she got over the anaphylactic shock, though nevertheless the words "For Animal Use Only" were clearly there for a reason.

After quite a few days travel we found ourselves ascending the Hoggar Mountains, which rise to nine thousand feet. As we ascended I sat in the spare tyre on top of the cab. In each tyre there was a certain quantity of smuggled booze hidden, and I was listening to Matt Johnson of The The singing merrily *This is The Day*. The vehicle appeared to cope admirably and bravely reached the summit at Assekrem. Assekrem is one of the highest points in the Hoggar and is where Pere Foucauld, later beatified by Pope Benedict XVI, made his retreat, the Refuge de l'Assekrem. He spent 10 years of his life studying the language and culture of the Tuareg before being shot dead in a revolt against the French at Tammanrasset in 1916.

We arrived at Tamanrasset a day later. Not for the last time in this trip, the truck faced a mysterious mechanical problem. It was announced that the gearbox had gone. I had not noticed there having been any problem with the gears and on the most difficult stretch of road up to the refuge the vehicle appeared to cope admirably. There was to be a delay whilst a new gearbox arrived from Bedfordshire, England. That night in my tent I overheard Veggy John, who looked rather like the pop star Robbie Williams, talking to the driver. He said he was heading off over the desert on his own, a decision which was going to put him in good stead. Something told me I should do the same, my intuition also being well founded.

So next morning, I made my way to the police checkpoint where soon I would have a lift into the deepest desert. I asked a Frenchman for one. "Oui, une place seulement" he replied. I still remember him; Bruno was his name, smoking a pipe containing sweet-smelling cherry tobacco. Veggy John was surprised to see me at the checkpoint and later he found a lift with a Swiss travelling circus. By the time I next saw him, they had him juggling and he was planning to join the Cameroon National Opera.

From the checkpoint, the well-metalled road south of Tamanrasset headed off into the deepest and most remote desert, where the hell of midsummer seemed frighteningly imminent. I was certainly glad to be there in January and not a few months later. This was no place to hang around in. Suddenly, a few miles on, the road just stopped and that, as they say, was "your lot". It was now getting quite warm, though it was January, and I was travelling in a convoy of a Volkswagen dormobile containing a German family, and a Peugeot 202 pick-up truck driven by two Frenchmen, including Bruno, and a woman. Soon I was earning my passage by laying the sand-tracks under the wheels. Even with the sand-tracks I still had to do a fair amount of what was, at times, quite worrying digging. The pick-up was able to carry their trials bikes, which were invaluable for looking for a way through what at times was impossible terrain, at least if one did not have sand-tracks.

The route was littered with the totally stripped shells of abandoned cars lying eerily across a swathe hundreds of yards wide. This must be one of those few places where you might expect to get a lift, and also be provided board and lodging, although I did have my own sleeping bag and a bag of very dry dates and figs. I was grateful nevertheless that they were happy to have me along. Funnily, apart from the original offer of a lift, the only thing I can remember any of these friends of mine saying was when one of the Frenchmen described the occasional maggots in my dates as "petit personnes".

After a few days, we arrived at the border-post: In-Geuzzam. This was where I hoped it would be apparent I had made the right decision to separate from the main party but I was yet to find out exactly how good a decision I had made. There were two huts at the border, which must be one of the world's most isolated frontier crossings. Soon it was my turn to face the Douanes (Customs). I would have needed to show I had bought £300 worth of dinar (which you couldn't, at least legally, change back). The only way out of this was to have an International Student Identity Card, which, luckily, I had, albeit out of date. The officer shouted at me in French "What's this supposed to be?" He then crossed out the card, tore it in half, threw it back at me and told me to go. Hoping he had passed me I moved towards the door wondering if I had got through.

Outside I felt a little relieved and thought I was now effectively in Niger – the country which borders Algeria to the south. I approached the police officer and feeling he would be happy for me to say something unpleasant about the adjoining country I told him what an awful place it was. Unfortunately I was still in Algeria as I now realised when I looked up and saw the Algerian flag fluttering gaily in the warm breeze. If I had then been shot dead I would not have been the first person to suffer such an end due to clumsy diplomacy. Anyway I would have been far more accurate if I had said what an awesome place it was. There was something magical about the whole country.

The policeman seemed very jolly and not at all bothered about my remark. Bruno asked me if I was through and we headed off over 'no-man's-land' this being a very wide expanse of emptier desert.

Chapter Five

Mana Mani

After a few short miles of no-man's-land we arrived at the Niger border-post. Reaching the policeman's hut wearing my Dread Broadcasting Corporation T-shirt (advertising a Ladbroke Grove pirate radio station) I noticed the officer stationed there had a considerable stock of beer stacked in crates behind the hut. The air of frivolity was unsurpassed and the policeman could not hear me banging on his door because of the Bob Marley tape he had blaring out. So I stuck my head around the door and he had his feet up on the table and a bottle of beer in one hand. With his other hand he stamped my passport like a highly contented Tom in *Tom and Jerry* and got back to the real business. The austere beauty of Islamic Algeria was behind me.

We moved off over the *reg* (hard, sandy ground), which was like part of Vauxhall's Millbrook test track in Bedfordshire, ribbed and veined for fifty miles, the way marked by the occasional oil drum. Eventually, after some time driving, perhaps days for all I remember, there was the most stunningly pretty 10-year-old I had ever seen just standing in the middle of nowhere pleadingly holding up a bowl waiting for someone to come along and give her water. She was an alien to behold and the whole atmosphere had changed completely from that of the previous country we had left behind. With pleasure we filled her bowl.

Approaching Agadez to within a fatal walk's distance we encountered what appeared to be some crazed lunatic casually ambling along in the opposite direction. We stopped to ask him if he was all right, taking a break for a brew-up. He said he was a Professor of Languages at the University of Mauritania and spoke 25 languages of which he was fluent in 14. He told us he had crossed the desert many times, which he did by reaching the last tree north of Agadez. He would sit under this until he spotted the distant dust cloud of an approaching lorry. At this point he said he would run like hell into the desert until the lorry came nearer. He claimed that without fail the driver would stop and ask him if he was a madman and would then order him to get in and take a lift over to Tamanrasset. Odd. I could hardly believe the bearded man. Perhaps he was the "Mad Professor" personified.

Eventually we arrived in Agadez and I said goodbye to my French friends who had fed and watered me over that death trap. Unfortunately my next drink of water was not so healthy and if I'd had a guidebook I would have known not to drink the water from this particular well.

I squatted there on the southern edge of the Sahara expelling fluids from every orifice excluding my ears, which would wait until Togo to exhibit similar behaviour. But it passed mercifully quickly; time being the only treatment available.

I started wondering what on earth I was doing here in Agadez, all on my own, and tried to recall the details of a single geography lesson I'd had on Africa back at school. I now made camp in a nearby campsite run by a Tuareg man with a Swiss wife. I went to the bank, which looked comparatively modern next to the rest of the town's architecture. When I came out, word had obviously spread that a white person had just gone in and now there was a small crowd of children waiting for me. Some of them were crawling along with flip-flops on their hands for shoes, their useless polio-ruined legs just dragging behind them. Perhaps I felt more pathetic than they did as they each said "Donnez-moi le cadeau Monsieur!" But what could I do? The French had a uranium mine up the road to fuel their nuclear bombs and power stations. Yet nobody had bothered to spend even a tiny fraction of that cost on some simple polio jabs for these poor creatures whose life expectancy must have been less than 20 years. I felt ashamed to be white.

I wandered around town a bit trying to forget what I had just seen, realising that despite having just enough to last five months in Africa, £300, I was in reality an extraordinarily wealthy person. There were no tourists here at all and in fact I seemed to be the only white person in town. I bought a meal for a few CFAs (about 10 pence) at a roadside stall. The enormous portion was served in a large metal dog bowl. I was to discover that eating al fresco like this was not without its hazards but on this occasion I suffered no ill effects and settled into a carefree rhythm as I now awaited the arrival of the truck.

I met up with Veggy John, now with the Circus. He set off to buy some ganja and eventually we found ourselves in somebody's house in the middle of Agadez. I think John annoyed the dealer who sank a nine-inch-long knife into the kitchen table and shouted "This is my house!"

I said goodbye to John. I never really knew why, but before we parted he asked me to look after a piece of African jewellery for him. It was a triangular-shaped garnet set in a silver alloy metal ring, and hung round the neck on a leather rope. I would not have a chance to return it to him until a year later.

The road north of Agadez was similar to the one south of Tammanrasset in that it was very good for a way before coming to an abrupt end at the turning for the uranium mine. It stretched to the liquid horizon and I stood there in the middle of the road staring along it. It felt very much like the film *High Noon*, except that instead of the four hours the film portrayed, this was weeks, the difference being a pretty good indicator of the sort of timescale, which seemed to operate in Africa.

One day, wandering around town, I decided to venture into the adjacent village of a local tribe who lived in small paillotes (reed huts) like the one I was lodged in. Outside one such paillot I asked the tribeswoman if I could go into her little house. This I now did, crouching down to get in, and inside her baby was asleep in its little crib, with flies crawling all over its face. So that was how she lived. I felt a bit meek about this and happened to have a baguette with me so gave it to her. She looked a little bemused. I returned to the campsite thinking of what somebody back in England would have thought if an African had asked to look around their house.

After a few days' wait, a sandstorm set in which made it difficult and very unpleasant to go out, the sand stinging my face so badly I could not open my eyes unless I walked backwards. I sat it out inside the dining hall of the campsite, where I was the only guest. Every afternoon at about three o'clock, a bat would fly out of its loft and lollop up and down the room, catching insects right in front of me.

I had already finished reading Sartre's *The Age of Reason* and, in the absence of anything else to do, other than write some letters, I read it again (I was even to begin a third pass).

I had taken two other books including Michener's *The Covenant*, a well-chosen livre for the journey to Cape Town, which I hoped to reach. But I had left some of my belongings, including *The Covenant* and Jimmy Boyle's autobiography, behind me in Algeria on the truck. The autobiography was notable in that it had some pages missing. Jumping to the rest of the story it became apparent I had missed a number of murders though I was too well *at the time* to imagine Jimmy Boyle had removed them himself and therefore that I was in a very powerful position.

I did venture out in the storm on one occasion but regretted it. I regretted not dressing as a Tuareg would with traditional head-covering to keep the dust and sand from entering my ears.

The sandstorm finished and on waking one morning I had the pleasant surprise of a hoopoe, an attractive bird with a crest, hopping around a few feet from my head as I lay there in my sleeping bag. My knowledge of ornithology told me there was a chance it may have summered in England, this possibility impressing me with the distance it had travelled to the campsite. I also knew that, according to tradition, and the Qu'ran, a hoopoe guided King Solomon across the desert to the Queen of Sheba.

I wandered into town and was beginning to wonder if the truck would ever arrive. At the police station they told me that the reason not one car had come down that road all this time was that the borders had been closed by the Niger State Security Service because of a UNESCO meeting in Niamey, the capital, down the road. Could it have been that, like the various officials at In-Geuzzam, they knew something about me I didn't and that moreover that knowledge had not originated in their own country? If so what might be in it for them? And what of my travelling companions? I continued my wait enjoying a regular midmorning bottle of Coca-Cola sitting in front of a shop which had large sacks of various foodstuffs outside, watching the trumpeter finches hopping all over the sacks. A Tuareg trader asked me if he could make me a leather wallet for my passport, which he then did, allowing me the convenience of hanging it around my neck when he returned the next day.

On one occasion I was walking along one of the main streets when I heard some jolly music coming from a shop. After having a carefree little dance in the middle of the street I enquired and bought a tape. Surprisingly for Africa, it did not even appear to be a bootleg. It was of a quite well known artist, Salif Keita, and the Ambassadeurs. Their music perfectly summed up the atmosphere in the town despite the horrors I had encountered there. The title of the song I heard is the title of this chapter.

I now produced some tickets allowing entry to le Théâtre Anglais and sold a number to the local children for a few CFAs. Not that I had any idea what the show was to consist of, and I eventually had to tell them the show had been cancelled and gave anyone who asked their money back, probably feeling as bemused by this as they seemed to be.

One day I was sitting at one of the tables in the campsite when two Frenchmen invited me over to share their red wine, which they were drinking in copious quantities with great chunks of ice. They told me they worked at the uranium mine, and were the only white people I met in Niger, apart from the Mad Professor. Meanwhile all the time, over and over, a distant reminder of Europe wafted across the campsite: the Swiss landlady's Rose Royce tape which played all day, every day, inside her house. It included *Is it love you're after or a just a good time?* and *Wishing on a star*.

After a couple of weeks, traffic started to flow again down the road from the border. I now heard how those on my truck (self-deprecatingly nicknamed by us the Wally Trolley) had all been arrested at the border for currency fraud, and taken by the Algerian Army under armed guard back to Tamanrasset.

Eventually, after quite a wait, they arrived in Agadez all eager to tell me their story, which did not sound altogether pleasant. They told me how, in some trouble and shame, they were put on display under open arrest. They were all fined £300 as well as having to also pay the original amount, though there was not an awful lot they could spend it on in Tamanrasset; so one or two were feeling the pinch, and one of the vets went straight home.

I also heard of how some nasty rogues on another truck had stoned Jerry in his sleeping bag. The rogues had also burnt his passport in the campfire, which meant he had to return to the British Embassy in Italy.

That night we went on the town for a few beers, the weather being a little unusual as it was cloudy and almost raining. I was asked if I knew the way back to the campsite: I said I did, though we could not see where we were going. I now said the 'immortal' words "It's all right once your eyes have adjusted" which it certainly was not because there was no light, no moonlight, no starlight, no houselights and no streetlights, just blackness. However, we did eventually get back though doing so rather like blind men. I was to be ribbed many times by having those words repeated back at me.

Next day we made for Niamey, and were soon installed by the swimming pool at the American Club. Somehow time in that city was reminiscent of *The Swimmer*[18] with Burt Lancaster: it was touched with the bitter taint of suicide. At the American Club I dived into the pool and at once felt some kind of shock and got out at the other end not to get back in. The force of hitting the water had done something not too pleasant to my ear.

At another swimming pool I overheard somebody saying "You can tell he's a swimmer by his shoulders." There seemed something deluded and jealous about this statement, as I could well have been a poor swimmer with my shoulders. I knew who was saying this, and it was to stick in my mind. The person who said it was to commit suicide – not, I hope, because of my shoulders.

Somehow this taste of jealousy seemed to reflect the sickly smell of the open sewers in the town, which was really rather appalling, human excrement being a more common sight here than dog excrement is in England. I noticed a lot of women laughed at me as I was an unusual sight, there being few white people here.

I went into a bar with a friend on his recommendation and decided I would like to get a copy of the tape playing. So I went to the local record shop where they ran off a copy illegally from their single disc. Next-door was the tailor's where, whilst I waited, he made me a pair of trousers, the baggy design and light material being perfectly suited to travel in these parts. Before long I was walking down the banks of the Niger in my new trousers listening to the Super Biton de Segou Band from Mali. It was all very African and mystical, spoilt only by the sight of a woman whose arm bone was visible, her flesh seeming to be falling off due to infection.

We hired a pirogue (a large canoe) from a chap wearing a T-shirt that said "California". We therefore named him "California". As the sun sunk into the haze I found myself in what had been a dream I'd had when I was nine. At that age the pied kingfisher had elevated itself in my mind to the level of a fetish object. Now I was really in the fantasyland of what was described in my *Hamlyn Guide to Birds of Britain and Europe* as an extremely rare bird. Here they were all around.

Again we moved on and soon were driving along a road built by the EEC in Upper Volta, one of the world's poorest countries. A few months later it changed its name to Burkina Faso, which in the language of the dominant Mossi tribe means "land of upright men", to distance it further from colonial days. The sight of the ex-army lorry seemed to give the impression that the second revolution in a year was going on as everyone would run out of their houses waving their fists in the air in jubilation. In Ouagadougou, the capital, we were ushered for security into a European's front garden, which somehow reminded me of the American Embassy in Saigon at the final withdrawal of US Forces in 1975.

Next day I consulted the witch doctor in the market place. As I walked up and down looking at the market stalls in the city centre, I found him sitting down on the ground with his stock of tools on display and wearing a very African hat. The palms of my hands were red for some reason: probably heat rash. I decided to show him them to see what he thought. I felt guilty of something as I saw him. It was as though my palms were red with the blood on the hands of British colonial power spilt over half of Africa and, because I was white, the French, German, Belgian, Portuguese and even Italian colonial powers too. He had all manner of snake-stones and other odd devices and in particular a bird's head with its claw stuck through it. Then he began to scratch a stone with a nail, making sparks fly over my reddened hands. Years later I would be able to say that I had seen a witch doctor privately. Unfortunately it was not as private as I might have liked.

A few minutes later (I have no recollection of paying him), I encountered two Australian vets from the truck whom I told I had just consulted the witch doctor. I did not laugh but he could not have seen my face if I had. The problem was *they* laughed, and he saw them laugh. I looked back hoping he had not seen them laughing but he had and was waving his arms around in our direction. I felt very uncomfortable, as I had not intended to offend him. If you believe in such a thing as a curse, or spell, then you would not have discounted the possibility that one was coming in my direction.

I did not really know why my hands were red although I did imagine a fungal infection. However they did not itch. Somewhere later in West Africa I also visited a conventional doctor who seemed the height of African jolliness and he prescribed me some cream for the hands. I did not pay him either.

Near to the witch doctor I saw a man with the most spectacular musculature, labouring under an actual yoke of postcolonial Africa. Lacking a beast to haul his heavy wagon he was doing so himself, like they haul lorries in the World's

Strongest Man competition. The market to which he was going was something to behold as well, in particular the butcher's stall, which was inside a very large cage with vultures walking all over the top and the leanest cuts of meat you would see anywhere. It was not my turn to cook but it was a rare chance to enjoy meat and we took it, most of the meals we had eaten being vegetarian. I had become quite proud of the meals I had served, all of which came out just fine with plenty for everyone.

I had sent quite a few letters to Amanda and now, at the poste restante in Ouagadougou, I received a reply. It said "Will write soon – next stop, Love Amanda." I also got one of my Great-Uncle Bernard's famous scripts. It began with the words "You Clive, are for sure one helluva news-wallah." I showed the letter to one of my fellow travellers, Sand, who was so entertained he convened the crew of the Wally Trolley and read it out to all with some enthusiasm. In the letter my great-uncle had used the phrase "Rapprochement not denouement". Sand found the whole script, and particularly this phrase, entirely amusing.

Of amusement to myself was the manner I got my own back on an Australian vet who said "Don't be stupid, you need an oven to make rice pudding." You do not need a degree in physics to know that the principal process in cooking is heating. But she had succeeded, though only for a few seconds, in actually making me feel stupid; so I thought about what she said, and with the meal finished and everything washed up I straightaway set to the task of showing she was wrong. I found some rice and milk powder and started to cook the rice in the big pot on the fire. One or two people poked their heads out of their tents to ask what I was doing. I told them "Never mind" but half-an-hour later I had a considerable quantity of very palatable rice pudding, which everyone ate with gusto, and my pudding became legendary. The vet who had made the remark ate some too – and was even impressed. Though she did not commit suicide having eaten my rice pudding, she did later complain to me about the dearth of mental health warnings for those travelling into the Dark Continent. Like me, she was to have troubles on her return.

There was another notable incident, I think in the next country, which resulted in us all being arrested for a couple of days by a disgruntled policeman. I find it difficult to remember which country I was in, and what actually happened, as the whole experience seemed to disorient me, but it might have been Togo. The driver, Norton, ex-army, was ordered to reverse at a checkpoint, which he did with obvious lack of care so necessary with a trailer. The policeman did not like it and even if it was not the tetchily reversed lorry and trailer, it might have been the illegal manner in which somebody had "dangerously brought the animals nearer with their optical equipment" as he laughably put it, or I laughably misunderstood. He did seem to think that because everything looked nearer through the binoculars it really was. We were taken away and none of us had any idea what was to happen. It was a little frightening for some of us. The policeman was very annoyed that somebody had said there were no elephants, "Pas des éléphants? Il y a beaucoup des éléphants – là-bas! Là-bas! Là-bas!" he said angrily, whilst pointing around.

He said he would show us the elephants but first of all we had to wait for about 24 hours for some big-knob police commissioner to speak to us. We gained the impression that they just loved having a go at us Europeans and in the end, all the Commissioner complained about was that somebody had been rude to the policeman. I never saw a single elephant in Africa, but if there had been collaboration between our driver and the Commissioner, that was massive enough.

Somewhere in West Africa, I saw the extraordinary sight of an African jeweller – both arms covered with watches for sale. In my mind's eye he was squatting in the centre of an immense African clock face one thousand miles in diameter. He was having a shit in the middle of the main street, and saying to me "Monsieur! Achetez-vous la montre!" Another interesting moment of street-life came when I saw a chap giving gentlemen shaves on the 'pavement'. Deciding I could do with one myself I soon regretted my decision as it became apparent he was using the world's most blunt razor blade. The dry soap he used to lubricate my face helped little and the pain was so unbearable my face screwed up and a tear ran down it. The barber assumed I wanted the same as everyone else and, looking in the mirror it was apparent that was what I had – almost. I now had a pencil moustache like all the locals, except mine was crooked because my face was so contorted whilst he shaved me. Everyone laughed.

Soon we were approaching the Atlantic seaboard whose vicinity announced itself by my hair taking on a horrible gooey feel. The desert had been so dry that one always felt comfortable, however dirty one was. But trouble lay ahead. After a dangerous swim without local knowledge in the Atlantic I went to sleep on the beach in Lomé and awoke as a wave crashed over my sleeping bag. I didn't need my sleeping bag again that night as the most extraordinary physical pain imaginable in my right ear overcame me. All I could do was wander around in excruciating agony.

Luckily I happened to be in the capital city of this country and next morning, with a friend, Annie, I set off to find a doctor. We were sent to what must have been the equivalent of the Togolese NHS. The previous evening I had seen the Presidential motorcade shoot by at some speed but the patients here certainly were not turning up in Mercedes with blackened-out windows. In particular, I saw one dying man being unloaded from a donkey-drawn cart. I felt deeply sympathetic to the Africans, having to make do with such humble hospital treatment.

At least I did not have to wait very long before the female doctor put some drops in my ear followed by a piece of cotton wool and then gave me a tablet, which I think was an aspirin. I was not charged for it but felt that surely I needed more than this; so set off to find a better hospital.

Soon I was standing outside a doctor's surgery at the main hospital where we had found the Ear, Nose and Throat Specialist (the French for this amusingly contained the word Rhino). We knocked on his door and he came out very angrily, pointing at the sign on his door showing he took emergencies only in the afternoon. He seemed like a French version of the *Demon Headmaster*, the children's television character with hypnotic powers that emanate from his eyes.

We returned that afternoon and the first thing he said to me was "Avez vous plangez?" Showing him which ear hurt he looked in the other one and began drilling with some electric syringe; this was exceptionally painful and tears rolled down my cheeks. He showed me black material he had extracted from my ear. It might not have been there if I had worn Tuareg headgear during the sandstorm. The pain was so great I was barely conscious for days. But I did spot a beggar on the white lines of a flyover in Lagos, Nigeria, and at the border of that country, the largest swarm of bats I had ever seen: the sky went black. This border was the only one in the whole trip up to that point where the border patrol asked how many of us there were, before collecting the passports. Good old British training you see. But this would become a significant issue when we got to Uganda.

The agony went on until, at last, we arrived in the Cameroon Highlands. Suddenly I felt a release of the pain in my head and then wetness. Pus was now pouring out of my ear like it was a runny nose, and the vets descended on me like they were ornithologists and rare birds were flying out of my ear. I was alive again. Waves of pain had become wings of relief.

Chapter Six

Highlanders

At about this time a Kiwi hitchhiker by the name of Kevin McGrath joined the party. Sitting next to me he pointed out that I had a single grey hair on the side of my head. This was news to me. I was nearing 23.

Soon we were in mechanical difficulties again, some welding being needed; though as before I could not see why. Luckily we happened to be near an agricultural college. The pupils said they would carry out the welding free of charge if we could raise a football team, which meant we all had to play. So we marched out into the baking heat, well into the nineties, to play the Cameroonians. There certainly seemed something of a sense of occasion about this matter and quite a crowd, several hundred at least, assembled to watch the game. Though perhaps one or two of our players did not really consider themselves ballplayers of note we were all "up for it".

Unfortunately we adopted the tactics more appropriate to a winter afternoon in the park back in England and soon we were 3-0 down. I declared half time unilaterally and gave the half-time pep talk, which I did with an authoritative delivery. During the talk I commented on the conditions and proposed to play a more Beckenbauer-style game with the occasional long ball to whoever would volunteer to go for it. This was to be me. Before long I scored my hat-trick and the equaliser, though the goalkeeper might have disputed it, and I went on a blazing run down the edge of the pitch, which was marked by the crowd. I shouted very excitedly "Je suis Roger Milla!", the Cameroonian hero of the 1982 World Cup in which they drew 0-0 with the eventual winners, Italy. During that game Roger Milla scored a goal, which was disallowed by the referee, the Cameroonians' wild celebrations proving premature.

I now made the faux pas of joking we had better not win or we might be going in the cooking pot, and they scored the winner to make it 4-3 to Cameroon (where I can report they had all heard of Bobby Charlton and George Best). Our lorry was duly fixed.

At some point around this time, the kitty was stolen and the driver blamed it on African thieves, though it was generally suspected he had stolen it himself in some dispute with the tour organiser. Various calls were made back to newspapers in England concerning all this. If they had chosen to come out to see what was going on, they would have been interested in a meeting, which was to take place not very long after this, at which it was proposed, not by me, to kill the driver. People travelling in Africa tend to think they are out of reach of the law somehow. Perhaps it is popular as a murder location. Certainly the declining behaviour of the group was somewhat reminiscent of those in Golding's *Lord of the Flies*.

Further into the Highlands we stopped near a waterfall. Whilst the others enjoyed a swim I just laid down in the grass by the road. The air, at least for a while, was fresher than it had been at any time since the desert. Lying in the grass I spotted a man walking down the road towards me. He was wearing a long flowing gown in shades of green. As he passed he spotted me lying there with a blade of grass in my mouth. A broad smile came across his face. He then said one word, slowly and deliberately, "Af-ric-a!" Without breaking his step he just continued down the road. This was a rare interlude to the heat, which was overwhelmingly oppressive, and became one of my favourite memories of Africa.

Later that day another man greeted me by running eagerly down his back garden, shinning up a coconut tree and picking me the freshest coconut available. My thoughts focused on our common ancestor and I wondered how many tens or hundreds of thousands of years ago he must have lived. What was certain was that he did live – somewhere in Africa. Suddenly many thousands of years of black and white history had formed a great loop described by the paths they had travelled. The ancestors of the great majority of blacks I had met in my life had gone to their tragic destinies in the Caribbean and America, many through one small door on the small island of Gorée, off Dakar in Senegal, and thence eventually to England. Mine had gone on a temporally longer and undocumented route to England through Europe – but it had all ended up with this exceptionally friendly chap with the coconut. He sliced it open with a machete and poured its milk into my mouth, my hands also around the shell. All the miserable pain in my ear had gone – it was a memorable moment.

Whilst we had dinner there was a giant thunderstorm. Torrents of beautiful fresh rainwater gushed off the roof of the truck, and I had the most invigorating shower in the tropics, courtesy of Bedford trucks.

Not for the first time during this voyage, an African told me that I had come there to write a book. The rainwater at dinner was just the sort of thing to inspire such a course of action. However at the time I dismissed their suggestions.

I had asked one or two of my companions if they had noticed how beautiful the women were in this country. During the African Nations Cup Final I found myself in a chap's house, and could not but help look at the lady I presumed was his wife or sister, lying seductively on the bamboo settee. I thought he said to me "If you want her then take her out the back" though I could hardly believe I had heard him correctly, as my French was not too good. He then said it would be an honour for him if I did, and I still could not believe him. Finally he came up to me and, pointing first at the banana plantation, then me and finally her, made a hole with the thumb and forefinger of his left hand and then stuck the forefinger of his right hand through the hole a few times. I was with 'Pam Ayres' and another girl, and was rather embarrassed by this, declining to accept his generosity with her sexual favours. On the radio, Cameroon had taken the lead over Nigeria and across the river the drummers began.

Next day we were in the Cameroon capital Yaoundé. It was a national holiday to celebrate the Cup win. In the street I met one of these attractive Cameroonian women. We went into a bar, which was full of Cameroonian Army officers. I bought her a drink and was asked by a well-educated chap from the US embassy, by the name of Harry Lawong, if I loved her. It seemed churlish, despite having only just met her, to say I didn't. The next thing, he was taking us all back to his house. I did not need a lot of pushing into what happened next, nevertheless I was. I had already been astonished by these people's attitude to sex; so what transpired did not come as much of a surprise.

I briefly read a bit of our host's copy of *Benham's Economics* prior to losing my virginity – within 30 minutes of meeting her. What a way to go. She was most beautiful. All she said during our brief relationship was "Do you want a wash?" "Oh la la!" and laugh a lot. I felt a bit guilty when I found out she was told by Sand that my mother had sent me to Africa to get a good African wife. We arranged to meet the next day but I did not turn up. I bumped into Harry in the street and he told me she had waited at his house all day for me. I gave him a cheap though partly silver trinket I had bought in Agadez to give to her. I felt both sadness and guilt. But it was a relief to be on the road again.

Soon we were in the Central African Republic. All I knew about this country was that its leader, General Bokassa, had spent several years of his country's generated wealth on his coronation as Emperor, and that he had been known to eat children.

We stopped at a village to camp, and after dinner headed off to discover the local nightlife. This consisted of an old gramophone, which the locals were happy to crank up for us. They even had some battery-powered flashing lights for it but the one soukous disc was astonishingly worn out. Nevertheless we had a good dance and found ourselves invited around to somebody's house. Here four generations were all sitting out in the front garden, though it wasn't much like an English garden. We all enjoyed the evening, with the rather grizzled senior member of the family sitting in his rocking chair. There was no barrier between us, though we had no common language. We were all just human beings. They had a barrel of mead from which we were disbursed copious quantities, though we had to remove the bees floating in it. There was plenty of honey, which was eaten in its combs, again including the dead bees, and the palm juice had fermented during the day to become palm wine, only having been harvested that morning. A young chap begged me to give him my dirty T-shirt, which I happily did, having one spare for the rest of the journey. Next day I saw him from the truck as we left. He had washed it and it looked very clean. He looked so proud of his new item of clothing and was walking with his chest out.

I would savour my time here by missing breakfast and walking down the road for many miles until the truck caught up. In the early morning the palm wine tasted like fruit juice and people would come out and give me some. On one occasion I came across a funeral, if it was not the wake, and the wailing was as spectacular as you could get, with drumming to match. The truck caught up and on I got.

Then, going through one village where, like everywhere, people waved and greeted us joyously, some children ran out excitedly and threw loads of fruit through the back of the lorry. The fruit included some very pleasant paw-paw, which I had not had before. Later, I developed a taste for the custard apple, a green spiky fruit with creamy flesh inside and black seeds which you remove, the skin not being eaten either. I have not seen one since, at least not in England. As we passed there was great mirth as a smiling woman sitting outside her house held up her not-so-black baby towards us. Everyone by her was waving, smiling and pointing at the baby. As she showed us the baby it seemed clear she was very pleased with it and even amused. It seemed she was telling us the father had come by on an earlier lorry.

That night somebody on the truck had their pillowcase stolen from the bush on which it was drying, with the result that we had to go back to the village to find it. On arrival the village elder appeared with the pillowcase, apologising profusely. They seemed a happy bunch.

Not far down the road at Boali we came to another waterfall. As I walked down towards it I saw the person who had remarked about my shoulders back in Niamey. Somehow I just did not want to see him, partly because it offended my delusion that no one else was travelling in Africa and partly for a reason I could not pin down. Really there was no excuse for this behaviour on either of our parts. Either way, I was not the one who, once we had passed each other, turned round and shouted "Ok, I know you have been having a great time while we've all been in hell!" or similar. This shocked me, but not so much as the news I received a few months after my return that he had killed himself, I think by jumping off a building. I knew of about 70 or 80 people making the trip (on three trucks) and we had met up on several occasions during the voyage. The death toll from suicide, including this chap's, would be two before the year was out: a considerable proportion experiencing post-Africa syndrome – a sort of culture shock with symptoms of clinical depression. I later wondered what difference it would have made if I had greeted him properly at that moment by saying "Dr. Livingstone I presume?"

The waterfall at Boali was wonderful. It was not so strong as to make it impossible to swim right through it; so there was little danger of drowning. Behind the torrent was the place to be, and soon there were quite a few naked Europeans screaming and shouting, and in my case catching bilharzia. At least that is where I suspect I got it, though I do not think our water hygiene was particularly good throughout the trip, making the journey more of a nightmare than a holiday for many of us. But it could have been worse because bilharzia, a parasitic illness caused by bathing in water containing human sewage, causes permanent blindness. Three hundred million people in the tropics suffer the disease, which can be fatal if not treated.

Some nutter organised a run, which did not impress me one bit. They all ran off in a temperature of one hundred degrees wearing walking boots – not very clever I thought, but then nor was I not using a condom.

As well as with some of the rest of the group, my morals also seemed to have 'gone out of the window' as I was now seducing the native girls with mad abandon, the chances of becoming infected in some way not even crossing my mind. But then what are a few shags in a country where one profligate leader was charged with eating children? I had read about a "Gay Plague" in *The Sun* newspaper before leaving England. But nobody told me where it came from. Despite my privileged position in society (I had more money on me than the average African earns in a year), General Bokassa declined to invite me around for afternoon tea and some barbecued infants' legs. If he had I would have had to go to the Ivory Coast where he was in exile. Instead I made do with some crocodile, gazelle and a little snake, which was very nice indeed – tasting like a cross between fried chicken and a cod fillet.

Two girls then appeared at the campsite and my friend Torq and I paired off with them into the showers, which was the only place to keep cool. Next to the showers was a toilet bowl, which was the most revolting thing I have ever seen, it being a seething morass of maggots coming up like lava in a volcano. I was fucking an African woman from behind and the campsite attendant pulled back the shower curtain and said "Ah, Bon." All within a couple of minutes of meeting. It never even occurred to me that the attendant was working for MI6 or that a sequence of events was now put in action leading all the way back to England with the result that Amanda went back to her previous boyfriend. Nevertheless, back in England Amanda did go back to him after the loss of her house keys. This, I imagined, was the price of my being unfaithful to her in Africa. If anything, it was just the price I paid for *going* to Africa. It was her I loved, not these African girls – however lovely they were. That night, I had a third and final most ill-advised liaison with an African woman. I had no idea there was AIDS in Africa and that it was the heterosexuals who had it. But it would take me 22 years to start worrying that I had some offspring in Africa I would never meet.

Soon after we arrived at the Ubangi River, which forms the border to Zäire. There was no bridge so we forded it. On the other side was the town of Zongo where we made camp. I went to cash an American Express traveller's cheque. This enabled me to return from Africa with the tall story that, after the cheque had been processed, the cashier had told me to take the pile of money heaped up, rather like a stack of baked beans, in front of the counter next to where I was standing. The currency of Zäire is the zäire, later revalued by a factor of three million due to hyperinflation. I would give one to somebody, a local, who looked at it as though they did not know what it was, not having seen one before.

Then I went into a restaurant for the rare treat of a fish dish. The room was so hot it was like eating in a sauna and it was also rather dark – darkest Africa.

That night we were woken up by one of our fellow travellers who had found a large hole cut in his tent, and his shoes stolen. We decided to post a guard at the fire all night and my turn came first. I gazed into the fire thinking back on all that had happened. England seemed years away.

Suddenly I heard a crack. Somebody had stood on a stick by a nearby building. I picked up the machete we used to hack wood for the fire. I crept off in the direction of the noise.

By the building I could clearly see an African standing motionless. It seemed he believed I could not see him, like a black cat does. I don't know for sure, but I have gathered the impression that completely black cats have learnt through genetic history not to move in the dark in somebody's presence unless they are in no doubt they have been seen. Other cats would just scarper immediately.

I raised the machete above my head and, running straight at him, let out a ferocious scream leaping over the undergrowth after him. He disappeared pretty damn quickly into the jungle.

We arrived at Lisala and discovered that it was a call of the Kinshasa to Kisangani riverboat. Reading the timetable, we learnt the boat had been due a couple of days earlier, but were told it had not arrived yet. One was not inclined to have much faith in the river-worthiness of such a vessel. It did arrive however, a couple of days later. Some of us decided to get the boat and meet the others in Kisangani. I took the boat.

Torq, who had helped make the trip enjoyable by bringing his Walkman, and various tapes to capture these times, kept losing his passport and cheques, though on each occasion somehow managing to retrieve them. This became a matter of some ridicule, and since this had just happened yet again, causing us all some stress, I now offered to take possession of both his passport and traveller's cheques. I assure you this was my own idea though it was a long time ago and I can't even swear to that to be honest. I was able to squeeze them in with mine, which had hung safely around my neck all the way from Agadez, where the neck wallet had been made for me.

We had only been on the boat a few hours when I took the opportunity to have a shower. In the shower I hung the wallet up on the hook behind the door and then, having finished my shower went outside to shave in the passing river. Suddenly I remembered the wallet and returning to the shower found it had gone. An African had gone straight in there after me and stolen it. I seem to recall seeing him. Now I had to tell Torq I had lost all his money and his passport. What an idiot I felt.

I went and lay on my third class bunk. Sharing the cabin were two Zäirian Army officers. They were wearing their regular uniform and on their feet brightly-coloured plastic sandals. The issue arose of whether I was allowed to take photographs of them, which I was not.

The boat was big enough to avoid the others for a while and I wandered around to see what was on it. Somebody was looking at me – I turned my head to see who it was, and there was a severed goat's head staring straight back at me at eye level. A woman had a large barrel and wanted me to sample some of the rather large maggots squirming in the soil it contained. I told her I had no money. She did not seem to care about that and a while later appeared at my cabin with a large bowl of them, fried up in her own seasoning and quite delicious.

That night there was another great thunderstorm, and the boat was navigated with the help of a powerful floodlight, which lit the bank. The boat therefore carried a bit of day along with it, the forest prematurely waking briefly as we passed along the bank. An enormous swarm of large beetles flew at the floodlight and the maggot lady scooped them all up and got frying again. The beetles were again most palatable.

I told Torq the bad news, which he took in the manner of a man who had known it was going to happen. *Maybe he did.* It meant he probably would not be able to get into Uganda and would possibly have to go back to Kinshasa. Of course so would I, and without any money in this remote place, it all looked a bit grim. Not so grim as the place we were heading for though, which 10 years later would be the scene of grotesque mass genocide. During three months in 1994 an estimated eight hundred thousand people, mostly ethnic Tutsis and moderate Hutus, were killed in Rwanda and Zäire. I must have met a number of them.

We were determined to enjoy our time on this strange vessel and the others made sure we were not short of a "Primus" beer or two, brewed in Kinshasa. We all sat in the bar, where the disco and the dancing began before 8am. The general impression gained was that dancing was as natural as breathing here.

The river was awesomely wide and long, with thick forest on either side, and looked as unexplored as it had been one thousand years ago. Only occasionally did we see any habitation, where it was apparent that the local economy was greatly oriented around the appearance of the boat, which became surrounded by a flotilla of vessels, all proffering their goods and comestibles.

Some poor chap without a ticket was arrested on the boat, and the Captain put into the bank in the middle of nowhere. It could have been one hundred miles either way to the next clearing, let alone habitation, and he was just thrown into the jungle in the night, struggling, as he was, like a condemned man, screaming in terror as they ejected him. Possibly he was the one who had stolen our passports and traveller's cheques. Possibly he had done it on orders and the whole thing was a display.

After the uncharted passage of a number of magical days on the river, all reminiscent of Conrad's *Heart of Darkness*[19], we arrived at our final destination, Kisangani, previously known in Belgian colonial days as Stanleyville. Kisangani looked like it had been left to fall to pieces back in June 1960 when the Belgians left and, in a bar on the wall, was a naïve depiction of blood and gore with Belgian paratroopers descending from the sky. It seemed the traffic lights had not been working for very many years.

I had spread sorry stories about myself on the boat in the vain hope that I might get my passport back but, should I be unsuccessful in this, I had decided to crash the border into Uganda somehow rather than go back to Kinshasa. That night we camped in the garden of a Greek-owned bar. The mosquitoes were extraordinarily unpleasant though somehow I had managed to avoid them to date. I had come to Africa without a mosquito net but with a piece of net curtain and had survived by sleeping in the tent, even in the hottest places. But I had no tent because it was on the truck, which had not arrived; so I set up my net over a table in the garden and went to sleep there. I was wishing I had a proper net and the mosquitoes began to terrorise me. Driven half insane I resorted to wandering around swatting and wondering what to do. I found that the shelf behind the bar was exactly the same length I was; so I lay on it with my piece of net curtain hanging down like I was in an open coffin on its side. I could see the mosquitoes landing on the net and trying to poke through it at me. The buzzing was horrendous, and when it stopped it was terrifyingly similar to waiting for the explosion of a World War II doodlebug. I lay there wondering if I was secure watching them all trying to get at me. Then came another buzzing. Then it stopped. "Damn it!" I said, one had somehow got in. It was a nightmare, as I waited to be bitten. Somehow though, I did manage to get a night's sleep.

The truck arrived and we were ready to depart. But before we did so, someone told me I was not going to believe what he was about to tell me. My passport had mysteriously reappeared, though not Torq's, or any of the traveller's cheques. This made me feel a little more awkward as we headed off down the road. I felt I did not deserve to get it back as I had picked the only custard apple in the tree in the garden of the bar. It was unripe and therefore, somehow, forbidden.

At this point in the journey, a long bend in the road of 50 miles or more on the map became a small corner in my memory. We stopped on this corner for lunch in a restaurant close to the Station d'Epulu, a zoo with one okapi in it and the centre for the conservation project for that animal. The special of the day was rice with spaghetti in a very thin tomato sauce – perfectly edible though risibly bland.

The air cleared perfectly, and the feeling of liberation from the torturous and oppressive heat of the massive jungle was a matter for some rejoicing. The angle of the sun gave the clouds a look you would never see in England, and the air was as crisp and clear as a glass of cool spring water.

Unfortunately I was now very ill again. I had however selfishly taken my malaria pills, so didn't get *that* illness. I say selfish because by taking the pills one only breeds resistance into the parasite causing it, with the result that the drugs eventually become useless. The mechanic declined them and became ill. But my alimentary canal was in a terrible state – I was really heading the way of fatality, and this time the problem was not going away. I did not consider what that problem might be. Instead I continued to gain the painful relief of diarrhoea at very many places first in the jungle and then savannah by the road from Kisangani to Uganda. Mucus was coming from my bowels. I moaned and I felt very unwell. But the change in weather was so welcome my memories of this time are good. During one of my many disappearances into the bush for relief, I found the most amazing bridge over a rivulet made entirely of ants holding on to each other, whilst the rest of the ant army crossed the bridge they, themselves, constituted. I could hardly imagine quite how they had gone about bridging the immense chasm without seeing them, not as individuals with little intelligence, but as a very clever brain on many legs for which no barrier would be too great – a small, but impressive, miracle.

Next day we let the Bedford truck really show what she could do as we ascended the steep track up to Mount Hoyo on the Uganda-Zäire border. As we ascended, a number of the locals, without so much as thinking of asking, climbed onto the trailer and began singing to earn their lift. Actually I do not suppose they were singing for anyone, it was just what they did. One of the obviously very happy women joyously singing obviously liked to wear her bra like a necklace.

Suddenly a body flew past the window as one of my fellow travellers, Tony, a plasterer from Bournemouth, fell from the roof. Luckily for him he did not break any limbs, and a while later we reached the village near the summit.

Now, mysteriously, it was announced that we were subject to another breakdown, though nobody had noticed anything go wrong. Suspicions arose that our driver was up to something, and the next thing we knew the truck's engine was dismantled and it was parked forlornly in the forecourt of a Greek expatriate's garage. It was announced, incorrectly as it turned out, that there was little hope of it getting to Nairobi.

I took myself for a walk through the town and up the hill, where I lay in the grass. If death had come that night then at least that day would have been a good way to reach the end of my life. From where I lay, I could see the snow-capped Ruwenzori Mountains across the border in Uganda. Everything felt totally peaceful and I was quite carefree. Then, a few feet away two friends appeared, enjoying the very same view, unaware I was there. I was about to say hello and then, deciding not to spoil their moment of discovery, just carried on chewing my blade of grass.

Chapter Seven

Blow

Back at the camp a number of pygmies had appeared and they lit a fire. Some of them had extraordinarily bad coughs and, together with a number of those on the truck, they sat around smoking their pipes, laughing a lot. I noticed Tony climb onto the back of the truck to lie down. He looked very unwell. Sand quipped that right then Tony was seeing more of the universe than I had through any telescope (back in my days at the Royal Greenwich Observatory). I was later to wish I had stuck with astronomy. For now I recalled getting a lift into work there. My lift told me his landlady had asked where he worked and when he told her she replied "Oh, that's where they do astrology isn't it?" to which he jested "Yeah, and we do alchemy and palmistry too."

In the morning, my birthday, Sand gleefully presented me with my present, a pipe bought from the pygmies that was made from some sort of hollowed-out root. It had been decorated with carved stars and had a clay funnel in the top. With it came a large leaf stuffed full of some plant material. Off we went down the road to smoke the stuff. I had once eaten a bit of cannabis resin and could not say I enjoyed the effect. I had given the rest to my great-uncle. He ate the whole lot, and claimed he did not feel a thing. It would appear he had a superior constitution to my own with respect to cannabis. Now I was to have to relearn that lesson.

At first we could not get it to burn, and so I was taking in huge breaths trying to make it do so. Now it was burning and I got a few lungfuls. In the space of about five seconds, I went from a carefree 23-year-old completely at one with the world (excepting my dysentery) to a frenzied zombie with a tumultuous volcano in my mind. "Oh no! Oh no! I have made a terrible mistake!" I exclaimed as I got up and walked off down the road feeling like my free will had been usurped, and I was just being marched into the jungle to die. At least I now knew it had been usurped.

Sand came after me and off the road I went, down a track. A woman came out of her house and saw the state I was in. Sand said back "Le soleil" as though that was what had got to me. Soon I was in the shade in the woods. Now I was on the floor. My whole body was convulsing uncontrollably, and yet I was fully conscious. Every muscle in my body was going into rhythmic spasms. I knew that was it. I was a goner. "I don't want to die!" I shouted, "Please God, don't leave my body here, tell everyone what happened!" I was now dead. Dead unconscious. Perhaps I really nearly did die. My heart seemed to be going at over two hundred beats per minute.

I woke up. I have no idea how much time had passed. Sand was stroking my arm to calm me. My skin had become ultra-sensitive, and the convulsions had stopped. There was a strange calm in the air. Where his hand was stroking me, peculiar waves seemed to be going through me. I got up. He did not seem to be there anymore. I was staring into a pool in which were many very large frogs. Seventeen years later I would read of the death of President Mobutu, whose nauseating regime ruled this vast country for so long. I would ceremoniously place the newspaper article announcing his death in the frog pool at the end of my parents' garden. It would gently flap in the breeze of an English summer's day and that would be my return to this strange moment in the jungle of Zäire.

Dinner had the blackest of black clouds hanging over it. It hardly seemed a consolation that I was still alive; I merely existed. I was deadly frightened. I was told a pygmy had explained, through an interpreter, that jungle spirits had entered me.

That night Torq slept in my tent to reassure me. I awoke in the night. I felt an animal the size of a large rat somehow moving under my body below the ground sheet. I was terrified. "There's nothing there" Torq said, but there was no doubt in my mind that I had felt it. However it was just an hallucination.

The Greek garage owner seemed mystified with our driver who had apparently abandoned the truck in his forecourt after dismantling the engine. Eventually I noticed the Greek mechanic set to putting it back together again, someone saying it was a Greek tradition to help out travellers. We gained the impression he thought our driver was nuts. Mysterious.

We reached the Ugandan border and began to feel the tension, as somehow we had to smuggle Torq through without a passport, deciding not to risk being honest. The plan was to mill around instead of lining up and get the girls to fraternise with the guards. As in Nigeria, though nowhere else, they asked us how many of us there were and collected in the passports. Now the milling began and before long we seemed to have got through. But then there was another checkpoint and we had to go through the same rigmarole. Eventually we thought we had done it and everyone cheered. But again we were cheering too early, as we drove around the corner into an Army checkpoint. They were drunk and carrying bottles and certainly swaggering about quite a lot. It was a bit frightening. But again we were through and now we headed to Kampala. It felt like we were at home already, what with the Ugandans speaking English and we even found a transport café where I dined on the menu's number 12: sausages, beans and chips. The prices were in "bobs", which also made one feel at home, as a bob was one shilling in old British currency or five pence post-decimalisation.

Driving along, after a brief view of the enormous expanse of Lake Victoria, we were stopped at gunpoint by a patrol from the Ugandan Ministry of Tourism and Wildlife. They ordered us to turn around and go back up the road where we had driven straight past the lions. It seemed there were not many tourists about as the war, in which 20,000 people had died, had only recently ended. They just wanted us to see the lions.

I felt most peculiarly unwell up top following the smoke and quite apart from that I was seriously physically ill. I told the Estonian vet my symptoms and he said "If you have been ill that long, it is probably amoebic (dysentery)." Out of his supplies came a drug Flagyl, which was like a miracle cure. Two mornings later I woke up hungry again and feeling quite reborn. Trouble lay ahead though.

Whereas before the smoke I was very happy now I was fed up with the trip and sick of the whole place. Game parks and Rift valleys now held no fascination for me. I just wanted to go home. I would not be going to Cape Town.

Torq got an emergency travel document from the embassy in Kampala and we arrived in Nairobi. I witnessed a ferocious argument between the driver, Norton, and the tour organiser, who had flown from England. I was later told the tour organiser had been found dead in an Algerian hotel room with his passport thrown on his chest. *Lord of the Flies* again. Looking back on the trip it seemed we had been very lucky that this was the nearest I got to experiencing any violence – it seemed a little like we had travelled in the eye of some kind of storm, all the crazy fighting having somehow completely avoided us. In fact, it was said after our return that there had been a coup in every country as soon as our truck left. There was more truth in the statement that we arrived just after there had been an uprising, as in Upper Volta the previous year and, only a few weeks earlier, when 1,000 people had died on the streets of Yaoundé in a failed coup.

I sat in the cinema and watched *The Eye of the Needle*, a wartime spy film set in the Scottish western isles. In the cinema there was still the feel of the glory days of the Empire, although at the end the Kenyan national anthem was proudly played with the Kenyan flag blowing smartly in the African breeze rather than *God Save the Queen* and the Union flag. My trip in Africa was over. It ended in a film set on a remote Scottish Isle. But it would not really be over until, years later, I arrived at the Talisker Distillery in the Isle of Skye and, in my imagination, the Station D'Epulu had been reopened underneath the crowding branches outside the gate at Her Majesty's Land Forces HQ, Wilton. To my mind, when I had driven in that gate, I had done so armed not only with my record collection but with all I had seen, learnt and experienced in Africa – including the witch doctor casting a spell on me.

I now needed to buy my flight ticket back and went to the post office to collect the tax refund for which I had put in a request before leaving England. My bank back in London was handling this. But there was no sign of the money in Nairobi. I was later to discover that whilst I had been in Africa there had reportedly been a fire at the London tax office and all my papers had been destroyed. I needed to telephone home and, still at the post office, was escorted around to make the call on a line, which, apparently, was already connected, making the procedure astonishingly inefficient in a manner typical of Africa. I succeeded in getting money sent to pay for my flight and soon was on my way home.

Part V

The Black Dog and a Seagull

Chapter Eight

Alioune Sissòko

It was a relief to get on the plane. I was fascinated by the man sitting behind me. For now, all I really thought was that he looked Russian and, after all, it was an Aeroflot airline. I would not forget him.

The plane landed a couple of times, once in Cairo and once somewhere in the southern Soviet Union. On this second occasion we were escorted into a room in which the walls were covered in Soviet propaganda and five-year plans. I little suspected that, five years later, the Soviet Union would be on the point of breaking up. Even less did I imagine it a planned event.

Reaching Moscow we landed again, and I failed to take the opportunity to have a guided tour of the city. Norton had told me of his stay in a Moscow hotel in which part of the building was out of bounds. Without the correct visa, the stay in Moscow was strictly monitored by Soviet State Security, the whole visit being under the control of guides. He told me there was a set of locked double doors, which had a curtain behind. A gap seemed to have been deliberately left between these curtains to enable one to see through. Through the gap, everyone appeared to be having a great time in a heaving bar, to which no access was allowed.

Tired from the flight we arrived back in London and I headed with Tony around to Amanda's sister's. Here I had my first bath since Khairoun. As I wallowed I thought back to my adventures in darkest Africa. Shortly I was speaking to Amanda and she sounded panicky at my arrival back, not having seen me for six months since the wonderful weekend we had spent together before I left England.

Hardly surprisingly my return was tremendously anticlimactic and I sensed an emptiness descending as soon as I returned. I can still remember putting the key in the door – nobody was there to welcome me. Coming back from the African theatre was dangerous, as I was about to find out.

A few days after my return I awoke in a cold sweat like I was having a horrible nightmare. Except the nightmare did not stop when I awoke; that was when it started. I had no idea I was now suffering from a recognised psychiatric condition. I simply felt I had severely damaged my brain by smoking the grass back in Zäire. Enormous fear that I could not shake off descended all my waking hours.

I broke into tears and told my mother I was frightened. This was not the moment when she asked me the most ludicrous of questions: "Where did you go to the toilet?" My immediate thought was of the chap in Africa squatting to have a crap whilst simultaneously trying to sell me a watch. I imagined him doing this in Bedford High Street, squatting near the site of Bunyan's prison.

Actually anyone who has not had a really good shit in the middle of the Sahara desert has not actually lived. It was worth going there just for that, though you need to get good advice from the travel agent on what to eat for maximum benefit. People talk of quack medicine but I am left a firm believer in extraordinary prescriptions for all manner of complaints. The answer to my mother's question was the girls went to 'port' and the boys to 'starboard'.

I took a job in the photographic department of Boots, processing people's holiday snaps. Standing behind the counter I felt like I was in a lift, being thrown about by the effects of gravity as it went up and down. It was difficult to conceal that I was experiencing this, and I went into a cold sweat and felt dizzy. In reality this was the combined effect of firstly having spent six months outside under the African sky with a continual flow of interesting things going by, the drugged smoke I'd had, the amoebic and bacillic dysentery, and now being cooped up below ground in the Boots basement. Oh, and not to forget the witch doctor. In the basement not a bit of blue sky was visible. Life was unbearable hell, and I could never wait to get out again. Things improved marginally when the driver of the van to the warehouse broke his leg playing football and I took over his job, meaning I was out of that hellhole bunker of a shop.

One day I took the train to London. I was continually rubbing the back of my neck as it had tensed up badly. When I got off the train at St. Pancras I was on the point of having a panic attack. If you have not experienced one you are lucky. I felt so bad I went straight to the UCL medical centre. I don't know why but they did not send me to see a doctor but a councillor who happened to be there. He pointed out the state of the back of my neck, which was red and sore with the rubbing. On the way out I bumped into my old friend Sîan Williams (not the newsreader) and this meeting afforded me some relief. She took me back to her place to help me calm down.

Later I was at my friend Dave Allen's. Again this was not the famous comedian – and yes, I would later have strange thoughts concerning the 1926 plan about why so many of my friends bore the same name as a well-known personality. You see I also knew an Iain McAskill, who shared his name with the television weatherman and, a few years later, I would have a girlfriend called Carol Barnes who shared her name with a newsreader. At David's place I told the story of my brain having been "fucked up" by the pygmy grass. Another friend nicknamed Cowpat, made an interesting remark that helped me survive the threat of suicide for perhaps 10 seconds, "Why don't you try to enjoy it?" I enjoyed the remark having, as I do, room in my philosophy for some masochism. As you will read later in this story: "True decadence demands masochism."

Eventually I got to see my GP who told me these were no longer Victorian days and he recommended I see a psychiatrist, Dr. Vasudevan. A friend (another sufferer from mental illness) and I humorously referred to him as Dr. Vas Deferens (the Vas Deferens are the tubes running from the testicles to the penis). Dr. Vasudevan came to visit me at home where I put on a display that everything was all right, which it most certainly was not. I saw him again a couple of weeks later. I was crying and obviously there was something wrong. He said "I apologise. I should have seen you earlier. I'm afraid you are going into a clinical depression"– this illness being aptly referred to by Sir Winston Churchill as the Black Dog. I don't know why he called it the Black Dog but British folklore is full of references to the Black Dog. The best of these springs from an event at Holy

Trinity church, Blythburgh, Suffolk, in 1577. A giant black dog standing on its hind legs was said to appear at the north door to the church (otherwise known as the Devil's door). Today, 'claw' and burn marks can be clearly seen on the door. The true explanation for these is now suggested to be the ultra-rare phenomenon of ball lightning. Since that time many thousands of people have committed suicide due to the Black Dog: clinical depression. I know why. Much better a small and friendly Jack Russell.

Being given this explanation was a great help as I had thought, up to that point, that the brain damage was irreversible. It must have been a classic depression. It had never occurred to me that I had an illness. I just thought there was something seriously and permanently wrong in my head. What I mean to point out is the difference between being badly pissed off and having clinical depression. The two are distinct states of mind connected by a continuum of mental states though it seemed at the time there was something very badly discontinuous between these. I was suffering a severe chemical imbalance in my head brought on by, amongst other things, smoking the ganja.

Despite the doctor's words I was confronted with the thought that, as life had become so miserable, suicide would be the unavoidable solution. I can still remember a terrifying moment as I left my parents' house one evening. As soon as this horrible realisation came to me so did the equally frightening quandary brought on by knowing I could not do that to my family. I felt horribly trapped in this thought. The only hope seemed to lie in the knowledge that I was going to die one day anyway.

The psychiatrist prescribed antidepressants, and as I was so afraid they would not work I did not take them, instead relying on his advice that I would recover eventually anyway. But the nature of clinical depression left me unable to believe his advice. This only made things worse. I struggled on through hell, eventually starting my Master's degree in October 1984. Mind you, I did manage to run the Bedford half-marathon during this time, in quite a fast time: one hour 27 minutes.

By November my condition was collapsing and I was unable to cope with the daily travel to and from London from my parents'. Desperate for the open air I would walk out into Hyde Park and near the Albert Memorial, tears streamed from my eyes. I was unable to cope, but somehow I had to.

I walked into the College doctor's clinic room, the skin on the back of my neck still red and sore from rubbing. I was crying before I even sat down. The doctor asked me if anything was wrong to which I replied in the negative. She asked me if anything had just happened and I said it hadn't. At once she told me, before I had even sat down, that I was clinically depressed and gave me a prescription for an antidepressant, telling me I was unfit to continue my course. It must have been one of the swiftest and most accurate diagnoses in medical history, apart from that for somebody whose body had been found under Beachy Head. I decided to go back and see the psychiatrist at the hospital. This time I seemed to have no choice but to try the antidepressant though still I was terrified it would not work.

That night, for the first time I took an antidepressant called Dothiepin. My lower body lost all sensation and I went to sleep, waking the next morning with a hangover and a dry mouth, the side effects of which I had been warned.

I put up with these side effects and persisted with the medication, which I was told would take weeks to work. I did not go into College but instead took to long walks including one right out into the country to near Rupert's house whilst eating the biggest Milky Bar I could buy. He was coming back into Bedford to do shopping and picked me up. Over a decade later I would pass this spot, again walking, where he and his wife had picked me up. There was a lone pile of manure there and my mind ruled in that the KGB had put the manure there to let me know how closely they had been spying on me during my life – they even knew where he had picked me up that day.

I was soon on the mend. But the pressure was enormous: my father had paid my tuition fees and I was not even at college. After a fortnight or so I was sufficiently recovered to get a small room in London and return to my studies. I took up Yoga, and found it particularly helpful to lie on the floor on my back relaxing every muscle as best I could every time I breathed out, as they taught me to at the hospital (this is called savasana or "the corpse" in Yoga). One night I was doing this when I felt what I can only describe as an orgasm in my head. Somehow the collective build-up of the drug was having an effect, and I felt real life flowing back into the actual chemistry of my mind. The drug worked! You cannot imagine what a relief it was. I felt like going down on my knees to thank Dr. Vasudevan. And this sudden recovery over a few minutes or perhaps even less did seem to show that maybe there had after all been a biochemical discontinuity in between my health and illness which was now suddenly reversed in the mathematician's catastrophe.

One day during my studies I went to the British Library reference department looking for some information for my Master's dissertation. Whilst the librarian looked for it I had a look around and found myself reading a Meteorological Office report about how an airliner over the Middle East had dropped some 10,000 feet vertically in a freak downdraught. Noting this, and seeing the librarian had returned with the information I required (something to do with ground-truthing radiometry) I went over to collect it. She handed me, I thought by mistake, a heavy tome down the spine of which was the word "Catecholamines", many of which, like dopamine, are neurotransmitters involved in clinical depression. You would not be surprised at what I later thought of this.

Outside the library I was waiting to cross Southampton Row at the traffic lights when somebody came running across whilst the traffic was moving off. He ran into me, bending my umbrella as he did so. I would not let this go and a situation developed in the Tube station. If the incident at the library wasn't enough, here was yet another, which my later schizophrenia would bring to bear a paranoid interpretation of. I would come to think it related to a jape of mine about the Bulgarians spying on me and my fellow students from their Embassy opposite the Applied Optics laboratory at Imperial College; the Bulgarian Secret Service having infamously assassinated the Bulgarian exile, Georgi Markov, using a poison-tipped umbrella in 1978. The policeman (whom the ticket collector called) got my assailant's address, which was in Essex. Such would be my delusion of grandeur that I later came to wonder if he was the actual "Essex Man" as it was only, it seemed, after this incident that I heard of Essex Man. On the escalator I was still having trouble with the adjustment back from Africa and found the whole Tube spinning around in my head.

After another month or so I was completely recovered from the Black Dog and able to come off the medication. I successfully gained my Master's degree and subsequently secured a position to study for a PhD. This time I had a grant. But my African trip was still not quite over (and in many ways it never would be).

I bumped into a school friend and was invited to rowing training. I was too unfit for the level of exertion made and my entire body was extremely stiff the next day, my urine brown. I visited the doctor who explained I had haematuria (blood in my urine) due to many small tears in my muscles from the training. He took samples. A couple of weeks later I got a letter from the Hospital for Tropical Diseases and Hygiene saying my test for the bilharzia antibody had proved positive and they would tell me when they had a bed available. By now I felt perfectly fine but turned up anyway.

Waiting for the nurse I had a rather heavy bag of books. When the nurse asked me to go with her I gesticulated as I picked them up, as they were so heavy. She said "So you're feeling pretty bad?" The opposite was the case.

I saw a young doctor who told me she was going to perform what was called "rectal snippets" on me the next morning. True enough that was just what she did and I can assure you it was even more embarrassing than it sounds, including in a way neither of us expected – judging by her remark as my bowels relaxed in response to this demeaning probing.

I heard one or two odd stories in that hospital about some of the diseases the other patients had and the treatments afforded. These stories were so odd I ended up thinking, 10 years later; the real purpose of her so-called rectal snippets was to install a microphone up my arse. In any case I was told they found dead ovii in the snippets but just for safety was given a large torpedo-shaped pill of antimony. This seemed preferable to having razor blades dangled in my gut, which I was told was what they did to one patient. They told me I was self-cured and I was discharged.

Chapter Nine

Cheduke Chose
(The Fish and Chip Song)

Having beaten the Black Dog on my shoulder I settled into my PhD studies at Surrey University. When I got to Guildford I did have a mild episode of clinical depression for which Dothiepin was again prescribed one year on from my previous depression. But this depression was very mild by comparison and I did not take any. It went and I would stay well for nearly a decade. The work involved writing computer algorithms for the Royal Aircraft Establishment, who wanted to obtain images of cracks in aircraft wings by sending electrical currents through them. The technique would also be useful for nuclear reactor casings or rail tracks. I was happy and well-suited to the work, splitting my time between my studies and rowing for my old college up in London.

I did meet up with some of my fellow African travellers on a few occasions. On one such occasion some of us, including Veggy John, met at The New Merlin's Cave, a club near King's Cross in London. I had worn, all the way across Africa, that silver-set garnet he had asked me to look after. Now, within minutes and yards of handing it back to him it simply vanished. I just could not bring myself to tell him I'd had it a few minutes, or even seconds previously, so made what must have seemed a rather rude remark about the stone. Perhaps the New Merlin took it.

Things simmered on with Amanda with whom I could easily see a future. But I also feared permanent commitment at this stage, and wanted to play the field a little longer. Our times together were few and far between, but no less the memorable for that. She sent me a passion fruit for Valentine's Day and this greatly endeared her to me. But I was crazy about her anyway.

Shortly after my return from Africa my father had told me of how AIDS was rampant out there and that it was not just isolated to the homosexual community. The penny did not drop until a year later. An attractive girl was working in the same office and with a lightning pick-up I had her back in my room where she told me she'd had hepatitis. This obviously put me off her but it also had the effect of making my father's words sink in. It soon became clear that I had a moral responsibility to go and get myself tested for AIDS, but first I had to see the professor at the Public Health Laboratory. I was quite a rarity as the full AIDS phenomenon had not at this point blown-up in the media. He pointed out that if I had the test it could mean I could not get insurance. I was surprised by his attitude as it was clear to me I had no choice in the matter. I had to have the test. Soon I faced the demeaning experience of visiting the sexually transmitted disease clinic and waiting for my number to be called out. I was told I would have to wait two weeks for the result to come through.

An immense black cloud hung over my head during this time – and it was no clinical psychiatric condition other than fear. I considered the possibility I'd had exposure to AIDS in Africa and realised that if I was tested positive it was either suicide or a life of abstention from sex – at least that was the way I saw it. I imagined the full horror of it and how I would have to tell my parents. It was just too horrible to contemplate.

The day of my test result came and after my number was called out at the clinic I found myself being asked to wait for a while outside the surgery room. My heart was thumping and right away I imagined the worst as I thought the explanation for the delay was that the doctor was composing herself to tell me the grim truth.

Soon I was sitting down in the surgery room. I was wearing a University College and Hospital (UCH) scarf, which Amanda had pinched for me and put in my bag. The doctor commented on the scarf saying she had studied at UCH going on to tell me that the result of my test had been negative. A huge smile of relief came across my face. I told Amanda who was pleased I'd had the test and that it was negative.

Although our times together were infrequent they were always magical for me. On one occasion I took her to see The Bhundu Boys, from Zimbabwe, at the Mean Fiddler venue in Harlesden, this band having written the song, which gives its title to this chapter. The band was to be decimated by AIDS, most of them being dead a few years later. In fact the singer, Biggie Tembo, did not wait for the AIDS to kill him but hanged himself before it did in July 1995, meeting his end in a Harare asylum after years of rootlessness and increasingly unhinged behaviour. Years later I would meet a Zimbabwean hotelier who had played with him. He related to me some of the singer's last words: "Women will kill you." On another occasion I sat with Amanda in The Spread Eagle, Camden. I had this warm magical feeling all over me that you could not beat. It was always like that when I was with her. It was always just so special, and I very much doubted I would ever feel like that again with anyone else, and nor have I. Just sitting next to her holding hands was a superb experience. I was privileged to know her as well as I did. Herein lay many of my future problems – if that is they weren't just caused by my drinking over twice the recommended daily amount for some years.

On one occasion when I went to London to see Amanda I visited my old workplace in Pimlico to see if Rashford was still there. He was. I told him of my African adventures and he said "So you've seen your bit of de world now." It was good to see him again. His words summed up the trip well – and I no longer had the travel bug. Thoughts of being followed by the Security Services were years away.

After one weekend in Bedford I was hitchhiking back to Guildford from a few miles away where a relation had dropped me in a heavy fog. The fog was so dense that I had little chance of being spotted by any passing vehicle. After waiting some time, quite hopelessly, who should pull up but the van of a local snail farmer. The difficulty of being seen would later mean, quite laughably, the snail van had been sent for me, the van being symbolic of the long and detailed plans the Security Services had subjected my life to.

Towards the end of my PhD studies a notable incident occurred. Amanda did my head in and not for the first time. She said "I wouldn't want to marry you or settle down with you." But I hadn't asked her! The thought of a cartoon character moping off with his belongings in a red handkerchief with white spots on the end of a stick came to mind. A huge weight had dropped in my head. But I did not let it show. I completed my thesis: *The Inverse Problem and Applications to Optical and Eddy Current Imaging*. I did this without any incidence of mental illness, apart from the mild episode as I began it, and a very black cloud of horrible rejection by Amanda in the days leading up to my viva voce. This I passed, obtaining my PhD, and took up my job as a contractor at RARDE, Fort Halstead in Kent.

Not long after I started work, my dad's operetta, *'Gainst All Disaster*, was performed. Dad gave me two front row seats for Amanda and myself. During the beautiful love song, *Stevington Cross*, a person collapsed in the audience and a doctor was called while the performance was briefly stopped. If I had not wondered why Amanda, a doctor, was not there and I had an empty seat next to me already, I did then. Once the person had been moved out the love song was sung again. Ever since I have wondered how things could have been different if I had invited her. We were meant to be, but it did not happen, and that is hard to take.

I did speak to Amanda on one further occasion and she called me a few times after I sent her a special Valentine's edition of my newsletter inspired by her. I had sprayed her copy in gold paint. If she had changed her mind she needed to try a bit harder. It would be easy to say I wish she, or I, had. But this has been my life, and what is to be gained by regretting anything?

I did not find what she had said very good for my pride, and did not answer her calls. I've still got one of them on a tape somewhere – after the fade-out on a Railroad Earth song. The song *Heyday* went:

> *Build yourself a mansion,*
> *Dig a hole you can't climb out of.*
> *Some situations were only made to bring you down,*
> *And this one's really done a fine job on you*[20].

I came across the tape one day and was surprised to hear the voice I still miss so much speaking to me from the past at the end: "Hi Clive – it's Amanda here... " followed by her sweet little chuckle. What could have been? I really loved her. She gave me some of the happiest moments of my life. Dolly Parton's song, *I Will Always Love You*, so famously sung by Whitney Houston, comes to mind but, thankfully, playing so far away I can no longer hear it.

For the next four years I would balance my time between top-secret work for the Ministry of Defence and launching my record label, Seagull without financial success. The truth was that I had fallen madly in love with Railroad Earth to the exclusion of everything else. But I wasn't the only one to. The highlight was when I succeeded in getting them slots at the annual New Music Seminar in New York. At one of these they played in the open air Amazon Club close to the towering World Trade Center. REM vocalist Michael Stipe was there and he watched me, the only one dancing to them. Our eyes met. REM's manager, Jefferson Holt, who signed them to Warner Brothers for $50 million, poached Railroad Earth off me in a rather more modest deal. I suppose that if I had been in their position I would have done the same. But the apparent lack of success Mr Holt had with Railroad Earth makes one wonder how different it would have been if they had trusted the instincts of one of the band and gone with me. To start with I would never have changed their brilliantly appropriate name to the insipid Ringo. Though to be fair they had done it so as to not get confused with the similarly named Railroad Jerk. But it seemed by most sedulous design with me at the centre that Holt's label was called Dog Gone Records. No doubt the CIA were involved.

It was all a bit like the song *Heyday* in the end, and my finances became quite a mess to be reflected in my developing state of mind. Perhaps it was the failure of my record label, coupled with a lack of direction in life, which led to what happened next. But whilst my behaviour was due to become erratic and bizarre one last incident would take place which, whilst at the time simply seemed very odd, would during my forthcoming illness. become personally significant.

The incident took place tantalisingly close to my workplace, DOAE, and here members of the K Foundation[21] arrived in a black limousine with darkened windows. Before members of the press they held an auction of small sums of money nailed or attached to objects, the reserve prices being higher than the nominal value of the notes. You can decide who was the crazier during the mad summer of 1994, the K Foundation trustees or me. For in the early hours of the 23rd August 1994, in a boathouse on the island of Jura, off the west coast of Scotland, the trustees of the K Foundation burned the assets of the Foundation: £1 million in £50 notes. The event was filmed and a book entitled *The K Foundation Burn a Million Quid*[22] produced. I don't know what the Bank of England would say but there, I later thought, was £1 million of the 10 I was looking for.

Part VI

The Summer I Thought I Was a Dog

Chapter Ten

Don't Worship Me

It's now the Sunday of the May bank holiday weekend 1994, the day after I drove to Wilton and made my crazy £10 million challenge. Now I can tell you a little more about the strange, magical and mysterious months prior to finding myself hanging off Chiswick Bridge.

I awoke. It was Sunday morning and I was in a state of shock. I decided to get in the car and after a while found myself driving along the North Circular Road. Soon I saw a sign saying Barkingside, which conveyed a meaning to me. MI5 would be laughing at me so much that they were barking – or splitting their sides. But to me, it was very serious. Again, I did not really know what was going on, nor where I was going, but found myself heading north. I heard on the news that an unusual weather phenomenon had been observed the previous day, a daylight meteor shower in Wiltshire, where I had made the crazy challenge. MI5 had got the message. This was another piece of BBC Radio 1 fake news like the one broadcast at midnight the night before they announced the disappearance of Prince Charles's dog. But this time it was in response to my challenge – of that I was certain. Very unusual indeed, I thought. It just seemed too big a coincidence. With the benefit of hindsight I can't be sure that both of these broadcasts – the one about a dog flying an aircraft that I mentioned earlier, and the meteor shower – were nothing but my own hallucinations. At the time they seemed very real – and extremely important. In any case for a meteor shower to be seen only in Wiltshire the adjacent counties at least would have to be covered in cloud. I'd like to know the truth.

Next, some black dude came on the radio and started speaking to me. His speech was directed at me personally and lasted several minutes. He was depending on me. Then I remembered that Whitsunday had actually been the week before that of the bank holiday weekend, Whitsunday being the day on which the Holy Spirit descended upon the Apostles. It seemed a bit was still raining down on them this following Sunday, which was an Ember Day, when people have prayers said for them as they enter the Holy Order. Some was raining on me too.

As this man spoke to me I felt I was being admitted to something. Maybe, I imagined, this something was the Holy Order of an MI5/Comic Relief cell for which the MoD had created the new security classification of Absolute Secret for the two files. Hence I too could enter this Holy Order, or at least shake hands with it. But there are loads of handshakes with all sorts of levels of secrecy attached to them. One night in Club Rich UK a chap would ask to borrow my matches even though he had a lighter. A few minutes later I would realise he had not given me the matches back; so I asked for them. But instead of returning the matches he gave me the lighter – quite a nice lighter. The MI5/Comic Relief cell was sending its agents into Club Rich UK, having given them apparently trivial tasks to undertake, these tasks obviously being born out of simple witchcraft. I felt I had shaken hands with both Comic Relief and MI5 using a box of matches and a lighter. Only years later did it occur to me he might have forgotten I had just given him a box of matches and was wondering about my audacity in pocketing his lighter.

The weight of a thousand years of British history was upon my shoulders. It was getting bigger. The power of all the magic and mystery possessed by the future King of England's dog was now mine. I felt massively humble and contrite. I later discovered there was plenty more power where that came from. What on earth to do? If I was not being followed before, then I was now. Soon I saw another radio transmitter, like the one at Bannerdown Hill. It was controlling me, just as surely as if I were on a Scalextric track. Then again, maybe it was just that everyone was being controlled, and only I knew.

I was nearing Saffron Walden when I came across a charity football match against an Arsenal team. I saw the poster announcing it. The poster seemed aimed at me. Perhaps, I thought, the £10 million was already being raised. Perhaps it had been paid! Some massive psychological change had taken place in my head: I felt that rather than the British music industry being distant characters, I was moving amongst them, like I was one of them. I could touch them even though they weren't there. The biggest most revered pop stars seemed ever so close in a way I could not quite put my finger on. It was a wholly new feeling. It was wonderful.

But I had the distinct feeling that from now on, if I put one foot wrong, I would be dead meat. My knowledge of Prince Charles's dog was proving very difficult to handle and, quite apart from being dead meat, I could easily bring a thousand years of bad luck on the Royal Family if I did not learn how to control that knowledge. I knew that Saffron Walden was granted a licence by Charles I to sell saffron, hence its name; and Royalty seemed all around. A group of people in the rump of MI5, the Special Intelligence Service in fact, were watching my every move. They were fiercely and almost insanely loyal to Royalty to the point where merely thinking of them terrified me, as I had not yet properly realised I was one of them, in this act of dog. Before I got to Saffron Walden I found myself at Audley End, and once again I saw a sign announcing a dog show. This was 10 million times more significant than it normally would be – in a way that felt like your lottery numbers coming up.

Owners and their dogs seemed to be surrounding me. I could only deduce that MI5 had a national database of dogs and their owners for defence purposes, which would account for why it seemed so many pelican crossing lights were red, with an owner and dog crossing. It was a very weird thing to experience this, I can assure you. There was a general mobilisation of dogs and their owners. All were standing in position in case the existential outcome of the collective free wills of those brainwashing me (using my MTRUTH) and myself led me in a different direction to that predicted. Some ludicrous procession was forming around me, and everyone felt incredibly important as they dutifully walked their dogs to precise command. When there was no dog or owner I reasoned that they, MI5, were just trying to keep me guessing. I was unable to disbelieve what I was thinking because I wanted to believe it.

A high proportion of drivers passing me in the opposite direction seemed to be subtly raising their fingers from the steering wheel and this had the effect of hypnotising me in a rather unpleasant way. Also, it seemed, people in the street kept saluting me. But their salutes were, it appeared, deliberately done in a way that left me wondering if, for example, they were just scratching their temples. Of course I soon deduced there to be little point in approaching any of these people whom I thought were sending me these messages. If I could ask, and had done so, they would have been sworn to secrecy so there was no point in doing so. I could keep a record of how many times this happened and become a new kind of spotter, but what would that achieve? One thing it might achieve would have been to remove my delusion that I was receiving messages in this way, or that dogs and their owners were surrounding me, and I did not want to do that because it would remove *the boundless potential I had suddenly somehow sensed*. I realised such a course of action would almost certainly leave me none the wiser, and probably even more uncertain. I really believed I was an SBS Reserve MTRU.

Then there was the business of "your" and "you're". As you will know people often sound like they are saying "your" when they mean "you're". Every time I heard somebody begin a sentence with "your" when they meant "you're", I would hear the voice of Prince Andrew in my head saying, rather disenchantedly, "my", followed by that sentence. At times this got a little much to put up with. I could almost imagine others, in the same circumstances, walking around cursing Prince Andrew and demanding he shut the fuck up. For my part I was rather endeared to him for his apparent adoption of the mannerisms of those at my alma mater as I discerned over my MTRUTH.

I found myself going to buy a hamburger as a mark of respect for the astronauts Chaffee, Grissom and White who had perished in the Apollo 1 fire. Now I was a CIA slave simply paying homage, with everything I did being watched.

I had heard about a bird called a lyrebird and it was said to make a sawing sound. I made the connection when, from outside my parents' home I could hear electric saws going. MI5 were winding me up by accusing me of being a liar for saying my body had been invaded by aliens. The fact that the bird's name was spelt differently did not worry me in the slightest. I went round to try and see who was doing the sawing and, at the front of the house where they were, in the bedroom window, were hanging, side by side, a Union Jack and an Irish tricolour. I only just noticed that, mysteriously stuck to the window between them was a playing card.

I was also beginning to experience some other odd psychiatric effects with what I saw. To start with I formed the impression that, certainly in my vicinity, many more drivers had their headlights on than normal. There always seemed to be a convoy going the other way (in military convoys vehicles drive with their headlights on to avoid separation, even by day). Everywhere I went the military were ordering people to drive in the opposite direction to me. I, of course, never saw the policeman standing by the road with the sign telling the drivers to put their lights on. But that was not all. I found myself imagining that some drug had been given to me to make their headlights look brighter.

I started hearing a voice in my head, the voice of my brother in the police saying, over and over again, "Mr Blobby". I heard this what seemed like hundreds of times over the summer. It seemed to convey to me the excruciatingly embarrassing and ineffectual extent of my progress – and yet only drove me on, even if only to get away from the thought of Noel Edmunds' irritating creation.

I reached Saffron Walden and for want of something better to do, decided to visit the museum. Seal was on the car radio singing "You're playing with fire without getting burnt." This seemed to be a warning to me. In the museum I read about the English Civil War. I asked the curator what the Royalists wore in their helmets, and he told me something bright, whilst the rebels wore heather. I chose to put something vivid in my cap, metaphorically at the very least. I learnt about the Lucas family in Colchester and decided to go there for help, as quite obviously there was something seriously wrong, and having been under the siege there during the Civil War I believed the family expertise might be useful.

On the way to Colchester I happened to pick up a hitchhiker I knew who was going to a festival. His name was Nathan Wiseman. This seemed to be prearranged, with his surname holding significance. I gave him no information about what was happening – for example, that I thought MI5 had asked him to stand there in the hope I would pick him up, apparently coincidentally. Of course if I had told him what I was thinking he might have simply thought I was totally off my rocker. So, in that sense, I now felt horrifically trapped, a bit like someone who is trapped in a place from which they know they will never escape because no one knows they are there. The heavy weight of responsibility was on my shoulders.

I dropped him off and headed into Colchester. I was behaving confusedly and oddly. This was because of my aberrant interpretations of the stimuli I was receiving. These stimuli made me react by going around in circles. My free will was looking and feeling rather poorly – an amusing medical diagnosis I feel. I had been de-existentialised if you like, as though I had been put in a psychological autoclave.

I decided to look for a pub. I was near a large and elaborate water tower known as Jumbo the Elephant. But it seemed much more like an actual 150 feet-high elephant than it would to someone who was well. I asked a young chap where the nearest pub was. He invited me for a drink there and we got talking. But again it seemed as though he had been sent. Afterwards I wandered around a bit looking for the Lucas family home without success and then headed back to Saffron Walden. It was the thought that counted.

As I came into Saffron Walden, a police Land Rover Discovery appeared in front of me. I was being escorted into town. I kept noticing people putting their dogs on, or taking them off, their leads. I only had a free will when MI5 had my MTRUTH switched off. They could control me or, at the very least, substantially interfere with my behaviour, my actions then being a jointly controlled pocket of existentialism. This pocket of reality would be created by my free will and whoever it was controlling me using my MTRUTH. Every single thing I did was now incredibly important and significant, even the name of each pub I visited. I had to choose carefully, so as not to offend those who were following my every move. They might eliminate me. Perhaps they had already in a sense.

I parked the car and saw a man walk by, holding a dog lead out in front of him but without a dog. Perhaps the dog had just gone around the corner, perhaps not. This meant I was off the lead (that is my MTRUTH had been turned off). Now I could do as I pleased, no information be it subliminal, supra-subliminal, or otherwise, being used to control me. What a relief!

Soon I was leaving Saffron Walden. On the way back a van appeared in front of me. On the rear door it said "Woburn Wild Animal Kingdom". Whatever the real explanation for the van being there, it meant I was to go to Woburn the next day. The van was quite a way from Woburn and I reasoned the further away you see such a van from its origin the less likely it becomes. I laughed at the possibility that Prince Charles had called the Duke of Bedford and requisitioned the van. MI5 had then, using my MTRUTH, conducted a mind meld between the Duke of Bedford and myself. I do not know if such a thing is a moving-traffic violation but Prince Charles had invited the Duke of Bedford to NATO Northwood to illustrate how British Intelligence and the military had managed to capture my imagination and make me go to Woburn the next day. It was now I imagined that the Church of Latter Day Saints (the largest landowner in East Anglia) might have got hold of MTRUTH technology and were using it to brainwash those in their ministry. This seemed a somewhat insidious, though relatively harmless use of such technology when you think of how some might employ it.

Next day, as I made my way around Woburn Park, the BBC Radio 1 DJs, Lynn Parsons and Bruno Brookes, seemed to be making apposite remarks, as they played the all-time top one hundred. I took my hands off the steering wheel, looked around the inside of the car in the steering wheel's vicinity and asked myself what the hell was going on. It indeed seemed I had some sort of military augmented-reality system, an MTRUTH.

At this time, as well as my MTRUTH, I thought something was coming from a brilliantly concealed invisible head-up display in my car's dashboard, unable at this time to realise that it was actually in my head[23]. Again it felt like my car had eyes quite apart from those of the monkeys clambering all over it. The relatively unknown band Secret Affair was mysteriously at number 96 in the chart. I could not quite believe this unless the band had an organised campaign or the record had deliberately been inserted in the chart by MI5 to wind me up – or send me a clue. Once again there seemed to be an astonishing number of high performance motorbikes in my vicinity.

Almost like a piece of flotsam, and completely hypnotised, I found myself caught in a whirlpool and dragged out of control in the direction of London. I arrived outside Broadcasting House at exactly the same time as Queen's *Bohemian Rhapsody* was playing, it having been voted the all-time number one. They had got complete control over me using my MTRUTH and made me drive all the way there. Here I put my name in the visitors' book and told the security guard whom I had come to see.

Had anyone else ever found themselves in the same position, I wondered. It was as though this was all just a standard procedure and I was merely the latest to be processed. I waited, and then after seeing Lynn Parsons go by with her assistant, actually met Bruno Brookes and shook his hand.

I was left thinking those words over and over in my head: it's got to be a windup. Somehow, shaking his hand enabled me to regain some insight and control of myself. Intuition told me someone had had one over me. I drove away again feeling really stupid and thinking, or even saying aloud, "It's definitely a windup!" Then I wondered: wait a minute, *what is* a windup? Having established what one of those is, I asked myself how big could it get? I even reached the conclusion that the universe itself was the biggest windup of the lot. So maybe, I thought, all of creation was just a gigantic watch with Prince Charles's dog in the movement, a rather unusual movement.

I drove to Barnes, pointing my forefinger around open space and trying to make logical sense of the situation. Soon I was sitting down in that same pub where, a few days earlier, the landlady had been putting out the lucky heather before I drove to Her Majesty's Land Forces HQ at Wilton. She did not usually do this and had been asked to do so by the brewery at the request of MI5. I regained some composure and considered the situation. My mind was fighting a logical battle with my illness. If anybody could get out of this it would be me.

That night I went to a pub in Chiswick. At the bar were some people talking and one of them told me he had known a member of the group Badfinger who co-wrote *Without You*, the number one hit for Harry Nilsson and who had committed suicide. He did not tell me the other co-writer had also taken his life.

Walking back to Barnes a very sassy-looking pick-up with an impossibly good-looking driver stopped and an attractive girl bearing an uncanny resemblance to Amanda got in. This seemed aimed at me in a manner designed to make me feel a total loser and completely excluded. It did rather. It was Everyone-Else-Is-Having-A-Wonderful-Time-And-I-Am-A-Complete-Loser syndrome. At this moment I felt wetness on my left ear lobe, which I touched, to find it was bleeding. I believed that a powerful laser beam had been fired at my ear at the moment I saw the attractive girl get in the car. Then I heard a voice in my head say "An old one" – as though I had just been a victim of a standard Secret Service dirty trick. In reality I think I just had a bit of eczema.

The next thing I clearly remember is sitting, a day or so later, in The Ship pub in Bedford with my friend Brent (a former paranoid schizophrenic who painted the cover of this book). My mind seemed to want to make anagrams of everything. So with Brent living most of the time in Donegal I found myself thinking "lane dog" whilst Nairac became "Can IRA". I decided that Nairac had not been the real name of the SAS spy shot dead by the IRA and said to have been canned in a meat factory. For the press his name had been substituted with an anagram of Can IRA by British military intelligence. Confused and mystified by all that had happened, I asked him "Is it possible for an individual to be completely controlled by the media?" Not apparently surprised by this question, he said "Oh yes, it's well known that the Security Services can do that but they will only do it under certain circumstances." I shuddered a little and said to myself "Well they've really done me." Then I recalled how supermarkets subtly manipulate their customers and now it seemed I was an MI5 customer doing some very odd shopping for Comic Relief.

In the gents, having washed my hands, I was trying to dry them in the blower but it kept switching off and I had difficulty turning it back on. I seemed to recall the same thing in an episode of *Some Mothers Do 'Ave 'Em*. This was not by any means the first time this had happened. I noticed the name of the manufacturer (or the purported manufacturer) on the machine. It was Warner Howard. My brother Howard being a police officer it did not take me much to read a meaning into this name. I was pretty sure that somebody was watching me, probably at a remote location, and they were switching the drier off and on. I felt sure that, when I had reached my goal, a hot consistent hand drying experience was mine. But how to reach that goal? I felt I was getting warm even if the hand drier wasn't – yet, simply by my having become aware of what was really going on. Every single hand drier in the country, and probably elsewhere too, was wired to a PC at Thames House (MI5 HQ) and from there they could be switched on and off according to the whims of a Security Service officer who, perhaps, would only be able to watch if the person at the drier had, like me, cameras in their eyes.

That night, back at home; I picked up a copy of my old 1973 school magazine. Opening it at random I found the following poem, which seemed as though it had been presented to me from "the other side":

Elegy for a Soldier Killed in Action

So, boy, they got you at last, eh?
I knew they would,
I thought you was dead when the card came through the door,
And before that, when they graded you A1 –
A prime joint, boy, a prime joint.
You looked good in uniform,
You really made me and your ma proud of you, boy,
Standing on parade with your boots and your carbine
And your forage cap crisp like your ma had starched it that morning.
Only she hadn't, 'cause we hadn't seen you for a month,
We saw the picture in the local paper.
When you got your medal we was proud, boy,
The whole town was proud of our son.
If you'd come home on leave then, you could have had
                    anything you wanted, boy.
It was a pity you couldn't make it for your twenty-first,
Your ma was broken-up a piece by that,
So was Annie, boy – she's left town now.
Every time she went shopping she had to walk
                    past the recruiting office.
Last we heard she was working in Vegas, but she don't write any more.
She was real shook, kid, you had a good one there.
She'd have made a good wife, you'd have made a great couple –
Prime joints, boy, prime joints.

Laos, they said you got it.
I thought you was in 'Nam, but they said you weren't.
People back here thought you were a hero, boy,
All this stuff 'bout it being a bad war don't take
                    much hold in these parts.
Your buddy Mike didn't go, you know –
To 'Nam that is, he went to Canada instead.
I reckon his ma's got it worse than yours,
You're both dead to them, but you've got your medal.
No – I mean you had your medal,
'Cause I've got it now, son, I'm keeping it.

Your ma don't like to see it no more,
'Cause when she sees your name on it she sort of hurts inside.
She's all right though, kid, she's strong.

They tell me you was buried in Laos, boy,
By an Army preacher.
Glad you got yourself a Christian burial, it eased your
                    ma's heart just a bit.
We couldn't neither of us stand the thought of you just laid out cold,
But warm and stinking in the sun,
You was a good son, boy, a prime joint –
You was a real prime joint.

I dunno, why I write this, kid, but I do.
Your ma ain't the only one broken up, only it don't show with me.
I keep stopping to think, and then write some more.
I don't know where you are, son, I don't know where I'd send this letter.

Ian Hughes

Few knew where Captain Nairac got it – but it wasn't Laos. The poem merely confirmed all my delusions that I was engaged in a military theatre.

Meanwhile anything remotely connected with dogs practically barked at me and I became obsessed with car number plates, which, if I looked at them, often conveyed a message making me think they were put there by MI5. I was suffering the number plate variant of what is known as Capgras syndrome – a condition, named after the first to diagnose it, the French psychiatrist Dr. Jean Marie Joseph Capgras, in which you see doubles of people and think they have been put there, very often by the security services. Often I would see number plates with the letters CRP and KRP in them, these seeming to be personally offensive messages. Furthermore it now seemed quite possible that MI5 would arrange for swarms of cars to move into my vicinity when I was next driving. Then, one by one, these cars would move right in front of mine, their number plates together spelling out whole sentences in front of my eyes, sentences nobody else would see which were for my eyes only. It also seemed that a large number of Ford Fiestas were finding their way in front of me. It seemed they were all the Popular Plus model, rather than feeling paranoid, I liked it. I was popular with MI5 and they were surrounding me with large numbers of them to encourage me. The coming fiesta only encouraged the self-aggrandising tendency the illness came with. I also kept seeing the letters SVS on number plates, which barked at me "Special Vet Service", and I was oscillating wildly and uncontrollably between one end of the mental spectrum and the other, like somebody failing to balance on a gymnastics beam. It's obvious, of course it is, it's the Special Vet Service, I would think, and then less than seconds later: I must be stark raving bonkers. Once again, I remembered the catastrophe theory, in which you were either a genius or a lunatic depending on the route taken to reach your current position. I recalled that the mathematician whose book on the theory I had read was named Arnold. This name was shared by DJ Tony Blackburn's dog, which continually barked out from Radio 1 in the '60s and '70s.

This tenuous link no longer seemed a coincidence, but was causally and deterministically connected with me through the elaborate conspiracy of 1926 in the most substantial of ways.

I was sitting in the Kentucky Fried Chicken restaurant. Some Bedford High School girls came in and sat down to eat. One of them said to her friends "What would you do if the Queen came in here now?" As far as I know she did not – but I felt her presence. A local doorman, Danny Ferguson, did, however, visit this takeaway as recorded on the shop's security video minutes before his death. Before he had digested the meal he was hacked to death in his bed with a machete. That put me right off fried chicken restaurants. I had some video of him shot at the Railroad Earth/Lazy House gig.[24] Watching the video it became clear that Danny was alive and well, living in Jamaica.

When I had eaten my food (I've since stopped eating factory produced meat), I decided to have a curry as well. I even went into the restaurant, which was close to the one I had just dined in, but demurred. Instead I found myself staring in through an estate agent's window. Inside the window there was a sticker, containing the word "Challenger". At the precise moment I saw the word "Challenger", a car alarm went off in the nearby multi-storey car park and somebody walked past behind me saying, I thought, "I'm a builder." I was being nailed into position, militarily speaking. Builders were no longer just builders; window cleaners were no longer just window cleaners; and decorators were certainly not just decorators. I was now party to the most sensitive piece of military intelligence there was. They were all MI5 agents and they surrounded me. They were building in my illusions and delusions. They knew I was reading the word "Challenger". I had been one at Wilton just as surely as a Main Battle Tank driving through the gate of HQ.

At about this time there was a big promotion for the "Pepsi Max Big One", the huge roller coaster in Blackpool (it was the biggest in the world at the time). I was now being put on the mother of all roller coasters in this MI5 psychological warfare experiment. But who was really running the show? Who was actually operating my MTRUTH? I have said MI5 but the truth was that, at any particular moment, I had no idea. All I knew was that the Special Intelligence Service had been running the show since 1926. Right now, for all I knew, somebody in the CIA, the KGB, MI5, MI6, the Army Intelligence Corps, the Army's PsyOps Unit, Naval Intelligence, 22 Mobile Bath Squadron or some kids at Brampton County Primary School (my old school) could be operating it. It was just a game they could play. Hence it was not difficult to imagine the Royal Family having a go. In the case of the Royal Family it was a game in which they did not realise the virtual SBS officer whom they were controlling was a real person – me. They had not been told for some reason. I even imagined the moment the CIA took over the controls from whoever was controlling me prior to that moment. If you fuck with the Special Forces that's what you get, I thought, as I begun to think I was one of their number. I decided to go to Blackpool the next day.

The next morning, before my departure, I went into Andy's Records. Because I was now so sure I was being controlled using my MTRUTH I decided to approach the cassette shelves without bothering to see which letter I was looking under and with my eyes shut to be sure I pulled out a cassette at random. I opened my eyes and in my hand in a pink case was *The Sport of Kings* by the Liverpool band Pele. At the time this seemed an extraordinarily meaningful event. When I heard the lyrics it seemed even odder, what with songs about the British Army and Special Forces operations, telephone tapping, and a visit to Buckingham Palace to meet the Queen, for example. It was just too appropriate and seemed to be a sign from the one and only God. I went into the bargain bucket and pulled out Tasmin Archer's *Shipbuilding*. The message felt positive and meaningful.

I headed to Blackpool. Now I began to experience feelings of immense importance again, and had this awful sensation that I had to go to certain places, otherwise important people would be disappointed. This is ridiculous, I thought, but seemed powerless to stop it. I picked up a hitchhiker who had a cat on a lead. The cat looked well-travelled, and once in the car it just curled up and went to sleep like it were home, unlike the average non-MI5-trained cat which would have gone into a wild panic in a car, or maybe just pissed itself. He had been told by MI5 to wait until I picked him up, as MI5 knew I picked up hitchhikers. I suspected his cat was an MTRU. Come to think of it I thought our cats at home might also be designated military personnel along with all these dogs I had heard about who were said to bark when their masters were on their way home. There was no intuition or farfetched insight involved – they were simply Mobile Tactical Reconnaissance Units with Electronically-Augmented Imaginations, which MI5 would use to tell them who was on the way. They could see their masters coming in their EAVs. Or perhaps this *is* morphic resonance, the process said to explain such phenomena[25].

Arriving in Blackpool I was soon thundering around the exciting roller coaster. It seemed symbolic of the mental ups and downs I was already experiencing and was yet to experience. I purchased a photograph of myself on the roller coaster sitting next to some huge fat bastard and, when I looked at myself, I seemed particularly unattractive. Some time later I would find the photograph, and on this occasion I seemed the exact opposite. I was sure the picture had been touched up. In fact in Capgras syndrome it is quite common for people not to be able to recognise their own image or to believe that inanimate objects have been replaced. More amusingly there is at least one example of a patient who thought their dog was an impostor. In *Phantoms in the Brain*, Dr. V.S. Ramachandran, director of the Center for Brain and Cognition at the University of California, San Diego, wrote about one Capgras patient who thought his poodle has been replaced by an identical but different dog.

It felt like I was now being followed by an ever so subtle "moving block" radio system. Was that remark aimed at me, I would think, as I heard something said on the radio? I could not quite tell for sure, which meant only one thing: yes it was, because I wanted it to be. I found myself changing radio stations to see if it would go away but it just would not – so I believed it. I felt famous and became drunk with that possibility. Just north of Blackpool I found myself in a car wash listening to Johnny Mathis singing "I'd like to be a great big movie star" (from the Stylistics' *I'm Stone In Love With You*) and it certainly was like it had all been planned, ever such a long time ago. It all seemed beyond a dream. My fame in intelligence circles had been foreseen in the pub one Friday afternoon 68 years earlier. I had been spied on all my life, more closely than Prince William had been.

I got to Ambleside and booked into a hotel. The manager, who took me to my room, looked mysteriously like a chap from *It Ain't 'Alf Hot Mum*, and he put me in room 7, somehow succeeding in conveying the impression that the number was significant and lucky.

After being shown my room, I drove up the Honister Pass. I had been there before in CCF training back in the '70s but it was nice to drive up instead. I remembered how a car with the registration plate A1 CCF was always parked near my GP's surgery. At the top of the Pass I got out. With *The Sport of Kings* tape playing at top-whack and the door left open, I began clambering up the mountainside until the car looked like it was in an advertisement on the back cover of *The Sunday Times* magazine. A little down the valley was one of this country's more spectacularly-sited postboxes. I sent Steve Wright a postcard. This was to acknowledge what had been his part in the most successful military operation of all time: my being brainwashed into driving to Wilton. Further around the valley I stopped again and got out. You will recall I thought that, as well as there being cameras in my own eyes, my car could see too. So I walked down the road in front of the car and started admiring some yellow gorse flowers. As if my car had indeed got eyes, through which events could be seen from far afield, a few weeks later I saw a man appearing to mimic me opposite the statue of John Bunyan, back in Bedford. He seemed to be saying "You were right, I'll have a bit of that" as, oddly, he examined the yellow gorse flower in the large tub by the site of the old cinema where The Beatles and The Rolling Stones had once played. He had been sent by the Security Services.

I went out for a drink, firstly in The John Peel. As explained to me by the barman, this was not the renegade BBC Radio 1 DJ, but a Cumbrian huntsman, the most famous huntsman in the country. He was immortalised in a song by John Woodcock Graves: *D'yer ken John Peel?* Like Sir Charles Lucas he might help me it seemed.

Then to a nightclub where I met a blonde who told me she was a helicopter pilot. In view of my work on the Apache anti-tank helicopter project, I had thoughts that her presence there was not mere coincidence. I had quite a few drinks and headed back to the hotel.

The next day was a big one: the BBC Radio 1 road show was in Bedford and I felt an overwhelming urge to be there. I had been responsible for this during the dying days of Seagull Records – when I had met Mark Goodier. I wanted my record label to work but in reality it was over. I was now under huge psychological pressure. I could not sleep and, however MI5 had done it, by hypnosis or through my MTRUTH, they had succeeded in getting the Radio 1 DJs to totally control me. Something was telling me my label was going to be a success after all. But it needed a miracle. I believed there was going to be one. The percentage of my behaviour that was clearly down to a healthy degree of existentiality on my part was just too low. This accounted for my position.

Not able to sleep I went out and got in the car, probably well over the drink-driving limit. This was something I was certainly not in the habit of doing and nor am I proud of it. I drove off, not towards Bedford, but to Barrow. I was still going walkabout and the Tasmin Archer tape was telling me where to go. I felt like a dog chasing its tail. I would feel like that for some time, 10 years in fact.

I drove out of town alongside the lake, past a waiting police car. A few miles down the road, I saw the flashing lights approaching rapidly and pulled over. The police Discovery shot by at a hell of a rate. Relieved, I drove off again.

A while later I arrived in Barrow. As dawn approached, and not know Barrow at all, I found myself pulling up at a partly opened gate in a wall, the gate leading to a derelict flat area of industrial land. The top of the wrought iron gate said "Vickers Shipbuilders". I drove through into the open land, which was by the docks. The waning moon was out overhead in its quarter phase. It seemed by design that I was there and had not driven around Barrow haphazardly but gone straight to this gate. A black cat ran across in front of me and through the gate. This meant good luck. The SAS had just released it from around the other side of the wall, out of sight. And *of course* my car could see; that is MI5 were watching everything that happened, and had been since some time before the "Ducks Crossing" incident.

I reached over and put in the Tasmin Archer *Shipbuilding* tape. The moment seemed extraordinarily poignant. I listened and then drove off with *Solsbury Hill* playing from a bootlegged tape a girlfriend had given me, it being an aide-mémoire on one hand and a film script on the other. That was how I was feeling.

I now headed north along the coast. I noticed the road signs had sacks on them with only one destination showing. I had an overwhelming urge to go to Workington but the signs had been hidden. MI5 had this done in order to send me the way they wished. I arrived at the M6 some while later, and a Kellogg's delivery truck came alongside as I joined the motorway. It was obvious it had been a co-ordinated move with money involved to help raise the £10 million, the game being to advertise in the most exotic area of military communications; that is in the cameras in my eyes – in my MTRUTH. I felt compelled to press on and get to the road show. I felt that something was going to happen. Taking frequent breaks I eventually got to the Bedford turn-off at midday, very tired. Really you could say it was irresponsible to do all this pointless mad driving but I was obsessed with the dog. And if the money had not been paid by the deadline I felt Prince Charles's dog was still very much alive: I would procure the money myself and the dog would never die.

As I pulled off the M1 a large lorry with a very long low-loader in tow pulled out in front of me moving very slowly. The lorry had been put there deliberately, this time to slow me down to a safe speed. They wanted to make sure I got back safely. In Bedford, the Borough Council had all its banners and flags flying. I was a hero returning and the bunting was for me. It seemed like a welcome home party.

Having arrived home I had a shower and wandered down to the river where the road show I arranged was. Large crowds were sitting enjoying the atmosphere.

I heard a voice of a passer-by say "I did not want anything terrible to happen." That might have been the case but it did not stop the Mull of Kintyre helicopter crash the next day, killing a member of the Rowing Club, which was only a 30 seconds' walk from this spot.

My fingers began to tingle in a way I had never experienced, and then my toes did the same. A terrible cloud now rapidly descended over me and within seconds I was in a blind panic. MI5 had decided there was a possible terrorist threat, did not want me there, and had poisoned me. To me, this explained the passer-by's remark. Although I could, right or wrong, easily deny its having anything to do with me, the remark seemed, because of my schizophrenia, to be aimed at me. But then what does schizophrenia become if it actually was aimed at me? Perhaps it was not really a passer-by who said it. I certainly did not see their lips move. Perhaps the remark had been virtually placed in their mouth using my MTRUTH to overlay a parallel reality onto mine. Of course in truth the panic attack was a combination, not only of schizophrenia, but extreme tiredness and no sleep, a hangover, stress, large amounts of caffeine and little water.

I instinctively headed for The Ship without giving any thought as to why. I asked the landlord Bill for a shot of whiskey. The whole world was caving in on me. "Get an ambulance Sheila," I said to his Irish wife.

I walked out to the beer garden and went down on my knees. I felt I was dying. Sheila came out to tend to me. I got in the ambulance. "Have you taken any drugs?" asked the paramedic. I could not keep still and was in a wild delirium. Every single nerve in my body felt like it was attached to an electricity supply. I could not keep my head still and the ambulance seemed like it was tumbling out of control in the rapids of a powerful river. We got to the hospital. I could hear sirens going off in every direction, as though every ambulance in the fleet had been told to drive around the block with its siren on.

Sheila and my mother appeared. I was all over the place. I was sitting in front of a panel of doctors. It seemed like a Civil Service board. I was falling out of control like a dive-bomber with a dead pilot at the controls, "I've let everyone down" being my last words.

I woke up, completely recovered, some hours later, having been knocked out with something pretty heavy. But how recovered was I? I lay there for some time wondering why the sirens were still screaming in my ear. Reality was that this being a hospital, there were bound to be more sirens especially as the psychiatric wing, the infamous Weller Wing of Bedford Hospital, was next to A&E. But my mind told me otherwise. They seemed to be continually going off to tell me something: this being that there was something seriously wrong with the situation. Well that was certainly true. I seemed to have just had an almighty stress-induced panic attack. But I also had the thought I had been poisoned at the road show going round my head.

I made a phone call to my old tutor. I didn't mention that I suspected I had been drugged somehow down at the riverside. I remembered that passer-by's voice again saying "I didn't want anything terrible to happen", and for some reason I thought the poison had been deadly nightshade.

Next morning I was invited to play Scrabble. I had never been a patient in a psychiatric hospital before, and I was in shock partly due to that. Double Word Score "Jew". I noticed a Cathleen Caddick painting on the wall and thought of the boat parties, as she was connected with the Woodland Trust, for which the parties had raised money. There seemed something mystical about the painting's presence, mystical enough to produce a slight movement in me. But if that was odd, what happened next was positively bizarre.

One of the patients, an elderly man, approached me and apologised. I considered this most likely to be a symptom of his illness, and accepted his apologies by saying "That's quite all right." Now he walked away, and came back for another pass. "I'm really sorry" he said. Again I held up my hand to acknowledge the apology. Back he came, again and again, probably five or six times. Then attracting my gaze, he turned his whole body in such a manner that I could only look where he was now pointing. This was at a copy of that day's newspaper, on the front page of which was a picture of the Queen holding her hands up to her face in excitement. The picture had been taken at Epsom the previous day, where her horse had nearly won the Derby. It was a message from MI5 underlining the sovereignty of events at Wilton the previous weekend.

The man's behaviour was a mystery. I imagined he was not a bona fide patient. I later deduced that the man had been Prince Charles in disguise. But then, as my imagination really started taking flight in response to the barrage of bizarre perceptions I was experiencing, I fell upon the conviction that John Lennon's death had been a faked event. He had gone to ground as part of a religious cult to return when world peace dawned on earth. The person in disguise was not Prince Charles but John Lennon! I fear Mr Lennon may have come out a bit early if it was him. But the man did not reveal his true identity – and nor has Yoko Ono called me to enquire of her husband's health.

After the game of Scrabble I was allowed home, though I was not officially discharged until a few days later.

Walking back to my parents' house from the hospital I saw a young chap putting up a poster in an odd place. He was securing it on the side of the moat around County Hall just above the water level. This reminded me of another painting in the hospital of a woman at the water's edge, my making the connection apparently being a symptom of schizophrenia. But it was a result of the exceptionally close tabs MI5 were putting on me. They had seen what had happened on the ward through my MTRUTH, through devices actually implanted in my eyes' own aqueous humour, the substance filling the remainder of my eyeballs. The stuff in the eyes might be called humour but it did not seem altogether amusing at this moment. Nevertheless I was rather satisfied I was important enough to demand MI5 attention. The poster was advertising a gig a few nights later of a band worryingly called Suicide Nation. I was not suicidal – at least not at that point.

Crossing the Suspension Bridge I saw two young girls coming towards me. When they were a few yards from me they stopped. Then one of them jumped from side to side a few times saying, as she did so, "I was afraid the bullets were going to go through you and hit me." I had no doubt this was an enacted scene arranged by the Security Services – to remind me of what had happened in the Six Bells a few weeks earlier. I could think of no other explanation for their behaviour. It was most mysterious.

I did not feel quite right. Tom drove me to a local pub, Ye Three Fyshes at Turvey. They had two homebrewed beers amusingly called "This" and "That", so Tom said "A pint of This and a pint of That please." It was a bit Alice in Wonderland again. From his demeanour, I imagined the barman had been brought in especially from Sandhurst just to serve me. I was sure that after my challenge I would be followed, if I had not been already. I turned over my beer mat. There was now a very loud clap of thunder, which seemed to be causally connected with my having done so. I heard the clap over my MTRUTH. But it was actually raining outside and it was not a film set either – I looked and it certainly looked real. In this beautiful summer of madness, I thought the clouds had been seeded, and somebody, the MoD or Pentagon, had created lightning at the flick of a switch for purposes of witchcraft and national defence.

Whilst the military was fiddling with the weather, Prince Charles had been recruiting attractive single girls to stand around on the pavement where I was walking. They were all told to look like they were waiting for someone but weren't told who it was. The primary purpose of this was that MI5 wanted to have some offspring of mine to spy and experiment upon in the future.

Tom seemed to be questioning everything I did. But what was so eccentric about insisting on going into the car wash before this downpour? I did not know it was about to rain. His head would still shake in vacuous disbelief weeks later about this, so I was not the only one suffering this disbelief syndrome. But I was the one who was really ill, not him, and nobody will persuade me that I was not now mentally ill. I turned over another beer mat and it said "Marston's Pedigree" and I had an unstoppable fit of laughter as it reminded me of dogs – which were the principal subject matter of my schizophrenic thoughts at this time. I could only deduce that I must now be considered mad. But what I had done at Wilton also now seemed incredibly amusing for a moment.

I bought a Fillet-O-Fish from McDonald's, and some bloke passing by said "Well done son." In my mind McDonald's was the 'son' of the United Kingdom as well as *the* symbol of Americanism. Again I felt he was talking to me, and not to someone else about something entirely unconnected. Of course there was no point in asking him if MI5 had sent him because, as I explained I had reasoned before, he would have been sworn to secrecy. Therefore, if asked, he would have behaved exactly as if he was not talking to me at all: he would have denied MI5 had sent him.

I went to the Suicide Nation gig. Did that doorman say "Hello Clive"? Yes he did. It had been noticed by MI5 in their incredibly detailed assessment of the situation that the doorman knew someone else called Clive. Somehow, even without this other Clive's knowledge, he had been made to arrive at the exact moment I did, and this would explain how it appeared the doorman was saying hello to me. On the other hand it was almost as though there were two Clives and this one was the 'other me'! Or maybe the doorman *did* know who I was and now I *was* famous. At the time, I did not want to spoil this delusion. All I knew was that he had said "Hello Clive." If there really was someone else called Clive there, then I imagined there must be other scenes being acted out. These performances would be such that it was a statistical certainty that I would observe a worthwhile proportion of them. I would then be in a parallel universe of schizophrenia in which I had been trapped by both my actions and those of MI5. In return MI5 would recruit ordinary people to play tricks on me in order to further this legendary manoeuvre. It just seemed so obvious to me. What had happened at Wilton was such a ginormously significant thing that I just could not conceive it being ignored. I was certainly expecting something to happen and was continually looking out for it to do so. But I did not know what to expect. I certainly had not yet thought of a book. As yet, I had not quite thought through recent events in logical progression; so I was extremely vulnerable to my own ideas, all of them driven by the strange disappearance of Prince Charles's dog. It was an intricate and detailed illness. I believed I was being bombarded with manipulated reality.

Next day another odd thing happened to me. I was sitting in the pub garden on my own when a young ex-army chap came up and started chatting. He said he had been working for the United Nations in Vietnam; so I guessed he might have been sent to spy on me to make my MI5 file look more amusing when it was released at the Public Record Office in 2044. Whilst we were talking, I found myself looking at a bright light. At this moment another chap in the garden made a sort of irritated gesture as though to suggest I was not to look at bright lights, it seemed because the sensors in my eyes would be swamped. Earlier I had seen a woman wearing a pair of spectacles with one lens so badly damaged that she could have seen through one eye only. I wondered if I too had a device in one eye but not the other. She seemed sinister.

Something took me towards Twinwoods Aerodrome, from where Glenn Miller had flown on his last, fatal, journey. I had once had my hair cut in a barber's shop in Castle Road, Bedford. He was an old chap and he told me how he had given Glenn Miller a haircut when the famous bandleader lived in Bedford during the War, so I asked him for a Glenn Miller haircut. On another occasion, as a child, I'd had my hair cut by an old man at RAF Cranwell, where Lawrence of Arabia had been stationed between the Wars. Therefore I may have had my haircut by both Lawrence of Arabia's and Glenn Miller's hairdressers.

Near the aerodrome a mother and child walked past. The child was rolling a ball. This meant I had to play ball, as though I was a dog who liked to play – again it was prearranged. There was nothing I could do about it. It reminded me of the ball incident at Northwood.

Radio 1 now announced that there were certain arrangements, which needed to be made before any public announcement was made. There was not really any doubt in my mind that this was aimed at me, and really it all seemed quite straightforward. MTRUTH or no MTRUTH, receiving these messages from public radio services certainly saved the need for a mobile phone. But something made me feel that even to think of answering back would constitute schizophrenia, because the way the statement was made meant that it could equally have a perfectly legitimate explanation, which had nothing to do with me. I was truly trapped by my thoughts though just for a moment I'd had some insight.

When I saw the ball rolling and thought it was deliberate, it reminded me of a Roy of the Rovers story from my *Tiger and Jag* comic when I was a child. It was the story in which a bomb was discovered on the causeway to the Melchester Rovers ground and in order to prevent the crowd from leaving, Roy had to juggle the ball while the bomb was defused. I had to provide similar entertainment prior to there being some enormous media denouement of my activities. For his part, I kept thinking that Prince Charles hadn't just got attractive girls to hang around near me but had arranged for the county youth theatre to enact little incidents in my vicinity (like the two girls on the bridge), in order to influence my mind.

The problem was that my senses seemed to be heightened in some way, which led me to the impression that all sorts of magic tricks were being performed on me. But then I almost expected as much after what had happened. The very substance of everything around me seemed to be imbued with some mystical wealth, and my hands moved through it like hands in a casket of gold and jewels buried beneath a castle floor for hundreds of years. I looked at Tom's National Rowing Championships medal and it pinged and started swinging without me touching it. But the window was closed and the room was empty but for me. I remembered the intangible atmosphere that my Uncle Louis, a professional magician, would conjure when he performed tricks at my grandmother's renowned parties in Cornwall Road, Ruislip. The atmosphere now seemed redolent of this. I thought of what the concrete there might be hiding.

A fly hovered in front of my face. It seemed like it was making a sanctified legal representation to me from the insect kingdom. I found two snails having sex, and it felt like I had been a blind man whose sight had returned. Nothing was disappointing. Everything was amazing. I was six and it was my birthday. I was five and waking up on the first day of my seaside holiday. It just got better and better. A spider's web found its way to my hands, and it felt like my own fingers had spun the silk. The atmosphere was sparkling and shimmering like the sun reflected in a babbling brook.

I went to the café in the park and found myself being shown photographs by a girl. She told me these had been taken by her friend; the singer Mark Gardener in the band Ride. The closeness of this pop star merely confirmed all my feelings of importance. And the concept of photographs of unknown people taken by famous people told me that everything was now totally inside out.

Later that afternoon I was walking through the arcade in town, and now more wholly paranormal weirdness fell about me. A child was on her hands and knees blowing a heart-shaped balloon along the ground. I imagined her blowing it through the miniature door in the arcade wall to a magical kingdom – not so much through the looking glass but the caretaker's cupboard. I thought of the line "Blew the heart right out of the arcade" from the song *The Word Is...* on the Pele album I had bought on the day I had driven to the Lakes. I imagined the child was acting on IRA instructions.

There was still a massive unresolved conflict in my head. On the one hand it seemed MI5 had fitted me with MTRUTH as a Comic Relief stunt to raise money and on the other it seemed I might be seen as just a dangerous religious cult member. Somehow I concluded I had to spend money to raise money, though how I could only imagine.

Information coming from the television and radio still seemed to be aimed at me personally as per the strong anthropic principle of the universe. The anthropic principle is the cosmological principle that theories of the origin of the universe are constrained by the necessity to allow individual human existence. Hence the strong anthropic principle is that everything is put there for humans. I had gone a stage further though and thought it was all put there specifically for *me*: call it the very strong anthropic principle if you like or, to use the basketball term, an Intelligence Service full press.[26] Put another way the principal says that "the party is only for those who get there, and aren't killed on the way." I had every intention of getting there – if I had not arrived already. I even found myself feeling guilty if I did not watch television in case somebody important had messages for me. When I watched the list of credits at the end of programmes it seemed to have been altered in order to hold some meaning to me. To think everything had been put there for me and me alone is a rather vain philosophy and was, of course, a symptom of my illness. But I loved it.

One day I noticed that a book, *Royal Wedding*, about the wedding of Prince Charles to Lady Diana Spencer, was sticking out on the shelf to the right of the television. It had been pulled out like this deliberately so that Prince Charles, who was on the left side of the front cover, was visible, peering from the bookshelf. MI5 had had the book pulled out. Then I foresaw that, as a result of their actions, a subliminal image of Prince Charles would appear on the right of the television screen, as British Intelligence wanted to augment the mystery of my actions that bank holiday weekend. Indeed this I now hallucinated. They would broadcast other information too in order to interfere with my behaviour, just as my friend Brent had confirmed they would, given the right circumstances. So, for example, I found myself believing that the gaze of eyes on the television indicated objects in the room around the set. I was not averse to sending out some messages myself and went into a motor store where, without batting an eyelid, the shop assistant took my order for a pair of new number plates: "DOG 1".

Then I went into an electrical store and one of the customers said "Everyone's got loads of money." This seemed to be aimed at me and I bought some things I did not need, still thinking I was in some Comic Relief promotion. I bought a two-week timer I would never use. It seemed to convey some significance as to what would happen in two weeks time. I also bought some sports clothes I did not really need either. It would always have been impolite to say anything back to any of these people who, my mind told me, were talking to me, so I gave no indication I believed their words were for me.

I was walking near the river and in my head I heard a voice saying "They're just people." Stella Rimmington, the then Director General of MI5, was talking to me and trying to reassure me about my strange feelings concerning these passers-by. Whilst she was the Director General of MI5 I kept finding myself thinking I was the literal 'head' of MI5, my head being packed full of electronics. She was trying to train me out of schizophrenia. But the reassurance soon turned to something else when I heard someone shout aloud nearby, and not in my head this time, "Simon should not have come back." The overheard remark gnawed at my mind. It reminded me of the day I had gone for a run with my old school friend Simon. I was a bit unfit and he went ahead but returned so we could run together. It seemed we had been followed. Such was the sensitivity of the computer modelling of the Apache anti-tank helicopter feasibility study that it was only natural the Security Services would want to know everybody I spoke to.

I saw a Borough Council rubbish lorry go by. It had a sign on the roof saying "Cleansing Hit Squad". I felt a mysterious paranoia, as it was clearly suggestive of the ethnic cleansing going on in Rwanda. The lorry had been driven past me deliberately on MI5 instructions and seemed to suggest more genocide was on its way. It was. I was an MI5 officer and this was the daily intelligence report coming in! The later news from Bosnia only seemed to confirm this. But somehow it had a strange effect on me in that I could not believe the report was real. A florid theory came to me concerning a doctor friend of mine who had been working in Rwanda providing medical relief. He had performed a huge Comic Relief illusion, perhaps using old film footage and the MI5 contacts it seemed he was bound to have. The genocide not having taken place was, of course, an attractive fantasy. But my knowing this somehow meant I could emerge as a mega-hero from what I subconsciously perceived to be a bit of a career dead end: my clearance would be removed. I was seriously ill, but not for imagining that.

Following the lorry was a car whose number plate was "PAY 10". Again I thought it was being driven past me on instructions. The 10 were the IRA hunger-strikers who, one by one, had starved themselves to death back in 1981 and, it seemed, I was to recompense them for their troubles. I was becoming more minded to do such a thing and the years to come would give me plenty of time as well as opportunity to think of doing just that. And of course the fact that the initials of the Bedford Borough Council were "BBC" seemed supremely significant – as did the parking of the BBC Dog Warden's van outside my local.

Then I saw a van, which said "Precor" on the side. My mind disregarded the possibility there was no significance in its driving past and instead I found myself thinking the Security Services had done this to brainwash me into thinking something fantastic was about to happen. Either that or it already had and nobody had told me yet. Later I even imagined this was sensitive intelligence from the Irish government advertising the imminent greatness of the band The Corrs. Thankfully, I now find it rather difficult to believe that anyone would go to such lengths to interfere with my mind, though the state of schizophrenia I was in at that time left a gaping hole for my deluded mind to fall into. Fall into it I did. I felt very important with my farfetched delusions.

About that time there was a film on television set in Italy during World War II. It was rather comical, and involved a certain amount of playing dead, which I found extraordinarily amusing. It seemed the room was full of laughing gas, as I could not control my hysterical laughter, and hoped nobody would notice it.

The instability of my situation coupled with the knowledge I had gathered earlier in the spring now showed itself. It did so in a way that was not to be the last demonstration of my perceived duality of mind. At some point during the film there was a break in the transmission. For an instant I found myself just sitting looking at myself in the television screen as though it were a mirror, and indeed that was all it was. I was just seeing my reflection in the screen whilst it was blank. I was sensitive to this and it made me climb back in the chair. For a moment or two I seemed to be inside the television. It felt eerie. I went from hilarious laughter to deep dread in seconds.

However unstable I was feeling, I was gratified to notice the bowl of marbles was still on the table in front of the television. I had not lost them. But later that day both my parents were in the room and, from the movement of their feet; I seemed to be receiving Morse code messages. In particular I noticed my mother's foot, which was tapping away like the telegrapher in *High Noon*, except I was sure my mother did not know Morse. Her knee just went up and down like a telegrapher's sending-key as she watched the news. I was damn convinced she was putting out messages. Moreover I thought the bowl of marbles had been put there by MI5. As for the cat, it was certainly putting out something. I saw it still for a second, looking towards the button which, when pressed, rang the old servant's bell. Then it gradually turned its head in a most extraordinarily paranoid-looking manner and suddenly ran off like the clappers, as though it'd had the fright of its life. Was it just a flea, I wondered, or had it got the same problem I had? Quite likely, the house seemed infested both with defence electronics as well as insects and I was being bitten to pieces but at least I had no fur for the fleas to hide in. I was so overcome with the mystery of this that I hardly dared think that the cat might have an MTRUTH too. So to have a quiet word in its ear by way of explanation was out of the question. But if the cat was an MTRU with an EAI how could I possibly explain it to the creature? At least its controller would then know that I knew, whoever they were, and this might facilitate an environment more suited to the cat's personal disposition. This might result in a very happy-looking cat watching a *History of British Cat Food Advertisements* production on its EAI in supra-subliminal mode, unbeknown to those in its vicinity.

A page of plans belonging to Tom now fell off the table. It tortured me with the knowledge my own paper records were poor. This filled me with suicidal dread. The falling of the paper did not seem to have been accidental. I felt ashamed.

Later as I was about to go out on my bike, the thought of Martin Galvin, the head of North American Aid for Irish Independence (NORAID) came to mind. My brain was like an open map on the table at the War Games Club back at school. This thought tortured me as I tried to confront whatever truth there was in it. I was totally naked. My mind was no longer mine. It was open for anyone to wander around, like a public park; and it was full of dog mess. I broke into a horrible sweat. But this seemed the right reaction because if I did not detest Martin Galvin beyond words I might be shot by MI5 outside the front door as soon as I opened the gate (my feelings towards the IRA would later moderate dramatically, in keeping with the peace process).

Then, through the paranoia in which my mind was swimming for its life, I saw a green ammunition case by the gate. It had a big white sticker on it with, in red letters, the word "SUBJECT". Subject is military intelligence speak for a person under surveillance. It referred to me. The case had been put there by MI5. Furthermore there was a brightly coloured plastic bottle top on the pavement outside the front door. It too had been put there deliberately by MI5 rather than just having been dropped. I was too frightened to realise that, if I was right and it had been MI5, I was, by the power of positive thinking, one of the world's most powerful men. As my delusions advanced over the next three years and I did see how powerful MI5's attention made me, I noticed that other people also seemed to have had bottle tops put outside their front door on the pavement. But I felt that, unlike me, they had no idea how powerful they were. I never found out if the ammunition case had simply been bought by Rupert at the auction or, of course, who the litterlouts were who dropped their bottle tops. I was practically existing on the power of positive thought so to say, that MI5 putting a bottle top on the pavement outside my house did not make me extremely powerful would be simply nihilistic.

At about this time there happened to be a few conversations in the house about the replacement of mercury amalgam fillings with ceramic ones. These conversations tortured me with the belief there was some kind of ulterior reason for them: everyone had to go to the dentist to have an MTRUTH microphone fitted in their teeth.

I had now bought two mountain bikes within a short space of time; one was a Raleigh Kalahari for which I ordered the sexiest and most comfortable black sprung Brooks' leather saddle you ever saw. I also bought another bike for my future girlfriend to ride, it being red, made in the USA, with the Stars and Stripes on the frame. I got on one of the brand new bikes and Tom got on the other.

Soon we were sitting in the garden at the back of The Bear pub with the bikes facing each other. The minutest detail of my surroundings had now become significant to me and, as the bikes faced each other, I felt strong powers of symbolism emanating from them, one British-made, one American. I got the drinks and Clint Eastwood was staring me out from the pinball machine, which Howard Marks, the king of marijuana dealers and former MI5 associate, was playing. Bizarre. Well actually it was not Howard Marks but I was mindful of how much he looked like him. This was one of the first occasions I experienced Capgras: very strange.

I noticed that the pub's new carpet had the pattern of equispaced triangles. The carpet had been chosen by MI5 as they knew this would make me think of discrete deterministic battlefield models and the cascading effects they have. They were just playing with me. All the time the carpet had been there but *only now* was I seeing it.

Back in the pub garden I looked down at the table on which somebody had carved a number, which I believed to be a file number at RARDE. Next to the number was the message "Sound familiar?" It certainly did seem familiar, but in reality it would be extraordinary if it really were that number. However at the time I was convinced the number and message had been put there by MI5. The Special Intelligence Service was unable to contemplate MTRUTH technology not being fitted to at least one subject without MI5's prior agreement.

In the lead-up to that most apocalyptic of bank holiday weekends the radio had been playing continually and, it seemed, most appositely, The Beautiful South's version of *Everybody's Talkin'*. I could only believe it was aimed at me because I believed I was such a genius that my course was already determined. Everybody was talking at me just as in the song and, it seemed, MI5 were teasing me with the notion that I could not hear a word they were saying but just echoes of my mind. It was a wonderful and most odd feeling. Even more strangely, my mind seemed to recall how a man who sang the song *Misty* had released before the song in question. Misty had been the name of my friend Simon's dog. Though this is now clearly an extremely tenuous connection, at the time it seemed *enormously significant*. Dogs seemed to trigger my imagination at the deepest level whenever possible. This was severe schizophrenia.

The Mull of Kintyre helicopter crash was still very much on my mind. I simply could not stop thinking that this had been a direct military response to what had happened at Wilton. I believed that, whether or not they were alive or dead, those on board knew what had happened. It seemed they might have been directly involved in what had happened to me. Knowing one of them, Michael Maltby, from the rowing club, only made this possibility seem more likely. Basically I was now suffering a disbelief syndrome, and it all went back to the dog.

One day I was driving past Marshall's car showroom in Bedford when I saw a Royal Mail van parked with its hazard indicators on. It seemed I was being told to go in and buy a brand new car. I managed to resist but felt really churned up. I had slipped into a ludicrously patriotic state of mind but despite this I now visited Hildark Motors, whose name itself sent me into a wild paranoia. It seemed like I was in a mixture of *It's a Knockout* and *Patriot Games*, in the latter of which a CIA analyst interferes with an IRA assassination and is targeted for revenge. I sat in one of the cars on sale, all of them being Citröens, almost as though I had been put up to it. I left the garage not having purchased anything, seeing the owner as rather like a Jewish businessman in Nazi Germany. Later I would have a wild vision of possible courses of action for Mr Hildark, who could not make a sale because the public had suddenly gone ultra-patriotic too. The possibilities were laughably farfetched, and though I have forgotten what most of them were, I was left picturing Mr Hildark running out of his garage on fire, having soaked himself in petrol and set fire to himself for not selling British cars. On another occasion my thoughts explored an avenue of logic, which led me to feel I had psychically penetrated the Japanese Secret Service, unbeknown to anyone. It was a peculiar feeling and one, which I could only dispel by shaking my head and clicking my fingers near my ear.

My Rover was due for a service. I took the car to Marshall's. Even the make of my car barked "dog" at me. When I collected it and drove off, I nearly lost control when I put my foot on the throttle. MI5 had had a turbocharged engine fitted to make the car a wolf in sheep's clothing. I hardly dared look under the bonnet. I was embarrassed. I thought of the Weber carburettor in my old Austin A35. Friends used to think, when we left the traffic lights, that the excellent acceleration this carburettor afforded in such a small and old car was a joke it was so quick. The insurance man did not know – a bit naughty. This serviced Rover was something else. But the engine had not really been replaced with a turbo; I was letting myself believe it had – inanimate Capgras syndrome. The service had certainly improved the performance of the car and I just went along with the belief because the idea was attractive to my deluded mind. What was strange though was a slow puncture. A previous puncture, as shown to me by the shocked mechanic, had been repaired with a patch from which the cover had not been peeled. Needless to say I suspected sabotage by MI5, or even the IRA, and I was rather paranoid, if not proud, about it. But maybe he was lying. And if he was lying why would he? MI5 had got his bosses to tell him to lie to me. It was inconceivable that somebody had put a patch on my tyre without peeling off the backing.

Chapter Eleven

Mystery

Cambridge's Strawberry Fair[27] had arrived, and at the Fair there was a man selling whistles, which you could use your tongue with to mimic various birds. This person, standing there right in front of me in a public place, was in the Special Air Service. There was some kind of magical power attached to him. I believed he could control trained songbirds and crows to fly where he wanted, like a falconer. Perhaps only hours earlier he had been observing me from afar.

I remember little of the bands, though Kingmaker was playing. It seemed I was being turned into a kingmaker myself hence, of course, the name held significance to me. At the regatta the same day, Bedford School's 1st VIII rowed by and it felt like it was doing so to order for my benefit.

I had not yet learnt how to prevent feelings of nauseous, massive remorse and embarrassment at anything less than utter perfection. It was like a 24 hours per day, seven days per week, Royal visit. I found myself turning my head away, excruciatingly embarrassed at the most minor fault. An ice-lolly wrapper lying on the pavement was perfectly valid and understandable grounds for suicide at the very earliest opportunity. Under the next bus would do. Now the Queen herself was watching through the cameras in my eyes. The fact that I would not even look at the toilet paper I had just used gives you some idea of how real this Cameras-In-The-Eyes syndrome was. I could not look at it out of embarrassment believing Her Majesty, or somebody, was looking, or maybe even being forced to look, through them using my MTRUTH.

For some reason, although it was the height of summer, my lips were chapped and split. I went into a department store and bought a rather expensive lip salve costing several pounds. Then I went into a record store. I was standing at the counter. I cannot remember to what end. Somebody, a customer, put down a cassette box on the counter next to me. The assistant asked if he could help me. I gave him the empty box although I did not know who the artist was. I did not buy anything else. I walked out of the shop, and on the wall in front of me was a poster for The Indigo Girls at the Corn Exchange. By sheer and uncommon chance I had just bought their new album *Swamp Ophelia*. The person who put the box there had meant it for me. MI5 traditionally recruit a lot of their agents at Cambridge, and this person was a potential recruit on a small errand for them. One could only imagine what the person really thought. Obviously the truth was that they wanted to buy that tape and perhaps I had got the last copy.

I got the bus back to my car, which I now drove into the City centre, turning around in front of King's College, and closeby a gentleman put his umbrella up despite there being no rain. This seemed nothing other than what I should expect: some sort of sign for me. I could only deduce that I was on the right tracks. Now I made for King's Lynn – where else to go? It had the word "King" in it and that sufficed. There seemed little doubt in my mind, at least for a moment that I should go there. This was a blissful release from many other situations I found myself in, where I was at an utter loss as to where to go on this wild-goose chase.

I put on the tape. A few miles down the road, for no apparent reason, I turned left down another road and then kept turning left, the whole manoeuvre taking no more than 15 or so seconds. I was now stationary at the end of a short cul-de-sac looking at its dead end. At this precise moment the song playing on the tape finished and the singer casually announced "I'll skate, now you reverse." As reverse was what I now had to do this all seemed most perplexing. I had almost expected something like this. I recalled how skating on the frozen fen was popular in winter round these parts. But I was in a *summer* Wonderland and had drunk from a bottle marked "Drink me" outside the gate at Wilton. I would hardly have been surprised to see a mad hatter go by. The term "dead end" would come to mean to me one of the greatest of all terrors and here in this cul-de-sac was the first. If you do not really know where you are going you are bound to end up in some. If you go on like that for long enough then each dead end seems more significant than the previous one. Soon, cul-de-sac was to mean I was practically a goner. Without wishing to remind myself, I now remember how, over the next few months, this performance just kept repeating itself again and again, over and over. I did not know where I was going. *I did not know where I was supposed to be going.* "Please God!" I would eventually cry out aloud.

I was staggered by this incident with the singer saying to me that she would skate while I reversed. What had it meant? I did not even know why I had turned left the first time, let alone the second and third, to hear her then say this. There was certainly no diversion and there was no person telling me to turn left. I formed the impression that, whereas a tape was playing, I was in actual fact listening to a live broadcast of the band by radio, my cassette player having been altered by MI5 to make it *look* like it was playing a tape. The singer was commenting real-time on my actions[28].

I made a half-hearted examination of the cassette player. It was half-hearted because what would have been the point? These people were so powerful they would stop at nothing both to manipulate me and conceal the truth. I even imagined that by the time I even so much as got near a copy of the tape which really had the recording on it, the section with those words "I'll skate, now you reverse" would have been inserted in order to conceal from me the fact she had been talking to me real-time and those words had not previously been on the recording. Then even the remotest investigation by me as to whether this strange broadcast in between the songs had always really been there would have constituted a symptom of mental illness, just like the dog that could not stop chasing its tail. They were simply and effectively putting the fear of God into me.

I still have no idea why I came to turn left at that moment, let alone how it just came to be that I had put on the tape when I did. But every day it is statistically certain that a very large number of coincidences will take place worldwide and some of these I was bound to see. Only circumstance had made me imagine that, for example, the words "I'll skate, now you reverse" were not on the original master tape. Not one person in the whole world would ever tell me that many thousands of Indigo Girls CDs were subsequently withdrawn and destroyed as a result of my making this observation, such was the inestimably profound usefulness to the Special Forces of these brilliant women, The Indigo Girls! Now it seems ridiculous. But then it all seemed to be caused by my MTRUTH and MI5 trickery. One day I might go back there to check the cul-de-sac is not called *Swamp Ophelia*.

I continued into the fens. My whole route through the Bedford Levels felt completely determined, SAS-trained birds seemed to fly by at every junction in the road and all I had to do was follow them. The SAS were controlling the birds' movements using the bird whistles I had seen one of their members skilfully demonstrating back at the fair. The essence of *100% Pure Love* was all around and it was alluring and lethal. Come to think of it *Love Is All Around* was also in the charts. But I was not stupid. Somehow I would get myself out of this, even if it took me years to do so. I took my hands off the steering wheel. I could say the car seemed to know where to go, not because I believed that at the time (though I did) but because of where I went. There seemed to be *something about the car*. Whatever it was it led me to think: what is going on?

Once more I saw someone putting their dog's lead back on: I was under MI5 control again – my MTRUTH was on. I was completely surrounded by the Special Forces, though I could not see them, just the birds. I could not get this charity stunt and the £10 million out of my mind, and although I was not hungry I went into a Wimpy feeling like I had done only days earlier in Bedford, when I had gone into the Kentucky Fried Chicken. I felt I was so important my mere presence there would raise money for Comic Relief.

Driving on towards King's Lynn, the whole world was with me. I was shouting "Come on!" and making wild military-style advance gestures with my arms. I was now in some massive great military convoy, which I could see forming around me as the sun went down. I had been sent in here by the Special Boat Service to find out what was going on. It seemed the only sensible approach to take. I remembered my interview at the Admiralty. Now seemed my chance to justify turning down my position at the Commando Training Centre, Lympstone. I was turning up now, late. Soldiers were all around, in the fields, and in their cars. But all I could see were the bright headlights in the fenland rain and the birds. Then I pictured one of the soldiers, whom I believed to be SAS and hierophant to boot. I pictured him remotely using the electronic implants in my eyes. I thought of a poem I knew[29], which seemed inextricably linked with this time and place.

> As I came through the level fen,
> The bells of Ely sang sweet airs,
> And the cry of a curlew gave amen
> To all my silent summer prayers.
>
> And as I prayed in the twilight gloom,
> I turned, half-seeing a shadow pass
> On that Saxon road to Willingham,
> Shadow without sun, reflection without glass.

And all about me, a cold mist came:
And lines of men with axe and sword
Marched by, some silently, some wounded or lame,
Some calling on Hereward, their lord.

Then, with all the certainty of Fate,
Came one whose step I seemed to know,
Stumbling towards me, through Time's gate,
Across the barricades of the long ago.

Nearer he came, and as he passed,
I saw the question in his gaze:
"Who are we, if not of the same cast,
The self-same soul, in different days?"

"And is it still the same with you?
Do men still war, and march, and maim
Each other? Still, is it true
That peace is but a fading dream?"

And so he went into the darkness,
Eye over his shoulder at his own ghost,
Shadows across the spaces endless,
Until form and face in the mist were lost...

I was onto something. Hereward's day was lost. But King John's gold[30] was there for the taking. Soldiers were marching, the self-same soul in different days, and nights. Untold riches beckoned. But I had my own war to fight – a war with a 25 per cent kill rate – and I was gagging for battle. I felt imperious and really engaged in a military theatre. However I did not yet know I was suffering from schizophrenia. I did however feel a strong sense both of danger and of a duty to survive. To do that I was going to have to summon all the resourcefulness of a member of the Special Forces – for special forces were what, I believed, I was up against. This was the noble art: a psychiatric boxing match.

Reality began to settle in again and I felt lost and confused. There was no convoy; or was there? There was no gold; or was there? Yes there was, there were untold riches. I had to be positive. Somehow I had to uphold the honour of Prince Charles's dog. But I was sane enough to realise that to MI5 the £10 million would be a minor matter. They had more pressing problems, like the Anglo-Irish one. But for my part, eternal salvation was perpetually around the next corner. I was on a colossal mountain, and each time I reached the peak there was a higher one beyond. Back and forth my mind went. I knew I had to expect the worst. These people were going to screw me for all I was worth, and there was no point in thinking otherwise. Another dog being taken off its lead: I had control back. And the fact that the England cricket team's wicket keeper bore the name Jack Russell was no mere coincidence – it was by longstanding design!

"That's where I need to go," sang the Indigo Girls on my car stereo. At that moment I was thinking of Castle Donington; so that indeed was the place to go and not King's Lynn after all. The Monsters of Rock festival was on there that night, and it seemed to be the elusive key to a door, which led where I could not imagine. Perhaps Prince Charles's dog was there – whatever that meant. The Russians had once put a dog, Laika, into space[31]. What could I do with one? I had found the dog, yet I was looking for it too. But I also had to look for my self – and had quite forgotten for now what might be buried at the foot of the garden in Cornwall Road, Ruislip. My dad had brought a measure of fame to an unknown dog by the name of Tatters. Thinking of his poem drove me on through the glorious and historical night.

Ode on the Decease of Tatters, a Dog personally known to the Poet.

Alas, poor Tatters, canine friend
This day is now your empty end.
Alas, your passing's premature,
You left no works that will endure
And such great dreams, as once you knew
Can never come again, for you.
Gone now, alas, sweet dreams of rats
Of buried bones, and chasing cats.
Gone, gone, alas, the well-torn slipper
The well-filled bowl, the well-chewed kipper.
How often, in the sun-lit room
Pleasantly, before the touch of doom,
Imagined you, some doggish heaven:
Biscuits and bones, sharp at eleven.
That place where is the Eternal Bone
Ungnawed, untouched, superb, alone;
Where gold-laced slippers are the coin
And all, in joyous barking join:
Where collars and leashes, are no more,
And dogs have wings, can fly, and soar...

Yet dreams are vain, and empty, still
Life is yet the unclimbed hill...
Alas, alas, my canine friend
This too short day is at an end.

As I passed the Kingthorpe turn-off, a police Discovery turned right. This was where Jo Hake lived. Back in 1988, I imagined, she had been passing copies of the Jones-Lanczos vectors I had developed during my PhD to her KGB controller in the Surrey University Russian Department. Her nickname was Zero K in reference to the temperature "absolute zero", the temperature at which molecules are motionless[32]. She was a rather cool customer, and the campus was absolutely swarming with Russian students like her. Again the Discovery seemed deliberate; they wanted me to know they had found something out.

I arrived in Lincoln and though I was not hungry I bought an Indian takeaway. I felt a duty to show myself at the restaurant as though I were on a Royal visit. I ate the meal in the beautiful light reflected from the floodlit Cathedral, which was towering over my car.

For whatever reason I now drove to Nottingham. When I got there I picked up another hitchhiker. He was going to a gig at The Marcus Garvey Centre and, as he was black, this was most appropriate. I joined him for the evening and he and his friends treated me like Royalty. It was almost as if the most powerful Black Force in the world had sent him as an emissary – from Comic Relief and his brothers in Africa. It was as if the streets had been swarming with black men sent by MI5 to hitchhike in the certain knowledge I would pick up *one* of them – one representative of the Universal Negro Improvement Association, to which Marcus Garvey had devoted his life. That was how important I thought I was. But for this story, you could say the wonderful company this chap's friends gave me for the night only played into my deluded thoughts – I believed it was all a set-up. And the set-up was wholly worthy of a fly-past by an all black UN helicopter, invisible in the famous night air. That was how significant this all was. How magnificent!

After the gig I said goodbye and drove north, towards the festival. I had bought one hundred packets of Superkings and some Capstan Full Strength, thinking this meant a payment to Comic Relief. The sun was coming up. The moon was going down. I was in a lay-by. I smoked one and burnt some rubber to see what the car could do.

Shortly after dawn I reached Castle Donington and drove around the festival site. As I approached the Control Centre a 4x4 appeared in front of me. On the back it said "Maverick". I thought this was there for me to read. MI5 had followed me all the way and I was the maverick. I wanted to see the main stage. "It's all over," I was told by the police. I still wanted to see it. I believed there was a revelation on it, or if not Prince Charles's dog: Laughable but true.

I was now seriously out of it and had been up all night. Where to go? Where better than Leeds? And why? Dog leads. I was driving around Leeds now and had been on the go since the previous day without sleep. The Radio 1 DJ Anne Nightingale seemed to be talking to me. She knew I had found the M1. "A1! M1! A1! M1!" went a voice over and over out aloud in my head. But which one? Some bizarre great convoy was developing all around me made up of any vehicle you could think of. Only I did not know where it was to be. "A1! M1! A1! M1!" over and over. It would be one of the two. It would be the biggest and most bizarre convoy in history and it would reach to Buckingham Palace led by me – the hero.

The light seemed incredibly bright. Everything was glinting from the cars around me. I seemed to be getting photophobia. I became firmly convinced my car was being 'crushed' under the foot of an extremely powerful satellite-based laser beam system that tracked me using GPS everywhere I went; either that or I was tripping on a mixture of LSD and speed. It was blinding. If I were on drugs that might explain why no one else was seeing it. Or were they all too far gone? At least I knew something was up. I danced my car wildly in and out of the traffic like it was *Come Dancing* with Angela Rippon. I shot up the hard shoulder and down an exit road. I was joyriding and did a handbrake turn. The car nearly rolled and killed me. It was Barrow-upon-Soar, and soaring I was.

Some kind of sense returned. I just carried on. The whole country seemed to be going to the 50th anniversary D-Day celebrations that day on the south coast.

I was dazzled. I could not stop. It was like being in the crowd coming out of Wembley stadium. I was being swept along. Now Heathrow got hold of my head. I would just go there and fly away. I saw the brilliant and blinding sunlight glinting from the wing of an airliner taking off. It was inviting me to get on board and just fly away in my mania. The impulse was irresistible. Again I kept hearing the old Fred Neal song *Everybody's Talkin'*. I was indeed going where the sun shone brightly and where the weather suited my clothes. The song had practically taken over my head. I was like someone ill in bed with a delirious fever. But my temperature was far more than 100 degrees. I was red-hot, in more ways than one.

My friend Peter had shown me his autograph book. Nobody had signed it since Neil Armstrong when he visited RAE Thurleigh after Apollo 11. Of course it could have been faked: Mr Armstrong might have only signed it the previous week. Nevertheless I had added my signature to it below Mr Armstrong's, impressed by the fact that Peter did not seem to mind me doing so. I could now travel to Cape Kennedy and hitch a lift outside the space center there. It seemed certain I would be picked up and find myself in orbit on the space shuttle. The world seemed a very small place in which I was easily as important as the first man on the moon.

I passed Heathrow but no, that was not the next place after all. Instead I was now heading into London. I put the car in an underground car park. A Rolls went by, number plate WW3, just west of Kebab Kid on the King's Road. This meant World War III and it had been sent by MI5. I had an insane fit of laughter as I recalled Tom once referring to the large lumps of reconstituted lamb you see on spits in kebab shops as "BSE loofahs". In Kebab Kid the spit was actually loaded with real cuts of lamb and it is therefore one of the few proper kebab shops around. I found myself thinking this World War III was one being waged by Prince Charles against junk meat.

I went to Buckingham Palace and looked around the gallery. I saw a picture of Queen Charlotte, wife to the "mad" King George III. At her feet was a small dog: it was almost barking at me. I bought some Sandringham lavender for my mother. Outside, I went up to a policeman on the gate, and asked if Prince Charles was in. I got back in the car and now I was off again towards DOAE where they could Stop, End and Finish me, these being the commands that ended one of the gigantic programs I ran there. I saw a blue tit fly past going in that direction. I imagined it was the one that had been nesting outside the office window. I wondered why the fuck it had been kidnapped, taken 15 miles away and released just as I happened to be driving past. It recognised me straight away. I was mad just to imagine that. An almighty battle was under way between the existential me and the me whose existence was completely deterministic because of the control my operator had over me using my MTRUTH. Right now I was hardly feeling existential, rather more like a software item in the Apache battlefield simulation, but at least I managed to get home. The £10 million was already looking like a smaller sum and my thoughts were turning to more pressing problems – like those of the six counties of Northern Ireland.

I got back to Bedford in the afternoon, exhausted physically and mentally. I went straight to bed.

Chapter Twelve

Colour-blind

Everything was different but nobody seemed to have noticed. If I had imagined nobody ever would notice one might have expected me to shrivel away like *The Incredible Shrinking Man*[33], there and then. But I was too deluded. I was sitting on the bench at the back of The Bear. When Andy had hanged himself six years earlier, in 1988, there was said to have been another Andy Woods who also drank there. This one, I was told, had got up one night, said goodbye to everyone, and walked around the corner to hang himself in the car park at the back of the Highways Agency. I imagined this second Andy Woods was just a false story put about by MI5 practising the black arts.

But I knew the first Andy Woods well. When I had the Black Dog back in 1984, I had met him one day, at the end of the hedge by the Bedford School playing field. Years later I was astonished to notice that, whereas the winter snows had nearly completely melted, there was still a patch of snow marking the exact spot we had passed that summer day. MI5 had been following me even then and knew the significance of this place. They had put a pile of snow there to get me thinking – or simply as a display of their power over me. Later, I would notice that things seemed to happen when I passed this spot but they were nothing to do with MI5. Things happen everywhere!

Still sitting in the sun at the pub, I imagined that Andy, like Jo Hudson, had been a CIA agent too and was alive and well living in America. It was too attractive an idea compared to his really having hanged himself. A tear came to my eye and I wiped it away. I had been at his funeral and everyone was crying. Who would put their family and friends through that misery I thought, unless John Lennon really was alive? I was just well enough not to believe his coffin had been empty. But I *wanted* to believe it had been. Being from Bedford School he would have had plenty of MI5 contacts and possibly knew Michael Maltby himself. I remembered the day our crews had dead-heated at Bedford Regatta. Under the Town Bridge I had caught a very slight crab and now imagined an SBS frogman had grabbed my blade from under the water – it was an initiation. Only MI5 would have the power to procure funerals with empty coffins I thought, as my mania went into overdrive. I could arrange a fake IRA funeral for Gerry Adams and, upon the denouement, peace would reign when everyone returned miraculously unharmed. I shook my head as though to stop these wild thoughts.

With a sudden and profound realisation I noticed that all the British Telecom junction boxes had been painted army khaki. I could feel some awesome power closing in on me: a power so strong I could be swept to my death in it. My phone calls were certainly being monitored, and to let me know they were the doors to the nearest junction box had been left open.

I went into the bike shop. Something was impelling me to buy a third mountain bike. I recalled that *Mountain Climber* was the code name for an MI5 agent in the six counties and I regaled myself with the delusion that *Mountain Climber* was actually me. A couple of years earlier I'd had a most vivid dream that I was on the most extraordinarily large mountain, so terrifyingly high I will never forget the dream. It had to be the biggest most difficult mountain in the world and, as Kipling would have agreed if he'd had the dream, this mountain was the home of Gods, for that was what he said when he visited the Himalayas. It was an MTRUTH dream. My having bought two mountain bikes was, *of course*, connected with all this.

There was a Glenn Miller exhibition at the museum the following week, as I was about to discover. At this moment I was standing by the old castle mound. Events like the unexplained pinging and swinging of Tom's rowing medal had led me to consideration of the possibility that the whole place, including my parents' house, had a maze of tunnels built under it. From one of these tunnels, I imagined, some specialist weaponry had been used to fire at the medal. In any case there had always been stories about tunnels from Bedford Castle to The Ship, and perhaps the landlord knew more about this than he was letting on when, as he often did, he spoke of the sealed-up caverns in the cellar. I had also heard there was one from there to the Town Hall.

Insects seemed to be swarming on me and any avenue of thought, however fantastic or self-persecutory, now came easily to me. I now imagined that 'the flies were on me' and the reason they were there was that I had been sprayed, by MI5 or the Pentagon, with something they found attractive.

I cycled around the Castle Keep mound where one night I had lain with Amanda, the result having been that she was on the ward the next day with grass stains on her dress. There, parked outside the museum, eerily and awesomely, was a very large US Army pick-up being unloaded of artefacts for the exhibition. There were so many possible explanations for the flies it hardly bore thinking about. What I thought was alternately unbearable and deliciously acceptable. Again I received what seemed to be some kind of sanctified representation from the insect kingdom. As before, an insect, which seemed to want to make friends, hovered in front of my face looking straight into my eyes. The next moment I felt I was not much more than a heap of dog shit on the grass. A Polish girl had once given me a blow-job on that mound and the next morning an honest gentleman, also Polish, came to my house with my wallet, having found it up there – a strange coincidence. Or was it a coincidence? Perhaps he had been spying on us.

The signals, imagined or not but indisputably perceived, were raining in on me. I was having my hair cut in My-T Sharp barbers but my brain chemistry was out and I could barely keep still in the seat. Songs on the radio seemed to have been chosen for me, and I felt some person knew exactly what the problem was – that person being the radio controller. He was choosing the music for me, one song seeming to tell me to go for a run.

Having had my haircut I cycled to The Bird in Hand pub, but not on the Kalahari, which I was thinking of giving the "cock horse" treatment, by riding it to Banbury Cross. My thoughts were becoming florid to the extent that the "fine lady on a white horse" there became far more real and alluring than she normally would be: she had become "The Bird in Hand". Thankfully I was not so ill that I was minded to walk to Banbury with the bicycle on my head, like somebody I had once seen in Africa. Presumably he did this in order not to get the tyres dirty in the puddles of tropical rain, or perhaps simply because he had a puncture, though I presume he wasn't going to Banbury.

I had no particular reason to get on the train other than the terror I had experienced at the mere thought of Martin Galvin, as I unlocked the bicycle in the passage that afternoon a few days earlier. I perceived that the consequences of my actions, all born out of patriotic responsibility had been amplified by what had happened at Wilton. My political standpoint seemed to be moving. Previously Mr Galvin had been just some obnoxious Republican on the television. Now, because of my actions, I had unwittingly forced upon myself the full responsibility to justify my behaviour in the light of his real existence. I would end up regarding him as a personal friend. At least two huge forces seemed to be bending my mind around to the point where a bloody enormous wave was crashing over my head. It was not planned but if you are surfing and something like this comes along you do not think about it. I had once heard of a great day's surfing somewhere and a particular wave they called the Tuesday Mountain. Well it was Tuesday now too and I felt I was surfing something enormous in the psychic-ether, the stuff of surfing legend. And, if you cannot surf, you look like "The Monster of The Id" in the film *The Forbidden Planet*, struggling in terrible pain and only vaguely visible in the mother of all force fields, itself hardly visible but terrifyingly tangible. That was how I felt at this point, only unlike Dr. Morbius in the film, I could hardly put the shutters up[34] and nor did I have an IQ of several hundred.

Soon I was at Bletchley. Somebody who looked like he was in 2 Para shouted out, from a waiting train, "Hey mate! How much did that bike cost?" Perhaps he was telling me I had not really paid for it; perhaps he was saying I had not paid yet and was going to do so in a big way. I wondered.

I got to Milton Keynes and decided to book a sleeper to Scotland. On my arrival I bought a copy of *Land Rover Enthusiast* to read on the train. Perhaps all sleeper-train journeys feel like something out of an Alistair MacLean novel and this was no exception. I found my cabin, read the Land Rover magazine and when I was completely satisfied with that, went to take my seat for dinner. I decided I would rather like to buy the ex RAF Strike Command extended wheelbase Land Rover with 22,000lb winch (which I had seen advertised in the mag) and getting a job at MI4, otherwise known as JARIC, turn up for work there in it.

At my table was a very well-to-do lady in tweeds who told me she was going salmon fishing, which all sounded much as I had expected for conversation in these surroundings. It was about now I began to experience a profound pressure never to say the same thing twice. It felt like the full press again. This made me feel I was permanently gazing into a merciless mirror, which revealed the most shamefully detailed and critical view of myself. This was of such remorseless insight it had a total and nearly catastrophic effect on my whole physical and mental state, sufficient to propel a significant proportion of the population from the top of the nearest high building or even better in front of the nearest fast moving heavy object. I had already met one person who had killed herself by jumping from a train and I was to meet another. This resistance to repetition was a potential threat to myself.

I said something, and a chap I seemed to recognise whistled, I believed to indicate he knew everything I had ever said and that I had just committed the fatal crime of saying that particular thing "yet again". And that was quite apart from the problem of my beliefs about my MTRUTH. *His* MTRUTH was attached to a database containing all I had ever said, documented throughout my life by the KGB, or whoever was doing this to me. From this database he could immediately tell if I was repeating myself. You see, unlike me, he had full control of his MTRUTH and its voice recognition software immediately analysed my speech and matched it to all I had ever said on the database it was attached to.

I completely enjoyed the dinner and wine, asked the night porter to make a phone call home for me and retired.

Whatever actually happened during the night, and where it happened, I will probably never know. But when I woke up the next morning deep in the Scottish borders, my cabin seemed to be on the opposite side of the train to the one I had retired in, though I appeared to be in the same cabin. The carriage itself had been decoupled during the night in a siding. It had then been turned around and recoupled before the rest of the journey. Whilst this was a ludicrous suggestion to make to anyone to me it was already becoming the sort of possibility, which I felt I would be mad to discount to myself; in fact it was just the sort of thing I was actively expecting.

I was disoriented but enjoyed breakfast, though the lady in tweeds was notable in her absence. No doubt she had been gruesomely murdered in her cabin and had not yet been discovered by the attendant, delivering her personal copy of *The Times* with her own obituary in it. He would find the door to her cabin locked and, there being no reply, would open it with his master key to find her bludgeoned body dangling upside down from the ceiling with the jugular cut, something of a torrent of blood flowing from the cabin.

Getting off at Inverness, without it even crossing my mind that this had been the supposed destination of the Chinook which had crashed at the Mull of Kintyre only a few days earlier, I now had to decide what to do next. Here, if anywhere, I began my survey of the Irish Isles showers. In my head I had personally renamed the British Isles and given that there is an Irish Sea and a lesser-known British Sea, more commonly known as the English Channel, this seemed perfectly logical. I can report that the Inverness Station shower did not have the thermostat temperature set according to the position of the lift in some offices backing on to Exeter Street in London. At least I don't think it was. In that lift, in my days as a security guard in 1983, I had once received an odd call into the emergency phone, and I was still wondering where this call had come from. Also, the Inverness shower did not appear to have any potentially fatal electrical fault, unlike those in most of the bed and breakfasts I was to stay in during this story. In fact, there is only one shower I have had which surpassed this one, which you will hear of later.

Hypnotised with indecision, I sat in Inverness Station staring at the children's ride for as long as two hours. Life was as simple as that but I was not putting the money in. I was soon to slip back, not for the last time, into that utterly sceptical and ill-advisedly disbelieving state of mind. In this state of mind I could so easily fail to recognise who some of the people walking by were, even if I heard it said right in front of me. I just could not see how amazingly famous

I was now bound to be. Eventually, as usual, I snapped myself out of this hypnotic state, these people being nobody in particular, and found my way around to the library. Here there was a database terminal of training opportunities in the Highlands. I typed in two keywords feeling I was being watched, and now received a short list of details of courses under "Film" in the Western Isles. At that moment I nostalgically recalled repeatedly seeing *Local Hero* on all the cinema hoardings in the Tottenham Court Road area back in 1983. At that time I had no idea what the film was about, but now it had to be about me, somehow, or my life would be meaningless.

I walked through town going into Fraser's Department Store where I got a store card and with it bought one plate hanger, made in England. The word "hanger" hung heavily in my mind with the black weight of paranoia. At some point I seem to recall gazing in through a garage window and for some reason it was clear the Rolls Royce was missing. There was definitely something not quite right in my head because I now found myself thinking that the Master of the Rolls had been shot dead by the Army, this ridiculous conspiracy theory in my head going right into orbit like Laika, or even Tatters, had done. I had to pull out of this somehow. I was on a relentless pursuit of the truth, which I might discover only by allowing my thoughts to imagine the ridiculous.

I wandered through a furniture store and then found myself in W.G. McPherson's Adventure Stores in Church Street. "Everyone's got loads of money," I recalled the man saying to me back in Bedford. Therefore I could hardly leave without buying a "Borders" Barbour, a Saunders "Space Packer" tent (made in England and which Mr McPherson personally recommended to me), and a new cloth cap especially made for Mr McPherson by "Olney". A new one was much overdue. Before my mission really began in earnest, I was on the train home from work when I left my beloved tweed flat cap on the train. It was a Dunne & Co. cap, with the usual inscription "Domine Dirige Nos" inside, had a popper attaching the peak to the top, and its material, Harris tweed, contained the tiniest dash of pink. It was size 7 3/8th and unique in that it had a fine dust inside the label which could only have got there if it had spent several months inside the trailer behind a (Bedford) truck that had travelled across the Sahara desert. I miss that cap. If you come across it, please let me know.

With my replacement cap I was now equipped to go to ground, as in the Geoffrey Household story *Rogue Male*[35]. But somehow I had the thought, which I would have again, that if I was in the SBS my CO would order me not to use my normal survival skills; so as it turned out I only used the tent a few times. I would however become something of a Rogue Male myself.

I already had a Swiss Army knife with a unique feature, which "only this particular knife" had. In reality it was a feature only this particular model of knife had. I purchased it in Harrison and Symonds' Gentlemen's Tobacconists, in Bedford High Street. Mr Symonds was an agent of the Federal Bureau of Firearms, Alcohol and Tobacco, United States of America. He was party to knowledge, unknown in this country outside of the Security Services, surrounding General Crush's spectacle at Waco in the "Gay 1890s". This was when General Crush put on a show of two steam trains crashing headlong into each other, several spectators dying from the flying wreckage. It was one of the most spectacular publicity stunts of the 19th century. Only Mr Symonds, whilst wearing his bowtie, and only then, could possibly have the imagination to recreate that spectacle. Only an experienced MI5 officer such as himself could ever be charged with the onerous responsibility of arranging the reconstruction of such a thing. But he would be mindful of the knowledge of the fatalities that day in Waco. As for more recent events at Waco, it had not gone unnoticed by my paranoid imagination that the Seventh Day Adventists had an office in Bedford. What was I thinking – he was just a tobacconist!

I made a weak and feeble attempt to visit Loch Ness but it was like one of those horrible dreams when you are trying to go somewhere but have to run harder just to stay on the same spot. Eventually I cycled off in the direction of Culloden, finding that my bicycle lock would not undo and deducing that it had been tampered with. This was no surprise as one of the bicycle locks had had the strangest thing done to it. The plastic covering was now configured in a manner, which easily flummoxed my entire collection of academic qualifications as to how it had come to be the way it was.

Somehow I did not feel I had to go more than a mile in that direction. I ended up just cycling around a small housing estate, which had no greater claim to fame than that a paranoid schizophrenic, me, had cycled through it one day. But I did not imagine the placing of a plaque to announce that exact fact. My thoughts were far more grandiose. Culloden, rather more than this estate, was still vivid in many a Scotsman's eyes. Then I tried going into a hardware store and bought a tube of Locktite glue in a pitiful display of humour aimed at those I believed were spying on me. I thought everything I did was noticed. I returned into town and bought a train ticket to Glasgow.

From the train, whilst enjoying the scenery, I noticed some American tourists whose conversation ever so slightly amused me, possibly, I do not recall, for some entirely deluded reason. Not everything I thought was the fruit of insanity.

I found myself sitting opposite a well-educated young lady whose presence there I hardly even considered to be anything other than a pointed and deliberate act; so her scrawled note of the telephone number of the Crest Hotel, Glasgow, could only be for my use. Whilst she went to the toilet I wrote it down.

Arriving in Glasgow I chose a Rocky Road flavoured ice cream from Baskin-Robbins on the station platform. It seemed prescient even then. Now I have to check on their website to see there is such a flavour. It is chocolate ice cream loaded with almonds and miniature marshmallows.

I cycled off to the hotel where my peculiar imagination had its way with me again, as I really believed the coughing coming from the room down the corridor was Eric Idle's own. I had seen a person I thought was a relation of his at a service station the day before the road show and thought *Monty Python* had been set on me.

Actually I had met Eric Idle once when working in a pub in London and was satisfied that my rudimentary humour had given him something to mull over. One of the barmaids had told me that the chaps from *Monty Python* were at the other end of the bar. My heart had immediately gone into overdrive as I felt I had to make their acquaintance – but only if I could say something original. Whilst being a barman, to make the job more amusing, I had distorted the whole geography of the pub to the point where doing a glass-run was more like a mountaineering expedition. You had to say where you were going; give your route and announce when you would come back. I would say, partly quoting Captain Oates, "I'm just going on a glass-run, *I may be some time.*" All this had caught on with the other bar staff. Occasionally someone would call to a glass-runner as though they were so far away they were only just audible.

The head barman was collecting glasses from the top of the fruit machine only a few feet away, almost shaking hands' distance. Eric Idle and Terry Jones were standing at the bar in between us. I called out in a manner mimicking loudness, cupping my hands to my mouth as I did so, "Hello, can you hear me, I can only just make out what you are saying, speak up!" The head barman reciprocated. I was chuffed to get Eric Idle looking confused and then charged him several million pounds for a gin and tonic to which he replied "And could you change this billion pound note?"

On the television they were talking about digging up and rebuilding the Euston Arch. I was a maniacal philanthropist who wanted to reinstall all the railings cut down for armaments during World Wars I and II. During the programme there was a shot of some railings that the cameraman was walking past. The cameraman was a Special Forces MTRU, with cameras in his actual eyes and, like me, nobody had told him. I felt I was not alone in this brewing reality war. I did not recognise the railings and ruled out these shots having been taken from my own eyes – through *my* MTRUTH. Thank God I did have *some* insight! But how could I possibly contact this officer and tell him what I had learnt?

It being only early evening I cycled off around Glasgow and somehow my path led me right up to the plaque commemorating the opening of a building by Prince Charles. It had been put in front of me; or rather my movements had been controlled to the point where the plaque might as well have been put straight in front of me. There was magic in my bike and this had brought me here. I saw a van going back into town, which said "Sage Builders" on the side, with an owl emblem. I decided I had better follow it. It was leading me. I had to be a Sage Builder too, in order to make something of this.

That night, at the hotel bar, it became quite clear to me that the KP nuts for sale were just MI5 telling everyone what they thought about Kim Philby. No, you don't understand – I actually believed that. The fact that you could also buy Planter's nuts obviously seemed by design. It was terribly exciting realising all this!

Next morning I went to Debenhams stores and bought a matching designer pair of "Mainsail Nautical Challenge" beach shorts and T-shirt, which seemed more than appropriate. They had been designed especially for me. Once again, I had been brought to them, my free will having been subsumed by my MTRUTH. The feeling was great. Then I went to see the film *Four Weddings and a Funeral*. It felt like everyone was laughing at me and I was getting messages from the film – for example that I had to be the Best of British and nothing less.

After the film I cycled down to Queen Street Station and observed a seagull so large I thought that it was either a top secret Pentagon robot or I was seeing things on my MTRUTH. Then, as I stared at it, I thought, yes, it is a real seagull but it is so big that it cannot be just any old gull – somebody round here has got a trained pet albatross. My thoughts went back to the SAS bird whistle expert at the Strawberry Fair.

So I sat down in the bar to wait for my train. *Blockbuster* by The Sweet was being played. At the moment when they sang "You'd better beware, she's got long black hair," a girl with very long black hair walked past the window outside the bar and came in; so I took the radio at its word and completely ignored her. I was used to such perceived messages and this was no longer unusual. But I was certain it had been arranged.

After a long and very beautiful journey I was in Mallaig, the port for Skye. It was late and I had not booked anywhere to stay. I walked up a landlady's garden path whilst her Scotch terriers ran to greet me.

Next morning at breakfast there were two young ladies with their auntie. They seemed an unlikely party and told me of the day before, which they had spent in Eigg (an island next to Skye). Somehow it seemed they were there because of me. But it seemed that rather than being there to spy on me they were there *as part of my team*. There was something alluring, pleasant and mysterious about their presence and this idea.

Reunited with my bike, which I had left on the train the previous night and which they agreed to look after for me at the station, I got the ferry to Skye and after a fair old bus trip arrived in Portree, the capital. The bus did not terminate there so I took it all the way to Kilmuir and booked into a bed and breakfast where the landlady brought me coffee and biscuits. I noticed she appeared to have a penchant for Alistair MacLean novels but I thought they had just been put there deliberately in anticipation of my arrival. I was completely suspicious of anyone without giving any indication of such. Even a couple walking down the track from the hillside together managed to get a handle on my imagination. I picked up *The Secret Ways*.[36]

Next day I visited the Museum of Scottish Country Life. Now I was really looking for Prince Charles's dog. This was the first time I had walked into a stranger's living room unannounced since an occasion in the Forest of Dean, during CCF training at school. My school pals and I thought we were entering a pub called The Balloon. However the pub had been closed for years and they had neglected to take down the sign. Inside I found a couple of old ladies watching television, and no bar. We apologised and made our exit. Here in Scotland the main exhibit was the occupant of the house: she had a nice peat fire going and a copy of the 1953 *Times Coronation Colour Supplement* amongst a plethora of artefacts well worthy of a trip to the nearest distillery at the earliest opportunity.

I took a lift south, back down the island towards Portree, and walked part of the way with a girl I met en route. We had coffee and then I set off for Carbost. On my way I kept an eye out for the golden eagles I had been told lived around those parts. I came across a lady with binoculars and then, across the valley I saw the most spectacular sight of an eagle, my school's emblem, soaring high above the heather. Truly magnificent.

My newly developed uncommon inability to trust the reality of various events taking place around me now manifested itself again. As I waited for a lift I counted, for no particular reason I recall, the number of cars coming down the minor road from Carbost. I then found myself wondering how many Munroes Mr Smith, the Labour Party Leader, had climbed since he 'died' and connected this number with the number of cars coming down the hill. So he was not dead either. He too had faked his death by joining John Lennon's cult and had chosen to bide his time until the exciting denouement by climbing.

In Carbost I found my way to the Talisker distillery, for good measure spotting a sea eagle over Loch Harport. As I queued up to enter the distillery there was an almighty roar as an RAF jet suddenly appeared at low level. No doubt this affected that particular batch of 10-year-old whisky which, if it was anything like the sample I tasted, was no less peaty than the lady's fireplace back up the road at the museum, and peatier than anything I had drunk before or since[37]. I had felt I was being spied on ever since Wilton, and suspected the RAF jet was making fun of me – either that or I was now a tool for military intelligence, probably both. After all, one thing I certainly could not believe was that MI5 did not have a sense of humour.

Coming out of the distillery I walked off down the road and was given a lift by an academic and his wife who, because of her looks, I thought was related to Amanda. They dropped me off and soon I was in Portree where I went to book a hotel room. First of all I tried The Portree House Hotel. The receptionist was on the phone and I waited politely for her to finish her conversation, part of which included her saying "...and there'll be a commission for the Ministry of Defence? Very good." I did not exert much mental effort on what she said. It seemed not in the least bit unusual because it was perfectly feasible that military personnel travelling to the St. Kilda firing range favoured the hotel. In this case the MoD might well have arranged a favourable rate to save the taxpayer from unnecessary profligacy. At the same time it seemed quite obvious that if some lunatic appeared who seemed hell-bent on raising £10 million for charity then ordinary military life would have to go on, more or less without any change. Her remark was aimed at me, and was pre-arranged. It was a bit expensive; so instead I booked into a hotel overlooking the harbour.

After booking in I walked around town a bit, and one of those incidents that left me wondering occurred. I went into a shop with the intention of buying a watch. Up a flight of stairs I went and, at the top, found myself facing a solitary stuffed seagull. It seemed to have been put in front of me, perhaps by being raised through a window as I entered the shop. It reminded me of my failed record label, Seagull Records. I found some underpants, which were difficult to obtain in this town, making me wonder about the old joke concerning what a Scotsman wears under his kilt. I bought a few pairs, so as not to miss an opportunity. I also bought a Timex dress watch. I asked about its origin and the assistant asked her boss, in a broad Skye accent, "Timex, that's out of London isn't it?" making it sound like a horse: a pretty big horse, as Timex is an American company. It seemed a strange thing to say because I thought she would have known of the Timex factory in Scotland, as there was a strike there, which was news that day. I also purchased a Walkman and a pair of Trophy binoculars, noticing that JJ Vickers & Sons Ltd had imported the latter. I thought back to my dawn trip to Barrow, where Vickers built submarines, imagining incorrectly they were one and the same.

I returned to The Portree House Hotel, bought a drink and put some music on the jukebox. The man opposite reminded me of the MR2 driver in Wiltshire. Perhaps it was him? He was thinking about my choice of music. I imagined that the way he was moving his head was intended to convey these thoughts in my direction. Perhaps it was nothing of the sort and he was just having a normal conversation with the person next to him. I had somehow become oversensitised to the situation, a condition that can be reflected in either direction, though not quite to the extent of full-blown schizophrenia being infectious.

My friend Caroline had once asked me if I had ever been to a ceilidh. There was one that night and with my new binoculars I had a look at the building from my hotel room. I spotted her lookalike coming out of the door at 1am. I was still drunk on Radio 1, and stayed in with my new Walkman, listening secretly to it whilst spying on the ceilidh. I felt like a child playing secret agents.

The next day I explored Portree though it did not feel quite like a holiday, more a mission. The different decors of the pubs reminded me of the Republican-Protestant rift over the water. I was now interested in Irish politics and particularly those of the six counties.

I watched the seagulls picking at the scraps in the harbour. Once again I had trouble accepting the seagull right in front of me was real rather than being some top-secret robot or MTRUTH illusion. I think I was still under the influence of that landlady's Alistair MacLean book collection. Walking up the steps from the harbour I noticed what appeared to be a raffle ticket and I picked it up imagining it had been deliberately dropped in my path. Turning it over there came the revelation it was a ticket to Balmoral, some one hundred miles away, and now I had one other force being exerted on my brain chemistry. It had indeed been dropped in front of me deliberately, only seconds before I got there, out of my sight. But that was not the only revelation.

In town I bumped into some friends from home, including one, a McAskill, whose family lived on the island just up the road. One of these friends, Rory, had won the Diamond Challenge sculls at Henley Royal Regatta and another, by the name of Wig, I had victoriously played rugby with at school, against RAF Brampton. They had all come along to run the half-marathon but unfortunately I did not have my running shoes, so I retired to the bar again. I rejoined them all later in another hotel where the Stornoway MoD Surplus shop was having a sale. I bought some trousers, which, during the sales patter, I was told were tailor-made for me. I believed they actually were. He also offered me a torch, and I decided I did not need one as I was already carrying one for Amanda.

Another of these friends was Miles Fellows, who had rowed for Great Britain. I made the connection with the headline, which had been in the paper a day or so earlier, about the Miles Messenger aircraft used on spying missions during the War. After the sale I went with Miles and the others in the car to Carbost. "You need to get hitched after all this is over," Miles said. Perhaps I misheard him and he was just talking about how to get around the island after they had gone but, whatever he meant, I did not feel it right to respond. Instead I decided to pretend I had not heard, should he say it again. In any case perhaps I imagined he said it. But the point is I believed I had prior intelligence about his remark from the newspaper article.

We arrived at Carbost and the weather was beautifully grey and still. A small dinghy was moored just away from the shore of Loch Harport so the crews of moored yachts could come ashore to The Old Inn. Somehow, with great mystery, the dinghy captured my attention. It was a special boat. Then the night's drinking began. Prior to university, some of the company I kept, which included these chaps, was always so replete with drink I had even chosen a different university to avoid it. Despite this there had been occasions when I had drunk with them, after which I had no recollection of the next day. But now there was dancing and I was glad to see them all.

Still, the next day did come and, after a good night's sleep, everyone was off south for the weekend. I got a lift to Skulamus, where I said goodbye and hitched to Ardvasar (Aird a Bhasair), from where the ferry sailed. A helicopter was taking off from the garage as we separated. Naturally, I imagined my MI5 spies were using the helicopter.

There was little traffic and I decided to walk all the way there: 15 miles. It was wild and barren with only a winding single-track road and I imagined, to the point of it almost being real, Gary Barlow from Take That walking past in the opposite direction. The delusional reality of this merely confirmed my feelings of importance. After some miles the Sound of Sleat came into sight but I was not even halfway yet. I saw a small cairn to the side of the road and went to inspect it. It turned out to be somebody's stash of cut peat drying on a pallet.

Arriving at Ardvasar, evening setting in, I discovered there was no ferry until the next day, and booked into the bed and breakfast, noticing it had storm-proof arctic windows installed. It did not occur to me this might be portentous of what would be happening to me over the next few years. It seemed simply an indication of the wild weather in the western isles. I took a walk around the island towards the Aird of Sleat, where I knew Prince Charles's dog was, admiring the view from the cliffs over to the mainland and in particular down towards the Mull of Kintyre, whose secrets had partially revealed themselves to me. Then I retired to The Hideout (the name of the bar of The Ardvasar Hotel) for pool and beer. I felt nice and secure in my hideout. And though I had not been all the way to the Aird of Sleat somehow it took on an almost mythical countenance such that a piece of my heart would always be devoted to it. Yet it was just an area of land of a few square miles with a few houses in the middle.

At the pool table was a brunette Kiwi girl traveller who made an odd remark to me about an Inverness newspaper, this preying on my deluded imagination. Perhaps she never mentioned it at all. I was drunk but not so drunk as to stop me taking her hand, but she would not have any of it. Her loss. I went back to my Radio 1 secret messages, unaware that within a year a new brewery would open on Skye producing amongst other ales, Cuillin Beast, for this very bar The Hideout. Legend has it that the great Celtic warrior, Red Branch Knight, and hero of early Irish literature, Cúchulainn, was accompanied into battle by a fierce dog-beast that lived in the heart of Skye's Cuillins. I too was in a battle, but accompanied by a rather more benign canine.

Next morning was beautiful. The sun came streaming in as I had my breakfast. A beautiful young girl with long flowing blonde hair playing her harp for me in the beams of the morning light reminded me of the baths back in Khairoun and I felt like I was on heroin – not that I knew what that was actually like. Who needs drugs when you can listen to a harpist play at breakfast?

I bought a batik shirt, and soon was on the train back to Glasgow reunited with my bike. After passing a tourist steam train, Ben Nevis came into sight.

I really have no idea at all why I decided not to get the train back from Glasgow too. Somehow I had reprogrammed myself to think that because of what I had done, I was like some sort of Renaissance Egon Ronay on a nationwide spying mission on behalf of the ignorant masses – and not just spying on restaurants. Either way, I flew back from Glasgow arriving at Heathrow in the late evening and found I was not allowed to take my bicycle on the Tube for some unexplained stupid reason. So I thought of a stupid reason. I thought it might be just to annoy me. Then I began to imagine some murderous

Indian and wondered how many members of his family he had dismembered, packed in suitcases, and sent to India. My thoughts were racing again. I felt deranged. I shook my head.

So I had to cycle to the next station, several miles away. On the way I saw one or two ambulances and police cars going by at speed with their lights flashing, quite possibly at me I thought. If, by this flashing, they were trying to shed some light on these imagined Heathrow trunk murders, I could be of no help, even with my imagined new powers. Again I succeeded in making it home to Bedford, wondering what the undetected murder rate was.

Chapter Thirteen

My Suitor

The morning of 21st June 1994 was warm and sunny with little cloud cover – it was almost telling me something, like a CIA or British Intelligence spy satellite could see me in the visible band. I was at a loss as I drove off the Bruges ferry because Radio 1 was only just coming through; so I could not receive my messages. Never mind, I drove off towards Brussels and soon found myself descending into a rather deep tunnel, feeling afraid I might not be able to handle the car, as my brain chemistry was so unstable. Still, I made it there all right.

I was wandering around at random again, somewhere near Rue Charleroi. The name struck the bell in my mind. I was right out of it and had no idea what to do. Then I was on a tram to Rue John F. Kennedy, and when the tram reached its destination I got off to look around. Walking back towards the town something made me glance back over my right shoulder. There, up on the first floor some 50 yards away was a man sitting in the window with a rifle aimed at me, or at least that was what I saw. It was the Belgian State Security Service, playing with me. Their agent was posing as Lee Harvey Oswald, President Kennedy's assassin. They had a cordial relationship with MI6, of course, particularly when an MTRU was sent over and, more especially, an MTRU who did not know for sure he was an MTRU. Naturally the Belgians would be happy to take control of me using my MTRUTH as a guest of the Belgian government.

I ignored this ruse, helped by the fact that he did not fire, and made my way back towards the centre where I found myself wandering towards some monument. From behind it came a man walking his Jack Russell dog, and I felt somehow obliged to see where he had come from. All I found was some graffiti and little else. The dog cocked its leg against the monument, and I declined the chance to get a bemused response to my question as to whether the dog was Prince Charles's. Returning to the street I found a bar and relaxed over a low alcohol beer. It did not seem beyond the realms of possibility that I might find Prince Charles's dog in Belgium.

I went on wandering about aimlessly for a scent. I boarded a tram going to the Heisel Stadium and again I was back in this tortuous avenue of bad omens and mutual embarrassments. Once more I was on a Royal visit and the Heisel Stadium was just too embarrassing a place to go to, a collapsing wall having killed 39 football supporters there in 1985. I got off again and headed back in the opposite direction until I reached the centre. Here I noticed one of those odd little things, which, to a person in normal circumstances would have meant nothing, but somehow I could not forget it. There was a woman at the back door to a bank. I saw her close it. This purveyed the meaning to me that there were no back-door sponsorships available there to help raise the £10 million. I went on and found myself in a magnificent graveyard full of macabrely styled tombs and mausoleums. I read one of the gravestones. It was that of a former pioneer in the Congo. Memories of Belgian colonial days were all around, and I thought back to my weeks in Zäire and on the Congo riverboat.

I really felt out of control of myself. It was not so much that somebody specific was controlling me. I just did not know what to do with the result that absolutely everything seemed to be controlling me. Not for the only time this summer I was just going round and round in circles, whoever or whatever was making me do this being wholly unaware they were, except my MTRUTH operator. Posters, shop signs, snatches of conversation, types of cars, anything was capable of making me just turn round and go back where I had come from. "Looking-At-Me-In-The-Wrong-Way" syndrome you might call some of it. I was in the railway station and completely stymied. I must have hung around there for a couple of hours trying to do something – anything, sensible. At one point I saw an Arab trying to make a phone call. Some sort of palaver preceded his arrival and I was drawn into a conversation about use of the public telephone. The Arab asked me if I could help him and he told me he was trying to call Kuwait. I did try to help him but after he had gone I was left with this excruciating feeling that I might not have completely satisfied him. Ridiculous really – but I felt like I was on a treasure hunt and this Arab was a key.

It was around here that I met an obviously talented singer with her guitar. We chatted for a while and she told me of her band before playing me The Indigo Girls' song, *Fare Thee Well*. I wandered off to get something to eat.

I found a hotel and booked in, noticing that I had been given a room very high up with all the windows open. I thought of jumping, or rather whether I was being invited to, and instead decided this was definitely my last trip on my own. This was just appalling. What the hell did I think I was doing? But I knew what I was doing. Or did I? Yes I did. I was looking for the dog. I was looking for myself. Whatever I had done I knew why I had done it. I resolved to contact Amanda.

Chapter Fourteen

Lonely Rainbows

Next day I made for Paris, near the border picking up a bloke with his German Shepherd dog. Over the border we drove and stopped for a drink. The dog was thirsty too and the waiter brought it a large bowl of water. The sight of a French waiter watering a Belgian's German Shepherd dog near the border seemed extremely significant in a way I can no longer recall. But this was valuable intelligence.

I parked my car at the Gare de Sud and took a TGV to Montpellier. On the train I read Dostoyevsky's *The Gambler* and, with the level of debt I was running up, this was quite appropriate. I still had the overpowering feeling something big was going to happen.

For travel on the train my bike, which I'd had in the boot of the car, had to have its tyres let down as the wheels had to be taken off and I couldn't do that without doing so. So when I arrived in Montpellier I found a bicycle shop where the owner proudly showed me the original yellow Tour de France shirt he had worn when, many years earlier, he had led the race. He remarked on my Brooks' saddle, which he described as "la mieux". I bought a Mt. Zefal bicycle pump and reinflated my tyres, wondering where Mt. Zefal was, and if I was now on it.

At the hotel the owner poured me a well-appreciated cold orange juice and soon I was cycling off to find the beach, which I failed to do as it was just too hot and the beach was too far away.

That night, my one night in Montpellier, I did some exploring and noticed a double of Gerry Adams walk by. This made me feel as paranoid as befits someone in a schizophrenic mania. True to Dr. Capgras I thought he had been put there by MI6. The restaurant did not take a credit card and, having no cash, I had to leave my watch while I went to find a working cash machine, which I eventually did, regaining my Timex that I had bought back in Skye.

Next day I was back in Paris and it has to be said slipping further into illness. I picked up a hitchhiker who soon after shouted "Attend!", as I nearly crashed at the traffic lights when blinded by the sun. I spent the night in a hotel opposite the Gare de Sud where I found myself under the spell of a radio station, Radio Energi. It was talking to me, even though it was broadcasting in French and I could not really understand what was being said. French Intelligence knew something, maybe rather a lot, about what was going on in my head. They had got hold of the KGB files of one or two French citizens too, and Thomson CSF, the French defence electronics company, knew all about this MTRUTH stuff. Next day, after a wander, I set off for Calais.

North of Paris and well on my way back to England I found myself driving through a huge thunderstorm on the Somme, which certainly got my more imaginative ideas going. A pick-up drove by with a very odd spectacular spiralling light display shining from the back. I was being invited to follow it, but I didn't. Who was it? I had no doubt it was some MI6 jester, or maybe some chaps in French Intelligence whose fathers had been in the Resistance. I thought of the Absolute Secret files. What with all these electronics in my body they had no choice but to follow me into Europe, probably carrying a briefcase full of surveillance equipment, monitoring my fancy car and me. Little did I imagine I would have eight years of flashbacks to this spiralling light display.

Eventually, after driving all night, I was nearing Calais as the French dawn approached. I remember the last three songs I heard Radio Energi play. They were: *Sleeping Satellite* by Tasmin Archer, *Ordinary World* by Duran Duran and *Return to Innocence* by Enigma. My mind was telling me this was France saying goodbye. I felt very emotional as I pulled up at the port to embark upon the Cat. Perhaps I have not stressed it enough. *I was the target.* Some short-range French Army unit pirate radio station trying to get into my head was following me. It was a while to wait for the Cat so I took a nap listening to my Take That cassette, which later disappeared – stolen for a lark by Robbie Williams or Gary Barlow I thought. Somebody else with schizophrenia might well have thought the name of the band was an instruction.

On the Cat, all announcements were preceded by the first three notes of what sounded like *Touch Me In The Morning*, which seemed quite appropriate even if entirely unintentional. I had this strange image in my head, I thought over my MTRUTH, of the vessel being some enormous floating cat. This was as vivid as Jumbo the Elephant back in Colchester, and very Alice in Wonderland.

I arrived back at my flat exhausted and determined not to sleep but to have a bath and get to Henley Royal Regatta to meet up with some friends. The bath was a strange experience, and weird hypnotic sounds seemed to overlay everything Radio 1 was broadcasting. Again I felt the broadcast had been augmented in some way, possibly in my near vicinity.

At Paddington I met an interesting middle-aged and very well spoken man while waiting for my train. He looked exactly as I imagined a Masonic grandmaster might look. He was very polite as he spoke to me and declined the offer of a trip to Henley, explaining he had a meeting. I supposed the meeting might well be between some rather special people, a Masonic grandmaster and an MI5 officer in the tabernacle near Covent Garden. There was no doubt in my mind this meeting concerned me – and what to do about my peculiar behaviour.

On the train to Henley the newspaper headline was about the theft of a baby, Abbie. This succeeded in making me guilty about an incident when I was a young boy. I had pinched the face of a baby in its pram and run off. I had somehow been sensitised not only to the media but everything that went on about me. I felt a little tortured by this news.

At the Regatta I was desperately missing Amanda, the entire place to my mind being inextricably connected with her. Happily though I met some friends. I found myself in the delusion that they were somehow going to see that Amanda and I got together again. I saw somebody point at a balloon basket by the footpath and say "He's seen the balloon." It was as though it was I who had seen it and he knew it. I had the wild delusion that a helicopter was at this very moment bringing Amanda to me, and we were going up in that balloon. How hopelessly deluded I was. I really felt sick in the head. Just how sick I was now and how sick I became is up to you to decide. It is also up to you to decide who was responsible for what was to happen later this summer.

I did see another old girlfriend of mine walking by in the enclosure, though decided not to speak to her. Then an amusing, albeit male thing happened, without which this story would never be complete. Then I saw a chap with a camcorder. Another attractive girl was standing there and I saw him scan the camcorder up and down her curvaceous body. The camcorder was a sign: amusingly, my MTRUTH controller was not in any way disagreeable to my similarly casting 'my' eyes up and down attractive female bodies. I really was the eyes and ears of the British Intelligence Service. They could see and hear through them.

As my friends and I drove away to Bedford after the end of racing, I saw a young man with his head in his hands sitting outside The Angel pub. It seemed he was sharing my grief that I was not with Amanda, though even now I was still imagining her following me in a helicopter, so as to join me later in Bedford. Not to be.

Chapter Fifteen

Standing On My Head

A few days later I found myself on the platform of Ealing Broadway Station. Why I was there I have no idea. All I remember was seeing the headline in *The Evening Standard*: "Another mission for Prince Andrew". At least that's what I recall. Somewhere I had read he had a new desk job, which I imagined was at MI5, and once I had read this I could only assume he was in charge of me and it was time to be off again. If somebody *was* in charge of me there seemed little harm in imagining it was him. Soon I was aboard the flight to Schiphol airport, in Holland, having taken the Tube to Heathrow. The truth I had imagined and rather liked believing in was that his older brother had been the one British agent who knew of my status as a KGB/MI6 double agent.

So it seemed the truth was out – but not very far. Ha ha, I thought – if it goes on like this the entire Royal Family will know the truth about Prince Charles's dog. So what was it? At this point I could not rule out Pooh's being an MTRU herself. She too would have a telecommunications harness (canine version) and EAI, of course. I imagined the dog had momentarily disappeared behind a magician's screen to provide the element of truth lacking in the majority of newspaper reports. I thought of Squiggygate (the incident involving a leaked recording of Princess Diana's telephone call to a lover) and wondered what might be intercepted on Pooh's MTRUTH: possibly ads for Pedigree Chum and other sensitive canine material. Perhaps the real Pedigree Chum ad was in fact a GCHQ intercept of a call to Pooh, this accounting for the interference I saw on the ad one day, Pooh now operating undercover since the announcement of her assumed demise, a demise which was greatly exaggerated. What was I on? Doolally!

Talking of Prince Charles, it was around this time that I imagined, or saw on my MTRUTH, Princes Charles and Andrew being taught a lesson by the Security Services. The two princes were wearing school uniform, including shorts, and having a wonderful time playing a computer game, which was disguised as being confined to virtual reality. In the game they were taking it in turns to operate a virtual robot in a car. They were doing this in the most irresponsible way possible, as one might imagine two schoolboys doing in virtual reality. But whilst they thought they were driving a virtual reality vehicle, what they were actually doing was driving me round the bend. I imagined they later learnt this and were sent to their rooms like naughty children. As for me I was the one and only person this was being done to. It was a lesson that had to be learnt at the highest level in British Intelligence – and I was the hero. What a hero I was – I was such a hero!

Once again I had little idea what I was to do when I got to Schiphol but it seemed I had little choice in the matter. After all, Prince Andrew was behind me and therefore, of course, so too would be the Dutch Royal Family. Soon I was over the North Sea, and happening to glance out of the window to port, a couple of hundred feet below I saw what I presume was a Royal Dutch Air Force jet flying past. It was certainly what would be classified a near miss – and I did not gain the impression I was seeing it on my MTRUTH. Obviously the pilot was a rather important person, it seemed, which could only make me wonder, yet again, how many other important people were going past me in the opposite direction but on the pavement, as on the Oasis album sleeve. My delusions of grandeur told me the picture on that sleeve was causally connected with events happening to me – like the passage of this jet fighter.

On at least one occasion, both during this summer and again later on, I would see a man walk past me who looked both extremely angry and, it seemed, reluctant to do so. He had been ordered to torture me through my MTRUTH but, having done so, was told by his CO what he had actually been doing and that I was in fact more important than he was so, to acknowledge such, he had to walk past me like this. Bearing in mind that, in reality, these passers-by had nothing to do with me, it is amusing to now imagine what they would have thought if they knew the truth! The sheer force of this delusion was most impressive. I cannot stress it enough – these people walking past me were extremely rare, talented, and special: SAS, SBS, IRA, Delta Force, members of the Magic Circle, high ranking Masons, High Court judges, you name it. I felt elite and extremely important in this delusion – the feeling was mysterious, magical and wonderful whenever it happened over the next few years.

I remember little of this sortie. In fact you might say I was never there officially. Of course I went to see *The Night Watch* in the National Gallery. There I had all manner of thoughts about what some of the other tourists were listening to on their Walkman guides to the gallery – instructions from their respective intelligence agencies. There was no doubt some of these people were foreign agents, and not necessarily just Dutch ones. The technology I possessed seemed an open secret in the world intelligence community where, at this time, not one person had correctly managed to deduce that their free will had been subsumed into the world intelligence playground. Only I was anywhere near that.

Then I went to see some jewellery being made in the local family outlet, and was thinking of buying Amanda a ring. Like Rufus May (a sufferer of schizophrenia who became a clinical psychologist and public figure), I believe schizophrenia is partly an experience-derived illness. I think it would be helpful for patients if it was seen that way, rather than merely a biologically derived condition. But at this moment I had not yet discovered she was married. In my case, I suppose, the schizophrenia was born out of my perceived loss of her, the failure of my record label, *and drinking too much*.

I took a boat trip. It was the first time the guide had done the tour. She was a member of the Dutch Royal Family, spying on me at the request of Prince Charles.

Nothing else too odd happened in Amsterdam, except for my seeing a copy of Herman Hesse's *Narziss and Goldmund* identical to my own in the hand of another tourist. This was apposite as I saw it in Anne Frank's house, where my heart thumped as Auschwitz seemed frighteningly close. It was being carried to order for me to see. This would enable British Intelligence to see it back home via my MTRUTH and the Dutch Security Services MTRUTH intranet. It was important this should happen because Hitler despised Herman Hesse. I would not have minded betting the book was my very own copy. I imagined somebody saying "If I ever find out he imagines that I will eat my hat." Perhaps it would be more realistic to expect them to have died laughing before they got round to it.

"Well – no Prince Charles's dog in Belgium or Holland", I said to myself. But then again perhaps he had never had one. It was all just a joke between Prince Charles and MI5 intended to set my imagination going. In that case it was just me and really I was like the dog in *The Herbs*, the '60s children's television programme, which ran in circles announcing its name, Dill, and proclaiming "Though my tail I'd love to get, I have not caught it yet."

I was unwittingly trying to catch my own tail, except my tail was becoming my *tale* – this story. *The Times* article announcing the dog's disappearance on April 22nd had described the dog as long-tailed. Maybe it was a misprint. That must have been it! Prince Charles had given them the copy designed to excite me into writing, and the newspaper thought HRH had obviously misspelt it long taled, but that, nevertheless was his prescription for me. The newspaper had 'corrected' Prince Charles's spelling. So now I knew what had actually happened. The rest would be history.

Once more I returned home to Bedford, another mission complete. Now I knew the truth about Prince Charles's dog.

Chapter Sixteen

The March of the King of Laois

Again it was time to be off and now I was imagining my parents had been to Buckingham Palace for an audience with the Queen to discuss my behaviour. I felt an overwhelming duty to somehow represent His Royal Highness Prince Charles in all of this, which meant I needed to go on what to my mind was a British Intelligence State visit – to Ireland. The lengths I went to. But looking for Prince Charles's dog in Ireland would obviously be a sensitive issue and had to be a collaborative exercise with the Irish. Questions would be asked about how it got there and what it was actually doing. And anyway you could not just turn up in a foreign country unannounced to look for a missing dog of this magnitude. But I assumed I was being followed and so if I went to Ireland those who needed to know would be informed ahead of my arrival. And if I didn't assume that (as some of the time I forgot) I was hypoparanoid[38] to the point of being an international criminal. This meant that every time I forgot I was being followed they could say it was a separate criminal act and I would need high-level round the clock legal representation.

I was not to leave for Ireland without showing further signs of the illness I was already deep into. Firstly my susceptibility to hypnosis had increased and near my house I was entranced by the sound of cars driving onto what at the time was the biggest Bailey bridge in the world. It was a temporary measure whilst the previous bridge, which had concrete cancer, was being replaced. Yet even that excited extravagant and farfetched ideas in my head about Mafia conspiracies.

Near the bridge was an old plinth, which had once had a trophy cannon on it from the Crimean war. As I lay in bed early one morning I was hypnotised by the noise from the bridge and, by autosuggestion, I began to hear the noise of the tumult at the Charge of the Light Brigade. And very strange it was.

I also became obsessed with what I maintained was the theft of police NO WAITING cones near my flat. Almost every other house had at least one cone in its front garden. I walked down Rocks Lane (where my flat was) removing all the twenty or thirty cones from the gardens. I placed them dangerously in the road causing a certain amount of traffic chaos for which, luckily, I did not get picked up. The sight of the chaos was quite an amusing one – all caused by my anger at the theft of traffic cones for personal use. Whilst I was doing this I saw a lady coming towards me. I had not yet heard of "thought broadcasting" and did not then know that the belief this was happening was a symptom of schizophrenia. As she approached I felt that thoughts were indeed being broadcast between our minds. I concentrated my thoughts on her mind. After she had passed, and was behind me, I was convinced I had made a direct connection to her head. At this moment I turned my head to see her walking away towards The Red Lion. She too turned her head at the same moment. It felt very odd – perhaps she was an MTRU too and, if so, it would be interesting to know what she had ground-MTRUTHed. Or perhaps this was morphic resonance again.

I wandered off to take a closer look at the Empress State Building. A friend had once told me it had a GCHQ outstation on the roof and I could feel beams of syrupy paranoia coming down from it, fit to make most people vomit there and then. I walked up Shorrold's Road and a rare Citröen Pininfarina was parked near the house at which Mr Kipper, with a bottle of champagne wrapped in a Union Jack, had met his victim. At the time I thought it was right outside that house and that MI5 had put it there.

Despite this immense globular paranoia ball I was in, I found it fairly easy to think: don't be silly, of course nobody is watching me. Then, somewhere near Jill Dando's house, I obtained a Snickers bar, which I never had any intention of eating but only bought to use as a weapon. It was a hot day and I set to melting the bar inside its packet. I felt personally threatened by the globalisation which led to its name change from Marathon.

I had been possessed by somebody on the Mull of Kintyre helicopter, whose occupants, if they actually existed, knew about the alien landing at Bannerdown Hill. I had been sent by them to investigate it. Strange, I again thought, that I had ended up in Inverness only days after they died since that was where they were said to be going when, I imagined, the SAS chucked all that spurious helicopter wreckage down onto the hillside to fake the accident.

Anyway, something put me into a massively anti-American mindset, which I had seen before in others, the day my firm was taken over by an American company. Walking up towards Hammersmith, the Snickers bar was getting pretty liquid. The idea behind its intended use was that you could not just walk into my house, take a Marathon from the fridge, and rewrap it as a Snickers bar, without asking me – another strange delusion of grandeur. Not that I would have had one in there as I didn't even like them. I dropped it deliberately in the revolving door of Coca-Cola headquarters, stood on it to make the wrapper burst, and let the door revolve a few times to spread it around the carpet a bit. I pictured the Coke executives up in the boardroom snorting cocaine (early Coca-Cola actually had cocaine in it) at that actual moment and eating their own supply of Marathon bars. I suppose this was a terrorist act. I am not terribly proud of it. Sorry America.

I was beginning to visually hallucinate when my eyes were closed and was tortured by the vision of Amanda in bed with her boyfriend. Not pleasant. Then, one day I took a drive and, finding myself near Dunstable, came across a village that bore her real name, the name by which her friends knew her. I headed for Dublin.

At Holyhead I found I had a few hours wait before the ferry left, and drove up to the cliffs to see the view. As I went up I was completely blinded by the sun; so I slowed to a couple of feet a second at most until I got to the top. Having MTRUTH, I had become some wondrous tool of the Freemasons. They were using me as an example of military technology with my MTRUTH connected to personal computers belonging to various musicians, who were using my escapades for inspiration.

I later found myself thinking that this incident was the inspiration for a song called *Blinded by the Sun* by The Seahorses. In fact I started believing the whole album was about me and had been inspired by intelligence reports leaked to the guitarist John Squire. I could see him vividly in my mind's eye. He seemed to be laughing at me; but there was nothing unpleasant about his laughter. I just gained the impression he had a highly developed sense of humour and that it was an honour to have him laughing at me.

So why do comedians not feel they are being persecuted when they are laughed at? Obviously because they know they are funny and it's nothing to worry about. Have you ever heard a so-called schizophrenic complain everyone laughs at them? Maybe they were just undiagnosed stand-up comedians caught up in a post-schizophrenia sociopathological system. But, nota bene, I was never convinced either way that it was actually John Squire or just my own good visual imagination, let alone my MTRUTH. It might as well have been Ronnie Corbett adopting the virtual disguise of Mr Squire without even one tiny variation in behaviour from anything other than utter amusement.

Although I was having these strange thoughts, if anyone had asked me some pertinent questions about them, I would have, whilst laughing, denied I believed them, especially I suspect if I'd had to put money on it. In any case it seemed too dangerous to tell anyone in my immediate vicinity. But my weakness was that I was thinking them in the first place, and the thoughts were just too alluring to me to be ignored. I had to go along with them. The thought of all my favourite albums over the coming years, and some others besides, being inspired by my antics really appealed at the time – it meant I was somebody. So it was easy to see rooms full of gathered well-known songwriters all remotely going through my record collection praying I had bought one of their records because the rules stated they could only enter my virtual world if I had. They need not have worried. They did not realise they had been chosen for the very reason that I had. Peter Gabriel loved it.

At the top of the cliff I could see the ferry I had missed now far out, almost halfway to the horizon with the Wicklow Mountains clearly visible, so high up was I and so clear the weather. It was a beautiful day. I had once seen a road sign in a pub, The Mill Hotel back in Bedford, indicating the distance to Wicklow and Dublin. It now occurred to me that the sign could have been put up here, the distance to these two places from the clifftops being as on the sign. I also noticed somebody had written on a dirty car windscreen "See you later" and imagined, of course, that this was a message for me from MI6. I headed into town and drank some beer while waiting for the next ferry.

Suddenly I recalled an occasion 12 years earlier during my time living in Kilburn, northwest London, where there is a large Irish community. I had found a £5 note on the pavement. But, most unusually it was a Bank of Ireland sterling note, made for the Northern Ireland market. I now had no doubt the note had been placed there in front of me all those years ago, perhaps by MI5, perhaps by the IRA, or a double agent, just to lead my thoughts where they needed them, if not then, all these years later. I imagined that perhaps they'd had to do it several times before I saw it. Not for the first time I now put together all manner of incidents in my life, incidents which at the time I thought nothing of, but which it was now clear had been of long standing design back to the progenitorial meeting of 1926. They wanted me to remember the £5 and I had, and now it was payback time. I wondered what lay in store for me in the Republic of the Irish Free State.

On the ferry I drank more and when I arrived at Dun Laoghaire on the Sunday morning, I was not in good health. In fact I was ripe for another breakdown caused yet again by staying up all night.

As we got off the ferry I noticed a young chap wearing a Pele T-shirt. Needless to say I felt this had been aimed at me because I had been listening to their album *The Sport of Kings* for half the summer. He had been told to walk in front of me with his back to me as, unusually; the familiar logo was on the back not the front. As you will recall I had bought the album at random the day before I rode the Pepsi Max Big One. I love that album. Somebody had told me Pele were Irish – which made it look even more fixed. In fact somebody also told me that one of them had won the Irish lottery – though I presumed he meant by my picking out their album at random.

The many vapour trails overhead reaching back towards London seemed to convey another meaning – almost as though they had been deliberately caused by the military. Being so tired I proceeded to enter a state of complete indecisiveness involving the overwhelming and unusual feeling that now I had to drive to Belfast, some one hundred miles to the north, and back again. I was on the verge of a panic attack, so out of kilter was my brain chemistry. Eventually I managed to correct this and headed into town believing my presence here had indeed been made known, as a matter of courtesy, to the Irish Government. Just as it was in Europe, the movement of all MTRUs overseas being one in which governments co-operated, I now had a new handler, this time of Irish nationality, to subliminally control my behaviour.

Meanwhile, on the matter of my MTRUTH status, there seemed some scope for humour in this situation. I found myself hearing the song *Getting To Know You* from *The King and I* in my head. My new MTRUTH operator seemed to be getting to know me and more often than not I tended to ignore any orders he placed in my mind. I felt that to do as he said would render me wholly deterministic and not in the least existential, this state of affairs not appealing to me. But is not the difference between the two just a question of human vanity? Well actually, according to the Dutch mathematician Gerard 't Hooft we only *think* we have a free will anyway and that underneath the uncertainty of quantum mechanics there is a deterministic order. John Conway, from Princeton University, says we are not really free to choose the chocolate cake over the plain one and suggests that someone who has been tracking the motions of all the particles in the universe will be able to predict with perfect accuracy which cake you pick. Or in other words he is a determinist.

I could see my new operator sitting down at the computer terminal and then casting his eyes down my files before taking control through my MTRUTH. None of this conflicted with my feeling that, at this moment, I was in the military and not a civilian. I told myself I was under orders to *not necessarily carry out my orders* – this way I could still remind myself I was a Soviet MI6 agent seconded from the Special Boat Service. I would not have thought I looked like a bucking bronco to the Garda controller assigned to me – more like a bronco that would not necessarily go left or right if he told it to. He would notice I seemed to be getting sent in circles all around Dublin by signs pointing to *The Flintstones* exhibition, none of which were any help whatsoever in navigating one's way to it. Typically Irish. You could only get there if you took a cab, which I did. In the exhibition it was apparent the Flintstones had not arrived yet, and I felt enormously embarrassed by the display as though I were, indeed, on a State visit and something had gone wrong with excruciating consequences. I felt similar embarrassment at the waxworks, which showed signs of the Troubles in the graffiti on the cabinets. All very painful – and Bono looked like the IRA had melted him during the night.

Actually, to date, I had seen few and infrequent items of information over my MTRUTH these including the visions of Amanda in bed with her boyfriend. By now I had deduced these to be some sort of immersion therapy in the emotional autoclave laid on for my benefit by the Army Intelligence Corps Psychological Warfare Department. Either that or some little known part of my head was doing it automatically. Apart from that, all I had seen were those black streaks in my vision. But I was keenly aware that there would be consequences dependent on what information I was made party to over my MTRUTH. If I was not simply being presented with benign concept image documents or text files the knowledge therein could be potentially dangerous to hold. One example presenting no danger to me appeared when I had found myself examining a plant back in Bedford. A drop-down screen had appeared in my EAI. It was obvious that the ultimate purpose of this particular screen was to give me a full intelligence report on the plant as in *Star Trek*. This happened a number of times and when it did I assumed that, should I go to America, my controllers would give me the full capability of my MTRUTH for my own intelligence purposes as regards flora and fauna. I would then be an expert ornithologist at a moment's command. However the screen contained no information. It was as though somebody was showing off the possibilities to me. I imagined I should click my fingers to bring up the required window – but did not try. It was just my imagination.

I wandered around town for a while, finding a pub where the doors still appeared to be open although it was 8am. Seated on the floor in the doorway was a young chap, the first Dubliner I had met on his home patch. "Hi, how are yer! Where were yer last night?" he said. He was so familiar that an independent observer might have thought he knew me. He really did sound like he had been expecting me the previous night. I imagined he was the person who had written "See you later" on the car windscreen back at Holyhead. *He was in the IRA.*

I had a full Irish breakfast in The Clarence Hotel before booking into The Ormonde Quay Hotel, as featured in the Sirens scene of Joyce's *Ulysses*. I put my car in the compound. I went out for a walk, short of sleep and unwell. Casualty and another massive panic attack were looming rapidly. I saw the letters "IRA" sprayed on a wall. I found myself in Archbishop Ryan Park in Merrion Square, surrounded by the busts of Irish literary figures. A tall man walked past me. As he passed he said "You need to relax" in an American accent. He knew I was in trouble and was talking to me. *He was a CIA agent.*

I retired to my room and went to sleep for some hours. I awoke. The World Cup was on. It was half time and I could not believe what I heard. The presenter appeared to say "Our friend with the parade has woken up for the second half." I thought it was aimed at me. Was this a joke? Did this go back to Wilton? I might have liked to confront him about what he had said, and why he had said it, but there remained a mountainous barrier of power and deception between us. This rendered even thinking of such a thing schizophrenia itself. Yet I had already come within a whisker of doing that precise thing to the two Radio 1 DJs. Again the thought that some parade was developing around me was overpowering.

I was beginning to think I knew what the results of the World Cup matches were going to be, and not just that – I could decide beforehand whom I would prefer to win. I believed the result of the match rested on my decision. It was not for money. It would just be a bit of a laugh if South Korea beat Germany 7-5.

I had broken my years-old promise to read *Ulysses* before going to Dublin but that was the least of my worries. Still, next day, I took the tourist bus trip around town. The weather was fine and the guide in top form. I had seen the statue of Molly Malone, and enjoyed the guide's rendition of *Cockles and Mussels*.

We were driving down one particular expensive-looking street and I happened to notice a man banging forcibly on the door of number 10 – definitely, it seemed, a real message. Downing Street knew where I was and had been informed by MI6 at a Cabinet meeting.

On the bus I noticed a double of Amanda. I say double though in reality I would say there was just enough about her to make me mindful of the possibility that she had been deliberately sent on holiday from England, on her own, and that she was to be alone on the same bus I was on. Going to work one day at RAE Farnborough a couple of years earlier, I had been sitting on the train when the inter-carriage door opened. I 'knew' the person coming through was extremely attractive to me before the door opened. Through the door came what certainly was a likeness, if not a full double of Amanda. She even shared one of Amanda's names. One afternoon I'd had enough of this. So I decided to track her down by hanging around on the appropriate platform for a couple of hours. She did eventually turn up and I asked her out without much success. In fact the next thing I knew she had left the country for Belgium.

Anyway, holiday romance. I summoned up the courage to ask this particular girl to go for a drink with me and she accepted. Soon I was drinking Guinness with her not far from the brewery itself. It could have been De Danann itself (the Irish folk band) playing in the pub. They played *The Banks of the Nile*, *Langstrom's Pony*, *The Tap Room* and *Lord Ramsey's Reel*, which I recognised from their first album, *The Mist Covered Mountain*. The girl could have had little idea how unwell I was – I concealed my illness well. She had no idea I thought she was an agent.

That night in The Ormonde Quay Hotel nightclub there was a gay disco with a number of transvestites present. The chap I was speaking to, who seemed to have a gammy leg, was talking about Bono and, whether or not he said he knew him personally, at that moment someone walked past and said "You will be meeting him soon at this rate." He offered me a cigarette. On the packet it said "Special Filter". This referred to the security procedures. He was an MI6 agent and knew exactly who I was. Throughout my trip I would keep seeing "Special Filter", not just on packets of cigarettes but also on advertisements. I was subject to the highest level of security the Garda and British Intelligence could muster – because I had MTRUTH. And the Irish are great dog lovers!

Next day I was much better and went for a wander around town. I saw a large advertising hoarding announcing "Good News Travels Fast". I was "in", as though I had joined a children's gang. I was a true Jack Charlton amongst Irish – or I would be. And I wore a flat cap. The sign had two meanings. The poster related secretly to the peace process and the momentous IRA ceasefire, which was about to be announced. I *knew in advance* of the statement, released on 31st August 1994. Here is the first paragraph of it:

Recognising the potential of the current situation and in order to enhance the democratic process and underlying our definitive commitment to its success, the leadership of the IRA have decided that as of midnight, 31st August, there will be a complete cessation of military operations. All our units have been instructed accordingly.

The IRA had recognised the potential too! I visited the General Post Office, centre of the tragically failed Easter Rising of 1916 organised by the Irish Republican Brotherhood, forerunner of the IRA. In the Post Office I saw the statue of the Cúchulainn. He was born Setantus, perhaps after the Setantii, a British people, though this did not really explain the very Victorian look of the statue.

I bought a train ticket to Galway. Tom had told me to go there for the festival. Standing in the queue for the train I noticed how tall I was compared to everyone. I felt freakishly large compared to the Celts.

I arrived in Galway in a far better state than I would have done by car. The Garda in Salthill accommodated me in an officer's bed and breakfast and that evening I inadvertently became an IRA fund donor when I bought a bootlegged tape of the U2 album *War* in the arcade. Little did I imagine that within six years I would attempt to provide their political wing a considerably larger sum.

That evening I found myself in a little emotional difficulty because sitting near me, in a fish restaurant, was a double of my friend Caroline. It was a little like when, during school days, I had attended the funeral of a rowing friend who had been killed in a car accident. Arriving late for his funeral, a fellow-mourner (the one who later had a sex change) had made a gesture with his hand towards a bouquet of flowers in the shape of a rowing oar. But when I looked at what he was pointing at I could only see a violin case – with a machine gun in it. I spent the whole funeral desperately trying to conceal the fact that I was cracking up laughing at this. I almost had to walk out of the church. Why I was amused I have no idea. Here in the pub I found myself having to cover my face with my hand and occasionally pretend I was coughing or something, anything but laughing. I imagined the comedian Dave Allen dressed as a Catholic priest saying to me "We all react differently to grief, my son" as I cracked up laughing even more.

The girl's mannerisms seemed extraordinarily reminiscent of Caroline, an erstwhile member of De Danann, with whom she sang and played her cello. Perhaps in my mind I am exaggerating how close a double she was and perhaps any confusion I was suffering was exactly what I imagined had been intended. I was certainly suffering mild Capgras syndrome. Or was I? You see with schizophrenia there is some truth in saying that if you believe you have it you can't be that bad. But at the time I had never heard of Dr Capgras. *If I was seen to laugh, my cover would certainly be blown.*

Amongst the others at the table was a redheaded girl who was giving somebody a tarot reading. Concealing my mirth I asked her to give me a reading and she agreed. The first three cards I drew were The Chariot, The Devil and Death and the others seemed no less prescient[39]. Amongst much else (which I forget) she told me that people had formed an unfair impression of me and that this was to be righted. She also told of an emotional relationship I was to have with a powerful man. Not being gay I asked if that was what it meant and she said no, to my relief, as I wanted to believe the cards.

If I was suffering Capgras syndrome then I also appeared to be suffering another, previously unrecognised, psychiatric illness: *Third Policeman's Bicycle*[40] syndrome. However I had not yet realised it as the performance of that play, as part of the festival, did not come until after I had been to the children's performance of *Alice's Adventures in Wonderland* and heard Diana Ross singing *I'm Coming Out* from a passing car. I did not imagine this was a secret message from the driver about a forthcoming announcement concerning his own sexual orientation but simply said quietly to myself "Ah, so you [MI6] are coming out [to Galway] are you?" More likely it was the CIA as down near the harbour I met a bearded tramp with an American accent. He told me I would not believe him but that he was a former astronaut. He pointed up at the moon in the daytime sky and, taking another swig of his whiskey, assured me he had been there. So maybe I was not the only deluded one... but then again.

I noticed the most spectacular swarm of flies I had ever seen, even in Africa, forming a miniature cyclone over a large steel drum nearby. I believed they had been brought in especially, God definitely knew what for, from somewhere in the tropics. This told me that, if anyone was going to have flies on them, there were some bloody big flies available in large numbers close at hand in Galway. The grass was ever so green and the mountains across Galway Bay invited me beyond where the salmon ran.

During the play I felt as well connected with the universe at large as the chain on this third policeman's bicycle. Every line in the play seemed personally pertinent, just like when I had seen *Four Weddings and a Funeral*. Actually, barring the fact that I had not murdered anyone, I think it probably was and for once I was not deluded.

I returned to my room and listened to my new tape of harp music, *Rip the Calico*, played by the master harpist Paul Dooley, which I had bought directly from him in the street. I lay on the bed relaxed, mental health being little of a problem during my time in Galway – the beautiful harp music bringing much needed peace and harmony to my mind. It would be easy to say it was merely my decision to take public transport, which improved things. But I still imagined the Princes Charles and Andrew wearing their school uniform having fun driving my car in virtual reality. However the car itself was back in the hotel compound in Dublin.

On the way back to Dublin the train went through a station that was having a new platform built. The worker standing proudly on the platform knew there was someone very important on the train, that person being me, and he looked a little frustrated the train did not stop.

Soon I would be back in Holyhead, to spend a night – but not before I saw a double, or even actual relation, of Martin McGuinness, at the Dublin ferry port.

At the bed and breakfast, I was put in the family room and was wondering about an Irish family who might stay there later. I sensed some sort of duty, as yet unfulfilled, to address the peace process, then a few days old, as I imagined the poster telling me to when I arrived in Dublin. On the top of the cupboard was a box of toys. This reminded me of a song entitled *Thinking of You Now* by the group The Box of Toys. I had once unsuccessfully tried to buy the record. So taking an envelope, I wrote a slightly altered line from that song: "We walk along the open *Sands* that inspiration bring," put some money in and hid it behind a picture hanging next to the cupboard. I remembered when I was in Canada in 1982, the year after Bobby Sands died. A bloke had appeared out of nowhere, found out I was British, and without me saying anything apart from where I was from, told me he was an IRA funder, spat at my feet, and walked off. I later wondered if he was employed by the CIA to recruit, or perhaps educate, agents from the British student population working the summer over there. It was a short lesson and I remembered everything he said. Perhaps he did a lot of spitting that summer.

Next day, driving across Anglesey I could not believe the large wind farm was real. Somehow it seemed to have been superimposed on my vision through my special eyes. I glanced back at it disbelievingly – not sure if what I was seeing was really there or not.

Soon I was in Portmeirion, where *The Prisoner*[41] had been filmed. The atmosphere was unaccountably odd, as you might imagine if you are familiar with that series. I booked into a bed and breakfast for the night. It belonged to a policeman again. There was one book (and one only) on the shelf next to the bed: it was entitled *Blindspot* and, bearing in mind my beliefs about there being electronics in my eyes I was particularly paranoid about it. The blind spot is the part of the fovea where the optic nerve connects into the retina. You can detect the presence of your blind spots by looking at a star and then looking slightly away from it whereupon you will notice the star to disappear. Somehow I found myself staring at the draw in the bedside cabinet. Feeling overwhelmed with paranoia I suddenly pulled it open. Instead of the Bible there was a bumper party pack of balloons and I immediately suspected this was a feature of every B&B in Portmeirion. I was happy to find the balloons and fully believed they were for me. I took them and still have them.

I went up Snowdon on the mountain railway and, at the top, had more ophthalmic problems, with seagulls. I noticed two bright lights down at sea level three 3,000 feet below. My knowledge of applied optics suggested holography to me, in which two laser "point sources" are used to create a hologram. Without thinking about it in detail, and given the surprise I felt in being surrounded by a flock of seagulls at over 3,000 feet, I found myself wondering if they were really there at all and were not just very impressive moving holograms. Perhaps this is not a common problem in schizophrenia. But with me it was often the main problem; this being not that I was hallucinating, but that *I was believing I was hallucinating*. Furthermore, as you already know, I was unable to believe some newspaper reports were not MI5/Comic Relief manoeuvres.

That night I camped out for the first time in my new tent, bought back in Inverness, enjoying a few beers in the local pub beforehand. As I supped my beer I thought back to the success of my 'Royal' visit to Ireland and the relaxation of listening to Paul Dooley's harp music, in particular *The March of the King of Laois*, in my own Garda bed and breakfast.

More notable events would take place before I reached Bedford and my own bed again. Next day, while taking a break from driving by Lake Vyrwny, a small Jack Russell appeared from nowhere. It was a friendly little dog, standing up on its hind legs with its front feet on my legs and licking my hand – but with no owner in sight. This, if not the dog itself, was symbolic of His Royal Highness Prince Charles's dog, Pooh, and I sensed a great friendliness in the animal. In my countrywide search for Prince Charles's dog I guessed the truth of the matter was that, with or without his knowledge, the SAS, or even the IRA, had kidnapped his dog for a laugh. Or at least that was what they wanted me to think. Likewise Prince Charles's having crash-landed a plane in Scotland did not somehow seem anything but a staged event. Again I found myself believing it had not really happened. By now, for sure, the prince would be aware that Pooh was still alive and would therefore have some hope. Or if not at least his dog had not died in vain. But I thought I had just met Pooh herself and there, unseen, the SAS or the IRA had released her in the nearby undergrowth. Mysterious.

An hour after Vyrwny I was walking by Lake Bala, Dr. Bala then being consultant psychiatrist at Bedford Hospital. He was fondly referred to by that name but actually his full name was Dr. Balasubramaniam. He was amicably referred to as Dr. Balasubterranean in the same manner Dr. Vasudevan was referred to as Dr. Vas Deferens[42]. At that time I had only seen him once briefly whilst having my massive panic attack on the day of the Radio 1 road show. He'd had to scrape me off the ceiling with a spatula whilst standing on a stepladder I was in such a state. I was to get to know him much better and as I walked by the lake I thought of him. His name was redolent of the fact that a monster similar, but less well known than that in Loch Ness, is said by legend to live in the depths of Lake Bala. But the monster was already revealing itself to me in the form of my mental illness though, if truth were told, I was enjoying this more often than not.

The next day I visited Llangollen, taking trips on a barge and a steam train. On the train some trainspotters were in my compartment and I found their conversation exceptionally amusing. Later that day I visited the Pillar of Eliseg, commemorating the eighth-century monarch of an old Welsh kingdom. A camomile lawn surrounded the pillar. Opposite the pillar, on the other side of the road, there was a sign announcing a car boot sale the following week. In front of the sign I supraimagined a rather lulu person dressed as a Saudi prince looking at it before getting into a Rolls Royce. This was very odd, and I felt a strong urge to go to the car boot sale imagining I could find a priceless work for a pittance. It seemed that untold riches were within my grasp if only I could hold myself together. I imagined the Saudi prince was on the biggest treasure hunt in history. His wildest dream was to unearth even more riches beyond belief: solid gold, silver, diamonds and coins of the most exquisite and beautiful type. He longed to dig his hands deep into the treasures and then let them fall back into the chest in which they had been hidden, a river of wealth worth millions of pounds flowing through his hands. In my MTRUTH or merely in my imagination, I then saw his chauffeur-driven car pulling up at my grandmother's old home in Ruislip. The owner was in and the wealthy prince bought the house for cash paying many times the market rate there and then, on the condition the owner moved out that second, to go to a hotel at the prince's expense.

Around the back he went, excited beyond imagination, to poke a stick through the 45 years of undergrowth at the foot of the garden to find it was true what he had been told. With the help of an Irish labourer he had seen drilling the road in Ruislip Gardens, the concrete was dug up. He believed nobody apart from the Irishman knew he was there though, in reality his elder brother had him turned into an MTRU during the night for a birthday present. In fact his older brother had brainwashed him all the way from Saudi Arabia, with the help of one or two documents, to find this place where a Cold War-sensitive divining rod would twitch right, left and all around. For under the concrete was millions of pounds of Nazi gold and this was the best paid half-an-hour's work an Irishman ever did. You see he was a Flynn, related to my magician Uncle Louis of that Irish surname – and he too was an MTRU in his case being controlled from Dublin. The whole operation had been scripted back in the pub that afternoon in 1926 – though, at the time they were not too sure where the booty could come from.

My father had told me proudly of the Soviet stout he had once drunk on meeting Russian Naval Intelligence during the last days of World War II. I ridiculed his claim, in 2002, to have laid the concrete with his father. I did not believe the USAF serviceman had lied to me and remembering his exact words to me that day back in the '60s when I was only six and he gave me a clue to the greatest treasure hunt ever imagined in history. I did not forget his words. Why would he have lied to me unless the Americans had spied on my father and grandfather? Nor did I forget Ian Curtis's words, whatever he was really thinking, KGB concept document or otherwise, and wondered what BBC's *Groundforce* team would make of this concrete. My imagination was in overdrive.

So I wrote to the Queen on a postcard of Lake Vyrwny and asked her, a little more realistically, to arrange a competition in Ireland with 50 prizes of trips to London, including a guided tour of the Tower of London. Minutes before the party arrived to view the Crown Jewels, I asked Her Majesty, the fabled Koh-i-noor diamond would be removed from Her Majesty's crown and replaced by a little cocktail stick held to the crown with a piece of Sellotape. On top of the stick would be a sign saying "The Koh-i-noor diamond was stolen by the Irish Republican Army in 1994. It has never been recovered." I also asked Her Majesty to arrange that the diamond be miraculously recovered at the car boot sale opposite the Pillar of Eliseg a few years later. The thought of the effect of this in Ireland left me drunk with hilarity. Legend has it that whoever has the diamond rules the world, and knows all of its misfortunes. But I was unaware at the time that the diamond is said to have a curse; I only found out later when I noticed a piece of *The Daily Express* in the street outside my house. It is said that the 105-carat gem, whose name means Mountain of Light in Persian, and which was mined in India around 1100, carries a curse lethal to male owners and "only God or a woman can wear it with impunity."

As night fell, I reached the Welsh/English border. There was a roadblock and diversion with police redirecting the traffic. I took this to mean the border into England was closed and I assumed this had to be a Welsh MI5 having a laugh – though the eighth-century King Offa, 81 miles of whose 149-mile dyke still stand, was not mentioned by the policeman as far as I recall. After the detour I managed to get to Shrewsbury feeling very tired and panicky. There I booked into a hotel and then took a walk. From a car parked by the road some young

Welshmen got out and one of them called out to me "There he is! In the cap!" and then "Hey, you're that famous bloke aren't you?" Next they all sang out together "It's not who you love, it's who you know" in a tune I did not recognise. This made too much sense to me. They had been sent, I was sure. They were probably just some lads out on the piss.

Tired, I once more arrived back in Bedford. Outside the house was a car with the number plate R594 UCL. My mind told me MI5 had put it there and the plate meant "Right, May '94, University College London". MI5 wished to remind me they knew what I was up to. Prince Charles had spilt the beans to them that I was a KGB agent, and now everyone knew – not just the Special Intelligence Service. It seemed almost certain they'd had a tracking device fitted to my car and the message was to remind me of, what I believed, was that fateful May bank holiday weekend.

On the day of the British Grand Prix I drove out to the northwest of Bedford, and found myself under the clear blue sky of a perfect English summer's day, with a strong breeze blowing over the Union flag flying at a garden centre. A little way down the road a voice in my head said "Damon Hill has won the British Grand Prix." So I switched on the radio and found he had. Then, a while later, at a service area, it felt like I had driven in on some major pop star's video shoot, when I saw a ridiculously good-looking couple jumping into a large '50s open-top American roadmobile in impossibly perfect condition, it seemed. They had not a care in the world and life, for them, presented not even the slightest problem at any moment of their lives, from the cradle to the grave.

Italy won their World Cup semi-final and that night I was walking down the Embankment by the Suspension Bridge watching thousands of jubilant fans going on their celebration march (14,000 Italians live in Bedfordshire). As I walked along I heard one of them say "I'm going to give you an extremely fat cheque!" I believed the message came from the Italian Prime Minister and was aimed directly at me. This was one of the incidents that rather "did my head in".

Chapter Seventeen

We Are the Diddy Men

B eing of the opinion that I should act in the most appropriate manner for a person who had lost his own free will, I began employing various ruses to impose randomness on my actions. This was to persuade myself that I had some level of control of the situation. You might understand how the fact that I'd had to make an electronic random number generator at university now became more than significant considering my state of mind. It was further confirmation that everything which was now happening was predetermined (within certain margins which I could, and indeed had, pushed back for the sake of my own mental health). This realisation was frightening indeed. I now looked back on my life reassessing various incidents in my memory, in each case in the light of the existence of my KGB file, imagined or not. It was, indeed, as though I had been the subject of a 68-year-old conspiracy. This alternated between being massively sinister, and then hugely magical and regal, and cause for universal rejoicing. As in the novel *The Dice Man*, by Luke Reinhardt, I now took to writing a choice of courses of action, and using the random electronic die to determine the outcome, I gave myself some free will back as best I could. The actual amount of free will would be something for Michael Ignatiev and company to debate in a post-Bedford Modernian existential light. As for Einstein saying "God does not play dice", I did not believe he had been correct. Which reminds me, the Right Reverend Professor David Jenkins, former Bishop of Durham, said "I wouldn't put it past God to arrange a Virgin Birth if he wanted. But I don't think he did."

One afternoon, a few weeks after I had stood on Solsbury Hill and watched that Hercules fly by, I saw a pile of old Rupert Bear annuals and opening one at random began to read. It was *Rupert and the Dog Rose*. Mrs Bear's washing line keeps coming down and Rupert discovers the reason why. He becomes ensnared in a dog rose bush, which he finds himself pulled to the middle of, where there is a tunnel into the Imps' underworld.

Rupert meets the King of the Imps and finds that the bottom of Mrs Bear's washing line pole is poking through the ceiling in the King's Hall and they keep pushing it back. The problem is resolved and Rupert returns to the surface. In my mind I, of course, did what many a good schizophrenic would. I felt, not for the first time, that there was some kind of divine intervention involved here, in that the word "dog" was involved. Schizophrenia never even crossed my mind however, and I found myself considering all the logical explanations: perhaps a magician had somehow secretly glued all the pages together except the one where that particular story started; perhaps the military had such complete control over me that they could even get me to find a particular page at their whim, using my MTRUTH and complete reality replacement. Either way, I did not have the impression I was in full control of myself. And this seemed supreme magic.

I got on my mountain bike and cycled off to Bedford Park. By the lake there are some landscaped mounds, which I cycled around. Coming downhill near the water's edge, I found myself ensnared in a bush and had a strong sense that there was some unseen but causal connection between my now being ensnared in this bush and what I had read. What was now to happen will, for the rest of my life, remain in my memory an utterly bizarre event.

I returned home and, not having any idea whatsoever where exactly I was intending to go, got in my car and began driving north. I ended up aiming at Liverpool though the reason to go there was no more than the fact it was a big place I had never been to, The Beatles' home city and the destination determined by my random number generator. This dangerous religious cult I thought I had become involved in, left my mind feeling it was being torn apart. I was not 100 per cent, mentally speaking, but in a sense I was, perhaps, bearing up quite well.

After a long drive I arrived near the Liver Building with, atop, the largest clock dials in Great Britain. I found a nightclub and briefly considered going in but for whatever reason decided not to. I got back in the car, and now it was raining heavily with great claps of thunder. Somehow, although there was water pouring down on my car, my mind was telling me it was not real rain. It felt like I was on a film set. I was confused and had no idea where to go now, so decided to follow the lightning bolts. I was not convinced they were real lightning bolts either and it seemed as though my car had a head-up display on the windscreen again. Either that or I was seeing this lightning on my MTRUTH. MI5 had given the go-ahead. It seemed the DISC had, at last, released the wooden bars and padlocks they had been using at the controller's keyboard to restrict the level of subliminality in my EAI. This allowed GCHQ full access to me by way of communications to my MTRUTH.

For weeks now I'd had the overwhelming feeling that I was on to something, but did not know what it was. "There's something going on here, and I am going to find out what it is", summed up my general state of mind. Such a thought led logically to a consideration of the nature of existence. After having done years of highly classified work for the Ministry of Defence, I had reached the conclusion (and this is very sensitive information) that life is a joke. But right now I was conducting a clinical study of the treatment of schizophrenia, though had not quite yet realised it.

I followed the bolts, be they on my EAI, or more accurately in this case EAV, until they stopped. The rain now stopped too. Suddenly *I knew* I was the victim of some enormous prank. I saw the road sign saying "Knotty Ash" and turned left. It is a real place I assure you. Soon I came across a pub, The Knotty Ash Arms, and went in. I had a drink and then returned outside. In the street I asked a jolly young bunch where Ken Dodd's house was. Who is to say they were not the natural manifestation of Ken Dodd's fictional clan of jovial small people, the Diddy Men? They rather reminded me of those youngsters I had met on Solsbury Hill too as they showed me the way, and within minutes I was parked outside Mr Dodd's house. I went up to the door and rang the bell. And only a few hours earlier I had been reading of the King of the Imps.

I have no idea what I had planned to say to Mr Dodd. But the feeling was similar to that I'd had the day of Solsbury Hill and my trip to Her Majesty's Land Forces HQ. I felt I was expected. It seemed an end to all this was imminent. By ringing on his bell I might have resolved my confusion. I imagined he might say something like "Ah Dr. Travis, I wondered how long it would be before you knocked on my door... let me put it like this..." Imagine for yourself what he might then have said in the light of his learning of my exploits from the Knotty Ash Intelligence Agency. Perhaps he had something sticking through his ceiling too, put there by the SAS.

But Mr Dodd was not at home, a man telling me he was away. Somehow I could not quite believe him and suspected Mr Dodd was hiding around the back. I got back in the car and drove off towards Manchester where I found a room at The Prince of Wales Hotel in Whalley Range. This seemed appropriate as I was thinking I was on the biggest Wally range ever conceived. At least I was not driving through the night this time. I suppose I found there to be sufficient aesthetic grounds in the manoeuvre to free me from an all-night job.

At the hotel a wedding reception was taking place, which as a hotel guest, I gatecrashed after time had been called. Upon reaching my room I found the sheets to be a little unusual in that they had dark navy-blue and white stripes, exactly the same colour as the knickers Amanda had been wearing one night when I slept on her floor. I felt sad. MI5, I felt, knew everything about me. But then again it was a privilege. It was also my privilege to have, gratis, a military state-of-the-art mobile phone – my MTRUTH.

Chapter Eighteen

London Loves...

During the weeks after Wiltshire I hardly went to my flat at all. It reminded me of too much and I felt ill at ease there. The room felt sickly. On one occasion though, I did return. From my rear window I noticed the Japanese woman again sitting mysteriously in the back bedroom of the opposite house. There was something about her. Looking again later I found she had left. I took out my binoculars and had a look at the room she had been in. Then I turned my attention to the room to the right. Suddenly a great shudder went through my body, about which Roman Polanski would have been very interested. For a moment I was in the film *The Tenant*.[43] This would not be the last time I would feel that I was in this film. I was no longer looking at the room. Instead, standing right there, looking straight back at me through another pair of binoculars, was another me, though metaphysically distinct from myself. A deep groan of fright went right through my body and I stepped back horrified. I was staring at my own reflection in the mirror in her room.

Leaving the flat wearing my "Surf Dog" shorts I was again convinced that my every coming and going from the flat had been watched from the GCHQ outstation atop the Empress State Building a mile or two away. The van parked outside my flat was not all it seemed either, and had intelligence-gathering equipment in it to monitor my movements.

I shook off the shock of what I had seen through my binoculars, as much as one could, and now I was off to the Glastonbury Festival. It was a sunny day. As usual the helicopters were out, and not just in my imagination. *Show You The Way To Go* by The Jacksons came on the radio and I felt the siren-like force as usual. I felt an onus was on me but really could not think what to do about it except become some sort of prostitute to humility. How the hell could I make £10 million? I felt pretty silly and massively empowered at the same time. It was tearing my head apart. Worse still I was wondering if I was Prince Charles's dog myself: some solipsism.

Somewhere on the way down I was passing an Army base and noticed a sign announcing "Charity Jumble Sale". I was embarrassed but the Army were trying to raise the dosh: I had made something happen. The IRA ceasefire being imminent I imagined an Irishman turning up selling some shoulder-launched grenades from the back of a Morris Traveller. But I was still pissing myself laughing at this Irishman, or a retired lieutenant colonel in the British Army, finding the Koh-i-noor diamond whilst rummaging through some odds and sods at the Llangollen car boot sale. I felt a strong force pulling me to it – but I continued to Glastonbury.

I imagined that, amidst scenes of great jubilation, Prince Charles's dog was going to be winched down from a helicopter onto the stage during Peter Gabriel's set. But what did happen? Our campsite (I had made camp with Tom and some friends from Bedford) was buzzed by an Army Westland Whirlwind helicopter that appeared only 50 feet above. The weird thing was that even though the tents were practically being blown away, it was as though everyone had been studiously reminded that if they so much as acknowledged the mere existence of a helicopter they could go down for 10 years. Only I acknowledged it was there even though it was so close. It flew right over our 'pub' sign, erected so we could find our campsite in the sea of tents that filled the field. The sign said "Bunyan's Onions" and reminded me of the adage that good security was like an onion.

Next day I noticed a fighter jet approaching at an altitude of 1,000 feet. It then went into a vertical climb straight over our flagpole, letting off a bright glint at the apex of its climb, where it looped at some 10 to 12 thousand feet. I was not wanted and was being told to return to the Dog Star. The plane indeed seemed to suggest the direction to go in. For the Dog Star, this was wrong actually: all rather embarrassingly tenuous. But don't worry – it was worse than that. This is just what I can remember. There seemed no limit to the puerility of my thoughts. My mind was assaulting itself with meaningless inferences. For example I ended up thinking Prince Charles was going to set me up on a date with Tara Palmer-Tomkinson. What with the way I was thought-surfing it was inevitable that the flight of the plane had another meaning: "straight-up" or in another word: "honestly". Why, I wondered, would I be made to think that? It seemed the reason was that somewhere there was a powerful individual who by now had become so sick and tired of having to either hear people say "straight-up" or say it himself that he had decided to say it to me. Over and over I now found myself imagining all manner of things I had done to make someone ferociously angry with me, to the point where I was going to be ground into the dust.

Car doors had seemed to be slamming at me everywhere I went. But I was never quite being bundled in and taken away, at least not yet. Then there were the reversing lights. Everywhere I went I kept seeing cars go into reverse as I went by. There was an endless barrage of them and my brain felt massive rejection as this only meant one thing. It was MI5 scolding me. But they were also testing and pushing me. I had to persist.

But not everything I thought was the fruit of insanity. I recalled a night's observing I had once done at the Royal Greenwich Observatory during my nine wonderful months there. Through a larger telescope than the vast majority of people are lucky enough to look through during their lifetime, I had observed the Andromeda galaxy, 10 million light years from earth. Now it seemed most improbable that there was no intelligent life in that galaxy *alone*, and I imagined the scene, with *a* sun setting and the local aliens there watching the alien band of the moment perform at the end of a perfect summer's day, which happened 10 million years ago. I'd just love to hear the music.

Soon after the festival, and in view of what I had done, it seemed that the thing to do was head *towards* Dublin again. I thought I was so powerful I could exert a positive effect just by going in its direction. Somewhere in Wales on what was a perfect summer's day, driving along I saw a sign. I don't recall it being an official Department of Transport sign but rather a homemade one, perhaps hastily put up shortly before I arrived, I could not be sure. The sign saying

"Paradise" pointed down a lane. With the mood I was in there was no chance of not investigating. The beauty of Paradise staggered me as I watched the bright rays of afternoon Welsh sun spear through the canopy. If the dog at Lake Vyrwny wasn't Prince Charles's I was pretty sure it was here, in Paradise. And if hundreds of similar signs had been put up all over Wales this was the only one I was allowed to see. But I knew I had been in heaven.

I took a break in Bangor, North Wales, home of the Schizophrenia Association of Great Britain, though I had not heard of them yet. I did not even know I had that illness. I saw a man in the street looking at his watch. Then he looked down the road. I was indeed at the head of an enormous procession, which was yet to arrive and he was looking to see if it were visible yet. I was an hour ahead of the procession, but I did not want to wait around and disillusion myself about it. Then again, I thought, perhaps I was so powerful it would just wait too, and evade my sight. But of course there was no parade anywhere. It was all just the product of my manic, deluded and quite frankly desperate imagination. I just could not see that or even imagine it.

So what really was it that I was imagining to be following me? It was beginning to seem rather like the balloon, which followed Patrick McGoohan in *The Prisoner*; it had followed me from Portmeirion. In my mind's eye this procession, or balloon, however you wish to see it, was my psychological impression of the manufacturers, operators and interested parties, of my MTRUTH. My best guess as to who the operators were was the Army Intelligence Corps, possibly operating out of the Defence Intelligence and Security Centre via GCHQ or perhaps more likely MI4. My feeling that they were an hour behind made me wonder if, actually, they were an hour ahead and knew exactly where I was going next. The more I made it known I was close to the truth, the closer some of them might approach me. Soon I had arrived in Menai and booked into a hotel. The inside of the car was a military disaster, and I tidied up.

In the hotel I went to bed and settled down to watch television. Without looking at my watch, I adjusted the time by one hour as accurately as I could. If I looked, someone would know what I had seen as they too could see through my eyes – through my MTRUTH. But again it was worse than that. They knew I had done this even though I did not look, so powerful were they. They could tell what I had done using lodestone chips in my fingers. For some reason I was now thinking of the film *The President's Brain Is Missing*. Whoever or whatever had taken mine, quite possibly mere circumstance, it did seem to have gone. I had lost it. I could not even switch channels on the television without inflicting on myself the most unbearable psychotic effects. It was as though everyone in the whole country had to watch what I chose, they weren't too happy about it, and the final straw came when I decided to turn over from some American World War II film. The responsibility was all too much and sitting on the toilet I looked at the large white towel. It was speaking to me "Throw me in! Throw me in!" My thoughts were screaming, even if I was not actually shouting at the top of my voice, "I would fucking throw you in but I do not fucking know where to throw you!" The whole game had been thrown to the Americans and the Delta Force was having a field day: driving my mind insane with the power they had, the level of which was just too great to coexist with. But I had to.

I had to leave the hotel; the torture was unbearable. It was around midnight and I was walking towards the bridge. First of all I walked down a steep lane of picturesque homes towards the shoreline. The bridge was lit up and very spectacular. With the bridge becoming foremost in my mind, the pressure eased almost completely. Lightly headbutting a Royal Navy destroyer might have had a similar effect. That room had been no good, at least not when I had just been in it.

I returned to the top of the lane. Various night sounds also aided my relaxation, and now I was walking onto the bridge. I sensed the danger of lines joining points of equal psychotic despair inviting me along the route others had taken. There was no intention though to follow them to the same, or any, mortuary. If anything, the bridge was giving me some kind of therapy, as anything had to be preferable to that hotel room. I was reminded of the way I had felt on the Itchen Bridge in Southampton years earlier: a peculiar vertigo had come over me, which did not seem to come from within. I went down on my knees as I felt an irresistible force just lifting me up and throwing me over. The force was so powerful I had an urge to measure it by gathering a group of potential suicides and people suffering vertigo. I would then measure the weight required to prevent them all being thrown off by this force. It almost felt that if I had found something to grab I might not have been able to hold on any longer than somebody dangling from a rope or a ledge.

On this particular night the force was certainly there but somehow dormant like a sleeping giant. I turned and wandered back off the bridge and down the little lane to the south. I came across a graveyard right beneath the bridge where I felt a great sense of security, which some people might find difficult to understand. I had almost died and now I was at peace beneath these trees looking up at Thomas Telford's spectacular construction, which was positively ecclesiastical.

Still in the graveyard I heard the distant sound of a car being driven aggressively at some speed, each corner bringing the sound of rubber on tarmac. Louder and louder the car motored as it got nearer, as if the driver really knew what he was doing. Eventually it was on the bridge, travelling at some speed. This, as in the song after which this chapter is named, was the mystery of the speeding car that London loved. The song was playing in my MTRUTH and the driver of the car was no mere joyrider but sent by MI5 simply to make the night that extra bit memorable.

I sensed that those doing this were not just content with merely augmenting reality through my invisible headset, but in my actual vicinity too – the car just spiced things up a bit. The scene was, indeed, just too memorable for there not to be a purpose in that car being driven so fast so late at night. Then, as I thought of the song going "London loves, the mystery of the speeding car" my mind told me that "London" meant MI5. In the corner of one office in Thames House the Special Intelligence Service had placed a monitor showing everything through my eyes. MI5 officers would wander over and watch during coffee breaks – bets being placed as to how long it would be before I turned up there in the uniform of a naval officer. I would go round from desk to desk angrily proclaiming I knew one of them was responsible for the cameras in my eyes as well as the rest of my MTRUTH. I addressed the likelihood of this and it seemed pretty unlikely. Then my mind went through a whole list of similarly unlikely possibilities.

Something told me that MI5, more than anyone else, enjoyed a good mystery and I was intent on providing them with that – somehow. Years later the television programme *Watercolour Challenge* would come from just this spot. I would feel the presenter knew I had been there.

I wandered comfortably in the graveyard for a while, hearing the express to Holyhead go by on the opposite bank, and then made my way down to the shore to walk across the sand where something curious happened. I can only liken it to the release of ultraviolet light from the glue when opening an envelope. As I stepped in the sand it seemed to light up in an odd way, which only confirmed my feeling to have been on some kind of magic carpet all these weeks.

I enjoyed the night for a while longer and returned to the room, having successfully exorcised the previous terrors, and now succeeded in going to sleep.

Chapter Nineteen

My Best Friend Paranoia

It had been a better than average summer, though perhaps not quite your homemade lemonade 1976 one. It was certainly hot, humid and sticky enough to allow some of it to disappear in the heat haze of my mind. Now, many beautiful fragments of it are still just visible on the eight-year-distant horizon of my memory. I wish you could have known just how wonderful it felt *most* of the time – it was hyper-magic. If I have not captured it then I feel Pele and The Indigo Girls came closest to doing so in their eloquent albums *The Sport of Kings* and *Swamp Ophelia*. I just wish I could remember more – so you could know just exactly how amazing I felt during those few months' best schizophrenic moments. Perhaps somebody who has had a good LSD trip might know what I mean.

Details of how I got to Stranraer evade me. Perhaps it was not even on that trip that I found myself in Warrington. I do however recall wandering out of a shop there, wearing a black badge on which were the words "The Games People Play" and looking at a rubbish bin outside a pizza parlour. My brain chemistry felt about as stable as a glass jug of water which was on the point of falling off the edge of the table. Maybe, I wondered, the bin was at the site of the one that the IRA bomb of the previous year had been in. The bin appeared something of a stumbling block, which would be difficult to get my head round. I did not manage to until sometime later when I saw a TV programme about rearguard terrorist cells planned in Britain should the Nazis have had succeeded in invading in the War. I did not then find it hard to imagine I myself might have been involved in the deaths of women and children, if I wasn't already because of Dresden.

Signals seemed to be coming in at me from everywhere and I felt myself being pulled to and fro, almost like a molecule in a Brownian motion experiment. But this was not nice.

At a garage I had just filled up and the driver of the car in front of me walked around to his passenger side. Now, a little oddly, he bent over and looked at his rear number plate in a manner that made me look too, putting his chin between his thumb and forefinger as he did so. The letters on his plate were GOL. Part of mine was DAV. I thought of David and Goliath and that this was as he intended, as though I was now in some battle of biblical proportions. The truth was I did have a battle on my hands – against my illness. He got in and drove off. Across the road was a lorry, which, on the side, said "Pal finger". I remembered my Cambridge University interview and the gig afterwards by the Northern Irish band, Stiff Little Fingers. The name on the lorry seemed, laughably, to have been put there by MI5 to indicate I had a pal in the band.

Scotland welcomed me with the pipes at Gretna Green and I felt the couple getting married were honoured to have their wedding filmed by my MTRUTH. I never found out if they had eloped.

None of these forces, to which my life had become prey (so that I was now hyper-sensitised to what I thought were others' thoughts about my behaviour), subsided in any way as Lockerbie approached. It may have looked as though I was driving a car: in reality, it was more like I was in a storm-tossed ketch, being dashed on the rocks of some distant uninhabited isle. I did not go to see if there was any indication there really had been a plane crash at Lockerbie in 1988. I did not want to disillusion myself about flight 103 and discover Jo Hudson was actually dead. If she was not dead then I was powerful and, besides, she was a nice girl anyway. But I thought of Jo falling from the sky and, horribly, wondered if she had been still conscious as the ground approached. Instead of going to Lockerbie I found myself speeding along through the Mull of Galloway apprehensive that somebody living in Northern Ireland might, at that actual moment, be laughing at me on one side of their face and weeping on the other. If Jo really was dead then my whole delusory house of cards would come down. All that would remain would be the mystery of what really happened to Prince Charles's dog.

As I drove, the strangely eerie music used to name this chapter played on my car's tape player. As in the song I was "dancing with my best friend paranoia" and, when I drove off the ferry at Larne, it felt as though I was coming out of the back of an RAF Hercules near Takrit, Saddam Hussein's birthplace in Iraq. What was I doing here in Ireland? It seemed a natural consequence of my having driven through that gate back at Wilton, and nothing to do with any mental illness – that didn't even occur to me. What I would achieve in coming here God only knew. I simply had to be positive and assume I could do something useful.

A mile or so up the road I came upon a car crash that had just happened. There was something strange about the behaviour of the drivers. It was almost as if they were admiring their crash for artistic value and wanted all the people going by to be aware of this, unaware themselves that the performance was solely for my consideration. I thought they were squaddies or even SAS. I might have got out myself to take a look at it. I felt like a kid.

I had seen similar before on the M6 roadworks. A labourer seemed as though he had been told to imagine that entire stretch of 10 miles or so of roadworks had been put there for a reason, which had little to do with improving the road. As I passed, he threw his hands up in the air as though he too realised, for a split second of complete clarity, that the whole thing was a bloody great "windup". Like me before, he could have said out aloud, as soon as I had passed, "Wait a minute, what actually is a windup?" I might have replied "Pretend you had a dog and it's gone missing – then make it front page news."

In Belfast I parked my car on the top of the multistorey near the BBC and went for a walk before finding somewhere to stay. I nipped into a pub on the Falls Road for a wee. This was a revelation. I seemed to have faced months or even years of MI5 abuse inflicted on me with supposedly faulty handdriers like the one back at The Ship in Bedford. This particular drier was covered in IRA graffiti but it produced a positive tornado of hot dry and consistent air which did not strangely go on and off for no apparent reason other than MI5, or rather local Special Intelligence Service, interference. I felt I was now on the right track;

there was no doubt about this. I was red hot.

I have no great idea why I decided to stay in the YMCA but found myself in a bunk-bedded room with some Germans. I could not hack it and, bizarrely, set up my bed so it looked like I was asleep in it. Do not ask me why, though if I could remember a reason it would surely be pretty schizophrenic. Instead I booked into The Europa Hotel where I cannot say I had a very pleasant experience. It felt more like the Mukharabat in Baghdad.

The hotel club was fine. A chap told me he had contacts but would not say, at first, what they were. He had a strong Irish accent but which part I could only guess: I had not even learnt the Northern Irish one at this stage. Somehow he seemed a little familiar though. I was familiar back in that I asked him when I had last seen him. The relevant information appeared down the side of my vision next to his face, it seemed on my MTRUTH, and this included exactly where in Ireland he was from. At least that was what I thought the information in my vision was. Much of it seemed to have been deliberately blurred to prevent me actually reading it. But MTRUTH knew where he was from not just from his file but also by recognising his accent. The consequences of being told when I had last seen this chap, an Army Intelligence Corps spy according to the information, had obviously been decided as undesirable by the Military High Command. Later, as he told me about his IRA contacts, I found on my EAV what appeared to be the chap's entire service record, again heavily edited with no information other than to confirm he had been in the British Army. I was standing there right next to him and pages and pages of information scrolled down my vision. I remembered seeing the empty screen of botanical intelligence next to a plant in my EAV earlier in the summer.

When I retired to my room it seemed like I was in some kind of torture chamber. I was hallucinating, or seeing in my EAV, Prince Charles, and the IRA, ordering me out of bed, in the most viciously evil and sadistic manner. He then demanded I go into the bathroom and masturbate in the mirror. When I refused, he ordered me to dive out of the window and was shouting at me to the point where my head was splitting. This was all very unpleasant indeed. I could only logically deduce that this was SBS psychological warfare training and as such, I was privileged to be experiencing it. If I could cope with this then I would be ready to exploit my proud service record in the school CCF Naval Section. I was certainly being prepared for something. Of course if you had asked me I would have truthfully denied it but it was the only way my mind could possibly cope with the situation. Why else would Prince Charles be torturing me? I had done nothing to him, apart from not turning up to Lympstone in 1975, carrying a copy of *An Phoblacht* to my interview at the Admiralty and attending one meeting of the University College London Communist Society as a fresher in the autumn of 1980. The reality of the situation was probably that, even if I had not a single blotch on my record this would still be happening, the IRA would just not have it otherwise, whatever the IRA actually meant at that moment. Prince Charles must just have a sideline in psychological warfare, I thought. Only later did I realise that, however successfully I thought I negotiated this I could have done it better by simply assuming I was supposed to laugh at his suggestions – maybe tell him to follow his own advice. But that's easy to say in retrospect. In any case how could I know it *was* Prince Charles and not the IRA themselves? This was, after all, the peace process. All manner of weird stuff must be going on, it seemed obvious to me.

Whatever the explanation, the torture eventually abated, and I got to sleep. It was just a little taster.

Next morning, relieved I had not been driven to suicide the previous night, I took my breakfast high up in The Europa Hotel with a view out over the famous Belfast Mountain. As I gazed at the mountain and again wondered about the MI5 spy codenamed *Mountain Climber* I thought: perhaps the Army Intelligence Corps know everything. With MTRUTH they probably would. However much they did know I have little recollection of the rest of that day – except of the mountain standing before me as seen from my breakfast table.

Chapter Twenty

I Still Haven't Found What I'm Looking For

Whatever did happen that day I do recall imagining the IRA having come into my hotel room during the previous night to delete parts of my memory. Not that I ever really thought this particular part of my memory was in my actual brain rather than a variety of databases and neural networks held in a supercomputer elsewhere and attached to it by my MTRUTH[44]. I do recall driving along a road near Newry and putting on my Abba *Gold* tape. It had 007 in the catalogue number. When *Waterloo* came on, a Volvo (also a Swedish product and therefore enabling me to draw a deluded inference) suddenly overtook me out of nowhere and went past very fast. I was certain it was not just a coincidence and that I was right that day at NATO – I had MTRUTH. One other thing I did notice that day was that some newsagents were advertising *The News Letter*. This, of course, had nothing to do with the Northern Irish newspaper, which I had never heard of. Even if it did it was inspired by my own newsletter, circulation a couple of hundred, which I had used to promote my boat parties back in England[45]. I was massive and now I was finding out just how massive. The reality of the world's oldest English language newspaper in no way impinged on my thoughts.

The next thing I remember it was late at night. I decided, on a whim, that I now had to go to Londonderry. So, along a wet A6, across which I hallucinated thousands of giant frogs as big as my car hopping, I set off. Being on the A6 in Ireland made me remember the Irishman, James Hanratty, hanged in Bedford for the A6 murder at Dead Man's Hill, on the same road back in England. I kept seeing the face of Peter Alphonse, a man who once confessed to the murder on a French television programme. The interview was bizarre because he was lying on a bed during the interview, like Paula Yates would do when she interviewed people on the British television programme *The Big Breakfast*. I had believed for some time I knew the truth of the matter of the A6 murder. I knew of the A6 murder victim's spying activities at the Building Research Establishment. I had become fascinated by this crime and again found myself thinking it was all wrapped up in a huge conspiracy, possibly the 1926 one. I decided I would later report to the police all the way back down the A6 in Bedford.

I arrived in Londonderry, or if you prefer, Derry, in the early hours, not quite sure why I was there or what I was doing. Some unseen force was impelling me, a force I had become aware of by driving through that gate back at Land Forces HQ Wilton. I booked into the hotel where I got some much-needed sleep.

Next day I took a guided tour of the city centre where I discovered why it was so-called, the city being set up principally by rich Irishmen from London, though Republicans tend to leave out the London part. I saw the bomb-damaged walls of the city hall, and the Czechoslovakian chandelier (which I was told was ordered from there instead of England because of a faster delivery time). I was taken up to the city walls from where the old house of Dana, the famous Irish folksinger turned politician, was pointed out to me down below on the Bogside. I now pictured her singing *All Kinds of Everything*, with which many years earlier she had won the Eurovision Song Contest. Bizarrely, as she sang, I could see in my mind's eye a woman repeatedly sinking a detonation plunger in time with the music, pointing as she did so in various directions towards the resulting explosions. This, to my mind, was Republican humour at its blackest. Perhaps it was just *my* humour at its blackest.

After the tour I got in my car and drove around the Bogside where I sensed I was in acute danger. Then I shot off into the countryside, and over the border into Donegal. The pressure was incessant. I felt something of a criminal once again going over the border – as well as in danger, perhaps forgetting the hope of round-the-clock legal representation at the highest of levels, in which case I was the international criminal during these minutes I spoke of earlier. I was frightened and drove back where I had come from like a cat running through its cat flap in a hurry. I now went along the coast. My mental divining rod began to settle down a bit.

Near Castlerock I came across a beautiful open beach on which I could see some cars parked in the distance. I drove down the beach in a world of my own, and as I passed the waterfall the song of that name by The Stone Roses came from Radio 1. It was a beautiful moment, and reminded me once again that in some respect Radio 1 knew exactly where I was. The feeling was magnificent. It really was a wonderful moment in my life.

I drove on down towards the cars but made the mistake of turning around before I reached them and became stuck in the sand. Two rather large men appeared, one wearing an All Ireland Hurling Team top and, after a few seconds, they pushed me out of the sand.

I drove back off the beach and down the road I could hear Michael Jackson's unmistakeable voice in my head. He said, in his own hushed and excited tones, "10 million pounds; 100 million pounds; 1,000 million pounds". It all seemed quite straightforward really. It was all going to happen.

Later on I found myself walking on the spectacular Giant's Causeway. The Causeway is a stretch of columnar basalt forming a promontory. It was formed when an outflow of lava cooled into polygonal columns during Tertiary times and is Ireland's most famous tourist attraction. I found myself talking to an old man who told me that long ago in Ireland lived a gentle giant called Finn MacCool who stood 52 feet six inches tall. Across the sea in Scotland there was a rival giant called Benandonner. The two giants hollered at each other across the Sea of Moyle, each demanding a trial of strength. This was agreed, and the hospitable Finn offered to make the contest possible by building a rocky causeway between the two countries – and, the old man told me, this was the Giant's Causeway. Right now I felt about as tall as these two giants put together. I felt legendary. But then some reality came back although it did not stop me remembering the adage "It's not the size of the dog in the fight – but the size of the fight in the dog." However, despite my excitement, I had not yet imagined how the disappearance of Prince Charles's dog could lead to a story. But with the future monarch's pet anything was possible. I had to pay it due respect.

That night I stayed at The Castlerock Hotel. The only news from these parts over the previous quarter of a century had been of the Troubles and I had not really thought of how attractive this part of Ireland might be. Along this stretch of coast I certainly found how very beautiful it was, as I already had in Galway.

As usual, there was a rowing boat sling placed mysteriously in the bedroom (a sling is used for a boat out of the water but not in the boathouse). I have since been told they were actually for putting a suitcase on, but that's what it seemed at the time. To my recollection there had been one in every hotel room I had stayed in that summer, this merely confirming to me that everything was planned, and that I was being watched. It seemed it was because I was in the 1st VIII at school and somebody wanted me to know I was being monitored, somebody in MI5, somebody who was involved in rowing: it was a message from Michael Maltby. I say recall because I was not taking notes, having received the message from The Indigo Girls in one of their songs some weeks earlier: "Don't write this down, remember this in your heart." It was as though I had the honour of every trick in the book being played by MI5 because of the one I had played on them. All I can say is how could I forget the hallucination of Prince Charles ordering me to masturbate in the mirror? I felt I was caught in a nice policeman/nasty policeman situation and the rowing boat slings were to keep me going.

In the bar there was a double of Amanda with her husband/boyfriend. I could not say it was also a double she was with, as I had never seen her partner, but with MI5 anything was possible.

Now, still in The Castlerock Hotel, I was standing in the hallway outside the gents. Intuition told me the couple had no idea who I was or that I was even there. Standing still with his chin held thoughtfully in his hand and staring pensively at a cabinet full of stuffed specimens of various birds was the man I had seen earlier with Amanda's double. But, unlike in Portree, there was not a single stuffed seagull present in this collection. Because of this, rather than despite it, I thought he was thinking about my record label, Seagull Records, and that, whilst he was married to Amanda, he felt some respect for me. Either that or he was wondering why on earth they wanted him to stand there looking pensive about some stuffed birds. I believed he was from MI5.

Whoever this person was, there did seem to be something familiar about him. He looked rather like a particular person I had met at Surrey University. This person kept popping up in the Students' Union and around the university, and hardly seemed to be studying for a degree, at least not there. One evening I had been chatting to Zero K and he came over. A little oddly, he succeeded in preventing our conversation from proceeding. This person also brought to mind someone I had met before in my undergraduate days. He was an anarchist and I had been the subject of his vicious taunts one night in the Union bar. He stole my prized Harris Tweed cap from my head, in the street by the college. I ran after him and rugby-tackled the swine outside the university gates, getting my cap back. He was such an evil bastard that I could only assume these sadists I had somehow become involved with had set him upon me for a bit of fun. That was their job and if they did not approach it that way they were not doing it properly. Here this strange person was again, now with Amanda's double. It all seemed so mysterious and perplexing. Years of disconnected insignificant incidences had now become connected in my mind – I had been watched all the time. Yet, once again, I felt privileged to be having this extraordinary experience. Somehow, I had to make sense of it all. *I had to know what was really going on.* I returned to the bar and had a few beers.

Next day I made for Newcastle, County Down. The voices in my head were getting bad now. Over my MTRUTH, somebody in the Maze prison, which later closed following the Good Friday agreement, was torturing me. It seemed the prisoner, a Republican, had been given a British Telecom phone card by the British government to give me a call on my rather exclusive telephone number – which I thought had only three digits. I had no idea if I was near the prison or not but I heard him say, referring viciously to my trip to Wilton, "Look you arsehole! What fucking good did that little trick do? You dirty little British scumbag!"

He did not really need to say this. My imagination was already like a barn whose door had blown off in a hurricane and I was rolling around in agony up in the hayloft with a hateful Republican shouting a wicked tirade at me. All I can remember of the rest of this tirade was his saying "What would you do?" I just had to release some tension and did it, looking rather like the Killing Joke singer on the cover of the album *Night Time*, where he looked particularly agonised. I hardly had my hands on the steering wheel, it was more like they were around my head, and I eventually managed to shout out aloud "I'd keep my cell a bit cleaner!" I did this in reference to the IRA dirty protests of the '70s when they smeared excrement on the walls of their cells. I was a bit behind the game I think, as by then the prison looked more like a military barracks divided between the two factions. Having said this, I would later appear rather hypocritical.

I felt rather pathetic in all of this. It was almost as though the problems in this part of the world were none of my business. Moreover I was being told they were none. What possible difference could I make? But by the end of this story I was to satisfy myself that I had made one.

Chapter Twenty-One

Revolution

I arrived I arrived in Newcastle, County Down, relieved to have made it without crashing my car. I headed for the beach.

I watched a jovial scrap going on there between some grebos. They addressed me and I replied politely whereupon an ice cream came flying my way as they careered towards me. One of them shouted "Hey! You! We're from County Kerry man! Go home! Now!" I was not minded to disagree with this sentiment but a Scotch terrier wearing tartan went past in the opposite direction, this being south; so I headed that way thinking of going into the Mountains of Mourne to convalesce before the journey.

It had not been the first time that an ice cream had been thrown at me. It also happened at the Italy vs. England game in Turin in 1980. I had hitchhiked out to the European Soccer Championships with Joss. Sooner an ice cream than the tear gas which got fired at us at the Belgium game though.

Now I found myself driving up a farm track just outside Warrenpoint in which town, on the same August day in 1979 that the IRA assassinated Prince Charles's uncle, Earl Mountbatten, they also killed 18 British soldiers. The track came to an end and I became surrounded by cattle in the road. I still had some Superkings left over from my earlier jaunts and sat back to enjoy one, wondering who the farmer was and whether he was a Republican. It did look a little like he had let out the cattle to hinder my progress – so I wondered if he was the IRA Commander for Carlingford Lough. I wrote a postcard. He could see what I was writing real-time. The CIA displayed my MTRUTH's view through my eyes, now I was on the island of Ireland, on his personal computer. I was using the most sensitive of all military technology.

The road into Warrenpoint and the "road slippery" sign took its toll on my mind. I should have turned off the bloody radio. The DJ's voice was pulling me back and forth in each direction. But I had a GB sticker on my car, which made me feel rather more secure here than if I'd had one which said UK on it.

I booked into a hotel and put some cash into the local tourist economy. For this I expected and received nothing other than the look in the eyes of my 'best friend' – a stranger, as she eerily and knowingly walked past the window outside the hotel bar, staring back through it into mine. She was working for either British or Irish Intelligence and knew exactly who I was.

Twelve hours later I was at an old castle clambering through its troubled history like some children who were there, also clambering over its stones. Even the children seemed to be following me, like the lenses' gaze on my face. I felt I was being watched from afar using optical equipment.

I went into the tourist office and booked a trip to a place I had not heard of before, the Silent Valley. As I journeyed on the open-topped upper deck up to a dam at the top of the valley I sensed the presence of the Irish Republican Army, or MI5, probably both, watching me, either from the hills or the bus itself.

As I walked across the dam a man walked past. I seemed to know enough about him to make me afraid of wanting to know exactly who he was. "You should be *absolutely terrified*" he said. I was, for a moment quite literally, beside myself and, for that moment, I was him and he was me. It seemed that, if he did not actually say this, it was one of the rare occasions when GCHQ, or here, as I said, the CIA, broadcast something into my ears over my MTRUTH. I was given the perfect impression somebody had said it in my vicinity – somebody whose lips I was not looking at.

The bus was ready to descend back down the valley. I'd had eczema on my right ear since six years earlier, when I had used hair gel. But now my mind was telling me that MI5 had been putting some astringent on my ear in my sleep. It seemed that they wanted to harness the power of witchcraft and not, of course, that I had schizophrenia. That had never occurred to me. On the seat in front was a child of seven or so who, from behind at least, looked like the Milky Bar Kid. On the top back of his right ear, exactly where I had the little patch of eczema, so did he. They obviously started them young over here, I thought for a moment. I felt very paranoid about the presence of the child and his ear. It was as though somebody was telling me they knew everything there was to know about me – and that they were going to continue to remind me.

I raced down to the ferry, which I just managed to board with some relief, the journey being uneventful. However as the Cat sailed into Stranraer I noticed, standing at the end of the pier, the unmistakable double of an old friend, Neil. I remembered the conversation we'd had about scales of secrecy. When I saw what appeared to be him, walking about on the end of the pier, it seemed like he knew of my activities and was following me. He had been put there by MI5. This was one of the better examples of Capgras syndrome I experienced.

Disembarking the ferry I saw a small hole in the fence. As I went past it, somebody made to fix the hole as though they knew I had in some sense gone through it. The hole seemed to signify the security breach, which was my gaining the full power of MTRUTH and moreover becoming aware of it. It seemed like Wonderland and I remembered the play back in Galway earlier in the summer. I felt great.

Leaving town I was, nevertheless, exhausted, and should have taken a break, but the wave of mild psychosis or, if you prefer, extended imagination, still very much had the better of me. So when I saw an attractive blue sign saying "Kirkmadrine Stones" it took me exactly in the direction I didn't want to go. An archaeologist getting out of his car at the Stones, was trying to work out my purpose. Perhaps he was just any old father taking his family around the St. Columba exhibition, St Columba having brought Christianity to Scotland from Ireland in the 6th century. The stones are amongst the earliest examples of Christian carvings in Scotland. But I was still very paranoid and it seemed that they had got there earlier specifically to wait for me.

Heading back towards the border more random spurious and unidentified signals got the better of me, whilst the ticket to Balmoral in Portree and the Scotch terrier back at Newcastle, County Down, were beginning to play on my mind. By the time I got to the border they were driving me quite insane. It was like being in the game on *It's a Knockout* where you are on an elastic rope and have to run over a slippery surface to deposit water into a weighing device. Only rather than this happening for all to see, it was just happening psychically in my head – or rather on my MTRUTH.

There was some delay, which I succeeded in outmanoeuvring and, once I got over the border to England, the feelings hardly subsided but got worse. It seemed it was the ticket to Balmoral I had found in Portree which was really doing it. I could hear Princess Diana whining on in my head saying things like "Oh he really must go to Balmoral; he simply must visit Chatsworth." Hellish thoughts of this ridiculous parade were in my head again, and when the biggest boat I ever saw travelling by road went past, I veered off down a side road. A "Knights of Old"[46] lorry went past on the bridge ahead, and everything was in a spin. I thought Prince Charles had sent it as he worked harder and harder to keep up with my exploits. On the side of the lorry was a knight in armour on horseback and it said "Service with Honour". I could hardly keep my hands on the wheel. I had to get to my friend Carl's. The signs were agonising to read. One said "St Helen's". I knew Hell. I was in it. I knew two Helens too, and they were both torturing me. But I was damned if I was going to be anybody's bloody saint. I had to pull over. I just could not drive another foot. I looked up at the sign I happened to have stopped by. It said "Crank", the name of a nearby village, and seemed to snarl at me like it was telling me that was what I was. So sick in the head did I feel I would hardly have been surprised if the sign had changed into a ferocious big mouth and eaten my head.

Somehow I managed to get back to the main road and push on. At last I arrived at Carl's in Stockport. Thankfully he was in, and happy to see me, though I had not warned him beforehand. He could not have known how relieved I was to get there. I was hovering on the edge of a calamitous panic attack, and my brain chemistry was about as balanced as an inverted cone. Too much alcohol, not enough sleep and too much driving again. Somehow I managed to feign ease and facility, but a close look at my face would have betrayed an inner panic, it being drawn and flushed. I had to have a drink. Everything would then be all right, and it was, partly because I was temporarily released from this suicide drive.

Carl's wife (she and Carl had once left several long and amusing "Who am I?"s on my answer machine) was in the Edie Sedgwick[47] mould and they had a blonde woman staying who appeared in the living room in the early hours. Perhaps she was more ill than I was, though that would be saying something, because I imagined that Jamie Bulger (the toddler murdered by two boys the previous year) did not exist except to some ludicrously tenuous extent. I found myself believing his death had not been real in this unreal world where Prince Charles had invented the story of his dog going missing. I imagined Jamie Bulger's part had been played by Carl's son Oscar, meaning this was actually a University College Hospital Dentist School psychiatric theatrics outstation. Carl had already been unique anyway in my university career because one evening at a disco he announced to me, one by one, the direction of every attractive girl in the room and the fact that they all fancied me, which I was grateful to hear. I'll always be grateful to him for that.

His wife and the blonde girl made some plan to go shopping the next day, and still attempting to feign normality, I made a characteristically vague agreement to meet up with them. This turned out to be nothing more than being in the same city at about the time they were there, and going to the Cathedral where I inspected somebody's VC that was on display. Given my own personal circumstances this, or a driving ban, was not entirely inapposite.

L reg cars were about to appear and everything seemed ready to be revealed to me, including what I dared not know or say, the truth about project "L Zero". I had noticed many security codes on products I bought started with L having no other letter and I thought this somehow related to me via the secret project all could see, but only I knew the meaning of. But what was secret L Zero? I decided it was that John Lennon was not dead – and that was lie zero or L Zero. The band L7, whose hit had been entitled *Pretend That We're Dead*, must be in on it I thought. At the time this did not seem in the least bit tenuous and, for sure, went all the way back to 1926. The power emanating from these notions seemed quite astronomical.

Getting home seemed nigh on impossible. It seemed my car was also mentally ill. If it could have clung to the nearest passer-by (as in Joy Division's song *She's Lost Control*) perhaps it would have done, with good reason. Each mile was a strain and each service area too far to reach without having to have a break to try and pull myself together.

In my head the voice was building to a crescendo "Me! You! Me! You! Me! You!" and it was truly unbearable: I should have been on my knees. I got to yet another service station and bought a coffee. Please don't drug me, I was thinking pathetically, or perhaps mumbling under my breath, my head in my hands it was so painful. At that precise moment a man walked by who looked like he could be in the Forces, though I did not dare look straight at him. I already have [drugged you], he *thought* back at me as I looked at my wrist, his thoughts audible in my head. Something similar had happened before during that summer. I had seen a man hold *his* wrist, and this infected me with the thought I had the controlled release drugs cabinet there, in my left wrist.

Luckily, having convinced myself that there was indeed some type of controlled release drugs cabinet inside my wrist I had the intelligence to imagine that ultimately it was to my benefit. Otherwise I would have hacked it out with a knife, there and then, resulting in a strong spout of blood shooting across the dining area into somebody's King Burger Deluxe, even their face, leaving a large pool of blood on the floor. I was not well at all.

Chapter Twenty-Two

Psychological Warfare [48]

Somehow I had to get home and the trip to Chester Cathedral did not help much. I was still damn sure there was some slow-release drug capsule in my wrist, which could be turned on and off on a whim.

At another service station I failed miserably to find respite. "Please don't turn it on" my thoughts begged out audibly in my head, my hands imploring. "I already have" a passer-by again seemed to tell me. It was torture, but once more I made it home. Still no sign of Prince Charles's dog though.

Part VII

A Drugs Trip

Chapter Twenty-Three

Complete Control

So now you know a little about my college days, how I met Amanda and of my African adventures. You know how, after the collapse of my record label I descended into illness, this culminating in strange events in Wiltshire on 29th May 1994. You know of those exceptionally strange hours of 5th/6th September of that year, my trip to NATO HQ and how I came to be hanging off the bridge. You know of the intervening months during which I roamed Western Europe in search of Prince Charles's dog. It is now late August 1994.

****

I thought I had achieved something since Solsbury Hill, but my brain chemistry was still going crazy. I really did believe that I might have been drugged by MI5 on a number of occasions – to heighten my imagination. I still needed to send in sick notes to conceal what I was up to. So I visited my GP and told him about a panic attack I had recently had when I thought I was going to die. He prescribed me a drug Imipramine (an antidepressant) and some Diazepam (a tranquilliser). I was surprised by the prescription, as I knew, from bitter experience, I was not depressed. I did not have the Black Dog. If I had a dog it was Prince Charles's. But it was invisible. I seem to recall thinking that antidepressants were not just prescribed for depression, but also bed-wetting and, indeed, panic attacks.

Anyway, I decided to trust my doctor, and began taking the antidepressants even though the reality was that I was experiencing a manic schizophrenia. How was he to know that? I concealed my thoughts well. But the visions of Amanda in bed with her boyfriend were getting more vivid – it was my MTRUTH. This was unbearable torture. Then one afternoon, for whatever reason, I put on The Beatles' *Let it Be* and lay down on the floor. In vivid colour, I could see Mother Teresa[49] with a wicker shopping basket in which was draped a Union flag. The basket was full of bread. I told Tom about it and he told me people pay to have hallucinations like that. On another occasion I played The Sex Pistols' *No Feelings* and where Mr Rotten sang "I pray. You pray to your God," I was sure he was actually singing "Ah Clive! You're practically God!" I felt a special mix had been done by MI5 and my copy of the album had been replaced – either that or he had been singing those words all along.

The trouble now was that, almost within hours of taking the antidepressant, I was rapidly descending into a total unreality with my senses becoming even more imaginative. The barrier between where I stopped and my environment started seemed to have blurred – things previously not part of me seemed almost joined to me. I booked an appointment with a private investigator. At the meeting, held behind an estate agent's office in Hampstead, I slapped down £300 cash on the table with my best photos of Amanda and told him I wanted him to find out if she was actually married or not. Very sad but true. I was so deluded with disbelief syndrome that anything was better than the truth. This was some affliction – I was practically stalking her. Outside the office a black man went past and shouted out "I tried to tell you!" I thought he was talking to me and I remembered how another girl I knew had moved to Reading, where Amanda came from, and how, when I called this girl one night her phone had been engaged. I thought this bloke in the street was referring to the engaged tone I received being significant and that this meant Amanda was getting married. He was an MI5 agent.

I went to see Tom's band The Flashapjacks playing at the open-air gig mentioned at the beginning of this story. Now we have caught up with the point where my tale began. I believed that I was *The Lion King* and the song, *Can You Feel the Love Tonight?* was about me. If you had asked me about this, I would have said "Don't be so ridiculous," but I was allowing myself to think these things, and they became real in my mind. The whole world was seeing it as I did and actually through my eyes – through my MTRUTH.

The day after the gig, Tom was cooking a stir-fry in the wok. I had the most overwhelming feeling that, whilst I was in the other room, Yoko Ono had crept through the back door into the kitchen to help with the cooking. A few days earlier I had been in Barnes and a Japanese food lorry had mysteriously appeared in front of me in Church Road, though of course I could not read much of what it said on the doors. I had imagined the lorry was Yoko Ono's harbinger. I ate the meal and was then violently sick, not because of the food but because of the state of my brain chemistry. As I was sick in the porcelain Victorian toilet bowl my eyesight was wrenched, by my MTRUTH, to the blue lettering at the back of the bowl. It said "Comet". Later this would seem strangely portentous of comet Halle-Bopp, which shone brightly in the northwestern sky in March, three years later.

I stared out of the window, and every car that went past seemed to be having the effect of sloshing liquid in my brain chemistry back and forth as though my mind were at sea. I experienced a ridiculous hallucination of Amanda in knight's armour turning up outside on a giant white charger. I was so at a loss for something sensible to do at one point, that I could think of nothing better to do than go to Banbury Cross, as I had planned to do on my bike. There I expected to see Princess Diana, or Amanda, riding past on a white horse – no doubt with rings on her fingers and bells on her toes. In fact later I would at least attempt to get there. As in the rhyme, it seemed as though I had indeed had music wherever I went all that summer – all carefully chosen by the MI5 music division. This was a wonderful feeling I can assure you. But it was as though Princess Diana and Amanda were in the same predicament as I – though only I could get us out. I do not really remember the rest of that day or night. All was confusion.

✳✳✳✳✳✳✳✳✳✳✳✳✳✳✳✳✳

It is now the day after I went to NATO HQ and found myself hanging off the bridge, though I will not tell you what eventually happened at the bridge until the end of this story. I was now in the car heading for Reading. A voice in my head kept saying, secretively and excitedly, "Classic! Classic!" I was not sure if this was more to do with my belief that Prince Charles had been having classic cars parked everywhere I went, or the possibility of a book being in the pipeline. Either way, at some point in the next few hours, which were nothing short of a heavy drugs trip, I heard, via my MTRUTH, Amanda on the phone to her parents, saying that Jeffrey Archer was going to pay. Pay for what? I had to see her father, Dr. Black, in person, to verify that I had actually spoken to him; to ask him if she really was married. I had to ask him *what was going on*. At least I knew that, since Jeffrey Archer was involved, whatever was going on it was massive.

My head felt like a bowl of puke, and it was getting worse, it was the antidepressants. I was in a wild mania. The effect of taking the antidepressants was like that of pouring petrol on a fire to put it out. I had strong thoughts of crashing my car at speed into a motorway bridge. But first I had to speak to Dr. Black. Soon I was in Reading. I had no idea what was going to happen. I may have got something to eat because I remember crossing the road where there was a takeaway near the cemetery gates. Whilst crossing I carried out a completely random assault of a passer-by, by allowing my right shoulder to barge his, and although he did not get close to falling he did remonstrate at me. This was the one and only occasion throughout the time covered by this story when I committed anything approaching a violent act against another's person.

I got in the car, drove up the road to Dr. Black's house, got out, and knocked on the door. I wanted to know the truth – had I really spoken to him on the phone? As I said, I had believed it was somebody else, speaking through a GCHQ voice-morphing box. But I wanted to *know*. They had been advised to be out, as trouble was heading their way, MI5 watching everything via my MTRUTH. Either way no one seemed to be at home. Excruciating. I got back in the car pointing towards London.

A man walked past and dropped a piece of paper through the sunroof! I saw the message written on it and suddenly had this feeling I was an electric train on a pantograph. Some force (it seemed somebody else) completely seized control of my mind, or rather my very limbs, and jammed the car into reverse. Now I saw in my rearview mirror another Rover identical to mine move into the driveway. I put the car into first, pulled away, and parked on the other side of the road after making a U-turn. I thought it might be Dr. Black and I felt embarrassed about my mere presence.

From my observation point, I saw the driver of the car repeatedly ramming it back and forth, perhaps as many as nine or 10 times, into the parked white Peugeot. Eventually the Peugeot was a wreck and smashed up against the corner of the house, there being some possibility of structural damage to the building itself. Now the Rover stopped, with a cloud of fumes and steam rising up into the night sky. The driver, who was taller than I, with a short haircut and smart casual clothes, got out and began to hurl everything he could find at Dr. Black's house. Some of the items were rather large, and I saw him, fuelled by adrenaline, hurl, from above his head, a large paving slab through the windscreen of the Peugeot and empty the dustbin all over it too. Then he turned around and shouted "Fucking Moonies!" towards the next-door neighbour's house. The reason he was doing this was that he knew I still loved Amanda.

It would be pointless not describing these actions as those of another person. But in fact it was me.[50] Perhaps, who could ever know, my love for Amanda had just saved my life. The neighbours came out and asked over the garden fence if everything was alright.

The police arrived, and I was taken away. The police report said I was standing motionless and I was described as catatonic. I was taken to Reading Police Station where I was put in a cell.

I stripped off almost all my clothes and tore up my nice German shirt, which I stuffed down the toilet. All I now had on was a pair of Union flag underpants, and I paced up and down on the bench like a psychotic monkey in a zoo. I pissed on the floor and then was put in a cell without a toilet. I was passed a drink through the hatch, which I threw back at the officer. Later some sausages and beans were sent in and I threw them on the floor. I pissed on the blanket and wrapped myself in it. I defecated and rubbed some of it into my hair and wrote "IRA" on the wall with most of the rest, happy to be seen as a member of the Irish Republican Army. A Sikh social worker came in and, my face decorated with excrement war paint, I did my best haka. He recoiled and looked somewhat frightened of me. The bright blue gymnastics mat-style mattress seemed to be electrified and I was getting shocks from it. Over my MTRUTH somebody ordered me to eat the excrement on the floor; it was in fact the two sausages. I was being tortured by the white noise emanating from the air-conditioning. More than 24 hours went by.

Eventually a number of policemen came into the cell and demanded "Are you going to come along, or do we have to take you?" Next thing I knew I was being carried out, rather like a cricket kit bag, and put in the dog cage at the back of a police Sherpa van.

I did not know where I was being taken, but remembered going to Wallingford Regatta in the back of a similar van in 1978 when I had arrived, very travel sick, to row in the school 1st VIII. We had raced Eton, agreeing the drinks were on the winners. They still owe us a round. I was vomiting now too. A voice in my head, seemingly from my MTRUTH, told me I was being taken to Windsor Castle. This was not the first time, and would not be the last, that I imagined somebody was going to get me 'out' of this though having already pondered what a windup was, I now had to address what 'out' meant too. Out of the van was about all I was to get as we arrived, after about half-an-hour's drive, at some ghostly Victorian Mansion. It was in fact Fairmile Hospital, the psychiatric section of the Royal Berkshire Hospital, deep in the nearby countryside. It was a Victorian lunatic asylum. I got out and was now prepared to walk without being carried and was ushered through a door I felt was little used. The door led into a tower and I was taken up the dimly lit, winding stairs.

> *The asylum doors open wide,*
> *Where people could pay to see inside,*
> *For entertainment they watch his body twist.*
> *Behind his eyes he says, "I still exist."*
> *This is the way he stepped inside...*[51]

What I then experienced is of the stuff that inhabits the most macabre shadows of the imagination. I was taken into a room in darkness in which there appeared to be a certain number of entities lying in beds. I was put in a room at the side with a mattress on the floor. I was asked if I wanted any Temazapam (a sleeping drug) and refused. I lay down on the mattress. The two workers sat on chairs outside the door. Some kind of projection device had been placed outside the room and it was beaming three-dimensional moving pictures into my mind through the doorway. Either that or straight through my MTRUTH. I could see the Coronation going up the aisle in Westminster Abbey. This must be the introduction I thought. The Coronation was the only solace I had. It was the induction. I was in the furthermost terrible corners of my imagination. I got up and went out to the toilet and saw deep suspicion of me in the workers' faces. In reality they were psychiatric nurses both on suicide watch over me. The toilet had a revolting, almost hypocritically clean odour in it, which seemed to conceal the most disgusting truth about this horrendous building. I drew a swastika in the mirror with the soap. I felt the establishment deserved to be regarded as a Nazi one. Beyond that there was no rhyme or reason for this and I returned to the seclusion room.

Those lying in the beds, quite apart from the 'nurses', could no longer be described as anything remotely human, and I had been sent here to uncover this ghastly factory, operating right under the noses of the Security Services, only a few miles from Heathrow. Why Heathrow? Because I had uncovered a farm where zombies were being created by John Lennon's Soviet cult for export to the United States. No one who entered this place came out in a condition to which the adjective alive applied and it was all being funded by the Unification Church, the Natural Law Party – and, of course the Soviets. Now I understood, and the Beatle, George Harrison, a large donor to that party, lived only just down the road in Henley. It all made too much sense. If you remember nothing else about this story remember the utter disgust I now felt when I realised the horrible truth behind John Lennon's 14 years of 'death' and the sickening hypocrisy of his cult in choosing the apparent perfection of Peter Gabriel's Real World Studios for their British HQ. For that was what they had done. Never had I felt so conned. Only such a vile enemy could briefly unite the British Army and the IRA. My brain chemistry had fabricated an utterly vile parody of the truth – but it seemed overwhelmingly real. Lennon had started out with the very best of intentions but so determined was he that he had compromised his goal. His cult members were no better than vampires.

I lay back on the mattress. The orange squash would be poisoned; at least I could not risk trying it. I poured it all under the mattress and hoped the workers did not notice. I could hear the breathing of the zombies in the 'ward' around me, and now, in ghostly and ghastly unison, they all left their beds and began performing a slow motion dance of the dead. They were all far beyond help. Yet I could not quite be sure this was what was really happening in the room at this time. But I believed I was watching the results of a top secret KGB medical experiment that involved the dissolution of the patients' minds to the point where their personalities had been totally removed, leaving only the operating system, their controllers now indeed having complete control. Oh my God! If it wasn't the original experiment I was watching they had now gone operational! But still I was not sure if what I was seeing was in my EAI, if it was being inserted into my vision some other way, or was actually going on there and then right in front of me. They were dancing around each other in ghoulish and sickly slow motion caresses. Now blood started streaming down the walls, seeping from the room above. There, even more ghastly horrors yet unimagined by me were being enacted, in a room that was the source of the truly unspeakable.

Then I became aware of a sinister scraping and knocking sound coming from behind me. But no! Somebody was on the other side of the wall trying to communicate! Slowly and painstakingly, the SAS were scraping away the mortar around the bricks outside the corner of the room. Simultaneously I now developed the ability (using MTRUTH intelligence) to see through the wall to my left as the outline of a soldier from either the SAS or the Delta Force very slowly, more slowly than a hunting cat, edged along outside. He had with him an A10 tank-buster gun[52] that was being held up to the wall, only a few short feet from where the workers were sitting. I really was part of the operation. I was right – this *was* a factory! Oh my God!

A massive blast would make a gaping hole in the wall, destroying the workers in their chairs. A smaller blast would create a hole just behind me where the mortar had already been weakened. This would enable my escape and, at that moment, the room would be entered by the last line of national defence, the Army's Absolute Secret Last-Ditch Human Infection Control Unit, on whom the very survival of the human race depended. They would put a single shot through each of the heads of this sick troupe at the middle of the room – none of them worth saving.

I was getting ready for the blast, and very slowly and carefully slipped over the edge of the bed and into the corner of the room. To protect myself from the impending blast, I pulled the mattress over me and stuffed the pillow around my bollocks.

I could now see *the whole awful truth* and realised this would probably not become public knowledge until several years later. I could see a room where, at some time in the future, three young women I did not know were watching the operation unfolding on television. They were all in uncontrollable tears because it was the most terrible and unimaginable nightmare being shown by the BBC, without any prior warning – the previous programme having been interrupted. A whole network of such factories had been uncovered, and it was just unbelievable that such a thing could happen. I was a national hero. I had been sent in by the Security Services and Military High Command, being one of the very few with the mental faculties to stand up to this. Together we had exposed this evil conspiracy.

I could now see the Army, in a simultaneous combined forces operation, driving up the gravel drive to Peter Gabriel's house at the Real World Studios. In they burst, the new recruits, having been ordered to take no prisoners at all. I saw, by remote viewing over my MTRUTH, all astonished, not just Peter Gabriel and Paul McCartney, but the wizened husk of the mastermind of this diabolical plan, John Lennon. His fanatical Soviet play-dead idealism had drained him entirely of his intellect to the point where he was as degenerate as those pitiful creatures on the 'ward'. I saw the musicians' bodies being dragged out of Peter Gabriel's house across the gravel and flung into the back of the Army Land Rovers – like pieces of meat. These were just carcasses. This was how close John Lennon's evil and misguided plan had been to ultimate victory. His revolution had failed. Elsewhere hundreds of military top brass were being summarily executed on the orders of Her Majesty the Queen. All the way down the Falls Road they were clapping, and I descended further into the abyss of time and space in the corner of the room as the Queen vomited violently and uncontrollably for all to see. When she had done that she continued to retch profoundly and rhythmically in absolute disgust at all this.

Now I could see the Queen herself staring out at me from a universe of paper money, fluttering by in the apocalyptic wind. She was snarling out at me, dog-like, from her portraits on the notes. I was slipping away, and soon I would be out. It was all being filmed. I now vomited again and rubbed the vomit into my excrement-caked hair having a duty to show exactly how bad it was. It was therefore only logical that I should start barking for the benefit of the Ministry of Defence MTRUTH film unit, and I did. That was about it and I became unconscious.

Chapter Twenty-Four

Confide in Me

T he next thing I knew was waking to a golden morning, the sort of morning to send vampires back to their coffins for the day and lie in for a week. It felt just like a castle in Transylvania at dawn. Though I did not see him, as I was still under the mattress caked in vomit and excrement, I believed that the Major, for I recognised his voice, came into the seclusion room in uniform and ordered me to get up. Eventually I did and the male nurse took me to the shower. Bright beams of sunlight, sufficient to turn a vampire to dust, shone through the steam and the nurse stood there whilst I had the shower. The entire geography of the ward seemed wrong and I was convinced I was now in a different building. The Major was now nowhere to be seen.

As I took the shower, which was as good as those at the Imperial College boathouse, hot and consistent, everything seemed upside down, inside out and back to front. The hot steam filled the room and through it I could see Amanda doing her hair, as she got ready to come and see me. But she was not really coming, even though she would phone to say she would. At least I recall her phoning me; I was now so ill I could well be deluded in that belief.

The nurse was a Capgras double of Bill Mason, the international oarsman and boatman at the Imperial College boat club. He took me to the cupboard and put me in blue overalls like John McKay, the original guitarist in Siouxsie and the Banshees, had worn. Or rather I wish he had. In fact he gave me a very badly-fitting pair of itchy trousers, socks and a shirt I could not do up properly, taken from a cupboard next to the seclusion room. I was strongly aware that such a tactic would be a standard technique in the Army Psychological Warfare Interrogation Unit. I had little doubt that many of the original owners of this stash of clothing were no longer alive. I do not know what happened to the only item of clothing I had been wearing when I arrived: the Union flag boxer shorts.

My memory of that day is hazy but I formed the desperate belief that I was the last person ever to come in through that old door into the tower. I had been sent in to end this reign of horror *once and for all*. That is what the Lieutenant-Colonel had told me I had been brought in for back at DOAE.

There was something terribly wrong with my brain chemistry. I am told the brain itself does not feel physical pain, for example if an object is inserted into it. Yet I could feel the most extraordinary physical pain there, though not one iota of the emotional kind. I was walking up and down the corridor outside the nurses' office, past the toilets and the bathroom from the lounge to the snooker room[53]. The pain in my head was worse than unbearable – but somehow I did bear it. The reality of the situation was that I was suffering very severe withdrawal symptoms from the Imipramine and time was the only cure. I did not ask for any medication and, for the time being, none was given.

I examined the other patients for clues as to what was going on. Over my MTRUTH I was being told the Queen was now my own mother and I had to hold on. I sat down next to one of the patients and concentrated on his mind, willing him to make me a roll-up. He did and I thought I had indeed controlled his thoughts. He told me he had been in Rampton, the secure hospital for sex criminals, for 11 years and had now been moved here. I found myself believing he was in fact a Communist agent and French railwayman.

The Americans were invading Haiti and therein was both my explanation for the extraordinary physical pain in my head and the hope that I would recover. Evil witch doctors in the Ton-Ton Macoute were to be "taken-out" and this nightmare spell, which had been put on me purely by accident that day in Ouagadougou, back in Upper Volta, would be lifted. I heard the news on the television and it seemed it was being broadcast straight from the CIA to keep me going. Yet there seemed no end to this mortal terror.

I found a "Gerard" plastic carrier bag and it conveyed a deeply paranoid feeling. It made me think of Gerrard's Cross, where my uncle, a SmithKline Beecham executive, lived. I did not even think of Gerard (Gerry) Adams – at this stage. Words which appeared before me easily conveyed intended meaning – and in the case of this carrier bag, that they had been deliberately placed before me. Any psychiatrist would understand how such innocent and insignificant things could become so upsetting and disturbing in the mind of someone suffering from schizophrenia.

From the radio I heard REM's *What's the Frequency Kenneth?* Clearly they were working for the CIA and this was just their way of asking humourously of Kenneth Clarke, the then Chancellor and one time health secretary, on which frequency they could get through to me on my MTRUTH.

Bill Mason's double told me he had worked in Broadmoor. One of the other nurses was Jean-Paul. He, I imagined, was working for the French too. I thought of the tortured lyric "This is the room, the start of it all" from Joy Division's *Day of the Lords*. Ian Curtis, who sang that song, would have been creatively at home here. He had worked in a psychiatric hospital and many of his lyrics were said to be inspired by such places, if not by KGB/MI6 concept documents. I certainly believed that something incomprehensibly terrible emanated from this building. I really believed I had uncovered some horrendous Soviet conspiracy to destroy the mental health of the nation. The NHS was so badly organised they were not even aware this place existed and again I imagined a file in Whitehall relating to this building, lost down the back of a filing cabinet. The Soviets had a free run, and again I thought of how, after their Union's apparent collapse, a KGB agent had sold my file to MI6, or the CIA. I believed this wicked conspiracy had come to light, but only I and the Special Forces could see it. I, more than anyone, was the one to stop it.

Again I remembered the words "I am associating my own physical and mental health with that of the nation." Right now neither the nation's nor mine seemed too good, and that was not an understatement. In my mind they were both inextricably bound together and it seemed that the health of the entire country depended on my being able to "get out" of this.

I remembered the day in Fulham, when I had walked past the Empress State Building. Now I knew I was right – they had been observing the front door to my flat from it. I remembered the stench of stale urine coming from that building which, it now seemed perfectly obvious to me, was occupied by the ghastly creations of this very room I was now in. It was like the whole of the Empress State Building was inhabited by the shells of former human beings all of whom had had their souls stripped from them in this God-forsaken place. This had made them totally compliant with the Soviets' and John Lennon's master plan, which Prince Charles had, unwittingly, become caught up in. The fall of the Berlin wall now seemed ultimately sinister and part of a long-standing Soviet plan to seize control of the West. This factory of a hospital was a key component of their plan. I was trapped in a nightmarish science fiction story. How close could their plan have been to success that the whole nation and even NATO itself would have to rely on me to doom their plans to failure? Every unusual piece of rooftop architecture had become the source of a profound dread of dreads in my mind that day in Fulham. In this rebel warfare I could see the positions of "thought snipers" broadcasting their thoughts at me, driving me to the limit. I could only shudder. I thought of Mr Kipper again and easily believed he had been working for the Soviets too. Prince Charles would not give an inch, for now he too was waging war on me, to see what I was made of. I imagined that Professor Dainty had cast a rainbow through the little grille below the doorstep of my flat. This he had projected from the GCHQ 'gondola' atop the Empress State building. The rainbow cast a little hope across the cellar wall of the ground floor flat and through my imagination – unseen by anyone but me in absolute secrecy through my MTRUTH.

Up and down the corridor I went. One of the patients, who was clean-cut with dark hair, I believed to be from RAF Benson just down the road, no doubt from an extremely secretive squadron. Perhaps his cover was even deeper than mine, how was I to know? Agents were everywhere. I lost track of the hours and days of pain. I saw him come out of the locked nurses' office where, I thought, the nurse had buggered him. "Did you enjoy that?" the nurse casually said.

I went to my bed. I believed the beds were numbered – I really was in a factory. I was terrified to see that I was now one of the zombies I had seen dancing their macabre embraces the night before. The possibility that they were now to remove my soul was truly terrifying. This bed was the next stage in the process after the seclusion room I had been in the previous night, wherever that had been, as I was still not convinced I was in the same building. Oh my God! Where were the SAS?

I lay down on the bed and had some kind of seizure. Everything was horribly black and I had no physical contact with either my body or reality. I believed I was dead. My existence was now distinct from my body, over which I had no control or even contact. It was an out-of-body experience. Then, somehow, I came alive again, but only just. I was shocked with the shock of shocks at what had happened. I thought I had been given electroconvulsive therapy without my consent. I was determined that nobody would go down this road ever again. I had to be the last.

The sash cord in the window by the bed was broken and it was cold. A new male nurse appeared. Paranoiacally, and yet with ever such a small grain of hope, I believed him to be a Wyckhamist Mason. He performed the usual time-honoured charade, as I imagined it to be, of pretending to try and close the window with the pole as though the cord had only just gone, whereas it had, in fact, been like that for very many years. *All was sickeningly moribund.*

There was a spike sticking out of the mattress into my back. It was painful. I pulled back the bedclothes and the waterproof mattress cover and found the end of the spring pointing painfully out. Next to it someone had written, on the mattress itself, "KU KLUX KLAN". I was already terrified, so this hardly made any difference now.

I lay there on my back in a strange fever, all sorts of religious images passing in front of my eyes. I could see many Moslems on their knees praying in my direction. I forget who else. I was severely dehydrated and still believed the orange squash to be poisoned. Nothing could have persuaded me to drink it, as I believed it contained a fatal overdose of tartrazine. I decided I would rather die of thirst than face that (I don't know how much I'd have had to take but it is known to cause aggression in children and is now banned).

Then I could see a great fleet of removal lorries approaching the hospital down every single possible route in a clinically coordinated manner. The psychiatrist shared his name with the removal company. They were coming to carry out the biggest damned removal operation in history. I had to keep up my morale.

Without my noticing, the other beds had become occupied. I now indeed had to face the terror of thinking I was back in that obscene dance hall of a hospital ward I had been in the previous night. Oh no! Oh no! Now I was to become one of them. I was terrified. Now my mind was to be reprogrammed and I would soon be just another zombie. How could I keep hold of what was left of me?

All the patients appeared to be masturbating. Perhaps it was just the sex criminal in the bed next to me but it certainly didn't seem that way. I could only join in. I was in bed fully clothed, a typical symptom of schizophrenia. My senses were greatly heightened in some way and I just kept having orgasm after orgasm. My brain felt so painful, wanking seemed the only sensible thing to do, especially as everyone else was. Whereas the previous night I was covered in puke and excrement, now I was sodden in semen and I felt powerless to get out of bed or stop wanking.

Outside, I could hear some kind of electric pump going on and off. I was in psychic communication with a girl in her bedroom at her parent's house. There was a plane flying in the airspace between us and every time the pump switched on we both started masturbating. I could hear her saying, over and over, "I'm in the back room." The plane seemed to be relaying MTRUTH intelligence between us. She was a back room girl. It would seem she might have been referring to her position as an MI5 agent.

The generator or pump kept going on and off outside the building in the courtyard. Off I went wanking again, as though the water tower above the pump was full of semen, a virtually endless supply. Colditz? I dreamt of being in Colditz. I could see no hope at all of ever getting out. Then, in the back of my mind, I remembered that the Escape Officer at Colditz had been to my school, though even that thought did not seem to console me, and they said little about masturbation in *The Colditz Story*.

What little hope I had of divine help was killed off when, attending the nurses' station, a paranoid-looking nurse (who incidentally was not masturbating, or if he was, managed to conceal it from me) told me that the chapel had been closed down many years earlier. This seemed disgustingly sinister. I felt horrendously trapped. I had never felt so religious in my life. I said the Lord's Prayer. I said the 23rd Psalm. What else could I do if I was not to perform the ghoulish dance?

By now, word had reached my imagination that everyone in Reading Police Station had been killed by the Human Infection Control Unit. Nobody who came out of either the police station or this factory could be allowed to live and armoured personnel carriers (APCs) were driving around near both the hospital and police station, shooting anyone they saw on sight. Too right.

I awoke. It was now morning again. I was still alive, even though I had relented and taken a few very 'ill-advised' sips of the tartrazine solution. I looked out of the window and, at the bottom of the water tower, which looked more like the sort of thing you would find in a military installation, a man was approaching the tap. He took what I believed was a sample, almost certainly to be taken away for testing at, if not Porton Down, then the Public Health Laboratory. "As I had thought," I imagined the Government scientist saying, "very high levels of tartrazine, and certainly a fatal dose for the great majority of the population." My mind left me nothing to believe in, other than that I really was a hero and actually had uncovered a Soviet zombie factory. I was alone in the world as I had never been before and, it seemed, only I could get myself out of this most unfortunate situation.

It was the middle of the night again. I approached the nurses' control room behind the plastic glass screens. I knocked and the nurse let me in. I said I wanted to make a phone call. The news that the exchange was closed until morning was as bad as waking up at nightfall to find oneself chained to a bed in Dracula's castle. Somewhere at a safe distance, Peter Cushing now took down a rare old tome on the occult from his bookshelf and Francis Matthews said "I've never heard such a load of balderdash in all my life. You surely can't be saying..." but was interrupted by Mr Cushing replying, "That's exactly what I'm saying." I was a little more occupied with my belief that Dr. Patrick Ainsworth (whom I'd read of a few days earlier in the paper, and who was the namesake of the acknowledged expert on Windsor Castle) had been here only a short while before me, and had then gone to France and committed suicide. I could see why. But actually *Windsor Castle* by William Harrison Ainsworth was merely an historical romance. And it wasn't even Patrick Ainsworth but Alesworth. Even the most tenuous link from a basis that was deluded to start with can feed paranoid thoughts in schizophrenia.

I never saw this nurse again. As for the two on duty outside the seclusion room when I arrived, I guessed they were probably cat food by now.

I retired to my living nightmare. My trouser legs were encrusted in an extraordinary quantity of dried semen, more than I would normally ever produce in such a short space of time.

Somehow I had to get a message out, and I had to do so without getting an electric shock from the telephone, believing for some reason that was a real danger. There was a light switch in the small vestibule between the 'living' room and the dormitory, with solid wooden doors each side. I reasoned that if the Delta Force or the SAS had really been there on the night of my arrival then I could certainly hope the flash-over in the light switch would be detected by GCHQ, just as Marconi had detected the first ever transatlantic wireless message. If I could have sent out bits of Spike Milligan's *My Part in Hitler's*

Downfall in heavily-encrypted Morse code, from memory, I would have done. My friend Caroline had once said she thought my brain must be wired differently from everybody else's but unfortunately it wasn't *that* different. So I just sent - --...--- or ...---... not quite sure if I was sending SOS or OSO. I sent it so many times they must surely get the message, I thought.

At some point during this week, one of the other patients approached me in the corridor with a newspaper. He had that haunted look on his face, familiar to anyone who had been in such a place. His facial expression was reflecting an apparently eccentric obsession with a particular aspect of reality, in this case the wording of a newspaper article. This, he wished me to understand, was obviously terribly incorrect. He told me he was an expert in semantics. It seemed he desperately wanted me to comprehend what he was saying about the article. So, although I was in a terrible state, I tried to understand him. Who was he?

That evening I picked up the newspaper he'd wanted me to read. I was hardly able to read any of it, but I do remember one small article. It concerned a Ministry of Defence inquiry into the death of a member of the Special Boat Service in training. Strangely, you might think, I made no connection between this news article and myself. But six strange years later I was to wonder if I had been that SBS person, and the article was merely poking fun at my predicament – in the manner for which the Special Forces are renowned.

One of the patients told me that Spike Milligan and Prince Charles were having a jousting competition, which sounded rather amusing. As he told me, I felt a sudden revulsion to the mere mention of MI5 or MI6, which I happened (as was all too often the case) to be thinking about at that moment. For some reason the band Lawnmower Deth [*sic*] came to mind. On their album there's a track entitled: *Sumo Rabbit and His Inescapable Trap of Doom*. Suddenly I felt a great sense of kinship with this sumo rabbit – whoever he was and despite my slim frame. As for "Inescapable Trap of Doom", if I was not in one now it did not seem one could exist. Then I wondered if Prince Charles and Spike Milligan had formed a breakaway movement from MI5, MI6, the Special Intelligence Service, or whoever was doing this to me – the movement being known as the British Sumo Rabbit Psychic Wrestling Society. There, that sounded much better than MI something. For a few blissful moments it seemed I would never be troubled again by thoughts of Prince Charles's dog or ultra-elite intelligence organisations spying on, and even through me. All I had to do was think of the glorious sight of two fearsomely enormous and furry black-belt rabbits in the ring, both locked in mortal psychic combat – no body contact allowed. I was, understandably, suffering from a very nasty and severe sense of humour failure of a profundity requiring some sort of elaborate Heath Robinson life support system; that is unless the serious matter of rabbit-honour could keep me going. I made do with rearranging everybody's shaving brushes, which the hospital had issued us all with. I put them into different pigeon-holes, thinking I was Mondrian as I did so, and getting even more deeply paranoid about why it seemed the condom machine had neither a slot to put money in, nor a place for condoms to come out. I still don't know the answer to this.

But it was not just sumo rabbits that were locked in mortal psychic combat. I seemed to have been locked, via my MTRUTH, to the SAS rookie I had read about in the second Absolute Secret file mentioned earlier in the story. He had adopted the tactic of saying to me, over and over, for what seemed like many hours, "Fuck off! Fuck off! Fuck off!..." and I could both hear and see him on my MTRUTH walking around almost at random as he did this. It was him or me. We both believed this torture would finish if we could drive the other to suicide. I adopted the tactic of thinking, though not saying out aloud, arseholes, bastards, fucking cunts and pricks, to try and cancel out his psychic MTRUTH attack on me, in doing so quoting the intro from an old Ian Dury and the Blockheads song. Having done this a voice of total gravitas now told me in similarly unrelenting style that I was a "dud". "Dud! Dud! Dud!..." I believed it completely. I *was* a dud. The effect on my morale was shattering.

For my next trick, I took out what seemed a very rare and much sought after table football game from the ward's box of games. It was a little like Subutteo. I laid it out in the ward living room believing that with it, anyone in the ward was capable of determining the outcome of football matches on television. I believed I had done so, only a few weeks before, during the World Cup, when I was in Dublin. I will tell you something else: I believed I was the only person in the whole world outside NATO High Command, or away from the BBC sound engineer's desk, who knew why each World Cup match was accompanied by the continual drone of helicopters above the pitch. It seemed to be a message from the Pentagon referring to my work on the Apache helicopter project.

Nurse Jean-Paul did not appear too impressed and asked me to put the football game away. But he would soon have more pressing problems.

I was asked if I would eat and, believing that I was testing the psychiatric facilities for the severely disabled, felt it right to be as troublesome as possible. So I ordered a vegan meal.

When it arrived, sometime in the next few days (my sense of time was severely distorted), I was sitting at the dining table about to eat it when I saw a West Indian walking down the hallway towards me. Once again, terror rose within me as I realised my desperate hope to be the last ever admission into this cesspit of humanity had not been borne out. Only there was still some hope as I knew he had not come in from the same direction as I had, but through the door at the opposite end of the unit. This implied the possibility, if I really was in the same place I had been brought to that terrible first night, that the door through which I had stepped into this Ballardesque[54] atrocity exhibition might now be sealed up forever. I hoped that nobody could reopen it without destroying the whole hospital.

Never in my life had I seen such an overwhelmingly paranoid expression on the face of a man. I was terrified of him and tried not to look, lest he tear my head off – or worse. I began to consume my vegan meal like a humble Negro slave myself, eating under duress the best quality human excrement from my specially made NHS plastic plate, carefully avoiding his eyes.

I retired to my bed and lay down. Suddenly the alarm bells went off – there seemed to be at least three going. So maybe, I thought, my message broadcast using the light switch *had* been received and deciphered by GCHQ! Thank God! There might be an end to this! I could hear an almighty struggle going on down the ward and a bloodcurdling wail was coming in my direction fast.

Now it was nearing my bed and I just saw the red and flushed face of Nurse Jean-Paul, who looked like he had been hit badly, politely pulling the curtain around my bed to afford some privacy. A deep rumble was only feet away, and then I heard the new patient despatched into the seclusion room and, after a delay of a few seconds, the noise completely disappeared and the door slammed shut. There would be no sound out of him for several days.

****

After perhaps a week I was noticeably improved without having been given any medication at all (they had taken away the antidepressants found in my car). I really was very much better, though perhaps only in the respect that I was through the withdrawal symptoms from the antidepressant and the all out trip was over. From the window I saw one or two people walking their dogs in the grounds. They seemed mysteriously connected with me. I also noticed tyre tracks across the grass to the door of the open unit. I deduced that ambulances that reversed across the grass delivered new patients unceremoniously. I imagined these ambulances being fitted with hydraulics so the back of the ambulance could tip the new patient out of the back in through the rear door of the hospital.

I had heard on the radio that an old hospital, which had closed many years earlier, was now being used as a film set. I believed it was this hospital and it crossed my mind that everyone in it, except me, was an actor – Capgras syndrome again[55]. And of course it felt like the filming was being done through my eyes. I telephoned the office of Hugh Grant's Simian Films and asked to speak to him. I have no idea what I might have said. The girl said he was out of the country, which I did not believe. And Kylie kept singing *Confide in Me* on the radio. The Aussies would not be left out of this and had thrown everything at it they could. This was the Queen of Pop's personal message. She'd been put right in the picture, the whole project having been put together in days, or maybe years, and here was its culmination. Australian Military Intelligence had cut the mustard. They knew they could be proud of their part in the operation. For my part I hardly needed reminding of the enormity of the situation but the Australian big guns exhorted me on, very few of who knew the actual truth about this song.

I wrote to the Queen to ask to be transferred to a military hospital. I confirmed I was not sure whether Prince Charles really had a dog called Pooh or not and I offered my sincere apologies and condolences if he had. But I would not entrust anyone with the letter and was determined to wait for the opportunity to post it myself. If the nurses had seen whom I had written to, they would have regarded me as more ill than I wished. I wanted to get out.

"Oh no," I imagined Captain Mainwaring declaring, "You can always trust our boys to maintain a completely objective view of the world. I used to be a bit of a dab hand with pen and ink myself you know" – referring to my book, which I had begun to write on the ward. I wrote about a hundred pages and following my release showed it to my sister-in-law, who made an encouraging remark. But then it disappeared, bringing back a horribly intractable paranoia worthy of my delusion that Peter Gabriel had been summarily executed by the British Army, and I had to rewrite it.

The staff must have thought I was recovering too, as they now gave me a leaflet outlining my rights under the Mental Health Act. The Act enabled them to forcibly keep me in the hospital for 28 days, longer if required. More worryingly they could give me medication, even against my will. But the very word "Act" enabled me to think all was not what it seemed in the building. I read the leaflet carefully and as, by now, I wanted to leave, I noted the line where it said "Only a doctor can release you." Therefore, without much consideration, I asked myself where the nearest doctor friend of mine was and telephoned Amanda's home hoping she, or her sister, would be in. What tragedy! Her sister answered, and no, she could not come and release me. But she said it very nicely – offering some thin excuse about her having to go up to London. She need not have worried. I was no danger to her – or anyone really. I had a fair idea of where she was going in London.

Several days later the maniac re-emerged from the seclusion room. It seemed a demon had left his mind and been exorcised from the vicinity. My farfetched thoughts led me to imagine that some kind of interference effect had taken place in the psychic-ether between the psychotic waves representing, on one hand, our arrivals on the ward from different directions and, on the other, our different skin colours. A bit like Yin and Yang forces our force fields had cancelled each other out, creating harmony in the psychic-ether – and leading to his dramatic recovery. Now it seems on one hand a positive statement of the obvious, or somewhat psychotic, depending on which way I look at it.

He showed me his letter, in business format, with the addressee's address near the top on the left. I had never written a letter like this and felt guilty my letter to the Queen had not been similarly presented. I believed that he, or someone he knew, was aware I had written my letter incorrectly. He seemed to have educated me and I felt the guidance came from a higher source: this was real business. I was somewhat impressed with his apparent complete recovery and soon after adopted the same style of writing for my business letters. He was a nice chap and I liked him a lot.

On a slightly more schizophrenic note, he also showed me a piece of graffiti on the wall near the snooker table. The graffiti was facing a brass plate on the snooker table which said "By Appointment to His Majesty King Edward VII[56]... Makers of Snooker Tables". I forget who made it. He professed to know something about the graffiti, almost like he was an Egyptologist deciphering some hieroglyphs. I could not quite understand what he was trying to say about these marks on the wall. I, for my part, was a little more worried about the blue mark on the carpet, which, I found, persisted in my vision one day when I went for a bath.

Watching the blue mark floating about in front of me I suddenly shot back in the bath, like in a scene from the film *Jaws*, as I realised I was lying in a bath with human excrement floating in it. It was no illusion either. I got out of the bath and with one of the green paper towels I picked a piece up disbelievingly. Looking closely, I satisfied myself that it was indeed human excrement. I said aloud "I don't believe this, I have just had an NHS hot bath with human excrement floating on the surface!" The only explanation, apart from there being a fault in the plumbing, was that it was a dirty trick played on me by a person hidden in the roof space. I was horrified.

I made my retreat from the bathroom (the whole unit still had that wretched psychic stench about it, which I had recognised the moment I arrived) and, walking down the corridor, noticed the office to be locked shut, with one member of staff and one patient missing. Once again I suspected they were having some sort of improper relationship.

One morning a nurse showed me how to make my bed saying "hospital corners" as he tucked the sheets under the corners of the mattress. He winked at me saying "You know, military-style." I took this to mean that my letter to the Queen, asking that I be transferred to a military hospital, had somehow been read by the staff, defence or otherwise. I thought to myself I knew exactly what a hospital corner was – I was in one, and it wasn't very funny either. During our conversation he used the words "Doolally tap" and asked me if I knew where the words came from. He explained that during the days of the Raj there was an infamous camp called Deolali, 150 miles north of Bombay. The camp was commonly referred to as "Doolally" by those unable to manage the Urdu pronunciation. Soldiers who had served their time with their regiments, very often after years away from home, were sent to Deolali to await the next available troopship home. The wait could be a long and boring one, and the Hindi word for fever is "tap". Hence "Doolally tap" was the term given lightheartedly to anyone in the British Army showing signs of mental wear and tear. This, the nurse explained was how it came to be that today "Doolally", without the "tap", came to mean someone showing signs of mental illness. Many times over the coming years, when I heard any tapping, I would recall this conversation and deludedly believe the military were the source of it. For now, his talking of the military gave me a delusional sense of security. Perhaps I had just gone a bit further "round the bend" than most; only later would I discover the origin of *that* expression at Telegraph Island on the Mussandam peninsula. The telegraph relay station there was a hot and lonely place and those sent to man it were said to "go round the bend" as the peninsula made a large bend in the straits of Hormuz.

During the second week of my visit this nurse asked me if I would like to go down to the village. I jumped at the opportunity to take the fresh air and the village now took on the same air as Colditz village. Fantasising, I decided to memorise every detail of the trip in case I needed to organise a mass breakout.

It was a bright sunny morning, and the nurse even took me for a walk over the grass on my own. Now was not the time to run. The main thing seemed to be to get my letter to the Queen in the Royal Mail postbox, this representing a form of escape and no little solace for me. I had to inform the Queen. Relieved, I placed the letter in the Royal Mail postbox[57]. If I needed to get a message out, the hospital's internal mailbox could not be trusted an inch. However I did choose to place the letter to Virginia Bottomley, the then Health Secretary, in the internal mailbox, to ask why herbal Kalms tablets were not available on the ward. I later got a full reply from a civil servant explaining that Kalms were not classified as a drug by the government. This I thought was a bit stupid – like saying salt is not a chemical. As we walked over the grass, the nurse asked me about my problems and said he suspected it had been going on a bit longer than I was saying. This did not make sense. I had been fine for nearly 10 years before the summer of 1994. But actually I now think I had been due to blow for some time, and the nurse had been correct: it went back hundreds of years.

I did not write just to the Queen and Mrs Bottomley. I wrote to the Broadcasting Complaints Commission too. I complained about the news item I had heard on BBC Radio 1. This was the one concerning the flight near Uttoxeter of a light aircraft piloted by a dog, which I believed had been broadcast hours before the news of the disappearance of Prince Charles' dog. I made some more pointed complaints about the BBC interfering with my body through implants. What is certain is that the recipient (if not told to disregard such letters from members of the Special Forces on manoeuvre) must have thought I was barking mad. Barking yes, at least in the previous chapter, but as I later concluded from the treatment meted to me, this country's psychiatric hospitals are populated entirely by members of the Special Forces under such deep cover nobody knows they are there.

A day or so later I noticed the Queen's personal staff, including her Secretary, Sir Robert Fellowes, introducing themselves in the newspaper. My mind told me that this was in response to my letter. I neglected to leave the paper open on that page. Nor did I recreate the strange incident of four months earlier at Bedford Hospital when I believed I had met either Prince Charles, or a rather undead John Lennon, in disguise. This would have entailed going up to a hapless patient and, with a weird look on my face, pirouetting around with my arm outstretched to point at the information in the paper.

A nurse told me he was going to Lincoln for the weekend. He knew I had been there that summer. He was going there because now everybody had to, as part of this ludicrous procession I had imagined forming behind me. Looking at it another way, I was a trailblazer, investigating new ground in the history of mental illness. Again the nurse mentioned hospital corners. Once more I thought it was just an allusion, this time referring to my desperate attempt to protect my wedding tackle from flying masonry when the Hostage Release Unit burst in on the night of my arrival.

I now felt very much better indeed but, on the other hand, thought I had noticed messages coming from the Pentagon via GCHQ on the stereo of one the patients. The patient told me how he had burnt down a doctor's surgery. I thought of asking him for tips as I had one in mind myself: the surgery of the doctor who, it seemed, had got me in here by giving me medication which, quite clearly, had sent me 'into orbit'. When he left the room I ripped out one of the cables from the back of his speakers to stop the Pentagon broadcasts. It seemed a perfectly sensible thing to do at the time so, although feeling much better, I was still obviously ill. Then I sent a letter to Griffin Audiotechnology in Birmingham (the makers of his speakers) to tell them what miserable MTRUTH transmissions I had to tolerate on this patient's behalf. Sometime after my release I wrote to him care of the hospital apologising.

Although better, things took a dive when, after a game of badminton, I was briefly taken to the open ward. I wondered if the lights had been switched off deliberately to make me feel how lucky I was to be in the secure section. But perhaps this was just the way it was. Goodness me, in there I would have thought you could measure in seconds the time it would take the average healthy person to consider ending it. Surely this could not be the home of a living soul – these dark and weird characters seemed so sinister it would hardly have been any more frightening to find out they really were just actors or it *was* a Soviet conspiracy. But I didn't wonder. I really believed the lights had been switched off for some reason to do with me. Again I thought that this was the mental health "Act". The whole thing was indeed a disgustingly sinister theatre performance emanating from the former Soviet Union though actually I was rather better than before and this was a momentary relapse. I was just remembering my arrival.

Around this time the doctor saw me, and though he claimed to have spoken to me before, I could not remember it. I sat there facing him and a nurse. I remember nothing other than his challenging me with some of my written material he had obtained. He did not seem very happy about my saying that his place of work was not a hospital. Whatever I actually said in reply I think I may have politely pointed out that they were merely written words and I was a little angry I was being spied on like this. He now committed the famous faux pas of turning his head knowingly and dismissively to the nurse as though to say "We have a right one here don't we?" Then he told me he was prescribing me a drug, Chlorpromazine (an old-fashioned antipsychotic). I was a little surprised at this as I felt I was greatly recovered, as indeed I was. Now, to my horror and disbelief, he said that "later on" I would be given something stronger, or maybe he just said a higher dosage. Either way this meant only one thing to me – that he thought I was suffering an irreversible and degenerative disease. I just could not believe that. It's rather interesting that he did not tell me I was suffering from paranoid schizophrenia because only after this story did any doctor tell me I was – otherwise they all seemed to think I knew or was so deluded there was no point. He did not think to tell me he suspected I had suffered a violent and catastrophic reaction to the drug his colleague, my GP, had prescribed me. Nor did he tell me this was not my fault. Even worse I feel it criminally[58] negligent of him to not say "Now I must warn you that this drug Chlorpromazine is extremely dangerous for some people. For them it can cause suicidal clinical depression and akathisia. You might be one of them. If you begin to feel depressed in any way you must tell me immediately and I will take you off it." But he did not say that. If it did not begin with my GP a few weeks earlier, here began years of what I see as criminal negligence at the hands of unacceptably incompetent psychiatrists. For him it was socially acceptable to force me to take, without any warning, this drug of death. Only an extremely resilient personality would enable me to survive taking it. It would be left to me, without any help or advice from a single person on this planet, to determine that I would be insane to carry on taking it – and this in the face of pressure from his colleagues to carry on doing so. This is not to say I don't think the Chlorpromazine had any positive effect on my schizophrenia – I think it did. In fact it removed it. Maybe it would have not come back either if I had not drunk alcohol again.

Next day I saw him driving past in the same type of car as the one I had crashed into in Reading a couple of weeks earlier. It occurred, to my deluded mind, that he was having an affair with the owner of that car (Dr. Black's wife), ridiculous, as that might seem – because they had the same type of car.

My real brother Tom visited (I say "real" as this place had brought everything into question). He suggested I "try to catch lung cancer" to calm my nerves and I decided it was good advice. I wish I hadn't – this was where I really started smoking seriously. But it did help me to keep going.

My mother and father also visited. This was an utterly unhelpful and damaging thing to have to experience. To have to sit there like a four-year-old with a smegma problem whilst they spoke to the staff in my absence. Naturally, I pleaded with my mother to come and look at the super-satanic condom machine. They left and good riddance to them I thought, because of my illness.

I also received a visit from a solicitor. I don't recall arranging this myself and, to my recollection I only had a single request. This was for him to complain on my behalf about the white noise emanating from the ventilation system at Reading Police Station, which by now I no longer actively believed had been paid a visit by the Human Infection Control Unit to eliminate all the occupants. Though perhaps something else had happened. He must have thought I was pretty ill and mentioned something about European Law. The solicitor's practice was in Oxford. The next day I saw the local newspaper. It said "Royals pay quiet visit to Oxford". The visit concerned nothing but this solicitor and me. They had told him I was in the SBS.

I was allowed out for another walk, and was taken down to the river where the nurse pointed out the disused boathouse to me. With what I thought was a knowing glance, about which I was paranoid, he said "Another underused resource." I was rewarded for not running off, with a crack about the assessed likelihood that I would have done. The nurse also poked fun at my footwear: running shoes. Now I was given the chance not only to use the gymnasium upstairs in the tower but also to go for a run on my own along the river, for which my shoes were returned to me.

It seemed as though nobody had been in the gymnasium for many years. I imagined that in fact nobody had been there since Cup Final day 1978, sixteen years earlier, when I rowed at the nearby regatta. Later I did find some evidence this was the case, in the form of a copy of the Broadmoor Newsletter, dated 1978, in what I saw as the thick and long-undisturbed dust on the windowsill. It was like the only remaining room of my school, the tower room in the Blore Façade, which now fronts the Harpur shopping centre in Bedford town centre. You hardly needed a good imagination to believe that the psychiatric equivalent of the Elephant Man[59] was still haunting the room above this one, higher in the tower.

So I did go for a run and found myself completely tortured by thoughts relating to Amanda, which made life really nasty, so that it was quite obvious why plenty of others had chosen not to run upstream by the river but float down, dead, in it. The Chlorpromazine was already making me depressed – a known side effect of this drug, as I later discovered at the library. If you could know how I then felt you would have felt very, very sorry for me indeed. It was not nice at all. I was still unconvinced the hospital's occupants weren't just a load of actors, staff and patients included. Meanwhile not far away I could hear a train on the Great Western Railway speeding along. General Crush loomed large in my mind – and I sensed extreme danger.

For some reason I recalled how one day at school I repeated "Mars Bar" to myself, not ad nauseam, but until it became stripped of meaning. I had continued this to the point where I practically became the Mars Bar myself and I was looking back at what had been me, rather like the day at my flat, looking through the binoculars at myself, reflected in the window opposite.

I did not enjoy the run at all, a slight understatement. I had read somewhere that Chlorpromazine, the drug they were giving me, had originally been derived from insecticide. I was minded to announce it hardly surprising I felt so bad, given that I was taking insecticide. I satisfied myself that a short course of anything like this could turn a fit marathon runner into a pitiful shadow of his former self in a matter of hours. Nobody taking this despicable drug could throw themselves off a cliff – they would be too depressed to get there. And all this after just a few days of medication. How could I possibly explain how bad this depression was? To start with I was reminded of how I had learnt, back in 1984 upon my return from Africa, why people kill themselves. Every time I had a thought it seemed to have a 10-ton weight attached to it and I was close to a black hole into which all the thoughts were swirling. I was being dragged in by the weights to be crushed into less than the size of an atom. The force exerted was so astronomically enormous that even the simplest task required superhuman willpower to carry out. Oh my God it was horrible!

After the run I saw that a woman was sat hopelessly in the corridor wailing and looking like she had become part of the hospital and, if not a full Mars Bar, on the way to becoming one. Obviously very few knew of this. It seemed like she must have been there for very many years. I heard the Queen's voice in my head saying, apologetically, "I didn't know." A man, it seemed another long-term inmate, was standing motionless in the corridor appearing to stare at a brick. I stared too and thought he was trying to tell me that was all I was: "Just another brick in the wall."

The next time I was allowed out, instead of running I walked down to the boathouse, where I was a little frightened at seeing somebody I had once rowed with, a Cambridge Blue, sculling by in the Wallingford Small Boats Head of the River. I was frightened because I thought he might have been there on MI5 instructions and embarrassed because I did not want him to know I was in the loony bin. I could not even manage the school 'Masonic' greeting: the claw (in this greeting the hand was held with its palm facing upwards and the fingers half-clenched whilst a high-pitched wail was made). So I just went back to look at the newborn calves and pick some blackberries.

Next day, in the Sunday magazine, I noticed a small picture with the caption "Goodbye Blackberry Way", alluding to the song by The Move and the September way to the river. Yes, goodbye, good riddance and maybe, it seemed, I had not been so wrong to imagine there weren't only moorhens in those long reed-beds by the river, but also the Special Forces spying on me. I imagined them, watching all I did through my MTRUTH. I felt they had seen my attempt to write the first chapter of this book. But if they had, surely they did not know that I had foreseen a head-on train crash on the Great Western Railway. It seemed dangerous to imagine, as though just doing that would make it happen. It later did. I imagined I was the "Master of Disaster" and, having had that thought, I wondered what that position entailed. I could only presume it meant that should it be required, for whatever reason, the responsibility fell to me to arrange enormous fake accidents.

Towards the end of my four weeks here, I was grateful to be able to polish up my snooker a bit, for which I was allowed to borrow a nurse's cue. It was only natural that the young doctor who turned up out of the blue, studiously avoiding my gaze as I chalked my cue tip, should make me think she had come to spy on my notes and report back to interested parties. She might indeed be a friend of Amanda's, interested to know not just whether I had stopped barking yet, but also whether I intended to be present at any further violent incidents involving motor vehicles. However, of course, I could only guess that, and I would probably have had a more severe medical condition if I had not imagined it.

The consultant told me he could not keep me there and asked me what I was going to do when I went; so I told him I would go back to the hospital in Bedford and ask to be admitted there. This now seems a little unbelievable, as I was substantially recovered, but instead I now had a beastly depression, caused by that 'insecticide'. When I had been out a few hours it would become a different story: it was "beg to be allowed in" time rather than merely be admitted. However, the reason I felt so desperate I put down mostly to the Chlorpromazine. But I thank the doctor for releasing me.

After four weeks of being deprived of my liberty for the first time in my life, I collected my belongings, waited for my medication, and now I was free again. But almost as soon as I was out, things started happening again. Not that the Army Land Rover waiting at Cholsey Railway Station made me ill at ease in anyway – in fact it made me feel more secure.

I got off the train at Reading and, still in some suspended state of disbelief, went to look through the wedding photos in the papers at the library. I was hardly in control of myself now, but this behaviour was fairly existential compared to the night I was arrested. I found nothing there about Amanda, and got back on the train to London, presumably demonstrating I did have some control over my actions. I was still finding great difficulty coping with the fact that she was now married. In fact the knowledge was unbearable to possess – and I was terribly depressed. Poor me!

If I was expecting some kind of response to this I now appeared to get one. On the train, an ugly woman who looked like she was Russian for some reason sat down opposite me. She had a black birthmark on her face and was carrying a bag from a chain of shops bearing Amanda's real surname. I was paranoid about her, her black birthmark, and her bag (in the same way I was about the Gerard bag).

Getting off at Paddington, I watched her walking away; I had no doubt back to the Russian Embassy. I showed great sanity by not enquiring as to the purpose of her mission, and her bag. But I believed her black birthmark was aimed at me simply for my conduct in getting off the train at Reading. It was a bit too much like I had been stalking Amanda. But it was not my fault Amanda had done my head in (or mine her's of course) and it would be several years if ever before I was cured of this obsession – several years of immersion therapy prepared by psychological warfare experts from the British Sumo Rabbit Psychic Wrestling Society and presented to me over my MTRUTH.

Part VIII

The Working Men's Club

Chapter Twenty-Five

Sun Bursts In

By now I had acquired a great distrust of any doctor's ability to treat me properly. I owe my survival to this distrust because by stopping the Chlorpromazine (as well as drugs given to me later, some of which I quite literally ran away from) I removed the risk of suicide. The only way of approaching the situation with the hope of a successful outcome was to assume it was all some kind of Top Secret psychological warfare exercise in which it was an honour to take part; either that or I was a national hero in some sort of Doomsday scenario. If I invested heavily enough in this belief then, I thought, I might have some chance of survival. In this exercise the trick was to see through this conspiracy between the doctor and the drugs companies, against all sufferers, and former sufferers, of schizophrenia. For the conspirators a patient who had even just one brush with the illness was easy meat for 40 or so years' profits, if the patient did not kill themselves first[60]. The same would hold true, with one exception, for the more modern drugs I eventually came into contact with. With only that one exception the drugs were all so horrible to take that I had to believe I could do without medication.

****

So, when I arrived in Bedford after my release from Fairmile, I was terribly depressed. As I already said, this was caused by the Chlorpromazine, but I had not caught on yet. That is I was now suffering an illness given to me in the hospital, an illness that had killed many others. When I had got home at least three car alarms were going off around the house and they were driving me mad. It was a welcome home from MI5, who had decided to experiment on me. However I had not yet developed my own schizophrenia avoidance procedure. This was to actively consider and then attribute a level of probability to things being the case rather than just the product of my deluded mind. This probability would be more accurate (and uncertain, if necessary), than that presented by mere intuition driven by either a healthy imagination or schizophrenia. This is called Cognitive Behavioural Therapy or CBT – I would not be taught this technique by the NHS until eight years later. I would work it out for myself.

In the hallway was a paperback of *The Valley of the Dolls*. Its presence was designed to cause me agonising paranoia, and though I had no idea what the book was actually about, I knew exactly what I thought it was, I had just been there. Outside the bathroom I saw the old mirror. It had been there since 1974 and only now did it become eerily significant to me. At the top it said "Registered Agent". I had been one all this time. Only now was I really being tested. Only now had I been turned on, like a hatchling, the KGB having spied on me since birth. Only now did I realise what had been happening in my home for 20 years.

The mirror was an antique promotion for a motorcar supplier advertising "Suppliers of Quality Motor Cars: Rolls Royce, Duesenberg, Mercedes, Hispano-Suiza, Delahaye, Bugatti et cetera – all leading makes supplied." I shuddered when, looking closely at the mirror, it seemed that the moustached gentleman leading his lady down the grand flight of stairs from the elegant building to the chauffeur-driven Armstrong Siddeley was in fact Adolf Hitler with Eva Braun by his side. I felt sickeningly paranoid about this mirror, which had gone virtually unnoticed by me for all that time. The mirror had been placed there as a personal assault on my psyche and its power had built each of the thousands of times I had passed it over those years. It reeked of a filthy conspiracy, leading back to what the concrete had been concealing at the foot of my grandmother's garden for 40 or so years. Here were the secrets, and riches; those buried there had taken, literally, to their grave. Suddenly I was back in my grandmother's bathroom one night 30 years earlier, Frank Sinatra was singing *Strangers in the Night* on *the Light Programme*, and I was cleaning my teeth using the Euthymol toothpaste she always had. More like "Strangers Buried at the Foot of the Garden."

Therefore, in October 1994, I saw my GP, who said he had heard I had been smashing windows. I said I felt I should be in hospital. Little did I know, when I saw him, that the drug he had prescribed to me before my hospitalisation was more responsible for the damage than I. Moreover, to some extent, the illness I now had was caused by the drug prescribed to correct the effects of that antidepressant he had given me. The medical treatment had been miserably incompetent. I also felt a deep sense of guilt at what I had done in Reading, guilt which some would not have been able to cope with. Eight years later, it is clear there was nothing to be guilty of. Some might even say it was part of my treatment. But I should have sued him. I did think of it but decided not to for two reasons: I wanted to put the entire episode behind me; and the prospect of doing so was too daunting.

I now wonder if I made the right decision in asking to be admitted as I was 'merely' depressed, restless and rather paranoid. When I came out of my GP's I saw the Vauxhall Frontera, registration number A1 CCF, parked, as usual, near the surgery. It had been parked there by British Intelligence, the number plate referring to my former unit, the Naval Section of the school's Combined Cadet Force. The message was to cheer me briefly. At Bedford Hospital I was given a rather bigger dosage of the antipsychotic drug eventually administered at Fairmile, so I was now taking 100mg at a time. I was also prescribed another antidepressant: Seroxat.

I was now experiencing terrible pain in my head, rather similar to that I had to endure shortly after arriving at Fairmile. A voice in my head said "You're going in the mincer" and that was just what it felt like, as though a great corkscrew was turning away in my head. The voice came from the Special Forces and was not the product of my own mind. I was being toughened up to address the Anglo-Irish conflict. I felt like the farm worker who tried to unjam a silage masher by kicking his foot into the blades which then dragged him through to a horrible death – except I was going in headfirst. I felt like Captain Nairac. I sat on the bed totally broken. Nurse Pauline came and sat next to me. She said "I've been here 20 years and I have seen many people just like you sat there, and they are not here now." This, I felt, was one of the most successful pieces of treatment I'd had. But, in my state of mind, I wondered where these people actually now were – I felt sure many of them were dead, by suicide. I was to discover this was indeed the case. Still, she was very nice.

I was now unable to concentrate, and just had to pace up and down. I had the impression that the reason my head felt so awful was that my brain was like a corrupted computer disk, and the drug was fighting some kind of defragmentation war in my head. At night there were red safety lights on in the ward and these seemed inextricably linked with the Soviet Union. If you could feel how paranoid I was you would vomit until you were bringing up bile.

One night, in order to console myself that I could still function sexually, I had a wank. When I came it was like a cannon backfiring in my bollocks – quite enough for many people to give up the ghost right there. A gay male nurse eventually diagnosed this extremely painful side effect: retro-ejaculation. To think that people had been receiving this vile drug for 40 years or more.

I was allowed out for a while and met one of the doctors in the street. He told me I could go home whenever I liked. I was feeling more composed than I had done when I arrived in Bedford, but desperately depressed and restless with anxiety to match. I sensed I should not even dream of asking any doctor if I could stop taking the Chlorpromazine. So I came to address the problem of how bad I was feeling. After some six more weeks of hell, one of the doctors suggested that he thought I could reduce the dosage of the antidepressant. I kidded myself he had meant the Chlorpromazine. But I would persuade myself that I certainly did not need to take this drug for the rest of my life, or even a few more weeks; that was unthinkable.

During the nadir of this most unpleasant experience, two particularly bad moments come to mind. The first of these was when I had not yet been discharged, and Tom drove me out to the layby next to the site of the A6 murder, the actual layby no longer being there, it now being buried under the road. The road, when it was built back in the 60s, was an experimental one – I even felt paranoid about that. What sort of experiment was this? I thought, conspiratorial ideas running rife in my head. Having parked we walked off into the trees where Tom believed there to be a rare wild service tree, which he went off in search of, though without success. A light aircraft passed overhead, and I thought that its presence might even have been denied if I had asked Tom why it was there. I suspect, however, that he would remember the RAF Harrier, which had flown over low and at great speed just as we arrived at the layby. It was there merely in response to my presence. It was an acknowledgement of my position inside the military's virtual version of reality, and I wondered about the style this might be presented in on the computer monitors at the DISC. I considered the style of this parallel reality might be impressionistic, pointillist, Pre-Raphaelite or, most likely, surreal.

The fly-by merely reminded me of my theory, developed a few years earlier before I became ill, that the military had been involved in the A6 murder. Once again, I found myself wondering if Peter Alphonse had been working for French Intelligence when he lay on the bed on French television confessing to the murder for which James Hanratty had already been hanged. I had, in the past, come up with all sorts of bizarre ideas about this murder, all when I was not mentally ill. I was driven to these strange and sometimes humorous theories because I could not believe a particular piece of evidence I had heard was given at the trial. The evidence was that the murderer had asked the surviving victim, now in a wheelchair because of her gunshot injury, how to change gear. He was also said to have driven away crashing the gears and furthermore was seen, or rather heard, crashing them at various places on the route to where the car was found. But James Hanratty was a known car thief who could drive. If he had no intention to leave any survivors why would he bother pretending he could not drive? I could not believe he had been convicted. It seemed blindingly obvious to me and, as a result, I had imagined all sorts of things including that no execution had taken place the whole escapade having been some outpouring of Freemasonic black humour prior to the ending of capital punishment. All that was required was for some joke detective like me to come along and solve the mystery, it seemed. I had expounded upon this subject in my newsletter writing in one a story about how Woody Allen was the real murderer.

But I felt simply awful. Somehow my South African sister-in-law seemed a great source for the sympathy and will I needed to continue. In the afternoon I would purchase some wine gums and then get one of only two buses in the day out to her remote village in quiet north Bedfordshire for her free therapy. I do not recall if it was then, the previous summer, or later, but I asked her a question, which may appear rather jocose: "Have you noticed a lot of dogs in the newspapers?" Her reply was that she had – which to me was an almighty relief. But that relief was part and parcel of my schizophrenia, however delusional or insightful it was. I could feel this massive great psychic energy bashing away at my head and it really was mesmerising, all-powerful and excruciatingly intolerable. All I can conclude was that this was what I referred to earlier in this story when I said I was finding Prince Charles's dog difficult to handle. This was "the power of the dog". I wonder what Barbara Woodhouse, the TV expert in training unruly dogs, would make of it. It seemed like I was being taken for a walk by His Royal Highness's dog, and not the other way round, whilst something about this was absolutely tantalising my brain in a manner which was nothing less than torture. Anyway I was probably the unruly dog not Prince Charles's, who was, I imagine, a good dog. It was just that I had not got enough experience yet to deal with it properly.

A few days later, having been at least partially discharged from hospital, I found myself with Tom and his girlfriend at a pub, again near to the scene of the murder. My state of mind was almost unbearable; though bear it I had to, and if somebody had decided, surreally, to put the pub's pool table into my head, I would have been most grateful, as anything was an improvement on this state of mind.

So, without anyone's advice or agreement to do so, I came off the Chlorpromazine, hoping desperately that I would be all right. Life was far too miserable to contemplate taking such rubbish for the rest of my life. I was still depressed though, so carried on taking the antidepressants. In my experience antidepressants work well – but only when the source of the depression is removed. As for the possibility of trying another antipsychotic, that was out of the question. I then decided I needed a change of environment so phoned work and asked if they had any jobs going at RSRE, later renamed Defence Research Agency (DRA) Malvern. I was feeling more positive already. I had once been offered a poorly paid job there, but never got around to turning it down (I could not bear to turn down the job as the work was so interesting). Now, I felt, was the right time to work in Malvern.

First of all I had to attend an interview at Fleet. The whole thing was torture. I still felt extremely uncomfortable with the side effects and simply staying in the building and putting on a front of normality was only just possible. At least I had not applied for a job in that particular building. If that was not building-sickness then I do not know what is. I got a job, not that one unsurprisingly, and after Christmas was on my way down to Malvern. On the way I called at my flat and felt overwhelmed by depression in its most desperate form: the "clinging to the nearest passer-by" type again (once more quoting Joy Division's Ian Curtis in his 'jolly' ditty about a soon-to-be psychiatric patient: *She's Lost Control*). I telephoned Caroline, thanking her for sending me a pre-release copy of her album *Spirit*, which had attached itself to the memory of my weeks in hospital. She sounded like she might have been a good nurse as she gave me the telephone number of her local, which I was to call 20 minutes later when she was at the bar. Speaking to her I was extremely tearful and asked her "Why is my life like this?" Somehow I was to survive this crisis. It seemed my depression was geographically-located and now I would get more evidence to prove that to be the case.

Now I was on the train down to Malvern, and already feeling a little better as, geographically speaking, I had left behind all the madness of the previous year. My state of mind was improving almost by the mile. As my new manager at Malvern had asked me to, on the train I was reading *Most Secret War* by Dr R.V.Jones, the story of the development of radar before and during World War II. Arriving at Malvern, I telephoned the house where I was to stay, the house being rented by my firm for its employees. One of them came down to the station to collect me.

To a great extent it seemed I had escaped from Nazi Germany and wanted to tell my story, though it was already too long to do that without writing a book – a book I had begun but for which I did not yet have a satisfactory ending or even middle. From the moment I set foot in this house I felt better. It was on the side of Malvern Beacon, which seemed to afford a great sense of security, and soon I was at the snooker table in The Malvern Wells Working Mens' Club next door – getting there felt like a homerun. The road outside was lit with old gas-style lamps. This reminded me that Malvern was the former home of Edward Elgar, and Nigel Kennedy, the celebrated violinist, drank in a pub in town. There was a sense of calm and peace and to all intents I had recovered completely overnight. I felt secure.

In the morning the sun filled my room as it rose over Bredon Hill and the view was an elixir. The person I was working with on the contract, Christopher, was previously known to me. He was precisely the sort of person you would expect to find in a place like this. He asked me politely how the journey down had been, recalling having made the same train journey himself many years earlier, asking me if it was still like something out of a P.G.Wodehouse novel.

Christopher was so intelligent it was a bit like standing on top of the Beacon in an intellectual hurricane. Luckily I had already encountered one person in particular whose IQ I could never hope to match: he was my PhD tutor back at University during 1985-89. However, I did elicit some useful information from him: not only had I stolen off like a jackal with a kill of a PhD, but also received from him a copy of James Joyce's magnum opus, *Finnegans Wake*, with the advice that I should not read it unless drunk. Happily he had himself, from his own expensive wine cellar, fulfilled that requirement before he gave me the book. I was impressed enough to actually read 19 or 20 pages before the train from his London pied-à-terre reached my station. I never touched *Finnegans Wake* again but drank more and more steadily for some 15 years after.

Somebody had told me no student had ever got a PhD under his guidance. Whether that was true or not, I remembered thinking quite early on in my course that I was going to have to be pretty thick-skinned and tenacious to get one myself with my own insufferable stupidity. I am sure he would certainly agree with the suggestion as to my IQ and when he eventually wrote my reference, he did tell me he had described me as tenacious. Perhaps he might have said very tenacious if he could ever have known I would get this far.

Anyway, back to 1995 and Malvern. The controller told me that from now on I must forget everything that happened, which I was well qualified to do. However I will not be arrested under the Official Secrets Act if I recall an incident during one of Christopher's many salubrious smoking breaks, held in the corridor of what had once been a military TB isolation hospital. I was staring up at the Beacon and casually remarked that there appeared to be somebody up there looking down. Christopher took a look himself and, perhaps as if to demonstrate there might possibly be something in what I said, remarked enigmatically "Yes it does look rather like there's somebody up there." I always remember his remark as though it were a little cryptic. However, he then also suggested security might not be too happy if I brought some binoculars in to see if we were right, there being no air of jocularity in what he said.

There was an incident, which, though not at the time, would later make me wonder if he was psychic or rather, that he too had an MTRUTH fitted. After all, I never imagined I was the only one, though I did sometimes wonder if I was the only one left to work it out for myself. In fact the incident was merely one in which he entered the room at an opportune moment and I read just a little too much significance into it.

He drove me up there, over the Beacon, to the pub for lunch that day. On the way up I spotted one person innocently, but a little eerily, walking a dog down.

Not only had my schizophrenia completely gone, at least for the time being, but also I had stopped taking the medication for it. I set to the task, for which I had access to the most sensitive of information, with some sense of relief. I spent much of the time working alone, though the atmosphere was given (what might generally be described as) an unexpectedly rustic air by a pleasant local chap. From his accent you might have bet a fair sum on his having been a Worcestershire farmhand rather than a person exposed to issues of such sensitive nature as he was.

I did not need the antidepressants and stopped taking them rather too quickly, simply because I had run out. This resulted in dizziness and a sort of "zapping" sensation in my head. My subsequent failure to get off the antidepressants was, to my considered belief, to cost me another severe, though spectacularly interesting, breakdown. The drug – possibly combined with alcohol, caused this. Instead of gradually weaning myself off them, as I should have done, I became mildly addicted to them. The fact that they impeded my ability to have sex properly did not override my fear that the depression would come back if I stopped them. The Malvern doctor, who doled out more of the drug without asking the right questions takes some blame here. The depression would not have come back because I had stopped taking the drug causing the depression. I have never had depression spontaneously; a drug always caused it: either illicit, as during my Africa trip, or later, prescribed. Other than my partial impotence though, it was almost as if my troubles had never happened. Nobody was following me anymore. I had forgotten such things. Thoughts of my having a British Intelligence MTRUTH fitted were far from my mind.

But however free I felt of all that had happened, and however normal things felt, I could not forget what had occurred that day back at Wilton. There had to be some extraordinary natural consequence of it not yet realised, I believed. It seemed it might all have happened simply as a result of an earlier incident – perhaps my being turned into an MTRU without my knowledge. It is clear though that events of that bank holiday weekend had elevated my level of thinking towards a Security Services mindset – one in which Anglo-Irish politics were to the fore. Schizophrenic logic told me that at the least MI5 had a file on me, possibly a very strange and comprehensive one taken from the KGB archives – and one that would get stranger.

But in fact only two incidents occurred which were in any way likely to make me look over my shoulder during the whole time I was at Malvern. The first of these occurred in a Worcester nightclub. I found a wallet, and it seemed as if it had been dropped from above. The wallet *just* succeeded in getting me to wonder if it had been put there deliberately. I took the wallet to the cloakroom and did not even look to see whose it was. Funny they did not drop it right on my head. I was told a joke: why was a bloke not hurt when a bottle of lemonade was dropped on his head? I had answered "...because he was difficult to offend?" but the answer they said was that it was a soft drink.

The second involved my driving licence. A few weeks after arriving in Malvern it was revoked because of mental illness. I had been allowed to work with some of the most sensitive information there was but was not considered trustworthy enough to drive a car. I carried on driving for a while without returning the licence. On the one hand I thought the DVLA would not know, though I might have been argued to have broken the law by not telling them of a change of address but on the other a strange area of reality seemed to take hold of me: I thought somebody knew *what the situation was*.

I sort of wanted them to watch me. My having to return it seemed due to the mistake my GP had made – by prescribing an antidepressant when I was not depressed, but had schizophrenia. I have since learnt that many people who suffer mental illness do not tell the DVLA. After receiving the DVLA letter banning me from driving, there was an unusual incident, which put the wind up me a bit. This involved illegal use of my car horn by one of my passengers outside another Worcester nightclub late one night. It made me a little paranoid as to his real motive for doing so, the incident providing a policeman an excuse to admonish me. MI5 were just making fun of me in response to my bizarre representation on behalf of Prince Charles's dog. Perhaps the feeling was mutual. I felt rather hard-done-by as I sent it off.

Other than those two strange little facets of my time in Worcestershire everything seemed just terribly normal. Even *The X Files*, the American television drama about aliens and the paranormal, was just a television programme, which did not seem in any way appropriate to my situation. This now makes me laugh and ask: how deluded can one get? If anyone was in the land of *The X Files* it was, in view of the work I was doing, me – and I was no David Icke.[61] At least I had come out of my breakdown with some sense of sanity – though I still had the sneaking suspicion that the disappearance of Prince Charles's dog had been a Masonic ruse to poke fun at me. Once again it seemed that any truth in the story of its disappearance would be a scintilla, the same as many other newspaper stories, this scintilla providing the necessary degree of truth to make it fit for publication.

I was keenly aware – though, amazingly, I had not actually been told – that I had been diagnosed as suffering from schizophrenia. I had been led to believe I now had it for life, though I noted there to be no apparent signs of being persecuted. However I did notice, at lunch, the bottles of Ribena spring water, which announced FREE in large letters on the bottle when they were not actually free, the result being I paid for something without realising I had. The fact that I can recall such a trivial event, and more importantly that it merely annoyed me a little rather than incite within me some fantastic and farfetched delusion, well illustrates how balanced my mind was at the time.

So, I'd had a serious nervous breakdown and yet here I was working with (alongside Christopher) some chaps making a visit from an extremely secretive Government department – the very ones who I imagined had obtained my KGB file. But mental illness can be found everywhere in society especially in such pressurised jobs as the Security Service. In the case of one senior naval officer I later read about who worked on the Royal Yacht – his schizophrenia, similar to mine, ended his career.

But I knew I was no threat to security. After all, what was I to do, phone them up and say I was a threat to the nation when I knew I was not? Hardly. Anyway my employer did report my condition to the Ministry of Defence Vetting Agency.

Because of the extreme sensitivity of my work I wondered if my telephone calls were being monitored. Other than that quite natural paranoia, I felt relaxed and at ease in Malvern.

Spring came and, before I left for Hampshire, it did not go unnoticed that next to the house in which I had been staying there was a sign pointing east saying "Godolphin" – the name of the stables belonging to the fabulously wealthy Sheikh Mohammed bin Rashid Al Maktoum, one of the leading lights in the sport of kings, horse racing. To my mind the sport of kings had become the search for the future King's dog and the name Godolphin was just enough to remind me of the madness of the previous summer and my trips around these isles listening to that wonderful album by Pele: *The Sport of Kings*.

Part IX

Stuck in a Parallel Universe

Chapter Twenty-Six

Turn To Red

Once I arrived in Hampshire I found myself living in the house of a jockey and his wife. I suspect they never realised that by the time they gave me my notice, as they were moving, I was on the verge of severe illness again. It was now almost one year since I was first sectioned. This second breakdown was again caused, or at least exacerbated, by an antidepressant, in this case Seroxat. Logic dictates that if you take antidepressants when well they can send you into a mania. At the time I did not in any way foresee what was about to happen.

The company security controller telephoned me at work and gently admonished me for the challenge I had made down at Wilton nearly a year earlier. He told me that "security" had called and wanted to know what pieces of work I had been involved in, before my strange appearance down at Wilton. If the daylight meteor shower announced by the BBC that day was not enough proof that MI5 (or the British Sumo Rabbit Psychic Wrestling Society) knew what I had done, then this was. Or perhaps the shower had nothing to do with me or never even happened.

That night when I got home I noticed a brand new saloon car parked outside my house. It was unusual in that on its rear it had the insignia "People's", which I had not seen before. The following night, when I came home, the saloon had gone (not to be seen again). In its place, its perfect paintwork covered in droplets of rain, was a brand new Aston Martin. It was "L reg" and the other letters were HRO. Now I thought the L meant "learn". I imagined these cars were parked there by MI5 and were meant to excite me by suggesting I was a People's Hero. I tried unsuccessfully to disbelieve this and shook my head in amazement. I decided to set to the task of bearing out this prescience, even if it had just been a spurious piece of background information. Next morning that car had gone too.

I had decided to do something, which had been on my mind since the summer of the previous year – decorate my flat. Then, during those strange months, my flat had become a place that terrified me. There had been an occasion during that mad and wonderful summer when I was of the extraordinarily deluded belief that, when I arrived at the flat, it would have all been redecorated for me. Let alone my beliefs I was a dog. Now more surreal thoughts would come to my head. I found myself imagining, bizarrely, that when I got to the flat it would have been filled with anything which amused the person who put it there enough to have actually done so. I imagined a rich sheikh, perhaps Sheikh Mohammed, playing ridiculous games with me, having heard about my joke over Prince Charles's dog. He could have filled it with anything from concrete to the ceiling, like Rachel Whiteread did[62], to something else even more bizarre. One such possibility was thousands of inflatable black pigs (with actual anal orifices), which my friend Robert Wickham had been successfully advertising in *Private Eye*.

I had not descended into severe illness again yet. However it was just around the corner, when I was invited to The Queen Elizabeth Hall where Caroline was launching her new album. After the performance, which I enjoyed with her brother, an old friend from Royal Greenwich Observatory days, we went backstage for the reception. This was rather more lavish than the coffee and biscuits you sometimes got from the Ministry of Defence, if you were lucky. Amongst the many messages and flowers was something that was more like part of the Royal Horticultural Society Garden at Wisley, though it was in a basket and came from Mr Vangelis. As I carried the basket of flowers to Caroline's car, I began to imagine, not just the largest basket of flowers I had ever seen, which it was, but also a veritable garden of delight. In this garden, by a pond and fountain, I was amazed to see a girl I had not thought of since I was 10, when I fell in love with her. It was Hatty from *Tom's Midnight Garden* just as I had imagined her 25 years earlier. She was wearing a long white dress and enjoying the swing attached to the bow of the tree. As Hatty swung merrily away she was enjoying the beautiful view over the river and the fields beyond. I felt 10 again.

My new jockey friend was happy to earn a few bob finishing off the decoration of my flat. So my flat *did* end up being decorated by someone else. As I would learn, there could often be shown to be some truth in any delusion. And perhaps it was around this time I began to hear, in my head, the descending electronic note at the very beginning of the *Dr Who* theme music – it seemed quite comical, though what was about to happen was not too funny.

Not having to decorate my flat left me free to begin to behave peculiarly again, because of the ultimately dangerous combination of drugs and alcohol I was taking – or possibly because of the antidepressant alone, which I should have stopped taking at least six months earlier.

The first sign of impending illness, if it was a sign, could have been my decision to have a St George's flag dyed into my hair for the forthcoming Rugby World Cup. I even got to speak to a hairdresser at Vidal Sassoon. I did not, however, get to have my hair dyed.

I remember beginning to think that something was going on again and taking train journeys to no place in particular around west London. I felt myself becoming hypnotised by what appeared to be a threatening amount of barbed wire fence by the rail-side of the west London rail network. I found my head going from side to side, like a nodding dog in the rear window of a car. As I did so I thought, quite mantra-like, the words audible in my head: "Concentration camp, concentration camp..." over and over again without it seemed much choice in the matter.

I now recall standing on the platform at Richmond again, not having any idea of where I was going or what I was doing. A paper bag from a nearby pâtisserie had been left on the bench. It contained a hot coffee and a Danish pastry. Somehow it was just too easy to believe it had been put there for me. So I picked up the bag and went over to the opposite platform by way of leaving the scene.

On the opposite platform, I began to eat the pastry and noticed a young girl looking at the bench in puzzlement though not quite putting her hands on her hips for fear of embarrassment. She turned around and was now facing straight at me on the opposite platform. She was not unattractive by any means. I took another bite of her pastry and sipped her coffee. Of course, it might not have occurred to her that I was eating her own pastry, and nor did she look as though she thought I was. Surely she could not have believed that.

My condition deteriorated dramatically, a wild and deluded mania descending upon me, apparently fuelled by the antidepressants. I found myself at Paddington Station. I got on the Birmingham train – calling at Banbury – and now it looked like I really was going on the Banbury trip. In my delirious state of mind, I hoped so much I was in with a chance of seeing a fine lady, either Diana or Amanda, upon the white horse. At the same time it seemed I could escape from the lunacy of that possibility by going there, and proving to myself that it was complete fantasy. Either way, I could not seem to help aiming in that direction, the train going through Reading, where an exceptionally sad and obsessive desire drew me back to be near Amanda.

For no apparent reason the guard lent over and looked at the coupling hook. I could only think he had been told to, and that it was to remind me of the passenger who had arrived at Midland Road Station, Bedford, back in the '80s, impaled on the coupling hook of a Class 22 Deltic locomotive. This had the result that several people on the platform fainted. The person impaled had been an MI5 officer who had seriously betrayed someone and paid the price, the bodies of Security Service officers often, if not always, being disposed of in bizarre manners following their deaths, as I suggested earlier. Later on I would dream of my own obsequies; a dream I would be rather proud of.

It was not just civilians though who had such weird obsequies. Whole rows of Army officers' bodies had been decapitated on the railway line near Her Majesty's Land Forces HQ Wilton. I had destroyed their conspiracy at the last minute back in June the previous year. This I had done simply by driving through that gate, the conspiracy having been against my free will. However, there was no evidence that my presence at that gate, and what I said, had been down to anybody but me. The operation had been perfect.

Moments before the train pulled out of the station, I suddenly sensed mortal danger if I remained on it. This is now terrifyingly apposite, as 38 people were to be killed on this stretch of line over the next few years. I got off with seconds to spare before the train pulled out, leaving my treasured Raleigh Kalahari mountain bike on it. It hardly mattered, it was replaceable, my life was not. I had foreseen a train crash at Paddington when at Fairmile and now it seemed I was again. I felt utterly tortured as my illness made me think there would be an accident simply because I thought of it. I wonder how many of the soothsayers down the ages had been suffering a similar illness – an illness that seemed to come with some sort of enhanced perception. Either that or General "Crush" was putting thoughts into my head again.

A fearsome Army Intelligence Corps officer ordered me, over my MTRUTH, to walk to Bedford. On this occasion, I was determined to carry out the order. I left Paddington, and walked right across London until I got to the A1, it now being very late. I walked all night up the A1. As I walked, there appeared a travelling party with me, which I was hallucinating vividly as I walked. In particular John Lennon was next to me sitting at his white piano. Now, it seemed, my intelligence gained in Fairmile Hospital 14 years after his reported death was itself premature. Perhaps what I had seen was yet to happen in this meticulously planned conspiracy. But he was still the mere husk of his former self I had seen then, as though the years in his cult of fake deaths had completely taken his mind away. He was a raving madman, so hellbent on his ludicrously ill-conceived plan to pretend to be dead that he was scarcely a human being anymore, and could hardly play the piano. He was, prematurely, a very old man. So this was MI5's greatest and most terrible secret: a file marked "L Zero", gleaned from the Soviet branch of MI6. Which L was Prince Charles's dog I wondered, and which L was I? My paranoid mind also demanded to know what Peter Gabriel's Real World really was. It had taken on the air of the sinister. When would I read my own obituary in the paper? When would my own death be faked?

Morning arrived. It was a very sick morning indeed. Jean-Paul Sartre would have loved it. By the road was a gymkhana field into which I walked, climbing over the gate. In front of the first fence was a sign with "10" on it. It seemed I was being awarded that score. I walked past and looked back and on the other side it said "9". Something had made me look around and the effect was typical: it seemed a point had been taken away, and no doubt more would be, until I was driven over a cliff edge. The apparent deduction of one point seemed to be a punishment in this gruelling SAS/SBS psychological warfare experiment. But if you think something it does have a habit of actually becoming what you think.

I had now been walking for 12 hours. I saw the wind waving in some long grass. The grass even seemed to speak to me – it told me a joke I had never heard: DNA stood for National Dyslexic Association. It was like an LSD trip – not that I had ever had one. It was almost synaesthetic[63].

I was wandering around, quite exhausted. The morning rush hour traffic on the A1 seemed to be the absolute essence of an unspeakable evil. The human race had descended into a mass of sick puppets all controlled by the radio through the conspiracy I had uncovered, with me at its centre.

Once again, the only way the human race could possibly survive, and even then it was just a long shot, was for the Human Infection Control Unit to arrange the biggest pile-up in history, at either end of the A1. Everyone using it during the rush hour was to be "taken out". All the puppets would drive straight into the pile-up without so much as putting their feet on the brakes, so far gone were they. The Army Air Corps would fly up and down, finishing off any survivors. I use the word "survivor" with some degree of reservation. Zombie would have been a compliment, such pitiful specimens of reality were these disgusting things. They had all been brainwashed by appalling musical compositions. Pop music was evil at this moment. The atmosphere was utterly dead and everything had the essential quality of nausea. It was more than Sartre ever dreamt of. Even the little-used footbridge over the road oozed death and vomit. It was a cull.

I pressed on, and at some point found myself lying down in the middle of a little-used country road, quite high up.

Most peculiarly, my legs looked like the wall either inside a pyramid or on the toilet wall in *The Tenant*. Etched patterns seemed to have appeared all over them. But how could this be? I had not lost consciousness, although I had been walking all night. I deduced that the only way this could have been done was by some very high-powered laser beam. This was so intense that it had instantaneously burnt the hieroglyphs or cuneiform, whatever it was, all over my legs as I was moving – a sort of expensive military sun tan. It might have come from overhead, possibly from a satellite, whilst I had lain in the road. But perhaps it was just some effect of exhaustion/dehydration, or perhaps I hallucinated it.

If I lay there long enough, Peter Gabriel, not really dead after all, at least not yet, and my friend Caroline (who had worked with him[64]) would soon arrive. At least my fear of Peter Gabriel had gone. But perhaps I was wrong not to fear him – perhaps John Lennon really had based his cult HQ at Real World Studios. Still, I was not afraid. I believed they were on their way right at that moment. In my head they were talking to me. They were in an Austin A35 pickup[65]. In the distance on the horizon I could see the NatWest Bank Tower. Soon, I hoped, they would arrive. But, of course, they didn't.

I managed to get myself up and push on. Walking along the A1 a police car stopped and the puzzled cop told me I could not walk on the hard shoulder. So somewhere I descended to another road. The day wore on and I was becoming severely dehydrated and had neither eaten nor drunk anything for as much as 24 hours. I had to get to the clay pits at the Stewartby brickworks. I had to see the Transport Corps dumping the millions of bodies from the cull into them. I had to get there by sunset. I wanted to see the full horror with my own eyes, only the Special Forces being aware of the absolute necessity of this – and I was one of them. The mentality of the population at large had descended irreversibly and this was the last horrible hope. The truth of the matter was that at about this time eight thousand victims of genocide were being buried in mass graves at Srebrenica, in Bosnia, just 24 hours' drive away.

It was hot and all day I pressed on. Again I was on a motorway. By now I was becoming completely disoriented. I began to believe that I was now on the M1, not the A1, and was near the Vauxhall factory in Luton. I found myself standing next to a strange tree, which appeared to have had another species of tree grafted onto it. I had been brought here by my MTRUTH. As evening came I found myself in Hatfield.

In Hatfield there seemed to be no escape and I found myself just walking around and around in circles, desperately trying to find my way to the clay pits which somehow seemed much closer than the 30 or so miles away they actually were. Through my MTRUTH, I could see the vicious Army Intelligence Corps officer whose order I was carrying out, slamming doors in my face and walking off. I had now penetrated into the inner sanctum of the Defence Intelligence Service, a place yet more secure than the one in which I had been down at Malvern – and that is saying something. My presence here was a severe embarrassment not to be tolerated. As a matter of honour he was trying to drive me to suicide. That was his sole purpose, and mine was to resist. Any suggestion of existential value in our actions had disappeared. We were just two war machines in a battle to the death. But if only I could keep going he would be the one to take his own life as a matter of honour – not I. And all the time I could hear the unmistakeable voice of Prince Charles, a Rear Admiral in the Royal Navy, caught between the KGB, Soviet Naval Intelligence, the IRA and the deep blue sea, saying "Truly grateful." I believed he was and that kept me going. Thanks Prince Charles!

I tried to go into a pub but its doors were shut even though it was full of people. I went to another and the same happened. This all seemed terribly satanic: a great lockout[66] in fact. I thought of the old school motto taken from Isaiah to keep me going.

Isaiah 40 vs. 29-31

He gives strength to the weary
And increases the power of the weak.
Even youths grow tired and weary and young men stumble and fall,
But those who hope in the Lord will renew their strength.
They will soar on wings like eagles.
They will run and not grow weary.
They will walk and not be faint.

I crossed myself and finally I found the Rotary Club into which I walked quite exhausted. I went up to the bar and asked for a pint of water. It was served with plenty of ice and I drank it in one go. It was heavy water with heavy ice. It tasted better than it should be possible for water to taste. It was silver. It was gold. It tasted like I was drinking the purest elixir.[67] It was expensive stuff. I had another pint and asked for a taxi to be ordered. Somehow I had just pulled out of the dive by disobeying my own orders. Life had just flowed back into me and I felt it flow back with the heavy water.

Chapter Twenty-Seven

Dead Man's Hill

The taxi arrived and now I was off, at least in the direction of the pits. However I had not focused on the more local reality of what I had been wildly day-maring about. This was the reality of the exact number of murder victims actually buried there, courtesy of Shanks and McEwan, the operators of this landfill site. Their green trains pass out of London every day to deposit everything from an empty Fairy Liquid bottle to part, or all, of a murder victim's body. For sure, now in a lucid state as I write, I feel there would have been examples of those, undiscovered. But now *every train* was full of the rotting and lifeless bodies of the dead taken from their cars by the Human Infection Control Unit in the cull on the A1 the previous day. It was a mixture of *Quatermass*, *Dr Who* and Auschwitz right in the middle of Bedfordshire. If this wasn't *Sumo Rabbit and His Inescapable Trap of Doom*-country I don't know what is. Let no one ever accuse me of being a *Quatermass* or *Dr Who* denier. What made my paranoia worse was that my father had coincidentally decorated the front of our house in the colours of Shanks and McEwan's livery, making me feel it was full of rubbish. But I knew this was just an Army Intelligence Corps dirty trick to make me think I was rubbish. They were just getting at me.

Somehow I felt I would be in great danger if I fell asleep. The danger seemed as acute as it would have been if I had been the one at the wheel. I was in danger of being culled myself. The car was just too dangerously comfortable and the urge to drop off was simply irresistible. Somehow the extreme state of mind I was in, caused by the Seroxat, the lack of food, water and sleep and the general exhaustion was such that I felt, once again, like I was indeed on a small dose of heroin. I had never imagined it was possible to feel like this.

Soon we arrived in Bedford and I asked the driver to wait while I went to get the fare. Getting out of the car, I briefly looked up at the sky in the south, it being late evening and not yet dark. Terrified at what I saw, I shuddered, looking away at once as the clouds, still clearly lit by the setting sun, had formed themselves into a scene from *Hey Diddle Diddle*. In an instant I saw the little dog laugh, and the clouds, which had formed the image of the dog, had a terrifyingly apocalyptic air to them. My free will was not in too good a shape. Whatever mechanism led me to see this, it was why I was too frightened to go back out to pay the driver and thank him. The little dog was laughing, the cow was jumping and if I had studied the sky again in more detail perhaps I could have flicked through *A Child's Garden of Verses* too. But I was just too terrified to do that. What a terrifying world: one in which that book is the source of fear.

I now conceived the most horrible thought imaginable. I had taken the wrong branch in some extremely rare and exotic bifurcation[68] in the space-time continuum. I had gone through some terrifyingly profound trap of doom in time, only understood by Professor Stephen Hawking at the Department of Mathematics and Theoretical Physics, Cambridge University. This had been caused (in the *Dr Who* frame of mind I had slipped into) by Absolute Secret experiments involving wormholes conducted, with unforeseen side effects, at the DISC. But really the bifurcation was where I went into this Seroxat hypermania and fell prey, once more, to my deluded belief I had been on the operating table to have my MTRUTH fitted.

I sent out Tom and his girlfriend to pay the taxi driver. I told Tom what I had done. Now I began making strange remarks about how there was barbed wire everywhere and my brother, or anti-brother, if you prefer, just shook his head as though to say "No Clive, there's no barbed wire – what are you on?"

"No, you don't understand, I've seen it, it's everywhere!"

But what I was saying made perfect sense to me and was based on as much truth as I dared tell him because I feared the rest would just make him call an ambulance. He was not in fact my real brother but, indeed, his doppelganger in this horrible parallel universe in which I was now frighteningly trapped. With indifferent despair at my state of mind, he now left, and later I went to have a shower.

In the shower I looked at the face flannels, which were held in three rubber sockets. But they were no longer what anyone else would see. They were three young boys crying their eyes out right in front of me, the flannels just becoming large handkerchiefs in their eyes. They were a message leaked from the real world, where I had been tragically killed, and these were my three brothers mourning me. Above the flannels was a bottle of Boots horse chestnut shampoo. I recalled a photo I had once taken of Amanda with her sister at Robert's house. In the picture they were looking at a photo album and on the page they were looking at was, just visible in the photo, a chestnut horse. There now seemed an all-powerful connection between the horse chestnut shampoo and the chestnut horse. The connection was so powerful that Boots had made the horse chestnut shampoo and I, together with the photo, was the reason. The strength of this delusion of grandeur was overwhelming.

I went to bed and was only asleep for a short while when I awoke with Amanda's voice shouting at me to come and rescue her. She was sitting sideways on my chest going up and down trying to wake me up, and I could actually feel her weight on my chest so powerful was the hallucination. If I was not haunted by Amanda at that moment I do not know what haunting is. How many hauntings were really just schizophrenia? This was a truly impressive experience – I even felt the bed going up and down underneath me, all apparently courtesy of SmithKline Beecham, who makes the antidepressant Seroxat, on which I was now tripping.

Hardly properly conscious, I got up and dressed and went downstairs, it being well past midnight and everyone in bed. There was still just a faint chance that I could return to the real world. But the chance seemed extremely slim and relied on getting back to the place where I had left it, in Hatfield. Even then, my only chance of getting back depended on some very unlikely event taking place at the exact geographical location where I had entered this parallel universe. There I had to find this strange bifurcation, wormhole, or gateway through which to pass. If I did not make it there, at the precise re-entry window, then I had no chance whatsoever. This was real. I was terrified. Others, for sure, had gone in here and never got back – I had to believe I was the first who would get out.

The delusion was powerful in the extreme. But the real truth was that the place I could get back into the real world was anywhere I could get to and still be alive when I got there, having negotiated this fearsome antidepressant trip, and then cold turkey, on my arrival. If I *had* gone down a wormhole I would not put it past the Special Forces to have gone in there too to have a look around. Furthermore, if there was a wormhole anywhere, in my clinical delusion I strongly suspected there to be one within the vicinity of the DISC.

I got my mountain bike and switched the lights on. The gear cable was loose; so it was not possible to change out of the lowest gear. This sent me into a most peculiar train of thought that the tampering was a trick played by a mathematician, the gears in some way driving the universe. Thinking in a manner as deluded as that, I made no attempt to mend the gear change mechanism and cycled off down the road, pedalling furiously in bursts. It almost seemed my pedalling was driving the weather – like Sir Steve Redgrave might do with a rowing ergometer. But to do that I think I'd have needed a somewhat lower gear still.

Along the Embankment the stench came over me. It was as though I had been sprayed with some ghastly odour. But if the truth were told I was not entirely unfamiliar with the subject of hallucinatory smell and taste. I clearly recalled a brief period during my sixth form days. Still nursing the morbid fear I'd had of the art department from the first day I arrived at the school, and afraid to go near it, I was walking down the corridor. Past the turning into the said department, I noticed some kind of pungent smell or taste in my nasal area. This was brought on by what I believed to be mild depression. It would have been around the time when Ian Curtis wrote *Love Will Tear Us Apart* with the line "There's a taste in my mouth, as desperation takes hold."

I was in a very thick cloud of this stuff now. The streets were all rotten to the core in this disgusting parallel universe and 'people' were retching heavily and uncontrollably as I cycled past them, such was the stench of decay and misery. Bodies, and pieces of bodies, all with putrescent flesh hanging off, lay convulsing about the road whilst others engaged in horrific acts in this Boschian nightmare.[69]

I had to find a route to Hatfield. I decided on the A6 and after not long I was heading straight for Dead Man's Hill, scene of the A6 murder. As I ascended the hill I saw a huge pair of hands in the sky rubbing themselves together like they were making something of it. I thought they were the hands of my old tutor. He was thinking he could make some money out of this experience. I hardly dared look and now sped down the long hill to the roundabout.

Chapter Twenty-Eight

Wilderness

I now took the left turning heading for Hatfield, via Hitchin, still pedalling furiously in bursts. I was descending into the sort of exhausted delirium from which I had partly recovered when I had come into this stinking, horrible parody of reality.

My thoughts naturally turned to The Bear, which, when I had gone there with Amanda 11 years earlier, had many hats attached to the ceiling. I had to get to Hatfield, to the time portal or gateway back to the real world and Amanda. There were only a few places I had been with her and I remembered everyone. She lit up the room the moment she walked in. Talk about the bloke who thought his wife was a hat![70]

Soon I was past Hitchin, and somehow now began to lose my conviction of the need to get to Hatfield. I was distracted by a number of things other than my deep exhaustion. I was on a long straight road somewhere south of Hitchin and started to think I should go to St. Albans instead, but I do not remember why, other than that there was a cathedral there, and I was in deep trouble. I needed God's help to get out of this. Then, from my left, I heard the terrified cries on the original tape from the Saddleworth Moor atrocity where Myra Hindley and Ian Bradey brutally tortured and murdered a number of children, recording their anguished voices. The Special Air Service was playing this tape out on a ghetto blaster, though how the hell they had got into this parallel universe I did not know. However I was keenly aware that they had a base a few miles back down the road in the real world at the DISC. At least I believed they were the real SAS, unlike these other anti-people I had met in here.

I could hear the voice of a young desperately frightened girl crying out "Mummy, where's my mummy?!" I knew I must not look or stop, as it was certainly an evil little trick to stop me reaching the gateway back to the real world.

They were making it as hard as possible for me. However horrible a thing was going on where the cry was coming from, I had a duty to ignore it. If I stopped now some kind of terrible instability would result in this area near the gateway. I say 'gateway' but I did not know exactly what it really was. I only knew that it existed, and without it, I would never see my real brothers or anyone else I knew again. My illness had driven me to believe completely and utterly that I was indeed in a parallel universe, a grotesque and evil parody of the real one at that.

Again I could see bodies lying everywhere both beside and in the road just inside this terrible parallel universe only a few miles from the portal back to the real world. I could not look because I believed they were alive. Even if they were dead, I did not want to find out. The bodies I was now seeing, lying in, on and around the road, were indeed every member of that Special Air Service Regiment that could be mustered at the gateway, pretending to be dead. They were doing this in deference to my persistence, this vain explanation leading to the 'actual' one which lay in the realms of a high-level meeting between the military top brass and Professor Hawking.

Now, as a little light came into the sky, a large disc-shaped gap appeared in the cloud over in the direction of St. Albans. It was so perfectly formed that I could only think that some kind of air-bomb had blown a hole in the clouds. It looked just like a very good flying saucer as the new dawn faded in. Perhaps I had now made it back from the actual Golgotha, where there was no real life. But I was still not out of the woods. Somehow, I now found myself cycling in completely the opposite direction back towards Hitchin, although I have no recollection of either stopping or turning around. I now believed the SAS had somehow done this to me. I could only imagine that in my exhausted state I did not notice them come up behind and somehow turn me round. Then again, perhaps I only found myself cycling back to Hitchin in my dreams. But that was where I found myself the next morning lying asleep on the grass, my bike by my side.

I woke up there like a tired Rupert Bear who had been deposited with his bike by some sort of whirlwind. Perhaps I'd had a couple of hours sleep and I was mystified as to how I came to be in that place as my calculated position was some 10 or 20 miles to the south. I shall go back one day to see if I can find that patch of grass where I found myself that overcast morning, as I am not even convinced it was Hitchin. All I know was that I was not far from a railway station where, standing on the platform, I perceived there to be a health risk from the overhead wires. They seemed to be causing hysteresis in my head. Then I noticed the wires on the fence, which did not seem to have any purpose other than to remind me of the art on sale in Bayswater Road, by Hyde Park, the wires inviting me to hang pictures from them. These wires told me art was all there was to fight this deadly menace. It did indeed seem there were concentration camps everywhere, though I could not see any. I remembered speaking to 'Tom', and still believed he was nothing more or less than what I had thought – his doppelganger. Perhaps he was! Perhaps the drug really had given me access to a parallel hell of a universe!

I took a train to another station. I was still in a deeply paranoid state, though now believed that I was at least back in the real world. At some point I remember hiding in the healthy growth at the bottom of a horse chestnut tree, some children playing nearby. I must have looked particularly eccentric.

I took another train, though I forget why, even if I had a reason. I recall I got off at a station called Meldreth. I walked. I was now entering cold turkey. I had not had an antidepressant for over 48 hours. I was withdrawing from the drug and beginning to leave the trip. The reason I walked was because there were sores on my backside from the cycling, which made it just too painful to ride. But I had sores on my feet too from all the walking I had done in the previous two days. Slowly I trudged along, miles and miles of delirious pain gradually disappearing behind me with no reason for it, other than antidepressant cold turkey and the other effects of the preceding trip.

At some point I passed an experimental crop station, the plants growing there looking as though they might start walking out into the road, enveloping the traffic, and strangling the drivers. It felt like John Wyndham's *The Day of the Triffids*.

I had left the unreal world of that parallel universe behind. In that world, to say the skull ruled, would have brought cackling laughter from your own anti-mother. Here the anti-Queen herself ruled. I wish you could know how it was. No words can fully explain how desperately trapped I had felt. If you were left behind on the moon at least you would know you were still in the same universe. I believed my own anti-brother really existed in that world. In that anti-universe I had looked at the moon, something which, seemed more dangerous than looking at the sun in the real world.

The immediate problem was that my mind, or what was left of it, was taking me towards some of the former doorsteps of those who somehow seemed opposed to me: the Cambridge spy ring. I was coming towards some of Kim Philby's old haunts like an unguided missile, both physically and mentally.

My feet were extremely sore and I was in poor condition like a stray unfed and unwatered dog. The outskirts of Cambridge gradually came into sight and I possibly walked past the home of Jeffrey Archer who may have known I had, but perhaps *he* did not like being interrupted when writing, so left me to get on with it. As central Cambridge approached, a torturous pain descended on my head. I was having the pain deliberately inflicted upon me by the old guard of the Special Intelligence Service, more and more of whom were being arrested, including Mr Archer of course. They were all being shot and driven to suicide, the longer I kept going. It seemed I was thwarting their conspiratorial plans. I passed a boarded-up pub and found myself thinking the ring had drunk there many years ago. I shuddered. The fear and disgust were far worse than deeply profound.

My teeth were gritted and I could do nothing but growl under my breath to fight the pain, both in my body from the sores and in my head from the withdrawal. The pain was being somehow beamed straight into my mind from some ghastly mind-rack with cattle prods: my MTRUTH. I felt similar to the way I had felt back at Fairmile Hospital on the first occasion I was taken off antidepressants I did not need. This time I had done it myself. I had become so deranged I simply got separated from them.

Finally I reached central Cambridge – in a very poorly condition. If a dog warden van had pulled up driven by a man with a grab I would probably have been happy to try and get in the back. Instead I tried to book into a hotel though my credit card was over its limit. I had begun to have deluded thoughts that the Special Intelligence Service would put money into my account but of course this was just wishful thinking and, as I now imagined, just what they wanted me to think. I would need to make better use of my MTRUTH than this before that possibility arose. Even though I was in such a bad condition I managed to make some vain excuse for my card not being accepted as one does in such salubrious environments facing severe embarrassment. Outside I noticed the number plate of a car going by was M15 TAB and I felt this meant I could go back into the hotel and my card would now be accepted – but I did not have the bottle to try.

Instead I parked my bike and went into Pizzaland, sat down and ordered a pizza and a beer. I must have drunk about half a gallon of water. The beer and the pizza arrived. I tasted the beer. There was a horrible stench coming from it and I realised that a large moth had taken over my body like in the film *The Fly*.[71] I knew moths have an extremely powerful sense of smell and now, again, I was having olfactory hallucinations – hence I now felt like the scientist in that film. The smell was so appalling I could have vomited. Porton Down had released something from the drugs cabinet in my wrist. This enabled me, like the moth, to smell the stench of something in the Holsten Pils. I could certainly smell something, but in reality there was nothing there. Nobody in the restaurant even batted an eyelid at this huge insect, me, sitting at one of the tables.

I heard the Queen's voice in my head, or via my MTRUTH, ordering me to "Get up and leave this place immediately!" So I did without standing on ceremony, or paying. I abandoned my second bike, though it seemed the credit card company were repossessing it, next to the restaurant. Now I made for the railway station.

Soon I arrived at King's Cross. I headed across London but, for whatever reason, did not go to my flat. Instead I went to Richmond and attempted to book into a hotel. But again I experienced the stench of another hallucinatory odour, which told me to leave the hotel without delay, as the Queen had done at the restaurant. I walked towards Barnes and my flat, reaching the Common in the early hours. I did not have my key so, unless I woke someone up, I could not get in. Then I remembered that only the estate agent had a spare key. So I lay down in the dry leaves on the Common and, making myself as warm as possible, tried to get some sleep. The night was warm and for a while I listened to its noises. Then I heard a rustle and standing right there, just a few feet away, was a muntjac deer staring towards me. I went to sleep as it turned and disappeared into the undergrowth.

I awoke just as it was getting light and got up to walk into Barnes. Here I sat on the bench by the bus stop outside the pub a hundred yards from my flat. A policeman asked me what I was doing up at that time of the morning. Perhaps it was not the time of the morning but the fact that I had a skinhead haircut that interested him, or maybe there was *some other explanation*. This was not the only time I was stopped by the police whilst I had a skinhead. It seemed my lack of hair may have resulted in them picking on me, but actually it only happened twice. I asked him the time and told him I was locked out.

I waited for a few hours until about 7.30 and then rang Steve and Helen's doorbell at the flat below mine. Because of Capgras syndrome I had thought that Steve looked like Shane Warne, the Australian spin bowler, more than he probably does, which caused me a little amusement, and I was not too paranoid about it. They let me go to sleep on their couch whilst I waited for the estate agency to open. When I awoke, they had left for work, and I made myself a beautiful cup of coffee, feeling much better as the antidepressant cold turkey seemed to have worn off considerably, now it being several days since I'd had one. My crotch was really sore from all the walking and the rubbing of my underpants, which had actually drawn blood, I had walked so far. I borrowed a pair of Steve's underpants and felt much more comfortable.

I recovered sufficiently well after gaining entry to my flat that, a few days later, I was able to get back to work in Hook where, upon my arrival, I was told that my company had pulled out of the contract. The contract was with the Canadian Army to produce a messaging system and I was working on the BFSM (Battlefield Frequency Spectrum Management System) the purpose of which was to optimise the use of their radio systems. The cancellation of the contract led me to suspect some sort of very high-level security breach to which I was party, and nobody else. It was as though I had known this was going to happen all along. It all seemed so incredibly conspiratorial. I was still ill. But however ill I actually was there would be those who would say there was some level of truth in my feeling – how much would depend on who you asked, this I feel being commonly the case in schizophrenia. The truth here was that my team had not been consulted. In schizophrenia the remotest or most innocuous element of truth becomes an overbearing delusion.

I was told I had an interview at Wavendon near Milton Keynes, and this I duly attended. The interviewer was incredibly uninspiring and I almost went to sleep. One thing happened though and that was when he asked me what the pins stuck in the map of the United Kingdom might mean. He did not tell me and all this did was excite my most paranoid thoughts. Years later I was to imagine he did not know himself and had been told to ask me to test my intelligence. I was also to imagine they were IRA and Loyalist informants' safehouses. They were probably just customers.

After the interview instead of either going back to my flat in London or to Bedford I found myself standing on the platform at Bletchley waiting for the train to Wolverhampton, which I subsequently visited for precisely no reason other than impulse. The only explanation was that I was still a little ill. But my second and last hypermanic drugs trip was over.

Part X

A Tin of Cat Food is Nicked

Chapter Twenty-Nine

Love Cats

At this point in my story, not for the first time, there is some uncertainty as to the actual order of events. The truth of the matter is that at the time I had become irrevocably confused because of my illness. You could say that, in many ways, this confusion would remain so until after the end of this story, until I wrote the postface in fact. The illness had been brought on, once again, by taking antidepressants I no longer needed. For the second time in this story petrol had been poured on a fire to put it out.

There was a tight deadline to meet in my new post. I then remembered the remotely tenuous truth that I was technically AWOL from the Royal Marines Commando Training Centre at Lympstone, Devon. Like a lot of people who go round claiming, incorrectly, to have some affiliation with an elite military unit, my failure to turn up at Lympstone gave me something to live up to in a way. Not that I was going around claiming to be in the Special Boat Service or anything; but it did provide me with a delusional tool to face up to the problems I was to have, the tool being the aspiration to their mindset. If there was going to be anything special or elite about me I was doing it my own way.

But to return to that tight deadline in my new post, I had to work all night to meet it. Whether it was that night or an earlier one, as my illness continued, my imagination took over and with some time to spare I began writing down whatever came into my head.

This was the first occasion when I'd had a funny feeling about the computer network I was using. Somehow, as soon as I began writing, rather than make turgid entries in a software traceability table, the conviction came upon me that somebody was watching what I was writing – via my terminal. On one occasion I had left the building for a break, and noticed a good-looking man wearing sunglasses enter it. I suspected he was spying on what I had written on my computer over the network. It did not occur to me that he might be quite innocent of this charge and was merely an ordinary employee. But I thought he looked American, and was from the CIA. Perhaps he was one of the ones said to have been expelled in the news over a passport issue. Perhaps the whole of that was just to get me thinking.

This was to be the last time I came to work for some while. When everyone arrived the next morning, I was thanked for getting the work done on time, and told to take a break, which I now did.

I took approximately two weeks' holiday. On the first evening of that holiday, I was walking down the street in Church Road, Barnes, when a young kitten ran into the road.

Two women standing there shouted that the cat might be run over if nothing was done. Being fond of cats, and wanting to avoid an accident, I said I would be happy to take care of the cat. I duly picked it up to take back to my flat. My fears about the flat since the peculiar apparition of Pepper at the top of the holly bush, with the helicopter hovering high above, had now substantially subsided.

So I took the cat into the supermarket to buy it some food. The person serving had been severely disabled by the drug Thalidomide giving events an air of unreality. She told me that pets were not allowed in the shop. At this point, having heard this, two horrible girls now began unpleasantly accusing me of having stolen their kitten. Because they were so unpleasant about it I had no trouble deciding that they were not fit to keep the animal. I left the shop to take the kitten back to my flat and there I now left it. Then I went out again to get the young puss some sustenance, a tin of Sheba. It must have been the hoopoe in Agadez that did it, though perhaps I was not quite ill enough to think I was King Solomon rather than somebody in, shall we say, my close vicinity being that particular monarch. This just goes to show that even in severe mental illness a person can form a balanced view of the various situations they find themselves in.

Just around the corner I heard a shout, as a police van mounted the pavement and headed towards me. A small jeering crowd now surrounded me. This reminded me of a crowd I'd had the displeasure of meeting in Turin Railway Station when I attended the 1980 European Soccer Championships in Italy. One of the crowd had stolen my St George's flag, perhaps on orders. As with the kitten, I was completely innocent of any wrongdoing. Even with a full rucksack I had caught the little Italian rascal up and grabbed the flag back. However, this was not without exposing myself to serious threat of death, there having been a stabbing that week in Turin centre. Knife-wielding rioters had surrounded me. Here, at least there were no knives.

Barnes did not seem very pleasant at this moment though, and the hostility from this group left me in little doubt about what scum they were. I was now arrested, spit and verbal abuse being rained on me as I got in the van and was taken to the station.

At the station I felt somewhat glad to have been arrested, as it was almost what I had been expecting, though actually I was expecting something much bigger than that. They wanted to know why I had, in my wallet, a NatWest cashpoint card for Mr A. Hanratty, a relative of James Hanratty. I was wondering what the ultimate explanation was myself.

But I could partly explain this. A friend from school, the one whose father had the largest collection of books on the occult outside the British Library had, strange as it might seem, introduced me to this member of the Hanratty clan. I had, a number of years earlier, visited this friend and seen these books. He produced, from one, what must have been a very rare example of a 7" vinyl disc on which was recorded what were known as "diode voices". One of the tracks purported to be a message from the 'other side': Sir Winston Churchill, owner of the Black Dog itself, saying simply and quite audibly "Mark you, make-believe, my dear, yes."

My introduction to Mr Hanratty had been one night in Club Rich UK. It was then he told me he was an actual relation of Mr James Hanratty. He gave me the card, which he said I could use whenever and however I wished. This was rather nice of him although he gave me no PIN number. But this I hardly expected. I was simply grateful. I had probably done far more odd things on many occasions in my life.

The next day something strange happened, something that a person who had never had any delusional involvement in Prince Charles's dog might have disregarded. I'd had my Barnes flat fitted throughout with an absolutely gorgeous Axminster and Wilton Carpet. I never paid for it due to the finance company writing off the cost, several thousand pounds, when I was ill. I was walking past the Castle pub in Bedford when, to my surprise, one entrance to the pub had been laid with a piece of carpet which I seemed to recognise as being of the same design – or even one of the actual off cuts left by the fitter. This had been done deliberately by the Freemasons to tantalise my mind. This it did, and I was even more tantalised when, a year or so later, this practically brand new piece of carpet, for no apparent reason, was removed from the pub doorway. I sensed powerful forces at work – even if they were no more than the product of my mind and my mind alone. Talk about magic carpet.

In the police station my schizophrenia now allowed the full power of my imagination to exercise itself on this strange situation. What with all this occult and the matter of Mr Hanratty's cash card I really did feel like somebody was trying to tell me something.

By heart, I knew the letter that James Hanratty had been supposed to have written to his brother on the night of his execution. But my illness seemed to be the opposite of more usual examples of clinical delusion. Instead of believing things to be true which had no basis in reality I kept believing things generally accepted as true to be otherwise. I had never believed in capital punishment: to me, the chances of a miscarriage of justice were always too high. I thought of the letter. It was simply too harrowing to contemplate that such an injustice had occurred.

Since then DNA proved he was guilty but I imagined, MI5 might have faked the result. My imagination told me an anonymous donor said he would donate a sum to charity if they printed a positive DNA test result in the newspaper delivered to me, and nobody else's. Either way, still nobody had explained why Hanratty had asked how to change gear and then crashed them after the crime. In my strange delusion, whether he was real or not, I felt for James Hanratty, whose relation's cash card was about to be confiscated from me on suspicion of theft.

Right now I was not actually facing execution. But in fact the ludicrously trivial crime I had been arrested for had not even taken place. I had simply saved the kitten from being killed.

"We'll be keeping that as evidence" I was told. Now, having had Mr Hanratty's cash card taken from me (which was put in a clear plastic evidence bag) I was transferred to Twickenham where I was put in the cells. The whole experience was exceedingly disorienting. There was a strange cupboard in the corner of the cell, which I was unable to open, and I formed the opinion that it must contain a large cosh in case an officer wished to release a little tension on a prisoner. After further cross-examination, I agreed to reveal my true identity and therefore the location of the kitten, as I did not wish it to die of thirst, and at least it might then have another opportunity to escape from what I felt to be an unsuitable home.

Next day, on remand for stealing a cat, I was transferred to Wandsworth prison and certainly would not say this was less interesting than tabulating traceability requirements for the BFSM, both in fact having their merits.

As usual I could only imagine this was all just the continuation of some probably very long-standing military joke in which I was caught up and, arriving at Wandsworth, I remembered my *Ruminations on the Nature of Windups*, a small pamphlet I had considered producing some time previously. Believing this was all a military manoeuvre seemed to be the only way to make sense of the situation. The cat had just been a tool to get me in here to see what went on. I was an HM Prison Service spy seconded from the SBS.

Checking in on remand at Her Majesty's Prison Wandsworth, I was in no mood to say anything, other than maybe offer my credit card. I had no doubt they would have deducted something from it for staying in this 'hotel' as the first thing they said to me at the desk was "You're an obnoxious cunt aren't you?"

"If you say so" might have been the only rational response. It seemed to me that this little incident might show how, rather than rehabilitate prisoners; the British prison system creates criminals. So I did indeed decide I was here at the prison on a fact-finding mission.

Taken to my cell, which had no minibar I assure you, I found myself in the bottom bunk with another person in the one above, already asleep. The bed started to gently shake and then, quietly at first, a groaning sound began to build. Over the space of about 15 seconds the groaning built into a horrible scream and the whole bunk was trembling dramatically. I got out of the bed and saw, lying on the top bunk, a person who reminded me of James Hanratty, apparently having an almighty epileptic fit. There seemed to be some danger of him falling off the bunk and being killed; so I held his fitting body in place and somehow rang the emergency bell. In came the warders and I said "He should be in hospital." It was not long before I began to wonder if he was in the Marines, had been taught how to fake a fit and had heard exactly what I said. Well I never got to the Marines – maybe they had come to me, I thought.

The following night *I* went on the top bunk and wondered just how privileged I was to have got a pinboard by it. I wondered: who had previously had the honour of the use of it – apart from the fitting 'Marine' the previous night? It could well have been my Uncle Samuel, hanged at Chelmsford in 1903, and who my illness told me with utter certainty had been in this very prison cell. Seriously, an uncle of mine was hanged. His surname was Dougal.

The day of my hearing came and I noticed the atmosphere in the prison to be similar to that of my old school boarding house near the end of term, at least in the holding-cells before being taken to the court. Now I was on the way in the prison van with piped music, which seemed just a little ludicrous as I gazed out on the passing London streets peopled by free drivers and pedestrians, and even the odd cat. I love cats, I thought plaintively, and the whole thing seemed ridiculous.

In the cell at the court I read the graffiti on the wall, which included some long tirade by an eastern European intellectual concluding with the saying "Stupidity is next to misfortune." It was most apposite.

In court I felt a little cheated. I was somehow hoping for an extended hearing involving in-depth cross-examination and a full discourse by a Crown Court judge into the legalities of removing a kitten from Her Majesty's Highway and taking it into custody. Instead I was just given a month's unconditional bail, which I thought, amusedly, might indicate there was nothing to stop me saving another cat. I did not want to leave the court and could not believe nobody looked amused.

I now went up to the desk run by Group 4 and said I was ready to go back to prison. I did not want to be released and got it into my head that I had the right to stay on remand rather than be discharged before the case. Somehow I felt extreme danger to myself which would be far less if I was in prison. They refused to take me and said I had to go. Then I said "But what about my belongings?" but they would not even take me back to get those.

I was now thrown out onto the street. I went up to the Group 4 van twisting and breaking its windscreen wipers. Casually, I set off on foot back towards Wandsworth, several miles distant. I feel like saying I left a trail of overturned rubbish bins all the way there, hurling abuse at passers-by on foot and in cars; so they could tell I was a real nutter – but I didn't. After the long walk (it was a hot day) I eventually reached the prison and rang the doorbell to ask for my belongings back, no longer insisting on being let back in. There was a wait now and eventually the voice came over the intercom that they had no record of my being there. So this is what offenders, and the innocent, have to contend with in the modern British prison, I thought, sensing some purpose in my having to experience all this. The only logical thing to think was that the head of MI5 had called the prison and asked them to lie, as I was an SBS trialist trying to escape from that particular Trap of Doom. Or maybe I had got in years previously and this was not the first time I had been court-martialled out just to see what happened. Without my money, cash card or keys I was now a little stuck.

It must have been around this time that I reminded myself of stories of bankers who had gone to the river and thrown in all their identity and credit cards to head off, Reginald Perrin-style, into another life. I had not forgotten that the prison, or more likely King Solomon, also had a tin of cat food amongst my possessions. In reality it was probably just some Mason friend of Prince Charles, or the concierge at the King Solomon hotel in Jerusalem. Failing that, the one in Golder's Green.

In the late afternoon I now headed back across London to Barnes. I bunked the train, having no money. I procured a key to my flat from my neighbour, found my chequebook, and decided to treat myself to a curry around the corner to cheer myself up. I was a good customer of the Monzil and they said it would be quite all right to pay by cheque without a cheque card, which I falsely explained I had left in my flat.

I then attended Barnes Police Station where I reported the theft of my wallet, some cash, my keys and a tin of cat food. The reply came from over the desk: "And where were these stolen Sir?" "Er well, in Wandsworth Prison actually." He did not seem terribly impressed.

I was fuming, and not just from the heat of the curry. It had been a long hot day, my temper was a bit frayed and none of King Solomon's wisdom had rubbed off on me. Should I have been inclined, I might well have imagined Peter Snow, the television commentator, who lived in Barnes, wearing an orange bandana and peering from the turret of a stolen APC, or more likely an updated version of one of King Solomon's thousands of chariots. The chariot would be crashing through fences and walls in the summer uprising of 1995, complete anarchy and chaos having set in since the day I saw him popping into the café for a croquette monsieur and coffee.

I now went around the corner and into the pub where, with the cashback from the Indian restaurateur, I drank a couple of pints. Having finished these I got up and left The Sun noticing a black Porsche parked by the road opposite the pub garden. Out got the guitarist from Status Quo – at least that's who I thought it was. Now I wondered if he had been put there deliberately – Capgras syndrome once more. Then, to my left, I noticed that the wall had a crack in it. I picked up the large chunk of loose masonry, possibly provided for me by the local Masonic lodge master and, running over the road almost automaton-like, I hurled the chunk through the Porsche's windscreen. On this occasion it was nothing like as obvious that somebody else was in general control of my actions as it had been in Reading. But it does seem the antidepressants were at least a contributory factor as this was very out of character. I felt that I was indeed involved with the Masons and that I was a bit of loose masonry myself.

Everyone was watching at the pub, and within seconds police came pouring around the corner from the station, and I was arrested again. At the station I had an interview and they said "You again eh?" They still had my Hanratty cash card and said I was on suspicion of theft. Ludicrously, I tried to explain that I knew Malcolm Gregsten, shot in the A6 murder, had been spying at the Building Research Establishment, quite a fantastic story for which I should have been congratulated. I had enough sense not to mention my suspicions about who took the tin of cat food but despite this I soon found myself at Queen Mary's hospital. This time it was not such a frightening experience, though I hardly feel like saying that about the Fairmile experience which was just too horrible to recall without observable adverse effects.

The hospital was quite nice and it was a pleasure to sit in the garden in the sun. To be honest I did not observe much evidence of mental illness in any of the patients, and certainly not myself. By now the adverse effects of the antidepressants had mostly subsided although I was still to have some moments, as you will discover. However, I was now facing another battle: I believed I was in some sort of legal limbo brought about by being consciously aware I might have augmented reality capability via my MTRUTH. I would later make some more deludedly ornate inscriptions in the legal avenue I was now pursuing but for now I just sat down to enjoy what I saw as a hotel. Bizarrely I had thought that about Fairmile but it'd had its advantages including the snooker table, there not being one here.

One of the patients was into halal meat despite being white and English and another, whom I suspected of not being a genuine patient, had a quite extraordinary ability to climb walls. He was not a large person but as I sat there enjoying the sunshine in that sheltered corner of London, I could not but help feel privileged to observe his skill. I ended up thinking that he was a Commando probably known as "The Fly" and had been put there by the Royal Marines to impress me. A little like me, he was not a genuine patient and seemed to come and go over the wall at leisure.

Soon I was coming into conflict with the doctors one of whom, it seemed quite obviously, was the grandson of Dr. Mengele of Auschwitz who conducted disgusting experiments on twins, killing them with injections of phenol. I spoke angrily to him the one and only time I saw him. Then, at a panel, one of the doctors said "I gather you have been writing to the Queen." I did not know how he knew this; so simply chose to deny it. In a later skirmish with NHS psychiatric care I was to point out that writing to people in positions of authority was not an indication of mental illness. In fact upon being sectioned I was given a leaflet explicitly stating that the patient could write to anyone except somebody who had asked they did not do so. The doctor then said that he had been told that I had looked like I had been hearing voices.

"Who said this?" I asked, leaning forwards raising an enquiring finger. "I cannot say" said the doctor. Comically, I asked if I had looked like I was hearing them at the moment the person looked at me, or whether they thought I had heard some earlier. "All I was doing was reading *The Winter's Tale*. Could you tell me what somebody reading *The Winter's Tale* looks like if they're hearing voices?" I asked.

I also found Lord Mountbatten's biography by Philip Zeigler. I became ultra-paranoid about a section in which it was claimed he had travelled over Africa in so many days. It would have been impossible to make this journey in the time allotted. Once more I had wild thoughts that I had uncovered some massive long-standing conspiracy – but this seemed no lunacy, I actually believed it. And all because of some MI5 officers having a laugh over drinks one Friday afternoon in 1926, the joke now being told in absolute secrecy by an MI5 long-term reality generation cell, the newer members of which were beginning to question what they had been told about Prince Charles's dog.

My eldest brother Rupert visited, and I told him about the impossibility of the journey in the Mountbatten biography, trying vainly to make him agree with me that something was badly wrong, but without success. Of course he could not understand my deluded viewpoint. I handed him a piece of paper saying that if anything happened to me then what I had written on the paper, which was that Philip Zeigler was a traitor of the highest order, was the explanation. I tried to tell him that he might be in danger too – quite ridiculous really. Again I told him how Mountbatten could not possibly have made the trip across Africa in that time and how that was "part of it".

I spent the days in the hospital quite happily though suspicious of why all the artwork was by French artists. One night I dreamt I became partially conscious, being aware I was being hurriedly carried down the corridor. The next day, whilst watching the television, my vision became blurred. I wondered if I was going to lose my sight altogether. Well, I had lost something because, once again, I now became convinced that there were indeed cameras in my eyes. My imagined explanation for this was that in the night they had anaesthetised me – hence the strange dream, but had not given me quite big enough a dose, the result being the anaesthetist getting disciplined. Having dreamt I was being carried down the corridor I believed I had, in fact, been transferred to the ophthalmology department for an operation on my eyes by military surgeons to upgrade my ocular implants – and have some more lodestone chips installed.

Now I really was a state-of-the-art MTRU. I was even aware an operation had been carried out to put the equipment in. It hardly mattered to me that there were no signs of invasive surgery. I had electronically-augmented imagination, electronically-augmented vision, complete reality replacement (known in the military as "wall-climbing reality" because of the effect it had on MTRU personnel when it was first used), first, second and third person thinking (brainwashing) and not only that but my operator could see and hear everything

I was seeing, and hearing, in authentic 3D surround vision and sound. The Special Intelligence Service could make me think what they liked. Furthermore my unit could all feel, smell and even taste what each other was feeling, smelling and tasting. We could not even sleep without them taking control of our subconsciouses, both visually and aurally, whilst not even a mumbled word as we slept went unrecorded, unclassified, unanalysed, misinterpreted and on occasions passed to King Solomon. For my part I thought that, in what I imagined to be SAS parlance, I was a "shit-hot" piece of military equipment. I had an MTRUTH. Oh, I almost forgot, I was also embedded in the parallel CIA virtual Europe and, whilst in this hospital, wrote to the Queen and asked it be the impressionist style one. This, I believed was my privilege.

Part XI

Escape from the Loony Bin

Chapter Thirty

Here Comes the Flood

My climbing skills were not so advanced as those of "The Fly" and I chose to go over the low fence into the neighbouring private garden. I don't know if anyone saw me, though I can easily imagine one of the patients saying "There goes another one who thinks he's in the SAS and has cracked a religious cult wide open."[72]

I ran up the lawn and down the side of the house. A woman was washing up in the kitchen and shouted at me "Oi! Get out!" chasing me up her front garden. Her gate was locked; so I had to climb over it being biffed by her with a large frying pan as I did. I ran up the road and zigzagged to evade anyone still after me, there now being the dilemma of whether to run, and look suspicious, or walk, and risk being spotted by any pursuers.

Almost within reach of the safety of Wimbledon Common, I decided not to act like Peter Rabbit about to reach the gate to the wood beyond Mr McGregor's vegetable patch. Instead I dived into a large bush in the corner of somebody's front garden. Perhaps this saved me from recapture, for a police car may have been driving along the Common road right at that moment. But hiding in the garden had its risks too, so I walked up to the front door and rang the doorbell hoping nobody would reply. Nobody did and I slipped back into my hiding place.

In the undergrowth it was dry and comfortable, and I was lying in a bed of leaves, which seemed like a million pounds in cash. I picked up the leaves and let them slip through my hands. I remembered doing this with sand in the Sahara. As the minutes passed, I felt safer and safer.

After some hours, darkness came and, emerging from my hiding place, I brushed myself down. I was on the Common in seconds. Wimbledon Common is the sort of place, as Geoffrey Household said in *Rogue Male*, where you find dead bodies when out walking the dog. Now *I* was the Rogue Male.

On the Common, I was close to where Rachel Nickell had been stabbed to death. In my state of mind there seemed some exaggerated significance in this. I recalled how, at the time of her murder, I had been very close by, being driven to work by a friend. The coincidence was too much and I found myself thinking there had, in fact, been no murder. Once more I was suffering this peculiar disbelief syndrome. A policeman, doctor, funeral director or coroner, for example, would just say I was lacking intelligence. On the other hand they might have said this was a common symptom of grief – not that I knew her, though again I think she was from near Bedford.

I did see a dead body once. I had been driving around the perimeter road at Surrey University, where many rabbits can be seen. I accidentally ran one over. Reversing back over the body to see what I had hit finished it off. The next day

I drove slower to the A3. On the slip road it was apparent there had just been an accident. If I had not killed the rabbit, and driven slower, I might have been *in* the accident, unless they had been waiting hours for my arrival. A couple of cars were stationary, and a girl was sitting on the kerb, her crash helmet next to her. As I got nearer I saw a chap waving me by. A 20-foot long section of the road was painted in blood and, at the end, there was a body lying quite dead, with a crash helmet nearby. I hardly dared look; he had been run over from behind. Later shock set in and I went back to see if I had imagined this, but by then a tent had been erected at the scene.

I was now on the Common with a knife I had stolen from the hospital, heading for the location of a murder I thought had not really happened. I have no good explanation for my taking the knife; it was just a whim – and my army fatigues had a calf pocket into which it fitted perfectly. But I think a Kalahari bushman would have thought nothing of it. However I seem to recall thinking along the lines of: this is what the others do and I would too, to make it real if you like – I had wanted to find out what happened to them. I now decided I no longer had any use of the knife and threw it in a small pond.

I wandered around the Common; failing to find any of the bodies mentioned in *Rogue Male* and made my way to a bus stop. My friend nicknamed "Edge" lived in Putney but, as he was not in my phone book, I felt safe to go to him without fear of being tracked down. I decided to give him some excuse about not being able to get into my flat until morning. Luckily he was in and he said it was fine for me to stay. He had an aquarium, which reminded me of my childhood. One of my guppies had gone missing and I had no idea as to what had happened to it, not having any peculiar delusions then about the existence of intelligence agencies running long term reality generation cells doing odd things with fish. I found it weeks later inside the hood, having apparently jumped through a small hole and been unable to get back.

It was all very relaxing at Edge's house and I felt at home. Little did Edge know I was on the run from the "loony bin". He was a creative chap as well as a renowned oarsman. He produced little pamphlets, which he sold to his friends. These were rather like my own newsletters. Here is an example:

> *I have put this stuff together*
> *So that I can ask for a quid*
> *Sponsorship for Look, the charity*
> *For blind and partially sighted*
> *Kids that I am running for*
> *In the marathon.*
>
> *It's not really worth a*
> *Quid, but, if you were to*
> *Sellotape 50p over each*
> *Of your eyes, then I don't suppose*
> *You'd think twice about either*
> *Leaving them there forever or*
> *Giving them away to help blind kids.*
> *From this point of view*
> *You are getting great value.*

You get to see, and maybe a
Blind kid will as well.

Edge[73]

Next day, after saying goodbye to him, I paid a visit to Drummonds Bank. Holts had closed, all the business having been transferred there. Drummonds did not have quite the same level of service but was, if anything, more grandiose, with a large and beautiful chandelier, though nobody to escort me to the cashiers. They had closed my account due to the size of my overdraft. But I succeeded in withdrawing some money from my father's account to get me back to Bedford.

When I got there I went straight round to my father's house. I was jabbering on about how the Hanratty family were following me everywhere I went. "No Clive, they're not," he replied. However unlikely that was, perhaps it was only as unlikely as the sight of me in my father's drawing room. But the whole cat incident and the Hanratty cash card had really got to me. Why, really, had I been in prison? It seemed like I was up against some unseen force trying to pull me down. I thought it was MI5 doing this, the rationale being that, if they sabotaged me, eventually I would do something sensible in fighting back.

"I need to call a friend, wait a minute," Dad said. I did not believe him for a moment and made a run for it as I was not prepared to risk being arrested in the next five minutes, certain he knew I had escaped and had not been discharged. He made a vague plea for me to wait but I would not have it. I could not face more Chlorpromazine. Nothing mattered more than avoiding it.

Outside the scaffolded house opposite a builder watched me leave in a hurried and suspicious manner. I also noticed Dad had bought a Volvo, registration number VRY 51S. I believed the plate was a reference to Lake Vrwyny, where I thought I might have met Prince Charles's dog the previous summer, and to the Special Intelligence Service. Again it seemed my own father was in the Special Intelligence Service. It seemed my life was all a big experiment in schizophrenia set up by MI5 and MI6 following the Berlin Wall being brought down and their subsequent hilarious receipt of my revelational KGB file. There was no doubt about this. They would manipulate me with anything – including my fear of drug-induced depression.

Near the changing rooms in the park, a Jack Russell dog was being walked – for all I knew it was Prince Charles's. That really seemed a possibility. I ran towards the café. Now was the time to make a decision. Either way it would be a gamble but I could not risk the helicopter and several police cars after me. So I put my immediate wellbeing in the corporate hands of J.C.Decaux, operators of the pay-to-use toilet, and luckily did not have to ask for change. Heart thumping, as though I had seen a ghost, I breathed a sigh of relief as the door of the pay-to-use toilet shut protectively behind me. Looking back I feel no less relieved. I had escaped from the hospital without being given what I was not yet fully aware of, this being the despicable effects of their *other* drugs for schizophrenia. I had, however, determined that Chlorpromazine was no recreational fun drug.

Now I had to wait for the coast to clear and just hope nobody raised the alarm. After a few minutes panic set in again, as the toilet door automatically opened, my time being up. This seemed unfortunate to say the least, especially when I now consider that I had very severe emotional constipation. This was caused by a number of things – including my intelligence about Prince Charles's dog. But what of somebody still sitting on the toilet when their time was up?

I would not have the toilet telling me my time was up, nor was I going to spend the next few hours pumping money in. What was this – some EEC-regulated takeover of the dominion of Mr Thomas Crapper, inventor of the WC? I had to put another payment in to get the door to shut again. It shut and now I attempted to jam it with any available material, though with little success. After my time was up once more, I felt the door trying to open again, and obviously this faulty TARDIS or most existential of toilets just did not understand what was going on. So I had to stand there holding the door shut, which I did for several hours until the faint glimmer of light at the bottom of the door disappeared, and I knew night had fallen.

During this time I realised again the Special Intelligence Service could have put lodestone chips in my body – including my fingers. Here my delusions were getting into *Star Trek* holodeck territory. But interestingly, having had the clinical delusion I was in an anti-universe, now I was addressing the possibility I was indeed in two universes at once: the real one and a virtual one.

I thought of what military intelligence officers refer to as asymmetric warfare. I decided an asymmetric war is a war fought using any asymmetries between the real world and a parallel virtual one. I would later consider how I was myself capable of affecting certain asymmetries between any parallel universes, which had been set up, and the real one. I would see myself as Arne Saknussem in *Journey to the Centre of the Earth*. In the story he scrawls "Arne Saknussem was here" deep on the inside of the earth. I thought I could leave some virtual aural graffiti in this toilet consisting, say, of the song naming this chapter. Only the rarest of the rare, those with MTRUTH capability, would hear it and, for reasons you will discover shortly, I imagined that piece of aural graffiti would be Peter Gabriel's *Here Comes the Flood*.

From my MTRUTH, or my own good visual imagination in my role as an SBS/MI6 psycho-spy KGB double agent nuclear war prevention spetznatz operative, I could see the new recruit to the 22nd Regiment of the Special Air Service being called in to hear the good news from his CO. But instead of being told he had passed the entrance tests he was told there was one more hurdle to jump – a hurdle which for him, but not me, would be easy though nevertheless rather mindblowing. This hurdle was to find the solution of what was really a rather simple problem though, as you will understand, this was a hallowed and time-honoured tradition in the Special Forces. All the new recruits were set this task. Oh, and talking of new recruits, agents and subjects, one of the first things that happened when they became known to the Service was that a 3D image of them would be loaded into "the System". Whenever they needed to be introduced during a briefing the musical box from *Camberwick Green* would appear with the music all youngsters of that era remember so well playing. They would then appear from the box, rotating just the same as Windy Miller et al did for a few years in the 60s. "Here is a box, a musical box, wound up and ready to play. But this box can hide a secret inside, can you guess who is in it today?" No doubt the voice of the briefer would be morphed for security reasons into that of Brian Cant raising issues of copyright at the highest levels: a whole new area in modern warfare.

The psychic-ether had been programmed so that somebody with MTRUTH fitted and tuned to the right channel could find the place in Great Britain where, on his MTRUTH, *Here Comes the Flood* (or the *Camberwick Green* music depending on operational conditions) was playing louder than anywhere else. In all directions out from that spot the music got progressively less audible. Only to make it more interesting the volume also oscillated so that it gave a ringed pattern, which spread out all across the country like the waves made when a stone is thrown into water.

The new recruit was ordered to leave SAS headquarters and not to return until he had something interesting to report. So he left HQ and, after just driving around for a while, he could have sworn he heard music in his head. That night he decided to book into a bed and breakfast in Malvern. Here he could not hear the music.

Next day he drove off again, and soon found he could hear the same music. He turned his car radio off – but, to his astonishment, he could still hear it. So now, he deduced, he had aural implants. After another few miles, to his chagrin, it had gone. Logic dictated he turn around and go back to see if it returned and it did. So he decided to make some notes to see where this all led. Now the task was quite simple of course but what he did not know was that the closer he got to the solution, that is where the music was loudest, it was actually affected by his proximity. You see he was initially being led to the J.C. Decaux public toilet in the park in Bedford – this being a demonstration of the linked consequences of people's actions. But as he got closer the solution moved too, in a way I shall describe. Though never having heard of Newton's approximation method (a well-known mathematical technique of use in such a situation) the new recruit deployed a die in his unstoppable approach to the solution.

Well, this chap's map began to show, quite clearly, the presence of the ripples from a 'water drop' in the ocean of Great Britain's psychic-ether and by the next afternoon he was heading in a straight line to Bedford ignoring the periodic disappearance of the music.

Anyway, so there I was, still in the toilet. Once or twice whilst in there, people tried to get in. On one occasion, I heard what seemed to be somebody's dog relieving itself against the outside of my TARDIS. "Come on boy!" said the dog's owner and it barked quietly once. For some reason, probably boredom, I now invented a new word: "cronym". Then I came up with a military definition of cronym. Basically it was a near-acronym. I have not heard if it's in the OED yet. For my first cronym I thought of GLOVEBOX for some reason and decided it meant Great Lovebug of Xymox.

My confinement in this TARDIS got the better of me to the extent that I pulled out every single paper towel from the dispenser. There was also quite a lot of toilet paper and I thickly carpeted the floor, already covered in towels, with a layer of it. God knows what Mr Decaux thought next day when he came to service the toilet, his van having a big Union flag down each side. He must have thought some "nutcase" had been in his toilet the previous day. As for me, I wondered who chose the toilet's colour scheme; it was decorated to a nicety.

With nightfall I casually yet intrepidly left the cubicle and made my way over to the Suspension Bridge across the river. Unbeknownst to me I would be followed by at least two entities: firstly by the intuition of a professional psychic my parents brought in to track me; and secondly by the solution of the problem which the new recruit to the SAS had been set to find. This might be years later, the next day, at the same time as I left the toilet, or my route may already have been traced by this or previous new recruits.

The new recruit's map of the ripples in Britain's psychic-ether emanating from the pay-to-use toilet was rough and ready. Either way, as he approached Bedford, with the aid of his map of the ripples, his career success continued to affect the solution of the problem. As his map was approximate he could not see this – though this did not affect the outcome. The solution, that is where the centre of the ripples was, moved down the path in the park along my route upon leaving the toilet. I imagined that, at Military High Command, the SAS rookie was codenamed Sumo Rabbit 37 and I Sumo Rabbit 38 – to give a break from dogs for the moment. This was all well and good but somebody in the Special Intelligence Service was a big knob in the British Sumo Rabbit Psychic Wrestling Society. When he found this out he felt his rabbits were potentially compromised by the codenames so, at the highest level, the SAS rookie was codenamed Egg 38 and I Chicken 37. I came before he did. Needless to say, all this was done with the approval of both Prince Charles and Spike Milligan.

I weaved my way, avoiding roads to evade the police, not fully aware my imagination was allowing me to be followed by these two entities: the psychic's intuition and the solution, as well as the new recruit. I imagined the person responsible for the position of the solution was retired and, pipe in his mouth with slippers on, was occasionally receiving, amusedly and interestedly, intelligence reports on my progress. If you like, think of the two entities as the odd balloon in *The Prisoner*. Nearby I heard a police car's siren and felt wary of the 'balloon'. Eventually, by a circuitous route, I arrived at The Phoenix pub. Inside were photographs of President Kennedy's trip to Dublin in 1963.

On the wall outside was a plaque on which there was a phoenix with its wings spread and, below, the words: *Level of Water Reached in the Great Flood of 1823*. Luckily I did not feel depressed, as no antipsychotic drugs had been given to me. I felt positive and had the urge to reinvent myself somehow. I would rise up, not with wings as the eagle in the school motto, but as the phoenix-like Jeffrey Archer did from the flames of his bankruptcy after a bad business deal. To start with I had to go to ground, as in *Rogue Male*, at least until things had died down and the police were no longer looking for me.

I had not fully appreciated the power of the Law in this type of situation. But I did, correctly, suspect that under the Mental Health Act I only needed to stay out of trouble for 28 days after which they could not put me back in hospital unless I did something ill advised. I had somehow been told this by way of my brother Howard in the police. This rule later changed, a fact which became significant in my desperate attempts to avoid some 10 murderous drugs, as you will learn. Each of these drugs would be like a strange privilege granted me by each of the IRA/INLA hungerstrikers, so I knew a bit what injustice felt like.

In the pub I ordered my 'last drink' again, a pint of Guinness. The solution did not come in with me. Instead it hung around, balloon-like, near the King's ditch (a ditch marking the mediaeval edge of Bedford, part of which can still be seen in the middle of the roundabout).

Now I realised how hungry I was, and did not have enough for some chips. I had to eat as I was in for a long walk. I could not dare hitch in the immediate vicinity, as there was the danger of being spotted by the police. But I felt safe from the police even though I sensed the presence of the balloon from *The Prisoner*, or the solution and the psychic's intuition if you prefer, using MTRUTH to follow my every movement. For delusional military reasons, which were accurate but delusional nevertheless, I thought the balloon would not betray me to the police. So, having finished my Guinness, I left The Phoenix.

At this moment I imagined an interesting moment in British lego-military history. Up in Scotland the Lord High Chancellor, Lord Mackay of Clashfern, was at home with his wife. He received a phone call from MI5 and, as a direct result of the call, he went out into his garden and, as an aide-mémoire for work the next day, drove a large stake into the middle of his cabbage patch using a grand sledgehammer. In the morning, being reminded of what to do by his unusual and purposeful action of the previous evening, he arranged a legal document which specified the location of the solution to the problem the new recruit was set to solve and which had followed me from the public toilet to the pub. The Lord High Chancellor decided that, until further notice, the solution would be geographically located at the plaque outside The Phoenix. Furthermore particular attention would be paid to any asymmetries in the vicinity of the plaque between reality and the model codenamed *Colchester* – the Defence Intelligence psychic-ether being accessible only to those with MTRUTH. The Lord High Chancellor knew all about MTRUTH.

With the pub disappearing behind me, I was fascinated at the impossibility of knowing when the new recruit would reach it – if he hadn't already. Perhaps it would be many years later.

Reaching Bedford the volume would become clearly supra-subliminal, suggesting he must be close. He parked up and wandered about town. The SAS rookie hardly needed his map now, the ripples in this parallel Great Britain being so close he had to just push through, the music in his head coming and going regularly. No bother here. He decided to go into the nearest pub, enjoy a pint of Greene King Lowes low alcohol bitter whilst enjoying the song, *Here Comes the Flood*, still playing over and over – though nobody else could hear it. Half an hour later, he felt pretty sure, he would be off back to HQ. He reached The Phoenix.

In the corner of his eye he saw the plaque on the wall outside the pub but walked past, noticing at once the volume drop, the sensitivity of the MTRUTH lodestone chips in his body to his position and orientation being exact, much in the way anyone who later got an iPhone would be used to, but more accurate. He stepped back once and up went the volume again. He looked left and the sound dropped to nothing. His whole will was completely subsumed in carrying out his order. He turned his head to the right and saw the plaque.

Many people would be so shocked at what now happened they would be in danger of stepping back and being run over by a passing car. Only a seasoned schizophrenic might simply be pleasantly surprised. For at this moment, without having heard of such a thing or knowing what it was called, the new recruit discovered he had electronically-augmented vision as well as hearing. At that moment his MTRUTH was operating in total reality replacement mode: "wall-climbing reality". Gone was the plaque, gone was the pub and what could he see but a traffic policeman in the North Bedfordshire Constabulary. The policeman, who he could see using the implants in his eyes, was telling him he had been recorded as travelling at 31mph down Mill Street, Bedford, using a speed camera hidden inside the eyes of the full-scale model fibre-glass United States police state trooper stood outside Bedford's old Fire Station as an advertisement for the mobile phone shop now there. Furthermore this had been ground-MTRUTHed using the lodestone chips in Egg 38's body, to 30.237mph.

He was given a caution and congratulated on having just become a member of the 22nd Regiment of the Special Air Service. Egg 38's normal unimpeded vision then returned and he headed back to Hereford quite flabbergasted at what had happened. As he drove, he felt a little like I had done on the day I came across the Dog Show on Bannerdown Hill.

As for what happened to Egg 38 on the way back to Hereford, I'll leave that to another's flight of imagination. It might have been some time before he actually did get back.

A lady in the chip shop gave me 50p so I had enough to buy some chips, proving there is generosity in the world. However, what might she have done if she had known I was on the run from the loony bin, the local psychiatric hospital being right opposite the chip shop?

Now I was in my own *The One That Got Away* and I felt a kindred spirit in the writer of that book, Chris Ryan. Seeing that as I was obviously trapped in 'Iraq', as in that story, it seemed sensible to walk out along the railway, just as in that book. I did not believe that anyone who wanted to arrest me would look there. So, as in the song Egg 38 could hear, I decided to take the old (rail) track, which had once gone from Oxford to Cambridge, though now only the Bedford to Bletchley part was still in use. I climbed through the hedge onto the embankment and then down onto the line. The ubiquitous style of fence elsewhere would have been far more difficult to surmount and was another entity I had developed a deep dread and unexplained paranoia about – it was something to do with the trident shape at the top I think.

A little way down the track I heard the last train of the night approaching from behind me. This was a potentially dangerous situation as I later imagined that my controllers had the capability to digitally subtract various sounds around me using my MTRUTH so I could not hear them. They had a better way to show off this ability – which did not involve killing me with a train. But that was for later.

As the train approached I dived into the undergrowth and played dead hoping the driver would not notice me and stop. If he had, I would have just run off across the fields. The rickety old train passed by and its sound faded into the distance, allowing me to continue my journey out of 'Iraq' SAS-style.

Here the track was single and it was just too easy to walk down the middle of it with the sleepers making good stepping-stones. Being involuntarily obsessed with spying (and, like Rufus May had done, thinking I was a trainee spy), I kept thinking of all the "sleepers" who might be known to me personally in this vast conspiracy, or 69-year-old joke, I had come to believe in. I believed I was one myself. I actually *had* been recruited by the Royal Navy at the interview for the Royal Marines at the Admiralty Arch that snowy day back in January 1982 – but it had not quite clicked until now. I noticed the smell of diesel from the sleepers and, as the miles went by, I became desensitised to it. Several times, ahead of me down the line, I saw Prince Charles's dog leading the way: it would stop and look back at me to check I was following before running off ahead. A secretive voice in my head said "That's how important you are."

After about six miles I arrived at Ridgmont Station. Here I tried to get some sleep in a dilapidated shed. It was too cold and I got little or none. So up I got and began walking across the fields in the direction of Toddington Service Station. In the fields I found the remains of what looked like an old-style gypsy site including a decrepit-looking horse-drawn wagon. Though it was still night I could see by the lights of the M1 and the little moonlight that, it seemed, the site had been ransacked and burnt down. This must be part of the conspiracy, I thought, and nothing more complicated than a group of British Nazis came to mind. Looking at the 'burnt-out' gypsy camp which, in reality, may not have been there in any form, I remembered what I had thought were openly broadcast MI6 intelligence reports from Bosnia: the signs on the Bedford Borough Council rubbish lorry saying "Cleansing Hit Squad".

Down country lanes I went, feeling very secretive and thinking few could know what I was up to. I felt a strong affinity for the night, which was now dark with the moon down and cloudy, but with no rain. I came across the headquarters of a private security company, Wing Security, deep in the countryside. I believed it was just a cover for the military intelligence operation – but could not quite make full, logical and satisfactory sense of it. Now, in my sleepless state, my thoughts were out of control again.

I eventually reached the service station a couple of hours before dawn, and tried to hitch south for a while. Eventually I gave up and crossed to the northbound side. Motorway service stations are lonely places to be in the early hours and though lonely I felt surprisingly happy to have escaped. I certainly had no thoughts of suicide.

Eventually a car stopped to pick me up. The driver was a Turk, probably sent from NATO allied command. I was off north whereas only a few minutes earlier I had been heading south, a mark of the chaotic state of my mind. Now I had a chance to get some sleep.

The Turk dropped me at Watford Gap, north of Northampton, and soon I was travelling to Morecambe with a vanload of drunks. And why not Morecambe? It seemed as good a place as any to go. I felt a bit like starting my life all over again, once more. Really this was just a huge mid-life crisis.

In Morecambe I booked into a bed and breakfast and the landlord took me to my room and made me a cup of coffee. He did not seem too worried that I did not have any money to pay him. "Social Security can sort that out tomorrow" he said. Back downstairs he told me he'd just had a big clear out because everyone in the house had been on drugs. His clear out obviously had not been too successful, as a very young chap asked me if I wanted any "whizz", showing me a plastic bag of white powder: amphetamine sulphate or something.

The Social Security office was in Lancaster, and I walked all the way there the next day. I was not prepared to give my real name, partly because I was afraid of rehospitalisation. So, rather hopefully, I gave my name as Charles Wilson, the Great Train Robber, claiming I did not know my National Insurance number. I thought MI5 were watching everything I did and would react positively to my humorous alias. However this was obviously a waste of time; so I made my way back to Morecambe, though I was not to return again to the bed and breakfast, which I had spent one free night in. I was sad not to return there as this meant abandoning my 1990 England World Cup shirt which I had been wearing the one time I entered Bedford's gay pub, the Barley Mow, one lunchtime that year. Perhaps the room has been sealed up, my shirt still draped over the chair, to see if I ever imagined that and could therefore trigger some event the nature of which I could not be sure of.

I walked and walked. At one point I walked along a disused railway track bed, which, as with the walk to Ridgmont, made me feel mysteriously at home. Perhaps my fascination with railway lines was due to their being laid by the Irish. I had substantial Irish ancestry on both sides, though was Church of England educated, and loyal to the Crown. All around me I now kept seeing disused old factories surrounded by tall brick walls. I felt deeply paranoid about them: they were going to be used as death camps.

I started hitchhiking again. Whilst waiting I read the messages on the back of the road sign left by those before me: "John and Annita – 6/6/92 – going to Newquay. Good luck." It seemed the message had been especially for me, after all it could have been read only infrequently, though there were other messages and the grass by the sign was a little worn by those before me. Next to this message was a small-unhatched chrysalis. I felt I was metamorphosing too.

I got a lift to the Midlands where I found myself wandering around another lonely motorway service station at night. Outside the shop was a large box of expensive gourmet crisps. They were past their sell-by date. I asked the attendant if I could have them and he said I could. So for the next couple of days I carried the box with me for an endless supply of what would become a rather boring though nevertheless gourmet meal.

With my box of crisps, I now got a lift all the way down to the southwest. Here I was dropped, in the middle of the night, somewhere near Torquay. As he said goodbye the driver told me there had been a rape in the vicinity. This reminded me of a similar story I had been told by a chap called Milton A. Monell in the same circumstances in America. All night I had waited for a lift – nobody stopping as a rapist was about there too. He later sent me his newsletter appealing for money for his ministry in the Soviet Union. He amused me by saying "My paycheques are evidence of your availability to Him."

With another lift, I was in Torquay itself where I made for the harbour. Here I spent the night walking around aimlessly, feeling rather chilly and fed up and with no money and nowhere to go. It was not that I had no money but the prison still had my identity documents as well as my cash card. Somehow I did not want them.

Dawn eventually came and I tried to get some kip on a bench, but without success. However I felt positive. After a couple of hours a man appeared and opened his coffee shop – Vaughan's Bar. I saw him putting out the tables; so I went over and asked him if he wanted any help. Next thing I knew I was the one putting out the tables and mopping up the floor. Then he prepared me breakfast and went out to buy me a packet of Old Holborn tobacco and some Rizlas. This all reminded me of when I was in America where, I found, entrepreneurial behaviour was similarly rewarded. He invited me back the next morning. This all made me feel much better and gave me the feeling that anything was possible. I could have asked him to help me find somewhere to sleep and no doubt he would have, but I didn't.

I remembered when I was the dishwasher in a rib shack in Lafayette, Louisiana, USA in 1982. The manager knew I had nowhere to stay and felt sorry for me. The owner, a very portly chap, would pull up outside the shack each lunch time, walk into the kitchen, and gorge himself on a large pile of barbecue ribs. Then one day he came up to me and told me to clock off. Outside we got in his air-conditioned Cadillac and drove off down the road. He told me he had heard what a good job I had done of cleaning up his pots and pans – which my predecessor had left in a state, that predecessor not necessarily having been in this establishment because you would have had to search the whole of the United States for a set of pots and pans that dirty. He also said he had heard I had nowhere to stay and now took me to a spare air-conditioned caravan he had. He told me I could live there at no cost to myself, that he would have me trained to cook, and that within two years I would be the manager of one of his restaurants. I had felt a little guilty at this offer knowing I planned to return to England at the end of the summer to complete my degree. I was a little tempted though. I actually had two jobs on the go at the time. In the other I was a busboy in a Mexican restaurant, Cisco's Hacienda.

I had arrived in Louisiana on the strength of a job as a roustabout in the oil industry but production had collapsed and there was no work. I spent my last $20 on some shoes, a white shirt and some trousers from Woolworth's to get the job. The manager of this other restaurant was an Argentinian and, the Falklands War having just finished, it was a notable situation.

Lafayette was an interesting part of the world. The "Cajuns", who lived there, had been kicked out of Canada by the British and dumped there in the swamps; so I might not have expected a great welcome. On the contrary one day I went into a Cajun butcher and the lady butcher christened me a Cajun too by making me eat some spicy "Bourdin" sausage.

One day I was clearing the tables in Cisco's when a chap said, referring to the Falklands, "Your boys did a good job out there" and gave me a $10 tip. I also met a few Irish Americans one of whom claimed to be another IRA funder. He spoke of the Troubles and said he had renounced violence.

Here in Torquay, 13 years later, I had been up all night and was tired. But the breakfast and hot coffee I had earned, which was far better than the gourmet crisps, had perked me up. However I badly needed sleep.

In a half-hearted 20-minute penetration test at the DSS, I used the name of Jeremy Jewson. I made an apparently hopeless and schizophrenic attempt to sign on under this name and, finding I got served very quickly, become convinced the Social Security officer had put me to the top of the queue because he was Jewish and my supposed surname was Jewson. For a moment I was posing as Christ and had discovered another conspiracy: a Jewish one[74]. Ah but no! All the chap wanted was to build a new Jerusalem in England (Torquay Branch). But at least there was some logic in my behaviour – I was spying on the State apparatus to determine if there was anything wrong, however small. I had indeed discovered something was seriously wrong: I thought I was the eyes and the ears of the Intelligence Services without my permission. Perhaps I had been pleased to acquiesce to this. Or I was subject to the Rehabilitation of Offenders Act 1974 for a sample case of making a premium rate phone call in a pub and not putting any money in. And I was still wrestling psychotically with the notion that I was Prince Charles's dog itself. I decided on the name James Longhurst as my next alias.

I took a long walk down to the beach. During the walk I passed The Winston

Churchill pub, not suffering from his Black Dog but very tired. Then I arrived at the library. It was the Carnegie library in fact. Carnegie was a Scot from near Edinburgh who became wealthy by setting up the iron and steel industry in Pittsburgh, enabling him to start a foundation with his massive riches. Through all of this I had the overwhelming feeling that some type of great riches were within my grasp too, if only I could keep going. The books on the shelves of this very library seemed to be made of gold – though only later did I wonder if what I wanted most was power, not money.

I began writing a letter to the Queen Mother relating the story of a small family bookmaker. His shop, which I had just visited unsuccessfully for lack of money, earned a million after a man came into it and placed a bet. The bet was large enough to bankrupt the bookmaker if it was a winner; so, of course, he used the bet as a tip, placing his own hedge bet at William Hill. I told her I knew about L Zero, MI5's greatest secret, and how Prince Charles had never really had a dog called Pooh. And if he did, Pooh was just an alias. If she ever read the letter she must have thought I was barking mad – but I hope she was entertained. Mad I was, and barking pretty hard too. I recalled Jerome K. Jerome's jolly jaunt up the Thames with two friends and a dog "Montmorency" in his *Three Men in a Boat*. Except it is well known they did not actually take a dog with them. Jerome, like I was imagining Prince Charles had done, had made the dog up. This, when I thought about it, only further excited my far-fetched and delusional thoughts in a way that seemed to make so much sense.

In the library I again conceived the wildly deluded idea that a huge celebration was afoot. When I came out onto the streets they would be adorned with much bunting including a modified Union flag which, due to the peace process in Ireland and a call I had made to *The Times* recommending unification of the pound and the punt, now had green stripes in it[75]. I was quite sick in the head, partly due to tiredness as well as the schizophrenia, though this enabled me to write this bizarre letter to Her Majesty. I was mortally disappointed when I came out to discover no bunting. So I consoled myself with the thought of the council bunting upon my return to Bedford on the day of the Radio 1 road show the previous year. Near the harbour I found The Queen's Hotel. One of the "E"s in its sign's light was not functioning. Eccentrically and ridiculously loyal, I went in to complain to the staff.

Back out on the street what seemed like the most sensible idea I had ever had came to me. You may know the poem "A Subaltern's Love Song" by John Betjeman about a lady called Miss Joan Hunter-Dunn. I had now neologised an MI5 operation named "Operation Joan Hunters Done". In it I was sure that every Joan Hunter in the country would be gathered together on some pretext and led into a room in pitch darkness. All the Joan Hunters would mingle around in the darkness bumping into each other until they had all discovered there was nobody in the room except other Joan Hunters. What the purpose of this madness was I never really found out. All I knew was that it seemed, with all certainty, to be an exceptionally sensible thing to do. What is more such a thing may one day have to happen for some reason.

I walked to the harbour again and approached the Harbour Master to whom I offered my services wire brushing and painting the harbour railings. He told me he could not give me that job because it was not up to him but the council. Coming out of his office I saw the notice. It said at the top "Section 45-48 Torbay

Harbour Act 1970". My eyes were immediately drawn to Part V, subsection 87 and it was as if the force of MTRUTH, if not God himself, had made this happen. For what I now read seemed, at the time, profoundly pertinent and the fact that I was reading it an absolute miracle. It said "Exercising Craft", "No person shall within an Enclosed Harbour whether or not on any vessel, except with the written consent of the council or in the course of the proper business of the Harbour *exercise any craft or skill* for hire or reward or in the hope of any gratuity or offer or sell, peddle or hawk any goods or things." I felt like I was being put down like a sick dog at the vet. I believed the craft I was exercising was witchcraft. I knew that, just like other members of the Special Forces, I could never make any money for myself from telling my story. There was no doubt one or two people would be having a pretty dim view of me if that were what they thought I was about.

I continued my walk around Torquay. It was a little wet and as I had no clean socks my feet felt uncomfortable, though not quite bad enough to get trench foot. I found a wall to a small overgrown garden, which had snails crawling all over it. I picked them all up and threw them back into the garden where I thought they were better off, as a passer-by could kill them quite easily if they got onto the footpath. I compared their position to my own. No doubt if anyone around me knew how ill I was, they would have thrown me back into hospital if they could. The only problem is that when you are schizophrenic, very often you do not *want* to be in hospital. You can only get into hospital if you bring to the attention of the authorities that you are either a danger to yourself or to others or are suffering from an illness of "a nature and a degree" requiring hospitalisation. I have never really presented a physical threat to anyone, other than the chap whose shoulder I barged outside the cemetery gates in Reading. So here I was, wandering about the country simply evading those who might discover there was in fact a warrant out for my arrest.

Continuing my walk about town I became obsessed with the standard of redecoration of the Town Hall, which I observed to be very shoddy, the redecoration still in progress. I went to the local newspaper and persuaded a reporter to come and look at it. He agreed and perhaps I even appeared in that week's paper – though I never saw it. I wondered if he decorated toy soldiers at home.

Some force seemed to be driving my mind to address farfetched military scenarios. It was almost as if some MI5 secretary had come into the room and put the document on my table. I had to produce a plan to evacuate the entire land of Great Britain in less than three days in case of biological attack. All sorts of images came to mind – including the Bretons coming back after 1,400 years in exile and claiming squatters' rights when everybody else was out.

That night, walking down the street near The Queen's Hotel I heard the sound of Marc Cohn's *Walking in Memphis* playing from a passing car. I felt rather sure that Christopher Reeve, the actor who played Superman in the films, was faking his infirmity and it was as though the music I was hearing had been arranged from America. Mr Reeve had walked in Memphis. Unfortunately for him there was about as much truth in this florid daydream as in the message received by a chap with schizophrenia I had read about in *The Big Issue*. He saw the station "Burnt Oak" on the Tube map and said he thought it meant he should go and set fire to an oak tree. Similarly, a poster I saw advertising the forthcoming gig by Van Morrison really meant that Jim Morrison was not dead but inside a van in the near vicinity. That is what I really believed and that is just how trapped I was in this fantastic illness. Perhaps I'd have been nearer the truth if I knew Van Morrison, or this van, was from Belfast.

Again I find it difficult to remember exactly the order of events. There had been so many happenings; it was impossible to recall them all. One incident I do recall though occurred when wandering aimlessly around Southampton in the middle of the night after unsuccessfully trying to find a bed. Somehow I came across a social centre with a children's playhouse outside that looked like a large dog kennel. In this, dog-like, I spent the night. Very appropriate.

The next day the friendly people at the social centre gave me a shower and a carrier bag full of food to keep me going. As I left, feeling clean and having had my laundry done, I noticed the plaque announcing *Opened by Her Royal Highness the Princess of Wales*. It felt like I had been personally presented with the bag of goodies including what I recall as a heart-shaped tin of ham.

Any ideas about there being sensitive military electronics in my body would often fade to the background – basically I would just get on with it. And my recall may not be as good as you might imagine. But I now formed the impression that, probably like the MI5 agent on the sleeper to Scotland 14 months earlier, my MTRUTH had voice recognition software listening to what was being said and heard on it. This would be of particular use when a translation was needed, or if my operator needed to pop out for a while and catch up later, for example. And even if I did not recall everything that happened MTRUTH did. I was seeing real-time responses by way of concept image documents displayed on my EAV in response to, for example, the conversation I was having with somebody. These concept images were being plucked from what I later would realise was probably an early Google image search, such a tactic by my handlers being a logical response to my persistence – the basketball full court press again. I had just to wonder how I could end this barrage of imagery and see just what I needed or wanted.

On one occasion I was talking to a chap in a club whom I told I could not hear whereupon the loud music suddenly went muffled so that I could hear him perfectly. Only I believed that in reality the music was still loud as I could tell by feeling the bass vibrating in the counter of the bar. It was clear that my handlers were monitoring the disco and, like I suggested they could have done with the noise of the train approaching me from behind, had digitally extracted it, using my MTRUTH, from what I heard. In fact I think the DJ or the original producer had just cut all but the bass.

At some point I found myself in a nightclub in Exeter though to be honest I do not even recall if it was on this particular sojourn. But I did go into a nightclub there and an incident occurred. In the club I was sitting next to a chap whom I imagined might well be in the Royal Marines, the Marines Commando Training Centre being at Lympstone just down the road.

Now, 13 years after my Admiralty interview, and rather longer since I went AWOL, I felt I had arrived at base in a sense, to report my position as an agent of the Crown. Basically I was free to believe whatever truth there was in my being anything to do with the SBS in order that I could proceed efficaciously. I asked him if he was in the Forces and he said he was. I passed him a piece of paper on which I had written "Terry Wiles is the Head of the Special Intelligence Service."

I asked him to give it to his commanding officer. "So who is Terry Wiles?" I imagined his CO asking.

When I was nine and my father was working at RAF Brampton, I attended a local school near the perimeter of the base. At the school I saw a truly horrific sight. It was a young chap of my age in a wheelchair. His name was Terry Wiles. He was illegitimate and apparently mixed race but those were the least of his problems. His mother had taken Thalidomide and as a result, instead of arms and hands he had just the wholly useless vestiges of fingers coming out of his shoulders. But that was not all. He had no legs but just the horrendously deformed feet protruding from where his legs should be. He used these feet as his hands. He was a lovely chap and was very bright and sociable. I noted that nobody ever made fun of him – possibly because they were just so shocked with pity[76]. He was a terrible sight for any nine-year-old to look at.

Now Terry was in my Cub Scout pack and he wore his uniform just like anyone else, though his jumper had no sleeves at all and you could just see where his 'fingers' stuck out from his shoulders. When we did our grand howl at the start of meetings and said "Dib Dib Dib, Dob Dob Dob, we will do our best!" Terry obviously could not join us in quite the same way. Instead, as we called out our motto, he would roll his torso around our circle. It was a great privilege for me to have met Terry in my life and he made me realise just how lucky I was. I would even go as far as to say he helped me stay alive in my darkest hours, some of which you have already heard of – with more to come. In the nightclub I imagined Terry in the uniform of a five star general wheeling in on his state-of-the-art 'battle' chair to a meeting of the Joint Chiefs of Staff at NATO HQ Northwood. This memory would put me in good stead. Heaven knows what this chap's CO thought of the message.

I found myself wandering down some beautiful Devon country lanes near the sea. They were just the sort of lanes where the hero of *Rogue Male*, hunted down by his would-be assassins, made his hideout in the bank of and, using his own cat[77] Asmodeus's gut, skin and an iron spit, shot his tormentor in the face from within his hovel in the ground, killing him and enabling his escape. I felt the excitement of possibility. Around here I noticed the road signs all had what looked like a Germanic cross on them and my paranoid mind told me this was some vestige of a secret German plan to invade here during World War II. There seemed to be a conspiratorial magic in the air.

I tried to sleep in a field on the rolling uplands near Start Point but it was too cold without a sleeping bag. As I lay there I heard the distant sound of some church bells. Then I remembered a poem[78] about another despairing traveller through life and time.

The Tomorrow Where Nobody Cares

As the traveller went over the windy wold, slow bells rang
From the cloud-grey spire in the little town,
Dream-cradled in a fold of hills: and a traveller's song he sang
About summer and love and greengage lanes, as he went down
That winding way, in a timeless time ago.

But the lonely traveller is chained to the treadmill of his own despairs,

Ever hearing songs of promise, glory other-wheres:
Each journey is a solitude, a kind of dying;
And there's no use going back, there's no use crying
For the remembered road in the mist, the loves of long ago.

For no road leads back to that sweet past,
No highway jumps the barricade of time:
Nor would you see what could not last,
Take back from the tolling bell one single chime
Of the gold-spun hours of long ago.

For the lanterned cobbled lane is gone for ever,
The cottage killed by a profiting axe:
Vanished the twisting summer hedgerow, the starry dingle by the river,
And Midas-money drips like a candle's spoiling wax,
Crusting with formlessness the shapes of long ago.

And there are those who cannot see what harm they do or say,
Nor ever know what purpose is in life's short stand:
But drear ambition drives them from day to ageing day
Counting pennies in a trembling hand,
Till Death's surprising finger a penniless gain shall show.

So the lonely traveller is chained to the wheel of his own despairs,
A man who moves like time, his steps all forward lying
Over the time-misty hill, the tomorrow where nobody cares:
And there's no use going back, there's no use crying
For the greengage lanes, and the songs of long ago...

I had my thoughts. I wondered what Amanda would think if she could see me here trying to get some sleep under this drystone wall. Again I remembered the day we spent walking on the downs above Beachy Head. I counted through every time I had seen her in my life and it came to 31. I thought of the Aborigines, and what they would think of my journey. "There's nothing wrong with you Pommy, you're just on walkabout!" I imagined one saying. Cold, I rose and instead spent the rest of the night walking.

Shortly after dawn I got a lift with a chap who told me of a terrible secret. This was that near the end of the War there had been an exercise on this stretch of coast in which 946 American soldiers lost their lives. Even now, he said, the Ministry of Defence were very cagey about all of this. This knowledge preyed on my imagination. Who was this man? Had he been sent specifically to meet me? God had certainly sent him – but who else? In fact he was referring to Operation Tiger. Admiral Moon, who was responsible for the exercise, had later committed suicide.

I found myself in Plymouth, having by now used the bag of food which had been given to me courtesy of Diana, and went into a supermarket where I asked the manager for a loaf of bread. Amazingly, he told me "Just take one of those loaves there" and, though the bread was stodgy stuff costing only 19 pence anyway, I was truly grateful, and was able to fill my hungry stomach, the thought that it was a conspiracy not crossing my mind. But I am not convinced he understood me, and maybe I risked arrest by just walking out with it. Perhaps there is somebody driving an Aston Martin around somewhere they thought they had been told they could have.

From Torquay I made my way to Falmouth. As I left Torquay I looked and felt cold, as well as feeling desperately tired. A young chap picked me up and gave me an old but expensive jumper trimmed in leather. I prized this, and was most grateful.

In Liskeard I took a working break from the hunt for Prince Charles's dog sitting on a bench by the road. A middle-aged lady, obviously realising I was engaged in a noble activity, asked me if I was all right. She went away and when she came back I was sitting on the bench reduced in spirit. She gave me a packet of ginger nuts and a round of sandwiches. I needed to clean my teeth and as I hated having dirty teeth I went to the dentist where they gave me a free toothbrush though looking back I can't be sure if she thought I had not stolen it too.

In Falmouth I went to The Samaritans and said I had no money and nowhere to stay, and they sent me to a hostel where I was able to stay the night and get dinner: a hotpot. The hostel, as I was to discover they often are, was a cheery place.

The beds were laid out in a dormitory and were very close together. I slept like the proverbial log but not without a strange experience as I fell asleep. I was still convinced in some respect that there was a conspiracy to overthrow the Royal Family. From somewhere near came the sound of the Last Night of the Proms, but strangely, the lights in the room did not seem to be shining constantly: they seemed to get brighter and brighter and then suddenly go out. In my tired and deluded mind, I thought that each time they went out, a rebel army unit was executing another member of the Royal Family. I could see Prince William pleading "You can't shoot me, I'm destined to be King!" I sensed that either there was nothing I could do to prevent this ghastliness, or if there was, I was the only one who could.

Next day I was told I could not stay another night, and was not given a reason why. So now I was on the street again. I still had an optimistic and manic state of mind, and found myself walking up the biblically named Jacob's Ladder (in fact just a long stairway). I had read that the story of Jacob's Ladder was actually a description of aliens landing in biblical times. In my experience mental illness is often tied up with strange beliefs about aliens and I was no exception though I sensed the beliefs were others'. Ever since my visit to Her Majesty's Land Forces HQ Wilton the previous year I had been obsessed with making logical sense of my actions that day and was convinced I had the duty to raise the £10 million myself. All these strange thoughts and obsessions about the Royal Family were also typical, I believe, and no doubt every day Buckingham Palace received letters from people as ill or more ill than I was.

I tried to walk out of Falmouth to find a good point to hitchhike from but found myself going backwards and forwards in a state of total indecision. All I actually had to do was get hold of my cash card, and I would have been able to book into a nice bed and breakfast, as I was still being paid. But I was afraid of getting in touch with my family in case that compromised my position and got me arrested again. The risk of forced medication was too great and had to be avoided at all costs. So it was out of the question to make any contact. I felt as though I could return only when I had regained my confidence by relaunching myself somehow, proving I was not insane. I was determined to succeed in that aim.

Eventually I got another lift, from a chap going to Newquay. He dropped me near Bodmin, in a lonely place, and I wondered in the dark how near the famed Beast of Bodmin might be. Eventually a chap who looked like my old friend Dave Allen picked me up in his Volvo. Everything seemed so secure and relaxed and it felt like I was receiving heroin from my onboard drugs cabinet; either that or he was a dealer somehow managing to give it to me, perhaps in a sweet. At the very least I found his company hypnotic. During our conversation he told me that, during the days of the Lunatic Act of 1845 and the Criminal Lunatic Act of 1860, his grandmother had worked at Bodmin asylum, and that her job title was "Lunatic Attendant". He was going all the way to London; so I just sat back and enjoyed the ride. I was convinced he was related to Dave but dared not say – Capgras syndrome again.

Somewhere we stopped and went to get something to eat. I had no money and he paid for me and then said, before dropping me off, that he was into random acts of kindness, and gave me a £20 note.

I walked up the slip road and found myself entering a 'hotel', passing a security guard. The building had a horrible sense of death about it, and I imagined it was otherwise vacant. As at Fairmile Hospital, it felt like part of a vast decaying business empire, which was so badly managed it had become infested by a sickly death cult. I sensed great danger there. It had that same stench about the place and once again I was sure there could not be anyone genuinely alive in it. I suppose if I had asked of anyone familiar with that building what was wrong with it, they might simply confirm it to be an awful place but my senses were heightened because of this sick mania I was suffering and it seemed far worse than merely awful. It seemed gut-wrenchingly awful. You could vomit for hours. I left and began hitchhiking back in the direction I had come from and did so all night until I got to some motorway services near Cardiff, where I locked myself in a toilet and went to sleep.

Nobody disturbed me, enabling me to get the sleep I needed. Luckily the door went all the way down to the ground; so no casual toilet user could think I was dead. It had been some time since I first conceived the idea of wanting to see my own obituary in the newspaper, but I certainly did not want to be found truly dead in a motorway service station toilet. Yet I was fascinated with the concept of pretending to be dead, as you already know from my conjecture about Prince Charles's dog, and my fake death here would allow me to read my own obituary. I even imagined my MI5 handler reading it and saying "Very impressive Captain Travis", using my naval rank as the only member of an Admiralty-selected Special Boat Service Reserve squadron on a 10-year operational mission into hell. This would result in being awarded the George Medal for valour. Actually I had only been an Able-Bodied Seaman and, laughably, imagined the Admiralty had court-martialled me *in absentia* down to Ordinary Seaman once again, this time for the original offence of not turning up for training at Lympstone all that time ago. Of course I could not win the Victoria Cross as I was only in the Reserve. Either way the Special Forces did not actually turn up. So my thoughts about my fake death were obviously premature. And anyway, I'd had my car serviced, so it was just the scrumpy I was looking for.

Next day I found myself hitchhiking near a golf course, feeling cold and miserable. A car stopped and took me a few miles. The driver felt sorry for me and gave me a nice black SAS-style jacket. I'm wearing it on the cover of this book except there it is painted green for compositional reasons. I fantasised that this very jacket had been used in the SAS raid on the Iranian embassy and had been given to me with some mysterious ulterior motive based in witchcraft. Maybe my fake death was still on. They dropped me at another service area and I felt much warmer and comfortable in my delusion, if it was a delusion, that I was something to do with the Special Forces. I was trying to think along the right lines to enable me to get out of this situation.

I found myself walking down a country road towards Abergavenny. It was much warmer now, as the sun had come out. A bemused passer-by saw me sitting in the hedge. As I sat there, I heard a female voice in my head say, excitedly but as reverentially as you could possibly imagine, "Prince Charles is King!" I believed I was the only person in the whole country or even the world outside of the Special Forces; of course, who knew the Queen had stepped down, or had died. Indeed, now I had got my black original SAS jacket it simply confirmed I was now in the position I had aspired to since the day of my Admiralty interview: I was now, indeed, the only member of my own Special Boat Service Reserve squadron, a position I intended to fully exploit.

I got to Abergavenny and went into a baker's shop where I bought some rolls. Sitting in a sunny spot by the road eating them I discovered some little spiders, which could jump many times further than their own body size. I believed these spiders were not native to Wales or even the United Kingdom and had been put there, again by the Special Forces, as a clue, so exotic did they seem.[79] It seemed they wanted to show me the full wonder of the world. It got dark and I lay down to go to sleep in the doorway of a derelict chapel.

Morning came and I looked up to see the chapel had no roof – but fortunately it had not rained. A man came up to me, though I was still not quite fully awake, and he placed a small iced cake beside me and said *"Croeso"*. Good Welsh hospitality. Prince Charles knew everything that was happening. In his position as a Rear Admiral, he was watching my progress and looking after me, though I had already found out that being looked after by a Rear Admiral on a psychological warfare exercise did not simply consist of being given fairy cakes.

I walked about all day more or less aimlessly and ended up in Pontypool. Here I spent a wet old Welsh night sleeping in the main stand of the rugby ground, so at least I was dry. The Royal dog, cocking its head slightly, looked into my eyes to discern if I would mind it jumping up and then it did and curled up on my lap. I could feel the warmth as though it were actually there. Still I was obsessed with the concept of pretending to be dead – as I thought John Lennon had done. I still believed that I had actually met him, or Prince Charles, back at Weller Wing, the previous year. I hoped that, at the end of all this, when I was a hero and everyone knew – I would meet all the undead to exchange our stories of years in the wilderness. No matter that, whilst I was at Fairmile, I had seen both John Lennon and Peter Gabriel shot dead by the Army at the Real World Studios. In my letter to the Queen Mother, as well as my story about the betting coup, I had related my plan that, like John Lennon, the entire Royal Family should pretend to be dead explaining this was the only way they could be saved from the coming revolution. Being under attack by circumstance and history they had to follow the tactic of a beetle which rolls over and pretends to be dead to save itself. I implored them. *I was Prince Charles's most trusted advisor.*

I visualised those bizarre moments when Princess Diana *et al* would meet their cell and be told that the whole world thought they were now dead. I could see Buckingham Palace getting fuller as more and more 'died' and holed up there. I even imagined the undead being allowed out to walk around the West End incognito – one or two of them asking, with amusing naïvety, if that was safe, as though it was like going back in time and you might kill your own parents before you were born. A wartime spirit prevailed in the Palace and a well-known politician was getting somebody to bring towels and hot water because somebody was having a baby – like they always do in the films.

Next day I found myself at another motorway service station wondering what to do next. Here I saw a Rolls Royce drive past whose registration number I thought was L7. The driver, who was probably a chauffeur as he was smartly dressed in a uniform and hat with sunglasses, looked like he might be Prince Charles's own chauffeur. Suddenly it seemed like half the dead rock stars were not really dead, and that they had all joined John Lennon's cult. I was the hero in all this, and not just because I was the only member of my own SBS Reserve unit. My cover work positions were in some of the most sensitive areas of military technology, for example at RSRE, RARDE and DOAE. But, you see, I also had my own record label. Therefore, I believed, my position at the interface of the defence establishment and the music industry made me unique. This, together with the fact that I had seen through the biggest illusion in modern history, if I had not planned it myself, made me oh so valuable to their plan, conspiracy or joke, planned as it had been in such detail all those years earlier.

What a hero I was! This was why I was not depressed because I was in a delusive mania born out of truth – a truth I was yet to fully exploit to justify my having been ill. I would think things like: there is always some truth in the delusion someone holds. Then I would think: who's to say some MI5 chaps *did not* have a drink one Friday afternoon in 1926 and even tell or make up some grand long-term joke? As for the foot of the garden in Cornwall Road, nobody could argue it was not concreted over – or that it was not a rather odd home improvement. Perhaps they *had* left plans to bury a case of 1926 Talisker single malt Scotch whisky there and things did not work out as they had intended, the result being three MI6/KGB double agents were also buried along with the Nazi gold and treasures, and of course the original 1926 MTRUTH file.

Only I could decide what to do with my unique position. It all seemed so obvious that this was why I was having all these strange experiences. Outside of the Security Services, only I knew the true meaning of L Zero and L7. But if Prince Charles's dog was a front, so too could be L Zero, the MTRUTH file and even the Irish peace process. But a front for what? The sudden realisation of the consequences of this was overwhelming: *MI5 knew where the Holy Grail was and they wanted me to find it for myself!*

At the service station there was another Capgras incident (which, amusingly, itself sounds like the title of a Cold War espionage novel: *The Capgras Incident*). In the car park there was a rubbish-hopper full of newspapers with the name McCreath on the side. Then, passing me in the restaurant (where I found a mostly uneaten plate of fish and chips which I moved to another table and ate) was a girl whom I thought was someone I had not seen since I was eight years old, Cindy McCreath. She was a fanciable girl and I had once kissed her whilst playing kiss-chase. I froze to the spot and was unable to say anything to her, but instead just carried on down the corridor. Then, when I thought of the rubbish-hopper, I decided fate, or MI5, must have sent her, and went back to look for her – but in vain.

I climbed into the rubbish-hopper where it was warm and dry but found it inadvisable to actually go to sleep as I had visions of being carried away in it and dropped into a newspaper-mashing machine. I had heard stories of a similar end befalling tramps; so I did not feel too secure and just dozed, not wishing to be recycled, at least not that way.

I got another lift and found myself back in Cornwall somewhere. I was wandering around at random with no idea what to do next. Walking through some woods, where I lost the path, I ended up fighting my way through undergrowth and found a rickety old rotten wooden fence. I walked through it like it was a thousand years old (it fell to pieces) to find myself standing on a deserted single-track railway line rather overgrown with weeds. Although the track was rusty it did appear, from the silver line on the rail, that there had been a recent train. Then, around the bend I heard the unmistakeable sound of one slowly approaching. I returned into the undergrowth, where I felt secure. The front of the train went past and then stopped, hundreds of yards up the line, the wheels in front of me shunting back and forth in enormous waves. I decided to hobo it and, sure I would not be spotted, climbed into one of the large wagons, having no idea where the train would take me.

Inside the wagon it was chalky (china clay actually) and I would later emerge looking like a ghost – in a marshalling yard in what turned out to be Cardiff. So I was back in Wales again.

After brushing myself down I walked into Cardiff centre as it was getting dark. I still had some of the money I'd been given, and went into a pub to have a beer and decide on my next move. When I came out it was obviously going to be a cold night, the first frost of the autumn, and I had nowhere to go. I found some broken-down boxes just lying in the street and discovered that, intriguingly, when put together they made a perfectly formed six feet two inch-long undraughty coffin sufficient for sleeping in a shop doorway. I chose Country Casuals. There I had wanted to have a fake funeral and return from the dead. Now, like I said, some truth had been born out of my delusional plan. The boxes had been left there by the military. As everyone made their way home from a night on the tiles I was the one really on the tiles, but quite warm in my coffin despite it being frosty. Some of them jeered or threw coins. One person ran up and gave my coffin a hefty boot but I was unhurt. Kicking somebody's coffin – have some people no respect for the dead?

Next morning, I got up and picked up the coins, value approximately two pounds. Walking around in the bright and crisp early autumn sunlight, I met a young chap who took me along to a hostel where I got a free cup of coffee and it was decided that I needed a place to sleep.

That night a strange incident occurred. I was sitting in the foyer whilst somebody tried to sort me out a bed. The security guard was dozing. Down the stairs crept a bearded man whom, with ease, I believed to be a former member of the Special Forces. He just looked like one. He crept towards me on tiptoe like a hunting cat so as not to wake the security guard. Then he gestured to me silently to follow him, which I did and we went upstairs.

Upstairs he sat me down in front of the television, asked me if I wanted a coffee, which he then made me before disappearing not to return. The famous Princess Diana interview with Martin Bashir was on the television. The good treatment I was receiving in Cardiff was because the Royal Family was watching over me. Prince Charles or Princess Diana herself had wanted to make me comfortable to watch the interview. That was how close I had got to them, proven by the obvious fact that the chap who got me past the security guard was a former member of the Special Forces: they thought I could do something massive, like make an application to the Prince's Trust for a negative amount. I woke up the next morning in the same seat with the television still on. I felt as though I'd had my most strange and mystical encounter with the Royal Family yet and, making my way outside, I noticed the plaque announcing: *Opened by His Royal Highness the Prince of Wales.*

Now I made my way over to the Salvation Army hostel where they told me I should not have had to sleep on the street and could have come along even in the middle of the night and they would have found me a bed, provided I was not drunk. I had breakfast, which I ate with gusto. Afraid of arrest, I gave the name James Longhurst, which would mean they would not be able to claim against my National Insurance number, but this did not prevent me getting a bed. I spent the day wandering around Cardiff.

Chapter Thirty-One

She's So High

After a good night's sleep and breakfast I jumped a train to London without a ticket. I sat in first class and the guard did not check me; so although I felt some trepidation that he might discover I was ticketless I enjoyed the journey and ordered a bottle of wine to my table – it was gratis as the train was late.

Now I was on the street in London. I believed I had received a personal message from the President of the United States of America. It seemed real enough for me to think it could have been one of those rare occasions the Special Intelligence Service broadcast me something above subliminal in my MTRUTH. I received the message from President William Jefferson Clinton on a bright-blue autumn day near Parsons Green. Here, psychiatrically destitute, I was walking towards Chelsea, and found a large apple lying on the pavement. It was a Granny Smith, very crisp, and having no bruises seemed it must have been placed there quite deliberately moments earlier. I was happy to eat it. The message was simply "Nice day!" which I supra-imagined him saying in a confirmatory way. The apple was perfect and reminded me of New York, "The Big Apple", which cheered me up.

Later I walked into Centre Point looking for a bed but it turned out to be the Confederation of British Industry and not the charity hostel of the same name for the homeless I was looking for. That night I slept in the entrance to Leicester Square Tube Station. During the night a wonderful feeling came over my entire body. Surely this could only be heroin, I thought. In reality it must have been a combination of the cold and the upset to my brain chemistry. But no, Prince Charles wanted to make me feel comfortable and he had sent a car down from MI5 with a marksman in it who had shot me with a heroin dose. The psychological war I had decided I was in was continuing, and this was the more pleasant side of it. Moreover there was no chance of getting addicted – as I didn't believe they would allow that to happen. But this would not be the last time by any means it felt like I had been given heroin.

As dawn approached the newspaper vendor woke me up as I was lying on his pitch, but he said I could sleep next to his stand – so I did.

Later on another down-and-out approached and asked if he could buy me a coffee. I had no money but he bought me one in Oxford Street. Then he took me back to his den (made of cardboard boxes) under the steps to the DSS near Charlotte Street. He invited me in and we both lay down to sleep. Only I did not feel very comfortable in his quarters and without thanking him or saying goodbye I furtively got up and left – hoping he did not notice. I wandered around Oxford Street for a while, stealing a pint of milk which had just been delivered, then made my way down towards Soho where I walked into a hotel and served myself breakfast. There seemed to be no check of room number and I got away with this ruse beautifully. As I enjoyed breakfast I wondered how many of the other guests were down-and-outs like me. Again I wondered how I was going to raise the £10 million for charity. Right now it was a long way off but I still felt optimistic.

I took a wander around the hotel and discovered it was quite a decrepit old building with communal bathrooms and little or no security. So I decided I would have a nice hot bath and then spend the next night in the bathroom with the door locked, which I did.

Next morning I wrote a letter to the United States' President and walked into the embassy handing it to the guard. In the letter I said the Queen was in danger and needed help, which I asked for. I seem to recall the guard was a serving British naval officer. Later I became paranoid about the United States' ability to keep my identity as an agent secret and assumed this guard was the last line of defence. Was I being followed? Or was it too late and the letter had got through? The letter was hardly interesting and I imagined may have been discarded – depending that is on what Aldrich Ames, the US spy who was caught selling secrets to the Russians, had succeeded in getting out of the KGB – like my name.

The President of Finland was visiting and all down The Mall the Finnish flag was flying. Now I needed to contact Prince Charles to warn him the Finnish President was in danger too. Why he was in danger I do not recall. I made my way to Prince Charles's office, which I identified by a notice announcing "HRH Prince Charles" next to his car park slot. But before I got there I realised it might be some time before he arrived, possibly days, and I was determined to wait at his office until he appeared – however long that might be.

On the pavement were the remains of a discarded hamburger. The challenge was on and the challenge meant I had to eat the hamburger like a pigeon. I wanted to go as low as possible as only then could I really find my way back to the top and my goal. I went down on my hands and knees and ate the hamburger by biting it and throwing it up in the air a number of times. I crawled around at random in a hilarious parody of the bird. I thought of the novel *Birdy* – about a Vietnam war veteran and psychiatric prisoner who thinks he is a bird. But I would argue, without having read the story that he did not really think he was a bird – he simply chose to adopt the posture of one, just like I was now doing in St. James's, and had when I barked at Fairmile. I imagined he had some ulterior motive for behaving in this avian manner. I was just feeling peckish.

I have always felt a strong affinity with feral pigeons, so many of which have chronic and unsightly problems with their feet – as I had done with a nasty fungal toenail infection. So I wrote to the Chairman of Burger King at Grand Metropolitan, on behalf of the pigeons of London, to suggest a uniformed Grand Metropolitan Pigeon Warden be appointed to go around putting lame pigeons out of their misery, or at least be taken to Switzerland.

After eating the remains of the burger without, as it turned out, any ill effects, I made my way into Prince Charles's office. Here I was greeted by three officers from the Royal Protection Squad who interviewed me as they searched my bag. One of them bore a striking resemblance to Pete Townshend from The Who and this was one of the best Capgras incidents of the lot. I could have laughed. Somehow I did not actually ask them if I could meet Prince Charles and no calamity befell the Finnish President. Talk about Prince Charles's dog. Now I was more like his pigeon.

I wandered through the nearby Robert Dyas ironmongers, feeling surprised such a humble shop was still going in such an expensive area. Then I went into the equally famous Lock and Co. Hatmakers, by appointment to H.R.H. Prince Charles. I was fitted for a bowler hat. Whilst being fitted, a procedure I noted to be carried out in an impeccably gentlemanly style, I noted an American was being fitted for another hat across the shop. To my then mind he was a very good double of William Jefferson Clinton himself. In conversation with his fitter he asked "How much would a hat like that cost?" To this the reply was, in the most convincingly respectful manner you could imagine, "In this style, about seventeen hundred pounds sir." Once again it reminded me of *Alice In Wonderland* where you might remember the Mad Hatter's top hat still has the price label attached saying "In this style 10/6d". Inflation you see.

I was staggered at how much you could pay for a hat. Impressed by the exquisite service I asked "Would it be all right if I left a £5 deposit and collect when I'm famous?" The fitter replied, without batting an eyelid, "That would be perfectly alright Sir, I shall make up your receipt." I gave him a £5 note I had found in my jacket lining. I didn't wait until I was famous, but went back two years later. The very same gentleman enquired "How are you handling fame sir?" I think he had read what the receipt said as I was not yet famous for anything he could have known about, unless Prince Charles had said something to him.

Walking around St. James's I noticed an old water trough for horses, which had on the side, the words *Metropolitan Cattle Trough and Drinking Fountain Association*, a flowerbed having been tastefully laid out in it, as they often are. I went to the library and found out the address of this peculiar body, which I then visited. An elegant mature lady opened the door at what seemed like a private address and directed me elsewhere.

I now decided I wanted to produce a national database of water troughs and drinking fountains. So I decided to go to the Millennium Commission to apply for a grant. I needed an old van and a laptop personal computer. I would drive from town to town all over the country with my grant, sleeping in the back of the van and drawing all the water fountains I could find. The job would keep me occupied for years and I could put my catalogue on the Internet. I thought there must be a lot of history to uncover associated with the fountains. At the Millennium Commission, who saw me without any appointment, they referred me to English Heritage who gave me the forms I needed to apply for a grant.

I walked along the river. Near MI5 headquarters I sat down on a bench. As the pigeons walked amicably about, I noticed that the water fountain was not working. It was a more modern type and I wondered if I would include it in the survey. I knew I would be a happy man doing it, and seemed to recall that Prince Charles was patron of the Water Fountain Association.

Suddenly, somebody unseen turned on the fountain; but the flow was not very impressive, indeed it was little more than a somewhat pathetic trickle. It seemed to represent the amount of success I was now having in my life. Amusingly, as I had been thinking about the Security Services so often, I was not thinking of MI5 even though their headquarters were close to where I was sitting. The already laughably weak fountain then declined to a dribble. Only later would I imagine that MI5 were watching from the windows of Thames House at that actual moment, and that they themselves had been adjusting the fountain's tap. I would have to try a lot harder to raise the £10 million immortality money. That night I slept well in the bathroom of the hotel again. Next morning I was off to Bexleyheath, carrying my plastic carrier bag full of English Heritage documents. There was another occasion when I walked past Thames House, though when it was I do not recollect. Only I do clearly recall noticing a screwed up tissue nestling against the wall. The type of tissue I could only guess.

At Bexleyheath, I went to the YMCA to see if I could get any accommodation from which to plan my way out of all this. I met a nice chap called Andy Braund. They had no accommodation – it was just a meeting place. But I told him some story, and he went straight to the cash box and took out enough to get me a bed and breakfast. I was truly grateful. He took me there in his car, paid the landlord and wished me good luck. I did not push my luck by asking how long I could stay. Later, when I emerged from this confusion, I sent him a postal order for the sum, courtesy of James Longhurst, which must have surprised him. Somehow I never got to the address the lady had sent me to.

Next day, whilst going ticketless through Catford on a train, I decided I would soon be so powerful that all I would have to do was ask politely, and Catford would become Dogford, whilst "dog-eared" would become "cat-eared". Sitting opposite on the train was a Catholic priest. He said "Top o' the morning to yer my son" and asked me how I was. I said "Fine" but explained that for some reason I was thinking I was so powerful I could change the name of Catford to Dogford and have people say cat-eared instead of dog-eared.

"Tell me son," he said perspicaciously, "have yer ever suffered from schizophrenia?" and I explained I had. "It's a terrible illness," he told me, "you'll suffer prejudice and discrimination." Then he told me a story about a dog he knew.

"The dog looked in a shop window and saw a sign which said 'Help Wanted. Must be able to type, good with a computer and bilingual. We are an Equal Opportunities Employer.' The dog went into the shop. He looked at the receptionist and wagged his tail, looked at the sign, and whined. Getting the idea, the receptionist went and got the office manager. The manager looked at the dog and was rather surprised, to say the least. However the dog looked determined and so was led into the office. The dog jumped onto a chair and stared at the manager. The manager said 'I can't hire you. The sign says you have to be able to type'. The dog jumped down, went to the typewriter, and typed out a perfect letter. He took out the letter and trotted over to the manager, gave it to him, and then jumped back onto the chair. The manager was stunned with the dog's skill but said 'The sign says you have to be good with computers'. The dog jumped down again and went over to the computer. The dog proceeded to demonstrate his skills with various programs producing a sample spreadsheet and a database, which he presented to the manager. By now the manager was utterly dumbfounded. He looked at the dog and said 'I realise that you are a very intelligent dog – however I still can't give you the job'. So the dog jumped down again and went over to the sign pointing with his paw at where it said 'Equal Opportunities Employer'. The manager said 'Yes, but the sign also says that you have to be bilingual'. The dog stared straight back into the manager's face and said 'Meow'."

I laughed. Then the Catholic priest looked out of the train window and exclaimed "Well bless me soul, if it isn't raining cats and dogs!"

We said goodbye. I decided to press on cattishly, rather than doggedly, though I was on the street again – wandering a little aimlessly around South London.

That night I found myself walking around late at night in Croydon shopping centre. In it was a Cadillac absolutely covered in cutlery bent by Uri Geller who, in my delusion, I did not trust. His tricks were all part of John Lennon's illusion which only one or two BBC staff, almost certainly Freemasons, knew about. All the cutlery was deliberately malleable, and the illusion would unfold on New Year's Eve 1999. That was why it was so important that the Royal Family had to pretend to be dead. After all the preparation, they surely could not avoid this plan of action. The question was: which L number had MI5 assigned to this lie – the Cutlery Lie?

In the shopping centre I found some tables, which appeared to have been used for some trade exhibition. The tablecloths were draped so that they reached the floor, providing a concealed place to sleep, undisturbed by the security guard. Lying securely and warmly under the table I thought of how disquieted I had been about Lunar House, where people seek asylum and which I had seen outside. Somehow my illness had made me incredibly paranoid about bad architecture such that it sent a nauseating shudder to the core of my subconscious. Laughing, I imagined Prince Charles saying "What was so ill about that? I feel like that all the time."

Next day I went to Ipswich and, being ticketless, was thrown off the train. The British Transport Police were called. Don't ask me why I went to Ipswich; really I have no idea why. I just did. The policeman said he was going to let me go, and said, "Looks like you got a result this time", which was obviously better than being arrested and possibly returned to hospital. I spent the cold night sleeping in a shop doorway until another policeman came along and told me I would have to move on. I found somewhere else and tried to get a bit more sleep but it was too cold.

In the morning I went to the library, which I felt was the only place I could really trust in all of this. They sent me to a house where I would be able to get a free lunch. Milton Friedman was wrong: there was such a thing as a free lunch after all.

Refreshed by the meal, I went back to London and walked into Birkbeck College where I knew there was a shower I could use. As the powerful and hot stream of water flooded down my body, I thought of the great riches, of whatever type, which would be mine when it became known that I was the only person in the world to crack this illusion: the illusion of John Lennon and MI5 named L Zero. And this was quite apart from "1926" and my KGB file. I set off for Scotland.

Chapter Thirty-Two

We Wait And We Wonder

I said goodbye to my lift from England at a roundabout quite some way outside Edinburgh. It was getting dark, a bit chilly and really not very wonderful. Soon I found myself in the car park of The Stakis Hotel and here I chanced upon their MPV whose sliding door was unlocked. In the back were some blankets so I slipped in and covered myself up, hoping the vehicle would not be used until morning. That was a bit too hopeful as it was not late, and sure enough a while later the staff politely asked me to get out as they had to go and collect someone. Again I began hearing the sound bite of Howard's voice saying "Mr Blobby". I was being ridiculed. It was an automated response from the computer my MTRUTH was attached to, the operator having gone home, or perhaps wishing it to appear he had.

So now I began the long walk into the city and, an hour or so later, found myself sitting on a wall opposite some waste ground. Not being familiar with Edinburgh, I had no idea where I was. One day I would return and recognise this spot though, near Holyrood, and "Little Ireland", noticing that an attractive building had been erected on the site. Sitting there wondering what to do next, a group of Scottish student types out on a drinking session, asked if I was alright and handed me a couple of quid. It so astounded me (I had not asked) I just sat there looking at the money in my hand. I felt quite emotional about their kindness. I would not say what happened next was like a Hogmanay celebration but it was nice to have a couple of coins. I wandered off back in the direction I had come from, noticing a plaque marking the birthplace of James Connolly, Father of Irish Republicanism, who was executed by a British firing squad on May 12th 1916 after the Easter Uprising. He had been taken by military ambulance to Kilmainham Prison, carried on a stretcher to a courtyard in the prison, tied to a chair and shot. With the other executed rebels, his body was put into a mass grave with no coffin. I would still be experiencing some level of delusion of grandeur upon my return here and associated the exchange of this small sum of money with the construction of the wonderful building – imagining the Masons had made something of it.

That night I found my way into a building site on Cowgate, close to the plaque and near the Royal Mile, one of Edinburgh's main streets. In it was a workman's hut with an unlocked door and I let myself in. There was an electric fire, which I switched on, and a fridge in which I found some not terribly fresh bread and instant coffee, but no milk. I put the kettle on and brewed up before settling down on the floor to get some kip. Before I had gone to sleep somebody threw a bottle at the hut and, as it smashed, I heard them say "At least he's got some bottle." They were from the Scottish Special Forces and had been ordered to do it. They had used my lodestone chips to locate me as being in the workman's hut, which was modelled in *Colchester*. Yes – I did have some bottle, and the next day I would prove it.

Next morning I took a train and got off at Dalmeny, shocked into doing so by the enormity of Sir William Arrol's Forth Rail Bridge, or perhaps because I could see the Heinrich Himmler of the Railway Revenue Protection Inspectorate in the next carriage. Just outside the station was a disused building. I had a look inside and decided it was a desirable property for an Edinburgh stockbroker, though at present it was obviously uninhabitable due to it apparently having been designated a graveyard for fruit machines.

I walked down the long path into Queensferry, admiring spectacular views of the bridge on which work was being carried out, as it always is. I was mindful of the possibility of being killed by a falling tool. Fifty-seven people had been killed during its construction alone and I did not wish to join them. More recently a famous escape scene was shot on the bridge in *The 39 Steps*. There was much of that film in what was now happening, or what I thought was happening, to me.

After a pleasant walk I was in the village and, at a loss as to what to do next, as I had been for some time, had a look around. For some reason I left my bedding, which I had been given at a social centre somewhere, outside the post office. When I returned, the bedding had disappeared. The long drop from the Forth Road Bridge, half a mile from the rail bridge, seemed to cast a shadow over my every movement.

I visited the museum where I imagined myself as a future Queensferry Burryman (a local folk character like a cross between a Morris Dancer, a Pearly King and a May Queen at a pub bun fight down in London's East End).[80] As depicted in the museum, he would be dressed up, covered in flowers and the fruits or burrs of the lesser burdock, and paraded around Queensferry with great jollity every August to safeguard the herring catch. Nationality restrictions would, I imagined, probably make thoughts of me as the Burryman a sensitive issue. Instead I took to spying on the distant Rosyth Dock Yard through an old pair of oversized Japanese Imperial Navy binoculars, now land-mounted.

As night fell, having few coins left, I went into the pub under the bridge to drink a beer, which I did at a ludicrously slow rate. Outside, just where Stephen Hendry, the World Snooker Champion, was to give a BBC *Grandstand* interview a year later, some joyrider appeared and tore up the street between the beautiful road and rail bridges, the latter being floodlit. It was an inspiring place – and I felt positive.

Now I had to find somewhere to sleep, a task I set to without even the slightest feeling of depression. Earlier in the day I had posed as a prospective housebuyer whilst looking for somewhere to crash later and managed to be shown around some new flats, some of which were already occupied. I was feeling positive about the prospects of my later actually buying one.

It was now late evening. I found my way back to these flats and bedded down on some discarded cardboard underneath the bottom of the communal stairs. Here there was no door through which I would be likely to be disturbed, and I went to sleep.

In the morning I was awoken by the sounds of someone getting ready to go to work in one of the flats above, and I lay there listening on my bed of cardboard, which was better than nails, though with no bedclothes. I heard this person shut the door then come downstairs. Somehow the noises made left me in no doubt it was a woman – but I was also left thinking she had not locked the door. I was now to discover that her boyfriend was not in.

When she got to the bottom of the stairs, just a few feet from me, she stopped, possibly because she had forgotten something, or perhaps for some other reason, and returned to the flat. Now she came out again and the sound the door made as she departed left me in no doubt she had not shut it properly again.

Perhaps she was just in a great hurry, perhaps the door needed a good pull or perhaps that was normal round there. Either way, after a while I decided to go and find out if I had been right, possibly out of nothing more than curiosity, and sure enough, one little push with my finger and it was clear the latch was not in the notch and the door swung open.

Schizophrenia goes both ways and I imagined Prince Charles had phoned up and asked the occupant to leave the door open. So I had little difficulty deciding to pretend, should I need to, I believed a friend of mine lived there and had told me to drop around anytime I liked. This meant that I could now go in, have a bath and a shave, continental breakfast including cereal, ice cold milk, coffee and orange juice followed by a relaxed morning going through their CD collection. Any worries about unexpected arrivals were adequately prepared by my plan to say, in an Irish accent for a laugh, that Patrick had told me I could stay, and if they did not know Patrick it must either just be a friend of their partner or there had been some mistake. I even planned to say "So you must be..."

I suppose I felt a little rude to use their razor and toothbrush but at least I cleaned the bath properly. I did take the liberty of borrowing a yellow polo shirt made in Mauritius but there was never any question of taking their Calvin Klein jeans, just not my style. I would have used my own toothbrush from Liskeard but it had disappeared, leaving me suspicious that I had not just lost it. I could not help but notice they had left their wallet and that it was stuffed full of coins to bursting point, but I did not feel inclined to take anything from it. It was a test of my honesty by Prince Charles. I could not however resist doing one thing before I left. An old friend of mine had once told me a story about somebody at a party. They had chosen to stick the host's toothbrush up their arse and photograph it there, using the host's camera, before leaving. The owner of the toothbrush presumably discovered this to their horror when, later, they had the film developed. I sensed that my mere presence as a person in possession of such knowledge put me in a very sensitive position. So to mark the occasion, there being a loaded camera, I took a photograph of the window to the street through the door into the living room; doing nothing improper with the toothbrush other than, admittedly, clean my teeth. I now left, the only signs indicating my erstwhile presence being that the chair was positioned to obtain the full stereo effect from the speakers, The Eurythmics CD was still in the stereo, the polo shirt was missing and the front door was properly shut, if not deadlocked. Oh, and of course the photograph.

Please don't gather the impression I am particularly proud of this behaviour. But nor am I ashamed. You see I really believed I was *supposed* to use the flat. Only fleeting insight had made me imagine somebody might catch me there and not be too happy about it. I should have visited the nearest Aston Martin garage like the bloke I mentioned whilst I was in this frame of mind.

I indeed now felt I was a prisoner in a book on a library shelf waiting for someone to release me by reading my story which was unfolding by the year, if not the minute. Like in *The Prisoner*, I was not a number; I liked to think – though whether I was being followed by a large MI5 balloon, a psychic, and a psychic-wrestling SAS sumo rabbit, I was not sure. However I later noticed all the BBC programme introductions were preceded by a shot of a large globe balloon floating over places, many of which I had travelled to in my attempt to find Prince Charles's dog, including here, South Queensferry. But this was hardly surprising since I had been to so many places. Nevertheless, I felt there was significance in these broadcasts which I was party to. And I might find myself into the bargain.

Refreshed from my free use of this 'grace and favour' apartment I now made my way back into Edinburgh and visited the Public Library. I picked up a copy of Wisden at random, and opening it found myself reading a short article about first class cricket in Israel. This was a remarkable story in that only two or three games had been recorded, making Scotland look like the home of the game, and one of these games had been abandoned when the pitch had been invaded by schoolgirls. At least that's what I recall. It did not say whether they were from St. Trinians. Laughing to myself, I thought of the question mark in *Jerusalem* again and wondered if I would ever be a member of the Lords' Taverners.

Picking up another book at random and opening it likewise, I read of how deported Irishmen had been driven to cannibalism in the Australian Outback, having escaped from the prison compound. This knowledge made quite an impression.

I was wearing a motley assortment of clothes which I had been handed at various points in my journey including, over the first pair of trousers, a pair of grey jeans which I had found spread oddly over the barbed wire fence by the National Stadium in Cardiff. They were a good quality pair except, mysteriously, all the stitching was undone from the bottom of the trouser legs to the crotch on both legs. Somehow I had procured some safety pins, I have no idea from where, and used these to hold them together. I took these trousers to the dry cleaning shop by Princes Street to be re-stitched – but never collected them. I wonder who's wearing them now. The possibility of begging never even crossed my mind and, should I have been inclined, I might have said at this time "I don't do that."

That evening, knowing it was too late to get help from the DSS, I made my way back to the Royal Mile where I slept in the workman's hut again. How many nights I stayed there I do not know, though I realised the workman might get a bit arsed off with my uninvited presence, and however it came about, I found myself walking across the Forth Road Bridge late at night. I felt a little bit uncomfortable to say the least. This reminded me of walking across the Itchen Bridge in Southampton, a few years earlier.

On this occasion, I did not have to go down on my hands and knees, though eventually felt driven to at least look over the edge. Doing this did not prevent me from reaching, with some sense of relief, the other side, where I now decided to pay a visit to the security gate of Her Majesty's dockyard, Rosyth. Perhaps, I thought, I was not the only person to be relieved I had got there – it being an inconceivable waste of the latest military technology that I should be found dead on the beach at Leith, downstream.

Soon I was at the dockyard gate. In my deluded state of grandeur I felt a strong duty to make a report at a Scottish military establishment, at least now I was here, having already done so in England. I reported to the gate and was escorted by a firearm-toting soldier into the office for interview. I told them how Philip Zeigler, the author of Lord Mountbatten's biography, was a traitor and had to be arrested, explaining how Lord Mountbatten could not possibly have made the trip across Africa in the time given in his biography. There was a policeman there who asked me if he could sit in on the interview. I declined to have him present and explained how I had uncovered a network of spies inside the Ministry of Defence. By now I do not think they could have arrested me simply for absconding as the 28 days had passed. They probably had a good enough excuse though by what I was saying. But a lot of people do not know about mental illness and they probably just thought I was "some nutter". They were right: how could I possibly be a member of the Special Forces looking for Prince Charles's dog? I was expecting a cup of coffee and a bed but that was a little optimistic. I gave my name as James Longhurst. They said it was all right and let me go, so once more it was the middle of the night and I had nowhere to go.

I walked north. At about one o'clock I saw a late-night runner who I thought was spying on me, and then, further on, I got a lift, which took me to Perth. I wandered around town a bit looking for somewhere to sleep and eventually walked into the police station. There were quite a few people waiting, so I went into the toilet, shut the door, and went to sleep. After some time I was woken by a policeman who objected to me sleeping there; so I had to get up. Not to be outdone though, I waited around and when the coast was clear I went into the interview room at the front of the station and then took part in the longest and most boring interview ever conducted at Perth Police Station. It lasted until next morning and only I was present – nothing being said. I sat at the table with my head on it. I was not disturbed. *I did not notice a tape recorder.*

Next day I found myself in Inverness. I had been there the previous year when first ill, and now revisited the library. Then I made for the Salvation Army Hostel where I got a lovely hot coffee. The atmosphere there was wonderful and they took me to my room where I immediately went to sleep. I slept all that day and night. I was very tired.

The day after, I headed north again with the intention of getting to Wick. It was late autumn and not very warm. I got a lift with a chap who took me to his house and gave me lunch near the Moray Firth. Next I found myself in a Land Rover County being driven along the spectacular coast road to Wick. When the driver described the road as the "track", this fed my old delusion that some sort of procession was going to form, and I was in it. If the Special Intelligence Service *had* fitted me with an MTRUTH and were only inputting information subliminally, I could not tell they were, it seemed. Fair play dictated they give me some clues. The "track" also reminded me, once again, that I could not be sure to what level my actions were down to my own free will, existentially speaking. Alternatively, I could not be sure to what extent I was on a well-defined Defence Intelligence *Wacky Races*[81] route a bit like a Scalextric track on which I was not, by any means, the only person. It was as though I were on an ancient pilgrimage route, now a Special Forces hierophantic assault course and I, along with the other members of my Admiralty-selected SBS and Army-selected SAS *Dirty Dozen*-style units, were all looking for Prince Charles's dog. "We're all mad now!" I said to myself.

Arriving in Wick, without paying, I watched Wick Academy play football. After the match I wandered around, gleaning the town's close links with Norway, as a result of once having been under Norwegian rule. I went into a pub where I got a beer either with a few coins I had or by pretending drinks in the glass collection area had been mine. If you are prepared to face the health risk you can get nicely drunk in a busy pub by collecting nearly-full drinks from near the dishwasher, especially late at night if it's busy.

Then I went to the police station and 'explained' my predicament. I told them I had lost my wallet in Portree and had nowhere to stay. I asked if I could "sleep in the cell", sensing a double-meaning based in espionage as I did so. Instead they said I could sit in the entrance lobby while they phoned up Portree Police Station. I imagined bumping into this policewoman later and during a chat she would joke "Oh you meant spend the night on the bench in the room we put people in after we have arrested them – why didn't you say? I thought you were from MI5." Of course my story was untrue; so I suppose I was wasting police time. She brought me a coffee, which was Scottish hospitality rather akin to the little cake I had been given in Wales.

On the pinboard, I noticed a picture of a missing girl. This was my latest Capgras incident as she looked rather too much like the Polish girl who had given me the blow-job on the Bedford Castle mound a few years earlier – the picture seemed to have been put there for me. I sat there all night dozing and next day made for Scrabster Harbour.

I was now as far north as it is possible to go on the mainland. I reached Thurso hungry, and without any money I went into the supermarket. I found some bread, which had reached its sell-by date and walked into the restaurant with it (so that I had not actually left the shop). The shop manager approached me and I complained that the bread was stale and should not be on display questioning the legal meaning of "by". He was not very nice but did not arrest me, he just threw me out of the shop.

However my fortunes now changed. As I was standing by the road at the edge of town waiting for a lift a police Land Rover pulled up. The driver was a mature policeman, ready to retire, and he knew what I had done. He told me to get in and asked me if things had not been going too well for me. He took me to the Church Hall where lunch was being served to the retired folk. There I was invited to join them and what a friendly bunch they were. I sat opposite an affable Glaswegian to whom I told some, but not all of my story. Life is only so long and, if you do not adopt an MI5 posture you can turn into a 24 hours per day storyteller. Filled up with a lovely hot lunch I continued my way along the north coast of Scotland, braving the rapidly approaching winter.

I walked a few miles along the road, admiring the desolate scenery, which became more beautiful by the mile, and then a young attractive English woman picked me up and gave me a caramel slice for sustenance. I asked if I could keep it for later but really I should have invited myself into her house as I quite fancied her; but on this occasion it was not to be. As she dropped me off she asked a strange question about a man we could see: "Do you know that man?" The air was heavy with the mystery of the Alistair MacLean books I had read back at the bed and breakfast in Kilmuir the previous summer.

I got another lift, this one from the director of the Dounreay "fast breeder" nuclear reactor station. This was the only fast breeder reactor in the country but had now stopped producing electricity and was out of favour, though I was always a bit of a fan of that type of reactor.

Now I really got into my walking with the inviting mountains of the northwest Highlands in the distance. I walked on and on, past deserted closed-down hotels and crofts. In places I found myself walking on bits of disused road, which looked like they might not have been used since World War II, the road having been upgraded, with pieces of road having become isolated, like ox-bow lakes. Eventually I found another lift and the driver pointed out "The Monarch" of Scottish mountains, An Caisteal (Ben Loyal), which is shaped like a crown.

I remembered the Absolute Secret document at RARDE, and the possibility that my MTRUTH included 3D sub-millimetric lodestone GPS chips in my fingers. From a command and control relay station in the back of my neck the Special Intelligence Service could not only see straight through my eyes but also monitor the movement of my fingers should I try to write with my eyes shut. The thought came to my head that I should write "36" secretly with my forefinger in my pocket, the 36 referring to the 36th Brigade of Ulster Volunteers who were slaughtered on the Somme and from whom today we have the Ulster Volunteer Force (UVF). This I now did.

Now I learnt the greatest secret of my life for how was it that I now looked up into the sky and there, within a matter of seconds and certainly not minutes, appeared a large vapour trail 36 in the sky? The answer could only be either that the 36 was being overlaid on what I saw using my MTRUTH or that the idea came into my head over my MTRUTH a few short moments before two RAF jets actually drew the 36 in the sky. Quite astonished and somewhat perplexed by this I now remembered how I had somewhere heard that wherever you go you are never more than 50 yards from a rat. At the time my mind was telling me there had been a deliberate dual meaning in this. Any radio emissions broadcast, or rebroadcast from inside a human body were not likely to be terribly powerful. If required at a remote location they would have to be picked up quite close at hand in remote locking terms: in this case by RATS (Rebroadcast Army Telecommunications System). This was known in the Special Intelligence Service as the Rehoming Animal Telephone Service (a charity for stray pets in Bedford). The RATS would have been laid earlier along my path or might even be carried along unseen nearby. But I was just hallucinating – it was all just wishful thinking and visual autosuggestion. How could that possibly be true? But it *was* true and what is more, the devices in my eyes also had motion sensors so that I could myself leave graffiti on the sky simply by writing with my eyes. So I signed my illegible signature across the Scottish sky. I thought of also leaving my Drummonds bank account number next to it but decided Scottish intelligence would wonder what the world was coming to if people could just turn up and leave graffiti across their sky like that so demurred.

Evening fell just as I came across a small village not far from Durness near Cape Wrath, the most northwesterly point of Britain. Here, on bonfire night 1995, a few weeks later, the K Foundation painted a contract onto a car agreeing to end the Foundation for a period of 23 years. The car was then ceremonially pushed over the cliff to its final resting place, some six hundred feet below.

I found a wonderful empty-looking house, which had long boxes against the wall outside in which it was obvious that fishing rods were stored, but now they were empty. Perhaps the occupants had gone fishing I thought – but they had not put a sign up. Whoever the house belonged to, I thought they must be very wealthy people to have a getaway like this. I could not find a way in, and was frightened by a dog barking in the distance as well as a light which seemed to come on inside, so I carried on walking towards Durness. It got dark and another Landrover stopped. Inside were a man and his daughter. They too must have thought I was a bit of a nutter. But they must have also felt sorry for me because they gave me a carrier bag full of comestibles to keep me going out in these wilds – but they did not remove anything first making me wonder if it had, in fact, been bought for me. Mysterious. I should have asked for some money to buy a beer when I arrived in Durness but I was not given to begging – at least not yet. Perhaps Prince Charles sent the bag, I thought.

They dropped me in Durness near closing time and I entered the pub. There was no chance of a beer without asking someone to buy me one and I did not feel like doing so. So I looked around the pub for a place where I might be able to sleep undiscovered, but without success.

I left the pub and instead found a field with stooks of hay in it, a rare sight showing farming here was still little more than crofting. I attempted to make a bed from one of the stooks. But the bed was not warm enough and I could not sleep. This was the sort of situation where I was going to pay for being AWOL from the Royal Marine Commando Training Centre. My survival skills were not what they might be. But I made sense of that, not by invoking what I had done whilst AWOL but by simply telling myself I was in the SBS and had been ordered not to use any of my usual survival skills. So catching a rabbit was perhaps out of the question – unless I did it in an unusual way. Anyway, there was no snow to dig a snow-hole in.

There was a high cloud base and it was quite chilly. So I got up and walked – and walked. I walked all night past the mountains Foinaven and Arkle. I suspected that Ireland's greatest steeplechaser, which won the Cheltenham Gold Cup in 1964, '65 and '66 was named after the latter so it seemed likely the 1967 Grand National winner, Foinavon, with two "o"s, was named after the former. The slightly different spelling held some transient and supremely significant meaning, which related to the 1926 meeting and the Torbay Harbour Act 1970 in a way that only reinforced my delusions of grandeur. It was a wonderful feeling. Like Foinavon I was miles behind in the field and at 100-1 I was all but out of the race. But I was starting my comeback. Here, in this remote and beautiful place, with nobody around for miles, the Special Intelligence Service had chosen to let me in on what was now my own all-powerful secret. Don't ask me what it was mind you – I was just convinced there was one.

But *there was a secret wasn't there* and as the miles went by, not a dog in sight, I again cogitated on the truth about Prince Charles's dog. I felt its presence close at hand, a Special Forces reconnaissance troop with the dog shadowing my every move nearby, unseen in the mountains, watching me through night vision goggles. Or maybe I had been partly right when I said to the Queen Mother that something was amiss. Prince Charles had every reason to fool the press and whilst they knew he had a dog, maybe it was just at a friend's house. He'd have found it easy to give them the run-around. Or maybe the IRA *had* taken it and it was living happily in Ireland having converted to Catholicism some time ago, its new owner also in possession of my prized Harris Tweed cap[82], so I knew what it felt like if I didn't already. He'd wear it whilst walking the Royal dog, now a Republican asset and IRA mascot, not with any sense of triumphalism, nor with animosity or to "rub it in" but with a sense of magnanimity to us which challenged some images of Republican ideology. He knew I'd understand. He just wanted the cap and the dog more than we did. Grandiloquently I realised that I could never swear I had ever seen Prince Charles with a dog *or knew that he had one.* Maybe I really was the butt of his joke, and to that extent at least *I was somebody.* I now knew it was no coincidence that my old form room was number 23, the same number as the fence at which events lead to Foinavon's victory. I was part of a plan there was no doubt. Like the great accident at fence 23, which was then named after Foinavon, though it did not fall, surely the peculiar accident of the May Bank Holiday weekend the previous year would have even more dramatic and perfectly mythological consequences. One of these consequences was that those who knew the secret of Prince Charles's dog would have its image discreetly placed on their gravestones as indeed some already had.

Whatever the truth was I accepted I would never know all of it, just the brilliant glimpses of it the Special Intelligence Service were allowing. I could only concentrate on what I did know, which was that I held a winning lottery ticket for a lottery bigger than any that had ever taken place by an invaluable amount. But the ticket did not belong to me: it was my duty to keep it safe. Prince Charles's dog was going to clean up for charity and I was just a facilitator. The ticket was really everybody's. I felt not the remotest sense of loss at the realisation the ticket was not mine. I felt so proud to be a member of the Special Forces, my compliance with the message imparted to me by Part V Subsection 87 of the Torbay Harbour Act, and at what was now bound to happen.

It was a beautiful night, and the stars occasionally peered through. I tabbed some 20 or 30 miles past Laxford Bridge until eventually, with dawn approaching, I was too tired to go on much further. Luckily I found a building site where they were constructing a short slipway down to the water and a dumper truck had been left with the doors unlocked. I climbed in and went to sleep. I was undisturbed inside the dry cab. The rain now arrived and I was saved from a quite dangerous soaking. I slept for some hours, thinking the roadworks had only been put there to make the fact that I had found this truck just in time, more believable. I was still given to imagining that Prince Charles knew of my every move and dreamt as to what this might one day mean for me. For his part perhaps he knew exactly where his dog was as he read the intelligence reports coming in. But he wanted to know of any intelligence which might enhance His Royal Highness's dog's military status – for example whether I had realised his dog was an MTRU or not. He wanted me to know but also wanted me to work it out for myself. He was egging me on and actively supporting me with his agents. I certainly felt many people in this most remote part of Britain were helping, and providing progress reports of the search.

After a few hours I awoke and the rain had stopped; so I climbed down from the cab and continued my walk. A lorry driver picked me up and took me to a junction not far from Ullapool. There was a large dead Scottish wildcat by the road, the only time I saw one. Apparently they do often interbreed with domestic cats but, by its size, this was obviously the real thing. But still I did not see Prince Charles's dog, yet I had imagined it there. Perhaps it had been closer than I had thought.

Ullapool was a beautiful place but without any money it had nothing for me that I could see; so I continued on my way feeling briefly sapped of initiative. I got back to the Salvation Army hostel in Inverness by the evening, where I found myself at home once more – again thinking I was on some officially recognised route. I had often wondered if any GP had ever prescribed a patient an Ordnance Survey map with walking routes.

I still did not really know where I was going, or what I was going to do – only that I felt quite happy to be on the road like this despite the fact that my socks were dirty and uncomfortable. It seemed like everything was mapped out and all I had to do was wait to see what happened.

At the hostel I was able to get clean and borrow some clothes whilst my laundry was done. There seemed to be no problem about National Insurance, and I was easily able to book in with a false name and without any identification. This was important, as I did not want to be put in hospital. The atmosphere was again homely and relaxing, and I was relieved to have negotiated my journey around the wild northwest of Scotland where I had faced no little danger from the weather.

After a great night's sleep I was off again to Edinburgh. Towards Dundee, a lady who ran a bed and breakfast in Skye picked me up. She dropped me on the motorway in a torrential cloudburst and even though I took refuge under a bridge I still got soaked. I felt very cold and uncomfortable. The rain did not last very long however and I emerged from my refuge at the very top of the concrete slope under the bridge, knowing I would soon be back in Edinburgh at 'my' workman's hut. The sun was strong and steam rose from my drying black clothes. Sure enough I was soon back in "Auld Reekie" (an affectionate colloquial name for Edinburgh). Coming back over the Forth Road Bridge, this time not on foot, I felt I had completed quite a trip. But it had not even begun yet!

I spent the night in the workman's hut once more, and next evening, after wandering around Edinburgh all day, I found myself at Waverley Railway Station having no idea what to do. Noticing a train was about to leave to London I got on, again without a ticket.

Part XII

I Borrow 50p

Chapter Thirty-Three

Ten Storey Love Song

In order that I could enjoy the journey without being thrown off the train I cunningly decided to approach the guard and explain that I had left my wallet at the café on the station concourse in Edinburgh. She phoned up the station for me to see if they could collect my wallet. But of course they could not find it and so she made me out a ticket to Oxford.

I could now sit back and enjoy the journey to London first class. The next few days are a haze. All I know is that I did not go to Oxford but I do remember lots of walking, no bed on any night, and sleeping on trains in sidings. But things were once again about to take a turn for the better.

In Brighton I walked around and around all day just staring down at the pavement. Occasionally, well maybe once or twice anyway, I would find a coin, so carefully was I looking, and it seemed there was a sense of magic in this as though the Freemasons had deliberately placed the coins there a few minutes earlier. They had put them in such a position that my foot stepped exactly on them, making me mindful of the possibility I was embedded in a virtual parallel universe – a universe which could run on ahead to predict where my foot would fall. I was impressed by my imagination and happy to find the coins, the exact number of which I forget, partly due to poor accounting, which was a thought: perhaps somebody thought I was a bank and they were deposits. One of the coins was a 5p and I was pretty sure it was the King's shilling, I could not imagine the Queen troubling herself with such a Masonic ruse so it seemed it must be Prince Charles's. The funny thing was it was one of the old larger 5p coins, which had been replaced in 1990: it seemed mysterious. Anyway the streets of Brighton were paved in sterling and my thoughts now turned to how I could procure some more without begging, or pretending I was a bank.

I went to the Job Centre. There was a job as a letter opener. This reminded me of my great-uncle's wartime employment in Denmark where he had what he described as the depressing task of opening, reading and translating letters from Germany. I lived in his house for nine months in 1980 when working at the Observatory. After a few days living upstairs with him I decided to clear out one of the 'unused' downstairs rooms and move into that. The furniture, in large amounts, was all piled up against the door, as I could see peering in through the garden window, and must have been pulled into that position with a piece of string. His civil defence corps uniform was still hanging behind the downstairs toilet door, a door I also felt I was the first to have opened in many years. I never mentioned the problems getting into the room to him (or anyone else for that matter) and whatever emotions he had about my getting into the room he did not show them. What possible explanation could there be for this if there was not some truth in Uncle's claim, when I was a child, that there was treasure in the old chest at the bottom of his garden in the decades of undergrowth he called the jungle?

Apart from the letter opener's job nothing much appealed. Then I went into a Burger King restaurant, and found a whole meal which appeared to have been abandoned; so I waited for a while until I was sure nobody was going to collect it and then, as I had done before, moving to another table to avoid suspicion, tucked in. I really did think to myself: how stupid could I be? The meal was obviously put there by the Masons. Sure enough no one returned to collect it. Mysterious. I had no fear of it being poisoned.

I found myself at the back of Tesco's. Somebody had left a load of furniture, including a bed, in the car park. I made a corral around the bed with the wardrobes and other furniture for security much like I was in the Wild West and surrounded by Red Indians. It was a cold night but at least I did not have to sleep on the ground and the bed was not cold though I had no bedclothes.

Next day I went to the library to find out what facilities there were in Brighton for those on the street. They sent me to the Resource Centre where I got something to eat and a cup of coffee, both free. I discovered they had a PC which I could use free of charge. So I started writing and soon I had one side of A4 written word born of my illness, my situation, and a completely fictitious story about a doctor who had been struck off. With my free copy I made my way into the Kall Kwik photocopy shop where I asked the man behind the counter to lend me 50p. He declined. I said "No, could *you* lend me 50p?" Then he reached into his pocket and gave me the 50p. I now asked for 50p's worth of copies of my newsletter which he duly printed off. This was another Capgras incident as I thought for some reason that he was the son of Jack Straw, the then Shadow Home Secretary. He had only just come through the back door of the shop, having been driven there by MI5.

What I now did would have no little effect on my pride. I went outside and within a few minutes I had sold the copies of my newsletter on the pavement for a healthy profit enabling me to go back into the shop with about three quid to make a whole load of copies, which I returned to the street with (he refused to accept the 50p I owed him). Within a few hours I found I had about twenty quid and, discovering that The Grapevine bed and breakfast was only 12 quid, knew I could easily support myself by selling my newsletter on the street with money left over to eat and get beer – that most important of commodities. However, it has to be said that in the six years or so before I first became ill I had drunk every night consuming at least twice the recommended safe amount. Perhaps this was why I had become ill in the first place.

I booked into The Grapevine bed and breakfast where I took a lovely shower after examining my pretty room, which had a beautiful view over the church. Downstairs in the café I enjoyed a cup of Camp coffee, an appropriately homosexual beverage given the enormously gay community in the nearby Kemptown area of Brighton (which is affectionately known as Camp Town). That night I felt quite well and was happy to go out and enjoy a few beers in The Heart and Hand. I would settle into this rhythm for the next few weeks, eventually discovering I could get cheaper photocopies at the Resource Centre, this boosting my income to an acceptable level.

Next day I went back to the Resource Centre and typed out another side so I could have a double-sided newsletter. I let people pay what they wanted for it which meant everything from nothing to, in one case, that of the rock star Bobby Gillespie from Primal Scream, nearly three pounds. I saw him walking towards me and recognising him straight away, said "Hello Bobbie." So having myself bought loads of his records, including a favourite, *Sonic Flower Groove*, I now got some of my money back.

Each time I got the print outs I noticed the font size oscillated strangely for no apparent reason. So I wandered the streets announcing "Little Big Issue with an oscillating font size" and probably other things I now forget by way of asking people if they would like to buy a copy of my newsletter. I declined to announce any beliefs about why my font size might be oscillating like that. I had great success with this – meaning in some way I had justified my existence and given myself my personal pride back. I had some suspicions about the PC at the Resource Centre though.

Of course just because I was gainfully self-employed this did not mean I was not ill, and nor did my remaining separate from my flat, my cash card and my salary, which was still being paid. But I was still having the occasional strange experience. One day I noticed the number plate of a Jaguar being driven down North Street. After I glanced back at the car I could have sworn that the rear number plate was different to the front. For a moment my schizophrenia was defined by my feeling that the Sussex Constabulary had done this. Or maybe it had just been badly ringed.

I was still thinking that the Security Services remained in full control of at least my overall body movements though with all my education I knew that I must be able to exert some free will – particularly if I *knew* I was being brainwashed. I knew of a condition called catatonic schizophrenia in which the sufferer remains stuck in the position they find themselves in. A more bizarre variation exists known as catatonic schizophrenia with waxy flexibility. In this condition, whilst the sufferer remains rigid, their limbs can be moved by a helper into new positions which they then stay in until the same is done again – rather odd, until you replace position with military posture perhaps (military posture is the degree of aggression presented by an army's positioning on the battlefield).

I thought my body was swarming with bugs and devices: mostly lodestone chips immersing me in virtual reality courtesy of three-axis accelerometry. The Special Intelligence Service was united against mental illness itself – and had been for many years. They thought everything was a consequence of the state of mental health prevailing. I needed to snap out of the one I was in but I just did not really want to, as I enjoyed being an apprentice spy. Only they could alter my posture for the time being. I laughed at the thought that, like baby pigeons, you never seem to see a baby spy. Then I remembered my KGB file full of early pictures of me – including one in which I was dressed, for the fancy dress at the village fête, as a guardsman, a picture which the KGB would have seen as a big coup at the time. Well I knew the secret with the pigeons, as I had once seen a baby pigeon in its nest. When they leave the nest they look practically full-grown.

Empathy with pigeons, ideas about secret organisations and especially thoughts that one is an apprentice spy are not, I suspect, at all uncommon in schizophrenia. I am sure Rufus May would agree with me. He too had been sectioned repeatedly, and thought he was an apprentice spy. Rufus May was interesting because, like me (at least at this stage), he did not believe medication was the complete answer to this problem and, as you already know and will see, I had great problems with medication, none of which I was currently taking. Rufus May was also relevant in all this because despite his having been ill he succeeded in becoming a clinical psychologist and, on one occasion, escaped from hospital without getting out of bed. If anybody was in my SBS unit perhaps it was he.

I had the bizarre thought that Yassa Arafat was hiding inside the clock tower, erected in the middle of town in 1888 (the year of the formation of Celtic Football Club) to celebrate Queen Victoria's golden jubilee. I could, should I have been inclined, have gone straight to Ladbrokes and placed a bet on it using all I had procured from the hawking of my newsletters on the street. The bet would be on it being found, by the end of the week, that Yassa Arafat was in fact locked up in the clock tower with a large supply of dog food, as well as provisions for his own purposes. He might even have been free to come and go, after a brief delay due to an admin error, to replenish his stocks. I might have had a side-bet on its being shown this came about due to a major international misunderstanding caused by an error in translating the Koran from Cornish to Breton. That's how bizarre my thoughts could get. I later discovered that the golden ball on the tower used to go up on the hour many years ago, controlled directly by a landline from the Royal Greenwich Observatory if you believe that, but this had been stopped because it whistled in the wind. I was unable to see a solution to all of this, other than knock the tower down, and that was an obvious waste of a good clock tower, problematic though the Palestine situation was.

So I wrote a new newsletter in which I described how the Queen and her armed forces were going to have to take over the Government of the country and sent it to Her Majesty. I met a chap outside the library. He was tall and impressive and asked me who would be giving the orders if the armed forces took over. I told him that the Queen would with her best advisors. I felt I had removed the Government's credibility entirely and made Parliament look like it was full of a bunch of gibbering idiots, so impressive was I. He seemed genuinely interested and I was convinced he was from the Special Intelligence Service, like my old tutor, who had helped me set up my now defunct record label, Seagull Records. He asked if I could possibly detail a little more accurately my plans for the complete military takeover and publish them in my next newsletter – saying as he walked away "And make sure they take over Brighton Borough Council – it's in an appalling state!" He seemed rather too much like the undead Michael Maltby – still waiting for me to produce the £10 million so he could then reveal he was not dead.

Inside the library I noticed that the big grandfather clock had stopped. Any normal person would have thought it simply needed winding up but to me there was no question that it had been allowed to run down and then set at a time of great historical significance in this country. I visualised something like this having happened: at twelve minutes past eight, the time at which the clock was set, the Joint Chiefs of Staff as well as the heads of MI5, MI6, the police and the Special Intelligence Service, had met in the bunker beneath the former Charrington's Head Office. There they had decided in some way that I had won my game with them. The game was to discern I was a military asset and part robot. At that time it was decided there would indeed be a military Government in this country, either that or the whole land had to be turned into a field psychiatric hospital. The time on the clock was the time of the occasion when Rear-Admiral Prince Charles entered the room – and it was decided, for reasons of national security, that his dog had to appear to disappear. Or perhaps it had to appear to disappear again elsewhere and the disappearance I knew of had been a highly localised event. I thought about it hard and was not sure anyone else knew of the alleged event except through me, apart from, *in some respect*, Danny Baker and the announcer I had heard on my radio that morning the previous year[83]. Even Danny Baker could have been a trial of the latest voice morphing equipment: and if it was him how could I know if he had done it of his own free will? It might even have been under duress. Not a single person had told me about its disappearance otherwise, and the newspapers could have been Special Forces editions produced for purposes of canine hierophancy. Either way I may have many years out: the hospital may have opened in 1926.

I found a copy of Kim Philby's *My Silent War* on the shelves and noticed that the gentleman with a stick in the queue in front of me, who looked like he could have been a close friend of Philby, had a blue hardback British passport. Of course, I wondered if the reason why he had a "proper" passport and not a European-style one was that he was a member of the Special Intelligence Service, not that he had got it before the European ones came in.

I sat down to read *My Silent War* in the library. I soon learnt that during the War, MI6 had set up the SOE HQ in Baker Street. Laughable as it now seems I was sure at the time this was causally linked with the almost incessant playing of the Gerry Rafferty song, *Baker Street*, in the Students' Union when I was studying for my PhD. I hated that song to start with. 'They' had been putting down a marker to make it clear later how much effort they had expended on me. Later the librarian allowed me to leave the book behind the desk for my convenience. I dropped in every day for an hour or so to read it before coffee and more touting of my newsletter. I discovered that when Philby had been recruited by intelligence, Burgess had given him the codename Dud. I recalled how the voice in my head back at Fairmile, as well as telling me to "fuck off" over and over again for hours had also said "dud" in a similarly unrelenting manner. Now it made sense. It was interesting to see how Philby's legacy had affected my own line of investigation decades after his defection to the Soviet Union. On a less insightful note I discovered that, during the war, a commander of the service traffic section at the Government Code and Cypher School, Bletchley had borne my own real surname. This really firmed up my delusions at the time for in reality, I am now a little sure, he bore no relation if, that is, he existed. What also fired off that wonderfully alluring feeling of supreme importance I had was that somebody had made little annotations with no obvious detailed meaning at points through the book. These I thought had been put there by the Special Intelligence Service to influence my mind. At the bottom of one page an hourglass symbol had been pencilled in next to "closer", the title of the second Joy Division album. Their singer, you will recall, I proudly believed to have been an agent. Then at the beginning of the chapter about the Volkov case where it said "a promising career" this had been changed, it seemed by the same person, to "*my* promising career". This raised the possibility that Philby himself had made these annotations. My knowledge that he was said to have died in 1988 did not get in the way of this in any way. I thought the particular book had been brought especially all the way from Moscow with the specific intention of it being used to control me. That it was.

I wondered if Philby had decided to settle the problem about the question marks in *Jerusalem* by going ahead and building it in England. But he knew the Soviet Union was bound to fail and ultimately it would need British people to help it survive as a peaceful country. He had not really defected but had sacrificed himself for the greater good, and now I myself had been drawn into his, and their, long-term plan, whatever that really was – the plan having been hatched all those years ago in that Friday afternoon chat over drinks. Perhaps it was not John Lennon but Kim Philby himself who had been L Zero, it all having been planned out so many years before. It felt like it was not I who was unstable but the situation. But of all of the people around me in the street, in the library, in the cafés and pubs, almost nobody knew what was really going on, and this was why I was in such a privileged position. This meant I had an enormous responsibility on my shoulders to do the right thing, there appearing to be some flexibility here. I had done the right thing by attending the recruitment meeting of the UCL Communist Society. Of course news of my presence at the meeting would have reached Moscow, to be received by Mr Philby with no little satisfaction. I should have thought it would have reached one or two other places with a slightly different emotion, but perhaps not really that much different.

So I worked out how much tax I owed on the selling of my newsletter in which I now wrote about my associate Mr Philby. I also became obsessed with the beaching at Brighton in 1980 of the *Athena B*, a ship carrying pumice. For a few days the *Athena B* had been worldwide news as crowds flocked to see its wreck right on the main beach in Brighton. The first tranche of tax was about £100.

I went to the post office and got a postal order for the exact amount having kept records of all the money I had earned from selling my *Little Big Issue*. I decided to send the postal order to the Royal Army Pay Corps at Worthy Down announcing that now there was to be a military government they would be handling the affairs of the Exchequer. A few days later there was a trailer on the BBC (on the TV in my B&B anyway) for some programme and an Army officer was being court-martialled for embezzling funds. That really got to me. I believed it was a direct response to my hardly, given what had happened to me and who I was, astounding actions. At face value somebody had been ordered to go and have an Indian meal and then a booze-up on it or something. Perhaps the money had not really been embezzled, but used to fund a plan to address the problem of the sectarian divide in the six counties. I was sure the Army knew I had breached a local bye law, which I had seen announced on a stout plaque attached to the railings on the sea front: LOCAL GOVERNMENT (MISCELLANEOUS PROVISIONS) ACT 1982 SECTION 3 AND SCHEDULE 4 STREET TRADING. They would without any doubt whatsoever exploit that fact for all it was worth, at a time and place of their choosing: I was not to have to wait long. They would not even see the 'tax' or the profound stigma attached to possession of the permit within the community I was operating in as mitigating evidence I was sure of that: why should it be? But what would another have done in my position? These were troubled times and it was more normal to break the law than obey it and visit the town hall to get the permit. They'd have probably thought I was a bit of a nutcase if I had, especially when they saw what I wished to sell: they may even not have let me have it and I had to fund my operation somehow. I might get caught up in long-term editorial disputes with the

Borough Council over the newsletter. I did not notice any Libyans buy my newsletter though I sold so many it would have been easy to miss, though I did not miss a monk in robes buy one for £1. I strongly suspected that I sold one to one of the real Big Issue community and the possibility arose that none of them had the permit either meaning they were all potentially double agents themselves and what is more one or two of them *probably knew more than me* too. Furthermore somebody must know they did not have permits in which case there was an extended conspiracy and it probably went right back to Moscow.

I sat on the shingle beach and in my head, whether by EAH or my own skills in psycho-espionage, I heard the voice of Stella Rimmington saying "At this moment in time he is sitting on Brighton beach smoking a roll-up." I looked around and found a piece of pumice. It had almost certainly been spilt from the wreck of the *Athena B*. I decided to make my way back to the library. Taking a running jump to surmount the groin, I got a painful knock on my shin.

I took the piece of pumice into the library and asked them if they had a file on the *Athena B*. Duly they brought out the old box file, which they dusted down and handed to me. I lapped up everything about the incident feeling convinced I had once again uncovered evidence of a long-standing conspiracy, quite apart from the one involving the Local Government (Miscellaneous Provisions) Act 1982, which Kim Philby had known all about despite the fact he was in Moscow at the time.

For some reason my illness led me to believe that there was some profound meaning in what news article was to be found on the reverse of each cutting, and not just about the *Athena B*. Only I could see this. I thought it a ruse of the Masons to control reality, and the outcome of the reality war it was now so obvious I was caught up in. On the reverse of one cutting, behind a picture of the beached *Athena B*, was an article about the death of an Army officer, killed supposedly by a falling branch in his driveway. I even thought this had something to do with Cunliffe v Banks in 1945, an obscure and tragic legal case I read about at random whilst sitting in a solicitors where I went one day to complain about the oscillating font size. I noticed that in one paper they said the *Athena V*, instead of *B*. Just exactly whose victory was this? I wondered. All, I believed, was not what it seemed and I had similarly delusional and mysterious feelings to those I'd had about the spelling of the horse Foinavon. I found a woollen bobble hat and formed the conviction it had been Brian Sewell's hat and that I *was putting on my Brian Sewell hat* with all that entailed as though I was to go round expostulating in a rather camp manner.

Next day in the news I heard of the Israeli internal security service, Shin Bet. I had never heard of that organisation and found myself thinking that Mossad had renamed itself as a result of the nasty bang on my shin the previous day. I even imagined some money had changed hands in this incident. But something else happened concerning Shin Bet. Somehow, and I forget how, I gained the impression I had foreknowledge of the assassination (on 4th November 1995) of Yitzhak Rabin, the Israeli Prime Minister. It seemed MI5 had carefully shielded me from the news in order to give me the delusion I knew he would be shot, or any other delusion they felt it might be of use for me to have. I had been led to believe he was going to be shot when, in fact, he already had been. Whatever the explanation I did feel I had prior knowledge – a strange feeling to have – quite apart from my usual ideas accommodating the possibility Mr Rabin was pretending to be dead and may also be hiding in the clock tower, not necessarily at the same time as Yassa Arafat but with his own supply of dog food. I do not recall the tower having any visible entrance above ground so access may have been via a tunnel, possibly from the adjacent bookshop.

At about this time I read an article in the newspaper about Prince Charles having bought a new and rather expensive stereo from a British manufacturer. The article said he was so impressed that he had bought two. He had bought the second one for me: I probably owned all sorts of things by now which I would never see. Somebody had probably done me the courtesy of writing my will too. This was because I was the greatest of heroes. In the whole of the world I was the only person, outside of the Security Services and Special Forces, who had realised exactly how enormously important his dog was, rather like the legendary Barcelos cockerel in fact. Legend has it the Portuguese cockerel came back from the dead. It has now become the symbol of faith, hope, justice and good luck. I pictured His Royal Highness as having my whole life and career sorted out for me right down to a place to live and call my own – he had even wondered if I would like the handmade wooden steering wheel for my Range Rover, price some £700, though reality might make this a somewhat insecure outcome. Again I recalled: I'd already had my car serviced, what more did I want? It was just "some scrumpy". Philby got little more than some vodka and I was not even sure he ever had a car to be serviced in the Soviet Union, hence the will. Prince Charles had, in his hand, passed to him from MI5, a copy of my Vale of Glamorgan by-election newsletter. He was trying not to completely crack up. Now that His Royal Highness had read my newsletter, and was clearly amused, anything was possible. All I now had to do was play my cards right and come and get the rest of my life. I gazed admiringly at a Triumph motorbike in the window of a shop. Everything was laid out for me.

I decided to go by train to Eastbourne one day to sell my newsletter there. On the back in the centre was written a quote from *Dad's Army*: "You have to change at Eastbourne when travelling to Warmington-on-Sea." I had always thought that Warmington-on-Sea was really Bexhill-on-Sea, where my grandparents had lived, my grandfather having served in the Royal Observer Corps there, and that was good evidence I was right.

A helicopter was circling and I imagined it was piloted by someone coming to see me, having been sent down to buy a copy of one of my latest newsletters by Prince Charles. I had been sending them with reports of my activities to Buckingham Palace so, in my state of mind, this did not sound so farfetched. Then a person wearing a badly fitting and simply awful suit, whom I believed to be Prince Michael of Kent (who had presented me with my PhD), came up and indeed purchased one for 50p. I was proud: he'd probably got it for some Libyan mate, if not for now possibly to go in his general present stockpile for a later date. Giving presents was just a kind of war really when I thought about it.

Returning to Brighton and having got drunk I returned to my lodgings again having, as usual during these weeks for some reason, purchased some sweets to cheer myself up. A voice in my head told me to go on thirst strike to the death: it was the byelaw, and that would be just for starters. I was pretty screwed up as a result though luckily I did not stick at this for more than a few hours. I was being tortured by MI5 having got people to hoot their car horns outside my window, if not leave branches outside my abode, to remind me of the unfortunate Army officer I had read about and the related case of Cunliffe v Banks. This thirst strike was my way of protesting. Everything was known about me and if I protested hard enough then the MTRUTH and otherwise torture would stop. They just wanted to get me to fight back and give them some fun.

I took an early-morning walk along the beach into the sunrise wondering whether to produce a new pamphlet: *Ruminations on the Nature of Windups Vol 341 No 26 or something* (the previous one was going to be *Vol 147 No 82 or something*.) but instead found a café where I had a lime juice pressé, coffee and read *The Times*.

I continued to have no problems selling my newsletter, which ran to three editions, or four if you include the early single sided version of the first edition. One day an enthusiastic young chap complimented me on the quality of them telling me he had the set, including the early single sided one. That boosted my confidence and coupled with the fact that no officials, like police, ever approached me, I could say the operation was a complete success. And they had another reason to investigate my performance due to the aforementioned breach of an Act of Parliament.

One cold wet night I was selling my newsletter in a covered alley near English's Oyster Restaurant. There was a shop selling glassware and lampshades. Disturbingly I found myself thinking of Crystal Nacht – 10th September 1938, when, at 01:30hrs, Josef Goebels sent out the order to begin the ethnic cleansing of Jews. The Jews were charged 1 billion Reich marks for the damage caused by the Nazis and 26 thousand were sent to camps. It seemed certain to me that in Nazi Germany I would have been sent to the gas chamber and not an asylum. For, before they started on the Jews, the Nazis began on their own: the disabled and mentally ill.

Before I left Brighton, sadly not staying on long enough to see The Stone Roses perform for one of the last times for many years, I had another Capgras incident when I saw what I thought was a double of Ian Curtis. Then I thought it might be his brother, though I don't think he had one, walking down the "Peace Lane". I also spotted somebody, aged about 16, whom I believed to be the son of Robert Wickham. Robert had donated to a sperm bank in Harley Street when we had been at University. Both these doubles or relations were shows of strength by MI5 just to amuse themselves with the incredible power they had. They had gone through entire sets of living members of family trees in order to find such strange doubles, as well as circulating secretly in the police and the military the images of those whose doubles they needed. That is how privileged I was. But it was better than that! They had a massive database of all the passport and driving licence photos to search electronically to find doubles using linear minimum variance morphing software (that's just maths for finding doubles). If they found no match they could always approach foreign intelligence agencies for help. A few years later and in my case they'd have mostly come back saying I looked like Roger Federer and not bother using their fancy gear.

Never once during my time illegally selling the newsletter did anybody say anything unpleasant about it – with one exception. One dark evening a chap in his fifties approached me and seized the copy from my hand. After a cursory glance at it, poking it with his forefinger, he told me he was from *The Sunday Times* and that my newsletter was a load of bollocks and a load of crap. I looked at my newsletter and felt sorry for myself, as he had said it with some conviction.

Some years later I would, by chance, return to this spot. Somebody had sprayed, using a stencil, the Saint logo (a stick man with a halo) on the pavement. Of course I imagined this related to this incident. Beginning to think I knew how the minds of the Special Intelligence Service worked it seemed possible Roger Moore had vandalised the pavement himself, possibly having driven there in a P1800 Volvo, as he drove in *The Saint*, the Bond-like 1960s series.

After I had been in Brighton wandering around The Lanes (part of Brighton consisting of alleyways of shops) with my newsletter for a number of weeks, selling quite a few hundred pounds worth, I became a little depressed at the thought that in one of these expensive restaurants Amanda's husband might have proposed to her. Then one day my landlady said she wanted me to move into the basement room for one night.

I found myself thinking she was a serial killer who got rid of backpackers in the basement where, no doubt, bodies were buried under the floor, never to be discovered. The basement room was very depressing and I cried knowing this was to be the death of James Longhurst, and I would have to say goodbye to my friends at the Resource Centre.

I hid all the remaining copies of my newsletters, including the masters, under the floor in the corner of the cupboard, left The Grapevine for the last time and began walking along the coast towards Beachy Head. You might call this a cover up.

It was already dark as I set off. Poor James Longhurst! I admired him for the success he'd had with his newsletters, and the criminal way he sold them without the correct permit. But I could not quite see him as me (depersonalisation again). James Longhurst had been murdered by the landlady of The Grapevine and was now buried in the basement. But I, Clive Travis, had to go on. I decided to have a T-shirt made up, on which, were the words "Been There, Done That, Got The T-Shirt".

As I walked, the lights of Brighton disappeared behind me and soon I was walking along the Telscombe cliffs. I had walked this exact route some 15 years earlier when I had been to see The Clash at the Electric Ballroom in Camden. I had seen a train come into the Tube station with "via Bank" displayed on the destination indicator. But it had already been there; so then I was heading north instead of south. I did not get off that train until Chalk Farm, and by then my fate was sealed – I would not be able to get the last train to Bexhill-on-Sea. So instead I had to take the one going to Brighton. In those days I earned £55 per week and was not used to the luxury which James Longhurst had of staying in bed and breakfasts. So when I got to Brighton I just walked down to the seafront and headed for Bexhill. I got a lift on a milk float ripe with the smell of sour milk and, high up on the wild downs in the early hours, I had flagged down a Mini Countryman to get another lift.

Walking up onto the Downs this time I saw a flash of lightning. But there was no rain or thunder. So I knew it was an hallucination. Either that or it was my MTRUTH. I wondered what Professor Dainty might think of this. I would see him in my imagination, looking like he was firing something very carefully and accurately in the direction of my retinae. This would happen again later and it seemed, when it did, I was somehow being given a small dose of heroin again. Again I would imagine all kinds of exotic delivery mechanisms for this involving the military. Really, of course, it may well have been some subtle effect in my brain chemistry. They can't have been giving me heroin all the time for a variety of reasons.

When I reached Newhaven I tried to get some sleep on a bench by the war memorial but it was now November and too cold; so I just carried on walking up onto the Seven Sisters. Just like I had sensed all those years earlier, there was something foreboding about this windswept place, particularly so at night. Perhaps it had something to do with all the people who had jumped, and even driven, off Beachy Head. I had no intention of doing such a thing but there were those who had fallen off, perhaps during horseplay, or even been thrown off. I had once seen a picture of somebody who had jumped, taken just after the point of no return.

When I reached Eastdean, it was still very dark but here a strange incident occurred. A man was standing at his garden gate at this unholy hour, and he pointed down his road raising his arm in a seemingly military manner, the road leading to the cliffs. I could only deduce that it was known I was here and that someone, if not Prince Charles then someone working for him, believed I was the sanest person in the world and was to be given every help including with navigation. I had seen such a thing many, many times in my EAI and had learnt to ignore it, finding I was just being sent in circles – the idea being to demonstrate to me I was really a free agent. Now I was seeing it for real, and I was a little frightened.

So I walked along the cliffs as I had done with Amanda that wonderful bank holiday weekend over 12 years earlier. With dawn approaching I got to Beachy Head with its sheer drop of five hundred feet where, every year, many people throw themselves to their deaths. I read the inscription on the old Royal Observer Corps post where my grandfather had been stationed during the War.

Out to sea I could see the Royal Sovereign lighthouse, which I had looked at through my telescope from the beach at Bexhill all those years ago when I was on holiday at my grandparents'. For some reason the light had been turned off and so was not sending out its beam every 30 seconds or so as it usually did. It had been turned off because of my activities as some kind of warning by the conspirators: the British Sumo Rabbit Psychic Wrestling Society. As if to confirm this paranoia, it was no longer called the Royal Sovereign Lightship (it used to be a ship) on the shipping forecast but "Greenwich Light Vessel Automatic" and, with the later change of name of the Royal Ulster Constabulary, I was to hit upon the deluded idea of making the North Bedfordshire Constabulary Royal instead, to compensate. Physicists, as well as ecologists, might call it conservation of Royalty. Similarly people would now refer to Northern Africa and North Ireland to see if that had any beneficial effect on the peace process.

Along the coast I could see Bexhill. On the sea front is the Sovereign Light Café[84]. It was too far away to identify it but I knew some light from it was impinging on my retinae. This seemed to say something about my situation.

I began making my way down from the cliffs towards Eastbourne and slipped on the wet grass. This gave me a bit of a shock and I wandered carefully over to the cliff edge, little realising how strongly a cliff would figure later in my life. Soon I was in Eastbourne and had enough money to go and get myself breakfast.

For the next few days I wandered about tired and hungry with nowhere to sleep except on trains in railway sidings again. Here I was occasionally disturbed and thrown off, pretending I had fallen asleep at the end of my journey, just climbing back on board later.

I made my way to Cambridge, spending a night sleeping at Gatwick airport on the way. Airports are a good place to sleep because (a) they are warm and dry and (b) you can pretend to be a jet-lagged passenger waiting for a connecting flight – so security does not disturb you. As I wandered around the airport I heard a voice in my head saying "Dog 9 to Dog 1." Another SBS or SAS dog, sumo rabbit or MTRU was trying to raise me, but I did not respond: it might just have been two other dogs I had overheard. How did I know which dog I was anyway? Over and over in my head I heard what became the very familiar voice of a young woman saying proudly "James Longhurst, he was..." and then stopping before revealing what he was; but this was all I heard. Best be my own dog I thought.

Lying in the airport lounge I felt rather dirty, uncomfortable and in need of a shower. When I woke up it felt like somebody had washed my arse during my sleep and for whatever reason I found myself thinking this had been done by the Queen Mother in person. Also, whereas my feet had previously felt grubby and uncomfortable, now I appeared to have clean socks and my feet felt all fresh and nice. Unless you have been on the street you might not know what an uplifting thing it is to get your feet washed and have clean socks – quite apart from having your arse pampered like a baby's by the Queen Mother. The truth was really not much more than my socks just having been able to dry out and perhaps the proximity of that dog I was looking for.

By the time I had reached Cambridge the little money I'd had was gone. I discovered a hall where sleeping bags and inflatable mattresses were supplied and here I could sleep for the night. The room was heated with wall-mounted infra-red lamps and the atmosphere, as usual in these places, was cheery. On the wall was a portrait of King Charles II looking down and I sensed a great deal of warmth, humanity, and some mystery emanating from him. I wondered what he knew of Robert Hubert, whose execution was during his reign and whose death warrant he may well have signed. They were different days.

Dinner was served and a lovely homemade pudding with hot custard followed. The inhabitants of this hostel seemed to be a mixture of tramps and dropped out academics many of whom had, like me, mental health problems. Maybe they had been looking for the dog, years before me. Should I have enquired they might all have thought various Royal dogs had been missing since a whole variety of dates. I spoke to one of them and he professed to be an expert in genetics, and I wondered what on earth he was doing there. I should have asked myself the same question. But then I already had – I was trapped in a book on the shelves of the library still, possibly a very special library, waiting for someone to open my pages and release me into reality.

In the morning we were turfed out onto the street, the hostel not opening again until the evening. I made my way to the library where I handwrote a new newsletter. Soon I had some copies, which I proceeded to sell, again without any complaints or interference from the police. So my spirits rose as I once again proved I could support myself without any state handouts – although it was supposedly true that I had nowhere permanent to stay. In any case, the hostel was perfectly adequate for the time being.

As I was writing the newsletter, there came a point when, having written a particular sentence, a number of people came into the room. Their purposeful entrance seemed to be rather like the entry of the judiciary into a courtroom.

They all knew what I had just written, via my MTRUTH. Their entry had been prompted as though they had been waiting outside the door for the right moment. This was a peculiar feeling but one which convinced me I had their full support in what I was doing. They were Cambridge academics in contact with MI5 and some extra parts had been written into the performance, this performance.

That evening, aware that I could not get into the hostel after a certain time, or if I was drunk, I went to a pub and had a few beers to cheer myself up. I thought it possible Prince Charles had drunk there when he was studying at Cambridge and, in my visual imagination, or EAI, his psychic presence confirmed he had been once or twice, wearing a fake beard. I was hardly even thinking that only some 28 miles away my family was wondering if I were still alive, not having seen me now for several months. It had been a good day and I had sold a copy of my newsletter to Professor Hawking's secretary for £5. I later wondered if she had wanted some change but she certainly did not wait for any.

That night I returned to the hostel for yet another of several nights I spent there. As usual, there was that cheery optimistic atmosphere and King Charles's eyes seemed to follow me around the room as in some old comedy horror film.

Next day I tried begging but did not enjoy it and gave up after a minute or so, picking my cap up and walking on. I sold a few copies of my newsletter near the station and, without a ticket, took the Norwich train. When the guard became aware, the train made an unscheduled stop at a remote country station in the fens called Shepea Hill and I was thrown off. The station was completely isolated and did not serve a village or even a hamlet. I climbed the stairs to the signal box and, noticing the warm coal fire which the signalman had to heat the box, handed him a copy of my newsletter some of which was about the possible reopening of the Oxford to Cambridge railway.

I wondered why Shepea Hill was so-named, as there seemed to be little sign of any hill or even a mound. I thought of calling 999 from the telephone box and asking for the Shepea Hill Mountain Rescue. Then I pictured Prince Charles's emergency hearse racing by again.

Now I started one of my long walks and eventually found myself sitting in a pub in Mildenhall enjoying a few beers. Then I hitchhiked back into Cambridge in time to get back to the hostel for another well-earned night's rest. As I lay in my borrowed sleeping bag on the stage under the portrait of King Charles II, I conceived my plan of action for the next day. Having conquered Shepea Hill, using oxygen, I would write a story about another Royal Geographical Society-sponsored mountaineering expedition, this being a rather more challenging one to the nearby Gog Magog hills. These hills, which are only a couple of hundred feet high at most, are named after an ancient Anglian king, Gog, and his kingdom, Magog. According to some these hills were the real site of Troy, and the Iliad and the Trojan war were actually about the battle for tin in England – and not as usually thought Turkey – during the Bronze Age. I slept soundly, dreaming of myself and Sherpa Tensing Norgay at the summit. It would be a good place to look for Prince Charles's dog and I decided to call Crimestoppers and let them know what I was thinking: I had a hunch it might be something I did not regret. They might be able to organise a search party for the missing Royal hound.

In the morning after breakfast I was ejected onto the street again for what would be the last time and made my way to Norwich round which I walked aimlessly all day. Although I did not keep copies of the newsletter, which James Longhurst had produced in Brighton, I still had all the documents in a plastic bag relating to my attempts to get funding for my nationwide water fountain survey.

From Norwich I took a train back to Wymondham and, admiring the old station's beautiful architecture, began walking along the main road to Thetford. As I walked in the dark with the headlights streaming past dangerously close, I identified myself with a monk whom I imagined had done this walk many hundreds of years before, when the traffic wasn't quite so incessant.

After some 10 miles or so I threw the carrier bag containing all my documents into the middle of the road and left them there. Better that than myself – there was no footpath and this was quite dangerous. I reasoned that my doing so lessened the chances of throwing myself into the road – or tripping and falling into it.

Late at night some 20 or more miles down the road I arrived at Thetford, where I found the chip shop had just closed. But I had no money anyway, and resorted to hanging about cold and hungry on the railway platform. As I waited I noticed a sort of squeaking sound every minute or so. This seemed to come over my MTRUTH to give the impression it came from the air above – but it did. It was the sound of migrating redwings, which fly at night during the autumn, as I later learnt from Tom, a keen twitcher. Though when he told me the heavy delusional air of Fairmile Hospital enveloped me, and the mere word redwing was all of the former Soviet Union. You needed specialist equipment to prove the truth in this one way or the other and furthermore you needed to believe your equipment.

I waited all night until the dawn train came, to take me back to Cambridge. I do not remember what happened that day – I was confused and unsure of what to do, as well as very tired. I do recall getting a lift from Cambridge the following night. I hardly cared where the lift took me and the young chap driving said he was going to Manchester; so Manchester it was, and I arrived there in the early hours. I walked to the airport and spent the night sleeping there like I had at Gatwick.

Next day I walked into Manchester past the old Factory Records (Joy Division and New Order's label) office in Palatine Road. Once again I did not really know where I was going, but somehow found my way to the city centre. On the way I found myself in a library. My illness had a strange effect on the way I interacted with books: For example the Rupert Bear annual. When I opened a book, which, with the exception of *My Silent War*, I did at random, then the page would present information, which seemed to have a special meaning. I was predestined to open the book on that page by some magical interference from the Special Forces. I had some second person's thinking coming in subliminally over my MTRUTH.

Outside the main library I began talking to a friendly, caring woman who took me to the back of a church where they were serving sandwiches, coffee and biscuits. Nobody rammed any Christianity down my throat, which was nice, and a young man offering me a biscuit asked, rather amusingly, "Do you take *a* biscuit?" In the computer world a biscuit, otherwise known as a cookie, is a computer program, which is sent down the telephone lines on the Internet to infest your computer. It seemed he might either be alluding to my behaviour really "taking the biscuit" or suggesting the Security Services might later wage an electronic war on my PC, if they had not already back at the Resource Centre and at work. From the church I went to the Salvation Army Hall where I had another free coffee, discovering there was somewhere I could get a bed for the night.

I got a bed with some ease and a false name, but found myself a little paranoid about the cross scraped on the back of my door which I felt had something to do with my trip to the church earlier in the day. Outside the hostel was a man with a German Shepherd dog standing on the grass – seemingly to order. I believed he was a relation of my hero Ian Curtis and even that the old dog may have once been Ian's puppy. I believed they had been told to stand there in deference to me.

I hung around town for the evening cadging a beer in a pub by successfully asking a few people if they could buy me one. Outside, I had a problem with an eight-year-old who seemed extraordinarily aggressive and wanted to pick a fight. What is more, his older friends seemed to think I was the problem, which made the situation rather unpleasant. I made my way back to the hostel for a much-needed slumber.

Despite a good night's sleep, I felt depressed and decided to return to Bedford and face the music. On the way I found myself in Ian Curtis's hometown of Macclesfield. Sure enough, as if all was laid on for me, I did not have to wait too long for a lift. A chap wearing army fatigues in an open top Land Rover took me very coldly some way towards Bedford. One more lift, in the form of a Tesco lorry, was sufficient to get back to Bedford. Of course I wanted to believe the lorry had been specifically sent by the Chairman of Tesco's, whom MI5 had told of my position.

Back at Bedford I decided to test the water by going, not to my family, but to a friend's, Budge, to find out if he knew I had been missing. Budge was interesting because his Uncle Victor had been one of the jurors in the trial of James Hanratty, and Budge had once told me that his uncle always said, correctly, he thought Hanratty guilty. I had my own ideas – as I have told you. Luckily he was in and Sîan, his girlfriend, served me wine. Indeed he had heard from Howard I was missing; so I telephoned my sister-in-law to say I was back in town. By now the 28 days had long passed – so there was no danger of automatic re-hospitalisation.

Part XIII

A Mere Trifle

Chapter Thirty-Four

Step into My World

Varsity Rugby day came a few days after my return. I felt the urge to visit the trackbed of the old Oxford to Cambridge railway line again. Having reached it I looked at my watch. The game would be starting. I needed to perform some ceremony to ensure the reopening of the line by appealing to the powers that be in those two cities. The boat race challenge had to take place on the balcony at Bedford Rowing Club, both captains having come by train from the two cities on the Varsity line, most of which had closed in the 1960s. Next to the bus station just short of the old St. John's Railway Station, Bedford, somebody had dropped an empty bottle of Turbo cider. There was something about it, almost like it had been put there deliberately and ceremoniously yet in an apparently random position for me to see. This was the nearest I had got to being personally presented with the scrumpy I had requested at Solsbury Hill the previous year, Turbo being the dog which, as you may know, featured in *The One That Got Away*. The bottle could only have been put there by the SAS, and I believed it – because I wanted to believe it. I decided to drink some scrumpy that night to celebrate.

I got back to my parents' house in time to see most of the game, and just as I switched on two people invaded the pitch. The commentator described them as "two idiots". This made me ask myself why, back in Brighton, two blokes in bear costumes had come skating down North Street, both making high-pitched wails whilst giving my old school Masonic "claw" greeting. One of them, for a moment, had partly removed his head to show he was, if not Prince Andrew himself, a very good, though obviously Capgras, lookalike. I now had little doubt who the other was and even imagined Mr Starmer-Smith, the commentator, knew exactly who these "nutters" on the pitch were, not only Prince Andrew but also Prince Charles himself horsing around to entertain me. Strange thing, the imagination. Stranger still, schizophrenia.

One day I decided to pay a visit to the hospital, where I had been unhappy with my treatment. The term schizophrenia had only been in use 83 years then and, it seemed, each patient was little more than a drugs company guinea pig. With this in mind you might excuse me for believing that my treatment was in breach of Health and Safety regulations. What other field of medicine took patients into hospital and made them suicidally depressed before releasing them? Yet I was to have more of this treatment – far worse than that I had already received.

In the street by the hospital's psychiatric wing something bizarre happened. I saw a young chap on the opposite pavement stop, and then start walking backwards whilst mimicking, with his arms, the piston pushrods of a steam engine. But he did not just reverse: he made a curving line into the middle of the road as though he was going into a siding. When I saw this I did not discount his having done so on orders, the intention being that I was to see it. To me this meant that I could do anything I liked, however bizarre, and it would not indicate schizophrenia. He, I imagined, was in the same military unit as I: the Special Boat Service Reserve – or perhaps even the regular unit itself.

Not to be outdone I now went into the hospital and asked to see a manager. Having decided that the FRU had taken the consultant psychiatrist's medical qualification certificates into their possession, I told the manageress that there was a 'doctor' in the hospital with no medical qualifications. I furnished the manageress with no other information and left, feeling a little fired up. A week or so later, I found an article in the local paper reporting that a doctor working at the hospital had been exposed as having no qualifications and had been sacked and deported. Did this mean I had some amazing power of intuition with respect to this doctor? I was bemused. I asked myself: did this mean I really did have MTRU capability? Did the Security Service know what I had said that day? Rather amusing, I thought, particularly when the person I spoke of could have been me, as I am a doctor without any medical qualifications. In fact I was split between thinking the story had been a spoof or just a great coincidence. It is not always clear where the dividing line is between the imagination and schizophrenia.

Around this time I noticed that, when I was sitting on the upstairs toilet, but not the downstairs one, I would hallucinate a 1/50th scale Prince Charles with some helpers, I presumed SAS, standing at the bottom of the toilet door. The bottom inch or two of the door had become detached from the rest of it and with his helpers Prince Charles was forcing this massively heavy and long gate open with some effort – as it was about 50 yards long and difficult to move.

One day I was in the record shop. The way the chart was displayed with 1-10 down one column and 11-20 the next alongside meant that number 5 and 15 showed up the name Amanda would have had if we were married made from the names of the two artists occupying those spots. This really got to me and reminded me that my main psychiatric problem was that of heartbreak, which had gone undiagnosed by the NHS. The surname of the first artist was Limerick so, thinking back to that first night I got sectioned, I wrote one.

> *There was a man from Bedford*
> *Whose father bore the name Edward*
> *With his head in a spin*
> *He upturned a bin*
> *It was Bedlam before he got back to Bedford*

I once heard of somebody else who was said to have cracked up because the woman he loved did not marry him. The joke was that his best friend *did* marry the woman he loved and he cracked up even more. Then there was the bloke who went into a pub and started buying everybody drinks. When asked why he was doing this he said his wife had run away with his best mate. Asked who his best mate was he replied "I don't know but he's my best mate now!" However, the killer anti-heartbreak joke has to be the one about the two ardent Yorkshiremen. At a match one realises he has left his wallet at home. The other offers to dash back and get it. On his return he looks pale and drawn.

"I've terrible news for thee Bob. Your wife has run away and left thee, and your house 'as burnt down to the ground."

"I've worse news for thee lad, Boycott's out!"

But now I was feeling tortured and thought what I had seen in the record shop had been arranged by the Security Services, via British Intelligence, to get me thinking. Then I saw a copy of the Suede album *Dog Man Star*. I thought of what I had said at Wilton about Sirius, the Dog Star. Could I possibly be correct in what I was thinking? Had they been told to call it that because of what I had done? The connections I was making were tenuous in the extreme and quite frankly embarrassing to recall. But *Dog Man Star* was not all I noticed. There was also the NatWest Bank television advertisement featuring a dog, which amongst other things, was flying away in a jet airliner on holiday. Was I being told something? There still seemed to be a lot of dogs in the media.

I had thought about the symbolic significance of my own record collection, each time discarding the notion, though I still thought I had a special copy of *Never Mind the Bollocks*. I had realised that when a person appears before a psychiatrist the psychiatrist can have only a limited idea how the patient got there. One way I had got there was by playing a Joy Division album at a guess 97 times – many of the lyrics appearing to be about psychiatric patients. So I decided to catalogue in detail every record I had. I gave up within about one minute sensing the action was wholly futile, as the KGB had photographed me every single time I had ever bought a work of recorded music – and still were. So why should I bother? They had done me that favour already. And anyway life was only so long. I had better things to do.

One day I was watching a Ride video entitled *Today Forever*. Noticing my binoculars at hand I focused them on the television screen. I now noticed an interesting effect if I looked through only one side of the binoculars so that both eyes were focussed on the TV but one through the binoculars. I then found the appearance was given of the band playing inside the room, my brain superimposing the video over the view of the room through the unaided eye. To make it more impressive I drew the curtains and watched in the dark. My mother came in and erroneously gained the impression I was behaving schizophrenically whereas, in fact, my behaviour here was easily explicable and devoid of mental illness in all respects. My mother did not see that and I was later to be accused by a psychiatrist of having behaved bizarrely on this occasion. In fact I was accused of performing a "bizarre ceremony".

On the chilly Christmas Eve of 1995, I was walking into town past the Woolwich Building Society near home when I saw a nice-looking ginger cat. Two blokes were walking near me. One of them picked up a stone and threw it at the poor cat, which fled down the passage. Little did I know that a few weeks later this cat would be living in our house. My mother held her account there and as, during the day, the bank looked after the cat, she had the chance to show some interest in it. A manager visited the branch and said the cat would have to go; so I went up to collect it. The cat had a lovely personality and would lie on my chest staring into my face – most therapeutic. We would call him "Grateful Cat" though his real name (or at least *a* real name) was Duncan.

I had with me my prized gatefold sleeve of Siouxsie and the Banshees *Join Hands* album. This was deliberate. I took it to St. Paul's Church and passed it through the railings, sensing enormous power in this action, especially when bearing in mind the fantastic contents of the record, albeit including an awful rendition of the Lord's Prayer, which I had scratched through deliberately to prevent it being played. I brought it back through the railings and left it against the door of the church for the bemused vicar to find the next morning. If you know the album, you will not be surprised to learn that by the next summer I would be deluded into thinking this action had resulted in hundreds of millions of poppies springing from the Norfolk countryside – noticing this on a visit. The enormous sense of power these actions had conjured also led me to think the subsequent removal of the railings around the graveyard was in response to passing the record through them.

I feel a little frustrated that words may not have been enough to describe how peculiar all these experiences were at times. Having said that, there was an incident, which perhaps felt even odder than all of the rest put together. The Phillips airship, with the words "Making a Better World" on it, had gone past the window at the front of the house. Airships still fly from the nearby Cardington base where the R101 flew from and one of the wireless operators, George K Atkins, was a relation. I once went to the library and got the box file out. The last message sent, in quaint English, was that the guests, having had a fine dinner, were enjoying cigars.

I could not rule out Phillips being technically aware of my status as an MTRU. Grateful Cat had been put to sleep (he had feline AIDS) and *Funeral March for a Military Hero* by The Crashing Dreams finished exactly as he arrived back from the vet. He lay in state before burial in a cats' cemetery in the garden and all seemed magical and most fitting. I looked at the Royal College of Veterinary Surgeons' leaflet Mum had brought back. It said "The best treatment for your pet is the Complete Treatment." I took this to mean Prince Charles's dog, if not Grateful Cat, was looking at immortality as a reasonable prognosis, if the course was completed, and the money procured.

Then something came over me like I had turned into some Warlock No. 1. I cannot stress enough, let alone accurately describe, how strange the incredible experience that now followed was. It seemed that a mysterious and magical cloud had enveloped the room. I set up a most strangely lifelike diorama in the room, consisting of a Sunny Jim rag doll[85] with an extendable office desk light in his face, interrogation-style. Also in the diorama was a Clint Eastwood film soundtrack tape with Mr Eastwood, in his classic pose, looking at Sunny Jim. There were other items on the table, all of which seemed to have become imbued with very powerful magic. Playing on the stereo was a very rare compilation tape entitled *Discreet Campaigns,* which was released on a friend's label: "Rorschach Testing". It included tracks by Eyeless in Gaza, James, New Order, The Cocteau Twins and The Wake amongst others. As the rare music played, and my witchcraft diorama exuded its spell, I walked in circles of reverential steps around it: High Priest of all I surveyed. So odd did this wake feel that I shook my head in disbelief. This was the alluring side of schizophrenia. I later saw the chimney at Kempston Hardwick brickworks had "Eastwoods" painted down its side. It had been painted like that because of Clint Eastwood's part in my ceremony – all of which had been seen by a CIA remote-viewing psycho-spy through my MTRUTH. The chimney would be coming down. I looked out of the window and the gnome in the garden seemed peculiarly sentient. It had been watching me for years – it was alive!

The carpet in the back room of the house had come from my great-uncle's house in Bexhill-on-Sea. In the front room, where I carried out this ceremony, there was a half moon-shaped matching rug. I had noticed that it always seemed to be rucking up to the left and became convinced the FRU had been coming into the room and moving it, always to the left, that is the west. Being a physicist I had a moment's insight. I was unable to believe the carpet's magical properties extended to its being able to do this itself. Also I ruled out, for the moment, the FRU's involvement. I wondered if my habit of walking in circles clockwise whilst listening to music might have caused it. So I decided to walk in the opposite direction whilst listening to the *Discreet Campaigns* tape. I got bored with the experiment and, eager to get a result, tried marking time. What did I know? I could see the carpet was moving with each step – always to the west. I decided that a snooker player would understand this phenomenon, as in snooker they allow for shots bending because of the nap of the baize. Less insightfully I believed that its movement was inextricably linked with the meeting in 1926, my great-uncle's wartime employment and the subsequent collapse of the Soviet Union. Except it was: it was *his* carpet. I sent an email to a friend detailing the phenomenon, and my previous suspicions about the FRU, from an Internet café. I noticed a chap making a mobile call outside the shop. A couple of days later I went to play a record and what did I see this time? The magic rug had moved east and was no longer rucked up, convincing me once again that Menwith Hill, GCHQ and the FRU were in play. I remembered a photo in *The Daily Telegraph* of a woman eating pizza from a new Pizzeria the Americans had opened in Moscow in 1988. Under the picture I had written an article exhorting NATO to bomb Moscow with Big Macs. In reality I think my mother had straightened the carpet.

This was one of those phases when I did *not* really feel I was being watched. Yet I did think: how wrong can one be? And who was the chap making that call? I was suspicious. I forget the deluded reasoning, if there was any, for what I now did. I came to the decision to leave a trail of damage to foreign cars all the way across Bedford that night. I set off, well after midnight, to wend my way across the town quietly bending windscreen wipers. I was not well. It was a bit like being a new recruit, tearing my tweed hat to the tiniest shreds, convinced I had lodestone microchip radio technology in it – destroying my own power with mad abandon and finding myself unable to channel my strength properly. I blame the antidepressants – even though it was months since I'd had any. I even thought Comic Relief had something to do with this.

I did still have some sanity though, and studiously avoided any Italian models, what with there being so many Italians in Bedfordshire. I could have waited a couple of years until the incredibly ugly Fiat Multipla MPV came onto the market. This looked like the designer had draped a cummerbund full of failed breast implants around the bottom of the front windscreen. Then I might have damaged only that model. Perhaps Jeremy Clarkson would have helped me.

After an hour or two of this I made my way up Cleat Hill, north of Bedford. The milkman had already been. I poured the milk over a BMW. I left everyone in the adjacent Graze Hill alone thinking I might get shot as, being in the country now, I thought there would be more guns around. Then I headed over the fields on public footpaths. But soon I totally lost my bearings. Eventually I came upon a large almost military-like farm complex, which I walked past, believing I was completely safe from detection. Under the floodlit entrance, I saw two or three Land Rovers pulling in. Briskly and purposefully, a small apparently military detachment and a man in a black gown looking like a senior judge got out and headed for the farmhouse, all of this clearly visible from my vantage point a couple of hundred yards away. They were there to discuss me. In fact it was probably just the farmer and some friends back from a late night out. With tiredness my imagination had taken over: the farmer was no ordinary farmer, not one bit.

I decided my secret was safe with the owls, and the odd horse on the other side of the fence, despite what I had seen. I was reminded of the famous scene in *The Night of the Hunter* with Robert Mitchum: the magical boatride down a river whose banks teem with fantastic wildlife. I was totally lost now as to my direction and location, but then I saw the familiar sight of the water tower appear, its silhouette just beginning to show against the morning light. Eventually I reached the road and, with a crisp dawn upon me, I walked towards town. The Life of Riley was playing that night at The Grafton Hotel, the local IRA pub.

Near the caravan site a speeding old R reg Ford Granada coupé with a vinyl roof went past. Inside were a black Labrador and a bloke who looked like he was in the Parachute Regiment. The driver was a double of Dennis Waterman – the actor in *The Sweeney*. The dog (who was really enjoying himself) and the bloke were riding shotgun some way out of the window. As they went past I thought he shouted "You're going to pay for that! I'm going to do you well and proper!" Or perhaps he really did shout something like that – I was very tired having been up all night walking and it was not the first time I had been shouted at from a passing car by any means. I was to form the impression I had paid, as I will shortly explain.

It was almost time to go out by the time I got up. Drinking my coffee I spilt some on a map of Wales I happened to be looking at. Without there being any rhyme or reason I found myself, childlike, tipping the map to make the spilt coffee flow around the page forming a track on the map as it went. Eventually the coffee flowed no more and by a random process had stopped on the map in Betws-y-Coed at the words "Fairy Glen".

Ffos Noddun (Magical Chasm)

On mossy mound where toadstools grow,
They dance in moonlight, row on row,
To music from the purling brook
Where Conwy dreams in secret nook.

Strange moonlight whisperings thru the wood
Where ancient golden beech have stood
And drowsed, thru drifting times of yore,
Steeped deep in mystic myth and lore.

Their bark with lichen garlands hung,
'Neath cobweb skiens with dew-pearls strung,

While knurled and knotted roots surround
To shield, from man, the hallowed ground.

That mist-clad land of whims and spells,
Floating music and tinkling bells;
A door lies hid beyond night's pale,
Wrapped in a glimm'ring, shifting veil.

But if that spell-bound caul you'll pierce,
Then drink the mead from faerie tierce;
The shade will fall away, and lo,
Into the elven realm you'll go!

Where pwca, sylph and woodland sprite
Trip light and skip in pure delight,
While imp and hob kick up their heels
And spin and whirl thru faerie reels.

A faerie woodwind's eerie lilt,
From fife that's hewn of wood and gilt,
With pulsing throb of faerie drums,
Through the glen at midnight comes.

Leila Sen

That night in the Grafton I got talking to the landlord, a staunch Republican if you ever met one. He brought me his album of cuttings about Kevin Lynch, the 8th IRA/INLA hunger striker, a customer of the pub, who had been martyred on the first day of August 1981.

A few nights later, whatever the combination of antidepressants and alcohol had done before my journeys around these Isles, it was to become more apparent that although I had got off them, I was still locked into an imbalanced mental chemistry they, or something, had caused. I needed something to put this right. Oh no! Not another disk reconfiguration! I might have thought – and probably did.

One night I decided to take my great-grandmother's cut-glass bowl containing one of my mother's excellent trifles and, in full view of some young anglers, despite it being dark, place it in the reeds at the edge of Longholm mere. What do you make of that then? I thought, and brushed my hands at a job well done – a *mere trifle* served up with a heavy dose of schizophrenia. Not a simple matter but a small lake with a pudding of sponge, custard, fruit, cream, jelly, nuts and a little sherry in a crystal glass bowl. The lake was later beautifully refurbished.

The only other problem was that it seemed my voice box had been hijacked by something and, rather like a scene from *The Exorcist*, somebody else's voice, albeit totally unintelligible, was coming from my own throat. I decided the only logical explanation for this was indeed some form of possession, and that I needed to be exorcised. Alternatively, it seemed it might be something was coming in through my EAH – and out from my mouth.

I visited a friend, Rich. Whilst still at school, he had his initials and date of birth (23rd March) on his moped's number plate: RKK 23M. This achieved some delusional meaning in my mind. In fact, perhaps, it was pure coincidence. If not, this sort of thing was probably going on at both discrete and discreet locations all over the country. Many years earlier, to his horror, somebody had shot his neighbour's cat and thrown it over his wall. This incident, you might be surprised to know at this stage, would later become significant in my view of the peace process in Ireland. Rich was probably the school's greatest and most renowned exponent of the art of mock-homosexuality, a talent he made no attempt to disguise. He was even known as "Gay Rich". Nor was it just for show, he just loved it, though he was not really in the least bit gay, it was all just a laugh.

At his house, those salad days of group mock-homosexual acts were a long way in the past, except in a Julian Clary Gay Nostalgia show. I managed to surprise this ghoul in my head by preventing any of its vocal emissions from departing my mouth and I also succeeded in preventing my head from rotating around and spraying Richard's living room with vomit, again as in *The Exorcist*. Perhaps it was Grateful Cat trying to get through. Soon I was off and bid his family goodbye, all of them probably blissfully unaware of his comically 'dubious and shady past' – or of how ill I was.

Now I headed for Kate's toxophily party where I might have been inclined to let it all hang out and have her shoot an apple from the top of my head, that is if I trusted her not to be too distracted by its rotations, the voices and the vomit. In actual fact I just got merely healthily drunk and decided to make a persistent and spirited attempt to seduce some woman who later went off with my knitted woollen skullcap. It would be a while before I saw it again, though as for my head itself I would now lose it completely.

Coming out of the party, a short way up the road I saw yet another stolen traffic cone in somebody's garden. I had imagined the whole Denmark Street area of Bedford descending into a guerrilla war zone deliberately imported for reasons of efficacy from Northern Ireland and believed that I was in deeply enough to justify some pretty extraordinary displays of behaviour. Perhaps picking up the cone at the pointed end, and smashing in the front windscreen of an L reg. Mercedes I now saw was not one of these, but maybe it was: I did not know whose car it was, but maybe the Special Intelligence Service did. I headed off home, my thoughts running wild.

As usual there were cars parked all over the pavement – this only being legal if the driver is instructed to do so by a constable in an emergency. But what about a detective superintendent? I had no knowledge that the drivers had been told to park off the road by a police constable as per the Road Traffic Act. If it was World War II and we were living in the Irish Republic, where World War II was called "the Emergency", this might have been an explanation for the illegal parking. This part of town, as I already had imagined, was being used for six counties military manoeuvres – this possibly explaining the widespread damage to street name signs, which allowed my mind to make deluded inferences concerning U2's song *Where the Streets Have No Name*. I did manage to just squeeze past one of the cars in the small gap between its door and the street lamp, without leaving a very nasty long scratch as I squeezed through.

I had visited the police station to complain about the illegal parking but they said they did not have the resources to deal with it. I did not give any clues as to my developing delusions of grandeur about myself and the problems of Ireland. Instead, it would appear, they would prefer I go to hospital for a couple of months at a cost to the taxpayer of £18,000 at £300 per day. This was a Catch 22 situation.[86] I did not ask the policeman explicitly how he would react if I now left the police station and did cause some damage. It seemed far more logical and a better use of taxpayers' money if he got in a panda car there and then and drove to the cars by the park to give them tickets – but he didn't. I had managed to restrain myself – but now I was going to blow.

The moment I got into bed that night a car alarm went off and in an instant I arose, driven, with an enormous surge of adrenaline coursing through my head. I steamed down the stairs, possibly making a wild and spurious 999 call and took a shovel from the shed. Rushing outside I attacked the car, the haze of the rage so great I could hardly even see what make it was.

I now thought some extremely adverse things about a chap I had seen coming from a house a few doors along. He looked like one of the chaps in the Railroad Earth/Lazy House video counting out what I imagined was a huge wad of drugs money, the chap with him being a narcotics dealer – this was Capgras once more. So thinking some equally adverse thoughts about his Ford Fiesta with fog lamps I decided it deserved a good seeing to. For eighteen months now, I seemed to have been in a swarm of Ford Fiesta Populars and Popular Pluses. MI5 had put them there and it really gets to you after a while – this craven servitude to the Security Services. So I smashed out his headlights good and proper, doing a better job than Bernard Ingham did when he smashed up his neighbour's car. I wonder why was he not put in hospital? I had forgotten that due to logistical problems they could not fit everyone in the ward.

I was not finished yet though and set off for a nearby street determined to demonstrate that if nobody had thought there was an emergency as per the Road Traffic Act, there was one now. Having done that job, with one or two bedroom lights coming on, I made off in the direction of the old Cambridge railway line trackbed again. I felt like relaying the track to Sandy single-handed.

Only I now saw a speeding police car coming along the bridge. So the police had plenty of resources to arrest me but not quite enough, without me, to stop the root problem – be that an Anglo-Irish conflict, illegal parking or car alarms going off, alarms which at the time I thought were set off by MI5. They were elevating me to my rightful position as a Soviet double agent looking at the six counties, if not Moscow. I decided to finish off a few more cars while I had the chance and spotted a new Clio, which looked like it could do with a trip to the body shop.

I went quietly. I knew the officer from school, leading me to suspect he was really just a civilian who had been ordered by the Masons to put on a constable's uniform and arrest me.

Thinking back to what appeared to spark this incident, the alarm, I thought it had been set off deliberately to trap me. This, I believed, was what that bloke in the Parachute Regiment had meant when he shouted "You're going to pay for that!" And I kept hearing the voice of my brother in the police saying that the Secret Service was winding me up. He knew what was going on.

At the police station they did not appear to bother taking into consideration my recent peaceful trip to the library. Of course they 'probably' did not know about it. There, as I imagined MI5 had seen via my MTRUTH, I had chosen, completely at random, a book on criminal law and, again randomly, opened it at a page detailing part of the Forgeries and Counterfeiting Act. This concerned "using a false instrument" – and conjured a picture of somebody joyfully playing an air guitar being arrested. That's interesting, I had thought, and having time on my hands had gone straight to The Engine and Tender pub. Quite officially I told the landlord that if he did not take down his notice of announcement of his refusal to accept £50 notes by the next Thursday I would arrest him under the appropriate section of that Act, which I fully detailed to him. He had leant over towards me dutifully. As he looked at his notice he seemed quite convinced that I was serious. It must have been the way I told it, as I did not bring an air guitar with me.

Part XIV

A Strange Dream

Chapter Thirty-Five

Tremble

Some time later, after being allowed to sleep for a while, I was awoken in the middle of the night to be interviewed. At the time this seemed like military-style interrogation. The officer said, rather loudly for that time of night when you're half asleep, "You work for The Ministry of Defence don't you?" This made me feel I was seen as having a level of mystique attached to me. Next I was in the interview room being spoken to by a Sikh social worker whom I told that the whole town was swarming with zombies and that I'd had enough. Of course his job was to sit there and say things like "No Clive, don't worry, there are no zombies" and other ludicrous contradictions of my own, quite valid, personal beliefs.

Confused between zombies and mummies, I was left thinking he really believed I meant that every other person was to be seen wrapped in partly unravelled bandages as they walked around the town centre, shopped, worked behind counters, drove buses, or even watched an old video of the *Monty Python* Bicycle Repairman sketch[87], all done rather stiffly of course. I wished he had just drawn a great sabre from his sheath with a swish and a glint and rained down the almighty power of the Amritsar Golden Temple, the Sikh's holy shrine in India, on all mental distress in the vicinity.

So what did I mean by zombie? I had just realised that the issue of human consciousness was simply one of vanity, enabling humans to recognise themselves and others. If something about a person has changed dramatically an observer will say "He was unrecognisable as the person I knew." They often forget that an animal can enjoy itself and nobody could deny that computers too, need to recognise each other. The town was populated by human computers doing no more than a series of not very complicated tasks: for example diagnosing mental disorders, which a real computer could probably do a lot better. Existentially, the town barely existed was what I was really trying to say. Perhaps this misanthropic streak was caused by the antidepressants – and was still there despite it being months since I had taken any. On the other hand I had not felt violent when I was away from Bedford on my roustabout so perhaps the town itself was a danger to *me*. Or perhaps my presence in the town made me confront the situation and that was the danger.

A given response from each of these computer zombies could have resulted from a certain input, or even no input at all in some cases. That is, all that the zombies said came from a tape loop set at the factory, a little like the sales school where they train pull-string Action Man salesmen. I presume there is one. This was a rather floccinaucinihilipilificational[88] view of society I grant you – though I have nothing against Action Men. Everything they ever said was simply a conditioned response[89] to everything that had ever happened to them. Perhaps I was seeing the town many years hence – when it really was populated, and run, by robots. The town was full of MTRUs, like something out of a John Wyndham science fiction novel, a common theme in whose stories is people's response to disaster, whether caused by nature, aliens, human error or one or two other things. On the other hand human beings were just robots anyway and the brain just a complex computer – anyone disagreeing with me on this matter demonstrating the characteristic vanity of human beings. The whole idea of existentialism *itself* is just a symptom of human vanity.

Next morning I was taken away into the deep Hertfordshire countryside, followed by a plainclothes policeman in his own car. He was verifying exactly where the ambulance took me, in case it was driven by an IRA double agent, or because *I* was one. I was now becoming afraid they might be going to inject me. I had not had one yet, if you ignore various inoculations including a quite frightening rabies jab I once had. If I had known what the effect would be this time my fear would have been worse.

I was taken to another gothic castle of gloom reminiscent of Fairmile, this one called Fairfield. It was more than a bit Mervyn Peake. Here paranoia set in, this including wondering just why it was that a nurse by the name of Tommy Trinder[90] was working in this hellhole. "What is this; a music hall?" I asked myself.

From the ward I could see the tower where no doubt, like Fairmile, a poor monster had once lived. I could hear his or her pitiable human spirit, groaning in despair and crying out to me, leaving me in no doubt as to the misery which had gone before here. I had experienced some of this misery myself – but worse was to come. Gormenghast would have been a breeze compared to this place.

Half the inmates spent the days sleeping on the floor near the radiator pipes, they were so drugged up and the dormitory being locked during the day. One of them was an extraordinarily obese Asian. I asked him why he lay near the pipes and he told me that was where the secret radio transmissions came from. Well they were not secret anymore. Perhaps, I thought, all sectioned patients were now given MTRUTHs on the NHS, these being the state-of-the-art treatment for schizophrenia and endemic community criminality.

There was a Ribena machine on the ward selling a number of different varieties of the drink in cartons. It seemed to present a strange aura: for a start, it was relatively rare compared to the ubiquitous Coke machine and all the cartons displayed the Royal by Appointment insignia. The fact that Ribena was made by SmithKline Beecham, of which my uncle had been an executive, rather assuaged my feelings. My then anti-American xenophobia meant the Ribena made me feel at home in that I sensed this was where the buck stopped, or rather did not get in, and I was reminded of my gran's house, where she always had Ribena, which my mother could never afford at home. The insignia meant I was safe in that I had the support of the Royal Family. In actual fact one of the Bowes-Lyon Family, from which the Queen Mother was born, was on one of the other wards – as I was to discover.

I put in an appeal to the Mental Health Review Tribunal for release. Prior to the appeal a solicitor visited me and I handed him a list. On the list were all the young people I knew who, for a variety of reasons, were dead, the clear suggestion on my part being that I was at the centre of some huge and murderous conspiracy – or at least that I was in mortal danger. He did not react to this as though I were ill, though of course he was paid by the taxpayer to take my instructions and no doubt he would lose his clients if he told them they were ill.

At the appeal the subject of Steve Treby arose. His brother had been the youngest Marine in the Falklands war. Steve committed suicide by hanging himself after slashing his wrists. After the appeal, and now fearing the worst, I went back to the ward and gazed out at the black squirrels, one of whom a patient told me kept appearing at the window. This seemed a little unlikely, given the height of the window and the lack of branches near it, especially as he was the only one who saw it. Nevertheless there are such things as black squirrels – they are a rare version of the Grey Squirrel. They are found in Hertfordshire, predominantly around the Letchworth area, where there used to be a pub called The Black Squirrel. Some, indeed, live in the grounds of this old asylum. Black squirrels are easily recognised by their attractive shiny jet-black coat and scraggier tail. So he might not have seen one at the window but, like me, he could have *from* the window. Perhaps he had seen the black squirrel from *one or two other places* as well, and was not letting on. In fact he might well have been seeing it round the clock for the last six months and had only just found out why. You could ask him yourself and he'd reply that he dreamt of seeing black squirrels and if he told you what he had been seeing the last six months you would not believe him so there was no point in telling you: he was board of telling people. He too had MTRUTH.

One of the nurses, an amenable West Indian chap by the name of James, came over and gave me the news my appeal had failed. This was not that surprising considering the damage I had caused. A cloud of despair came straight into the ward from the local Health Trust and stopped right over my head.

Now I was sitting at the dining tables. Everything, including the one-piece tables and chairs, was fixed in place in case somebody got a strong case of feng shui. All the plastic plates and cutlery were put away in between meals. I saw a group of the nurses approaching. Each of them had a supermarket labelling gun in which the labels said "PARANOID SCHIZOPHRENIC".

I was not prepared to go down without a fight – I did not want to be labelled by them. Yet at the same time something just made me realise they were only doing their jobs and I did not feel like being violent in defence, though I easily imagined others would.

Now I was looking straight into the eyes of one of these nurses, and the sight was shocking. I saw a vicious evil in his face. I am sure the feeling was mutual. I allowed them to take hold of me, and then started screaming and struggling, like I was a wild cat at the vet. I wanted them to know how I felt about what they were doing.

Now I was in the seclusion cell; they had my trousers down and the injection of Clopixol went in. I felt like I was being gang buggered. They all left, leaving the door half open. I lay there crying a bit. Soon I could tell something a little unusual was in me. I left the seclusion room quietly and sat down to watch television, resigned to whatever they would do to me next. But they had already done it. It would be some years before I was convinced I needed *any* medicinal treatment, rather than just a period of calm reflection. Nor, at the time, was I convinced the injection did me any good – in fact the opposite, or at least it made me ill again in another way. In other words it was impossible to take on an ongoing basis since I preferred the original condition. A vet, when talking to me later, used the cliché: "Sledgehammer to crack a nut" to describe this treatment. But if they had given me a drug, Olanzapine, which had been licensed in the previous month, this book might not exist, as you will learn after the end of the story.

Quite apart from the life-threatening dangers of the illness I was suffering, or more to the point the treatment of it, one might have thought the hazards of life on the ward were not inconsiderable. After all, some of the patients were supposedly there because they were a danger to others, quite apart from themselves. One of the patients did attack me for turning off the radio even though he was not listening to it and the TV was on. It was not a very concerted attack though. He had just been out on leave and maniacally walked up and down the room with his hands outstretched describing the "huge great orb" he had just seen in the old orchard where the patients had once harvested their own fruit. Then, word for word, he sang *Wonderwall*. I was to meet him again briefly, years later. But it would be unfair to describe the atmosphere in there as violent – this was the only occasion there was anything like violence. Actually you see more trouble in the High Street on a Friday night. As for that illness I am still reasonably convinced it had a lot to do with the antidepressants. After all, with the exception of one of Tom's headlights the following year I have not committed a violent act since.

Supper arrived and the familiar sound of the kitchen blind going up and promptly down a requisitely short period later did little for my appetite. I was, and still am, unable to explain the strange buzz in my head when my stomach rumbled: I was a bit like Pavlov's dog, a pretty sick dog at this time. Still, I managed to keep this little secret. But food was no pleasure, and come to think of it I said little about that either.

Each night, at eleven o'clock, we were all herded up ready for bed. We waited outside the locked door up to the dormitory and, when it was opened with the big old set of jangling keys more than a century old, paced up in file. As I cleaned my teeth I would enjoy the fact that the pigeons were roosting at eye level right outside the jammed open window of the communal washroom. One of the pigeons would stare straight back into my eyes from its doze as I cleaned my teeth, its head drawn partly into its neck to conserve heat. I had a friend. And the Department of Health pigeon loft was another little secret of mine.

I placed a few coins on the windowsill out of sight from inside the washroom. The Chancellor of the Exchequer knew about this (and the pigeon loft) via MI5 and my MTRUTH. He ascribed an M number to my pile of coins, and would use it as one of his major monetary indicators as to the strength of the economy. The extreme sensitivity of my MTRUTH, and its use, would then be capable of macroeconomic effects, including wealth creation, only a multinational corporation or a nation of shopkeepers would otherwise be able to achieve. The only ones party to this, outside of MI5 and the Treasury, would be those pigeons watching me clean my teeth.

There was no pleasure in getting into bed, the medication made sure of that. Honestly! Can you imagine getting into bed being devoid of pleasure? It would make no difference who you were getting into bed with feeling like this. There was however some much needed comradeship with the other patients.

Something strange seemed to be happening to my eyes, though I soon fell asleep. Suddenly I awoke. My pyjamas were ruffling in the wind and I was dangling. My eyes felt like they had been replaced by those of *The Demon Headmaster* and the ciliary muscles seemed to have developed a life of their own (probably a side effect related to ocular gyric crisis, in which the eyes turn up making the sufferer look, bizarrely and alarmingly, as though they have no irises or pupils). On top of that my eyes seemed to be focussing quite out of control and independently. But that was the least of my problems, as I appeared to be dangling at an altitude of some 2000 feet below a World War II barrage balloon with the lights of a large town – Bedford, laid out way down below. I must be directly above the Meteorological Office outstation at Cardington, I thought. I reached behind my head to see what was holding me, if anything, and found what appeared to be a lead for a medium-sized dog. I should have thought of this earlier, if I had not been only semi-conscious, as in any normal circumstance this would be exactly where I would wish to be, and now I was, courtesy of the SBS. This treatment, I felt, was infinitely superior to a depot injection as that made me clinically depressed. Dangling there, I fondly recalled the Indian summer of 1978 and sitting on the roof of my old school gazing out towards the village of Haynes, my geography master having instilled into me a strange fetish about the instruments hanging from the old barrage balloon – of which I was now one.

The wind waved again in my winceyette pyjamas, just like those I had put on uniformly, dutifully and a little resignedly that first night at the school boarding house all those years ago. Still dangling from the balloon, I heard a phone ringing. It seemed to be coming from the breast pocket of my pyjamas and at that moment I became aware of the weight of a mobile phone in that pocket. I took the phone from the pocket and answered "Hello." Presumably through a GCHQ voice-morphing box I heard the unmistakable voice of Betty, who was Frank Spencer's wife in *Some Mothers Do 'Ave 'Em*.

"Frank? Is that you? I heard you were having a bad night" she said.

"Having a bad night Betty? I'm dangling under a barrage... Betty? Are you there?" but the phone had gone dead.

Whether it was vertigo, just pure terror or an NHS novel drug delivery system hijacked by the military, I went unconscious again, the Special Forces tending to drug people they dangle under barrage balloons – using such methods to leave them unsure they really had been.

✱✱✱✱✱✱✱✱✱✱✱✱✱✱✱✱✱

I woke from the dream, freezing-cold and lying on the linoleum floor in the corner of the dormitory, two of the night nurses telling me to get up and go back to bed.

Chapter Thirty-Six

Hope Springs Eternal

Almost immediately after coming out of the seclusion room, I had felt that unbearable akathisia and anxiety coming over me. I found I could hardly sit still for a minute and ended up pacing up and down the ward corridor endlessly. I had no idea how long they were going to keep me there but reasoned that it should not be forever – though feeling like this, any length of time became that long. This was horrible torture. It really was. How did I get through it?

As well as walking backwards and forwards like this I found myself smoking incessantly to calm my nerves, and very slowly and unsurely the days went by.

I gave the psychiatrists the same list I had given my solicitor. It included Jo, Andy and Steve. The difference in outlook between myself and the psychiatrists concerning the list was a seemingly unbridgeable gulf. I had a clear military view of the situation. So many were now dead in my immediate sociological vicinity that only a fool would deny that I too was in mortal danger. But all the psychiatrists did was deny this. There was no doubt in my mind, as I had originally sensed, that I was fighting a very dirty and dangerous war with a very high kill rate. I now feel even more strongly I was correct. *I was walking in the steps of the dead – including those of others who could not hack the treatment*[91]. I had been forced into a situation where I was no more than a profit figure in the drugs company accounts – perhaps I should have been more paranoid about the SKB Ribena machine, instead of letting it make me feel more comfortable. After all, Coca-Cola do not make drugs which; when you take them, make life desperately unliveable, forcing suicide to be perpetually top of your in-tray. Perhaps I would take over Coca-Cola, fill the laboratory animal test centre with dog trials of new Coca-Cola flavours instead of antipsychotics, I thought. The possibility that a dog had to feel like this for my supposed sake was a piece of information I found unbearable to possess. I felt capable of breaking into the test centre to release the poor animals. I looked at myself in the mirror and imagined I had the head of a test Cavalier King Charles spaniel. And I looked very sorry for myself. I had to make sure I did not become a profit figure in the undertaker's accounts too, at least not before my time.

The hospital, which like Fairmile was a huge rambling building, had once held several thousand inmates. Most of these patients had little chance of ever leaving, so heavily labelled as lunatics were they. The hospital used to have its own railway siding and according to the history books, those who got women pregnant out of wedlock would have them ruled "Unsound of Mind" and put on trains to be brought here, many for the rest of their lives – quite shameful treatment. Not surprisingly, in my state of mind, I saw the place as a concentration camp even though almost all of the vast, sprawling building was now empty. This, if anything made the building even more frightening, the long corridors being haunted by 136 years of tortured souls, with three more to go.

One such tortured soul was an artist friend of mine (he painted the cover of this book). He had been in and out of this hospital and others, for 10 years from 1969. He has described to me not only how they were still using straightjackets (on him) during those years but also how he was hosed down and given cold baths by the nurses as a standard procedure. He has not had any antipsychotic medication since 1979 and has stayed well. He is an ex-paranoid schizophrenic.

The views from the windows were glorious though, and even in winter as it was now, there was sunlight in the ward almost all day if the sun was out. The only problem was that during all the time I was there I was only allowed into the walled garden once.

I got to know some of the patients. One of them was a prisoner transferred for some reason from HMP Bullingdon in Oxfordshire. He claimed to be a Jehovah's Witness, which unnerved me. Great, I thought, I am locked up in here with a religious nutter, though he showed me how I should dry out my Clan tobacco before smoking it and he seemed all right. Although he had a bad limp, he did not seem to be suffering any illness. One of the other patients was a Scouser who had a manic and tortured air about him. A year or two later I was in a pub when one of the nurses who had held me down told me that Scouser was dead after jumping from a train. Frighteningly for me, I was told that Scouser too had begun writing a book, but had not finished it when he died. Rest in peace Scouser.

The injection was making me depressed already, *and that was on top of the restlessness and anxiety.* One of the nurses, female, whose brother had mental illness and later committed suicide, sat with me. I could hear ticking coming through on my SBS MTRUTH. The idea had been to give me a tick when I did something right. But MI5 wished to give the impression they had given up ticking like that because they wanted me to realise I was not under orders. Now they were doing it at random. I said "I just cannot bear this ticking in my head" to her. I was ashamed to have told her this, to have given away this secret, and could imagine others would have killed themselves such was the shame of it. It was my deepest secret, that I was in the SBS – and I had given it away. In reality, you might think, the ticking was probably just caused by the joints in my neck giving whilst my neck was stiff from the stress. Then I noticed that the diagonal lines on the shower curtain were also present as interference on the television screen. MI5 were doing this to see what I made of it – like produce an intelligence report for them citing spatially sensitive witchcraft. As for the expression "What makes somebody tick", with both great excitement and fear I realised this had originated in the 1926 MTRUTH file. It had been deliberately inserted into the English language then by being placed in a few well-chosen locations in the media, perhaps like the title of this book. This would mean that one day "Looking for the dog" will have come to mean suffering mental illness.

Talking about the shower it might seem a minor point considering the medication was making me suicidal but due to health and safety regulations the shower was only lukewarm – a psychological war was being waged against the patient by the Health and Safety Executive. They were trying to grind us all down whereas when they went home they all had nice steaming hot showers and baths – the murderous bloody hypocrites! As if the torture from the medication was not enough! I wrote to the Secretary General of the United Nations in New York about the torturous state of the shower explaining that I was doing my best to find Prince Charles's dog but that being confined in a psychiatric hospital was limiting my progress existentially somewhat and asking him to accept my apologies.

One morning I woke up to find I had small cuts on some of my fingers. I imagined not that a member of staff had done this to but that it was one of the other patients – after all, I had pulled out the speaker cable from another patient's stereo at Fairmile, so I could not rule out some form of comeback. Something had been put into my fingers through the cuts, like new sub-millimetric lodestone microchips, and now it seemed certain the Special Forces had paid me a trip during the night. Quite possibly, it seemed, without the staff's knowledge or, if not, the rest of the staff.

During my time at the hospital I hardly ever saw the doctors but when I did, the atmosphere was confrontational. With the exception of Dr McInness at the open unit back in Bedford, the psychiatrists, though not the nurses, seemed very cold. On the other hand there was a jovial Frenchman on the ward. He showed me how to escape into the roof and explained his absence at the weekend was due to his being a consultant psychiatrist in France and having to see his patients. He requested, inviting a response, that I take note of the manner in which he vomited on the carpet – making precisely no attempt to rush somewhere or maybe do it in a bin or something. So that was what he thought of the place.

For my part, other than the fact that, because of the medication I had to pace up and down like a zombie, I behaved perfectly sanely during my time there. Because there was no chance to get any exercise, I tried doing some sit-ups using the radiator pipes to hold my feet and also completed a few press-ups. However as the Clopixol began to work on my schizophrenia, the depression got worse and worse. There was a danger of my brain falling through the floor into the ward below so heavy was the weight of the illness.

One night, as I lay in bed, I noticed I could hear tapping coming from the pipe. It's not difficult to recognise Morse code, only I could not read it, and it probably just sounded like Morse. I wondered where exactly the pipe was being tapped like this and what the root explanation was. What indeed was the message? For all I knew it was a bit of an Enid Blyton story or, more likely, *The Dark Side Of The Moon* – a nightmarish true account of the plight of the Poles during World War II, compiled under the guidance of the famous Polish hero, General Wladyslaw Sikorski. I remembered what the Asian sumo had told me on the ward that day about the secret messages coming from the pipes. For once, it seemed, I was not deluded. But, I wondered: was he? For all I knew he was under the orders of General Musharraf, the Pakistani General – who took over the country in a coup d'état three years later. I was not in the least averse to a military takeover of this place.

I began to find it harder and harder to get up in the morning but really there was no choice in the matter as we would all get thrown out of the dormitory to go down to breakfast. Meals began to appeal less and less. You really don't want to know how bad this was.

The statistics of the place were truly gruesome. I was already surrounded by suicides, and many times I had read about the death, which emanated from this hospital. I knew the only hope of survival from this terrible affliction was if I could summon all the resourcefulness and resilience of a fully commissioned officer in the Special Forces. Anyone who has suffered from schizophrenia will know what I mean – it can be a fearsome and life-threatening illness. However the problem I was having did not seem to be so much the illness but the treatment of it.

One day I was excited to hear the drone of a helicopter approaching and racing to the window I caught sight of a Chinook through the trees over the old orchard. It was the SAS flying over from the DISC to cheer me up by a show of strength. They knew everything that was going on in here, through my MTRUTH, including how to escape. Yes – escape, how was I going to do that? Like in wartime Germany it seemed to be my duty to escape. I noticed the trapdoor into the loft above the book cabinet, which the French 'psychiatrist' had shown me days earlier. I decided that if I hung around in the television room at bedtime I could climb onto the book cabinet and from there get into the loft replacing the trapdoor so that I could remain there undiscovered during the ensuing search. From the loft I could carefully make a hole through the roof and, climbing out, shin down one of the drainpipes, which I had surveyed from the window by the pool table. From there it would be a simple matter to escape across country in the night and by the time dawn came, I could be many miles away.

Of course the danger of being caught on top of the book cabinet would mean I would almost certainly be kept here longer; so I decided to bide my time and hope that, like at Fairmile, I would be released for good behaviour. As for the French 'psychiatrist', as was my wont, I had tremendously deluded thoughts about his having been sent to meet me by the French.

Then, one evening, when I had been there four weeks, one of the nurses, Harry, came in excitedly and told me that I was being transferred to Weller Wing, the open ward back at Bedford Hospital. Home was now in sight. Though depressed by the medication I was joyful – and he shared my joy.

After a delay until the next morning I was driven to Bedford. By the road I noticed an Army Land Rover. Its presence gave me support in my struggle – it had been put there for me to see. The Army Intelligence Corps psychological warfare experts knew everything there was to know about my struggle. They would not make the mistake of underestimating my value to them, I was sure.

After a week or two at Weller Wing, during which time I wrote an amusing letter to the authorities about the lack of English mustard at dinner, I was released from the Section and allowed to go home. No further injection was given but instead I was put on oral medication: a drug called Melleril. This led naturally to thoughts about the state of the mental health of David Mellor, the politician and Chelsea fan. I thought messages were coming at me from every possible direction. I decided that if I could I would inflict on him, a fellow Chelsea fan, the same medication-induced pain I'd had to endure, in a short burst so he knew what it felt like. Then I would hijack the 6 o'clock news for two minutes during which he would announce, from a top-secret location at Stamford Bridge, that the whole of this country's psychiatric units had, for the last six months, been full of patients from the SAS and SBS. For reasons of national security, all consultant psychiatrists would be put on medication from midnight. The broadcast, interrupting the normal transmission and having had no introduction, would finish with the sight of the Chelsea mascot and *Blue is the Colour* playing, the broadcast beginning and ending entirely abruptly with no explanation anywhere in the media. This would be with the exception of Mr Mellor at The Duke's Head in Putney, explaining why he was feeling so suicidal. In this pub he would explain that he was finding it difficult not to think either that he was caught up in a military psychological warfare exercise or that he was, like all the patients in the psychiatric system, also a member of the Special Forces.

It was now the spring of 1996 and it had been two years since I first became ill, though I certainly had not been ill for all this time.

Part XV

Going Nowhere

Chapter Thirty-Seven

The Heat in the Room

So once more I was released from hospital. Again, in one way more ill than when I had gone in. I had been battered into submission by the treatment, and was now clinically depressed, resorting to that well-known posture, crouched on the settee with my head down smoking roll-up after roll-up, one of my knees going up and down. I was being kept like this because I had been made to believe I needed to carry on taking this shit, the Melleril, for the rest of my life. I would lie on the couch all afternoon under a blanket turning my back to the whole world with the exception, for half-an-hour or so, of *Lovejoy*. Even that I could not enjoy properly. I was beginning to connect the Melleril with the length of my life. It could be long or short.

This was where I began to feel some legal issues impinging in my career – these would later become rather more involved. Upon release from hospital the consultant psychiatrist had told me it would be therapeutic for me to get back to work. As such I was free to collect a form (Med 3, otherwise known as a sick note) from my general practitioner with "You should not refrain from work" circled, though I did not find this out until later. I would then be free to attend work subject to any security restrictions forbidding me from entering the building. However, previously I had gone straight back and been immediately sent down to the Defence Research Agency Malvern, without any problems. This was not to happen this time. April came and I called up work to say I was ready to come back. They told me they would call back in a few days when a job had been sorted out for me.

I waited at home for the call but it did not come. Meanwhile I was dangerously ill with the depression. Still I would lie on the settee all day motionless. I went to play golf with my mother's man friend and felt the depression so badly that it was all I could do just to get to the next hole, and away from where I was. But this brought no solace – only the horrible realisation of the abject futility of getting there.

This went on for a few weeks and I recall I was too afraid to drink alcohol with the Melleril, the possible consequences being too unthinkable to risk.

After a few weeks had passed, I telephoned again and this time I was told that the person I had previously spoken to had left the company. So now I had to chase around to find out who was now dealing with me. I discovered it was a chap in "Human Resources" – or Personnel. He told me I had to produce a medical report before I could be allowed back to work, which was not strictly true, as this depended on where I was working.

I joined the Rowing Club and got in a crew, though I had not rowed for nearly 10 years. This helped as rowing is hypnotic, but my stamina was severely impaired by the drug, which prevented me from running much more than a mile without just coming to a hopeless stop. I could not wait to get away from the club to smoke. Likewise on the golf course, I continued to have a restless urge to get away from the present and this showed itself in a very poor approach to my game. To say I could not enjoy it properly would be a slight understatement. I was perked up a little by the observation that the course was on a military air route, as I could tell by the regular fly-pasts of low-flying RAF and USAF jets. For my part I felt I was on my own bombing range – bombing schizophrenia and what people thought about it.

Summer came and I was getting more and more depressed – suicidal in fact. I was driven to make desperate phone calls to people just to tell them the state I was in and to gain sympathy. At one point I was staggering down the Embankment by the river in a near delirium of depression accompanied, almost as though it were my funeral, by my father. What was enjoyment? I'd had to call him despite the fact that we never really got on like a house on fire, but it was a feature of the depression that when things got really bad I would appeal to him.

Still I had not got back to work, and by the time the medical report was produced months had gone by since I had come out of hospital. It did not occur to me, at least not yet, that I had to get off this Melleril stuff. The trouble is that doctors seem to think that, because you are depressed, all they need to do is give you some antidepressants. As it was I went on without them but I was later to find out that whilst antidepressants work very well for clinical depression (as I already knew) they do not work so well, or at all, if something is actually causing the depression. In this case it was certainly the Melleril – a drug that would later be withdrawn from use. Little did I know that it would be withdrawn at the time, or how many people it had killed. Still, I soldiered on with it, trusting the doctor's advice, which I should not have done as life was intolerable on it. But whilst I found this drug, like almost all the others, so intolerable, the consequences of taking prescribed drugs (and not just those for mental illnesses) proves fatal for thousands of NHS patients every year.

I managed to make a couple of regattas and won two pots at one, though the whole exercise just became an awful chore. Dad left me a note saying it was a "double triumph" though was not sure if he was talking about a success in the MI5 Capgras section or not. There was however the single exception of perhaps a split second as we slipped over the line first to win the final of the IVs and a jubilant hand came down on my shoulder from behind. Then I won another pot in the VIIIs. The words of my school song came back to me:

Bedford Modern School Song

> *When hope is young and our hearts beat strong*
> *And the blood runs warm in our veins,*
> *How we long to race at a swinging pace*
> *In the boat that carries the black and red.*
> *Hold on to the last till the goal is past*
> *For the boat that carries the black and red.*

> *Sons of the spreading eagle's crest,*
> *Nurtured here in our homely nest,*

Till the time draws nigh
When we long to fly
North and south and east and west.
Let us honour the name,
Let us cherish the fame
Of our school of the black and red!

I had to hold on, as in the race, but an enormous blackness had come over me in which I felt unworthy of the company around me. I was hugely inferior it seemed and felt I was being punished for being so. But ambition had not completely gone and at least I could see a rung on the ladder back to normality.

I became physically sick and rushed to the toilet after Paul Gascoigne scored his famous goal against Scotland in the European Championships. Life was truly wretched. Even this great day was marred by the terrible depression, and it has to be said that whilst my schizophrenia had often been almost enjoyable and fascinating, as it was for much of the summer of 1994, this depression certainly was not. The developing dilemma was coupled with the fact that I had been told, both to my face and via the medical report, that I would have to take this medication for the foreseeable future – a truly horrible thought.

August came and I was a very lonely and frightened man. I was longing for an end to these days of misery. I remembered my Dad's words as we walked down the river: "Keep going no matter what."[92] My memory is blurred, but at some point I went to the cinema to see *Fierce Creatures*. I had lost confidence in my ability to survive, and now found myself having to make a lonely decision. Why had I done what I had done? What would happen if I stopped taking this stuff? Would it happen again? Would I end up damaging more cars?

In the darkness of the cinema I took all the medication I had left and just threw it on the floor. This would have to be my secret, as I knew nobody would support my decision to stop taking it. But life was just too miserable whilst taking it to make any other course of action something I could possibly consider and now I was sure it was the drug making me feel so bad. I could already see the days, weeks and months of my secret mapped out ahead and I pictured myself walking down the street, fingers crossed, using plain logic to avoid getting into trouble. I felt exposed, lonely and insecure, and just had to hope the Gods were still on my side.

Another thing which kept me going was an unusual golf round on winter tees where I nearly broke one hundred. On another round I noticed one of the military aircraft flying over the course to be an A10 – the "tankbuster". Remembering the first draft of the beginning of this story concerning the death of Peter Gabriel and the use of the A10 tank-buster gun inside Fairmile Hospital, I wondered if the pilot had been responsible for the draft's disappearance – as though the writings were of key military significance.

I knew that, having stopped taking the antipsychotic medication, I must soon also stop the antidepressants too, because not having done so on the previous occasion, I had ended up hallucinating the hands at Dead Man's Hill. This had to be done very slowly to avoid withdrawal symptoms including sickness, dizziness and an odd buzz in my head. I could only describe this buzz as feeling like Bill Nelson's *My Intricate Image* was playing in my head. This would go in a matter of minutes if I took something smaller than a quarter of a tablet. I think

I had stopped too quickly a few weeks earlier – very likely my nausea had been because of this. This meant I was dangerously confused, and I lost sight of how easily that particular problem could be solved. But now I was doing it properly and within a fortnight or so I was completely clean and totally well.

My golf improving, I sought the advice of an old chap at the 19th. I told him I was getting better range and accuracy from the rough. He said "Listen to me son. Golf is life, golf is my life, and golf has made me my living. You have to play it like you play life – like you mean it. If you don't live your life like you mean it nobody will trust you. They'll think you're a liar! The reason is that your mind has told you, without you even thinking about it, that you have to play your shots from the rough like you mean it. Have you ever seen a fireman turn up to a fire without a fire engine but just a glass of water? No. Well that's what you look like when you play your shots on the fairway! I know, even though I have not seen you play. Play them like you mean it. Play them like you're in the rough. Only when you have got used to playing them like you're in the rough can you then even begin to think of playing them like you're on the fairway." Then he told me to wait and left the bar. He returned a couple of minutes later and handed me what was obviously a rather old golf ball. In fact it was a Dunlop *Warwick*. "What do you make of that then?" he asked me. "That is the actual ball Arnold Palmer used when he won the United States Masters for the first time in 1958. Put it in your bag for luck, it will make you play better – and play life like you mean it!"

Now I was able to enjoy my golf properly, as demonstrated by knocking 11 off my best score getting 90, putting for 89, and I was enjoying life again. But even the professional had not told me the full story – which did not sink in until a few rounds later. When I was playing shots in the heavy rough my leading arm was straight, at least at the moment of contact. When I eventually realised this and, moreover, kept it straight throughout my swing, including on the fairway, I was hitting the ball as much as an extra 50 yards.

But there was still the worry of the secret I had, that I was not taking my medication. This made me feel guilty. I almost felt I was actually supposed to feel ill because of the label I had been given though, as I said, the only way I knew what diagnosis I had was from what the drugs I had been given were indicated for.

I seemed to have become a full-time golf professional, courtesy of what I saw as fraudulent insurance payments, which my employer had obtained for me. I saw these as fraudulent because it seemed so easy to get a sick note when really I wanted to be back at work and, moreover, felt fine to go back. Meanwhile my employer did not seem to want me back and they were just too happy for me to keep taking the payments. I was alive again. But I seemed to be a full-time cripple. I refused to accept it. But hallucinating various golf professionals coaching me round the course hardly seemed a disability. Nor did the vision of Prince Andrew, a keen golfer, telling me I was playing at the Royal and Ancient (the club at St. Andrew's from which the game is governed).

It was about this time that I first began receiving visits at home from a community psychiatric nurse (CPN) and, on one occasion, a social worker. These visits were not something I looked forwards to or even felt the need for. In fact in the case of the CPN the whole exercise seemed a waste of time merely designed to check I was taking my medication. Now, years later I am angry about these visits – as they did nothing to prevent the later loss of my flat and mortgage.

It became apparent that I was not going to get back to work unless I pushed even harder for it, my employer appearing quite happy to leave me on the permanent health insurance. So I arranged a meeting at the company office because I now realised they had deluded me into thinking they were sorting out a position.

At around this time I saw an advertisement on television, which asked, "Have you had the privilege?" I found myself wondering if the question related to me and that the advertisement had been prepared in collaboration with the MoD. I asked myself if the question was about my being a Special Forces/MI5 MTRU, with full MTRUTH, EAI, EAV, EAH and complete reality replacement capability. I reasoned that somebody was bound to be given that honour without being told as, for example, an experiment in schizophrenia, the word "schizophrenia" having been coined only as recently as 1912, and its study therefore being in its infancy.

One day I went for a walk in the country. Across the fields I reached the church in Ravensden and found myself looking at the noticeboard. I received something of a burst of energy; it appeared from Prince Charles's dog, when I read on the noticeboard the announcement of an application for planning permission for a dog kennel. This both amused me and made me feel that my presence here was not solely the result of exercising my own free will.

Instead it again seemed that I had been guided here using simple brainwashing techniques broadcast over my MTRUTH. At the moment I finished reading the application I looked up to see, high above, a jet's vapour trail. It seemed, not that the trail was winding because of atmospheric conditions, but because the pilot had been ordered to weave across the sky high above me. I thought it was signalling to me. As for the identity of the dog which would live in the kennel I imagined Prince Charles's dog might be moving to Bedford and it would do wonders for house prices.

Towards the end of November I had a meeting with a chap in Human Resources, whereupon he chastised me for not taking my medication – medication that was subsequently banned from use. He didn't have to take it himself and I would just love him to have had to go through what I had. Then he would not have spoken to me like that. The meeting was held in a building from which I was supposed to be banned – a breach of MoD regulations by him, not me. He waved the confidential medical report at me; I thought it was only to be seen by the company doctor. I felt bitter. His behaviour made me loathe him. The way he was speaking to me was belittling and insulting. I imagined an out of season mad March hare running past the window behind him. But later, worse would be done. I heard from the MoD Vetting Agency that if I got ill again and it was shown to be because I stopped taking my medication *I would never be given my security clearance ever again* as this showed how "irresponsible" I was.

Finally I was sent to a position in Milton Keynes. I had tried to get to work for some nine miserable months after I had been cleared to go by the psychiatrist. All this time I was sending them sick notes from my GP, notes that said I was ill when actually I was perfectly okay to work – at least once I stopped taking the Melleril. I had the perfect right to just turn up to work like anyone else would. I did however eventually get there. I found myself back on 10th December 1996, walking up the gravel drive to the front of the old country house where I was to work, the crows cawing peacefully in the tall trees above, and I felt a sense of relief to have made it. I was very happy to be back at work and felt no enmity to my employer.

I was taken to my new office, O14, with a distant aspect over the border into Bedfordshire from the window. I hardly objected to breaking down some cardboard boxes inside a cold computer room, though I did wonder exactly why I was doing this. I noticed my room number was alphanumerically similar to MI5 and checked to see if it had been changed recently. There was no sign it had.

Prior to my return to work I had been told I would have to sign a contract forcing me to take my medication. A multinational corporation forcing a person to take a drug which makes his life unpleasantly unliveable is a recipe for suicide, and brutally immoral. At work I was put under pressure to sign it, which I did under duress, having no intention to comply. If only, I imagined, those pressurising me to sign the contract could know what these miserable side effects were like, then they would know how disgusting their murderous little contract was. Now I did feel enmity, and lots of it.

I was now given the task of designing and building a Customer Survey Database, a task I set to with a new found zest for life. I would listen to the Spice Girls singing *Two Become One* on my Walkman on the walk into work from the railway station. Not having taken any medication now since the summer, I was newly fortified with the barrier of time I had erected with myself when I made the lonely decision to stop taking the Melleril. I would count off each full moon as the barrier of time became greater and the proof I did not need the drug became, it seemed, more evident.

Everything seemed normal, nobody was following me, I found a new girlfriend, Sue, and the only real problem in life was that I found myself keen to get away from her to have a roll-up. She told me she had once met the Princess of Wales, but I was well enough not to read anything deluded into this. She was obviously just one of Princess Diana's cupbearers.

I joined the Conservatives and began helping with their campaigning. Thoughts of being followed and of dogs had long been forgotten – or rather pushed far into the back of my mind. I started running again. I found that when I got to Cleat Hill I could see my imagined personal trainer with a stopwatch. He was a black man standing outside Bedford Rowing Club. I could also see a helicopter-load of fat men being left on a Scottish Island with minimal provisions.

The only problem now was a little nagging suspicion that I had somehow "been done" with respect to work though I felt that realistically I just had to try and keep out of hospital. If there were any symptoms I just had to reason them away, which, with spring approaching, I managed to do.

But trouble lay ahead. With the arrival of spring I ended my new relationship with Sue, and having put myself forward as a council election candidate, this being announced in the local paper, I had a bad experience. I decided to go in to the Party just to give them the courtesy of knowing that if I stood then there was likely to be press interest in my medical condition. This I did. The Party official, a well-known and upstanding member of the community, told me that somebody, having seen news of my prospective candidature in the paper, had already telephoned to say that I was not a suitable candidate; so the Party would not be going ahead with my nomination. I asked him who this other respected member of the community was and he refused to tell me. I left the office with a lump in my throat. I felt mistreated and sensed something seriously wrong with what had happened. But that was not the end of the matter.

The very next day, as I walked down the street, a boyfriend of a local Labour councillor, both friends of mine, called out laughing at me from the opposite side of the street "I hear you have been thrown out of the Conservative Party!" I felt bitter, particularly as this was not true.

I persuaded myself I did not want to be a councillor anyway, and if that was what politics was like, I wanted nothing to do with it. Subsequently I discovered that mental illness is no bar to standing for Parliament, let alone the local council. Some would even claim that mental illness was a positive requirement to be an MP. Years later, I would tell all this to one local Labour councillor in the pub. He said to me "Come and join the Labour Party, we're all mad!" But at the time I just wanted to put all that had happened behind me and concentrate on my job. And anyway, perhaps it had been nothing to do with my mental illness but a debt I still had from my record company days. Either that or they somehow knew of my idea to call Crimestoppers about looking for Prince Charles's dog in the Gog Magog hills, a call I never made.

Chapter Thirty-Eight

Stairway to Heaven

Summer was approaching – it was over a year since the end of my previous, second, forced hospitalisation. One evening, sitting in The Ship, something interesting happened. I found myself sensitised to people's laughter. I had to forcibly reason my way through the feeling I was having that their laughter was aimed at me. I did this by considering who they could really be laughing at, either in the other bar or nearer at hand. Having done that I was able to put my mind at rest. I did this by reasoning it simply felt like they were laughing at me because it was a mild symptom of schizophrenia. The symptom then seemed to entirely evaporate – without any drugs – until one evening as I sat alone. Who should appear but the Spice Girls! They came and sat down at my table. They were not actually there, but my imagination seemed to have got more vivid than usual. It seemed my MTRUTH was in operation again. Then something a little strange happened to my vision. I noticed what I was sure were the effects of mutual interference of white light – something I did not remember to have happened in the past. I knew only few people would recognise what it was I was seeing – those with training in Applied Optics. Even fewer would imagine it had something to do with their having an EAI. But actually it was just an optical effect of my eyelashes. White light, like laser light, is coherent over short, wavelength-sized distances and therefore interference fringes are possible. If you have ever seen attractive mysterious patterns on a wall onto which the sun is shining through a tree in leaf then you have seen the effects of mutual interference of white light – in this case the light from the gaps in between leaves interfering to make these patterns.

One day I was enjoying a drink in The Mill Hotel. Whatever was on television it amused me to the point of laughter. I was sitting on my own – a bottle of prescribed pills (of I forget which type) standing on the table next to my pint. The Irish landlady came over and asked me to leave – which I did, again with a lump in my throat. A couple of weeks later, thinking the landlady would have forgotten the incident, I visited the pub again – she still refused to serve me. This meant I had been banned from a pub three times: once for laughing; once for crying; and once for pulling down a scale model of a Gemini space capsule. It was about three feet high and was to promote "Lunartic" [*sic*] beer in one of the Firkin pub chain. The occasion I was asked to leave for crying was when I was the intermediary between Tom and his girlfriend who were splitting up.

There was in fact a fourth occasion on which I was asked to leave a pub and, I have to say, it was rather odd to say the least. I went to a pub I had not visited for some years – The Crown: "Established during the reign of George IV". Enjoying my beer, I noticed a woman wearing a headscarf sitting in front of me.

Even then I was thinking there was a Royal similarity. She was haranguing the poor chap sitting facing her across the table like it was something out of *Eastenders*. He just sat there meekly, barely saying a word. Eventually I'd had enough of listening to this tirade and called out "Why don't you give the man a break?" whereupon she turned her head in a slow, deliberate and exaggerated manner to face me. At this moment my blood ran cold because it did appear she bore a remarkable facial resemblance to Her Majesty the Queen. I have to say the target of her ongoing verbal assault did not look very much like the Duke of Edinburgh though. I forget what she said but whatever it was it did not feel very nice. It really felt like the situation had been a set-up. The landlord asked me to leave, which I did. Walking down the street outside I let a judicious shiver pass down my body, shook my head, and wondered what sort of witchcraft I had just experienced.

At work my database project neared completion, but I began to have trouble staying in the office, and stress started setting in. One evening after work I was waiting for my train in The Station Hotel at Woburn Sands, where each of the station's nameplates barked "Bobby Sands" proudly and effusively at me. On the bar was a newly poured pint of Bateman's beer. The light above was producing a shimmering, scintillating and sparkling look in the froth. *Stairway to Heaven* was playing on the jukebox and I was astonished to see hundreds of sailors swimming around in the beer's head. They were shouting at me for help as they floated up and down in the foam and the swell of the high sea. Be this in my MTRUTH or otherwise, I knew I had to do something, but short of calling the Coastguard, I had no idea what. Instead I looked around at the other drinkers in the bar, bemused. I thought of Revelation 20:13:

and the sea gave up the dead that were in it...

I left my expensive pen deliberately, as I had done with my mountain bikes on earlier occasions – a sign of relapse into schizophrenia. Soon the train arrived.

Next day in the office the atmosphere was becoming more and more oppressive. I wrote an email to my manager on the subject, but did not quite dare send it. There was no proper ventilation and I felt like I was being steamed out. Off came my jacket and undone my top button. The whole area began to take on an air of unreality as had happened during that long hot summer of 1994 and again in the days before my arrest for the 'theft' of the cat. It was now summer 1997. I saw a knight in armour sword fighting like a practising fencer in the corridor. This was a little bit more than just the product of my visual imagination. The vision was involuntary – and clear enough to mean it was either hallucination or MTRUTH.

I began to hope desperately that something would be done. Soon there were large numbers of workmen in the building, and all the doors in the corridor were wide open. The workers were moving between the courtyard and the outside grounds, where a colony of feral cats scampered around guarding their domain around the old country house, which the offices adjoined.

With the receptionist I booked a room in the old tower for a meeting with someone important and imaginary, though I knew not who. I felt I was now the real president of this multinational, and now I was going to have to justify my perceived seniority by acting the part properly. But it wasn't just that I felt that. I also felt somebody *was making me think that*, deliberately. I did not mind this. So I attempted to channel my feelings of awesome power efficaciously. Prior to the appointed time I arrived for the meeting with myself. I turned over a new leaf on the large paper drawing book attached to the board and wrote, in big letters covering the sheet so as to make it perfectly visible at the back of the room, SBK, the EMI publishing company. My state of mind allowed me to see some deluded meaning in SBK being an anagram of SKB, the drugs company that my uncle had worked for. I then sat down to enjoy a coffee and a cigar. I admired my career success, as I knew I really had arrived. I had realised my power – the power my MTRUTH afforded me. It was a mixture of delusion and autosuggestion.

By now I could not stay in the office for long without breaking for a roll-up. Then, one afternoon, I just had to get out of the building completely as the tension was becoming unbearable, quite apart from the heat in the room. I began to find myself thinking that anyone in the building not employed by my company was somehow an agent of an American religious cult – very likely an extremely wealthy, powerful and sickly one. The raid, by the Federal Bureau of Firearms and Tobacco, on the Branch Davidian Church of the Seventh Day Adventists at Waco was uppermost in my mind once again. This I found suggestive of what was now happening. Somehow this cult seemed to have reached here.

I was sitting in the smoking room when a garrulous American came in and said to his colleague "It's all in the ears." In reality EARS was a piece of company management software but I thought the cultists had got hold of MTRUTH technology. This had gone so far that the military apocalypse scenario had arisen again: these people were being lured here to be exterminated by the Special Forces – the same as the day of imagined mass slaughter when I walked from Barnes to Hatfield two years earlier.

It was frighteningly real. All the employees in the building were very sick members of this extreme religious cult. I sat down in the smoking room and this was the signal for the entire building to vacate their seats, though I had not been told. Suddenly large numbers of people were all moving down the corridor in an eerily orderly manner, a little like the Eloi in H.G.Wells's *The Time Machine*. They were heavily infected. Only I remained seated.

It seemed as though I was back at Fairmile Hospital and, like the Eloi, everyone was being farmed again. There I had believed everyone in Reading Police Station had been killed by the Human Infection Control Unit. But, however ill I was, my imagination now allowed me some insight via the full scope of the meaning of the word "kill" from being actually shot dead to simply becoming party to certain information – or being made to die laughing. But now there seemed no doubt the former was going to happen here, and I could see the BBC's Brian Hanrahan standing in front of the Army road block with, behind him, the smoke ascending from the compound – which was really just another Waco. Then it seemed the latter would happen and it was all just a huge joke. But there was a logical battle going in my mind as I tried to reason my way out of these thoughts. I thought that the man wearing the white coat spraying weed killer or something around the base of trees in the grounds of the offices was also an infection control specialist from Porton Down, spraying concentrated SKB Ribena. I shook my head briskly in bemused approval. This was seriously schizoid. Either that or I was moving towards horticultural homeopathy.

At lunchtimes I would walk to a pub The Tawny Owl and on one occasion felt overcome by a sickly sense of glory as though, in some sense, I were now the richest person on the planet. I just could not handle it in my brain, biochemically speaking. These feelings were accompanied by thinking that any unexplained behaviour of my PC was down to somebody having hacked into it once again.

I sat at the machine motionless, and looking at my mouse in a strange way. I then pictured a terminal with some large rat of a mouse connected to it. This other terminal, at some distance from mine, was showing exactly the same as my monitor. My thoughts really got carried away and I imagined its contents subject to British School of Motoring (BSM) dual control. Perhaps now the iron bar across the distant keyboard would be removed – the bloody great padlock on its end to prevent the dual control being used (bar exceptional circumstances) now being unlocked. The circumstances enabling this to happen were surely as tightly controlled as those which allowed for the use of nuclear weapons. These were such circumstances, I felt – and now, maybe, I could have full EAV. Perhaps now I would be able to watch television without there being one near my eyes – but in them. But in fact I never really saw what I might call a full-scale hallucination, or "wall-climbing reality" before me. Either I saw what was really there and did not believe it, or I saw a ghost of my subconscious. One exception to this was the Mother Teresa hallucination. Also, beyond this story, whilst taking the antidepressant Zispin, I found myself in bed hallucinating a premiership football match in full colour. I assure you it was most impressive. But this was a listed side effect and not, I feel, a schizophrenic hallucination. In other words somebody not suffering schizophrenia could also enjoy *Match of the Day* without paying for a television licence.

I found myself wondering if the person at the other screen was American; so I typed onto my screen something combative and then "Microsoft, Crown Property." No doubt they had a keystroke monitor at the very least, I thought.

I abandoned my machine for the purposes of the task I was performing and now, sitting at another terminal, began to experience the same feelings. The vast quantity of archived documentation stored in the old bus station now seemed to be somehow weighing me down like it was attached to my mind through a massive yoke. None of the figures on the screen seemed to make sense and I found myself believing the amount of disk space available was impossibly big. I reeled away from the terminal in the oppressive heat, everyone else having now deserted the office, the corridor being very quiet. I wondered if they were already dead in the recreation hall.

I now doubled up in the corner of the room behind the filing cabinet, laughing desperately and uncontrollably. The old bus station was now fully ablaze. Everyone in the whole area, now sealed off, was dead – with the exception of me. I was going to be the only one to come out alive. After a hero's welcome I would be rushed away to Special Forces HQ for debriefing. I pointed hysterically at my PC like it was the funniest thing on the planet. My stomach muscles had not been exercised this well since rowing training the previous year. But I still had sufficient control of reality to realise that if somebody *was* alive in the vicinity and now entered the room I would have to pull myself together pretty bloody quickly, possibly by pretending I had a very serious attack of hay fever.

Luckily nobody came in, and only once did I give anyone the slightest reason to suppose there was a problem. This was when, having had problems with my scroll bars, I imagined the cause was that they were connected to the large levers in the signal box at the nearby railway station. So I casually complained to someone in the room "I sometimes wonder if my machine is connected to an outside signal box." Again, to my left in the corridor, I vividly imagined two knights in armour having a swordfight.

My feelings had at first been accompanied by guilt and embarrassment when I perceived that somebody had realised I knew they were there and had hacked into my PC. These feelings were a bit like those experienced by a mother who finds her six-year-old downloading top secret documents from the Pentagon or enabling nuclear submarines to target their local shopping centre. But I soon realised that there is a big difference between an aide-mémoire, a deliberate message, and hundreds of pages of telephone conversation transcripts, possibly taken from cassette tapes, which throughout my life I had found unravelled in the street and in trees. I supposed they had been put there by MI5 as part of their regular review of stocks in an act of witchcraft. So I now imagined I could type anything on my screen, even send myself strange emails and create, in the mind of my imagined jousting partner, exactly those symptoms which characterised the illness I was suffering. The matter of Tolstoy's *War and Peace* would then be just an 800 page aide-mémoire, piled up in stacks like tins of baked beans in supermarkets, Prince Charles wondering if it was a message aimed at him. I was just talking to myself. Only somebody knew I was and what I was saying to myself.

A few days after that, and holding the belief somebody was out there, I typed into the machine the short story of my last Capstan Full Strength cigarette, and my escape from this situation. By way of a challenge I deleted the story right in front of my eyes – eyes I also suspected were *their* eyes. That would put the wind up them, I thought. British Intelligence was thinking: how could I possibly know they were watching every little tiny aspect of my manner at the machine? It was a great little short story but I destroyed it thinking that MI5, or whoever it was, still had a copy for posterity.

Again I found myself reasoning that the only logical way out of this was to imagine everyone working in that building lying in rows in the recreation club with their bodies covered by blankets. I would leave it up to someone else's imagination as to whether they had committed suicide, had all been shot, or were simply performing a quite spectacular display of Masonry worthy of a change of name to Joinery for security reasons.

Having deleted the story, I left the office early, flicking a defiant V at my PC as it powered-down. I passed the Infection Control officer from Porton Down in the garden, still spraying the Ribena around the bases of trees, probably, as I suggested, a little more diluted than normal. I felt like my head was about to split because a sniper had his perfectly sighted rifle trained right on it from up in the hills near Woburn Golf Club.

I wandered down through the housing estate until I got to the railway. Reaching the railway I placed a fifty pence coin on the track and moved away to the end of the field, as, in the distance, a track maintenance gang happened to appear. The atmosphere was strange. The train passed and I waited for the track gang to disappear so I could return to inspect the damage. I stood still and did not think they had seen me. I kept my eyes fixed on the spot where I had put the coin to see if they picked it up. They didn't. Reaching the track, with the crew now further up the line, I picked up the coin, no longer on the rail. I was surprised to see that the Queen's head was entirely unscathed other than a little mark on her shoulder, which looked like her sash, whereas the linked European hands on the other side were severely damaged. This seemed to be a miracle, showing the Queen to be untouchable. I placed the now damaged EEC commemorative coin on top of the fence post of the stile by the nearby rooky wood. That strange feeling was back as though everything I did was being watched from nearby. But I liked the feeling – it meant I was important. The coin would be collected, I was sure.

Now I ascended the hill through the woods where I had imagined the sniper had been. Soon I arrived at the Golf Club where, by accident, I left my umbrella. It had been manufactured by the British Umbrella Company, Brixton, making it seem, to my then mind, very powerful. A few days later the golf club announced the forthcoming construction of a new course, the Marquess' Course. This was witchcraft. Simply leaving the umbrella had resulted in the announcement – a strange delusion of grandeur of the same type which made me foresee the death of the Israeli prime minister.

It was probably around this time that, when lying in bed, I would notice what sounded like the occasional tiny stone being thrown at the window. In reality I think the noise was caused by energy being released in the process of "glass creep". Glass, as you might know, is a very viscous liquid and gradually flows. But I thought the SAS were firing micro-bullets at the window from underground tunnels outside the house.

The next day I did not arrive at work until the afternoon, my manager criticising my timekeeping without saying anything about all the extra hours I had booked in the security logbook at weekends. He refused to pay my travel expense claim for a later train, which was cheaper. On his desk I noticed a letter from a particularly sensitive client, which looked like it had been photocopied a ludicrous number of times, this seeming significant. I worked late until dark.

Leaving work I had a moment's strange 'insight'. It occurred to me that MI5 must have wound down the operation quite some time ago, the strange file on the disappearance of Prince Charles's dog and my involvement in it having been long put away. I felt my presence in the office where my MTRUTH was being controlled from. Nobody was near the terminal and though people were nearby I could only hear voices in the background and could not make out what was being said. MI5 may have wound down the operation but the Army hadn't. That night I found myself standing on the platform waiting for the train and, just like they were flying out of the oppressive heat of the room O14, there came the drone of a swarm of Army helicopters over the horizon near the golf club. I thought: am I imagining this? No, I definitely am not.

At first there was just one – I saw its lights come up over the horizon from the lower greensand ridge, then another and after the next few, I lost count. I really could hardly believe what I was seeing but of course it was nothing to do with me – or was it? There must be something massive going on at Fairfield Hospital, I surmised, and of course it was to do with me. I had now become an integral component of these military operations. I felt proud. I did indeed have an MTRUTH fitted. Total in-body virtual reality with remote operation –

possibly via a British Telecom-disguised Army Intelligence Corps van. It was like the Oasis *D' You Know What I Mean?* video. Half the Army Air Corps had turned up for this manoeuvre.

Talking of Fairfield Asylum, it was about this time I decided to take a trip there voluntarily to concentrate my mind on the thought that I would do nothing to justify being put there again. As I arrived at the Victorian building an old man walked by and for some reason called me Oliver. What was this – the Civil War?

It was also about now that I decided Defence Intelligence had created, for military exercise purposes, a building double of my parents' house in a computer. This meant you could walk into the house virtually and, for example, pick up a book – possibly whilst a member of the FRU did the same in the real world. Why this would be done was merely a matter for conjecture. A strangely magical and alluring feeling descended on the house – rather like the day I set up the voodoo diorama with the *Discreet Campaigns* tape.

At that moment a card came through the letterbox and hung there tantalising me. My imagination told me this was happening simultaneously real-time in the model. I read the card. It said "The CD you ordered: *Oh Crikey! It's Lawnmower Deth* [sic] has arrived in the shop." At this moment I sensed an enormous force requiring me to get a copy of Joni Mitchell singing *Both Sides Now* on board. It was almost as though the house was going on some long voyage and no more stores or supplies could be brought aboard once it had set sail. There was something utterly Alice in Wonderland about the whole thing and I thought of the line in that song about "Ice cream castles in the air." Everything seemed mysterious and magical.

Now I saw somebody in the SAS drive an ice cream van out of the back of a Hercules aircraft over Salisbury Plain. Somebody dived out after him and, reaching the van at 100mph in free fall asked for a double 99 with raspberry sauce. At this moment the SAS ice cream man realised he had not put the handbrake on as ordered, which he now did, and then switched on the chimes, which began playing *Greensleeves* from the plummeting van. The other parachutist now got his ice cream, paid, and received his change. Then he began eating the ice cream, with a little difficulty, and the SAS ice cream man left the van. Both SAS men landed safely, the van, being well bombed-up, causing a huge explosion on hitting the ground nearby, one of the chaps still licking his ice cream as he took off his 'chute – the whole incident being observed from a grandstand, full of military top brass and defence contractors. This might sound laughable but it was a military exercise based on my deluded belief in 1994 that the United States Defence Secretary, Warren Hastings, had been in England working covertly as an ice cream man with MI5 and the Pentagon.

Next morning, when I got off the train, there was a large Class 22 English Electric Deltic locomotive waiting at the signal, though why, I could not imagine, other than saying I wondered if a homeopathic doctor, (or Liz Hurley) drove it in Army fatigues. It seemed to have been laid on for me specially. I had for some weeks been having feelings about the other people on the train. Irish Republicans were on the same small train I was on as part of the peace negotiations. I was getting messages again, though to write down what was happening would have stopped this and removed my delusion. I did not want to do that because I was enjoying the power I was feeling in this state – deluded or not.

As usual, I walked to work from the station along the road and past the church, though I did on occasions go through the fields passing some llamas kept there. On this occasion I entered the village shop where I bought a copy of *The Herald Tribune*. Passing the Methodist Chapel I noticed a rare *Z Cars*-style Ford Zephyr parked down the lane by the side of the chapel. I noticed that its number plate contained the letters AVC. This was a coincidence because only that week, after having fallen behind in my Additional Voluntary Contribution (AVC) pension payments, I had managed to get the pension fund up to date. This made me shiver just ever so slightly as I passed the car, which looked a little eerie down the lane. MI5 knew all my business affairs including those of my pension and were trying to tickle my imagination. They, or the Special Forces, would wage some sort of low intensity war against me because of what I had done that bank holiday weekend some three years earlier; the 1926 meeting, or experiments in homeopathic horticulture being conducted by Porton Down. As I had in the story, I decided to smoke the last Capstan Full Strength cigarette, still in its box in the moleskin pocket of my Barbour.

A couple of days later, passing the Chapel, I noticed the Zephyr had gone. But further down the road outside the house named *Ponsgon* was another Zephyr. It was parked with the driver revving the engine up furiously. I was paranoid about the name of the adjacent house *Ponsgon* as I thought it was a reference to Professor Stanley Pons, who 'discovered', a few years earlier, the mysterious cold fusion process, which brought the false promise of boundless energy. Getting closer I saw the driver, who had a very short haircut and was leaning forwards at the steering wheel. He was looking eagerly at the sky all around him, moving his head across his field of view as though his life depended on his spotting any "incoming" (to use military parlance for incoming enemy fire). He hardly needed uniform and, without thinking about it, I took his odd behaviour to mean I was the one in extreme danger and not him. I thought he was trying to spot this "incoming" on his MTRUTH. I was being brainwashed by the military using all means available. His presence meant that if I did not consider my every movement with precise logic I would be taken out. His foot went down and off tore the old Zephyr with burning rubber tyres to disappear in the direction of the village. The Special Forces had just been in action before my very eyes. The driver was in the SAS.

Next day, on my way to work, I noticed, where the car had been parked, a small number of cigarette butts in the road. It was Ash Wednesday and, it seemed, the driver had put them there to challenge me to stop smoking. I never bought a packet of cigarettes again – or rolling tobacco for several years.

At work I logged on to my machine and began typing in, aide-mémoire style, the Sherlock Holmes and lemon curd joke that my friend Patrick had told me, which I do not feel is suitable for publication. When I got to the punchline I replaced it with "It's quite simple Watson, you and I have solved the Greatest Mystery Known to Mankind. Tonight we shall raise the dead!" It seemed very serious. I believed I was going to raise the dead and make a lot of money doing it. But (should you ever hear the joke) I grant you that such use of lemon curd is a funny way to do it.

I was still fascinated with my idea about L Zero being the first lie by MI5, the lie that John Lennon was dead. Within months this obsession would have serious consequences.

One evening I was in The King's Arms pub in Bedford. Here I was, having a crap, feeling that somebody was looking through my eyes. It was very powerful. So powerful that I was still unable, as had been the case since 1994, to look at the toilet paper I had just used: An intolerable state of affairs to have to put up with. So now, having just wiped myself I held the dirty piece of toilet paper deliberately close to my eyes as a demonstration of what I believed to whoever was watching what happened over my MTRUTH. Next day at lunchtime I went to The Plough in Wavendon for lunch. I was just coming out of the pub. Next to the corner of a colleague's house (which he had told me had been clipped, during World War II, by a tank coming round the corner), a strange thing happened. I saw a chap walk down the street holding a screwed up piece of what looked like toilet paper close to his face, exactly as I had done the previous evening. Such behaviour seemed most mysterious the only explanations being: (a) I had an MTRUTH fitted and (b) somebody was watching everything that happened through it or alternatively (c) he was just blowing his nose. The level of mystery in Wavendon was palpable during these days.

Next day I was walking past the spot where I had seen the man looking at the toilet paper when a double of Peter Gabriel walked by. I could hear the real Mr Gabriel singing *Come Talk to Me* on my MTRUTH whilst, on my EAI there appeared, supra-subliminally, a dial whose pointer was registering something as I walked past him. It felt most strange and therefore, I can only presume the dial was indicating how peculiar this incident was. On future occasions the dial would appear registering something on each occasion I walked past this spot. It would be interesting to see what somebody made of this with a divination rod.

I was a bit peeved that my claim for travel expenses had been refused, and something had to break I suppose. Certainly my brain chemistry was not now all it should be. My experience working for the MoD and the Army in battlefield simulation, together with my intelligence about Prince Charles's dog, was to now have an interesting side effect. I have already mentioned the possibility of virtual realities or parallel worlds created by Defence Intelligence, these being a little different from those I had worked with. I now imagined the one they had of my actual house was so detailed it went right down to a leather bookmark left at some time in the past at a certain page in a tome written by Amanda's grandfather. The book (which was the acknowledged work on the organ, entitled The Organ) had a personal inscription from the author inside the cover to my father, whom he had met.

The presence of this book, and another of her grandfather's, seemed like witchcraft and caused me some concern. This had allowed me to believe there was something romantically predetermined of a 1926 nature about the book's presence and my meeting Amanda. I had to get over this.

Somebody in the music industry had learnt of the status of my home and its "building doubles". Their latest CD dropped eerily through the letterbox: hand-delivered in person. They wanted to affect a momentary asymmetry between my home and its doubles whilst the Security Services inserted another copy of this album both in the real and virtual doubles of my house.

I had once written a document inspired by having read *The Glass Bead Game*. In this I made reference to *The Organ*. In the document I proposed the game actually be played. The uncertainty of what was beneath the concrete at the foot of the garden in Cornwall Road caused me to think, once again, that one or two people had been playing it already, possibly back at the 1926 meeting. I imagined they had formed a dating agency, which, at no financial cost to myself, would arrange my betrothal to somebody, Amanda, who would not be born for another 35 years. Ha! Ha! But the best laid plans! Even MI5's designs could be disrupted by one single MI6/KGB double agent. I was not destined to marry her. Instead I was to end up making these tragically tenuous and bizarre connections between imaginary events and insignificant facts.

So there it was, more wildly deluded thoughts. I was thinking the CIA not only had a virtual double of my house and all its contents but also that they might even have created a real double of it and the pub, perhaps in collaboration with the British Army on Salisbury Plain. This would mean they could recreate the acoustics of the pub and overlay my reality, using my MTRUTH, with the sounds from their building double. These possibilities allowed in my mind for all sorts of lego-military manoeuvres, these only being limited by the imagination. The glider I had built in my teens was in the attic; there was also one in the attic of Colditz Castle. So obviously it was some Colditz veterans having a laugh at my expense. Again I thought of the Escape Officer there, who had been to my alma mater, and wondered what he might make of my position.

On one of the last days I attended work, as my train approached the summit west of Lidlington, I noticed a motionless silhouette against the skyline of the lower greensand ridge. It was a man standing in a gap in the hedgerow. He was looking out from the top of the hill in the direction of the train, if not directly at myself. I would normally have hardly thought about this silhouette, but now it stuck in my mind, and gave me an odd feeling. Was he the same person I had seen in the Zephyr? I certainly believed he was in the SAS, whoever he might be. So what else to do but go up there myself one day?

Sitting on the train the next day I now began to actively believe I had been constructively dismissed. I had certainly heard of such a thing. I did not remember you had to resign first to claim this. I got off the train at Lidlington. It was miserable weather; that was why I liked it. But it was not raining, it was just overcast, and my judo belt had not been put to the test for some time. Unnoticed by the British Rail Board, I left the station and bought a pasty in the butcher's. My judo, or my schizophrenia, was so advanced I was minded to the possibility that the little village butcher's had been kept open deliberately – even though it made no money. This might be either just this (normally early closing) afternoon or for many years, the opening being entirely for military purposes, for example to burn the roof of my mouth if I was not careful – the pasty was that hot!

Without a map I headed off in the direction of that hedge, a good mile from the station along the public footpaths past the local Army Cadets Headquarters. Across a couple of fields I found myself in a small wood. I heard the loud distinctive sound of a Chinook taking off to the south. The density of the vegetation prevented me from seeing the helicopter as it faded from earshot. Climbing over the fence out of the wood, I noticed it had a lot of barbed wire wrapped around it, although it was a public footpath, as the map later confirmed to me. It was not the wire which pierced my skin though, but just a small splinter, which I decided required hospital treatment and a tetanus injection. Part of this treatment would consist, whilst waiting the usual required period, of the sight of a young Asian doctor staggering out of the treatment room in probably the most delirious example of clinical laughter I have ever seen. He had been made to take laughing gas before being told about me, and my being an MTRU.

But I still had to get to the hospital before the tetanus got hold. It was not clear where the footpath now led; though later examination of the map showed it was straight across the ploughed field. But the ploughing confused me, it having been done deliberately with that very intention, and I did not want to sprain my ankle against the heavy clods. So I made my way along the top edge of the field, over the fence and down the hedge to the place where I had seen the silhouette from the train, the place I was obviously meant to be. I stared down on a passing train, imagination being the only limit as to who was on it. The roles might now have been reversed; perhaps the next in this Special Forces production line was looking up at me; maybe Roman Polanski, as eerily as in *The Tenant*, could have been the one there sitting in the very seat I had been in a few days earlier. Or perhaps there were some youngsters making their way home from school or some folks coming home from shopping, one of them perhaps noticing my own silhouette against the skyline in the gap in the hedge and wondering if I was just a cut out, as I always seemed to be there. Whatever the truth this was again exceedingly strange.

The sound of the old train disappeared, like the helicopter's had done, and I now sat down in the gap in the hedge and surveyed the Marston Vale all the way up to Twinwoods aerodrome on the horizon. I wondered if there had been *another person* on the train.

Now, in the corner of my eye, I spotted a Land Rover coming down the edge of the field where I had just walked. Somehow, I could not discount its having been driven out of the back of the helicopter I had heard, but not seen, only minutes earlier. If correct, I could not then be sure just exactly who this farmer was.

Soon it was near me and out got the Head of the Farmer's Union, or whomever he was, possibly a well-known Irish Republican not known to me, and very angry he was too. He might have come to test my judo I thought, to see if I still deserved my belt, and I noticed that he needed some expensive dental treatment to correct his badly aligned teeth.

I declined a fight and, careful not to sprain an ankle, headed off down the hill, at the bottom of which I had spotted where the path reappeared at the railway line. It would have been a shame to negotiate the hole in his hedge, only to break an ankle. I headed off to get back to the very important job of psychiatric patient in partial remission.

Chapter Thirty-Nine

The Omega Man [93]

It was now three years since I first imagined that the Major was about to knock on the front door. Thank God he did it quietly, I thought, as I didn't want to have heard him – not yet. I remembered lying on the bed thinking he was about to knock. I was just wallowing in the strange atmosphere of the room. But then, unlike now, I was not yet fully familiar with the symptoms of schizophrenia. I was to become used to enjoying them. The Major and I were the actual inspiration for *(What's the Story?) Morning Glory*. "All his dreams were made", as well as mine, both of us having MTRUTHs, these operating in dream-machine mode.

One day in Club Rich UK a funny feeling came over me. I was looking at the way the room had been decorated and the penny dropped. Clearly it had been designed to look like the sleeve graphics on the *Discreet Campaigns* cassette, which took part in that most magical incident of witchcraft involving Clint Eastwood and Sunny Jim, as I described. My eyes were drawn to a picture on this wall in which three chaps were sitting around a table discussing something. The one to the right was clearly Noel Gallagher, and to the left was Paul McCartney. But the one facing the camera was me circa 1989! Jesus Christ, I thought, this is serious witchcraft! The picture reminded me of earlier KGB tactics in manipulation of the populace using photos that had been tampered with, by the removal of Trotsky for example.

Around this time I received a new order. The last loud and obvious one had been in 1994, when I heard the voice say "You are associating your own physical and mental health with that of the nation." On this occasion it was "You are supposed to be forming an intelligence cell."

Now I was lying on my bed in that same room. I'd had no sexual experiences of any type for months – because of the drugs, sex and psychiatric drugs being a rather taboo area unexplored in my treatment. Now MI5, the Special Forces, or even the Masons, had really got inside my head. I was being subjected to some bizarre teledildonics loyalty test. I was being ordered to masturbate to the image of a somewhat unattractive person. For my part I was at once deeply afraid my sexual powers had gone forever and keen to verify they would come back, but it was difficult: I felt I was being imposed upon somewhat. I passed the test – fearing the consequences if I didn't. But then I had to do it again, this time to the image in my EAV of a rather more attractive female from the music world. I managed again. At least it was not Nigel Kennedy – I would have failed!

I turned onto my back and then thought of an occasion back in 1986 when lying on my bed in Kenilworth Court, Putney. Up on the pale wall to my left, though only for a moment, I distinctly saw spiders crawling. What had brought this on was not alcohol, because I hardly drank any then, nor was it drugs, because I had not taken any. So what the cause was I did not know, and was not worried about it either. But I certainly saw some creatures larger than your average house spider even though they weren't really there.

Peter (the one with the autograph book) had told me, years before, how he came out from a house in Bristol and at that moment, as he walked up the garden path, his whole world became a shattering pane of glass. I had felt shocked by this information and the torment he experienced. He told me he had thought he was a spider on his mother's dressing table. I lived to regret not keeping my mouth shut about this, because of an incident not long before I saw the spiders myself, in a basement flat in West Kensington. We were cooking dinner and I went out to buy some curry powder. I left my friends Peter and Steve alone to get on with what was already cooking.

When I returned and entered the room, it was like they had murdered somebody in the intervening minutes and were just not well prepared enough to conceal the fact. I waded through the air in the room like it was a particular drama lesson I recall at school with Dan Dickey on the last period on Saturday morning back in 1973. I loved Saturday morning school. It was perfused with a sort of sporting optimism Friday afternoon never achieved – a bit like the end of term each week. And Dan Dickey was such a magnificent character, just as you'd expect to be teaching in a British public school. He was famed for his story about baling out of a crashing Lancaster bomber at low level and having his parachute inflated by the force of the explosion from the bombed-up plane. Anyway what I mean to say is that I knew something had gone terribly wrong since I had left the building to get the curry powder.

If it was not then, it was soon after that Peter succumbed. I asked Steve, very sensitively, what had happened and he cringed and apologised to me for making the biggest faux pas of his life.

"What was it?" I asked, fearful of the reply.

"I casually asked him 'What was it like to think you were a spider?'" he said, as I stirred the curry. Peter did not get out of the loony bin for six months. He came out dreaming of having simple arachnophobia. Steve went on to be an alcoholic – a far worse one than me.

Back to 1997 again, I was still on the bed. It was years since Peter's mother's dressing table, and a few since Kenilworth Court and a scratch in my *Atmospheres for Dreaming* LP caused when I was drunk. There, in front of me, the lampshade was certainly not now what it might have been. It seemed to have morphed into the head of a wise man looking out of the window it was dangling next to. My mind told me, although I could not actually recognise him, that it was the head of Lord Mackay of Clashfern. I imagined that one day it would be quite normal to have MTRUTH. All thoughts and perceptions would then, should the person desire, be ground-MTRUTHed from a central Borg Cube – the giant cube-shaped cybernetic humanoid neural net computer in *Star Trek* capable of assimilating the human mind. I even found myself thinking of a PhD title: *The Role of Game Theory and Chaos in MTRUTH-disseminated Knowledge*. But as much as anything it was just a spurious thought born out of the Lord High Chancellor's name, which contained the word fern, ferns being a good example of mathematical chaos in that they look the same on different scales. I looked at the lampshade again, and now it was just a lampshade as though the Borg Cube, which had a link to a spare Aldermaston supercomputer, had overridden my aberrant perception.

Then, in my mind's eye, I could see the Major getting out of an Army Land Rover outside the house and coming to knock on the front door again. At this moment I felt an overwhelming sensation that, through whatever means they had available, MTRUTH or otherwise, I could hear somebody talking to me. However it was not clear enough and I said out aloud, in a frustrated manner, "I can't hear you!"

As I said, my employer had refused to pay my travel expenses. Eventually the day came when I was without enough money, unless I borrowed some, to get to work. Not being prepared to do this, I easily came to the decision not to go. Up and down the country truant schoolchildren will laugh at me. I did not really know what was going on, at least not yet. Eventually I wrote down that I felt it was neither right to go, nor wrong to stay away.

So I got a summons form from the County Court without even considering exploiting the official complaints procedure of the firm more fully. By mistake I filled in the form so that I was suing myself on behalf of the company. Either way I was a little worried about all this when I next saw the psychiatrist. I told him that I had been seeing doubles of people I knew, including members of my family. On one notable occasion I actually had seen somebody I was convinced was a double of a family member to the extent that I could not look at him. I did not dare take a second look the experience was so profound – and I was embarrassed. But then I never went back to Solsbury Hill, where I had conceived my response to what I was then convinced was Prince Charles's fib about his dog. Instead I had to desperately conceal the nuclear amusement I was experiencing, and not just because it was outside The Dog and Trumpet pub in the West End – the name of the pub being enough to crack me up.

No matter that this was a recognised medical condition, Capgras syndrome; it was still amusing, but a little frightening too. But whilst realising that I had developed a habit of categorising people according to whom they most resembled, I discounted the possibility that others would agree with my categorisations. But I did not discount the possibility that the Grand Master of the Masonic Order had wilfully, with Masonic chalice and aforethought, arranged for a certain proportion of these people to draw my gaze, even if only momentarily. I was sure that the Masons would go out looking for doubles with whom to make fun of all manner of situations at the drop of a hat given the technology to do that. I knew they could easily go to a doubles agency but reasoned that only MI5 would have the resources to find doubles of less famous people known to me. But to reveal I thought this was happening seemed far too dangerous. Simply raising an amused smile would put me in danger. My cover would then at once be blown to any watching members of an Irish Republican Army Active Service Unit. This was the lesson I had learnt in Galway in 1994, when I saw what I thought then was a double of Caroline. I really did feel it was dangerous to laugh or my cover would be blown – quite hilarious I am sure you will agree. To a certain extent I still found it funny but however ill you are, if you can see humour in it you are not doing too badly. Now I was to turn this lesson to my advantage. For having mastered the illness it had now become a skill, should I choose to use it as one, and write this book to prove that schizophrenia is an illness you can have and recover from to look back on objectively.

Therefore, though not without obvious hazard, I chose to tell the psychiatrist of some of these experiences and he agreed it might be a good idea if I came into the hospital for a while.

Unfortunately I did not quite anticipate the full consequences of agreeing to do this. I had not thought about the fact that I was not taking any medication, and as soon as they found out I was prevented from leaving the ward. I do not know if it would have made any difference if they had known I had not been taking it for some time but they simply could not conceive having a patient without giving them any drugs. I was mortified. I'd had no drugs for approaching one year.

And now I was worried about the company legal secretary writing letters to the County Court announcing that he was the bona fide legal representative of my employer and not I. There was only one logical thing I could think of doing, and though I did not realise this at the time, it did not matter that I mistook his first name, Ruaridh, to be that of an Asian and not a Gael. In any case it had been some years since I had deduced that life was just a big windup. I hardly now cared if Ruaridh was a Belgian name; so I resubmitted my summons against my employer from the hospital as Clive "Ruhr Raid" Travis. Maybe, it seemed, he was Asian after all but in fact Ruaridh *is* a Gaelic name: it's pronounced "Rorie". Either way I thought the Ruhr Raid connection might explain why, when I was eventually released, and saw a dandy flight of tweeds walking down the street, I imagined they were a reunion of 617 Squadron, the Dambusters.

But I was still stuck in Bedford Hospital's psychiatric wing. At least it was not the secure wing in the countryside. But I had the terrible threat of forced medication hanging over me, as well as the threat of being sent down to the asylum again for punishment. This was quite a frequent occurrence as I had often observed. I had to keep my head together to prevent that – something I only just succeeded in doing. I walked out of the doctor's clinic room having been told I was now being sectioned. I was so enraged I nearly picked up one of the chairs in the smoking room and hurled it through the window, totally unprepared to go down without a fight. All that stopped me was the fact that I had known somebody, Peter, whom I have already mentioned, stuck in that hellhole for six months. Towards the end of his time there he had been allowed to sit on the bench below the window to have a cigarette. It would be a little unfortunate to nearly get through that and then be killed by flying furniture.

I was to be saved by my GP and a social worker. My GP owed me that at the very least – bearing in mind his having dangerously misprescribed me antidepressants three years earlier. I thought, incorrectly, I knew what was coming when he told me he had to be honest with himself. His whole delivery bore that reverent impartiality of a man about to consign me to doom. I nearly fell off my chair when he told me he thought I was well. I walked back to the smoking room, which I entered like a professional soccer striker who had just scored, and those in the room were at my home end. They all shared my joy. Now the hospital couldn't give me any medication.

I then felt bemused that the nurse wanted to see me. My original motivation to get admitted had not in any way been entirely fraudulent. But now it seemed I was unwelcome, simply because I did not want to take any medication. What might have happened if I now refused to go? I doubt if I would have been the first; and I knew of people who had turned up at night and banged on the door to be let in; I had virtually been one myself. It would seem churlish to complain about being thrown out of a psychiatric hospital, though that is what happened. Upon my release I learnt my expenses had been paid, out of court. Perhaps they thought I had acute untreatable personality disorder and were trying me with those.

Now I was free again and, Capgras syndrome or not, there was certainly an odd feeling emanating from the drivers of some of the vehicles going past. I thought of the stand-ins Queen Victoria was said to have sent across Battersea Bridge to make Whistler's famous painting *Nocturne in Blue and Gold* more interesting. These doubles were as tangibly mysterious as the stand-ins in that picture and I imagined Prince Charles, the Masonic Grandmaster himself, commanding these doubles to strangely pass me. Have you ever driven your own car and not noticed somebody had changed your number plates? I am not going to say I saw such a thing because I never believed I had – apart from the Jaguar in Brighton, which I believed had different plates on each end. But my imagination was getting a bit like that. To some extent this was my most serious problem – I could not channel my imagination properly. What I was really doing though, as this book again proves I hope, was investigating what this schizophrenia thing is all about.

I was now back pretty much where I had been three summers earlier, though I was now more experienced in these things. I was stricken, or strengthened, whichever way you want to look at it, by the belief that my letter of the previous year about the Royal Family pretending to be dead was so indisputably ludicrous that something massive was bound to happen. But how many people had really gone through schizophrenia, survived, and come out the other side to talk about it accurately and objectively? At least I was not driving around in that ghastly imagined procession I had miraculously extricated myself from, as I still had not got my driving licence back. But I was still given to wondering, for example, if the apparently rather shortened BMW boot design had something to do with the damage I had done to Mrs Black's Peugeot and *the 1962 Toybox Annual*. In it was a description of the experiment whereby one can insert a whole egg into a bottle without breaking it (You soak the egg, with the shell on, in vinegar for a week to make the shell pliable. You then heat up the bottle and place the egg on it and the egg gets sucked in as the air cools down and contracts. Then you fill the bottle with water and the egg goes back to its original shape. Finally you pour away the water and the egg hardens again). In my paranoid state I could not help making the connection between the shape of the egg when it was halfway in and the shape of a number of cars on the market whose bodies, specifically around the sills, were similar, most of them being made by foreign manufacturers. The similarity somewhat terrified me to the point where this could only be some very longstanding conspiracy to overthrow England – the 1926 conspiracy. I imagined a secret file which had somehow survived its journey both to and from, in the last hours of the War, the Führerbunker itself. I believed the file was a revelation. I wrote and told Her Majesty. I presumed she actually got to see the letter and had said to herself "Ah, another one has noticed, I always wonder how long it will take before each MTRU does. I had better ring Chancellor Kohl." Her Majesty would then make the call, saying to him "If I were to say to you 'can you imagine what your BMW would look like if Clive Travis rammed it from behind repeatedly with a rather nice Peugeot coupé when you were out one night?' I don't suppose that would mean anything to you – would it?" So that explained it. What I can also explain is that a lot of people with mental illness do write to the Royal Family out of desperation, sometimes not appreciating that the Royal Family themselves see few, if any, of their pitiful letters.

Soon after this, I decided to visit a solicitor specialising in employment law. He was Irish and from Donegal. Funnily his name was Oliver, the name the chap had said to me the day I voluntarily visited Fairmile. As I arrived at his office I got a massive great slug of what I could only presume was heroin again, the stuff being somehow shot into my ear as I arrived. I had not felt like this since I was in the Volvo of the chap who gave me the lift from Cornwall. In some sort of reality I think I must have just had an ear infection. I put my finger in and there was a load of pus reminding me of my African trip. But I even thought the pus had been fired in. The solicitor told me the words, which, in my delusions, I would come to ridicule. I could not get it into my head that you had to first resign to claim constructive dismissal. I just thought I had been constructively dismissed and that was that. I think I was trying to imagine something positive about this unusual type of dismissal – call it constructive dismissal syndrome if you like. Whatever the sense in what he told me I simply decided he was wrong and whatever my employer was going to do, they had already done it.

Eventually I did get my driving licence back and took another job as a delivery driver whilst on holiday and picked up a Transit van, which I refused to drive because the offside mirror was broken. I eventually drove off towards Saffron Walden in another van that was mostly empty. So were most of the other white vans, of which there were obviously a large number. I deduced that most of the heads of the drivers of these vans were pretty vacuous too and the whole thing was some huge con. This made it obviously ironic that when I got to Saffron Walden railway station there was a car service centre right next to it but the station had closed many years earlier and the parts all came by road. I visualised my psychotic friend Peter wheeling a new engine on a trolley over from the station to the service centre – the station having been reopened.

I began my deliveries and soon wondered what the hell I was doing this for. To start with, the various postmen, who obviously knew their rounds properly, had already been to each place once that day, without having to zigzag back and forth like headless chickens reversing over bus queues and drawing abuse from other road users.

I was a bit hot under the collar and, approaching a junction, another multi-drop van pulled out in front of another one. There was a very loud screech of rubber followed by a huge bang. The two other multi-drop vans had crashed right in front of me! I had left a big enough gap to miss them. Was it my fault that not only had far too many railways been closed down but that the Post Office monopoly had been broken? Was it my fault that hundreds of thousands of vans were driving around more or less at random in this madness and mostly empty?

Most of the parcels I had now delivered, one way or another, and there was only one left, which I had left until the end because it was away from the main target area. I imagined MI5 had sent me on this mad exercise and had, in fact, organised the whole caboodle, hoping I would spot the apparent lunacy.

To get directions for the last parcel I called at the R.A. Butler Primary School, named after the former Conservative Chancellor of the Exchequer, Baron Butler of Saffron Walden: "Rab Butler". A woman gave me very clear instructions to the village in question, and I obeyed them to the word only to find I was lost. I now had to reverse several hundred yards down a dirt track from a horrible wire gate with a security dog patrol sign on it and another saying "No Entry". This made me feel rather more stupid than I was already feeling. In my deluded state I believed it had been deliberate. Now I put the teacher down to be one of those unfortunate people who, when you ask them where somewhere is, although they obviously know the area, seem incapable of pointing in the direction they are thinking about. Either that or Prince Charles, had, via the trade unions' high command, ordered her to send me in the wrong direction, I thought. I have noticed some people's inability to point where they are thinking about on many occasions in my life, and have inadvertently embarrassed a number about this. I now knew that the direction of the final recipient's village was opposite to the direction the lady indicated. There was also something about the name of the person to whom this last delivery was to be made – something rather fishy.

Now I was back on the main road, somewhere in the Ancient Kingdom of Magog again. Stopping a passing car at the crossroads I asked the driver where this village was. He had no idea, so I went into the pub on that crossroad and found it entirely deserted, like *The Marie Celeste*. I even worried if all was well; so went behind the bar and upstairs – not a soul was there. That made sense. The clientele of the pub were the retained Gog Magog Mountain Rescue Service, and had obviously been called out, possibly to Shepea Hill further north – a giant and dangerous fenland mountain at least two feet high. I knew, of course, what they were looking for.

So driving down the country lane at some speed, still not any the wiser where the recipient lived, and nearly crashing head-on with a passing removal van coming around the fork, I'd had enough and decided to take it out on the package itself. I reached into the back and hurled the package, for a suspiciously named Charles Rae, over the passing hedge into a field. It was worse than that though. I did not have a driving licence. Mind you nobody had asked me for one so it must have been another conspiracy. But I don't recall thinking there was anything wrong about driving the van other than it being a little silly to drive such a large and empty object around the English countryside. Not having a licence hardly if at all occurred to me.

No longer worried about delivering it on time and getting back to the warehouse before the staff bus left, I was now free to finish my journey safely, at my leisure, without undue danger of crashing through the wall of some, no doubt mysteriously empty pub again. However if I had done, I would not have hesitated to serve myself a drink; a gin and tonic would have done nicely. That may sound improbable but I had once made an unscheduled bar visit on the way to Henley Royal Regatta. Our boat trailer became disconnected from the Land Rover and carried on in a straight line on a bend, knocking a pub's car park wall down and coming to rest in a parking space by the pub entrance, none of the boats sustaining any damage.

At the job centre, I saw a job requiring Access database skills and turned up for the interview. The interviewer wanted me to demonstrate my abilities without using a wizard, some of the work including keeping a record of street-side furniture. At this moment in time I was a little averse to making Microsoft wizards redundant and just got up and left. Instead, and just for a laugh, I applied for a job in hospitality at Henley Royal Regatta.

Chapter Forty

Roll With It

I got the job and was told to turn up the next day at one o'clock. First though, I took a walk in the country out to Twinwoods aerodrome and its old control tower – now the Glenn Miller Museum. From there I could see, in the shimmering haze, the mirage of a floating wood many miles away to the west. I briefly saw myself as a Red Indian woman, and this was the first thing I had seen after giving birth. Because of Red Indian tradition this meant my child was called *Floating Wood*, a rather more romantic name than the one in the joke about the Red Indian called *Two Dogs Fucking*. That night I got wonderfully drunk thinking about my child and then thought of a manoeuvre of the local Combined Cadet Force in which the cadets were ordered to find a floating wood before the day was out.

Next day I turned up on time and I was given my uniform. I soon settled into the job and what hard work it was. That night there was a celebrity charity dinner with guests including Jenny Agutter, by whom I was fascinated, and Simon Williams, another well-known actor.

Afterwards I made my way to the campsite and proceeded to get drunk in the bar. Time came and I headed off to put my tent up in the dark, which became quite a cliché of a comic exercise. The main thing though was that I was not depressed. Not being depressed is a great gift, and however ill you are with schizophrenia not being depressed is a blessing. Unless you have actually suffered clinical depression, which is not to be confused with simply being very upset or pissed off about something, you could not possibly truly appreciate this. I got the tent up.

Next morning in the shower I could hear somebody whistling the old East German national anthem in the adjacent cubicle. You might be surprised to know I do not remember thinking it was aimed at me though very likely I did. What a rousing tune!

At work in the large marquee it was quite hot and it really was a beautiful day for rowing. But my managers kept contradicting each other in how they wanted me to do things: For example how to hold the champagne bottle when serving it. Each manager got irritated when they found me doing what the other had told me to do.

I was enjoying providing the hospitality though and standing by the veranda-style doors of the large marquee one of the guests asked for a gin and tonic. I served it with a flourish without measuring it: "One gin and tonic sir – a rather large one!"

Later on it occurred to me that everywhere I went I kept seeing my fellow catering workers rolling circular tables, without the legs, along the ground, and every time I saw this, the memorable tune with which this chapter is entitled began to play in my head. I felt good.

In the late afternoon, I was serving a large tray of coffee when something caused my right arm to twitch. I spilt the whole tray including the cream down the blazer of an American oarsman. I made myself scarce in case he hit me. I was convinced that I had some implant in my elbow, which had made me do this. The implant was almost certainly put there by MI5 – I had got drawn into a dirty tricks war with the CIA for whom he was obviously an agent. If there was no implant then a concealed sniper must have shot a micro-bullet at my elbow to effect this operation. I was sacked which was not terribly upsetting. At this point it is worth saying that one of the traps of schizophrenia is believing what you want to believe – perhaps because you are simply dissatisfied with your life. There has to be something better and you just choose to believe rather unrealistic things. But if you believe in something strongly enough things have a habit of coming true. There is some indication of this towards the end of this story.

Now I believed I was a fully-fledged secret agent once again, seconded from the Special Boat Service of course, and I spent the rest of the Regatta providing an entirely delusional security service to all the important revellers.

In the river by the bridge at The Little Angel pub I saw some bubbles come up, and then a small feather appeared. I found myself thinking that the Special Boat Service was on duty as a counter-terrorist measure, and the feather was a personal message from Prince Charles. I was uncertain if a dog had ever been fitted with SCUBA diving equipment and left it at that, unable to rule out that possibility and viewing it very seriously indeed if they had.

Sitting in the Bridge Bar (at the particularly beautiful and quintessentially English south end of the Stewards' Enclosure) as I slowly sipped a pint of beer, I saw a man whom I thought was Christopher Ryan, the SAS officer who wrote *The One Who Got Away*. Years later I would see a picture of him and realise my mistake. As a matter of fact, like in other situations I have previously described, if you had asked me who I thought he was, I would have denied that I thought he was Chris Ryan, or that I was in the Special Boat Service. But the possibility that he was Chris Ryan, and I *was* in the SBS, was just too attractive to prevent my going along with the thought.

At another table between us were some attractive girls wearing hats. They were the classic Henley/Sloane Ranger type and 'Chris' lobbed an ice cube at one of them and called out, seemingly referring to me, "He wants to buy you all a drink!" It was as though he was telling them off because they did not realise how important I was.

I wandered off to where I could watch some racing further down the enclosure. A couple (dressed very much as you'd expect) in a small rowing boat with a Jack Russell arrived and moored close to me. They cranked up their gramophone, which was playing a jolly old jazz record, and cracked open the champagne. Something made me focus on the cork gradually bobbing its way down stream toward the start. I felt hypnotised by it. Then something distracted me momentarily. When I looked back I was shocked to see the cork had disappeared! I stood up almost appealing and looked at those around me, none, it seemed, aware of what exactly had just happened. The lady in the boat took a sandwich from the hamper and gave it to the dog. It was loving it. I thought I recognised the dog's face but I'd never seen it before.

I went to celebrate the cork incident in the Fawley Bar over a pint of Pimms. Here, helped by the alcohol, and not sure if there was a hyphen in broken-hearted, I wrote a little poem:

Heartbroken or SBS Officer?

What difference would it make if there were a hyphen in broken hearted?
If there were, to me it would mean the world
And I think there probably is.
And I think it might be both.

Realising my problem was not heart disease but that I had lost someone I loved I imagined there should be a hyphen. However later examination of the dictionary showed the words joined together without a hyphen leading me to imagine a condition exactly halfway between heart disease and love sickness in which a hyphen was used. I was wondering who decided that broken-hearted was one word whereas free will was two. But then I picked up another dictionary, which had "broken-hearted". I put the poem in the breast pocket of my blazer. I later took it to the dry-cleaners, never to collect it – because I was again off running around the country looking for Prince Charles's dog. I now left the enclosure and wandered off into Henley town. There was a funny incident as I walked past the police station. I saw an officer was holding his helmet out through the window at above head height and upside down. Now the strange feeling descended on me that someone knew what was written on the piece of paper and they wanted me to start passing information to the police. So, seeing the helmet, I took the poem from my pocket and deposited it in the helmet, whereupon the helmet was withdrawn into the room atop the police station. Odd! Very odd!

Sitting opposite the jetty in front of The White Hart pub I saw India Hicks, the granddaughter of Lord Mountbatten and former society debutante, disembarking. In my head, I could vividly hear her thoughts – thought broadcasting again. She was counting what she believed to be MI5 security agents guarding her, and I was one. My delusions were a little more than entirely tenuous; after all I had rowed at the Regatta and was a member of the Stewards' Enclosure. As for my connections with the military powers that be – quite apart from my interview at the Admiralty, these all attained exaggerated significance. I looked so cool, casually guarding her wearing my blazer and flannels. And yes, I looked superbly good-looking, as you would expect of an SBS man, now elegantly clothed in suitable regatta attire. Well that's what I thought.

On the final day of the Regatta I heard someone say there had been another Real IRA attack. I saw a chap whom I recognised from years earlier rush by looking extremely angry. I guessed he was one of my colleagues though this was obviously sensitive information. I could not know the truth otherwise my integrity as an agent would be severely compromised. I could only guess. It was fun being deluded. And my delusion was only fed when I noticed no Real IRA attack came until weeks later meaning that, most unpleasantly, I had been informed in advance of the Omagh bombing.

Part XVI

Three Pieces of Sellotape,
a Magic Key and a Levitating Bed

Chapter Forty-One

Waves

My conviction concerning L Zero and that something massive was now bound to happen was to be finally justified on the night of 31st August 1997. The previous Saturday, wandering around town, I had come upon a wedding. I can't recall if I imagined there and then that the whole wedding was an act. What I do clearly remember was the presence of an Army officer and a Gendarme both of whose uniforms I noticed to be impeccably smart. Whilst at the wedding I had believed I was on Secret Service duty but events the following night left me in no doubt that the wedding was fake, put on by Comic Relief.

How much I had already achieved seemed to come down to little more than hallucinate the lampshade above my bed to be the Lord High Chancellor's head, and spot a West Indian holding a bucket outside the old school. He had been put there by Comic Relief and was helping raise the £10 million I had demanded to make Prince Charles's dog immortal.

Perhaps I am being a little negative in suggesting I had not achieved anything yet. After all, I had been successful in writing the first chapter of this book, which mysteriously disappeared. That only made me more determined to tell this story. And of course I was still alive. I remembered the list of dead people I had handed to the solicitor the second time I had been sectioned. Since then the list had got longer justifying my disregard for the psychiatrist's remarks that I was in no danger. Also, I had noticed in the Old Boys' newsletter the picture of the esteemed leader of Comic Relief, Lenny Henry, make a visit to my old school. Of course that could easily have had nothing to do with me but Bedford Modern certainly did, it was one of the country's oldest public schools and my alma mater. I thought of my KGB file and the line in the Paul McCartney and Wings song *Jet*: "Alma mater, born traitor."[94] What was Lenny Henry really doing there? I could only reason it was because of my gamble that Prince Charles had not really had a dog, Pooh, go missing. Talk about delusions of grandeur. But at least it was a sign. It looked like he might be on my tracks. I was not the only one with Aboriginal skills, I thought.

I was just dozing off to sleep when the newsflash came over that Princess Diana had been seriously injured in a car crash. I did not draw any conclusion until the following morning. As I awoke and it was announced that Diana had died it did not even cross my mind for a moment that she might really be dead. Once more I fell into the trap of schizophrenia in that I now believed what I wanted to believe because the belief gave me power and meaning in life. What is more I even believed the unusual music they played that morning had been commissioned in advance for this specific purpose – to conjure an air of mystery.

That it did. In fact it was a version of the music played by the musical fob watch in the classic Clint Eastwood film *For A Few Dollars More* (a rare example of a sequel film which is better than the original). All I could think was: Jesus Christ, they've done it – they've really done it! I was actually thinking that MI5 and the French Security Service had faked her death – whilst on the other hand Mohammed Al-Fayed thought they had murdered her (and his son). Many times I imagined the person to whom the responsibility of faking her death fell to, giving the go-ahead for this stunt, suggested by me, saying, "Let's do it!" There was simply no question in my mind. They had faked her death as a charity stunt to raise the £10 million. It hardly mattered that it was three years late. I had passed all the torturous Special Forces tests that I had been set – so far. History was being made and I was part of it.

I got up early, shocked by what I believed I had done, and went for a run. I had a slight niggle in my knee. As I ran along I could see, next to my knee, a one fiftieth-size Bill Clinton and a medical team standing on a platform discussing the knee. At the top of Graze Hill overlooking Bedford was a man pensively gazing over the town. He looked as though he was probably in the Parachute Regiment. I thought about him long enough to realise he knew what I was thinking, even if he did not himself know the person he was thinking about was the one just running past. I did not even remotely consider telling anyone what I knew. But I had to do something because now I was really trapped: I was armed with some knowledge, which would hold no value in another's mind. This was unless I could realise it fully in my own. I imagined he was thinking: now he can't be sure she's dead, even if he thinks he's sure she's not. Then I remembered the Sherlock Holmes lemon curd joke and how I had finished it wondering if the Central Intelligence Agency knew yet: "Holmes, tonight we shall raise the dead!" So!

Faking the death of Diana was the most serious joke I had come across and it deserved full respect, firstly because when I had originally proposed faking the deaths of the entire Royal Family I had singularly failed to mention Princess Diana, this now sinking in and making it an even more natural addition to this constellation. I even imagined her anger at my neglecting to mention her. The only question in my mind was: who would come next? Would I find that by New Year's Eve 1999 or even 2000 (given that was the real millennium) that the entire Royal Family had been killed by a *Monty Python*/Comic Relief double whammy, only to all reappear together miraculously undead at the expensively hired Royal Albert Hall? Okay, I was in quite a state fully believing Diana was not dead. But really this was not to compare with that of Norman Bates in *Psycho*. I had not stabbed Diana to death, or anyone else. Nor did I have her dry body in a wheelchair in the cellar. My psychosis was more of a romantic affair.

The day of what I believed was Diana's fake funeral came and I took the train out to Aspley Guise. I entered the village church and made my entry in the book of remembrance writing "Wishing you a holiday in the sun." Ever since then, whenever I picture her hearse driving along, I instantly visualise the marching boots intro of the first track: *Holiday in the Sun*, at the beginning of the album *Never Mind the Bollocks, Here's The Sex Pistols*, now wondering whose boots they were.

I got down to the motorway to see the hearse and, as the road was empty for a change, I walked out and lay down in the fast lane. Here I imagined the *Monty*

Python team having a tea party near Toddington services, further down the motorway. I could not decide what exactly was in the coffin. However it seemed likely that Diana was actually in it breathing through a straw rather than watching the proceedings from afar. Nor was I exactly sure what would happen at Althorp, her family seat where the coffin was going to. But I had my ideas, Diana emerging alive from the coffin to the joy of Viscount Althorp, her brother, who would then react like Rowan Atkinson in his famous takeoff of the *Game for a Laugh* television programme. In this sketch a man's wife had her head cut off and when it was revealed to him it was actually *Game for a Laugh* he mimicked the usual amused reaction of the victim of the prank. Hilarious. I felt emotional as the hearse went by and cried for Amanda. It was a real miracle that neither Diana nor John Lennon was dead.

I had once been told that a family was taking the coffin of a family member to his funeral in another part of the country, and had it on the roof of their car, under a drape. Taking a break at Toddington services, they returned to find the car had been stolen. I never heard what happened to the body. You can imagine the shock of the car thief when he inspected the box's contents. Luckily this did not happen to Diana. I did however notice the procession included a spare hearse in case of a breakdown, or some other magical, mysterious and historical reason! Or perhaps somebody hitchhiking in a coffin.

It had been some time now since I did Jefferson Holt, the manager of REM, the courtesy of sending him a 1p cheque, on a Holt's Bank cheque. Then I remembered how a chap, Gerard Nove, had insisted on lending me $20 when travelling in America some years earlier. Now seemed like a good time to pay it back. So I wrote to my employer outlining some crazy scheme for the paying back of over claimed travel expenses, suggesting the results be sent to Gerard Nove, Churchill Associates, San Jose California. I enclosed the $20 I owed him plus interest making $77, adding that anyone who thought that it did not matter anymore if Princess Diana was alive or dead had better be very careful about saying it. Now I had the impenetrable cover of complete lunacy. But however bizarre my behaviour it hardly matches, for complete lunacy, that of one old technique of psychiatric treatment: patients used to have a birdcage with a bird in it put over their heads. Their insanity was thought to be removed by the bird's pecking. And, as you can imagine, there seemed something mysterious about this "Churchill Associates".

I remembered the party Prince Charles had had a few days before her death – a party I felt I was psychically present at through my MTRUTH. Now I imagined the party had been to celebrate the go-ahead for this crazy scheme. Either way it was time to pay another trip to Northern Ireland.

But first I made my way to London. I was sitting on the balcony of The Dove pub in Chiswick when I heard a voice in my head say "Whatever you do – don't go to Ruislip!" So I finished my drink, feeling I could hear civil aviation radio traffic communications coming in on my MTRUTH. On the train to Ruislip an obviously Polish woman sat down opposite me. You can often tell: thin pencil-plucked eyebrows. But why? It went back to the chat over drinks in 1926 of course because, as you will recall, the Kroger spies lived just behind my grandmother's house – down the passage, two turnings and you were there. It was no coincidence this Polish woman was sitting opposite. Reaching Ruislip I got off the train and wandered to my grandmother's old house. I was disappointed to see the original "between the wars" frontage had been destroyed and the beautiful rising sun, stained glass window by the front door had gone. I wondered where it now was. The garage had been converted into a room meaning only one thing to me. KGB, or now FSB agents could no longer be smuggled, inside the boot of a Beetle via the garage, into the kitchen, as they had been into the Kroger's house. I walked down the passage and around the back, eager to see if the strange garden-foot I imagined had been sung about by Ian Curtis in *The Eternal* was still there. I could not see. As well as the Berlin Wall coming down, a wattle fence had been put up at the foot. My mind made the connection. But the question was: was there one? Again I laughed at the idea of bringing in BBC's *Groundforce* team. They could remove the concrete, exhume the bodies of three KGB/CIA double agents, take away the Nazi gold and treasures, the original MTRUTH file and the case of 1926 Talisker and send it away in a Brinks Matt van, pinching one bottle to give to me. There was an air of mystery in the alley. If you had a Cold War divining rod you could not have held your stance – let alone the rod. I was quite convinced I was being watched.

Now I wandered round to see the Kroger's house. As I approached it I saw a 1920s Morris Cowley coming tootling down the road driven by a bloke who looked like he had come through a time warp. He was smoking a pipe and had a deerstalker on. Following it a little old Austin saloon drove past. Then I saw a 1950s Beetle driven by a bloke who looked like Paul McCartney. He turned into the Kroger's garage. He was probably just a Capgras double and along with the others was off to a rally.

I decided to leave the scene of this paranormal weirdness. Back down the passageway I was in Cornwall Road again. Outside my grandmother's old house a person walking a dog passed by. It was grey with a silky coat – the type of dog, possibly the actual dog, which was used in the BBC *Watchdog* programme.

Soon I was back on the train into London. A bloke sat down to my left and casually glanced at me. He had a briefcase on the chair next to him. I wondered if he had a camera in it sending pictures of me back to MI5 HQ real-time, possibly via the now defunct Rabbit Tube telephone system. I amused myself with deluded and convoluted thoughts of their reasoning for this, feeling a mere exercise a little uninspiring and therefore that this was the real thing. *I knew somebody else knew what I knew.* The Italian section of MI6 wanted the shots because of the Armani spectacles I was wearing – wanting to sell them to the Mafia. I was rather proud of them actually, not just because they were inspired by 1920s fashions, but you see, I was always a bit anti-*Designer*. On deciding to buy some glasses, being slightly shortsighted, I had gone into a shop in 1991, and actually given up on the idea, as I could not see myself wearing a single pair of glasses that were on sale. As I left the chap asked me to wait a minute whilst he went around the back. It felt as though I was in an edition of the BBC *Mr Benn* programme where magical trips start in the clothes shop. A moment later he came back with a boxful of quite preposterous glasses you would only see Peggy Guggenheim[95] wear or if you asked for a pair modelled on the rear of a 1956 Studebaker. There was one pair in the box he had in mind: the most expensive pair in the whole shop. I immediately took a shine to them and said I would have them. I came back a day or two later when the lenses had been fitted and put them on leaving the shop to see Rocks Lane looked a bit sharper – rather good. Back at the flat I found, down the inside of the temples, the words in white

"Giorgio Armani". I was rather pleased and self-satisfied to see this, thinking smugly what good taste I had and *Designer* stuff was great after all.

So off to Northern Ireland. I had difficulty in saying it at the time and had not yet thought of avoiding the problem by saying six counties as Irish Republicans did. I would later mistakenly say "Five counties" in a whole list of rather unsecret communications to the landlord of The Ship, circulated to the Chief of Staff, Irish Republican Army and others involved in the peace process such as David Trimble. They must have thought I was a nutter. Then again.

The reason to go there was, quite apart from my delusion that I was working for the Special Forces, that I had read in the newspaper how a man had been shot in Portadown. Ever since the news broadcast on Radio 1 about Prince Charles's dog, I'd had severe difficulty not only in correctly interpreting what I learnt from the media but also in believing that it was necessarily true. So, in my dutiful state of mind, I decided to visit Portadown to see if I could ground-MTRUTH what I had read in the newspaper. I really did feel I was an integral part of the peace process, though this was sometimes tempered with a little embarrassment at myself.

I took a train to Glasgow and on the journey I had what I thought was another heroin experience. Somehow somebody had given me heroin, possibly from the same micro drugs cabinet I had in my wrist back in 1994, or through some other novel drug delivery system. I sank back into my seat to enjoy it and watched the mountains of the Lake District sailing by from the glorious comfort of my first class seat. MI5 had decided I was a terminal case and so had put me in the Royal Army Medical Corps Palliative Care Hospice for the Terminally Ill, or in my case insane.

On arrival in Glasgow I booked into a hotel for the night. There was an international junior girls' hockey competition on and they were also staying at the hotel. They invited me over to join them in the bar and I spent the evening with some very pleasant young females. Little did they know that I had been seconded from the SBS to MI5 for another trip to Northern Ireland as part of the peace process.

The following night I headed for Holy Loch, home of the British atomic submarine fleet. As I got off the train I got talking to an attractive Scottish girl whom I imagined had been sent specifically for me by Prince Charles. I let him down by not asking her out and did not feel particularly proud of my behaviour. This made me seem ungrateful, though this was not true, I *was* grateful – however deluded. I had long learnt to assume I was being followed though not to worry about it, instead seeing it as a privilege.

That evening I saw a strange and unusual ice-crystal rainbow in the sky over Gourock, and on the news the sacking of James Shayler, the renegade MI5 officer broke. He had alleged that MI6 had a plan to assassinate the Libyan leader, Colonel Qadaffi. I took this to be a warning that I could be liquidated too if I did not play my cards right. I did not for a moment believe he had really been expelled from MI5: he had merely been posted to France as part of the Diana death illusion. Yes, I really believed she was not dead – I wanted to believe.

Next day I made one or two strange telephone calls from Glasgow Station, thinking they were monitored and wanting to provoke MI5 into response. Then I was off to Stranraer Harbour to get the catamaran to Larne. Once aboard I got talking to an Irishman from County Kerry. He seemed to wish to educate me, being a mere Englishman, and as he lectured me on the Troubles he poked my forearm with his finger. I sensed the whole history of the Troubles had come down to this. I felt touched and also admonished by the apparent suggestion that I should not get involved. I was not far wrong. Other than that the journey was uneventful. The catamaran was a magnificent vessel. Its architecture reminded me of the roof-bar in The Marriott Marquis Hotel in New York where I had stayed when I took Railroad Earth to the New Music Seminar.

In Belfast I chose a hotel, which had been decorated in orange. Everywhere I went there was the ever-present sense of danger, which the Troubles had engendered. Somehow the hotel reminded me of *Fawlty Towers* with strange staircases throughout the building as in that comedy.

Next day, the tension had grown, and as I had not faced any torture the previous night, unlike on my previous trip here, I once again imagined I was facing "nice policeman/nasty policeman" treatment. This time it was "nice policeman" and, as I had been given heroin as a treat on the train, I knew MI5 had got hold of me. I had succeeded in passing the horrible tests I had been subject to on my previous Belfast trip when I stayed at the bomb-ravaged Europa Hotel.

I walked west out of the city noticing the tension produced by the passing Army vehicles. As I passed through Republican and Loyalist strongholds I sensed, as a stranger, that I was being spied on and followed by the local defence forces. At the cemetery I turned around and pensively leant on a junction box outside The Rock pub. I really was being watched, not just from inside the pub but also by an SAS officer who, via a tunnel, had found his way into the actual junction box. From there he had an ideal vantage point to spy on the pub, in the upstairs room of which the Irish Republican Army no doubt held meetings, and were probably having one then. It was after 11am, but the pub was still not open.

Feeling I was dressed up like a member of the Special Forces it seemed unlikely they would open the pub while I was there; so I walked down the road past the Children's Hospital to find one which was open. I was in a strongly Republican area, and if anyone knew who I was and where I had worked, I might have been a valid target for a sniper. To shoot me would have been a mistake, for later I would at least attempt to help in the peace process, as indeed I was now, albeit in an entirely deluded manner, by trying to place Prince Charles's dog on the negotiation table.

As I passed the Children's Hospital on the Falls Road, not far from the Sinn Féin headquarters at number 53, I saw a distressed-looking middle-aged woman pass by. The look in her face gave me a strong sense that I was not unique in being an MTRU. She too was an MTRU, a Sinn Féin supporter, member of the IRA, and was being brainwashed through her MTRUTH, not by Great Britain but the CIA. MTRUTH was being used to solve the problem of the six counties.

I spotted a chocolate Labrador, which seemed to have a very good grasp of where it was going and how to get there. It had, like me, an Army MTRUTH receiving accurate commands in its not so subliminally augmented imagination for which it knew rewards were available, and which it obviously was unable to tell anyone about. The animal even sat down and waited for the traffic to pass before crossing the road, accepting commands from its remote handler in supra-subliminal mode.

Walking through the deserted streets of an estate, I heard a whistle go off and once more gained the impression my presence had been noticed by the local volunteer defence force as I had briefly walked through a Loyalist area and back into the Republican one.

It was a warm sunny day, and I found an open pub where I ordered a pint of Guinness, which I drank on the pavement in the sun. I noticed the price of the Guinness to be at least 50p less than in England, wondering if this was a Guinness peace dividend in response to the IRA ceasefire.

A large number of taxis went past, each one occupied by IRA members spying on me, and going off to complain somewhere about my presence. Since I had an MTRUTH fitted and was a British agent it seemed rather brave to drink in this pub. Either way, in my delusion of grandeur I imagined this meant that, as a result, a whole series of pop stars would likewise be visiting the pub as part of the peace process.

That night I again set off up the Falls Road. Having drunk in a Republican part of town, without any adverse comeback, like being shot, my feelings towards the Republicans had improved, not only towards Gerry Adams but also Martin Galvin. But I did not have any unrealistic thoughts that I could solve the problems myself, only about what I might achieve in trying to.

Down the dark and deserted streets I walked, effecting interference on, and even transmitting messages to, the television screens of people in nearby houses, whose windows I briefly saw through as I passed. An Army patrol drove by. I remembered the words of the chap during the sea crossing. I turned right and found myself walking towards the steel gate and barricade dividing the two sections of the community. I was able to walk around the gate and soon I was in the Loyalist section of town, where I entered a pub and settled down for the evening's drinking.

Next day I caught the train to Portadown. At the second station lots of people got on. They had all been ordered to by MI5, and to follow me. In reality, of course, no one was following me, unless you believe I was an MTRU. Either way the feeling was compelling and exciting.

Soon I was in Portadown, which was decked out with the usual Loyalist bunting. I wondered what they would do if there was anything more recent to celebrate than victory at the Battle of the Boyne in 1690, as they could hardly put up more flags. I went into a Loyalist pub and bought a drink. As I sat outside, I noticed the tall kerbstones, like some near Union Street in Bedford. A connection I easily made, all those hundreds of miles apart. It all made too much sense. The Union loomed large in my mind – as did the Act of Parliament of 1801, let alone the cross of St Patrick in the Union Jack and the Government of Ireland Act 1920 as well as one or two other things. I decided to paint three kerbstones red, white and blue on my return to Bedford.

After my drink I walked back into town where I entered another Loyalist pub. I asked the landlord if anyone had been shot recently and he replied in the negative. Perhaps he meant not in his pub but I took this to mean that the newspaper report was incorrect, and had only been published in order to lure me here on a fact-finding mission: to do some ground-MTRUTHing in fact. I also thought of writing a book entitled *One Hundred and One Ways to Ask a Portadown Landlord If Anyone Has Been Shot Recently*. The question had been a challenging one, I sensed that he did not enjoy.

I headed for the graffiti-covered underpass, which obviously led into the

Republican part of town. As I walked through it, I knew many would advise me against this. After all I was loyal to Her Majesty the Queen and was working for MI5. A dog-walker went past and I suspected, possibly correctly, that he and the dog were, as earlier, from the local defence force and spied on everyone who came through this underpass. No one could deny the six counties to be suffering massive sociological schizophrenia. I now believed I could somehow become an antidote to this: the power of positive thinking.

Further along there was an incident, which left me in no doubt as to the possible dangers of the situation I was in. Some children approached and one of them, with his hand partially covering his mouth mumbled "Are you anything to do with the paramilitaries?" He seemed to wish to leave me uncertain that he was actually talking to me – this bearing out my feelings about certain parallels between my state of mind and the local sociological dysfunctionality. This also proved to me that the Troubles were real. I wondered what he might do if he had known what I was thinking, or who I was. There seemed no doubt I had been noticed and that I was being spied on again.

I went into the Fish and Chip shop for supper. Still ringing in my ears was the sound of someone on the opposite side of the road in Belfast three years earlier, shouting out some joke I thought was aimed at me, about the IRA and saying "He still hasn't had his fish and chip supper." The true meaning of "fish and chip supper" had become blurred in my mind, and seemed to represent some danger as well as no little intrigue. I recalled how I had got out of my car outside the Gaelic football ground in west Belfast and taken money from the cash machine next to the chip shop. I remembered how I got a strange tingling sensation over part of my face and had believed this was caused by some SAS ray gun fired at me.[96] Then, as now, the tension had been electric.

I ordered my fish and chips and went to the toilet. It was very exposed to anyone spying from the distant houses and I was the possible target of a sniper in one of them. I imagined the underpass was where punishment beatings had taken place. Strangely though, I had felt in more danger back in Milton Keynes where, upon leaving work I had on occasions felt extreme tension as though the bullet of a sniper was poised to enter my head, fired from the woods above Woburn Sands some distance away.

Finishing my supper (and finding I had not been poisoned) I continued my walk through Republican territory up the Garvaghy Road. A beautiful woman approached and we caught each other's eyes. She held my gaze as she walked past saying, as she did so, in a beautiful and seductive manner, "I...N...L...A..." I turned round to see her disappearing off towards the underpass, noticing as she did so what an attractive behind she had. I had made contact with the Irish National Liberation Army. My mission to the six counties was complete.

Chapter Forty-Two

The Headlight Song

I returned from my tour of duty in Northern Ireland. On the train, coming through the Lake District, I noticed I was not given any heroin. I assumed I had been sectioned in the Palliative Care Hospice for the Terminally Ill only on the way there. It was clear I'd had a spectacular remission. Now, for what seemed like the thousandth time, I heard the voice I had come to recognise (and like actually) of some retired military historian in my head. He was always defining a type of war in answer to somebody whose voice I was not party to: "A reality war? Ah yes – a reality war is a war fought using..." and then he went on to define it with no little expertise. It was clear that to him absolutely everything was just a war and there were times when he explained, in my head, some pretty extraordinary types of war and how they were fought. I imagined a dictionary containing definitions of all manner of types of war – no doubt he was the editor.

News of the death of Diana had hardly died down and I went up to London to see where the flowers had been placed outside Kensington Palace. The funeral had been staged – the florists had cut Comic Relief in on the huge profits they had made. But by the time I got there, all the flowers had been removed. Only the odd piece of Sellotape remained on the fence. I peeled a piece off and, for luck, stuck it to my Army fatigues which I had bought back in Portree three years earlier.

Again I was suffering disbelief syndrome, quite a common affliction in grief. It was just too alluring to believe Diana was not really dead – it gave me all the power I needed to believe that the British and French security services had faked her death as a charity stunt with Comic Relief. By now she had probably met Jo Hudson and Andy Woods.

I remembered my strange meeting with Jo Hudson on the plane back from the States in 1988. I did not go to her funeral. Now I found myself wondering if there had ever been one. I was correct – she really was a CIA/British agent gathering intelligence from me. If I had gone to her funeral I would have found myself surrounded by MI5, MI6 and CIA actors. The same, I found myself thinking, had been the fate for Andy Woods, though no doubt when their families read this they will say "If only you were right", Princes William, Harry and a girl I knew whose uncle, Michael Maltby, had died at the Mull of Kintyre, concurring. I recalled Andy's wake: somebody was wailing in the other room and *Brothers in Arms* was playing. It was one of those moments you just don't forget. This was how far they had gone: putting his family through that for the ultimate prize. Andy now knew I knew.

One Sunday morning, back in Bedford, I had an argument with my brother about his smashed car headlight and I lost my rag and went and broke the other with a hammer. I was about to go for a run. I then picked up the phone and called the police who were rude to me. The officer on the other end said something I could hardly believe: "It's Sunday morning and I have got better things to do." Still, I now realised I was in danger of being hospitalised; so I set off on my run, along the disused rail track towards Cambridge. Later it seemed clear the phone in the house had a hot line to an MI5 desk – and it was MI5 to whom I had been talking. Examination of a Victorian Ordnance Survey map of Bedford shows the modern day police HQ is close to, if not on, the site of a Victorian lunatic asylum. "That explains a lot!" I imagine some saying.

I ran for quite a few miles and eventually took a rest in some fields near Blunham. I saw a dead weasel by the road. It looked fresh, and had been put there moments earlier by the SAS, to somehow warn me about the danger I was in. Tenuous yes – but that's schizophrenia for you.

I felt it was no longer safe to stay in town, so I decided to get away until things had quietened down a bit. Of course there was no point in telling anyone that Princess Diana was not dead: they would simply think I was mad. At least I realised that. But what was I to do? The knowledge I had was a great responsibility upon my shoulders but one which all my Special Forces training in the NHS system had made me fit to stand up to, and capitalise upon.

The only problem was that I needed to get back into the house to get some things before I left town. Money was also a bit of a problem as I had overspent in Northern Ireland. I decided to seek help from Marek. I had Stalin to thank for having Marek as a friend: his parents had both been in Soviet labour camps during the War and I knew, given that he was a manic-depressive who drank a lot whilst taking his medication, he would understand my predicament.

I crept into the house, as I had no idea what the situation was and whether the police had been. No one seemed to be in. I went upstairs, again quietly, in case mother was having a rest. I went to the rear bedroom and carefully looked out into the garden, much as I had done all those years ago when I had poured the bucket of water on the Vice Warden's head. I could see mother doing some gardening. I should have time to have a quick shower, grab some things and be off. She would not even know I had been there.

Soon I was at Marek's, still in Bedford, where he was happy to have me stay for a few days. As soon as I told him that I was on the run from the hospital authorities he was sympathetic. It was not a problem. I could take what I needed to eat from his larder and he also lent me some money.

One day I visited Putney and was walking past the hospital for the severely disabled. Like me, one of the patients had also been secretly fitted with a virtual reality headset. He was so severely disabled that it was impossible for him to make this experience known. The staff did not know. In addition he was party to intelligence about my situation that I was not. He was watching everything I was, through full reality overlay mode on his MTRUTH. I bought a can of Red Bull and left it outside the hospital. He would receive it, and had seen me put it there. The whole episode seemed cloaked in magnificent secrecy. He was living my experiences to make his life more interesting.

Having perceived myself to be on the end of a barrage of bad luck, dirty tricks or whatever they were, depending on how lucid I was, I now decided that the time had come to fight back. I thought these tricks were designed to make me do that – to create a sensible and logical response. I had been forced out of town and at some point decided that the very next time something went wrong the only way ahead was to get some material into the filing cabinet at the Court Service. I had to do something and saw the Court Service as the only way out. I headed for Brighton without a train ticket.

At Balcombe Station I was thrown off the train and began walking. It was early Sunday morning and I'd had to escape Bedford where I was paranoid about the CCTV cameras. I imagined my brother's colleagues in the police scanning their screens to try and catch me. This meant that when I had gone into town with Marek we'd had to take a circuitous route to avoid them. He understood.

As I walked down the road a terrible pain erupted in my head. It was driving me to suicide. I could feel the whole weight of the world trying to make me throw myself in front of one of the passing cars. All that seemed to keep me going was the certain knowledge that I was the only member of my own Reserve SBS unit. Like me, everyone in the Special Forces had had their heads wired up – eyes and ears included. I could see on my MTRUTH the SAS rookie who had built his own electromagnetically-sealed den, that was preventing his MTRUTH from receiving incoming information.

However I hoped that, knowing the transmissions to be intermittent, I was to be rewarded for my persistence in facing up to them head-on, rather than adopt his tactic. But the pain was terrible and I only just succeeded in not throwing myself in front of one of the cars. The occupants of the cars seemed ghostly. They had all been told there was an SAS operation on and, as they were all former military, they had been ordered to drive past me. It was a game of death.

Then I wondered if I was not the only one in this unit after all. I saw my comrades as a Dirty Dozen of outright losers – we had nothing to lose – and we were the last bastions of the British Empire. If we died, so would the Empire. We were all being used to set some sort of example. If we could put up with this then why could others not put up with far less painful problems? The whole lego-political system of the country was on the verge of collapse and it was only we, this Dirty Dozen, who were keeping it going. Truly we were all heroes – we had to be. But I was a little different from the other members of this specially selected unit, as I had not got into it through the usual channels; I had a doctorate in physics, which would lend a little finesse to this rough outfit. That was why I was of such value to them.

After a long and mentally painful walk into Hayward's Heath I had breakfast before getting back on the train. The torture finished. I had won another great psychological battle in the history of the unit. I was still alive to fight on and somehow get myself out of this.

In Brighton I booked into a cheap bed and breakfast just outside the station. I did not really want to go back to The Grapevine, as I knew that James Longhurst, my alter ego, was dead and buried in the basement. He was in my past and would never return. But still I could hear that female's voice in my head, proudly proclaiming his name as a national hero. James Longhurst had set a great example.

The room was small but nice and I began thinking of decking-out the small roof outside the window with some flowers. I had a strong sense that, quite apart from my duties in raising the dead for the Special Forces, I needed and wanted to rebuild my life. My position as a member of the Special Forces gave me great power, as I believed I had already proved by getting this far, and this would put me in a strong position to face whatever torture was ahead. I did not for a moment think there would be none. I was to be proved correct in that belief.

There was a grease mark on the wall by the bed, caused by somebody's greasy hair resting on it. I felt a little paranoid about it and imagined the room had been used as a homosexuals' trysting-place. I could see a man on the bed with his head against the wall, being feverishly buggered by some rampantly gay HIV carrier without a condom. However it didn't put me off the room and I enjoyed a nice bath. At least I had proved, on my previous Brighton sojourn, that I could survive without the cushion of my bank account. My priority now was how I could best help raise the £10 million and Diana pretending to be dead would be a great help in this. But when would the next member of the Royal Family have their death faked? I would just have to wait. There was still two-and-a-half years left until New Year's Eve 1999. Plenty of time for arrangements.

During these days I noticed that GCHQ, Menwith Hill or whoever it was that fed me these concept documents through my EAI, were leaking a number of representations from Saddam Hussein. I was clued up well enough not to imagine it was the real and actual Saddam Hussein. But I did think he might find out what the Security Services had done with his image. If I were a Soviet MI6 agent, it would also be natural to make me a psycho-envoy in a virtual visit to Baghdad. I recall little of these psychic teleconferences other than that the whole episode seemed rather salutary. Thoughts of opening up Eurostar services to Baghdad were mentioned. The Conservative MP Robert Adley, on a visit to Saddam Hussein, had requested a trip to see some of Saddam's steam trains – a request he granted. I was rather in fear that the presentation of Saddam's image might incur the most appalling ones on the Internet reaching me on this psycho-net. But they never came. This was generally the case over some seven years of heavy-duty brainwashing through my MTRUTH. The source of any virtual torture, without exception, appeared to be my own country's Security Services. They would drive me to seek solace, using my MTRUTH, in the virtual worlds of foreign intelligence services. MI6 had actually handed over control of my MTRUTH system to, for example the KGB – if it was not the other way round.

Faking your death would become all the rage in Royal circles and Comic Relief would have a brochure of faked death scenarios. The well heeled could flick through this to choose their preferred stage exit from this world, into the secret world of the Comic Relief undead. I heard the posh voice of a Lady phoning up the secret phone number from her hairdresser's to rearrange the date of her fake car crash.

I had to wonder of course, if Diana were not dead, where would she most likely be? She was probably on board a British nuclear submarine and was being revealed to this country's potential aggressors in *Ice Station Zebra*-type prank disclosure meetings, which were part of the nuclear arms reduction and six counties decommissioning programmes. By the time of New Year's Eve 1999 every country's secret service would have met her and every country's leader, as well as Gerry Adams, David Trimble, Martin Galvin and a number of others, would have mysteriously been 'killed' as part of the illusion, just like John Lennon had been. Thoughts of the Beatles' famous live satellite transmission beginning with the French national anthem came to mind – I could see what a hero I would be if only I could put up with the torture and see this thing through to the day of the denouement. But then I remembered what my friend Sand had said back in Africa in 1984: "Rapprochement not denouement."

I decided to revisit Lewes where James Longhurst, my alter ego, had once spent a cold, penniless night in a pub very slowly drinking a pint of beer. I booked into The King's Head hotel. I had the luxury of my bank account and I was still being paid amply for what I needed to do.

That night I ate wild boar steak with garlic courgettes. I had been annoyed that the bath had not been perfectly clean and now I found myself further irritated that the knife was not British-made and was not a proper steak knife. I saw myself as an Arthur Price cutlery salesman and decided to do something about this.

Next day I went to the County Court and collected a small claim summons form. I'd had enough of these dirty tricks – or whatever they were. What with car alarms going off outside my house and dirty baths, I had to be careful not to get into trouble again, and the legal process seemed to be the way ahead. I had the full might of the legal profession at my disposal – Lord Mackay of Clashfern was the only member of it who knew either that I had a state-of-the-art virtual reality set embedded in my head or that Diana was not dead. This gave me great power, which I had to somehow realise, in order to raise the £10 million. On one occasion I saw him on my EAI suggesting that I wanted to stay in this legal limbo for the rest of my life. I filled in the summons making complimentary remarks about the wild boar steak and garlic courgettes, claiming damages of £2.80. I had also been annoyed by a builder who had done some damage to my bathroom, so I decided to sue him too.

Firstly though it was back to Bedford and Marek's for a few days until my pay came through. I had to live off ham salad sandwiches in the mean time. One night I was daring enough to go out with him to Club Rich UK feeling sure I would not bump into any of my brothers there and risk arrest.

My pay arrived; so I paid Marek back and was off to Brighton again. At the railway station there was a notable incident. I was sitting down on a bench on platform 1 as the InterCity northbound train pulled out. At the window at the end of one of the front carriages was a woman wearing African national costume. As her carriage passed she called out to me that she had left her wallet on the telephone inside the booking hall. Hurriedly I turned to see the wallet inches away from me tantalisingly close on the other side of the glass. I got up, ran into the booking hall and picked up her wallet. Back on the platform the end of the train was passing as it gathered speed on its northbound journey. I could see the lady looking out at the front of the train a couple of hundred yards away. Then I noticed that the window to the final door of the final carriage was open and, running at full speed to aid my accuracy, I threw her wallet into the train. The incident was set-up by the Special Intelligence Service Comic Relief department to test my initiative and honesty.

Back on my seat catching my breath I thought back to the African trip: *they* had been responsible for the lady from SOE in Paris, for the mysterious appearance of the beer jug in Messina and for the wooden 'rat' being pulled under my tent at Mount Hoyo, as well as all sorts of other incidents during those six months of Special Intelligence Service magic all coordinated from between the wars. There was no doubt about this and with a realisation weighing a hundred tons it was now oh-so-consequentially clear that "Pam" had in fact been faking anaphylactic shock in the desert meaning the Australian vets must have been in on it. "Rapprochement not denouement", Sand had said over and over quoting from my great-uncle's letter and it was clear I was by no means unique amongst my fellow travellers, whose KGB files were also in the hands of the Service. My uncle had worked for Danish Intelligence during the war so I could be sure the incident I had just witnessed, and all that I was now recalling, went back to the 1926 meeting in this deterministic unfolding of events. My cartoon depiction of the theatrical goings on during the trip had been frighteningly yet gloriously accurate and where the rat going under my tent was concerned I could not rule out the French and, because Torq was Jewish, Mossad as well as the very best of MI6's African contacts being involved too. And yes! The Russian sitting behind us on the Aeroflot flight from Nairobi: it was clear he knew about the secrets the foot of my grandmother's garden hid!

Back in Brighton once again I found myself wandering around on the main railway station platform. I noticed a pigeon in an absolutely pitiful state. I suppose my condition was not too good either, though I had not seriously considered having my feet amputated – yet, despite severe athlete's foot. As I wandered around the platform on a rather pigeon-like locus, I suddenly became aware the pigeon had disappeared; culled by somebody in the local gun club. I put together a psychological profile of him: ex-Special Forces, collection of vintage motorbikes and drank in the Six Bells, Chiddingly. I briefly imagined this person having dinner with the pigeon, not dead after all, in a quality Italian restaurant in The Lanes but ruled it out. Then, using the eyes in the back of my head, courtesy of my Special Intelligence Service MTRUTH and a constantly updated CIA virtual Western Europe, I saw him put the pigeon's body in a Special Forces pigeon body bag. He now took it to lie in state at the local branch of the pigeon fanciers' club. The well-defined and achievable military goal of this operation was to demonstrate my potential as a mover and shaker – not an earth-shattering one some might say, but they would be mere sociopathological nihilists. But that was not the end. I now kept getting the feeling that pigeons were disappearing all around me and had a strong intuitive belief there was a bloke nearby with a well-silenced handgun. Then I thought I saw a pigeon which had been fitted with an artificial lower leg, making its way successfully around the concourse. I don't recall it having a patch over one eye. And whilst on the important subject of pigeon chivalry, during World War II pigeons were trained by the British military to fly suicide bombing missions. They were taught to pilot flying bombs into targets by being dispensed seed when they pecked at an image of their target, their pecking being used to direct the flying bombs.

In the station there was a magical atmosphere, which, in my experience, can be caused by one of two things: either a pleasantly mild dose of schizophrenia or somehow having become accidentally involved in a long-standing Special Forces operation. Perhaps, I wondered, the military had become party to my letter to the Chairman of Burger King, either by interception over my MTRUTH or by Royal Mail from the Chairman. But why did I not hear the gun? This depended on its range and the silencer's effectiveness. I deduced the explanation was that my MTRUTH was being tested. As before, by monitoring the discharge of the gun, the sound could be digitally removed from what I heard through my MTRUTH.

Again I remembered the Saturday morning drama lesson at school. Our teacher would give us a part to act out. He never asked me to act out this one though – this was for real. Soon there was not even one pigeon in sight. I had read that somebody was harvesting pigeon's in Trafalgar Square and selling them to butchers. Maybe they were doing it here too.

My favoured hotel had closed down; so I had to find another one, The Madeira. I asked them if they had any Madeira in the bar but they did not; so I decided to sue them for a small amount too, deciding I simply had to consider this a Special Forces dirty trick – to test my initiative. Even the slightest sign of such and I would resort to the law. I saw this as the only way of staying out of trouble and not getting arrested, which to an extent was correct. But vexatious litigation is a common symptom of schizophrenia, either that or an unfairly attached label. You'd have to know exactly what had ever happened to each patient to know the truth in this.

I asked the receptionist to telephone the builder and to get his address (so I could sue him). I wanted to sue him for putting up ordinary white tiles in my bathroom. You did not have to be a master builder to realise it needed either matching tiles or, if none were available, complete retiling. Acting as my secretary she was happy to do this and I asked her to tell him I had a bill to pay. When I returned to the hotel she told me he had been funny about this, and she complained that he had traced her number and had phoned back angrily.

I went out again for a drink. When I returned there was a police car parked outside the hotel. I decided she must have smelt a rat; either that or she was not happy with the builder's manner. I was frightened off by the police car and went to The Victoria bar at the pier where I started drinking. I decided it was not safe to go back to the hotel. I did not know exactly why the police car had been there but the danger of being arrested and put back in hospital just seemed too great, and I was not prepared to risk it. I was well and truly on the run again.

At the hotel I had abandoned my bag. In it were: a rather expensive pair of Sir Ranulph Fiennes Clark's sandals; the Army trousers I had bought from Stornoway military surplus stores in Portree; and, inside a sealed Berkshire Constabulary evidence bag; the video of Danny Ferguson at the Lazy House/Railroad Earth gig. The murder of Ferguson, a few years earlier, with a machete, had set my most paranoid thoughts running and I had gone to the police with the video in which Danny said, "The police are coming after us." I believed his murder was inextricably entwined with the situation I now found myself in. No doubt the police would be suspicious when they found my bag – and do a search for me on the database, realising they could force me back into hospital.

In The Victoria bar I listened to the album *Happiness* by The Beloved playing. As you will recall it was this CD which had been in my ghetto blaster when it was stolen from my flat in a break-in a few years earlier, and I had not heard it since. The police were definitely after me I thought, and the fact this album was now playing seemed too much of a coincidence. It was the FRU who had done my flat, I was sure. MI5 had had the CD playing and it was the very CD, minus the case (which I still had), that had been stolen from my flat. They knew every way there was to get into my mind; they knew my happiness had been stolen; so what more logical thing to do than steal my copy of the album with that title? But of course the chances were I would have heard that album again somewhere in the years since it was taken – and this just happened to be that time. Really it was just wishful thinking.

I came out of the bar when the record had finished and began walking towards Hove where I took a train. From the train, whilst it was halted at a station, I saw a man (presumably a drunkard) precariously balanced on the live rail. I thought he too was in the Special Forces and was demonstrating how much danger I was in. Late that night, ever so slightly paranoid in a pleasant sort of way, and still on the run, I booked into a hotel in Salisbury, where luckily there was a late bar.

Next day I made it to Exeter where I lodged in a bed and breakfast. On the street were some rather unusual performers wearing silver, metallic space-age-type costumes, and who had large amounts of white makeup. They moved around in an enigmatic slow motion display of complete sadness. Unusual. They could have been mourning my imminent death. If they were they had been lied to. Off to Newquay.

Chapter Forty-Three

Boats

My decision to go to Newquay was based on the most laughably tenuous inference from the recent news about David Shayler, whose surname I considered was a message. I believed shale was once mined in Newquay and, right or wrong, was reminded of this as the train pulled into Newquay Station the next day alongside the unusually long platforms once used, I thought, to take the shale away.

The first thing I heard after getting off the train was a passer-by saying "You're going to become a junky, then you're going clean," but I did not see any lips move. To tell the truth I do not recall if I really heard someone say this, whether it was a voice in my head, or whether it was just me thinking. This was often the case. I gave consideration to the possibility that I heard it on my MTRUTH – through my EAH. If such a thing really existed, I thought, then the sound could merely appear to emanate from an unseen mouth in my vicinity. If that person had been an MTRU as well, and I had looked at their mouth, I'd have seen them mouthing words. These words they would have been reading, but not actually speaking, from a cue seen in their EAV. I felt like the Terminator, though I was a rather more benign entity. I was now in a world of my own. And my arrival in Newquay also coincided with hearing the very beginning of the original *Dr Who* theme music again. Also I could see on my MTRUTH the Major (I had not seen him for years) holding a clipboard, which he seemed to be using to mark my progress.

Suddenly I felt like somebody in the Royal Army Medical Corps Palliative Care Hospice for the Terminally Ill again, or possibly a bloke dying laughing in the Star and Garter retired servicemen's home, as a heroin slug again hit inside my right ear. I could feel the wetness. I looked but could see no gunman. I had no idea why; it was probably just to get me thinking. What was the real explanation? On this occasion all I can say is that I suddenly felt something on the inside of my ear and then I had the most wonderful feeling. This led me to suspect there was a wound through which the drug got into my blood stream. But it was probably just a drop of rain, which had got into my ear – causing a pleasant sensation.

Whatever the real explanation for this, it seemed possible at the time that some mysterious person kept giving me the "gear", often in only barely perceptible doses. Sometimes I would feel a small pinprick within my body followed by a most glorious sensation emanating from it. I thought that somehow I had been given a speck of heroin again, in some sort of coating, possibly in my food or drink. This led me to think that heroin is not in the least bit addictive if you respect it. I respected it to the extent that I never even considered going to procure extra supplies to take as I required. In reality, as far as I know, I have never taken heroin in my entire life.

Lying in bed one night with my eyes shut I could see a window cleaner and it was like he was doing a really good job on my eyes with one of those rubber things they scrape across the window. It felt very relaxing. Then, in my head, I felt what I deduced was a very small dose of heroin again. I went to sleep.

Whoever it was giving me this "smack", I had to respect him. I still had the memory of the wrist-mounted micro drugs cabinet from which I had been tortured with ill-suited, unpleasant drugs. But surely I was not really being given heroin? It must have been just my brain chemistry playing up again in an oh-so-beautiful way. This reminded me that Dostoyevsky had said that immediately before he had an epileptic fit he experienced the most beautiful of sensations. Given that I was also predisposed to excessive electrical brain activity maybe this was what I was experiencing too.

Right or wrong, I did indeed reach the conclusion that novel drug delivery devices had somehow found their way into my body. But I was only guessing, these devices also being able to trigger the release of the heroin to order, in a designated position. I knew modern palliative care medicine to be getting increasingly sophisticated in targeting drugs to specific parts of the body. New developments in nanomachine technology were only likely to increase this sophistication – and further my delusions. On one occasion I was sitting in a cabin-style bar, in fact called The Cabin, where they served a homemade tasting beer, the badge for which showed the Prince of Wales's feathers. At the moment I began raising the glass to my mouth, a lady resembling Princess Diana entered the bar. This was real. Simultaneously, I felt a gorgeous rush of heroin through my whole torso, making me hesitate from tasting the beer, and dangerously relax back into my chair to puff on a Hamlet. I say dangerously because my intuition had taught me not to display any emotions. I sensed danger in enjoying this too much lest I be seen. It was like when I saw the Capgras double of Caroline back in Galway in 1994 – I felt I must not betray what I was thinking.

After a few days in a dingy bed and breakfast I booked into a more salubrious hotel not far from the station. I was of the mind that it was an MI5 joint, and though I was not sure as to the full implications of the hotel not having the licensee's name displayed above the threshold, the place did seem rather like an unmarked police car.

In the room I sensed I was being watched, though thoughts of cameras in my eyes were not as intense as they had been on earlier occasions. But I found myself examining the television set suspiciously.

That night I took *The New Testament*, soaked it in water for five minutes and then tore it in half before throwing it out of the window. If you ever happen to try this yourself you will find that it develops a nice wrinkled and bloated look. I shut the window feeling better about things. The next day, now feeling guilty, I went down to the bookshop and bought a copy of Tolkien's *The Return of the King*, which I now cunningly put in the place of *The New Testament*. I thought this was portentous of the forthcoming fake death of Prince Charles – and his subsequent miraculous re-emergence on the day of denouement. Once again I remembered Sand quoting my Great-Uncle Bernard's "Rapprochement, not denouement." A few days later I was thrown out of the hotel supposedly for "getting up too late".

I looked in the window of the newsagent's by the old level crossing and found another place for rent. I then placed my own advertisement: "Small group of former international oarsmen looking for gym", not that I had ever been one. I found the flat advertised and the landlord, Hugh, a builder, had moved from Windsor some years earlier. He showed me the flat along with his very large bulldog, McCoy. McCoy seemed eager to inspect the flat just to make sure all was well, making periodic trips in to say hello to me, for which I was to repay him with packets of Real McCoys crisps. Of course it did not go unnoticed that Hugh and his dog had come from near, or even at, Windsor Castle. It was a set-up – the psychic proximity of Prince Charles in this military manoeuvre I had accidentally got involved in was most powerful. This power was never more noticeable than when I bought a lovely new designer "Big Star" jumper. It was the only one ever made and had been brought to me rather than I having found it: that was how important I was. The jumper had a large but rather understated star on the front with B and S on each side. This had the dual meaning of British Standard, for that was what I was. I probably had my own ISO accreditation.

Next day, now installed in a flat, which during summer would cost a lot more, I found that the gymnasium was closed for a few weeks; so I went for a run on the long beach. Some surfing was being filmed below a cliff, which was to become crucial, as you will see. It later seemed they were filming the famous Guinness white horses advertisement. Moreover it seemed important to me that they were, in a highly delusional way. But in fact the advertisement was shot in Hawaii.

I was now in a good position to start fighting back. This first of all demanded familiarising myself with the local drinking-holes, a task I set to at once. This went without any problems except that, being on my own, I became rather sensitised to the following: when I sat down, people kept asking if anyone was sitting in the chairs next to me. As a result I invariably found myself isolated on my own table. However, in The Red Lion, overlooking the harbour, I had a roaring wood fire to cheer me.

Newquay was a truly beautiful place in which to go to ground. The whole place was swarming with military intelligence. I was being plastered with subliminal virtual reality over my EAI. And my MTRUTH was being used passively to watch all that went on through my eyes – yet its being used in this way was none of my business. I'd had the privilege – as that television advertisement said, to have had someone see through my own eyes. To complain would be churlish. I was nothing more than a roving police camera. I quite literally had a photographic/videographic memory – not that I had access to it. As for what I would see in my mind's eye over the next few months, believing it was over my MTRUTH, I could never tell where my imagination ended and where, if anywhere, my EAI started. Regarding what was really just the product of my own mind as some electronic augmentation of myself, who could possibly predict how I would react to any particular set of inputs? I certainly never foresaw what would happen – and I am not talking about a perfectly executed bicycle-kick goal I saw at the local football ground one Saturday.

Whilst all this happened I felt an extremely powerful force telling me I now had to live up to something and it seemed no doubt, it was the reputation of the Special Boat Service. Then one day somebody walked past me who, I thought, had been to Eton and maybe owned a tobacco company or investment bank.

Then I found myself being told I had to walk like him, by holding my index fingers against my thumbs. This was how, I thought, another Etonian also walked. I had rowed against him at school in the race I mentioned earlier in the story. So I dutifully observed some level of thought about my own gait – it was a little bit embarrassing to be honest.

I began hearing the Queen's voice in my head – not a tremendously groundbreaking observation in the history of mental illness. She only said one thing, and I estimate I heard her say it, in an optimistic way, fifty to a hundred times: "Getting warmer, every day!" I sensed I was indeed getting warmer, and would indulge in my SBS fantasy. She said it in the tone one imagines Her Majesty, or any other dog owner, talks to their pet. So how was I getting warmer? I was on a journey to the centre of British Intelligence and the closer I got the more congratulations were due. These congratulations were in the form of 3D EAH MTRUTH broadcasts of a large number of people clapping, the news I was "getting warmer" or even, on my EAV, "the Queen fetish." Aware Her Majesty did not smoke, the fetish was the video image on my MTRUTH of the Queen taking a drag on a cigarette and then almost studiously stubbing it out in an ashtray. To see this was a rare honour in the field of asymmetric virtual battlefields – the asymmetry arising between the inconsistency of the representation of reality in the virtual world and reality itself. The Queen had been filmed smoking just one cigarette, this having been done for military purposes. I was the only one seeing it.

Another great compliment I believed was paid to me was an image of Mel Smith, the Comic Relief stalwart. This I saw many times. He would approach me looking like he really meant business – as though he were thinking, let's show him how it's done. After a few steps he would then commence stuffing himself with large chocolate Swiss rolls as fast as he could, looking like he really wanted to impress me. I was – nobody would have failed to be impressed – and the way he did it was so reverential, it would have been most unwise not to assume it was meant to be a compliment. You had to see it to believe it. I saw that, oh, perhaps a 150 times, and you see "food", I believed, is intelligence-speak for just that: any information, however small, of a sensitive nature, right down to the most ridiculously trivial joint and several tort involving chocolate Swiss rolls. But perhaps the most significant of all these hallucinations was the face of the black man who would appear before me momentarily and then keel away in divine amusement.

Inspired by this thought, be it down to either my MTRUTH or own very clear visual imagination, I decided to write to the Queen to complain about the chairs in the pub being moved. Writing to Her Majesty was just a tool to satisfy my imagination and, I believed, certainly no indicator of illness on my part. I did not believe it very likely she would actually read the letter. In fact I imagined it being opened much closer to hand. My post was being intercepted as soon as I was out of sight of the postbox, most probably by an SAS undercover postman.

That night in The Red Lion I sat down in a big leather armchair and noticed the barman tidying up. In doing so he moved the other large leather chair to my table, the opposite of what I had previously been used to. This left me thinking perhaps my letter had already had an effect. It was pleasant and alluring to think it had caused this to happen. Also, I was not completely certain if it had anything to do with my uncertain belief about the framed photograph on the wall under which it said "The Visit of the Prince of Wales in 1918". I found myself thinking that strictly speaking it was King George V (who ascended the throne in 1910) and Queen Mary, this being a deliberate mistake – *a joke*. This was evidence of the conspiracy to overthrow the monarchy that was unfolding before me. Reality itself was being chipped away at in this most sinister manner. The residues of my paranoia from 1995 told me that it had all been designed so that I was the one to unfold it. Whether, in 1926, the plan had been to actually overthrow the monarchy or just tell an elaborate joke to prevent a holocaust in Berkshire, the Security Services were now fully aware of what was going on – so that I was now seen as some sort of amusing historical anomaly. They knew I was a loyal subject and had no desire to be compliant in such a conspiracy – but a joke? Why not?

Seeing the picture announcing the Prince of Wales's visit, I once again felt I was on some sort of a treasure hunt or Magical Mystery Tour. Joke or otherwise, I decided to wrap 50p in a piece of paper, address it to Michael Winner, the film director, and hide it down the side of one of the armchairs – all seen, of course, via my MTRUTH. Again I sensed the presence of Prince Charles, now sitting in the other large armchair. It had been placed there on the express orders of Her Majesty the Queen, or more likely her representative, in response to my letter. No doubt Prince Charles was finding the whole episode extraordinarily amusing – but out of politeness was not letting on.

The tide seemed to have turned, if only momentarily, as I went on to enjoy my pint of Doom Bar Ale, forgetting for the moment how much dog excrement had started to appear on the pavement outside the British Legion club. Why was this? Surely not because I had written "Ardoyne" on a map on the wall of my flat? Perhaps, I thought, it was because I did not then know for sure whether the Ardoyne was a Republican or Loyalist stronghold. The Security Services somehow knew this, and had seen me write it through my MTRUTH. At the bar, as I waited for my next pint, a chap showed me an intricately folded £5 note which he had folded so that the Queen was clearly committing an obscene act. I could not decide whether MI5 or the IRA had sent him. But I knew it was one of them.

I also began wondering exactly why and how, still in The Red Lion, I could quite clearly hear Prince Andrew talking to a couple of military-sounding chums. Obviously they were not actually there and yet I could hear them. British Intelligence had built a double of The Red Lion somewhere, as with my parents' house and The Ship back in Bedford, this enabling the acoustics of Prince Andrew chatting to these chaps over a couple of beers to be overlaid on my reality via my MTRUTH. Their conversation was hearty and made me feel I was getting close – but they never addressed me. I wondered where this double of The Red Lion was and, as with my parents' house and The Ship, thought it too must be on Salisbury Plain. Of course it went without saying that the Special Intelligence Service had a speaker rebroadcast characteristics map of the town. Using this, and without my MTRUTH, they could send anything they liked into my head, and those around me, disguised amidst the pub chatter (you will have experienced this process if you have ever heard interference from, for example, taxi cabs, on your stereo).

Once more I could see Professor Dainty on my MTRUTH. He had his tongue stuck out like a nine-year-old playing with his toys and really enjoying himself. Again he seemed to be loading some sort of crossbow, with which he was perpetually about to fire something into my imagination.

I was standing outside a launderette to the north of the town. There was a rainbow but I did not believe it was really there. The rainbow was to the south, which would mean, impossibly, the sun had to be in the north. Suddenly, I realised I must be seeing this rainbow through my MTRUTH, courtesy of Professor Dainty. Whatever the reason I had been seeing him, it was unlikely he knew who I was, as the secrecy of the SBS was too great to allow that.

I felt I was trapped timelessly in a Ladybird book, *Adventure at the Harbour*. The place was just dripping in mystique and the town crawling with military intelligence. But it was just *my* military intelligence – *my* imagined MTRUTH run by MI5, the Army Intelligence Corps, GCHQ, the DISC and the Special Intelligence Service. Quite a big just. I felt I could hardly move as if I were just a figure in one of the Ladybird book illustrations. A brand new Coast Guard Land Rover pulled up on the little road going down to the harbour. It was a show vehicle for presentation to British Intelligence through my eyes in passive MTRUTH mode. British Intelligence was just showing off.

Each day I was reminded of that afternoon in Inverness three years earlier. There, in the railway station, I had stared mesmerised at the children's ride. Now I passed the wagon and horses ride, which had Jerome Moross's rousing theme music from *The Big Country* playing. It was almost as if this had been a concession to the CIA who were not actively involved – or at least did not wish to appear to be. It seemed cute and inspiring – as it was meant to be. The ride finished. I went and put 20p in myself – ghost-rider! They might find out later you see.

Two or three graves overlooked the harbour, and on the horizon an ancient burial mound overlooked *them*. I just sat there in The Fort Inn listening to The Verve album, *Urban Hymns*, drinking my coffee and smoking my Hamlet. I felt subject to the strong anthropic principle again and wondered as to the identity of the person who put this album on each morning: somebody at MI5 in order to give reality a little flavour and inspire me. I was the centre of everything. It would forever be 11am and I did feel like The Verve's Richard Ashcroft, when he sang "I hope you feel like I feel" in *Weeping Willow*. The whole message of the album spurred me on.

Down in the bay I could see a man who, I supposed, was not merely appearing to have trouble getting his windsurf board to stand up, but had been ordered to pretend he could not get it to. He was telling me how well my mission was going – despite it seeming impossible to attribute any level of certainty to my actions being of my own free will. I was the combined existential effort of MI5, Newquay Rowing Club and the Cornish Tin Mining Industry, all controlling me through my MTRUTH. Come to think of it, the last working tin mine, South Crofty, was closing; so I got an envelope from the bar, put enough in it for a pint of beer, and addressed it to the pit manager. I'd seen some graffiti on the wall outside the mine on the previous night's news. It said "Cornish lads are fishermen and Cornish lads are miners too. But when the fish and tin are gone, what are the Cornish boys to do?"

I thought of the chap who built himself the burial mound overlooking the bay. He was overlooking both the windsurfer and me. His spirit was helping the windsurfer decide whether to carry out his order, if he intuitively felt it was the right thing to do. Ludicrous possibilities were liquid in my mind. What on earth would the windsurfer have thought if he had known that somebody watching him was thinking these things? I decided to hide a pound coin inside the lifebuoy in the bar; suddenly it was World War I and this was my last drink before going to the front; if I returned I would retrieve it for my next pint, and that thought kept me going.

I finished my coffee and biscuit. On the wrapper it said "Produced in a factory handling egg". Some egg I thought, not noticing the colon after "handling". Later, elsewhere, somebody showed me their peanut packet that said "May contain traces of nuts." I could not believe it, and assumed it was an MI5/IRA one off.

One day, walking along the road, an affable looking black guy appeared in my mind's eye – if not my MTRUTH. He showed me an orange, and started peeling it. He said "Zest!" and held the orange towards me. I was utterly mesmerised and felt like just lying down in the street, but sensed the danger of being run over. I could smell the zest[97]. I knew I must keep walking. "Always walk positively and look like you know where you are going" as I had once been advised to do in Manhattan. It went without saying he knew every detail of my African trip, quite apart from the contents of my Security Service file. After he held the orange towards me, always doing so momentarily before continuing his mesmeric peeling, I sensed another smidgeon of heroin entering my body. This was certainly not enough to leave me lying, like Howard Hughes or somebody, amongst my own excrement, in a darkened flat with the curtains drawn round the clock, receiving a dial-a-pizza every couple of days. But it was just enough to feel I was a seriously "shit-hot" individual. I would have this experience again – always when walking down the street past The Fort Inn. It went without saying I was not to go looking for this guy, or even hope to bump into him. It was just a nice, though dangerous, experience. He was a heroin dealer.

I wandered amongst the fishermen, who were mending their nets. One of their boats was named *Restorick*. "Surely you know who Restorick was", I said to someone back at the pub above the harbour. "He was the last British soldier shot by the IRA." Further down the beach I found a cave with two large rock formations. I found I could jam a pound coin between them. I wandered further round the bay. In the cliff, at the height of a basin to wash my hands, was a little bowl of sand. I stuck some coins in it.

Shortly after my arrival in Newquay the suicide of INXS singer, Michael Hutchence, was announced. Of course I could not be sure about this, after all there must be some real deaths taking place. So I was not quite so certain he had faked his death as Diana had done.

Sitting in the Fort Inn, I picked up my coffee. I was breathtaken by the beautiful view up the coast. Diana stood before me, "Has nobody told you? Nobody dies – we all just go up to a higher level. Death is just an illusion put about by the Security Services in order to maintain public order. Charles has just told me. Isn't it wonderful? Apparently the Ministry of Defence has got everything under control and we should all be going through the boundary layer in the next few days. Of course everyone has to wait their turn. Oh, I am so excited – aren't you? Let me buy you a new outfit. You must look your best. And remember to send me a Christmas card. You're the only one who knows."

I did send her a Christmas card, possibly the only person in the world who did. Whoever received it must have thought I was bonkers. But I genuinely believed she was alive; so no offence should have been taken. It was a postcard and showed a picture of a seagull asking "What have I done?" and underneath: "Public Enemy No.1."

I succumbed to the delusion that Michael Hutchence and indeed Kurt Cobain, who committed suicide by shooting himself in the mouth, were in John Lennon's cult. I noticed that the former's surname is pronounced "Hutch Ents", and I saw loads of rabbits coming out of their hutches and playing on a bizarre rabbit playground. Barking mad I was – but no! I was only just beginning to exercise my thoughts on the Anglo-Irish situation; to address the problem you have to start somewhere and this was my first attempt, not as a schizophrenic, but a Grade 1 psycho-spy. I concede this was probably not the most helpful observation in the history of the peace process but it did at least remind me that a United Ireland was likely based on the different breeding rates of Protestants and Catholics.

I took a walk around town to see whose houses had got dog excrement outside (I had imagined MI5 had dogs which would make a mess to order for use only in rare cases where national security was an issue). Back in Bedford, I had noticed how the whole of one side of Waterloo Road, where the All European EEC Reich-Chancellery was (actually just a Europhile's house with a little Union flag/French Tricolore plaque on the wall), had been inexplicably sprayed with some sort of glue. I had presumed this indicated French cricket was being played and it was on a sticky wicket. And that was all after a night when it appeared to me the entire staff, current and present, of the Royal Logistics Corps Bomb Disposal Service had each turned up with a bag of snails, covering the pavement with them. I reached home severely traumatised, as the walk back from the pub was more bizarre than the *Monty Python* Exploding Shrubs sketch. In fact the stickiness was just the resin dripping from the trees and a wet summer night had brought the snails out. If there were any truth in the snail delusion it was that *Helix Pomatia*, which lives in chalky areas of southern England and is protected by the Wildlife and Countryside Act 1981, was brought to this island by the Romans as a delicacy. The thought of a joint British/Roman military operation crossed my mind and I shook my head at the insanity of it all. I had not checked to see which species these were and whether I had committed a criminal offence by stepping on them all.

Cats came up to meet me, and I wondered (having nothing better to think about and knowing of the occasional professional cat you read about in the papers) what the MoD regulation distance for cat-greeting was. Cat-greetings, as you will know, consist of, amongst other things, raising the tail in salute. Could the Pentagon change the weather in the six counties of the Irish Republic by tampering with the mean distance at which cats raised their tails in greeting? It seemed to me that they could and, given that possibility, it did not take a great leap in my imagination to believe they already had.

One day I met a poor bedraggled cat, which had the most pitifully matted fur you could possibly imagine. It was miaowing as though to say "Won't anyone help me? I don't know where the fuck I am and I feel shit". I had a very strong feeling the RSPCA had brought this animal, the worst case of animal abuse they could find in the entire country, and just plonked it down at various places in Newquay until I came across it. Jesus Christ of cats for a few days. I called the RSPCA and gave them the information.

I wrote to the Deemster Cain, an Isle of Man High Court judge responsible to the Lord Bishop of Sodor and Man (the Queen's representative), about my employment position, the laws for which did not apply in the Isle of Man. In the letter I asked, on behalf of the extraordinarily homosexual Queen's Head pub in Brighton, to bring back capital punishment for homosexual acts for fun. This would enable many happy years of fake executions of homosexuals in the Isle of Man if a pre-agreed fee to Comic Relief were paid. The fee would be means-tested for the person who wished to fake their death, entry into the Isle of Man for gays being only available through clandestine methods entailing a gay Special Boat Service. There was nothing homophobic about this. I felt I was on the side of homosexuals and that they might enjoy sex more if it was punishable by death, as it was until recently in the Isle of Man.

The day after writing I saw a cat with no tail. I had no idea if it was a Manx cat or had lost its tail in combat or an accident – either way I had no trouble imagining the cat to have MTRUTH (feline version) status. Being locked into my MTRUTH, I imagined myself as a cat in The High Court, taking action for years of abuse, including being locked in the garden shed.

"My Lord, in evolutionary terms the animal is not nearly as advanced as a fully-fledged human being and cannot be expected to have mastered the finer points of etiquette. I would agree the animal displays some socio-pathological tendencies, but really I cannot accept the treatment was as warranted as docking its tail after an accident might have been."

A letter from the House of Keys dropped onto the mat. As for the cats' greetings, I made a note, and later that day dropped a line to the Cornish County Surveyor asking him to conduct a survey into this. I also asked him to forward the results to the Ministry of Defence who, I said, were compiling an official compendium of cat-positions as there was no proper standard means of making anyone aware, friend or foe, or in court, about which cat-position they were talking about.

I kept imagining Stena, the Irish Sea ferry operator, would start running a catamaran service into Newquay harbour. On one occasion I was thinking this when a person stopped near me in the street and lit a cigarette as though he had learnt something about me, liked it, and this was his way of indicating it. Furthermore it seemed he might even know what I had just thought – not impossible if you think about it (in the absence of MTRUTH, something would need to have been placed before me, or said near me, which made me think of that). I had also become sensitised to people touching their noses. I thought this meant they *knew* something about me, and came from British Intelligence, *or the IRA*.

In Wesley Yard, a street in south west Newquay, I decided to leave a message for General Wesley Clark, the United States Army General, Pentagon Joint Chief of Staff and Supreme NATO Commander. I had written "Yard" and "King Ink", the titles of two of the songs on a BBC Radio 1 John Peel session by The Birthday Party back in 1983, the other song being *Figure of Fun* appropriately. I was now wondering if I might be one. I put the message, Arne Saknussem-style, down the pole of the road sign at the southwest corner of the street. With my knowledge of deterministic computer battlefield models I sensed somebody watching, saying "You don't surely think that will make any difference?" the joke being that in discrete deterministic battlefield models very small events can be shown to be the cause of far more dramatic ones. This is known as the butterfly effect and is a consequence of chaos. The next day, in a street near Wesley Yard, I saw a large 1950s American car in quite perfect condition. My mind refused to allow me even consideration of the possibility there was no connection between these events or that no causal line of evidence existed between them. It was the Neighbourhood Watch, the Army Intelligence Corps, and NATO Supreme Command who had done this – as proven by a file in each of their filing cabinets. I just stared at it – impressed.

Again I imagined the £10 million had been paid – perhaps by Mr Getty. In all likelihood, given the extraordinary fact that I had eye implants enabling me to see remote events, not only had it been paid but grants to needy causes as well. But the Special Intelligence Service was keeping their cards close to their chests to see what I did along the route. I was being fast-tracked into the peace process; hence at this stage grants were all made anonymously. And like back in Bedford, the Troubles were being imported in highly managed homeopathic quantities to Newquay using the dosh – or the £747.47 I was about to send Comic Relief myself. How the distance at which cats greeted you was of any use in the Anglo-Irish peace process may not seem too obvious – but I had to start somewhere. I was to start by proposing to measure the distance both before and after central Newquay had been secretly declared part of Ireland. I was positive there would be a tiny but measurable and significant difference – even if only by virtue of the anomaly of a cat with no tail.

I met a grey cat sitting on the junction box in the pedestrianised High Street. I stroked it and noticed its address, hanging around its neck. It said "1 Cheltenham Place" and, being that Cheltenham was the home of GCHQ, I thought it might be a GCHQ MTRU cat with, like me, cameras in its eyes etc. No doubt, I thought, it had completely adjustable greeting distance. Nor could I rule it out being used for anti-drugs surveillance. It was a very unusual in that few cats are seen in the High Street – sitting on a junction box as it did. It jumped up onto a parked scooter and sat there looking at itself in the mirror. On my MTRUTH, a strange cartoon world manifested itself. In it the cat could actually drive the bike up the High Street in the direction of Padstow, for lunch in Rick Stein's restaurant.

Having settled in, I now had to get my bag back from the hotel in Brighton. An apparently insurmountable barrier seemed to prevent me doing this. Everyone whose help I asked seemed disinclined to assist, on one occasion refusing to even speak to me. The bag seemed to become the key to something. I was very sensitive about its legal sanctity, as it contained the Danny Ferguson video. I had written to the police saying I wanted to see the pictures of the murder scene – as I wanted to know if it was real or not. I felt the bag was his secret and I had a duty to him.

The court began returning my summonses citing legal reasons why they could not be served. I did not care how many times they sent them back. I just wanted someone to know that I was unhappy. I was not getting complete satisfaction concerning the matter of the bag. I consulted several local figures but none would help, even on one occasion reacting as though there was something exceedingly peculiar in my request, perhaps because they thought the bag contained drugs. The matter of the bag seemed utterly jinxed. In reality this was the Danny Ferguson murder investigation.

I called Red Star Parcels. They told me I could pay cash to have the bag transferred if I visited a Red Star office, the nearest being in Truro. So I set off for Truro and, arriving at the office, the jinx continued. The man told me he could not take my money because the computer had just gone down. The anger was now building to a critical level because I was now completely convinced somebody did not want me to get the bag back. I wanted to say "Look you dunderhead, it matters not one jot if your bloody computer is working or not, because if you want to keep your job you can take my fucking money now and give me a handwritten receipt. And if your pen does not work then mine does. You can then get my bag delivered to this address tomorrow and if you fail then I will personally come around and burn your fucking office down!" But I concealed my anger well. He told me he could only accept cash if I wanted to *send* a package but not receive one.

I returned to Newquay. I had already realised the agent handling the management of my London flat had ripped me off by £900: charging me, simply for sending the New Year's contract and continuing to hold the deposit. But I was not going to have that. I did not need to be a legal expert to see that however many times they repeated that the contract specified the commission to be 10 per cent they simply had not carried out the work they said they included. For example, I still had the same tenant, so they didn't need to get another one. I could not believe anyone was prepared to be victim to this scam and began to think I was the only person in the whole world who had received this contract. It had been written up especially by the Lord High Chancellor as the logical extension to the Diana prank to check I could see through it, and find the proper way out. This delusion led me into a particularly pertinacious state, which eventually lost my vital place on the housing ladder.

I got even angrier with their solicitor to the point where I felt like teaching her a lesson too. I then set up some strange legal phase-conjugate mirror (a mirror you can see yourself in wherever you look from) around them. They probably thought I was off my head, but I was completely happy I had done the right thing at every step. I was rather proud of the legal prose constituting my 'mirror'[98]. They paid me back the money I had claimed and I went down to the bank and paid £747.47 to Comic Relief, in memory of Jo Hudson, hoping the sum would ward off what I sensed to be an increasingly powerful MI5/CIA magic full press. The sense that something extraordinarily sensitive was going on was only heightened by the appearance in my MTRUTH, on quite a number of occasions, of Martin McGuinness. Every time I saw him he was taking off a balaclava and saying, in a hushed and secretive manner, "Nobody knows I'm here!" But I would also see Gordon Brittas, from *The Brittas Empire*, and he was saying, equally secretively, "I'm not dead!" I was greatly encouraged by this too, and looking forwards to a new series, wondered for some reason if I had missed the final episode of the last.

One afternoon I went drinking in a pub near the sea at the north end of town. Sitting in front of the fire getting a little drunk, unusual for me in the day thankfully, a chap who looked like the man with the orange appeared. For security, I was not treating this period as though it were an experiment conducted by the British Society for the Study of the Paranormal; that is with meters, records and cameras, keeping a moment by moment record of what happened. If I had, it would have been readily obvious I was an Army MTRU and be banned from the pubs. Anyway there he was appearing to be shovelling loose bank notes into the fire whilst *Rain or Shine* by Five Star was playing, either in my head or on the jukebox. From then on, all I had to do was think of that song and he would dutifully appear, shovelling away. I wondered if Five Star's manager had been a heroin addict and these were the band's funds he was burning; either that or I was expensive to run.

In my legal actions I asked that the sums I was claiming be payable to Comic Relief, but knew that somebody was going to say "No, no, no; he can't go around doing that!" The Diana Princess of Wales Memorial Fund was in fact an intelligence cell in Comic Relief, and really the fund was just a matter of hilarity. I did not just imagine it – I believed it, because if she were not dead, that was the only logical explanation. Having made a number of representations on behalf of Comic Relief, as was my duty, I deemed it no longer necessary to even mention that charity. So I just wrote at the bottom of the claims "The Defendants cannot be sure where the Plaintiff puts the damages" and, signing the application "Newquay le test pilote Copyright Comic Relief 1997", sent it off. I really did not care what people thought because all I wanted was some peace of mind in case I was right. If I put a toe wrong, let alone a foot, I would be punished ruthlessly and remorselessly on my MTRUTH – simply by the mere existence of the Special Forces, who hardly needed to move to have an observable effect. If I did not take this chance I would forever regret it. Once again, it was as though I were back at the gate at Her Majesty's Land Forces HQ, Wilton, and trying to make sense of my actions that day. But the point was that the defendants could not be sure if the money would go to Comic Relief or the Diana Princess of Wales Memorial Fund because they could not be sure if she were alive or dead. As for where I got the idea of calling myself "Newquay le test pilote", I felt like I was the post-modern battlefield equivalent of the pilot of Enola Gay and it hadn't been my idea. It had come in over my MTRUTH from MI5 and, by giving Comic Relief the courtesy of attributing the copyright to them absolved myself of any accusations that I had claimed the credit where none was due to me – I was just doing my job.

I remember one of the writs I issued – against Mick Jagger. It went something like this:

The Defendant is a well-known recording artist. The Defendant has an "all-day breakfast" two weeks on Friday, upstairs at Sizzlers, Newquay. The Plaintiff is a passer-by, passing by and, on occasions, actually entering the aforementioned restaurant. The Plaintiff cannot be sure where he will be on either that day at that time or on any of the adjacent days at any adjacent times. The Defendant will make no attempt whatsoever to either approach the Plaintiff, refer to him or discuss him and will not even be aware of his existence, the Plaintiff not being sure, or able to be sure, if this is conducive to the level of satisfaction that might be reasonable to expect at that moment in time, the Plaintiff, this being so, not as a result getting any satisfaction whatsoever, this surely being to his detriment. The Plaintiff therefore claims damages. The Defendant cannot be sure where the Plaintiff puts the damages.

It was probably one of the most benign county court actions ever seen at Truro County Court. A couple of years later Professor Hawking's secretary would answer a letter of mine addressing me as "Cher Monsieur le test pilote", which heftily amused me and made me suddenly ambitious, as she suggested I write a book. I re-began writing this book days later.

Eventually I telephoned the police station in Brighton and they said that the contents of the bag were disgusting and that the bag, together with its contents, had been incinerated. This was not true as I was eventually reunited with some of the contents via my brother in the police. I did not believe what I was being told and, as a result of the later mysterious reappearance of those contents, but not the video, I am not sure the person who told me this believed it himself. I was left hopelessly confused to the point where I even began to wonder if there had ever even been a bag, let alone a dog called Pooh at Balmoral and a car crash in Paris. Either way I would never see the video again – and that broke my heart for business reasons as well as delusional ones.

Down in Newquay, things now felt a little more pleasant as I felt, for a while at least, I had distanced myself from the litany of dirty tricks in Barnes. There, on a three-day break from Newquay, I had made the call to the Brighton police, the officer being the suspiciously, or auspiciously named, whichever you prefer, PC Barry Barnes.

Then, one day whilst I was sitting on the toilet, I clearly saw on my MTRUTH Bill Clinton in front and to one side of me. The way he stood indicated he was acting the part of a care assistant and I was not fully capable of managing my toilet affairs. On this occasion it was quite clear that it was not my own imagination but my MTRUTH, and I ruled out the possibility that it was a schizophrenic hallucination. But that was what it was or at least might have been. This was a bit more than just your everyday imagination. It seemed they had taken the padlocks off my MTRUTH full-reality-overlay keyboard and turned up the level a bit. He bent over a little artificially making me mindful of the voice I had heard in my head, way back at Fairmile Hospital three-and-a-half years earlier. It had suggested I was going to do a lot for disabled people. I also thought of my imagined friend with MTRUTH at Putney Hospital – totally isolated in his body though able, as I was, with the television screens in his eyes, to live somebody else's experiences. The way the image of Mr Clinton bent over was a little awkward and unnatural, almost as though the person who sent this message wanted to give me the clue it was not Mr Clinton in person. He looked like a cutout on a stick as used in a shadowplay. It was just a CIA virtual reality intelligence officer indicating what was really going on here.

About this time I began seeing, each night at exactly 2100hrs, the image of Count Dracula rising from his coffin. This was the Special Intelligence wake-up call to get down to the pub and see what was going on – for example heroin dealing. I have to say it never got to the stage where I sat looking at my watch ready for the message to come through. This vision was rather more subliminal than that of Bill Clinton and, at the time, I thought it was just my mind's eye, and nothing to do with either schizophrenia or my MTRUTH. This leads me to ask when, in the absence of an MTRUTH, or an MTRUTH being used, is an hallucination schizophrenia; and when is it just evidence of a good visual imagination? The answer seems to me is that it becomes schizophrenia when the person experiencing the vision cannot bear what they are seeing – or acts inappropriately in response. Also there is a continuum of states, which tends to be forgotten, traversing the ground in between the two conditions. Finally, only psychiatrists attached to the military are in any position to diagnose a person as being a Grade 1 psycho-spy of interest to Her Majesty's armed forces rather than somebody to be left at the mercy of the NHS and the drugs company. It was quite clear that somebody suffering unpleasant hallucinations could indeed benefit by having MTRUTH, calming images being provided to expunge their more unpleasant visions from their mind. This was why, back at Fairmile Hospital, I had been told over my MTRUTH that I was going to do great things for disabled people – schizophrenia is classed as a disability.

Another thing I saw on my MTRUTH was the sight of the Major holding himself tightly up against the other side of a glass screen, like somebody trapped. Except this was not what I understood to be happening. It happened when I was smoking or eating, or drinking something nice, and he wanted to get a bit virtually or give me the idea that I was very lucky to be having, e.g. that cigar and I was to know he, or somebody, was jealous. It was a strange Masonic game and he had not been allowed a smoke in days.[99] And perhaps it was around now, though to be honest I do not recall exactly when this began, perhaps to within years, but I heard what became a very familiar voice of a woman in my head, with the sort of accent I somehow imagined was one of the more 'traditional' accents at MI5 and the voice always delivered information in only one format without any exception. First she would tell me something that had happened, was happening or was going to happen or was the case and then immediately she would say it again preceded by "You don't surely think that..." This was an interesting tactic and raised shall we say, a few more than one or two possibilities about the existentiality ratings in my immediate vicinity.

One night an odd thing happened whilst I was asleep. I found myself completely conscious of what was going on and yet unable to do anything about it – like move or wake up. Standing over my bed were three blokes whom I believed were Royal Marines. One of them had inserted a dildo up my arse and I could feel it there but not do anything about it. Very odd. This was just another of the tools they had to interfere with my mind – ritual degradation. I notice I had precisely no sex drive and hit on the theory that red squirrels become impotent merely at the sight of a grey one and did not make good porn stars. In my case it was more to do with my alcohol consumption as well as being merely shy about having sex when all could be seen via my MTRUTH. Also it seems I'd had something of a male menopause three years earlier.

In the morning I went to the barber's. Whilst he cut my hair I noticed that on his price list he offered "Friction" for a very reasonable price: 50p. I had never seen, heard, or had any friction so I asked for some. It seemed it was just a pleasant scalp massage and I was very happy with my haircut. But that night I was sitting in Sailors' nightclub with my cap on when a bloke came out of the gents looking a little deterministic, with a fired-up look on his face. He grabbed my cap aggressively and turned it around forcibly on my head. His top made me wonder if he was in the Fire Brigade and was under orders from the military. The reason seemed to be that, outside my imagination, things were a little quiet. My controllers wanted to frisk things up a bit to justify the expense of the full press on me as an experiment in Cornish pasty-rich military theatres. This all came about following the confession of Prince Charles as to his being the only MI6 officer in the country who knew that, as in my delusions about the Wings song *Jet*, I was a born KGB traitor whose life had been completely determined from birth. I was still strongly prey to this delusion. If the song, inspired by an intelligence concept document leaked to Paul McCartney in Nigeria in the '70s was correct, so were all those schooled in my alma mater. Now I could see right into the KGB archive over my MTRUTH and the original lyrics to the *Band on the Run* album acquired by the KGB in Nigeria (where, in reality, the lyrics went missing, having to then be rewritten). This was in return for the courtesy of Mr McCartney in accepting from the Soviet Union their concept document linked inextricably back to the famous Friday afternoon drinks in 1926, the last days in the Führerbunker and the strangely concreted-over foot of my grandmother's garden in Ruislip.

Now I became the subject of vocal abuse from some women with the bloke who had turned my cap and it felt rather unpleasant. So I complained and called the police, two of whom arrived outside, one appearing to be homosexual. As I stood there on the pavement, the person who had started the incident came marching out of the club and walked straight in between us. I said "There he is" but they did not look in the least bit interested, and I seemed to be the one under investigation. They just stared back at me. It seemed they had been ordered to. *Perhaps they knew who I was.*

I stormed off, hurling abuse at some passers-by as I did so.

When I returned the next night the manager would not let me in. I complained to the police. On the way home from the nightclub I flicked a V at a passing police car. They came round the block and stopped. The two officers came towards me one asking if I was supposed to be taking medication. It was an insightful remark.

Whilst I was continually forming convictions, which, for my own safety, I should have discounted, I was in a game of death. I got up in the dead of night and made straight for the beach. I stripped off and now I was in the water. Nothing could persuade me that they were not watching even the slightest details of my behaviour via my MTRUTH. I dived through the waves and soon was out in the swell. Now I would find out for sure how far they would go, and I knew exactly where I was going. I swam for miles and though it was midwinter I started to feel warm. Soon I was far enough out to know I could never get back; so I swam on to make sure of it and then further still. Now I would teach the bastards who were doing this to me! When the strength was finally sapping out of me I could barely lift an arm and I was stiffening. I could hardly feel my limbs any more. Now I took my last breath, which I would hold forever and dived. I was diving with a Special Boat Service squadron. We were diving to the ancient lost Kingdom of Lethowstow to seek political asylum. I had proved what I had set to... whatever that was.[100]

****

I woke up, it was a bright windy morning with not a cloud in the sky; the sash window was knocking quietly in its frame. I leapt from my bed and had a bowl of Special K sitting at the breakfast table in the bay window. I thought of the music for the advertisement which had been taken from the first track on Caroline's first album, and now it came on the television. A chap was addressing the ball on the 5th fairway; behind him I could see the beach where I had run into the water in the dream. Details of my childhood came back to me. I was in my pram outside by the house, which was number 1 – the old show house. The sky was blue, and light clouds sat stationary in it whilst my pram and the house moved past them; my father had come home from work at the Ministry of Defence and was talking to me.

A few years later, aged five, I would watch, on the other side of the house, a man building a brick wall. One day I would sit on it and wait for the fire engine, which had just gone past, to come back. I waited for a long time but it never did. Twenty-three years later I would dream of that wall and in the dream it was being knocked down. A few days after that, I was driving along and was astonished to see the wall had indeed been knocked down and replaced with bollards. What possible explanation could there be for knocking down a perfectly good wall? The coincidence seemed too great and I was staggered by it. At the time I had no thoughts of MTRUTHs, EAIs, EAVs, EAHs or dream-machines. But now I knew I had an MTRUTH, through which I dreamt of the wall in dream-machine mode, even then, in 1989. If my KGB file showed me as the wall was being built, and later sitting on it, this was exactly the sort of trick I could expect MI5 to play. The fall of this wall was a strange portent of the Berlin Wall coming down, which it did six months later. Albeit a planned event! I was now party to that plan through my MTRUTH – to which the KGB, if not God himself, had access.

Now I remembered being on holiday when I was eight. My father had brought along an RAF inflatable lifeboat and I was rowing it in the sea at Bexhill. A Westland Whirlwind flew right over heading for the Royal Sovereign lightship. I could feel the down draught. I was as far out as I dared go and now made for the shore where I got out my telescope in time to see the helicopter landing on the ship platform miles out to sea.

With Christmas approaching in Newquay, I wrote to the highest legal authority in the ancient fiefdom of Sark. I soon received a reply from La Seigneirie, the abode of said official: the Seigneur, informing me that I could bring an action there from anywhere in the Kingdom. I put up my only Christmas decoration, an advertisement for Usher's Ale cut from the newspaper, the advertisement showed a Christmas tree and wished festive greetings to all drinkers of Usher's ales.

That night I got a taxi out to a nearby village pub. There was a simply enormous dog of a size and variety I had not previously encountered resting in the back. It was so large the cabbie had had to fold the seats down. I looked at its face and it moved its eye up briefly in a marginally interested way to set its gaze upon me, in that way a dog does, before sighing and going back to its business. Talking to the driver about his dog, an Irish wolfhound, I did not catch something he said and he repeated it, this time without the Cornish accent, or even dialect. I immediately shouldered some guilt at the death of the Cornish language, a death it had been driven to by prejudice, discrimination and stigma and which I felt I was personally, in fact, entirely to blame for and had just presided over. Really, it seemed, I had just put the last nail in its coffin. On the pub juke box I played *We Fly So Close*, by Phil Collins and with the regular apparitions of the Chief of Staff of the Irish Republican Army, Mr McGuinness, it seemed we were. There were other dogs in the world apart from Prince Charles's. But perhaps this had been his too, or rather one of them, though what would have been the point in asking the driver? I suppose I could have asked him how he got other passengers in.

One day I was in a shop near The Cabin buying a packet of Walkers' crisps. Later, perhaps the next day, I went to look for a packet of Golden Wonder ones instead, as I felt massively powerful and it seemed like Golden Wonder were having a bit of a rough time of it. They might help me. So off I went to look for a packet – but the whole town had been cleared of Golden Wonder crisps to see if I noticed. The more I looked for a packet without any success the more convinced I became I was on to something. Eventually I went into a shop right above the harbour, The Original Harbour Lights Fishing Tackle Shop. In the window I had seen a small ad for some club concerned with the Queen drummer. I made the Royal connection though there was none, bar Brian May playing the national anthem on the roof of Buckingham Palace five years later. In this shop I did at last find a Golden Wonder product. It was a single pink packet and contained Golden Wonder "Pink Panther" snacks. I bought the packet and ate them. On the packet there was a promotion for a 007 watch. I was left feeling very wise having made my decision to send for one, and when it arrived, and was strapped to my wrist, I sensed that I was so impressive that if the chairman of Golden Wonder knew, he would be the happiest man alive. Not a bad bit of fishing. Next day I saw a Golden Wonder sales girl carrying a Golden Wonder blue portmanteau. I was rather sorry for her and wondered what she would think if she knew what I had done. She had hidden all the Golden Wonder crisps in Cornwall inside the old tunnel where wagons were once winched from the harbour, right under my nose. I was just a big kid.

The whole atmosphere of this town was now one in which it felt like something enormous was going on. Any of the fishermen down by that quay would confirm in private this was indeed the case, I thought. One of them told me that before the quay was built there was a community there called Newis. This made me think: New Intelligence Service. So my next story may forever be cloaked in mystery.

I took to creating newsletters again, for private circulation only, sending one or two to Her Majesty the Queen. Something really seemed to be going off in my head and I was quite pleased with the new publication. I developed one or two catchphrases like "I know this isn't particularly funny, but that's not my job" – which seemed exceptionally amusing at the time. On Christmas Eve I happened to be looking at one of them. To prove to those spying on me that I knew it had been read, possibly by somebody entering the flat when I was not there, using a camera pointing through the floor of the flat above – *or through my very own eyes,* I decided to destroy my own creation. At the time the first two explanations for my feelings just did not come into it. So, on a windy Christmas Eve I marched down to the harbour. Here I held up the newsletter for the benefit of all those I believed were watching and, with my arms outstretched, tore it into tiny pieces. I let the pieces blow away into the waves – feeling proud that I had almost penetrated the highest level of security in the British armed forces. I say "almost" because the whole point of this experiment was that I was not actually sure I had – to the extent I would put my life on it. So on this occasion, I did not jump in after my torn-up newsletter. Nor did I suspect arrest by the Army Special Investigations Branch if I did – but certain death in the rough swell.

Back in the pub The Pogues' *Fairytale of New York* was playing, and I wondered if my life would be any different now if I had sent Amanda a copy the year it was released. The lads at the table next to me began singing along and, since there were no girls with them, it seemed they were all heartbroken too, and what was wrong with that? They were having a great time. I believed they were there by *and* with design. MI5 design. I remembered receiving the passion fruit from Amanda on Valentine's Day after I came back from Africa. I still loved her. I had built my dreams around her.

The next morning, Christmas morning, I found a present outside my door with a small Christmas greetings card, which did not say who it was from. The present was a jar of pickled walnuts, by Appointment to Her Majesty Queen Elizabeth the Queen Mother. It was the only Christmas present I got that year. I had never eaten such things before but really enjoyed them. I never did find out who they were from.

New Year's Eve arrived. Everyone in Newquay wears fancy dress on this night and I had hired an old RAF uniform for the occasion, supposing this to be a criminal offence. But I did not feel well and stayed in, having a bad headache. I wondered if the Special Intelligence Service had a drug which was known to produce an extraordinarily bad headache and this was their way to prevent the offence taking place. As I lay on the settee there came to me the vision of a beautiful blonde woman lying with her head on my chest like my now deceased pet Grateful Cat used to. Was this a portent of what was to come?

With the New Year a few weeks old I took a walk up to the cliffs behind the Atlantic Hotel. For some reason I could not fathom, I kept thinking, during the time I was in the town, that Rod Stewart was going to pay a visit, and would stay at the hotel. On the clifftop, overlooking the harbour and the Celtic Sea is a small white building looking not unlike a small folly in the estate of a large country house. This 'folly' was in fact a huer's house from where, many years ago, a man would keep watch for the shoals of pilchard – which could be spotted from it, high above the water. He would then call "hewa hewa" down a megaphone to the waiting fishermen in the harbour below, who would then set sail the short distance out to catch the fish. Sitting in the white hewing tower I had a brief moment of insight: what was I supposed to be doing now in my life, and in particular with my job? But, gazing out to sea, the sun sinking with beautiful alacrity for the evening's drinking, I thought: what were Captain Cooke and Charles Darwin "supposed" to be doing when they made their voyages? I was on a voyage, no less glorious than theirs.

Around this time a huge storm blew up. It got very windy and the roof began to blow away; so it was too dangerous to go out. I decided not to pursue my complaint against the police and, perversely, as though it was some kind of reward, I developed a new complaint, which was that I was being given pasties which had deliberately not been heated up properly. I asked for them to be put in the microwave but they came back no warmer. I issued my usual court summons, against the Crantock pasty factory.

I went to a nightclub and got extremely drunk. A transvestite sold me a rose and we started talking. A while later 'she' was violently sick in front of me; so I got 'her' a taxi.

Next day I had one of the worst hangovers in my whole life and did not get up until very late. But it wasn't the worst. I once had a hangover so bad I got on a train to try to get away from it. The train happened to be going to Kettering and here I wandered painfully and forlornly into town and into a pub, where I explained my problem to the landlord. He knew exactly what to do. He showed me a bottle, like a Tabasco bottle, containing something called *Endorphin Rush*. He now made me a ludicrously strong virgin mary and then, with his forefinger, applied the *Endorphin Rush* directly to my lips. Then he said "You've now got about as much chance of having a headache as somebody who was dropped into a bath of concentrated sulphuric acid five minutes ago!" He was not far wrong.

So that night in a pub I ordered a large tomato juice with Tabasco. I was told there was no Tabasco. I pictured large quantities of Tabasco in the close vicinity, removed from the bar in the previous few hours. The barmaid seemed genuine but I was suspicious. I went to another pub. Same story. Eventually I got back to The Red Lion and a very large bottle of Tabasco appeared which only had enough in it to provide a few drips into my tomato juice. Delusions of dirty tricks again.

Next morning at the breakfast table I could see out over the golf course to the crashing Atlantic shores, a good no. 1 wood and an iron away. There, a hundred new recruits to the Royal Navy (as I imagined them to be) could hardly believe their first posting included learning to surf. I reached into my pocket, or perhaps I reached to the floor. Either way I found myself looking at my now severely bent Yale key. I had the most peculiar feeling as though I had been briefly unconscious. It reminded me of the day I found myself conducting that voodoo-style ceremony back in Bedford. The room's countenance seemed inexplicably odd. I know not how, but it seemed some person had bent the key right in front of me whilst I was in some cataleptic trance worthy of a reread of Edgar Allen Poe's *Premature Burial* – as well as dropping a line to Ray Milland, who starred in the film. It was like time had been parted as in my dreamt dive through the waters down to Lethowstow; and whether this was the first time this happened or not, I soon began to add up the minutes of my life *these people were taking away from me in such trances.*

I looked at the panelled wall by the electric fire, and now found myself searching for a secret panel through which somebody had reached into my pocket and taken the key. All manner of explanations came to mind, from midgets hiding somewhere in my flat to my very existence being a complete fiction. I contemplated picking up the nearest object and asking a passer-by in the street, in an absurdly bemused and metaphysical manner, what matter really was. I went over to the door and tried the key. *It no longer fitted even though I had just let myself in with it.*

The door had not been open when I returned and the only explanation seemed to be that someone had been in the room with me. For whatever reason, and I have no idea what that might be other than my Uncle Louis Flynn having been a professional magician, I now found myself imagining the key gliding serenely down a length of thread, from my pocket. I do not know what happened when it reached the end of the thread because neither my imagination, nor my MTRUTH, revealed that. All I knew was that the key no longer fitted the lock it had just opened! I had no knowledge of having the same ability as Uri Geller and so was deeply mystified and fascinated by this incident.

I wondered if Uri Geller really did have some power I did not understand and actually could do what he claimed to. If that were the case, it seemed possible that the explanation for the key bending was a massive burst of psycho-mechanical energy transmitted through me. But really I just thought a magician had bent the key or replaced it with another whilst I was in the flat.[101]

That night in The Red Lion there was a magician doing card tricks at the table next to mine. He had some sleight of hand. Taking some money from my wallet I looked at the picture of Bruce Forsyth I had cut from a magazine, a picture in which he was holding some very large playing cards about five feet high. The magician knew what I had in my wallet. *He knew my hand.*

I could not but help overhearing the conversation at the table behind me. A chap had raised the issue of the percentage of married couples who had each seen their spouse's anus. I staggered away to the bar cracking up laughing, wondering how many times man and wife had, on average, seen their spouse's anus. What, indeed, was the record? Then I felt a bit stupid when I thought of a married couple one of whom was disabled.

In bed that night, there was heavy incoming on my MTRUTH, and I found myself psychically present in some control room whose location I could never know. The room kept being busted, and set up again somewhere else with a different unit – with the exception of one person. I seemed to have some remote sensory capability brought on by drugs. But I had not taken any drugs. So if any were involved, they must have come from the drugs cabinet in my wrist – or some other way. The control room was entirely populated by blacks. They had a limitless supply of new recruits who would dutifully torture me psychically in the most unpleasant ways. Life was too short and there were just too many of them to enable me to do anything other than let all hope drain away. I could feel it draining from my limbs too. It was truly unbearable. But I had to believe the control room was surrounded by the Special Forces. In that thought lay my only hope at the last line of defence of my tortured imagination. I had to see the torture as a privilege to face – I was being admitted to the Black Brotherhood, whose ranks themselves included members of the Special Forces.

Morning came. As usual the sash window made the quietest of noises as it gently rattled in the Atlantic breeze. I lay in bed and it began to hypnotise me. The slightest sound took complete control of my mind. Noises started emanating from a room in the adjacent house, noises I believed were as loud as the sound made by the broken sash cord in Club Rich UK hundreds of miles away in Bedford – zero watts. Even if it was that quiet, I was keenly aware from my training that it took the same energy as the entire cheer at the Cup Final to boil a cup of water. That's how sensitive the human ear is. But just how quiet was it really? I kept seeing, in my MTRUTH, Matthew Thomas, the owner of Club Rich UK, being carried out on a stretcher under a blanket. I did not believe he was dead, or that he was going to die, but that this was what was going to happen soon. Michael, the doorman, was the only one in the vicinity who knew the truth, which was that it was a Comic Relief stunt. Matt was going to have his death faked. He was going to join the Comic Relief undead. Now he was to be admitted to the New Order.[102] This, I believed, was actually happening as I saw it. But what was the correct interpretation of this vision? Matt, like me, had been given the privilege of having an MTRUTH fitted, his doorman, unknown to Matt, being the local controller.

I seemed to be facing a mountainous barrage of dirty tricks again. Even a printout of my bank transactions seemed to present strange patterns of figures and odd correlations. As I looked at those figures my face would have betrayed confusion. There seemed to be something odd about the statement. Maybe it wasn't *just* the statement and the explanation was that I was surrounded by such farfetched oddness that a baffling effect was *bound* to become apparent in those figures. I had another look and was not imagining it. The statement was quite clearly populated by a large proportion of figures like 999, 666 and 111. I was mystified and decided MI5 had put my bank account into some humorous freestyle accountancy mode. I imagined Professor Sir Roger Penrose[103] might be interested – interested enough to procure a divining rod for his sole use.

Coming back from the bank I saw a tall and very tired-looking chap wearing several layers of clothing coming along the pavement. Something told me he was an SAS MTRU and, rather like me, they had brainwashed the fuck out of him – but he was still going, though he did not look too good on it.

Odd things seemed to have happened in the NatWest Bank over the road from the building society too, when I enquired about my tenant's rent money, and now the music from the NatWest bank television advert seemed to be coming out of the sash window[104]. I had my head in my hands in the bed. Somebody seemed to be sprinkling dust through a hole in the ceiling. But I could see no hole. The room was becoming a perfect torture chamber. I was sneezing uncontrollably. Others may have flung themselves head first through the window, as in *The Tenant*, and not even bothered getting to the cliff edge. I could have checked the putty to see if it had dried yet after the previous victim of this terror machine had thrown themselves through. Perhaps there was even a dress in the cupboard, as in the film, put there by Roman Polanski in person for me to put on before the final act. I hid a letter to the police under the settee for a bemused surfer to find the next summer.

I decided to cut myself. If I picked up the knife and did cut myself, the Special Forces would burst in, and the experiment would be over. I was caught up in the furthest and most extreme regions of the Masonic Order and wanted to force the issue by flushing them out of hiding. I took the bread knife, which was not sharp enough; so I had to saw, and began sawing into my left hand somehow stopping just short of the vein. I now felt massive self-shame and horror. I could have sawed off a couple of limbs, maybe three, with a chainsaw, before death arrived and nobody would have found me until a couple of weeks of rent was due. Who came first, me or that soldier in the six counties on the sleeve of my Stiff Little Fingers *Alternative Ulster* 7"?

Ainsley Harriot, the television chef, began to appear in my mind as head of the Black Secret Service – the Black Brotherhood; who would suspect him? And I found myself, half-running down the High Street, shouting out aloud "Ainsley fucking Harriot! Please leave me alone! Fucking leave me alone!" The sudden massive sense of enormous realisation was too much. *He had been the witch doctor in Ouagadougou!* The silicon MTRUTH chip inside my head had switched to overload.

I had decided to end it, and was now running down to the place where there is a short stretch of fence by the old harbour railway. The drop was as much as 200 feet to where I had seen the filming. I talked angrily and then shouted "I am going to punish you for this!" I was tortured by the voices and hallucinations. These I could only reason were caused by my having accidentally got involved in a top secret Royal Navy psychological warfare experiment. This was waged by MI5 through any means, from dog excrement on the pavement outside my flat, to the witch doctor in Ouagadougou, to my MTRUTH. It was only the latter which had kept me going this long, as the belief enabled me to see my pain as a privilege, true decadence demanding masochism. I had learnt this from the master copy of some photocopies somebody had left on the photocopy machine in Brighton two years earlier – thinking at the time this had been deliberate in order to give me a clue about future events. But now I'd had enough and was determined to finish it, as I could see no end other than this one last thing I could do to punish my tormentors – MI5, so they would never forget it. I would make them regret what they had done by taking my own life.

I had already taken a running leap over the wishing well further along the cliff the previous night but had found myself balancing on the edge of the well, staring down the precipice, and not quite brave enough to jump. I now climbed the fence, wearing my black 'SAS' jacket. I was extremely angry and determined to finish it off, as a number of my friends, like Steve Treby, had already done, in other ways elsewhere. But I was not thinking of them now. I had believed it was not real, and felt sure I had seen Steve soon after his suicide, begging in a shop doorway near the Admiralty. I dared not say hello as I could not risk it *not* being him – sensing danger if it was. A little oddly his sister's boyfriend had the name "Pothecary", with one "a", by name (apothecary is an old name for pharmacist). Steve knew, like me, what shit the drugs were.

Right now my MI5 controller must have been looking at me as though I were a bucking bronco. I'd had enough of this MI5 MTRUTH prison. "This time you've gone too far!" I shouted. As my head came up above the fence, my attention was momentarily distracted by a white light at sea on the horizon in the direction of the *Lusitania* wreck – hundreds of miles away across the Celtic Sea, a mile or so off the Irish coast. Whatever the force was which the light exerted on me, I now climbed down the cliff side of the fence and walked along the narrow strip of crumbling tarmac. I climbed back over the fence at its southern end and walked away, somehow having succeeded in saving myself from falling to my death. I went and drank a couple of pints of Doom Bar Ale in The Red Lion.

The shock of having almost thrown myself to my death seemed to shake out of me the schizophrenia that had nearly killed me. I felt completely recovered, for a while anyway. Then up to The Atlantic Hotel, where I had never felt the victim of any dirty tricks, on this occasion having a pleasant conversation with an Irishman, the only one I met in Newquay. This strange psychic cloud now seemed to clear. I enjoyed a cigar.

The truth of the matter was that I was hovering in some kind of *Boys' Own* adventure story limbo, and I was finding it difficult to focus on a way ahead in my life. I would soon find a way. That night I had a vivid dream that a plaque was being reverentially placed at the fence where I had so nearly thrown myself to certain death. The plaque read something like this:

At 21:32hrs on 22nd February 1998, during a top secret Combined Forces Psychological Warfare Exercise, this fence was climbed by Captain Clive Travis, a member of an Admiralty-selected Special Boat Service Reserve squadron. Tortured into submission by a British Army Intelligence Corps Psychological Warfare Unit, Captain Travis had had enough and was determined to commit suicide to punish his tormentors as his last act. As he surmounted the fence, determined to jump, and face certain death, he was distracted by the light, on the horizon, of a Royal Navy ship that was being used for intelligence-gathering purposes. At that moment he was under the complete control of Her Majesty's ship. He now climbed down the cliff side of the fence, walked along the crumbling cliff edge, and climbed back over at the south end, returning to have a drink of Doom Bar Ale in The Red Lion, having narrowly cheated certain death.

Captain Travis went on to successfully engage the Irish Republican Army during the war against British Occupation of the "Six Counties" of the Irish Republic. As a result, and under Ship's rules, Newquay was secretly designated, on a 99-year leaseback agreement, to be part of the Irish Republic. Negotiations with the Irish Government relating to the future of Newquay were completed in 2099.

Captain Travis was awarded the George Medal for valour for serving on operational duties in the face of the enemy over 10 years and refusing to commit suicide. Within 24 hours of his death, as he requested in his will, his feet were hacked off using a black axe by the newest recruit to the Special Air Service Regiment in an ecumenical service conducted by the Chaplain of the Fleet. His feet were then buried down the wishing well with full naval honours, an Irish Republican Army Cadre firing a salute just inside the Irish Newquay. His body, without feet, was donated to Medical Science after a Church of England funeral a week later. His remaining ashes are now held in an Erinmore Empire Grown Tobacco tin, a gift from the family of Gerard (Gerry) Adams, the then leader of the political wing of the Irish Republican Army. The tin now resides inside the bottom left coat pocket of the Utilitarian, Jeremy Bentham[105], at University College London.

Ministry of Defence, 22nd April 2101

"I am the Master of my fate. I am the captain of my soul" – William Ernest Henley

The reason I dreamt that my feet would be so-treated made sense when I thought of a line in the song *Wishing Well* by Free: "The only time that you're satisfied is with your feet in the wishing well" and I had found this song playing on my mind in the same way the question mark in *Jerusalem*, if not *The Question* itself, had been. Actually Henley had one of his *legs* amputated. He was the model for Stevenson's Long John Silver for that reason.

I am not sure if the plaque should also say that during the half-an-hour after I climbed the fence so did Captains Unman, Wittering and Zygo, their perpetual absence from the school register in the film *If...*[106] now being explained as they were in the CCF and had been assigned to special operations – the procedure I was caught up in being timeless and continuous. It was a Special Forces initiation.

I now became convinced I should take my employer to the Employment Tribunal. Except I later thought I might better have sent a copy of my claim to the employees to raise morale, and claim a pay rise for the quality of my prose, if not the chances of winning my case. Either way, there remained the possibility that a moment's reflection could dissipate all my most terrifying delusions, if that was what they were, and not MI5 concept documents downloaded from a massive image database to my MTRUTH by a Cray Twin[107] supercomputer or

Google search.

I visited Newquay library, as I often did during these Cornish winter months and, as usual, picked up a book at random to see where it led me. On the very last page of one book I found a rather unusual and little-known organisation said never to have been convened. Well, I had my own ideas about that. It was the Wireless Telegraphy Tribunal (WTT) and was part of the Department of Trade and Industry. It seemed this organisation might prove very embarrassing to a certain small group of MI5 officers – those in the Special Intelligence Service. In Greek mythology there was the "Mare of Steel", anyone unlucky enough to be sent for a ride on it being sliced in half as it was like a children's playground slide but with a razor edge instead of nice wide and smooth stainless steel. Not surprisingly I was finding their MTRUTH to be the modern military Mare of Steel. They had expended so much care and attention into driving me out of my mind using this Mare of Steel I had been put on, and strapped to with the Mobile Tactical Reconnaissance Unit Telecommunications Harness, that if I failed to succeed brilliantly they would fail too. But, this being Great Britain, surely there was plenty of room for fair play and, in addition, I was sure there was also scope for some pretty heavyweight legal representation. This was why I always felt so comfortable in the library. I was enjoying high-level legal representation courtesy of all the authors whose books were on the shelves and transmitted a field in *Colchester*, which the WTT was sensitive to. That's how *Colchester* had been programmed.

Now, via my MTRUTH, the legal representatives of the authors knew I was aware of the WTT and therefore fair play dictated it be convened. Perhaps it already had and perhaps it was not true it had never been convened. Perhaps they had been continuously monitoring everything broadcast into my MTRUTH from day one, whenever that had been, or perhaps only now had they got access and were trying to catch up as a matter of great urgency. There might even be whole volumes of breaches of WTT orders to go through; including every single piece of virtual reality I had ever received. I wondered what they had made of the chap in Putney hospital's "incoming" – deciding they might not have been told about him. In any case, he was only receiving it like an hour's soap opera each evening at 7.30pm instead of *Eastenders*, the theme music being one of the tracks on the 2nd Skin *SAS battle-cries* demo tape, which the band (formerly on my record label) had recorded at their last-ever practice.

I had sent the tape to the SAS headquarters. I imagined an SAS language laboratory in which a variety of pieces of music were played to SAS recruits. They were asked to say which piece they most closely associated with. The reply would be, in a very high percentage of cases, the second movement on this tape: *SAS battle-cry II*. However one recruit would choose *Ernie* by Benny Hill – and be immediately sent on special operations.

A perfect calm descended on the world like nothing really mattered at all – when the Cray, Internet, *Colchester*, MTRUTH or whatever was unplugged. For maybe a minute-and-a-half in seven years my mind felt free of this electronic Mare of Steel. I decided my near-suicide over the cliff was solely due to further breaches of WTT orders pertaining to documents reaching me over my MTRUTH.

The calm having descended, I found myself following a sign to the nearby village of Porth Joke, sensing the presence of Princess Diana. She was wearing a Barbour. Enigmatically and unseen in the country lane, thick hedgerows on each side, I said out aloud "I think the Duchess of Cornwall might prefer it now she's 'dead'" feeling I was being listened to over my MTRUTH. This was a rare incident as I had maintained radio silence throughout this escapade (that is I did not talk to myself). Despite my intuition that I was indeed an MTRU, I believed I was in no position to go round making demands.

I still thought Diana's death was a real joke, and she was really alive but simply out of the press. Then I thought I saw Prince Charles's dog, Pooh, run past in the direction of Porth Joke. I was not sure the dog, or for that matter the Joke, was actually his – though it *was* in Cornwall. Perhaps they were one and the same and he'd never even had the slightest involvement other than in his position as Duke of Cornwall. Except Porth Joke was no joke, nor was it a village or even hamlet. It was a place, a place where the only inhabitants were wild animals, birds, fish and plants. Here, all was serenity. I later found there were even pictures of the Joke on the Internet.[108]

Somebody had left the gate open and a person resembling Victoria Wood walked past me. She had a Jack Russell on a lead, though again I was not sure whose it was. But this time I was quite sure the dog was really there. Either way, having found the Joke, I felt a deep sense of calm completion and I was at one with the world.

There were some people with their dogs sitting on a bench overlooking the Joke, and they said "Nice Day!" to me. There was another Joke nearby, unless it was the same Joke, or perhaps the same Joke from a different direction. All the signposts had led to the same place, a joke, for some time in my life. My presence here seemed fitting. Life was a joke and now I had even found one on the map. A piece of my heart would always be devoted to the joke much as it was to the Aird of Sleat back in Skye and Paradise in Wales.

Next day I would look up "joke" in the dictionary. It said "joke: a thing said or done to excite laughter; a ridiculous thing, person or circumstance" At once the table was completely cleared of every intelligence organisation I have mentioned. It seemed an all-powerful force, more powerful even than the Special Intelligence Service, had determined that I be here, at this time, in these circumstances, from the moment I drove in through the gate at Wilton some three-and-a-half years earlier. Only occasional bursts of existential behaviour of my own had succeeded in producing deviations from the path which led me to this place. Here, indeed, I found some completion; some closure; almost enough to effect a change in the weather – the change being effected by the erection of a sign saying "Ministry of Defence Joke. This Joke Is Subject To The Official Secrets Act, 1994." Here, as much as anywhere, I had found Prince Charles's dog – at a place said to be a joke.

Chapter Forty-Four

Come On

I fled Newquay early one morning, no longer able to stand my own presence there. I only had another few weeks' residence anyway, before the summer season began. I had filled in a court summons on behalf of my landlord from Windsor and his dog. The summons mentioned trespass, but not criminal damage to my key, and I left it on the table, with the fee, for him to submit. I was still convinced somebody had been in my room to bend the key, possibly Uri Geller, or the spirit of my magician Uncle Louis Flynn. I was sad not to say goodbye to McCoy, who had been most companionable. It was still hours before dawn as I made my way through town for the last time. Anyone seeing me by the road that morning would have seen a madman shouting a certain amount of abuse at nobody in particular as they drove past. It seemed many of them had been told to drive past and have a good laugh at me, as though I were an entertaining inmate of a Victorian lunatic asylum, ogled at, as they were, by paying families on Sunday afternoons a hundred years earlier. I felt I had been "got at" in Newquay. Appropriately, a district nurse gave me a lift out of town. Later I imagined she'd been sent to assess me. Whether she had or not I experienced a strong MTRUTH replay of Amanda, on one of the last occasions I had ever seen her, throwing herself at me from the driver's seat saying "Oh Clive!" as she did. This was happening over and over and it was difficult not betraying the reality of this to the nurse.

I headed for Falmouth and things were no better there, in fact there seemed to be even more dirty tricks ready, including the disappearance of my pen. In the face of these imagined tricks, I decided to buy myself a pair of new purple socks like those I might have been awarded by the University of London Rowing Club, if I had been a slightly better oarsman. I felt a little naughty in buying them, as I was not, officially, allowed to wear such socks. Wandering around town I noticed an old brick chimney. Someone told me it was the King's Pipe where Customs and Excise used to burn contraband tobacco, some of which the King would smoke. In the current state of things I was surprised it was not emitting smoke right then. I was sticking to my few cigars per day, UK duty paid.

At the bed and breakfast I hallucinated what looked like it must have been about four-and-twenty blackbirds flying out from under the sheet, whose elasticated corner had just pulled away from the mattress. I did not want to pay the full amount for the room feeling certain things were wrong with it – like the kettle not working properly. So I asked a policeman to be present when I paid the landlord the reduced amount: All most troublesome. Surely, I thought, things could only be better in Scotland and that was where I now headed; perhaps I might even find a wife there. In fact I was to find somebody else's.

Just after the train had gone past Essendine Summit, where, at milepost 90¼, the Mallard steam locomotive, LNER A4 Pacific No 4468, had set its still unbroken record speed of 126mph between the wars, I went to the toilet. I could see on my MTRUTH a chap in a black gown seated behind a desk. Then I noticed I was thinking in the second person and it seemed the questions were coming from him. Mind you I suppose thinking in the second person is not that unusual – I had often got up in the morning thinking: sort your life out! But there was something a little more acoustically vivid about this – and it seemed to come from the chap in the gown, not me. I did not feel inclined to answer the questions verbally, as I did not want to acknowledge that I was experiencing this "second person thinking"; so instead I answered the questions by moving my right knee for "yes" and my left knee for "no", making it quite clear the movements correlated with the questions. Of course my controller would have seen this, even though I did not say anything. When this had gone on for a few minutes the chap in the gown came around the table and started pushing on the side of my right knee; so I moved it in response. Then he pushed the other side and so I moved it in the other direction. After he had set my knee in motion back and forth he gestured as though to say "So what's going on there then Captain Travis?" Then he picked up a clipboard from his desk and ticked something on it.

This was most odd and I left the toilet, whereupon the second person thinking stopped, and I took up my seat again – wondering how much of what had happened had been really down to me. The implications of events in the toilet were obvious: if they could make me think in the second person they could make me think in the first person – and I'd never know it wasn't me! So I wondered: had the second person thinking in the toilet been a clue from the Special Intelligence Service as to how much control they had over me? I settled back in my chair to enjoy the journey to Scotland wondering what lay ahead for me.

Just after the train crossed the border a woman and child appeared near me in the carriage. "Come on Bethan", the mother was saying. This enraged me as I felt it was meant to show power was being wielded over me – yet conflicting thoughts were at work in my mind. I wrote "Fuck-off Bethan" on a piece of paper, screwed it up, and dropped it near her, placing the hyphen so as to create the fashionable complimentary adjective[109] and a get out. I did this because my policeman brother had a daughter by that name and I was paranoid, if you like, or exhibiting well-founded battlefield intuition if you prefer, that I was being followed, and not just via my MTRUTH. I had long before adopted the posture that the world was in conspiracy against me and, at this moment, I both did not want to be followed and yet realised the power it gave me if I was. Anyway I am not very proud of this, though nobody would have noticed this witchcraft of mine. But sorry Bethan, if it wasn't a compliment you were caught up in the Troubles for a moment, not the first completely innocent person to be. What more evidence did you need that side effects could poison relationships? There would later be more evidence the Bedfordshire Police had followed me.

I happened to be in a carriage in which was seated, opposite me, an expert in employment law. I was minded to tell him how I had encountered a man I imagined to be the Chief Of Staff of the Irish Republican Army posing as a farmer near Lidlington in Bedfordshire, the man in question having, it seemed as you will recall, driven out of the back of a US Army Chinook, unseen behind the trees. I thought of telling him how only my expertise in judo had enabled me to retreat unscathed in the face of a ferocious assault, only requiring hospital treatment for a small splinter in my left forefinger. I was not sure the Employment Tribunal would recognise the relevance to my claim for constructive dismissal of this legendary battle on the lower greensand. But you see my view of the world had become like a weather map on which the isobars had been replaced by lines joining points of equal influence of the establishment. As my employer was such a large company, and this incident had been not so far from one of its offices, it now became relevant to the spatial sensitivities of my mind.

I was also minded to tell him how, before I had gone to Edinburgh, there had been an incident at the building society in Putney, an incident which, would blow up in my schizophrenic mind to become part of the most damaging setback in my life. What had happened was that I had given some money to my friend Roger in order that he could make a payment for me on his credit card. Somehow the money went into limbo, my friend not making the payment. Instead he sent me a cheque to Newquay. But I never returned there. I had a discussion with the bank staff about this. At the same time a single payment of something like £177.77 had mysteriously appeared in my account. I asked the member of staff what this sum of money was and she told me it had been paid in at Colchester the previous week. But the previous week I had been in Newquay and I had not been to Colchester for four years. I was already convinced that somebody else had paid the money into my account, either by accident or, it seemed more likely, quite deliberately. The 'fact' that it had been paid in at Colchester meant that, if it had been deliberate, it could only be one organisation and that was MI5. *Colchester*, I still thought, was the codename for the virtual reality populated by the ultra-elite: those MI5 had chosen to be fitted with MTRUTHs. I believed I was caught up in a civil war – such beliefs gave me feelings of power and grandeur, which compensated for what I saw as insufficient success in my life.

Instead of speaking to the lawyer I asked a question of a man reading *Intellectual Property Monthly*: "Excuse me, who would I contact if I wanted to copyright next week?" He replied, a little dismissively, "You could not copyright next week – it wasn't your idea." So I asked him whose idea it was, and that was the end of the conversation.

Next to him was a geologist. I asked him which geological era we were in and he replied the Cenozoic era of the Quarternary period of the Holocene epoch. When does the next era start? I asked. He did not seem very interested so I said that you waited for ages and then two came along at once so maybe it was the Schizophrenician era. That was the end of that conversation too. I later discovered that in 1800 we entered the Anthropocene epoch.

I booked into a bed and breakfast in Dalmeny, where I once took a bath and served myself breakfast in somebody's flat. It was nice to have some money this time, though that was not to last long. I was suspicious of the room and poured away the water in the kettle. Something also seemed amiss with the window. I felt the urge to protect myself legally in some way, wondering why on earth North Bedfordshire Police Force was on Scottish television. They seemed to have followed me and, thinking of the Bethan incident on the train, this came as no surprise. If I was an MTRU such a media incident was not surprising – they were trying to get through to me. Fair play dictated I be given the opportunity to choose between appearing schizophrenic by claiming I was receiving messages from the television – or doing something more intelligent about what I saw in the media. Since I had poured the water away I felt it would be reasonable to make a legal record of having done so. This would justify my appalling lack of confidence in the cleanliness of that water – which, might have been poisoned.

After the television news item with the Bedfordshire Police, a very peculiar, but quite explicable thing happened. The set had no remote control and a problem with the vertical hold. Having no way to stop the vertical hold "going" without getting up from the bed, I gazed relaxedly at the screen, my eyes no longer focused on it. Then, after a while staring at what would have been a point far behind the screen (if the set was not there) my gaze passed to a point just above the set. At this moment a spectacular effect became apparent: the bed convincingly seemed to start lifting off the floor! The bed was levitating! But this was no schizophrenic hallucination, it was a well-known psychological effect: the waterfall effect. A similar effect is apparent if you stare out of the window at the ground just outside a train you are on. When the train comes to a halt the ground looks like it is moving in the opposite direction to the one it had been. You can also observe this effect when the aerial photo at the start of *Eastenders* stops revolving and when you dismount a running machine at the gym. It occurred that if the vertical hold had been "going" in the other direction then instead of the bed apparently levitating it would seem to be sinking. I briefly toyed with this observation as having a marketable value: perhaps I could patent such a bed. It might be particularly useful for manic-depressives.

At random I picked up a book of poems and epigrams by Alexander Pope and begun reading:

> *Engraved on the Collar of a Dog*
> *which I gave to his Royal Highness:*
> *I am his Highness's Dog at Kew;*
> *Pray tell me Sir, whose Dog are you?*

I wrote it down and put the copy in my wallet deciding I would go to Kew and hide it as a little present somewhere for MI5, watching as they would be, on my MTRUTH. It seemed that, here in Scotland, I had a clue as to the whereabouts of Prince Charles's dog again. What is more I needed to let people know. And yes they would!

Next morning I encountered yet another dodgy shower likely to cause a massive social uprising, the overthrowing of government, and nationwide anarchy. I determined to ask for a partial refund again as I had obviously not enjoyed its full benefit. The landlady was not at all impressed by my request, and ordered me out of the house even though the time to vacate the room had not been passed. She then called the police. I apologised to the child in the room for her behaviour, noticing that their cat looked rather more like a pine marten than the majority of cats. If the Scottish Secret Service had any sense, she would have had to experience my ultra-mythical presence behind a screen in the Sheriff's Court, where a Mr Billy Connolly (star of *The Man Who Sued God*) would give evidence for me. Life, I was now as certain as anyone could ever be was a joke, so Mr Connolly was welcome to represent me or even pose as me. This would be a unique occasion. The High Court in Edinburgh had never before required the presence of an employee of the Ministry of Defence to demonstrate, using modern morphing software, that a litigant was right in his evidence that an animal did resemble a pine marten more than the majority of Scottish cats.

Later that day I met a simply beautiful girl who invited me to meet her in a pub near the High Court. In the evening I went to the pub determined to take her out for a curry but she did not turn up. Oh well. That night I had a dream. I had met the girl as planned, and we were now married and it was the year 2030. I was now a retired motorway policeman. We were driving around the M25 when I spotted what appeared to be an enormous pile-up on the opposite carriageway. "Looks like a job for Retired Motorway Policeman darling!" I said, as I pulled over onto the hard shoulder. In the boot I had some road traffic accident (RTA) screens, which I had kept from my years patrolling the motorways in the Thames Valley Police. Hurriedly I set up the RTA screens around our car during a gap in the traffic and through a spyhole in the screens I watched morbidly all the goings-on on the other carriageway, trying to discern if the accident were real or not. There were flames and thick black smoke was billowing into the sky whilst the screams of those burning to death trapped in their cars assaulted my ears.

"It's a good job we were going by. You can never be sure if these accidents are real or not darling. You know it takes years of experience to tell a real motorway pile-up from a fake one. Ah no – they won't fool me. Quickly darling hand me the checklist could you," I said, almost unable to see the smoke was so thick. I was running through the check list, developed over many years experience at the scenes of real and fake RTAs when suddenly, a full race trim high-powered motorbike shot past on the near carriageway driven by a German Shepherd dog. Riding pillion was Prince Charles's missing dog, Pooh. Heaven knows what it was doing in 2030. He must have got another one. "Good grief darling! Did you see that? These Security Service people know no bounds when it comes to concealing whether RTAs are real or not. It's probably just a diversionary manoeuvre."

Then, following the motorbike in hot pursuit was an enormous procession of emergency and military vehicles including Princess Diana's hearse. The Princess was fed up of pretending to be dead and was trying to get out of her coffin. Overhead was a swarm of helicopters including one for each national newspaper, all in pursuit of Prince Charles's dog. Even Max Hastings, once editor of *The Daily Telegraph*, had somehow made it through to 2030 and his helicopter was piloted by one of his Labradors... the scene was bizarre. I woke up. I got up, remembering a chap I had met in hospital who told me he kept seeing road accidents that weren't really there.

Within days I was making further enquiries about the sum of £177.77, and the sum of £55, which had also gone into limbo. I was also intrigued by the way, having left a bag of clothes on Roger's doorstep back in Putney, somebody had bothered to open the bag and take all the CDs at the top – including *Urban Hymns*. Their disappearance had further upset me psychologically. I demonstrated I was ill by complaining about the theft of the CDs at the police station – four hundred miles from where they were taken. The officer looked annoyed and I could see why, but my behaviour was explicable[110]. This issue, along with the reappearance of *Colchester* in my thoughts was making me very angry, and not only that, I became convinced I would be wrong to discount the possibility I'd had my drink spiked in The Last Drop pub. Outside this pub, on the Grassmarket, executions once took place. I felt I was being subjected to some pretty severe punishment too. The cigars tasted like they had been dipped in arsenic (as well as the rum they were supposed to be).

 Maybe the cigars were alright, I thought, but rather something in my blood was making them taste like that. I was like a moth and therefore could detect tastes nobody else could. But this was not new; I had experienced hallucinatory taste at least twice before, years earlier. But if I *were* in *Colchester,* why had I not met anyone in it? Well actually I had: for example the chap in the black gown and the chap with the orange. I was reminded of the shortsighted librarian in *The Twilight Zone* who somehow survives an apocalypse only to be left crawling around in the rubble of the library having lost his reading glasses. But the truth about the cigars was more likely that if you smoke too many, they do not taste so good.

Things were getting ridiculous, and sitting in Maggie Dickson's pub, an incoherent old man offered me a sweet, which I took, I imagined, in the manner of a man with his head down the throat of a gift-horse. The pub is named after a woman hanged in 1728 for concealing the fact that she was pregnant with an illegitimate child. However, two miles into the journey to take her body back to her native Musselburgh for burial, noises were heard coming from the coffin – and Maggie was found to be still alive. The case threw up an interesting quirk between English and Scots law – if the case had occurred in England, Maggie would have been put to death, as the law there required the condemned to be hanged until dead. But in Scots law, Maggie was legally dead – and at liberty. She became known as "Half-hanged Maggie". I was beginning to wonder if *I* was being executed.

I was of the opinion that whatever the reason, I had been given some form of amphetamine in the sweet. I began parading around the streets as only Ian Brown (from The Stone Roses) would do, making pointing gestures at the ground and to passing police cars, demanding £100 be delivered there and then. If I were an SBS officer seconded to the Special Intelligence Service, why were they not paying me, I asked. There had to be something in this for me and maybe I was just not asking hard enough. I had quite forgotten my car service and the Turbo cider.

A car drove past and from it I heard Bruce Springsteen singing "'cause tramps like us, baby we were born to run." I had little doubt this was a careful MI5 manoeuvre with me as its target. I dialled 100 for the operator concerning the £100, thinking MI5 were monitoring the call, and the lady asked me politely, though somewhat panicked, where to put the money. I hung up. I now apologise to her for the alarm caused. I walked past the sign under the George IV Bridge announcing the birthplace of James Connolly, which I had noticed on my previous visit. I had to check another me had not hurled his self in my direction off the bridge. There, above my same old workman's hut, was a twenty-by-twenty feet projection of the cover of the former Stone Roses singer Mr Brown's new album, *Monkey Business*. Everything that had happened, including this, now seemed astonishingly prescient of magnificent future events.

I had not seen this type of advertisement before and could hardly have been more astonished if, in reference to a line from one of the songs on that album, the biggest chandelier ever made had smashed through the sky destroying the hut, together with the Cowgate down-and-out centre along the road, leaving me untouched and barely ruffled, because both were now empty. After all, what did I expect? I was sure the projection was aimed at me and they had so much control they had psychically frogmarched me up to it; having as I then did, as much free will as a carefully chosen sheet of newspaper blowing down the pavement in the wind. I felt totally taken over by Ian Brown's persona.

Fearful of forced hospitalisation, this being part of the reason for my presence in the Scottish jurisdiction, I reasoned that the Edinburgh Royal Infirmary database would not indicate anything concerning my mental health. So I went there and made the risky request for a blood test so as to be able to know if I was schizophrenic or had been poisoned. As for what "schizophrenic" meant I was beginning to formulate my own beliefs on the matter. You see I had symptoms, which I surmised were due to both speed and heroin in my blood. On one occasion I could see an Army officer on my MTRUTH saying "Really rubbing it in." And at the same time, rubbing something into my vision, which felt like very pure heroin being released, using some novel drug-administering device suitable for somebody with ocular cancer. The feeling was extraordinarily pleasant and, apart from being the same sort of effect as described by Dostoyevsky, I could only deduce I was indeed, once more, being given heroin: *in my eyes*. However as to how I had no idea other than by having been put by MI5 into the Royal Army Medical Corps Palliative Care Hospice for the Terminally Ill again.

After a short wait the usual tests were performed. These included noting: whether I was in a wheelchair or not and whether any limbs had very recently been severed – including my head – a six foot fountain of blood shooting from my neck over the curtain to soak the patient in the next bed a bit like in the *Monty Python* "Anyone for Tennis?" sketch. However these tests did not include one that showed whether my toenails had a nasty fungal infection, which made my presence in Scotland a criminal offence. The attractive young female doctor was staring into space over my shoulder as she examined me. She was a Scottish MI5 MTRU, reading my medical notes on her MTRUTH.

My request for a blood test was refused. My trip to the A&E was not completely wasted though because I discovered that in the patients' toilet was a tap in the plumbing which, I conceived, turned off the water supply to a whole ward full of water-driven life support machines. I thought of turning off the tap – and the consequences of doing so. This would have the result of cutting the waiting list for treatment considerably as I might see in the next day's newspaper, where the ruling politicians would claim credit. I think I just turned it down a bit.

The problem would not go away though and I was forced to return in some desperation the following day. This time I encountered a real scumbag of a Registrar who could not even diagnose me as wanting to have a crap. He looked like he would grab me by the scruff of the neck and remove me, not just from the hospital, but also Scotland. Funnily, I seem to recall he was English.

I now attempted to get help from a private hospital, which I called from a public phone. In an intelligence service full press, the controller can 'walk' his cell from phone box to phone box (or cell to cell) as the subject moves around, in case he makes a call and it needs to be monitored. It seemed perfectly clear that, when I called the private hospital, it was a bit more private than I had anticipated and that, in fact, I was talking to a member of an MI5 amateur theatricals group, posing as the hospital receptionist. She had also posed as the operator when I asked for the hundred quid.

Next I made my way to the police station again. Being deluded, I might have expected a better welcome, including perhaps a wee dram; after all, I had told them Bedford Rowing Club had been burnt down by the Masons in an insurance fraud to enable them to build a better one – a constable who was a member of the club strangely being the first on the scene having set fire to it for a favour, I opined. I had told them this by placing a scrap of paper announcing my paranoid suspicions down the hole in the top of a traffic cone outside the station, watched, of course, by Scottish MI5 officers using me in my passive MTRU mode.

An officer tapping his forehand with a biro came out to the front of the desk. I told him I wanted the police surgeon to take a blood sample to which he replied that there was no police surgeon. This statement sounded somewhat blasphemous, having as I did, augmented my begging outside the Episcopal Church of Scotland in Lothian Road by actually worshipping inside on Sunday. Not that the police surgeon is generally regarded as a religious figure. I threatened to call 999 for an ambulance once released if he did not let me see the police surgeon and asked him, as though I was from MI5, if he was party to the operation of British Telecom systems. At this point a number of other officers of the Borders and Lothian Constabulary, one female, appeared and I was subjected to some kind of ritual Masonic torture. Perhaps there was a hidden button to be pressed whenever somebody was about to be given this type of treatment. I was forced to the ground where kicks rained in on my body. These I counted out for the benefit of MI5: fifteen of them. They could see the situation through my MTRUTH, if not then, on the day's intelligence briefing at 7.30pm, this also being seen by my friend in Putney Hospital on his MTRUTH. I now suffered excruciating pain from the handcuffs.

I was dragged through to a cell where my head, held by the hair at the back, was smashed to within a fraction of the floor, my body held in a painful jack-knife contortion using the handcuffs. They left the cell. I think they were probably just showing me who was boss.

On the back of the cell door was a yellow notice announcing the existence of the police surgeon, whom I was not to see. Now I took the opportunity of making a representation to the Deemster Cain, in the Isle of Man, whom I had previously written to, and Alan McGee, the Scot and founder of Creation Records. In desperation I spoke out aloud to both of them, imagining they could hear me, either via my MTRUTH or bugs in the cell. There was no reply – perhaps they weren't in.

Then, a while later, I was ordered out to the charge-desk where the most ludicrous ever trumped-up charge of assaulting five police officers was made on me – to my mind a bit like arresting six million Jews for punching Mr A. Hitler. Sometime later I was taken to another police station, not on this occasion being in a state of mind sufficient to imagine all the occupants having been shot following my departure – as I had done following my visit to Reading Police Station in 1994.

In the cell, any voices in my head stopped. Instead I could now hear *Amazing*

Grace being played on the bagpipes over my MTRUTH. This went on for the next 24 hours, including in the Court House where I was granted bail to appear again in a few weeks time. I sat there and thought, Jesus, I'm not imagining it, I can actually hear *Amazing Grace* playing over some reserved military communications system, not from the room, or through the window, but from inside my head! I moved around the room to see if it made any difference and it didn't. I imagined the tune was being played real-time in a glen somewhere. This was my welcome by Scottish MI5. There was some justice available. I was free again. I was ecstatic! The rest of my SAS/SBS Dirty Dozen unit would hear of this over their MTRUTHs, and all come flooding north of the border for the blissful release from the voice transmissions with which they too were being tortured. I had done it. I walked around the cell with my arms in the air elated that the torture was over. I felt like a film star receiving his Oscar. Only a very small percentage of the population would have the technical expertise to realise, not that they were schizophrenic, but that they had been turned into an MTRU and, wherever they went to the day they died, that they would always be in *Colchester*.

So when I heard the music playing, and it did not go when I blocked my ears, you can imagine what a relief it was. I also learnt, when I covered my ears, that Scottish MI5 had no desire to prevent me from knowing I was actually listening to a radio transmission, as they could have done by say interrupting the transmission with silence when I put my hands to my ears. This decision could only have come right from the top – Lord Mackay of Clashfern. Of late, whenever something had happened which I was not sure of, I had hummed the tune *Can't be Sure*, by The Sundays. This was my way of using standard Special Forces schizophrenia avoidance techniques (a sort of musical CBT) whilst displaying a bit of English pride (the lyrics start with "England my country, the home of the free"). This brought my Englishness to the fore and being that Lord High Chancellor (as opposed to just plain Lord Chancellor) is a position only available in Scotland this, therefore, was a major international incident.

How would they have known if I put my hands to my ears? Well, either by watching with hidden cameras in the cell or those in my eyes. Simply monitoring the movements, not only of my head, but all my limbs, including my fingers, all of which had a number of lodestone chips inserted in them would also suffice. I remembered the Queensferry Burryman and decided, once again, I had been the only ever English one – even if this was in no more than a purely virtual world it was nevertheless *Colchester*.

I believed at that moment that I did indeed have radio equipment fitted aurally and subcutaneously, and that a Scottish doctor, probably in the Army Intelligence Corps working from Army HQ Scotland at nearby Kirkliston had prescribed the music. The dose came with dramatically reduced subliminality, to be taken forcibly under Section 3 of the Mental Health Act (Scotland) 1983. I could see footage of the doctor writing out the prescription, which a member of the Band of the Black Watch collected for me, as I was too ill to collect it myself.

Amusingly I remembered how, under that section of the Act, after three months of the treatment one can seek a second opinion. Much as I was enjoying listening to *Amazing Grace*, three months seemed a bit long to wait to find out that a mistake had been made in the prescription and I was only supposed to listen to it for three days. What sort of doctor would think anyone could listen to *Amazing Grace* for more than three months constantly without some sort of adverse consequence? The patient might be a concert pianist for example and *Amazing Grace* would be something of a distraction during his performance, particularly if the whole orchestra had the same problem and were sworn to secrecy. Perhaps the director of one of those Japanese television torture programmes might be interested in all of this: it was WTT (Scotland) territory. As for the Public Health Laboratory I wondered how long it might take them to realise what was going on in this circumstance, or the one where many people were complaining somebody had put a branch outside their abode, an action I was now quite obsessed with. Anyway I'd choose *Amazing Grace* over anxiety depression and akathisia any day, and that was why my unit were headed this way.

During the night I was transferred to a cell beneath the Court House. *Amazing Grace* was still playing away and, after what I had been through, before deserting Newquay, I loved every minute of it. But I felt that not everything was what it seemed. I imagined the police in Edinburgh West End Station had taken me quite seriously, and suspected I was now an English/Scottish MI5/KGB double agent MTRU. So I pissed in a polystyrene cup and left it on the toilet so the police surgeon could test it – the result being unknown to me.

Next day I was released and went to the aptly named McCourt's solicitors on George IV Bridge Road where, free of charge, he filed an official complaint for me. Whatever had happened in police custody I seemed cured of the problem upon release so I did not pursue the complaint. As I left the solicitor's office I overheard a conversation about a case, which included the remark: "At the end of the day we'll find out this morning." The remark became still more amusing when nobody laughed – so I let off a huge guffaw as I left the office. Perhaps the remark was a little more pertinent and considered than I imagined.

I saw myself as an SBS/MI5 sociological stinger missile raising funds for Comic Relief. Whether I had allowed myself the luxury of being 100 per cent certain Princess Diana was not dead hardly came into it, though I *was* 100 per cent certain. It seemed I had the duty to discount the possibility she really was dead, as, if I did not, I would be unable to adopt the desired military posture.

Wandering around after the appointment I came across the statue of the piper from the Band of the Black Watch. I noticed a small piece of Sellotape stuck to the black fence in front. It reminded me of all the tape still stuck to the fence outside Kensington Palace where thousands of flowers and messages had been left following Diana's car crash. I peeled one off and stuck it, again for luck, on the front of my army surplus trousers next to the piece from Kensington Palace. I thought I might have been being watched as I did this – as you will see.

Now it has to be said I was seeing pretty wild things on my MTRUTH around this time, following *Amazing Grace* playing perfectly audibly in my head for 24 hours. For example I kept seeing Lord Mackay of Clashfern. Every time he was making that quick swivel of the head to one side and back which a person does when impressed with something. In my case it might have been the line from the song entitled *Erin-go-bragh* sung by Dick Gaughan which goes "Yer all turn to Scotsmen as soon as yer here." He wished me to know he agreed with that sentiment and also that I was obviously a good example, which could be well exploited for reasons of Scottish national security.

Then, after another unsatisfactory encounter at one of the building society branches I felt so angry that I marched off straight to the George IV Bridge and balanced precariously on its fence shouting "Is this what you want?" as a strangely disinterested traffic warden passed. Dangerous.

One day I found myself in a pub by the Forth in Leith. The gloriously appropriate *Step into My World*, by Hurricane #1, was playing on the jukebox and I hallucinated a bloke I thought was in an elite army unit, walking his dog and throwing a Frisbee for it to catch. I felt a wonderful wave of grandeur breaking over me – MI5 were entertaining me! Once again there was no limit to my self-aggrandisement.

Later that day on the Royal Mile my mental state was proven in a less pleasurable manner when a running chef (wearing chequered chef's trousers) spat right in front of me. It did not even occur that it might be an ancient tradition (there was) that it was bad luck not to at that exact spot – whether I was there or not. And the fact that I had once had my written-off engine replaced at the chequered flag garage enabled me to make a deluded inference about his trousers.

A few days later, as I sat on the bench by a statue of a dog called Greyfriars Bobby, an Irishman who later gave me money while begging, sat with me. Our conversation seemed like a small play worth staging, my cap being the nominal subject. I wish I could remember all that we said. What I do recall is what he told me was his palindrome "Detail of Eden: olive evil one defoliated". I thanked him for letting me know; asking would it not be better if the word for palindromes was a palindrome itself. He looked thoughtful for a moment before furnishing me with the word "retrovorter" which, he assured me, fitted the bill etymologically. I later lost this second cap, bought from Mr McPherson, Church Street, Inverness and with it went my memory of the play. A pity. I still had my life however. I went into a bookshop and picked up a book about "Greyfriars Bobby". According to the book it was nothing to do (as my illness told me) with a policeman back at Greyfriars Police Station in Bedford, but a dog, the statue of which I had sat next to with the Irishman. The dog belonged to "Auld Jock" Gray, a Pentland Hills farmer who each market day dined at John Traill's restaurant in Greyfriars Place. After Jock's death in 1858, Bobby supposedly continued to turn up for food at the restaurant when not pining on his master's grave in the nearby churchyard, a grave the dog is said to still haunt.

Amused by this, I wandered off to try another branch of the building society. There they told me that, in order to tell me who had paid the sum of £177.77 in, I would have to make a payment myself. I felt convinced there was something very much amiss, and refused, though perhaps that was a mistake. I was ready to consider I had merely imagined MI5's involvement, and therefore the possibility arose that I had simply received someone else's money by accident, most likely because their account number was very similar. But I wanted to believe they had paid it into my account deliberately because I wanted to believe in my delusion that Diana was not dead – and I did believe it. The fact that I had been told the money was paid-in, in Colchester just reinforced my delusion. An interesting combination of psychiatric symptoms, not believing the Princess of Wales is dead or that the Prince of Wales ever had a dog called Pooh. Quite aside from schizophrenia itself, hopes, beliefs and a desire for power and meaning in life are a very potent combination, none of them to be discounted in a search for the cause of this illness. Diana was helping me from beyond her own grave, from her holiday on the island of Mystique, and she helped me write this book, hence my reward to her of her charity being one of those all my royalties go to. So had MI5, by being there and making me think they had arranged the building society Colchester malarkey, even though I'm now sure they did not. I'm not giving them any. My reward to them is my loyalty.

As I had gone straight (by resorting to the Law instead of smashing up cars) I was going to continue that way, as I perceived there to be no hope otherwise. You see I did not think the money was mine. A member of staff now told me that the sum had not in fact been paid in at Colchester but at the Newquay branch, which had a similar number. Then I found myself experiencing the florid belief that the staff at that branch had had a whip-round – why else would they pay some money into my account? I still did not get it because now I was told it was the manager who had paid it in and not I. It simply did not cross my mind that in fact I had paid in the money. I just felt I was being buggered about. The penny had not dropped, or had it? I sensed *a danger* that the money really was mine, which I did not want, and intuition told me to go and pay it as follows before I found that out.

So I withdrew the money and went over the road to the post office, and paid the money into the Diana Princess of Wales Memorial Fund, being now the standard-bearer of the Diana Princess of Wales Own Canadian Regiment, one of the regiments of which she was Commander-in-Chief.

I took the payment slip, went to another branch of the bank and, picking up some of the building society's customers' rubbish by the cash machine, put it all in a payment envelope into the fund. I now went into this branch and tried to find where my £55 was. I had a very amenable conversation with the assistant manager during which it arose in my head that he wondered if I was running some fraud. After some persistence I now received my £55, which was of use as, little known to me, I was soon to be on the street and penniless. I was absolutely staggered and at that moment I experienced a well-recognised psychological pathology: I almost did not want them to give me the money. I was so conditioned to my delusions of people being against me that it just did not seem right: I almost felt cheated. I now discovered that there had in fact been two payments, not one, and then the penny dropped. The money had been mine, had been from Her Majesty's Paymaster General and I had paid it in. It was money returned to me by the court in Truro, to which I had made representations under the name "Newquay le test pilote" giving me, I hoped, some credibility in the French Intelligence community, *Colchester* branch.

Next day I went back to the other branch where the member of staff told me that I had paid in rubbish to their cashpoint and I got the impression they might call the police. But what had actually happened? Well I was ill but I had been dangerously confused by the building society's mistaken (if it was mistaken) invocation of Colchester, I had lost over £100 and now was told that a payment slip to the Diana Princess of Wales Memorial Fund was rubbish. If there was any rubbish in that payment envelope it was the building society's, dumped on the pavement by its customers. But I had asked for it. Still, I was rather perplexed and had forgotten my earlier conclusion, which I had come to more than once, that the £10 million was "nothing" and would sort itself out. Diana was being held hostage in a parallel universe, and £177.77 would not go far to releasing her back into reality. But really it was I who was in the parallel universe.

I sat in a pub where I calmed down with a coffee and a cigar. I thought back to the day of the funeral. I knew Princess Diana was interested in people on the street and felt I had to do something about it. Having delivered my deluded case against my employer to the court, I was rather upset as I approached some lawyers in the lobby of the Sheriff Court. Here I said something marginally outrageous about being a refugee and having nowhere to stay. As I approached Scotland I had begun thinking I was in an open MTRUTH court rather like when the jury is taken to the scene of the crime but here augmented by a state-of-the-art military communications system. I saw these lawyers as being like-minded to myself – as MTRUTH jurors. But I might as well have delivered my case to the kilt shop. I did not think the situation could get worse, but it certainly did. However, speaking to this group of helpful solicitors resulted in me being on the phone to the landlord of a flat they found for me, advertised in the evening paper. I spoke to a Willy who told me that if no one was in, I was to kick the door down and leave the rent money with the chap across the hall and he would collect it later in the week. Justice was available.

The room was not far away with the kitchen overlooking Arthur's Seat, the rocky core of an extinct volcano and, sure enough, to gain entry the door had to be kicked in. The chap I was to leave the rent money with was a friendly type and he brought me in a television set with all the knobs missing, so I could only watch one channel. The bed, I was to discover, was a later development of the one back at Fairmile Hospital and had a spring sticking up through the middle, so it could only be slept on near the edge. What sort of justice was this? In the kitchen the chap made me a coffee. I told him the palindrome the Irishman had told me to see if it amused him whereupon he went to his room and returned with pages and pages of very strange English. The first few lines went "Star? Not I! Movie – it too has a star in or a cameo who wore mask – cast are livewires. Soda-pop straws are sold, as part-encased a hot tin, I saw it in mad dog I met. Is dog rosy? Tie-dye booths in rocks." The last were "See silliness, else we'll ask Cornish to obey deity's or god's item. I, God, damn it! I was in it! To Hades, acne trap, sad loser! As warts pop, a dosser I – we – vile rat, sack! Same row, oh woe! Macaroni, rats, as a hoot, tie. I vomit on rats." He let me note down the beginning and end of the palindrome to go with my mounting pile of legal documents explaining he was a bit of a palindrome fan and had a whole file full of them. Check it if you don't believe me. Noticing it had dog in it, this merely played with my illness. So I asked him if he had any more dog/God ones to which he replied, "Dog sex at noon taxes God"!

What I now did was in the realms of street performance. I had developed something of an interest, though not yet fully developed, in the strange and extremely sensitive lego-medical interface between the world at large and the State. Right now, my not yet fully thought out obsession with this gave me something of an interest in cash machines, and their occasional theft using JCB diggers. Of course I did not have a JCB; so had to take something of a different approach. I had already dabbled, in a throwaway manner, tapping my old Holts account number into a Royal Bank of Scotland machine. I found it did not then empty itself of hundreds of thousands of pounds onto the South Clerk Street pavement[111]; so I had to try another approach again.

Even in those early days of my third Scottish foray, I felt the situation was more sensitive to the location of events than might generally be considered. Therefore it seemed fitting that my next attack should take place on the building society machine at the branch where the pink receipt for the payment into the Diana, Princess of Wales Memorial Fund had been branded rubbish. I sensed they were not Royalists there, but I could have been quite wrong in that belief, as I hinted. Either way I could not get out of my head the idea that the business about the money being paid into my account in Colchester had been humorous MI5 mischief making.

So I set to the task of making account enquiries all night long and did so with some determination, having no funds in the account large enough to remove without a more unusual procedure than normal. Occasionally a queue would build up and I would tell anyone behind me that the machine appeared to be out of cash and there was another machine down the road. This enabled me to casually continue my line of inquiry though perhaps I was no nearer the answer to all this than I had been in, for example Holland back in 1994.

The hours went by and, monkey-in-a-Sputnik-like (the Russians sent into space monkeys which were trained to press a button to get nuts), I just kept banging in my inquiries. At one point I had a break and tried another society's machine. Here I was spooked at some point, this particular machine seeming to run out of inquiry slip paper after which it closed down, the shutter coming down like in Dr. Morbius's house in *The Forbidden Planet*. I felt a bit naughty at this and returned to Lothian Road.

Here quite a queue built up again and somebody asked me what I was doing. Mindful at the time that they could well have been sent to ask, I said I was giving a street art performance in a demonstration against a building society/MI5 corporate conspiracy. I even announced, mischievously, that other people in the queue were demonstrating with me, and one or two in the queue looked at the others in a funny way.

I did have a guess at how many inquiries I made. I thought it was about six hundred and I did not rule out the possibility the programme that ran the machine announced counts of unusual numbers of inquiries from one person at the building society HQ, though that hardly put me off. Come about 3.30am I decided not to still be there when the staff arrived the next morning, and felt I was satisfied with the performance sufficiently to go back to my bedsit to sleep.

There is a line in the song *Lucky Man* by The Verve, which sounds like "Watch my beaver growing". I had listened to it in the Fort Inn back in Newquay. Somehow I conceived that "Beaver" was the code word for my fundraising activities north of the border and not being Scottish I felt I should modify my approach, doing so without any frills and in a manner which was to the point. I felt my "Beaver" was indeed getting larger. In fact it was just what had been my own money: the £177.77 plus the £747.47 I had paid in, in Newquay. The real sum would be heavily geared to this and could be millions already! Having delivered a copy of my legal documents, deemed by me in my capacity as acting Lord High Chancellor to have no legal basis south of the border, I soon discovered that the Scottish court system was far more attractive to my untrained legal eye. Instead of putting "The Defendant cannot be sure where the Plaintiff puts the money", I said that the money for all my various legal claims, all held in a large Post Office carrier bag, should simply be paid into court. I also replaced Defendant with Defender, as that was what was required in Scotland.

It made it sound like a football match.

I had paid Willy a week's rent but within days of arriving in Edinburgh I found my employer was no longer paying me. I had a piece of paper signed by him telling me what to do with the rent, this constituting evidence that I had a week-by-week contract of a type covered by the Eviction Act (1977).

Unfortunately Willy unsurprisingly assumed I was taking him for a ride and he threatened to thump me if I did not pay him the rent when he came for it the next morning. I had to complete my initiation into the street-life by requesting police assistance to prevent my being evicted at 9am. No police presence being there as 9am approached I decided to make myself scarce. A while later I dared make an appearance, and two enormous labourers wearing kilts came in, put a transistor radio on the floor tuned to BBC Radio 1 and proceeded to smash up the wardrobe with sledgehammers whilst, by coincidence, The Damned sang *Smash It Up* was on the radio. As I watched them I sat down on the small occasional table that collapsed, making me feel a right prat. Then they removed, but did not replace, the lock in the door. I let them know this was my legal abode. Willy was there and told me I had to go, but then left. Still no police. After they had all gone the police arrived. An officer who looked more like the vet in *Daktari* (the '60s television series set in Africa starring a Land Rover, a lion and a chimp) informed me that I was in Scotland and that they had their own laws "up here" clearly informing me that I was the one in the wrong. Before I left the flat for the last time I noticed there was a small piece of Sellotape stuck to the lock. I drew the *extraordinarily farfetched* conclusion that I had been seen peeling the piece off the fence at the Black Watch statue as well as at Kensington Palace.

I went to the library and read the Eviction Act (1977). It seemed to be identical in Scotland, save there being some explicit recognition of intra-Scottish geography which appeared to make no difference to my situation other than that it was recognised: that is, it mentioned, the burghs of Edinburgh. So I went to a civil law solicitor below Mr McCourt's office, who happened to be an English lady. She looked like she could have been the sister of a bloke I knew at University who got a first in electrical engineering. This person, despite his first, did not know why there was less interference on FM than AM, making me think he might have cheated in his finals.

The solicitor wrote a letter informing my landlord it was my legal abode and he could not evict me without going through the correct procedure. I felt somewhat fearful of returning to deliver the letter, though I did, finding the lock had been changed. I hoped it would count for me someday if I sent him back the key to save him having to throw away the lock.

So now I had no money and nowhere to stay, and having no inclination to return home, either to my own, which was occupied, or my parents', I conceived I now had a duty to perform. It is a little difficult to know the real truth about the homeless if you are a Princess, even if you shave your hair off, put on a caftan and smoke roll-ups on a street corner to disguise yourself. I imagined Diana doing just that. The media thought she was dead. Few knew the truth and I was one of them. So therefore I had to go on the street too. Diana would not just spend her time as the undead in a nunnery, not to my mind anyway. I had seen a picture of her in the paper after her funeral. I drew a caftan on her head and gave her loads of heavy punk make-up to see what she might now be looking like. With her new image she could wander the streets unnoticed, perhaps passing me begging, dropping a single 50p coin into my hat. I saw another picture of her in which she looked much older than her years. This was how MI5 thought she might look by the time my actions rescued her from her media isolation.

I tried to see the film *Titanic* but could not afford to and found myself sitting in The Greyfriars pub scrounging a coffee off a Norwegian, and wondering what to do. I told him I would write to King David of Norway to thank him for the charity of his subject. Selling my writing on the street seemed to be cheating as I had done that before, or James Longhurst had, and I formed the impression that it would be wrong not to do what everyone else had to which was to beg. Diana needed to know what would happen. I asked a passing policeman to lend me a fiver and he called me a "cheeky bugger".

This was when I first believed I was in contact with the Ancient Order of the Beggars of the Orison (official uniformed beggars granted rights by The Monarch). Soon I was enjoying the warm sun of a bright and bonny Scottish morning in The Ark, a place I think The Duke of Kinnaird set up, where down-and-outs could get breakfast. It felt like some kind of great party no one else had been told about. I had only been invited to it by virtue of the fact that I had been seen sitting in the street forlornly. Armed with my free invite I was able to enjoy a full breakfast with copious quantities of coffee. Here I was overlooked by a portrait of the Duke. After breakfast I picked up a copy of what seemed like an appropriately titled book from the small but quite adequate library. I opened it at random and was mildly astonished at what I now read, as usual when opening books in this manner. I had been predestined to read this page. God was watching me. He was something of a philanthropist.

I chose somewhere to beg where nobody was around and put my cap out. I had not been begging long when an Army chap, rather older than me, appeared sitting next to me. He was eagerly operating an old-style wind-up calculating machine. As usual I had no idea if I was seeing this on my MTRUTH or if I simply had a vivid visual imagination. However it was clear that, whoever he was, he was not actually there. Where he actually was would be an interesting question. But what I was sure of was that there were accountancy issues in an operation to raise £10 million whilst begging on the street. I was not so sure as to the taxability of gifts received by way of begging. Either way I decided to keep a record of my beggings and, whereas previously I had sent the tax on my income in Brighton to the Royal Army Pay Corps, this time I decided to send my tax to Buckingham Palace. The sum was returned from Buckingham Palace with a compliments slip, which I felt to be rather a powerful document.

Whilst begging one day, I saw my SAS buddy again on my MTRUTH. He was the same chap I had seen years earlier in his electromagnetically-shielded den on Dartmoor, which he now appeared to have left. He was now using a top secret MoD "begging lever", in a classified MoD film, to enable potential donors to put coins in his hat without having to bend down, the Heath Robinson lever apparently being used inside a secret Army base somewhere. I would try to mimic him by hiding a £1 Scottish coin I had begged, behind the moss outside the Episcopal Church, where I noticed one of the stair-rod holders was missing. I would later write to somebody who seemed remotely pertinent, the landlord of The Ship Bedford, addressing him as Captain, announcing the missing stair-rod holder was to be replaced free of charge by Golding's, the local ironmongers in Bedford, established during the reign of Queen Victoria. This would be done whilst *Stairway to Heaven* played, Golding's making a small payment to charity for the inestimably powerful consequences of being advertised in the top secret DISC virtual world named *Colchester*.

Providing a free advertisement like this would later become a standard form of behaviour. Trying to make sense of my MTRUTH capability, I saw myself as a light aircraft like I had once seen flying along the beach in La Jolla, San Diego, U.S.A., with a banner trailing behind. Payments would be made to charity automatically by the company being advertised when the banner was spotted by computer through an MTRUTH in passive mode. I was not sure of the actual implications of providing this strange 'free' publicity though did feel the Grandmaster of the Freemasons would be more than just a little amused. So next time you see a beggar, don't forget he or she might be in the Special Forces on a mission.

Sitting on the step outside the Episcopal Church I wondered whether I could pray for monies and therefore argue in court that I was not begging. Then I noticed what I thought must be a fairly rare sight in Scotland: a Rastafarian on a bicycle. I would often see this chap going past. Years later I would hear that a tablet was held inside the church, which the British Army had looted from Ethiopia many years previously. It was being handed back. I thought of the chap on the bike. He was the chairman of the Dread Broadcasting Corporation whose T-shirt I had worn in Africa thirteen years earlier.

Then who should I see coming along the pavement but the Irishman with whom I'd had what seemed like a set piece conversation in A-level literature when we discussed my cap. He put a Dublin postcard in my cap, smiled, and moved off. But then he turned and flicked, most accurately, a coin from his forefinger using his thumb. I saw the coin fly through the air, the moment sticking in my mind. I could see the coin turning in slow motion before it landed in my cap. On the card I found he had written: A Famous Poem by a Pimlico Poet[112]

Who Are You?

If pomegranates make you hot
And you fling yourself in chairs a lot,
It might just be that you are filed
Under the name of Oscar Wilde.

If, in the past, you think you missed a
Sneaky chance to fuck your sister,
It could just be, you have to chew on
The fact you're Ian McEwan.[113]

If an omelette sends you reeling
With a dreadful sickly feeling,
Your egg's essentially a martyr
To the cause of Jean-Paul Sartre.

If red-haired girls and poetry
Make you drink excessively
And your lines don't always rhyme:
I rather think you're Charles Bukowski.[114]

Pimlico Poet

I noticed the coin was most strange: a 1994 2p coin, which had the same colour as a 10p coin. Most peculiar. It reminded me of Wilton. The coin had been minted especially.

After I had begged a few pounds I headed for the Cowgate Centre to get lunch. When I turned up again later that evening to get somewhere to stay that night they gave me a bus fare from the kitty and sent me to a hostel. But before I left I hid a piece of paper, Arne Saknussem-style once more, down the side of one of the new chairs. The chap with the poem was from the IRA, so I had written "Sandline GB" on the paper (Sandline is a British company which provides military services on a hire basis. Many of its employees are ex-SAS and Parachute Regiment). The hostel was for people with psychiatric problems and the next morning I had to speak to a psychiatric counsellor. I chose not to admit I'd had any psychiatric problems; so I was asked to leave as that, supposedly, was not a suitable place for me. The next night I was back at the centre, which I believed to be some sort of peace process negotiation office, and was sleeping on the floor with "Panda", his friend who looked and behaved like Oliver Reed, and various other characters, not all of whom were to kick me where I lay trying to sleep, shouting "English bastard!" as they did. Panda told me a joke. A panda went into a bar and ordered drinks and lunch. The barman said "We don't serve pandas." The panda pulled a gun on him, so he took the order. The panda took a seat near the pianist. The barman brought over his lunch and drink. When he had finished the panda got up and shot the pianist dead. The barman rushed over and said "What was that for?" The panda took a dictionary off the shelf, opened it on the page with panda, pointed at the definition, and left. The barman read the definition: "panda: black and white furry animal, eats, shoots, and leaves."[115]

I sought help from the DSS and the council, and gained the impression I was trapped in a suicide machine. It certainly felt like every single person in the process had been instructed to tell me the exact opposite of what I needed to do in each case, from the wrong place to go to, the wrong person to ask for, and the wrong form to fill in. One of the people I saw bore the name of the well-known Scottish Nationalist, Salmond, which again aroused my suspicions that the word windup was not new to the Scottish language: I was not quite in the state of mind to see this as a compliment. She told me I could not claim benefits because I was not unemployed, even though I was not being paid. I just seemed to get sent back and forth from office to office and building to building in a never-ending series of emotional flagellations, leaving me shouting angrily and abusively at the staff that half the time seemed to be deliberately annoying me. Of course the reality was that I should have been contacting my employer. But the truth was that I was enjoying my psychotic freestyle too much.

Back on the street I saw my SAS buddy once more on my MTRUTH, sent by Scottish Army HQ nearby from the Royal Army Medical Corps Palliative Care

Hospice for the Terminally Ill – or in my case Insane. He appeared to be driving a specially modified car, which had a super-accurate speedometer. I wondered what this all meant and came to two conclusions: (a) The Borders and Lothian Constabulary were using my MTRUTH to automatically dispense speeding tickets to the registered owners of passing speeding cars and (b) Army HQ Scotland had an extremely accurate novel drugs-administering device. Hence they kept similarly accurate tabs on their top agent in the Ancient Order of the Beggars of the Orison – me. I had been admitted to the Order. I was six feet two inches, sitting 33 and 24/1000th of an inch south of the missing stair-rod on the steps of the Episcopal Church of Scotland in Lothian Road, on 21st May 1998 at 15:21hrs and 31 seconds. At this time I was given, on orders, an extremely accurately administered dose of speed (amphetamine sulphate). On other occasions it seemed to have been heroin; another drug which made Hamlets taste appalling and a third drug known by the Security Services to produce a monster headache: A strange present from Scottish MI5. I had been given it to see what I was made of. I also found myself thinking I knew the name of the drug administered that gave me this extraordinarily bad headache: Clembutol. I went to the library to find out about it. I could only find a drug called Clembuterol along with, disturbingly, its LD50 test statistics on mice and rats. I was beginning to think I was in an LD50 test of my own. I was reminded of my crazy 1994 convoy as I saw a Sherpa LDV Convoy van drive by to order. I wondered just how bad this headache had to be to provide a lethal dose to 50 per cent of test MTRUs and masochistically imagining the unthinkable – a headache worse than the one I already had. I am still mystified by the apparition of the name of this drug in my mind – let alone the morality of finding what it takes to kill half a group of animals for no reason.

Sitting in Princes Street with the monster headache, I sensed I had caused a bit of a scene in the Scottish Security Establishment. On my MTRUTH, through the mist of pain, I could see some sort of situation outside a Scottish castle. The whole thing seemed some big act to empathise with the pain and keep me going in this "Inescapable Trap of Doom". On the other hand it might have been exactly what I saw. Some Scottish Laird was formerly of Army HQ Scotland and did not want a suicide on his conscience after seeing me, on his MTRUTH, balanced on the George IV Bridge. But some madman, madder than I, overruled him by force of arms to enable me to receive the Clembutol. I could not hear a thing, Amazing Grace had stopped weeks ago, but I could easily imagine his broad Scottish voice shouting "Stop this madness before somebody's killed!" The reply to this, from Sean Connery, revealed here for the first time as the Director of Intelligence Operations Scotland, was "That's exactly what we're trying to do by carrying out this exercise."

Despite my more unpleasant experiences of the DSS section of the British Mare of Steel, I did succeed in being offered a council flat which I turned down, feeling uncomfortable that I had gone to the front of the list and not sure if I wanted it anyway. I thought the Scots quite proud of the authority they had successfully exercised, making my dealings with the DSS as troublesome as they could in every little way possible. It was not just British this Mare – this was the Scottish bit and they did not want me going home without me knowing they were the real master of sabotage as they dogged me every inch of the way round Scotland. I could see the looks on the faces of the DSS workers when they were told what Scottish Intelligence wanted them to do and replied "You want us to do what?!" I was sure I was not alone in this. A few hundred members of the Special Forces had been sent out to ride the British Mare of Steel through the Special Forces Inescapable Trap of Doom. They were ordered to do this in order to uncover inefficiency in the DSS.

"Let's suddenly put him to the front of the list and see what he does then", I imagined the DSS officer saying, already knowing they were going to put me in a flat I had heard about. Its windows were all smashed and had been boarded up, some of the boards having been pulled down for light, and the whole flat was full of pigeon droppings. The toilet? Overflowing with excrement. People said "You should have seen it." I had no desire to, though I suppose it could have won the Turner Prize.

I was more interested in firing off small legal salvoes at anyone who even remotely pissed me off. This was not for any reason to do with the heroin slug I thought I had got in my ear when I first went to that Irish solicitor. I had to do this to justify Diana's pretending to be dead. If I didn't do this for her, the exercise would be hollow – and I would have no chance of raising any money. I pictured the day of denouement again – when all the people who had deliberately annoyed me would discover both why I had reacted in the way I did, and even why they had been told to treat me the way they did – on that day I would be a hero! Diana was depending on me!

I had not discounted the possibility that my cerebral hemispheres had been completely separated in a trendy psychiatric cosmetic procedure to which I had not given consent, an operation that has been performed on some psychiatric patients, as had tens of thousands of lobotomies. Also, I once saw film of a chap who had one of his cerebral hemispheres removed. He walked very oddly but the redundancy of brain operation across the hemispheres was certainly partly demonstrated by this.

I now began to develop an interest in the law of begging which I was to happily see through to a quite ludicrous conclusion over the next few months. To start with there is the law of the street with which anyone who had begged will know about. I had little trouble from other beggars. "The Kaiser" did pay me a visit though, the Kaiser being the person who appeared to be the most notorious of those on the street. I discovered this when I went to the library and asked if they had anything on begging and, strangely, was told by the librarian that the begging law had been repealed the previous year. However what he now presented me with showed precisely no evidence of this, and even if he was right, then quite clearly nobody had told the police.

So I took the boxfile of cuttings on begging, including plenty of photographs of the Kaiser and other local characters, as well as members of the Ancient Order of the Beggars of the Orison. I formed the impression that there were one or two people out there who, though not on the street, rather deserved certain aspects of their own lifestyles looked into. Like the paper had done with The Kaiser. And one of them was the British Transport policeman at the main station. An ambulance crew in his office verbally assaulted me; he jumped over his desk as though he was about to lay into me – then I was thrown out of the office. Strangely I was yet again dramatically cured of the problem which led me to go there – it must have been the adrenaline. I stood at the top of the ramp down to the railway station where his office was, defiantly displaying a salute of two fingers at the ambulance crew and calling out "Fuck you!" They were horrible, one of them in particular appearing to be quite evil. Bastards. Sorry, I forgot for a moment the whole episode was the latest excruciation on the British Mare of Steel – and it was all my privilege to experience. They might have known exactly who I was: after all it was an SAS (Scottish Ambulance Service) ambulance.

This Orison of which these beggars were members was a funny thing. I kept seeing it as being held in the grand pillared building on the road up to The Scottish High Court: The National Gallery of Scotland. On some signal, or at some time, all the beggars would march in there: Slowly, dutifully, submissively and ever so slightly forlornly from all directions. They would, again, look just like the slave Eloi in *The Time Machine*, as they went down into the underworld, some to be eaten by the Morlocks who farmed them. In they would go to the Temple of the Ancient Order of the Beggars of the Orison to worship the prayer, which controlled them and to which they were devoted. In reality the *Big Issue* office might be the place I was thinking of.

I was innocently collecting coins on which to survive, this necessarily including a few beers in the evening. Unknown to me, my pitch was on British Rail property, the Waverley Bridge over the west end of Edinburgh's main railway station. Further along the street was a traditionally dressed Scotsman playing the bagpipes. It seemed the stretch of road leading up to the bridge itself would not be British Rail Property. This meant his toes, which were on the pavement, were impinging on part of the Queen's highway, or at least council property. Even though he was not on the bridge, the greater part of his body was inside the airspace recognised by the Civil Aviation Authority as part of the property of the owner of the shopping centre adjoining the Balmoral Hotel. This, I believed, might well also have been British Rail Property.

As the piper played, mostly, but not all, on what was probably British Rail property, I saw a British Transport policeman storming towards me like an angry relation of Mr McGregor in the *Peter Rabbit* story and shouting "Beat it! Beat it!" at me. This I did without any help from Michael Jackson, though I was beginning to wonder about the actual legal source of some of the currency coming into my hat. It seemed terribly unfair that the piper was allowed to carry on.

Later a young chap who looked more like the well-known Scottish snooker player, Alan McManus, began talking to me in a condescending manner, at some point kicking my cap enough to empty the money it contained, and likewise my mind of any morale. This money included the £1 he had just given me, which I was minded to give him back with interest. He found it far too easy to tell me to sort my life out as if that was something that someone could possibly do in an instant. I imagined that many of those who passed silently were thinking the same. He did not even know what he meant by "sort out" because he had never needed to do this himself. I thought of a family of lottery winners I had heard of living on takeaways in one or two rooms of an otherwise completely empty country mansion whose stables had been devoid of horses for some time. What was "sorted out"? All I wanted to do to sort my life out now was to click my fingers and have this arsehole disappear. There was something odd about his line of questioning. I could see him thinking of what to say next, and watched interestedly as he did this. Of course he could not know I had schizophrenia: unless his brother Alan had told him and had sent him along to wind me up a bit at the request of Steve Davis. Being a little angry isn't always a bad thing.

I thought this must be as low as it gets. I was in the gutter. As before, lest I forget, I actually went and laid down in the gutter itself outside The Balmoral Hotel. I must have looked a sorry sight. But I was happy and, as Oscar Wilde said "We are all in the gutter. Only some of us are looking at the stars."

I settled into my begging routine for quite a few weeks. My favourite place was on the church steps in the Lothian Road. I did spend one or two cold nights out on the street whilst the Cowgate Centre was briefly closed, prior to moving down the road towards Holyrood. One day I saw the Irishman again. Perhaps he thought I was studying for a begging qualification as he set me some homework:

Minimalist Dada Poetry Exercise

Finish the following poem, entitled Her Eyes by selecting just one word from each column:

	(column 1)	(column 2)
	yellow	tigers
In her eyes were:	burning	summerhouses
	painted	sunsets

Feeling a little anarchic, or if you prefer, rebellious, I plumped for "In her eyes were burning summerhouses" putting the completed work in my pocket until I saw him again. This exercise only confirmed my feeling he was from the IRA – and that I had been dragged into the peace process. I was quite sure I was in communication with the IRA – if not the Sons of Glendawr (the Welsh terrorist group active in the '70s, when they were infamous for burning down the holiday homes of the English in Wales).

I found that if I begged hard, I could earn enough to pay for my food and beers in the evening. Sometimes other beggars begged from me, which I found hilarious, on each occasion acceding to their requests. Often people just stopped for a chat and on one occasion I was given a piece of paper with the following written on it:

An Irishman's Philosophy of Life

In life, there are only two things to worry about, either you are well, or you are sick. If you are well, there is nothing to worry about, but if you are sick, you have two things to worry about: either you will live, or you will die. If you live, there is nothing to worry about, if you die, you have two things to worry about: either you will go to heaven or to hell. If you go to heaven, there is nothing to worry about, but if you go to hell, you'll be so busy shaking hands with your friends, you won't have time to worry!

On the May bank holiday I begged hard and collected £55, giving me enough to go and stay in The Albert Hotel, North Queensferry. Room 6 has the most spectacular outlook of any hotel room in the country, and I was a truly privileged beggar being able to stay there, the enormous span of the Forth Bridge, a leviathan of Scottish engineering, filling the sky outside the room. So you should always remember, when you're on the British Mare of Steel, solace is usually at hand if you use your head.

Staring up awe-inspired at the Forth Rail Bridge, a small boat sailing under it, I thought of the "wee boat that sails on the Forth", as in *Erin-go-bragh*. I had also kept thinking of *There She Goes* by The La's and whenever I did it just seemed to confirm that Diana was not dead. She was on this wee boat – just keeping a watch on me – and this "Rapprochement, not denouement" would become perpetual. It was like the television programme *This Is Your Life* but instead it was *Her Life* and various people would be approached by presenter Michael Aspel, and just when they thought it was their life Diana would appear – quite undead. A bit like *Game for a Laugh* really – except it wasn't because she really was dead. Very sad. Though I wasn't having any of that at the time, I would proceed as though she were alive. The only way forward was to banish from my mind any possibility she was not a prisoner of a complete press blackout, this being the tool to inspire me to succeed. In fact, I did not need to banish it. I believed I had directly caused her disappearance.

Meanwhile I was visiting the poste restante where I had all the mail associated with my crumbling life coming in, not only from the poste restante in Newquay but also the one in Hayward's Heath. This was not very funny. My Post Office carrier bag was getting fuller, and not just with bits of palindromes.

But staying in the hotel was a blissful, serene relief after having to sleep on the floor in the Cowgate. There were other occasions when I begged enough to stay in a bed and breakfast, but this was not often. On one occasion, a well-to-do man got talking to me in the rain. He told me that the assertive way I was saying "Any spare change please Sir?" made him think I was in the military. He said he was, in fact, a knight. After our conversation he said "Go and get yourself a bed and breakfast for the night", handing me a crisp Scottish £20 note. On another occasion, when I was begging loudly, some nice policemen approached me saying I would have to be quieter. Hidden in my jacket were some documents, which, at the time, I felt were incredibly sensitive. I read into his words and thought he might be giving me a message from MI5 about my fund-raising activities – my "Beaver", which the documents pertained to. But, of course, there was no beaver[116]. I had misheard the lyrics anyway. In reality it was fever.

One day a passer-by with a heavy Scottish accent came up and hurled abuse at me telling me to "Fuck off back to England!" He spat in my face then said, right in it, "You're just a fucking tourist!" So I got up and kicked his shopping bag, the contents of which spilled out, some, to my amusement being run over by a car. I chased him down the Lothian Road. Perhaps it was this day that an old school friend saw me begging. But instead of coming and saying hello he ignored me. I would later learn that, back in Bedford, he had gone into The Ship and told everyone what he had seen – so much for the old school tie! And it was only years later that I recalled The Tourists were an earlier version of the band, The Eurythmics, whose album I had played that morning in the flat in South Queensferry. The flat had been bugged; possibly not only by this MTRUTH I had received on the NHS. It was also being monitored by a private detective working for the Soviet Navy, whose founder had close connections with a nearby monastery, as I noticed on a tourist leaflet I found lying on the pavement, and had cause to pick up and read.

Returning to my pitch I saw a mediaeval jester coming towards me. As he got closer I realised it was my Irish friend. I laughed at his outfit, gesturing as if I didn't know what it was. "Ah, it's nothing to worry about my friend. I'm simply dressed as an owl-glass for a fancy dress party tonight. Now between you and me an owl-glass is a mediaeval jester or buffoon – the lady told me in the hire shop. Tell me, did yer complete the exercise I set yer?" he said, in a very heavy Irish accent.

I handed him the completed minimalist Dada poem: "In her eyes were burning summerhouses." As if it were something rather longer he said "I'll need a couple of days to mark it. I'll get back to yer then. Top o' the morning to yer", and he was off.

I never did see the marked version but I did see this chap one more time whilst I was in Auld Reekie. I was begging in my usual place on the steps of St John's Episcopal Church in Lothian Road when the annual Republican march went by, celebrating the birthday of James Connolly. I saw him in the procession and he called out "Hi! How yer doing? I've not been able to mark yer work! Terribly busy! Terribly busy! I'll get 'round to it one day! See yer around!"

Cheered by the sight of him I decided to have a shower at the Cowgate Centre to further boost my morale. Yet again I found a shower which did not work properly. It had a lot of red lights, which came on as the temperature went up. The only problem was that the temperature would oscillate between freezing cold and boiling hot. The lights looked like the floor indicators of a lift. I thought of that lift I mentioned earlier in which I had once received the wrong number call on the emergency phone 15 years earlier. The fluctuations made me think the temperature was controlled by the position of that lift. As the lights first went on one by one and then off again I could see, on my MTRUTH, the lift going up and down at that very moment all that way off in London! But salvation was at hand. After I got out of the shower, having decided it was part of the British Special Forces Mare of Steel – or suicide machine if you prefer – it was closed as being too dangerous. I wandered down to the main Edinburgh Station and had a coffee, where I learnt that there was a public shower for hire. A few days later I tried it.

I was feeling grubby and disconsolate but had done my laundry so had fresh underwear and socks ready to put on. The shower was so spectacularly good I would give it 10 out of 10 and then change the scale to 12 out of 12. It was a positive cyclone, worth travelling the entire length of the land first class to get to. It seemed the most glorious demonstration of the fact that true decadence demands total masochism. I believed I had discovered the only remaining responsibility of British Rail. As well as all the places I had found Prince Charles's dog to date, then I had certainly also found it in this glorious torrent of perfectly hot water of perfectly steady temperature with complimentary extra large clean warm towels and toiletries. The shower should be a tourist attraction and I wondered if it was a station in its own right. I don't suppose a dog would normally be allowed in but, from what I later learnt of dogs, imagined some would enjoy a good hot shower.

After the superb storm of hot water and steam had enveloped me I visited the library to search for MTRUTH on the Internet, to see if my secret knowledge had gone further than the Absolute Secret file. But no terminal was available –

it took another four years before I did the search. When I finally did I was schizophrenically astonished, given where I had usually begged, to see the very first entry:

MTRUTH Episcopal Church: Meditations on Truth. Christian Quotation of the Day, 27th October 1999. The idea of "conviction" is complex. It involves the conceptions of authoritative examination, of unquestionable proof, of decisive judgment, of punitive power. Whatever the final issue may be, he who "convicts" another must place the truth of the case in a clear light before him, so that it must be seen and acknowledged as truth. He who then rejects the conclusion which the exposition involves, rejects it with his eyes open and at his peril. Truth seen as truth carries with it condemnation to all who refuse to welcome it... B. F. Westcott, The Gospel According to St. John [1882].

It was in a hypertext mark-up link file called mtruth.html. I hope you feel I have borne these words in mind in the writing of this book: in for example the appendix definitions of "criminal" and "murderous".

That night, asleep on the floor in the Cowgate Centre, I was nearly killed when the heavy light fitting fell from the ceiling. Luckily it only hit my leg but I had a very severe bruise to my calf and went to the doctor in Chester Street. I felt there was some significance in the name "Chester Street". It seemed to have become "Chest ER Street" and, ludicrously, this played on my mind as I had a chest infection, quite apart from the peculiar apposition of Elizabeth R. I could have been killed if I'd slept the other way round. I showed the doctor the bruise and told him how I got it. I described what had happened as a joke and then demonstrated the urge to prove it by asking him if he knew any. "I do actually" he replied. He said a bloke in a hospital bed said to the doctor "Doctor, doctor, I can't feel my feet." The doctor replied "I'm sorry, we had to amputate your arms."

The next night I met an ardent Scottish Nationalist. I thought a Sean Connery-type director of MI5 Scotland had met him. He invited me for a beer, which was pleasant, especially as he treated me like an honoured guest. I noticed that one of the beers on sale was called Titanic and asked politely if I could try one to see how it "*went down*". He duly obliged and remarked, "Well you *sunk* that one pretty quick!" and "without ice". He spoke proudly of his family's Army record and nationalism. He would not have imagined I was wearing a Golden Wonder 007 watch in which MI5 had put a transmitter. Though, to be honest, I did not see if he had one on too.

The legal official in the black gown who'd appeared in the train toilet now came to me again. In reality I saw him on my MTRUTH many more times than I have recalled here but that is not to understate his significance to me. I was living in a liberal democracy in which even a legal non-event was anything less than profoundly significant. Everything that happened, for example the most minor tort, had the potential to help me make sense of my quest to find the dog.

Sitting on a stool talking to this Scotsman, I found that where I wanted to rest my foot, one stanchion was missing. I had to dismount the stool, turn it through 90 degrees, and get back on it. The said legal official then produced a tape measure with which he proceeded to make measurements of the vicinity of this incident, entering into learned discussions with colleagues before a forensic science team appeared taking photographs from clinical angles including from directly above, using a step ladder. Not for the first time I first realised we were all living in a joke continuum, each point in space and time having some overall level of humour attached, positive or negative, before God. *Colchester* was the complete joke. Moreover God afforded me round the clock legal representation.

Back on the street an hour-or-so later someone gave me a box containing half of a super-large pizza, which I gratefully tucked into. Then somebody gave me a fortune cookie from the Chinese restaurant they had just dined in. I ate it whilst reading the message: "Look at everything as though you were seeing it for the first time or last time. Then your time on earth will be filled with glory." I looked over the road and two drunks were having a fight. A lady walking had stopped before them. Her dog (if it was her dog) was barking at them. Next, staggering from a nearby pub came an hysterical Scottish drunkard who approached in a slightly worrying way which should not have alarmed me. He was crying with almost incoherently inebriated laughter. From his words I gleaned that he had just spoken to a lady who looked like one of the Queen's ladies-in-waiting. She had told him a horse went into a bar and asked for a gin and tonic. The barman had replied "Sure, but why the long face?"

What might have been more amusing than the unrepeatable joke he *actually* told me was the look on my face. I laughed it was so bad and he went staggering off towards The Balmoral Hotel, leaving me a bottle of Becks beer. As my stomach rumbled slightly I thought of another joke I did think funny. A man went to his doctor and said Doctor, Doctor, I've eaten something that disagrees with me" whereupon a voice came from his stomach saying "No you haven't."

Next day I begged on the fire escape doorstep of the Town Hall. I had been chased away from there one day by three policemen but on this occasion I looked round and noted the door was slightly ajar. I sensed I may have somehow exercised some sort of social leverage or at least somebody wanted me to think I had. It was an open door policy. So I decided to leave the 007 watch there as it was not me they wanted to spy on so much but the eight-year-old son of an Auld Reekie cocaine dealer. Midsummer arrived, and a key moment in my life was just around the corner.

Part XVII

I Meet Emily

Chapter Forty-Five

Forever Young

It was about eight o'clock on the longest day of the year when I was begging, not in my usual place, but outside Jenner's on Prince's Street. I was used to being approached by people for a friendly chat. One had even given me her address and invited me to come and stay with her family in Linlithgow. I could not sign on because according to the Job Centre I was still in employment. I felt trapped, as I feared re-hospitalisation. Now who did I see coming towards me but one of the world's most beautiful women. I instantly stood up and invited her for a coffee.

We went off to an expensive coffee house near the High Court. Ron Wood from The Rolling Stones had an interest in the shop, as we read in the menu. We talked avidly and, as I had £15 on me, I invited her for a pizza, which I paid for. I fancied her no-end and gazed up and down her arms. Her name was Emily, Emily Barker. It soon transpired that she had once met Prince Charles at a Pony Club ball at Somerleyton Hall, family seat of Lord-in-waiting to the Queen and Master of the Horse, Lord Somerleyton. She had asked if one of her friends could dance with Princess Anne. Later she told me she was somehow connected with Dick Francis, the horsey novelist, whose son had mysteriously collapsed during the Boat Race one year – something that had left me once again suspecting some extended conspiracy. Either that or he had been subjected to a Masonic punishment by way of some poison before the race for a minor transgression. It must have run in the family as his father's mount, the Queen Mother's horse Devon Loch, had also famously collapsed in the Grand National one year, yards from the finish. But Emily was so impressively well connected. Now this seems mere namedropping. But at the time all Emily's connections were grounds to indulge my schizophrenic fantasies.

In my state of mind, I saw her as a close friend of Prince Charles who had been specifically sent to help me get out of this unfortunate situation. I was willing and able to help her do this. However the thought did occur that the Special Intelligence Service had trawled around to see who had the most attractive wife and offered them a £1 million cheque made out to charity in return for sending her on this operation. Either way it was not long before she realised that my problems were a bit more than the mere fact that I was on the street and staying at the Cowgate Centre. I knew Prince Charles had sent her.

She took me around a hotel showing me the swimming pool and the jacuzzi, as though she was showing me how much better things could be. Next we went to a pub, Whistle Binky's, and there we danced 'til the early hours – though not literally of course, people only do that in competitions. She told me how her father had won the George Medal, the highest decoration for military gallantry when not in the face of the enemy. He had been a lieutenant commander in the Royal Navy Reserve in the War, was the Mine Disposal Officer for the east coast and had won the medal for defusing a mine in Dover harbour. I naturally decided she was a most important woman, especially as her father had actually met the King, and she the future one.

By dawn we found ourselves near the coffee shop again. I said something about jumping off the bridge whereupon she flung herself at me and we kissed for the first time. Things were looking up. We sat together on the bench for some time. She was English, very well spoken, and as if to confirm my thoughts about how important she was, she told me she had bought her horse from the First Sea Lord and knew the Chief of Defence Staff. Her husband was a senior Defence Director. This only fed my fantasies about the Special Intelligence Service. We arranged to meet the next day.

I went back to the Cowgate Centre where I was able to get a couple of hours sleep before being turfed out, as usual, onto the street for the day. I went straight to The Ark for breakfast, sensing my life was about to take a different course.

At two o'clock I waited for Emily. Sure enough she pulled up in her top of the range turquoise blue Land Rover Discovery. She was wearing a tartan miniskirt, tights and an expensive looking black cardigan. Twenty-four hours earlier this would have been a complete fantasy. She drove me to Perth where she bought me lunch and then took me shopping, buying me a new pair of jeans. Then she took me down to the beach in Fife overlooking the Firth of Forth. We cuddled sitting on the dunes.

That night England was playing Argentina in the World Cup. When Argentina scored the level of joy expressed by those in the Cowgate Centre was impressive, which I felt a little odd about as I, like a lot of English people, enjoy seeing Scotland do well. The reverse was obviously not the case. This seems even more unfortunate, though unsurprising, when I recall the Scottish Falklands' War veteran I had just met over coffee in the other room.

Over the next week I saw Emily again frequently, enjoying her company each time. One night I had begged enough to get a bed and breakfast and she came back with me for the night. The thrill of making love to her was all I needed. Could this be the woman I had hallucinated on New Year's Eve the previous winter? But the only problem was that as I made love to her, on my MTRUTH the room seemed to be full of black men. For once though, they were not taunting me but encouraging, almost as if she was my prize for not succumbing to their tests and passing out as the only white man ever to become a member of the Black Brotherhood.

The money for the rental of my flat had not come through, quite apart from my pay (I presumed incorrectly I had lost my job); either way I decided I simply had to invite this beautiful woman to Henley Royal Regatta. This she seemed made for, and I decided to collect my rental money on the way to finance the excursion. Already her companionship was helping me find my way back to normality. As we sat over coffee and tea waiting for our train, I was clearly aware I was supposed to be in court at that moment on a trumped-up charge of assaulting five police officers (this was dropped and replaced by breach of the peace). As they had duffed me up I had no intention of giving them the honour of my presence, a factor which would later be of significance, and nor did I tell Emily how I was now even more on-the-run than she thought. But she could see

I was not right.

I tried to persuade her to buy us first class tickets to Henley but she refused saying she never went first class. This caused a bit of an argument, which was to presage quite a stormy relationship. Either way, soon we were on the train to London. Strangely, Ross McWilliam, the BBC Look East presenter was in the seat behind us, though I decided not to say hello, thinking instead my usual paranoid thoughts about his presence. The train sped safely through Scotland and England and I felt happy to be with Emily. For the moment at least, I was off the street and a step closer to sorting my life out.

That night we found a bed and breakfast in Richmond. As we were getting ready for bed we had our first big argument. I had said something stupid and unrepeatable I hadn't meant. Emily became quiet and went into the bathroom. She spent too long in there and my suspicions were aroused. When she came out she was dressed and, picking up her bag, left. I went after her in my underpants begging her to come back.

Now I was out on the street in my underpants and the door to the bed and breakfast had shut behind me. I was crying to her saying, over and over, "I did not mean it. I was only joking." Eventually she came back in after I had woken the landlord.

Next day we met the tenant of my flat who, offering us wine and very gentleman-like, explained that he had made the payment of £800. As there seemed to be some problem with it we all went to his bank to find out. Eventually I got my money and, turning around, discovered Emily had gone. I raced outside but there was no sign of her. I was mortified and began to cry. I headed over to King's Cross, where I thought she would have probably gone to get the train back to Scotland. I wanted at least to give her back the money for the tickets. I put the money in an envelope on which I wrote her mobile phone number, which was switched off. As the train pulled out I noticed a vicar getting on. I read a schizophrenic significance into this. I ran up and down the train looking for her through the windows but without luck.

As the train pulled out I handed the envelope to the guard. So much for the honesty of train guards – she never got the money. Depressed by this I sat down amongst the pigeons in King's Cross Station. Somebody had dropped their chips and I watched the pigeons gorge themselves on them. Alone I decided to head for Henley, wondering if the guard had known about my ticketless journey from Edinburgh to Oxford in 1995, let alone all the other journeys I, like the average traveller, had not paid for. I went via Kew, hoping to amuse MI5 by hiding the Alexander Pope epigram in a BT junction box door hinge.

Chapter Forty-Six

Somewhere

I reached Henley disappointed that I could not show off Emily to the other Regatta-goers. As I felt I would be watched I had wanted to be seen with her: she was so beautiful, her presence was demanded by my sense of aesthetics.

I did not have my blazer, flannels or a shirt though; so was unable to go into the Stewards' Enclosure, despite being a member. Instead I wandered down the course as was my wont, past all the stands until I got to the Steve Redgrave Enclosure where I sat down to enjoy a pint of beer.

A woman entered the Enclosure smiling and I thought she knew who I was, and was smiling at my situation which she knew everything about. I was not unduly disturbed by this. In fact, although I was missing Emily, I felt quite happy, and was thinking of having a baby with her. Schizophrenia is not all torture and the deluded state can be quite pleasant. In fact as you can see I enjoyed being ill most of the time.

I met up with some friends from Bedford who were going out that night for a curry. I joined them. I tried Emily's telephone number again but still it was switched off and I decided she did not want to hear from me. But she would do. I sat and watched the rowing from the General Enclosure.

That night we drank in The White Hart Hotel. Losing Emily as I had done only allowed the memories of Amanda to come flooding back. She and the Regatta were still inextricably connected and probably always will be. After quite a few beers my thoughts turned to where I was going to sleep for the night. I asked at the bar and they lent me a sleeping bag.

When I got to the campsite and into the bag (it was not raining), the lining had fused together in big lumps. Furthermore the lumps were such that I was reminded, quite bizarrely, of the piece of ground I had slept on at this campsite 16 years earlier when I had spent the day with Amanda. The local branch of the Special Intelligence Service had been spying on me all those years ago. Noting precisely where I had slept that night, they had moulded the sleeping bag to the exact contours of that piece of ground to influence my mind.

The next night I decided to stay in a bed and breakfast in Reading. A ridiculously good-looking bloke who said he was in the Parachute Regiment gave me a lift there. I imagined he was related to Amanda. The morning after, hitchhiking back to Henley, who should spot me and stop but my good friend Budge, an intelligence officer in the Bedford police. His boss was my brother, Head of Intelligence. Interestingly he actually *was* an intelligence officer and not just some figment of my imagination. But beliefs back in Bedford about my demise were not proven premature, as he did not tell anyone he'd seen me, as he didn't know I was missing. His girlfriend was living in Henley during the week and we went back there for coffee.

I spent a pleasant Sunday night in a pub bed and breakfast in Henley. I could afford to pay as I still had some of my flat rental money, but unfortunately my tenant was moving out. If I'd had my head screwed on properly I would have made a simple call to arrange to get a new tenant but I didn't, partly because of my illness and partly because I was not happy with the management of the tenancy.

Instead, the next morning, I marched into the Henley branch of the building society and, armed with my beliefs about the current situation, deluded or otherwise, I handed the keys to my flat in, mouthing off some remark about the building society security department. I believed they had tarnished Diana's image by playing a dirty trick on me. This principally concerned the Colchester incident. I wondered paranoiacally as to the real truth about the building society's confusion of Newquay with Colchester. The girl must have been truly shocked at my behaviour. This act lost me my most important investment, my flat and the mortgage, which went with it. Due to county court orders I would not be able to get another mortgage, at least for some time. Furthermore, I was one step closer to the street again; the only difference being that Emily was now involved in my life and as it transpired she was going to stay involved. All I had to do, as Emily had told me, was to get a new tenant and this would have easily covered the mortgage. But I wanted to believe that MI5, the building society and the agent for my flat were in some conspiracy, because that made me important. My delusion was not helped when the building society began an Internet bank called "Cahoots".

On the Monday after the Regatta I headed for Reading. I was standing by the road trying to hitch a lift. There was a fair amount of traffic and I recognised some of the drivers, one of whom was a rowing friend of Amanda. Then somebody shouted something at me that put my back up. I began to get annoyed and felt persecuted. I began shouting things back at the drivers going past and must have presented the look of being off my head. I was – but somehow pulled myself together.

Eventually I got a lift into Reading where I still had enough money to pay for one more night in a bed and breakfast (Henley can be quite expensive and I had put some of the money in the envelope). That day I hitched to Dorking and, without an appointment, visited the medical insurance company who, I felt, had been victims of a fraudulent insurance claim for me when I had been certified fit for work. I informed the director of the fraud. He was polite and told me I would not have to pay the money back.

Penniless, I was on the street again, and spent a night sleeping in a shop doorway without even a sleeping bag. The next day I decided to book into the Salvation Army hostel where they said they would help me fill out my claim for housing benefit in order to pay for my accommodation there. The fact that it had not gone through yet did not prevent me from getting a room though, where the previous occupant had been allowed to stay with his two dogs. The room stank of dogs and I, of course, presumed somebody was having a laugh at my expense, probably Prince Charles, though if it was His Royal Highness I was compelled out of politeness and loyalty to find it all excruciatingly amusing.

At dinner I had another Capgras experience. One of the guests looked like

Dr. Black, whose wife's car I had crashed into at his house four years earlier. Naturally, I assumed he was a professional double who had been put there deliberately.

In order to keep myself going I needed to beg. Though I was not being paid I could not legally have lost my job but this was far from my mind. I had found a sort of drop-out happiness being on the street. The fact that it was summer helped and I really enjoyed my cups of coffee from the taxi rank along with the Hamlets I smoked. I was as happy as an ark lark.

One day a policeman arrested me for begging. As he marched me off to the car I was calling out "Sieg heil!" and doing a Nazi salute. Later that day I was bailed in the Magistrates Court to appear again a couple of weeks later. Outside the court I went straight back to beg in my usual place outside Vision Express. As I sat there I noticed one of the Stewards of Henley Royal Regatta walk by. I recalled an occasion when I was stroke of the school 1st VIII in training at Henley a day or so before the regatta in 1979. Near the start I spotted the Great Britain National lightweight VIII. I spoke to our cox, "Muddy" Waters, and asked him to try and get us on the start at the same time as them. We had a fast start and I fancied our chances. One of the National crew was heard saying to their coach "They're not coming with us are they?" Our bowman, Simon Taylor, replied "No, *you're* coming with *us!*" We set off for one minute, they for two. When we "wound down" after a minute we were clearly ahead by a canvas and my wiliness as stroke had borne fruit. That night, news having spread of the victory of us schoolboys, we were invited up to Leander Club[117], where we were congratulated by some of the most archetypically upstanding members of the British nation.

Now, 19 years later and on the street, my actions that day seemed for a moment to have become a benchmark for divine happiness. I was determined to earn enough money to easily afford a Range Rover Overfinch[118] and drive around all day trying to get to the traffic lights at the same time as standard Range Rovers. Then, without fail, I would "burn" them all up, like the school VIII had done to the Great Britain National VIII that day. This all seemed extraordinarily amusing and any passer-by would have noticed an extremely amused-looking beggar shaking his head in jocular disbelief at his own thoughts. On the other hand on one occasion I could be seen begging out aloud for my MTRUTH to be unplugged.

Meanwhile my housing benefit claim failed because I had given a false name. As a consequence I was thrown out of the Salvation Army hostel and had nowhere to go. That night, when the pubs shut, I headed off to look for somewhere to sleep. I found a block of flats. In my mind a friendly Rastafarian lived at the top and something told me to sleep outside his door but, for whatever reason, I did not, and bedded down (without any bedding again), on the cold floor outside the ground floor flat.

I was just dozing off to sleep when the occupant returned. I apologised for my presence and he said it was quite alright but obviously it was not because a while later I was woken by the police who moved me on. I should have simply returned when the occupant had gone to bed. Instead I resorted to walking around town. Another police car pulled up and I accused them of harassment and hurled abuse at them. I shouted that their job was to maintain the Queen's peace and they were not doing that by harassing me. I had a delusion of grandeur born out of my beliefs about Prince Charles's dog and Princess Diana. I felt very powerful.

I asked some passers-by where the YMCA was, and they merrily gave me directions. When I got there a West Indian security guard was on duty. He told me to come back in the morning. So I headed back into town and slept, undisturbed, under a stall in the Market Place.

Morning came and it was the day of my court appearance. I had no intention of turning up. I booked into the YMCA spinning some yarn about my situation and they agreed to process my claim for Housing Benefit. Once more I had a bed for the night.

I got to know the other inmates, one of whom was a pleasant chap with a polio limp. However the place was rife with drugs, and, esoterically, I wrote to the Court House to complain. The security guard who had been on duty had an impressive hypnotic voice which deceived me into thinking he was a nice chap but I was later to discover had, shall we say, a slightly different side to him. He became part of the reason I had to leave Reading and get out of the immediate situation, back towards some normality.

Next day I was begging in my usual place, called Smelly Alley, when, out from the department store, I was shocked to see a cousin. She did not appear to notice me but no doubt if she had done, there was a good chance she would not actually recognise me as I had grown a beard, which I usually did on the street. Sure enough, I later discover this to be the case because, despite the fact that I had now been missing for nearly one year, news of my presence in Reading again did not filter back to my family.

I had three further brushes with the Law one of which resulted in no more than a ticking off from a female officer. I was begging with a notice which said "Law is the essence of freedom: licence only leads to tyranny." She was a bit of a philosopher, it was clear, as she expostulated for some minutes in a laughably intellectual manner on the significance of my sign. As she went she said had not seen me begging and was "sure" I would not. On another occasion the policeman who had previously arrested me came by off-duty, and promptly headed off to a phone box, no doubt reporting me to the station. I made myself scarce and, finding a phone box myself, made a 999 call and complained that he was harassing me.

As I sat begging outside Vision Express I pondered the legalities of it. The Law as I understood it forbade me from begging in a public place, though not being sure what the definition of public place was I applied my own analysis. Where I was sitting, I decided, was not a public place but private property belonging to the shop or the leaseholder. My begging could only be *heard* from a public place, the High Street itself, and therefore I was not actually begging in a public place but a private one. I don't think the Magistrates would have been too impressed with my argument. It hardly occurred to me, and I would hardly have cared, if they had – but there were now not one but two warrants out for my arrest, both for failing to appear before the Magistrates, one in Edinburgh and one in Reading.

But these were happy times. I felt no pressure to sort out my life and I was simply going with the flow. My legal thoughts led me to think of begging down the inside of a long tube from my private place or even my own flat. Would anyone arrest me for begging from my own flat?[119] I started seeing people come up to me and looking down my tube, the end of which was in a public place, saying hello down it, before dutifully turning their heads to hear my reply emerge from the end of the tube. Bizarre. Emily came along on horseback and, dismounting, did the same, many times. "Ah you alright down there Clive?" she would say. I was amused. And almost as if to make me think I had not been forgotten about a group of black youths went by and one of them said "Rupert". I was left unsure if even another single word had been uttered, Rupert, apart from being my brother's name, was military derogatory slang for a junior army officer. On the third further brush with the police I had a strong sense some youngsters had been told to be there and watch.

Towards the end of my time in Reading I went out begging with my friend (the polio victim). Realising how lucky I was compared to him, I invited him for a drink with me. His manners were not very good and I took him under my wing for a few days. Perhaps I was a fine one to talk.

It was now getting on for two months since I had seen Emily and decided to give her a call. It was a perfect August day and I was sweating in the hot phone box. She sounded pleased to hear from me and I said I would call again though we did not at this stage arrange to meet. Sitting in a doorway smoking a Hamlet I wrote her a short poem on a piece of litter lying near me:

Miss You

Miss your face.
Miss your grace.
Miss your hair.
Miss your care.
Miss you bare!
Miss you fair!
Miss our hour.
Miss you flower.

I drew a small flower beneath the poem, wrote how I still loved her and sent it off.

An American had booked into the YMCA and he was put in my room. At the library one day I had picked up a copy of a book entitled: *Secret War Time Missions*. Opening it at random (as usual), I discovered that a United States Air Forceman had crossed the Channel by sea alone during the War, landing in Salcombe. The American staying in my room was his son and had been sent over in direct response to my opening of this book on that page, as they could see what I was reading through my MTRUTH. The Secret Services knew everything about me.

Little did the American know I was schizophrenic and heaven knows what he might have thought about sleeping in the same room if he had. For my part I had little idea if *he* was safe to spend the night in the room with. Either way we got on well, and I had my usual deluded thoughts that he was from, for example, the United States Drugs Enforcement Agency and had been sent along in response to my letter to the Court House. I did not get the impression he was too impressed with this particular YMCA though.

I bought a packet of commemorative stamps: "The Queens Beasts" and, imagining I was one of them, hid the stamps in the drawer for the American to find. I do not recall why I did this but the true reason would probably sound too farfetched anyway. I had a book, which had been given to me to read by a passer-by on the streets in Edinburgh. I decided to send it to "The Commanding Officer, 2 Parachute Regiment". Heaven knows why – apart from "messages" I seemed to have received from the book and the fact that this CO was Prince Charles.

Next day I went into the church and asked if I could beg on the path through the graveyard. My request was refused by the verger, and this enraged me as I felt God should be helping me. I did another Nazi salute and marched out of the church, again crying "Sieg heil!" as I went.

Trouble was brewing back at the YMCA. I knew that soon I was likely to be thrown out when my Housing Benefit claim was refused, because they did not have a National Insurance number for the name I had given.

That night, as I watched television, the security guard came in to vacuum. Without asking me he just turned the television set off, I thought, so he could plug the vacuum cleaner in. He was not amused when I didn't go to bed. The next thing I knew we were wrestling and my judo came in handy but he was very strong and we continued to fight up the stairs.

I had written to Kraft about the broken Maxwell House coffee machine, recommending they employ a young black girl who was domiciled at the YMCA. I had told them I thought she had sales skills. She now appeared from her room and called to us to stop fighting. The banister broke and the guard narrowly avoided falling to his death down several flights of stairs: All because I wanted to watch TV? I do not think so. He had a chip on his shoulder so big I am surprised he could stand up straight, if at all. We fought all the way down to my bedroom, which I succeeded in getting into, and locked the door. But I could not risk him going down to get the keys and killing me in my sleep. And this was the YMCA! So I grabbed my things and shinned down the drainpipe. I had evaded this nightmare but was on the street again not having contacted my family for a whole year.

That night I slept in the doorway of Vision Express again and in the morning went to the church hall to get a free breakfast. I recognised one of the diners as someone who had been on the same degree course as me. I do not know if he recognised me but decided not to introduce myself. I spent the day begging and that evening decided it was time to leave Reading and head north to Scotland where I hoped to meet up with Emily again. But I was not to get very far before trouble struck again.

A very well spoken black man picked me up and gave me a short lift down the road. He was on his way back from playing football. Somebody hooted at us and I made a V gesture with my fingers. At the traffic lights one of them came up to the car and tried to open my door but I had locked it in time. My driver got out and going up to this person proceeded to kick him and generally duff him up. He got back into the car and amusingly said to me "Sorry about that". He was apologising on behalf of his black brethren for the incident the previous night. Since he was obviously so well spoken, he must have been sent by a black MI5 outfit, I thought, in a deludedly elitist moment.

I liked him and during our brief conversation he helped me develop my modern political theory that the whole country was clinically obsessed with spending more and more money on bigger and bigger hospitals. As an antidote to this I formed an independent movement to get ahead of the game and turn the whole country, and then the world, into one massive secure psychiatric ward. As I got to know the patients I would conduct bizarre and perverse experiments on them by identifying individuals with levels of psychiatric health most closely resembling various world leaders. To start with, that security guard in Reading YMCA closely resembled Robert Mugabe and the nice young black girl under his sick guidance a good Costa Rican prime minister.[120]

Now it was evening and I was headed towards Oxford. Many of the cars seemed to be driven by tearaways and drunk drivers, whose passengers hurled abuse at me whilst they flashed their lights and hooted their horns. This really wound me up. I picked up a stone and decided, ill advisedly, to throw it at the very next car whose occupants abused me. I did not have to wait for very long. I landed a direct hit on the nearside passenger door. The car screeched to a halt up the road and, with more burning rubber, dramatically went into reverse and raced towards me. For a moment I thought it was going to run me over as it mounted the pavement and stopped. Out got five angry young men.

My attempts to get away were hampered by the fact I had my plastic carrier bag full of documents. Other than the bits of palindrome these were either the bizarre but amusing writings of a person suffering schizophrenia or official documents which together only meant one thing: I was mentally ill. But I believed they were my proof that I was a victim of a conspiracy, and as such were my means of legal escape from this situation. It would take me another two years to accept that the contents of this bag were more a reflection of schizophrenia rather than any real conspiracy. Whatever the merits of the bag's contents, and there were some, beyond the end of the story I threw it away. I was rather sad about this, as I confronted the insanity of what the contents represented.

Soon the five of them were nearly on top of me, the truth being that they, not I, had cast the first 'stone'. Normally I would have been able to simply run away but I was hesitant. I tried to make my way to the Wimpy but tripped on the kerbstones. Now blows were raining in on me and I had no real choice but to roll up in a ball. Then I felt a large hard boot hit my head and they ran off. I was dizzy.

I staggered into the Wimpy, blood streaming from my head, and an ambulance was called. The ambulance driver asked me if I wanted the police called, but intuition made me decline the offer (which, although I did not think about it, may have resulted in hospitalisation in the psychiatric unit). Soon I was at the Radcliffe Infirmary where stitches were put in my head. I was hoping for a bed for the night but was told to go, though not until after I had given a false name and refused to speak to another police officer.

Still dazed, I wandered around Oxford until dawn. It began to rain and I was getting wet and depressed. I found where I could get a hot drink for free and they told me where the down-and-outs' hostel was. Here I spent the next two nights. I was no longer in the mood to go to Scotland and decided it was time to show my face again in Bedford, where I had long been given up for dead. I phoned a friend, Paul, and asked him if he could possibly come and collect me. He told me he had read in the newspaper that my brother was in prison. This simply fed my conspiracy theory and though he could not tell me which one, I thought it might be my brother in the police. Actually my friend was wrong; it was simply somebody else I didn't know with a variant of my surname who had killed somebody drink driving and later very nearly killed me too doing the same.

Of all the voices I had heard in my head during this time my policeman brother's seemed to be the most common, often saying the same thing: "He's topped out." If he had really said that he'd have been wrong – I'd actually bottomed out, or more accurately was all over the place. Paul did not turn up to collect me, later apologising that he had got drunk and was not able to contact me. It was then I realised he was not my Polish friend Paul, but another Paul, a taxi driver. I decided to save up my beggings for a first class ticket back to Bedford via Coventry and after two more hard days' begging I reached the sum of approximately £66 without being interfered with by the police.

After over a year away I was on my way back to Bedford. At one point the train stopped next to a signal so I could see the number. The Special Intelligence Service wanted me to remember it for later reference. I wrote it down and it became just another tiny piece of an enormous amount of written material in my possession, all the product of my mental illness. Soon I would be home. But my problems were only just beginning.

Part XVIII

On The Run Again

Chapter Forty-Seven

Runaway

It may seem hard of me to not contact my family for a year but you have to remember I did not trust them, most of all because of the terrifying possibility they would have me sectioned. What happened next showed I wasn't completely wrong in this fear.

However I did not feel particularly proud of myself when I returned to learn that they had all given me up for dead. Still I was back, at last. However I can't remember if it was before or after my Newquay adventure that I called the police asking who I had to speak to in order to get the house swept for bugs.

A day or two after my return I was astonished to see a person whom I thought was the ringleader of the gang who attacked me near Oxford. I believed he had been made to walk past me by the Masons – who had seen all that happened that day, through my MTRUTH of course. More likely this was just Capgras.

I telephoned Emily and she agreed to come down to visit me. Soon she was flying down. From the airport she got the train, and I met her at the station. She came to stay at the house.

All I had to do was leave the room and the door would be quietly closed behind me so that my mother could explain to Emily that I was very ill. Emily later told me that mother had met her on the stairs, and said to her "You do know that Clive is terribly ill don't you?" I felt that the general impression given to Emily was that I was a dangerous person to be with. But as I have no record of violent behaviour towards individuals, apart from the throwing of a stone at a car under deep torment, and lightly barging the bloke in Reading years earlier, this did seem a bit unfair. But for now Emily contented herself with suggesting that she knew things about me but would not say what they were. I also later discovered that my mother had arranged a meeting with her over coffee in town at which she told Emily they were going to have to try and get me into hospital. She explained how some incident would have to be arranged at which I would appear to be the aggressor, maybe at Club Rich UK, and that the police had done it before. But it was to be a lot easier than that for them.

Emily decided to leave her husband and rented a country cottage just outside Bedford in the hamlet of Scald End. I moved in with her and her dogs Lucy and Polly, both Cavalier King Charles Spaniels, said to be allowed to go anywhere by Royal decree. The local was called The Jackal, meaning that during those happy months in Scald End every day was the Day of The Jackal – or every evening anyway. There were some postcards behind the bar from customers on holiday. One of them was of a man in a flat cap with a ludicrous grin on his face about to bite into a giant pasty. I could not be sure the postcard had been sent by an *ordinary* customer and thought back to the import of my winter in Newquay.

Meanwhile my mortgage was not being paid but I was a little closer to getting my life sorted out. Emily called into question whether I still had a job and I maintained I did. I persuaded her to go to my employer and ask them face-to-face. They told her I was still in their employment. It was explained to me that if I sent in a doctor's report my medical insurance payments would start again to the value of 90 per cent of my salary with the rest covered by Incapacity Benefit. But I did not seem to have much interest in sorting out my life and certainly did not want to entertain any involvement with my flat, which I simply didn't care about any longer.

At the time the relationship with my family was stretched, and I believed they would conspire against me to get me into hospital. Thoughts of the conspiracy involving witchcraft were not far from my mind. However Mum was giving me £50 per week to survive on until I was sorted out. If anyone was a witch it was me. And anyway what's wrong with a good bit of witchcraft? You can't beat it. The witch doctor in Ouagadougou market had to be on my side. I could harness his power. To me witchcraft was all about the law of tort.

I attended an appointment with the consultant psychiatrist, Dr. Balasubramaniam, and he prescribed me a drug called Respiridone, then rather more expensive than it is now. As I sat waiting for the prescription, which I had already decided I would flush down the toilet, I saw a notice by the dispensary hatch. I wrote on a piece of paper words from *Suburban Relapse* by Siouxsie and the Banshees, swapping the word "Suburban" with "Subramaniam", part of the consultant's name. Now it said "I had a relapse, a Subramaniam relapse." Too true! I hid the note behind the notice and deludedly thought this would later become legally important. Dr. Bala' had signed the back of the prescription so I could get it free as I had told him I had no money. In fact I was not eligible for free prescriptions as I was in employment, though not yet being paid again. I went down to the police station and as esoterically as before reported him for giving me a fraudulent prescription. I did not seem to be taken very seriously but luckily they did not search the National Police Database, which showed I was arrestable on two counts of not turning up in court. If they had, maybe they did not feel like it, or had something more important to do.

Each evening Emily and I would walk with the dogs down to the pub for a few drinks. Emily is extremely loquacious, whereas I tend to be quiet; so I just sat there admiring her good looks. Then as we approached home one night she said that she was going to give birth for me to a beautiful kitten.

Strangely, the next night, as we were walking near the farm, I said to her "Did you hear that?" She said she had not heard anything; so I decided I must have heard an owl. But on the way back I heard it again and, going over to the hedge under the old oak tree, I found a tiny little six-week-old kitten miaowing in the hedge where its mother from the farmhouse must have abandoned it.

I picked it up and its whole body was quivering with fright. It was a lucky little cat as it would not have had to wait too long before an owl or a fox took it. We got back to the cottage and, putting our new little baby down on the kitchen floor, it was immediately apparent that it did not mind the dogs. Nevertheless, it still seemed a little frightened but it did enjoy tucking into a tin of tuna. The dogs really took to it, licking it, and that night the little kitten slept in the dogs' basket with them. For the first time in my life I was actually living with a woman and a beautiful woman at that. Thoughts began to turn to sorting out my life, though if the truth were told I did not really know what that meant at this stage. I was quite directionless but suddenly felt, for once in my life, I had got something of a family.

Next day our new cat went into the garden, climbing a tree that looked like a witch's broom stuck in the ground. My imagination told me it had been grown like that, with its branches trained peculiarly and besom-like, quite deliberately. It seemed my being here in this cottage was predetermined from the time the tree had been planted by KGB Freemasonry. For sure, the planting and nurturing of this strange tree was directly linked with the MI5 drinks in 1926.

Now I saw the young cat take off on the witch's broom and fly all around the hamlet. I could not believe this was simply my imagination rather than what was supplied to me over my MTRUTH. The fact that the village of Broom was almost visible miles away down the valley seized my mind with thoughts of witchcraft.

I decided to write to Prince William, imagining that if not now then later, he would have full supra-subliminal EAI on his own MTRUTH. As far as I recall it was a rather peculiar communication with a reference to *The Glass Bead Game*. Later I was amused to see the post box from which I sent it had been moved, for no apparent reason, some 50 yards away. This seemed to demonstrate a degree of shyness in the Royal Mail, brought about by my daring to write to a future monarch. Where there's a *Will* there's a way, I found myself thinking, and wondered what I would have to do to get the post box moved back. Now another thing happened which made me mindful of the possibility I had an MTRUTH fitted, through which the Security Services could see everything I did.

Remembrance Sunday came and I laid some money ceremoniously on the ground at a post box near the river. Later I would notice the path leading up to the box had been newly remade. I assumed it had been partially financed by me.

One day I was at my parents' house listening to the Peter Gabriel track *Shaking the Tree*. Walking in the park later I saw a beefy chap shaking one of a line of newly planted trees. "Oi!" I called out to him, realising the strange coincidence. This provided me with further evidence I had an MTRUTH. So quite possibly did he, it seemed, as he looked like he might have been in the Parachute Regiment: A real meat-head!

We did some house-hunting near Bedford. On one occasion we were to look at a flat to rent in Bedford itself. I was a little shocked when we turned up at the appointed time to discover the landlord was a psychiatric nurse I knew. I was hoping he would not tell Emily how he knew me, though by then, it would not have been news to her. He took us to another place where he described his tenants as animals and told us how he had a baseball bat to control them – not a good sign I thought, especially for a psychiatric nurse! Then, a few days later we had another appointment with him and were late. He left a very aggressive message on Emily's answerphone. I called the police to complain and a constable came around to listen to it – though without taking any action. If I had made the call I'm sure action would have been taken. It seemed an unfair world. To be fair though I have always thought him a good nurse and he treated me well down the years.

We went to the rugby one day. A man walked by whom I thought looked like Michael Maltby, and as he passed in the opposite direction, he said "feeling a lot more comfortable." It was probably his new Pringle jumper but it seemed to be a message for me.

Emily wanted to go back one last time to Scotland to collect her belongings. So one wet Saturday afternoon, having hired a van, we set off with the dogs and our cat, newly named "Eryngo", all inside the dog-cage in the back of the van. I had got his name by opening an encyclopaedia of plants at random to find a kind of thistle called Eryngo Eryngium. I also learnt that Eryngo was the candied root of the Sea Holly, reputed to be an aphrodisiac – which amused me.

That evening we arrived in Windermere. We had dinner and then after a few drinks had one of our arguments of which there were quite a few, possibly born out of Emily's frustration at my situation and how little I seemed to care about it.

Next evening we arrived in Edinburgh having admired the beautiful autumn colours of the Lake District. If you've not seen the Lake District on a sunny day in autumn you've missed something fantastic. I had no doubt Prince Charles's dog was walking with a friend high above on the fells, a proud and wistfu glint in its eye as it took in the view.

We visited Pets R Us where we bought a lead and harness for Eryngo as we were afraid of him running off. I had a quick look for Prince Charles's dog whilst we were there, but no luck. That night we stayed in a hotel, which took animals; so it was nice to not have to worry about them being cold in the van. Instead Eryngo could play with the dogs in our room and that he did.

In the morning we went to Emily's house to collect her belongings. Her daughter was there and I was a little surprised that she did not show more distress at her mother's imminent departure. I helped pack and load her heirlooms into the van and we drove off for the last time from her family of some 30 years. Even I felt sad about the end of a marriage but it really was not my fault. I also felt sorry for her that she had collected so little in all that time. But I loved her and she seemed genuinely happy and relieved to be going.

As we drove south through the mountains of the borders the snow turned to rain. Eryngo was having an eventful little life. I considered writing an anthropomorphic child's book about his adventures, from a cat's point of view. I could be his MTRUTH controller to do it.

We spent that night in a lovely hotel at Shap Fell and again the animals were allowed into our room. Emily was looking optimistic about her break and having her with me did my confidence no end of good. We sat talking by the log fire until late. Outside the wind howled on the fell and I felt glad at my change in fortunes. Sometime in the next year or so, an RAF jet would come down on this fell, leading my imagination to uncertainty: there had not really been an accident – it was simply an RAF clue as to the level of surveillance I was, and had been, under.

Next morning, after a nice shower and breakfast, we were off again after loading the animals up for their journey back to Bedford. As we passed Northampton, and Althorp House, seat of the Spencer family, Emily made a fist as she realised that the years of misery of her marriage were over. Soon we were back in Scald End and I cooked supper, as I often did.

I sought help from a solicitor about the current situation and began sending him odd letters about the service Emily had been receiving at the garage. News probably reached back to my parents about my behaviour.

Around this time there was a wonderful meteor shower with spectacular and almost audible streaks of light shooting across the whole sky. It was the Leonid shower. We gazed up at the display into the early hours before finally going in to warm-up in front of the roaring fire with Lucy, Polly and Eryngo all enjoying the warmth.

Then, a few nights after my mother had suggested to Emily that an incident would be arranged in Club Rich UK, one did indeed occur. I was sitting with Emily when a bloke stuck the mouth of a bottle of champagne to her mouth. Diplomatically I asked him whether he was going to give her some champagne or not. He now feigned falling over and knocked my bottle of beer. Instinctively, I grabbed the bottle to stop it falling over whereupon he and his friend attacked me. Matt stepped in and they were all thrown out. Had it been a set-up? Emily seemed to have little doubt in her mind, and it was now she told me about the meeting with my mother. The reality almost certainly was that it was not a set-up but it was certainly a frightening experience particularly as they may well have had knives. We left and went home to Scald End. I called the police who came round the next morning. I showed them my injuries. Nothing transpired and I did not see my assailants ever again.

As winter set in I began to think that the hum of an aircraft going over each night was an RAF Lancaster bomber brought in to get me thinking. Anyone who knew the sound of Lancaster engines would recognise the drone, I thought. This merely demonstrated how farfetched my thoughts could get. I even imagined some of the original crew were on board in one last mission. This was how important I felt. It was later suggested to me, by another psychiatric patient who seemed otherwise very poorly, that it was probably an Argosy Royal Mail flight. Being in a paranoid schizophrenic state does not exclude the possibility of having some objective thought about the world at large.

What I was *not* deluded about was that Emily's and my bed was ever so slightly and subtly rocking back and forth and yet no one was staying next door. I thought of whether to tell Emily but she was fast asleep. It seemed the only explanation could be that somebody was pushing against one of the old beams of the cottage to make the whole building sway. I crept out of bed and went downstairs thinking that perhaps some kids were playing next door. But it was the police, the Masons, MI5, the KGB or the nearby Thurleigh Women's Institute who were playing games with me.

I pushed the door open to the next-door cottage and went in. I was determined to find out what was going on. No one was there and I went upstairs with some trepidation. One by one I went through the rooms but there was an eerie emptiness in all of them. Frightened, I returned next door and to bed unnoticed by Emily, who was still asleep. Back in bed, I found it was still happening. Our bed was rocking back and forth ever so slightly but unmistakably! I decided that the only explanation was that somebody had indeed been next door but had known I was coming and gone out before I went in, returning as soon as I left! Or failing that, they were outside the building doing it. There was no wind and no other explanation, other than the possibility this very old cottage was haunted. I liked the idea it was haunted and, with the witch's broom in the garden, the abode seemed steeped in mystery. I did not tell Emily because I knew the response I would get would be that I was paranoid.

One day we were driving into town in Emily's Discovery when a policeman with a traffic gun stopped us. I had a feeling the whole speed trap had been aimed at me. Neither Emily nor I had seen any speed limit sign. The policeman was acting alone, perhaps in more than one way, standing with his camera at the bottom of the hill. It seemed to me that since he could not see the speed limit sign from where he stood, and the reading on his camera did not show an image of the speed limit sign on it, there was no evidence any speed limit was in operation. The SAS had dug up the speed limit sign just before we came around the corner, carried it round behind the hedge in the bucket of a JCB, and then replaced it after we had passed round the bend down to the speed trap. I wrote to the police about this, not mentioning the SAS, and was refused the refund of the speeding fine I had requested on Emily's behalf.

Christmas came: Emily, the dogs and I got ready to set off for the Lake District again. But there was no sign of Eryngo. One of the farm labourers was washing down the hung turkeys and said something about shutting a cat in a shed because it was showing too much of an interest in the turkeys. But his north Bedfordshire accent was so heavy I could hardly understand what he was saying. We looked everywhere for Eryngo but could not find him and were forced to set off without him.

Near Northampton Emily cut up a lorry. It said "Blakeley" on it, a family name on my father's side. The driver was angrily gesturing at us from his cab and chased after us in a classic display of road rage. I was frightened – he was a squaddie in our own MI6 Soviet section MTRU convoy. We pulled in at the next service area and so did he. I thought he was going to come after us. I called the police and told them what had happened.

We arrived in Windermere, and booked into our bed and breakfast. It snowed and felt Christmassy. I soon started going down with a bad cold, which spoilt Christmas morning for me. Luckily there was an American girl also staying there who had some Sudafed tablets, which greatly relieved my problems and enabled me to enjoy the rest of the day. We wondered what had happened to Eryngo.

It had not gone unnoticed that with New Year 1999 approaching, no more members of the Royal Family had 'died', and I was beginning to concede no more were likely to. On the other hand the real end of the millennium was not until a year later. Perhaps there was still mileage in my theory about faked Royal deaths, I thought.

I was still a little ill, though it did not seem to upset Emily too much, and certainly not ill enough for hospitalisation – I thought. She was just too grateful to be with me. However she was aware that I was going to Windermere library and writing letters of complaint, for example about the shower in our room. I had been continually annoyed by bed and breakfast showers not working properly and had resolved to complain about them. This seemed preferable to ripping them from the wall and getting sectioned. On one occasion I went into Windermere Police Station and reported my family for a fraudulent medical insurance conspiracy, which got back to Bedford Police Station.

New Year's Eve came – and up on the fells we met a wonderful old chap. He was like the ghost of Emily's father, now working for the Secret Service. I had recovered from my cold and we enjoyed the evening. I was more or less free from my conviction Princess Diana was not dead so I was sad. But I had to make sure her holiday on the island of Mystique never ended. There she was receiving the same reports that Prince Charles was on our progress. Very detailed reports: she even knew which aisles of Pets R Us we had looked for His Royal Highness's dog in and how close I was each day to having to look in the asylum again.

After the New Year we set off back for Scald End. We were listening to Emily's wonderful *Talk on Corners* Corrs album[121], which I had bought her for Christmas.

It was dark and raining when we arrived back from the Lake District. I opened the door to the cottage and as soon as I was inside I heard the sound of a cat miaowing. I opened the window and in jumped a very thin and tired Eryngo. Eryngo had obviously not eaten anything in two weeks and was terribly hungry. I fed him without delay then lit the fire and we all sat down in front of it, happy to be reunited. Even the dogs were glad to see Eryngo again. It had been a terribly hard time for him, as in the song *Erin-go-bragh*, and he had obviously found very meagre pickings whilst we had been away. But we were grateful he did not give up hope that we would return.

Chapter Forty-Eight

Princess of the Sands [122]

We had only been back from the Lake District a couple of days when I found myself in Bedford alone. On something of a whim I went to the police station to report the shooting of Gay Rich's neighbour's cat near the Irish Club. In the street I had met my friend Lizzie, who like a sizable proportion of the population in Bedford, was eastern European and in her case heavily involved with RATS, the Rehoming Animal Telephone Service (but not the Rebroadcast Army Telecommunications System). She just loved her cats: she called them her babies. I told her about the shooting of the cat, though did not reveal to her how long ago it was. She was appalled and encouraged me to go the police.

Most people would say I was ill advised to report this old incident at the station but my state of mind was putting me on the attack. I sensed something was wrong and here was evidence of it. Irish sovereignty had been infringed near the Irish Club. But what about mine? Had I an MTRUTH fitted without my permission? I was about to find that the Scottish police were trying to extradite me back to Edinburgh. True, I must have looked mad to report it – but where was the harm in it? I was just using my innate Aboriginal tracking skills to determine there was indeed something wrong. There was something significant in the fact that the cat had been shot near the Irish Club. When you are schizophrenic you make connections between things which, in reality, have no connection whatsoever, which the average person would see. You can make the connection as much as you like – but if you over-make it you are getting ill. For my part I was feeling persecuted and wanted somebody else to feel the weight of the Law.

That evening Emily and I were at the family house. My mother said something which absolutely enraged me. I was cutting the bread and infuriated by her remark, pointed the bread knife at her. Most unfairly I would later be accused before a psychiatrist of having threatened her with the knife. All I did was point it at her and it was in my hand anyway.

I stormed out of the house and decided to call the Samaritans but discovered that the number was not free. I had no money. So I went back to the police station where I reported my family for a medical insurance fraud conspiracy yet again. A police officer appeared from the back of the station and said "Clive, could you come through?" My fate was sealed.

The officer told me he had a warrant for my arrest from Edinburgh West End Police Station (where I had been roughed up). I was going to have to see the psychiatrist. I heard the Charge-Desk Officer talking to my policeman brother on the phone, which only made the feeling of persecution worse. In fact they had waited until after Christmas to arrest me so I could spend it with Emily.

I saw my GP who told me that if I wanted to report animal cruelty I should have gone to the RSPCA and not the police station. He said "We do think you are ill." I did not want to be in hospital – and nor did I feel I needed to be there. I was terrified, as I knew what being sent there meant. Emily had to go back to Scald End with the animals but without me. She was depressed and uncertain what would happen. She got some of my things together and wrote me a letter saying she would stand by me.

So I was sectioned again under the Mental Health Act for the first time in three years. I did not deserve to be but who does? You have to be a danger either to yourself or others and that I certainly was not at this stage, or ever really. But you can also be sectioned if you are suffering from an illness of "a nature and a degree requiring hospitalisation"; so that's how they got me. They just did it to get me off the charge of not turning up to court in Scotland and that meant I would not get a criminal record. To some extent I was just being punished for what anyone would do which was to flee a foreign country where I had faced brutal oppression. On the other hand I was not taking much interest in my most valuable possession: my flat.

Next day at Weller Wing (at least I was not taken to the asylum on this occasion), Emily turned up. I was terrified, as I knew that an injection was imminent. It was not the injection itself that I was terrified of, but the effects it would have on me. I was put in the seclusion room after being allowed to finish my letter of complaint; I think it was to my dentist. I felt like a condemned innocent man. Emily was talking to the young female doctor. I walked in and told the doctor I would not forgive her for this. I had been diagnosed as having the clinical delusion I had a job. But it was no delusion – I did have a job, as Emily explained to the doctor, having driven down to London and asked my employer face-to-face. I sat praying out aloud to God as many as 50 times. The doctor was too late to intervene as the consultant had already given the order that I should be injected. I believe she did try to intervene whilst she found out if it was really true I had a job, but she was too late. I went like a lamb to the slaughter. But even though it seemed my pleas were falling on deaf ears I would discover (six years later) that one of the nurses refused to take part in this. She would become my community psychiatric nurse. Another was minded to give me 20 quid with the instruction that I should scarper at the earliest opportunity. I was not to wait for the 20 quid.

Emily lay on the bed with me. I could already feel the depressive effects of the drug coming on. Then I sensed a strange feeling in my throat and my voice began to go. All the muscles in my neck and mouth began to stiffen up. Soon I was actually speechless. A nice Asian doctor was called and he examined me. Amusingly, his name was Dr. Sain! But nothing seemed very funny at the time. The stiffening had been caused by the injection of Clopixol. He gave me liquid Procylidine, a drug for Parkinson's disease, which counteracts the side effects of antipsychotic drugs. It worked very well and within half-an-hour I could speak again. But it had been a frightening experience despite Emily's presence helping me through it.

The depression was already getting to me after a matter of days and I was pacing up and down the corridor with uncontrollable restlessness. I had also been prescribed an oral medication, Olanzapine. I hid it under my tongue and went to the toilet. There I saw the figure of a friendly Rastafarian on my MTRUTH who was working for MI5. He was gesturing to me that the pill was shit and that I should flush it down the toilet – which I did. This was unfair on Olanzapine, whose effects I did not discover until after this story – but the point was I believed I did not need it[123]. I was already desperately depressed by the situation in the non-clinical sense of the word and wrote a letter to the founder of my employer's company in America.

Amanda's husband seemed to be after me and was being prevented from reaching Bedford by the police. In the toilet, I cried desperately to God for help. But the Special Forces knew I was not sufficiently ill to be in hospital and were going to spring me from it. I kept seeing my old SAS buddy on my MTRUTH briefly entering the corridor of the ward and looking down it. This gave me hope – the hope that the Special Forces did know of my predicament.

But the truth was that, yet again, the only person who could get me out of this was myself. However, since I had been misdiagnosed (however schizophrenic I was, I did still have a job and therefore could not have had the delusion I had one), it might have been worth waiting for my appeal to the Mental Health Appeal Tribunal. I did not – and you could put that down as a mistake. As it would transpire this meant I could ground-MTRUTH what happens to absconded patients. I wanted to show how their rights are ignored. I believed mine were and I was just being flushed down the psychiatric toilet again. I thought of the other tribunal, of which the public are not generally aware: the Wireless Telegraphy Tribunal, and how broadcasts to and from my MTRUTH were subject to it.

My imagination allowed that strange tribunal to sit at a moment's notice to provide me with some lego-sociological protection from what, at times, had been a rather trying input of concept documents and images on my MTRUTH. I could not rule out these having been emailed to me at the address of my MTRUTH by the Iraqi State Security Service, the Amn al-Amm. This was because the documents' contents were not covered by the usual cinema certification. The Special Forces, the Security Services, the KGB and, by now even the CIA were very interested in my latest predicament.

In the hospital I met Melanie Jones. She'd had trouble with manic-depression and was obviously hyperactive but was a very pleasant person in her 20s. When I got out I would very nearly meet her again.

After a couple of weeks, I was allowed out for an hour's leave. Emily was coming in every day to see me but I could not sleep because of the terrible droning noise from the hospital's generator. I wrote a letter of complaint. The one-hour was just long enough to go for a walk and have a low alcohol drink in the pub, The Horse and Groom. The landlord looked more paranoid than I did. According to the local newspaper the pub had recently been attacked.

That night I had a dream I was hitch-hiking back to an asylum following Section 17[124] leave when Michael Ignatiev, the Canadian philosopher, intellectual and television personality, stopped and gave me a lift. He said to me "Existentially speaking, what do you think of the proposed plans to forcibly medicate patients in the community?"

I replied "Speaking as a post-Bedford Modernian it seems unlikely that I would now be asking you to drive me to the hospital if, upon my release in a couple of weeks, I would still be forced to take this despicable poison."[125]

"Did it ever occur to you that when a patient appears before a psychiatrist the psychiatrist cannot tell if the patient appeared there spontaneously or was *driven* there?" Mr Ignatiev said, as he tuned his car radio into a station where Joan Bakewell was expostulating in a ridiculously intellectual manner about Marzipan 25mg injections.

At the hospital I was sitting in front of the psychiatrist, whom I recognised to be Jean-Paul Sartre. With him was a big circle of mental health professionals, as is so familiar at ward-rounds to anyone who has been in a psychiatric hospital. In this case, I could see those at the ward-round were a collection of the world's most famous philosophers all avidly examining every detail of my countenance.

What they said to me was something like this, Karl Marx starting first: "You believe you have been enclosed in an MTRUTH harness. We, the vanguard, are here to shatter your false consciousness."

Then Descartes said "You are living in a world of total MTRUTH illusion, which you take to be reality. The Special Intelligence Service is using your body to feed their MTRUTH machinery. Are you to be deceived by this semantic and epistemological nightmare? Are you to succumb to the all-powerful demons in the MTRUTH who manipulate the course of your experience?"

I replied to them "I don't care if my beliefs are false, so long as I'm enjoying my experiences. Why shouldn't I sacrifice my life to MTRUTH and enjoy false knowledge?"

Nietzche interjected "There is no pre-established harmony between knowledge and happiness. You cannot justify the knowledge you gain from MTRUTH by suggesting it has happiness-inducing qualities."

Already bewildered, I now listened to Plato asserting "Knowledge is the supreme value. But I won't explain why, I never do, I just harp on about the knowledge of the Forms, those abstract, universal, timeless entities it is your duty to discover and love. If I had heard of *The Glass Bead Game* I would harp on about that too."

Confucius he say "Dog that runs halfway into wood already halfway out other side."

Finally Dr. Jean-Paul Sartre said to me, whilst swigging from a bottle of absinthe, "You have been driven into psychiatric hospital by a well-known Canadian philosopher, intellectual and television personality. My girlfriend is having an abortion in an extremely dingy and depressing illegal back-street clinic and a dark, angst-ridden post-Modernist neurosis is hanging heavily in the clinging, almost psychotic, midsummer Paris heat wave. I would like to impose a radical doctrine of human freedom on you: I want to try you on absinthe. Fancy a swig?"

A week later, my leave was extended to three hours so Emily was able to take me back to the cottage for the evening to see the animals. Eryngo had put on weight dramatically and was looking very well. Polly had a bump with a car so she had to go to the vet for the day – Lucy and Polly were not road dogs[126] – and her bump was my fault. After a quick drink in The Jackal, Emily took me back to the hospital for the night. I could not make love to her properly anyway because of the injection.

I had been in the hospital four weeks when the young doctor, Dr. Bude, whose name prompted me to make connections with my days near Bude, in Newquay, told me that the next day I was to be given another injection. To make it worse my CPN visited, telling me he had been on holiday in Newquay, the connections making me more unsettled. *I was mortified and decided there and then there was only one thing to do.* As well as the depression, anxiety and akathisia was also now setting in as a result of the injection. Who knows how much worse I would have been if they had discovered I was not taking my Olanzapine – quite likely they would have increased the dose of the intramuscular injection. One evening the nurse had asked the patient in the queue in front of me to open his mouth to see if he had swallowed his pill. The Nigerian nurse, with a very therapeutic voice, did not ask me the same. A relief. If he had and had made me swallow it I would just have made myself sick anyway. I sensed he was gently goading me, and knew I was not taking the pill. He had been acting on the instructions of the Nigerian ambassador to the United Kingdom by not asking me to swallow it.

That night Emily came in as usual. She was going to Tesco's and left me in the car. As soon as she had gone I got out of the car and, hoping nobody would see me, went to hide in the bushes nearby. This was a bad move as if somebody had seen me behaving strangely they might have called the police. But nobody did.

I waited some time until I was sure Emily would have discovered I had gone, brushed myself down and began a long circuitous walk to Marek's, hoping that Emily would not raise the alarm. I simply was not prepared to face the further effects of another injection, and if I had to be on the street again, then so be it. As far as I was concerned they had misdiagnosed me – I was a victim of medical negligence.

I did not know how Emily would react to my disappearance or if she would hand me in or call the police, as I had not told her of my plans.

Marek put me up on his floor for the night. I felt safe with him, following the persecution his parents, and grandparents, had faced in Russia. I knew I could trust him.

I got up at 4am and made my way through town avoiding the CCTV cameras. I was worried that a lookout might be posted at the railway station; so I decided to head across country until I was well away from Bedford.

Walking down an alleyway my way was blocked by a van pulling up at the end. It was guiding me; its ghostly presence so early in the morning meant it must be the SAS; so I turned around and headed back up the alley coming out by The Three Cups pub. Turning right I walked past Peter's house and then, horror of horrors, what did I see but a police car, but it did not stop. I now gambled on walking to the right of the roundabout hoping they would turn left but, more horror, they came all the way around and passed me. Of course by now the alarm must have been raised at the hospital; so the station would have been aware; but they did not stop. The drivers knew who I was but were on my side in this, as I had bombarded the police station with letters of complaint, none of which had offended them, in fact the opposite. The order to simply observe me came from the usual desk. I was now a farmed free to roam psychiatric patient – for the moment.

Soon I was on the disused railway line to Cambridge. I decided to walk all the way to Sandy, eight miles to the east. I had been very lucky, and now I knew it would be safe and my escape was certain. There seemed no possibility of being recaptured: I was thinking about staying away for good and, under the bright moonlight the miles went past. In the trees above I heard the "twit twoo" of an owl. I fancied I might be able to see it against the moonlight if I moved and, sure enough, I briefly caught sight of its silhouette before it silently flitted off into the owl-light.[127] The gap between my psychiatrist and me was the same as the gap between the hunger strikers and Margaret Thatcher.

A cold February dawn eventually broke with the sinking moon fading from prominence. It took me some hours to get to Sandy, the former rail track eventually becoming unnavigable; so I was forced to take the road.

It was about eight o'clock when I arrived there, once more on the run. Without a ticket I took a train to London. When the guard asked me to show him my ticket I told him some story and showed him a letter from my company. He left me alone.

Upon arrival in London I found myself wandering aimlessly around. I had gone to my friend Roger's house, but he was not in. Once more I was on the streets but hopefully not for too long. I was going to telephone Emily and take the risk of inviting her to join me. But first I decided to go and see my old tutor from my undergraduate days. I explained to him how they were trying to make me take a medical insurance claim and how it was fraudulent. Sighing, he advised me to accept the claim. He let me make some calls on his phone but I failed to get through to anyone.

That night I waited in The Half Moon and The Duke's Head for Roger to come back from work, but by midnight neither he nor his wife had arrived and I was forced to give up. I walked up to Chelsea and sat down in the A&E waiting room of the Chelsea Hospital. On the wall I noticed a small poster. It depicted a nurse arriving at the pearly gates. St. Peter came out and asked why the nurse should be let in. The nurse explained how she had worked in the hell of the NHS for many years and was duly allowed in. I laughed and drew a bubble from St. Peter's mouth, which said "Of course, come in and sit down – there's a six-month waiting list!"

I was tired after all the walking, between ten and twenty miles in the previous few hours, and went to sleep as best I could. At about 3am the security guard woke me and threw me out of the hospital, as I was not a genuine patient. If he had known who I was! I went to Chelsea Police Station and, explaining that I had been accidentally locked out, asked if I could spend the night in the cells as it was so cold. They said I couldn't but could wait in reception where it was warm. So there I sat until the next morning. As a Chelsea fan it was nice to see the night pass without any unwanted intrusion – though I would have liked a cell so I could lie down.

Morning came and I went to Putney Bridge Tube station and began to beg to get enough for breakfast and coffee during the day. Soon I had £10 and I set off to eat in The Bedford Café on the Lower Richmond Road. After breakfast I went to the library to see if I could find a bed for the night, eventually finding a hostel in Richmond where I could stay, but for some reason only one night. Still, I had a nice hot bath, got something to eat, and that night, after a couple of drinks in the pub over the road, I slept well.

Next day I tried to see if Roger was around and, waiting outside his house, he eventually turned up at about nine o'clock and we went across to The Duke's Head for a few beers. He lent me £100 and said I could stay until the weekend. The problem was that the injection had given me clinical depression again and

I needed antidepressants. I felt quite desperate. What terrible injustice!

On the Thursday I telephoned Emily and she told me that the police had been around looking for me. I asked her to join me and we arranged to meet the next day. I trusted her not to hand me in to the police though if she didn't she could face up to two years in prison for harbouring.

I made an appointment to see Roger's doctor and was mindful of a police car parked outside the surgery. The police, or MI5, knew everything I was doing and this whole thing was an experiment in schizophrenia to see what happened. After all, they knew I did not have a record of violence against individuals' persons and maybe they were sympathetic to me.

After booking the appointment I went to Putney Station, and enjoyed purchasing a platform ticket. I had this bugbear, not only that I could not buy a first class ticket from Bedford to Bedford St. Johns to show to a friend for a laugh but also that, in Bedford, I could not buy a platform ticket. Armed with my platform ticket I went down onto the platform. Thoughts of throwing myself in front of a train arose. But really this was only because I knew I had depression – not because I was so depressed I was suicidal, as I wasn't. Mind you, if you have never had depression and could experience what I now was I think you might claim you would leap in front of the very next train as that is the only way to explain how horrible it is. These thoughts of suicide were as much to do with transmissions I was picking up from the psychic-ether left by previous suicides at railway stations as any intention I had. It was just that I felt so bloody awful with the clinical depression they had given me at the hospital that I had to adopt the belief that I was in the Special Forces under orders not to commit suicide, in order not to do so. I had always been amazed at how few people on the Tube had obviously just read a Cold War espionage story in which a double agent is pushed to his death in front of a Tube train. I stayed well back from the platform edge and went into the impressively good coffee shop, the purpose of my being there. Caffeine should help I thought.

They served excellent coffee with a choice of syrups from hazelnut to mint. I chose vanilla. A chap was giving the stallholder some guidance. There was something impressive about him. He was a former MI5 officer who had been laid off following the collapse of the Berlin Wall. I pictured him in an office in the Admiralty Arch being advised by his former boss that he wanted him to take over a chain of coffee shops. These MI5 was planning to turn into one ward of the open psychiatric hospital for those caught up in the Troubles in Northern Ireland or, come to think of it, any conflict that remotely interested the intelligence services, including in the drugs deal theatre. If they had been out of any of the syrups I might have dropped a line to the director of MI5 or the Admiral of the Fleet.

On the Friday morning I attended the appointment and I did not tell the doctor the whole situation; I simply told him I was depressed and wanted a prescription for antidepressants. He told me I was not depressed, which was ridiculous, as I am a seasoned expert on it and I know when I am clinically depressed. Perhaps saying "clinical" might have swung it but I do not remember if I did or not. The depression was very definitely caused by the Clopixol. He refused to give me a prescription.

I came out from the doctor's wondering what to do. I bought a platform ticket for Putney railway station, as I had done the previous day, and went to the café.

I drank loads of coffee to try and alleviate the depression. In my head I heard the only voice I had heard for a while. It sounded like a senior barrister or an unusually sympathetic Army officer saying once, and once only, nothing but "Soldiering on." It was almost as though he felt as bad as I did. To know how I felt, he would not only have had the same injection but also a similar metabolism.

Then I remembered going to a Chinese acupuncturist when I had a chronic headache back in the '80s. It had lasted, on and off, for several years and I never worked out what was causing it. I still owed her £5. I noticed there was a Chinese herbal medicine doctor's surgery by Putney Bridge and, as I owed £5 to The Chinese Peoples' Liberation Army Medical Corps, I decided to seek his advice as a matter of honour. I also decided that, if he was wearing the uniform of that Army, I would ask him if he would prefer me to put the apostrophe before or after the "s" in "Peoples", to see if he was a communist or not. It turned out I could not afford to see him but I'm pretty sure that, if I did catch a glimpse, he was wearing a white coat and not khaki with red.

As I could not afford an appointment I asked the receptionist if she could sell me anything for depression. She offered me some pills called Jia Wei Xiao Yao Wan and I paid £8 for them. I spent the rest of the day drinking coffee and playing Roger's records including the beautiful and cheery song by the Sundays, *Hideous Towns*. This illness was hideous city Arizona. I say this because of the habit of a chap I worked with at DOAE. He had a way of expressing something to be the absolute limit in some way, good or bad. To do this he would say words describing the concept he was referring to followed, in every case, by the words "City" and "Arizona". Well I can assure you this depression, which came bundled with anxiety and restlessness, really was 'Hideous City, Arizona'. I hope it brings a legal action from the society of Arizona mayors against the consultant at the Bedford hospital at that time, who had diagnosed me as having "the clinical delusion I had a job". You do not need to be the best private detective in Arizona to see his diagnosis was incorrect – however ill I was. Anyway, in that song there's a line going "Out of the Army 'cos it drove me barmy and it didn't help", which seemed rather apposite. I fantasised I could now, in fact, join the Barmy Army[128] and, with a windfall, travel the world following the sun and the England cricket team. The song also went "I'd like to be in history". I felt I already was.

Emily arrived in the evening and we went out to dinner with Roger and his wife, Paula. I was a little cagey about what I was up to but in any case Roger said I could only stay two more nights. Emily agreed to take me to meet my employer's Human Resources department (lovingly known as Human Remains by many employees, including the one I mentioned, who called it Human Remains City, Arizona) the next day. I was terribly depressed with very unpleasant anxiety and was *having trouble keeping myself going*.

Next day we drove the short distance to Uxbridge to meet the Company and they saw us without any appointment, confirming I still had a job and would need to produce a report from my psychiatrist before I went back. I do not think they realised I was on the run and could be arrested. I was now taking the Chinese antidepressants, which were showing no side effects at all, unlike western antidepressants, which similarly take a while to work but often cause immediate side effects.

I persuaded Emily to drive me to the West Country the next day to meet two dear old friends of mine, husband and wife and now practising GPs near Exeter. That evening I could hear some music insinuating its way through the wall from the next house. I had this firm feeling that it was the very same music which had been played during the Cold War in an operation behind the Iron Curtain and had been chosen for that very reason. We were being spied on. For some reason Eryngo got stuck behind the fireplace during the night and in the morning, when we got him out, his grey and white fur was covered in old soot, so he needed a good brush-down. He looked a sight – like Tom in *Tom and Jerry* after he had caught fire.

We said goodbye to Roger and Paula and set off for the West Country. The anxiety, depression and restlessness were terrible and almost unbearable. The Clopixol was like a hundred ton weight attached to my brain. I wanted to just lie down in the road and die but the car was moving so it meant just opening the door and falling out, hopefully hitting a lamppost or being run over from behind. But I had Emily with me to nurse me through the damage the hospital had done to me and could see a way to get back to work. We bought Eryngo a new litter tray from the pet shop by Chiswick Bridge. Here I had left myself hanging off hypermanically four-and-a-half years earlier – and still have not said what happened next!

After what was a painful drive in cramped conditions we arrived in Exeter. There was an event in town at which I saw a chap dressed as a World War I fighter ace walking along the street in his fighter. He was such a brilliant actor, engaging passers-by in his jocular banter, that for a few moments I forgot how terrible I was feeling. Tally-ho old chap! For our parts Emily and I were like Pamela and Richard Hannay in *The 39 Steps*. There was no doubt Emily had been sent by the British Secret Service Bureau, and looked as good as Madeleine Carroll too!

I telephoned my friend Joe, the GP, and left a message, pretending we were just driving through rather than coming for help and advice. Sure enough Joe called back later the next day and invited us around for dinner.

So, leaving the animals in our bed and breakfast room, we set off for dinner. By the time we arrived it was snowing heavily, a white carpet covering the road. Joe was cooking the meal, a mushroom risotto, and as he cooked I explained the situation I was in without actually telling him I had absconded from a psychiatric hospital. To do so would have been unfair on a friend, ethically speaking, as he would then be party to a criminal offence. He told me that as far as he could see I was well, and certainly in no need of hospitalisation.

We sat down to dinner, Joe explaining to me about a patient of his who had schizophrenia. Apparently this patient was rather more ill than I. We briefly met Joe and Andrea's son, Alexander, and then Andrea had to go off to work, as she was on-call. I finished off the superb wine and with Joe promising to write a letter of support, it was time to go (he did not let me down). Before we left Joe explained that it was not actually the psychiatrist's report I needed in order to return to work, as my employer had asked for. Instead it was a simple doctor's note Form Med 3 (a sick note) from my GP with "You should not refrain from work" circled that I required. I think this probably gave me a slightly false view of the reality of the situation because the Official Secrets Act was involved at my workplace. Joe did not know this was the case. He also explained that it was quite common for psychiatric patients to change consultants. I do not think he said it explicitly, but he put into my head the idea that, as things seemed a bit hot in Bedford, it might be a good idea to move to another part of the country. There I would register with a GP and get the go-ahead to return to work. The reality was that I was far more ill than I was letting on to Joe, and that was quite apart from the anxiety, akathisia and depression, which were really crippling me, even though my sexual prowess had returned. I put on a tough front. In my case I could because Bill Mason, the ex-Olympic oarsman, had been my coach for a couple of years. You did not retain his services without being pretty hard. On the other hand, apart from the beastly combination of side effects, I did not believe I was ill so how could I say I was?

Next day we drove to Dartmoor and did a bit of sightseeing. I complained to Emily about my horrible anxiety and she continued to comfort me in my distress. We booked into a bed and breakfast and all I could do was lie on the bed and put up with it – however miserable it was – having nothing to rely on but the medical knowledge of an associate of the Chinese Peoples' Liberation Army Medical Corps. I make no apology for repeating the name of this organisation as it helped me to think I had the medical might of such a massive military machine behind me.

The next night we stayed in a much nicer bed and breakfast in Totnes and walked into town to spend the evening. In a pub we got talking to someone who explained he was a former employee of Mrs Shand Kydd, the mother of Diana, Princess of Wales. He told us how he had taken a horse and cart on a charity mission to Eastern Europe. He had been put there by MI5. As we walked back from the pub after a pleasant chat with him, I started having further strange thoughts about what was going on around me. Including wondering if each pub in town had such a similar person that night, for I did not recall his having arrived before us.

It was time to set off for Sussex where we decided to go and house-hunt for Emily. Bedfordshire was obviously out of the question so we had to hide somewhere, to avoid our both being arrested.

As we went past Stonehenge, we were listening to *Moon Safari* by the French group Air. I saw two soldiers strangely hacking around in the undergrowth. The Chief of Defence Staff had ordered them there. This was serious military humour with a well-defined and clearly achievable military objective. They had to appear to be looking for Prince Charles's dog to remind me what this was all about. I could not provide any other explanation for why two soldiers would be bush beating near the henge. I did not put the Army above telling jokes for purely military reasons, and remembered the *Monty Python* sketch about the funniest joke ever told. The joke was so funny it had to be broken into bits. A soldier died laughing when, by accident, he saw two parts of it. But this humour was deadly serious.

That night we stayed in Sevenoaks, and it was now that I began to feel a little better with the anxiety subsiding. Also I was not so restless, as the Clopixol was working its way out of my system. The next day was like a breath of fresh air in a rehabilitation clinic. Emily booked us into a place called Three Ducks Barn at Telscombe in the middle of the Sussex Downs east of Brighton, and not far from East Firle. This was as deep into the South Downs as you could get and it was really a private psychiatric hospital Emily had opened for me. I felt better almost from the moment we arrived. The residence was a converted barn with a gas boiler on around-the-clock to keep it warm. The ample double bed in a loft area with a ladder leading up to it made it feel like sleeping in a hayloft. Eryngo was able to climb upstairs, which the dogs could not, and he would jump onto the roof through the open skylight and from there down to the ground which came up to the roof on one side. So Eryngo was a happier cat than maybe he had been recently, cooped up inside various bed and breakfasts. He was at home again in the countryside and took every opportunity to explore, meeting the horses in the racing stables, once home of the 1902 Grand National winner, Shannon Lass.

I was truly happy at Three Ducks Barn and hardly if ever switched on the television. Instead we listened to Radio 4 all day and, after we returned from the pub, a round walk of some four miles, heard 'Sailing By' and the shipping forecast at 12:45am. In the morning I would go for a long run down to the main road and back, about three miles, whilst Emily fed the animals and had her bath. The Chinese antidepressants, Jia Wei Xiao Yao Wan, really seemed to be working; they certainly were not causing a dangerous clinical mental illness which the Clopixol had. Emily and I made some long walks across the beautiful downs and these further improved my mental state.

As I ran down to the main road one day I wondered what hell my departure had let loose back in Bedford, some one hundred miles away with all of London in between. It also occurred to me that MI5 and MI6 were 50 miles away in the same direction but somehow, despite all my delusions about them; I could not quite connect these delusions with their actual existence. Somehow my delusions transcended the reality of both these organisations – into the realms of the Special Intelligence Service.

Little did I think that, at my flat, letters were mounting up from the Building Society. I did not care, though did briefly wonder if there was now an extra for sale sign in the pile in the alleyway round the back. Although I felt perfectly happy and well, I was not quite right. Let us say I was not quite interfacing sociologically as well as I might have liked. But at least I was trying! I was writing what must have seemed strange, but harmless, letters to people in positions of authority including the director of my former workplace, RARDE. I also sent a deluded breakdown of my intelligence activities on behalf of my employer. This included my dutiful meetings with the American at the Reading YMCA the previous summer. I also wrote to "The Editor", the Special Air Service Regiment, at their HQ. I could see him in full combat fatigues but wearing one of those typesetters' caps with the peak. This was a joint operation and we badly needed a successful outcome.

But peacefulness had returned to my mind, and one evening I set off as usual for the pub, The Abergavenny Arms in Rodmell, with Lucy and Polly, Emily planning to meet us there later. Telscombe is such a beautiful place situated in a hollow and as we reached the edge of the hollow, the lights of Lewes were clearly visible some eight miles away down in the valley of the River Ouse[129]. Far in the distance I could see, but not hear, a speeding police car, its lights flashing through the darkness and no doubt its siren blaring. I followed its lights all the way along the Ouse valley down below, all those miles away and all the way to Newhaven. The sight of the police car so many miles away gave me a feeling of security up there on the Downs. The Special Forces knew exactly where I was right then. The distant speeding police car was intended to make me feel better, which it did. My assigned fellow KGB/MI6 nuclear war prevention agent was watching everything through my very own eyes at that moment, through my MTRUTH. If not, he would be watching from somewhere pretty damn close, like in the nearby gorse bushes – maybe both.

As I approached Rodmell with the dogs, which were really enjoying the open countryside, I visualised Mel Smith relaxing, fishing for the £10 million in the River Ouse in the valley down below. Hi Mel, I thought, on the Comic Relief psychic-ether British Intelligence Messaging System that no doubt, Comic Relief would never either confirm or deny the existence of, well not officially. Eventually, after some 10 minutes, the police car disappeared behind me into Newhaven. But I would not forget it. Many a Rastafarian would tell you that a police car is like the bagpipes: it sounds better the further away it is. This one was so far away I could not hear it at all.

We reached the pub and Emily later joined us. There was a disco and we happily danced. The singer put the microphone to my mouth and I marginally impressed Emily with my deep voice. 19 years earlier, accompanied by the pier organist, I had sung *Love Will Tear Us Apart* to the pensioners on Eastbourne pier a few miles down the coast. Afterwards a glamorous-looking lady, who must have been a real cracker in about 1942, asked if I was going into show business. Somehow I did not think she would get a job as a *New Musical Express* hack.

In the pub was a display of vintage shaving tackle including a rare collection of old razor blades. I thought of Caroline's friend Ken, ex-SAS, and his motorbike collection, which included a Wilkinson, made by the razorblade company. Being in a different constabulary had altered my feelings towards the police in general and, it seemed, there must be the possibility of asylum, if I spelt it correctly. This I did not, writing "psychiatric assylum" in one or two oddly desperate letters to Captain Mainwaring, Warmington-on-Sea Home Guard c/o Bexhill-on-Sea Police Station.

I had recovered from the side effects of the Clopixol. That was all I cared about, even if it meant having to survive without any money other than Emily's. Happily, her generosity extended to buying me a beer each night. The next evening it was raining and we left the animals behind to get the bus into Brighton. I told Emily about James Longhurst, and she was proud of me. We went into "Charlie's Bar" on the seafront. I wanted her to buy me a cigar and we had an argument. A man sitting nearby told me not to "speak to the lady like that". The next thing I knew he was walking towards me threateningly. I sat still and ignored him. He didn't hit me and just walked past. Emily and I made up, took the bus, and soon were walking down the unmade road to Telscombe where, in our loft bed we listened to the shipping forecast for the last time during our truly happy 12 days stay. I noticed the BBC World Service broadcast was not playing the usual music (*Lillibulero*) but something more modern. I hit on the theory it was written by The Other Two; Stephen Morris, and Gillian Gilbert of New Order fame, and that a secret Army Unit had jammed the signal from the Lord Camoy's attic[130] and overlaid this more up-to-date-style World Service music. I wondered if this was not a full reflection of the real state of affairs – perhaps Emily, the dogs and Eryngo were all MTRUs, I thought. Either way, though I am a bit of a conservative, I liked that music and still remember it. I never heard it again – as *Lillibulero* was brought back for some real reason.[131]

In the morning Emily filled in the visitors' book to say how much we had enjoyed our stay and I finished reading a book I had found about the Raj, and the lead-up to Indian independence. We packed up and now we were off to Camber where Emily had found us less expensive accommodation from which to house-hunt. She never said a word about the night I called her Amanda by mistake. I was not even thinking of Amanda but the word just came out. Happy as I was with Emily it seems the thought of Amanda was never far away, but further than in that beautiful place in the Downs.

As we drove down from Beachy Head we could see all the way to Hastings and Dungeness. It was clear that Emily was not feeling well. On the road where I had cycled to work at the Royal Greenwich Observatory, Herstmonceux Castle, 19 years earlier, Emily parked for a rest. I took the dogs on what was, for me, a nostalgic walk along the road to the Observatory, remembering the happy times I'd had there in my very first job after leaving school and before going to University. I had only earned £55 per week but with rent-free accommodation provided by my Great-Uncle Bernard, I'd had plenty of money to enjoy myself. They had been wonderful times.

I walked for over an hour though I had no money to buy myself a beer in our old haunt, The Lamb, at Wartling. I thought of how I had cycled one warm summer night through the Observatory grounds on the way back from Chiddingly. I thought of the badger I had trapped in my bicycle lamp beam and how, every time I steered the wheel, it kept running back out of the light to the middle of the road in front of me. I thought of the fireflies I found myself lying amongst as I collapsed off my bike, exhausted at the top of the hill in the Observatory grounds. I thought of how I wished I knew then what I knew now. But they were good times.

When we returned to the car, Emily was asleep with the headlights on and the battery was dead. We tried unsuccessfully to bump-start it. As we were now parked at a funny angle, a passing driver stopped to ask if we were alright. Luckily they had jump leads and soon we were off to Camber. The prompt appearance of the car got me thinking, once again, that we were being watched by the local defence forces – after all, her father had won the George Medal, and her grandfather ran an aircraft factory before the War. My girlfriend was a very important person and not just because she had once met Prince Charles at a dance – that is what I thought, and still do really.

We unpacked in our new hideaway and Emily went to sleep. That night I took the dogs for a long walk along the Camber Sands. The air was crisp, fresh and clean as the stiff breeze blew in from the sea under the moonlight, whipping up the sand in the dogs' faces. But they loved it. The tide was out and the moon was glimmering on the waves. We walked out some way to the breaking waves and the dogs excitedly played in them. Special Boat Service frogmen were only feet away in the water spying on our every movement in an exercise to test their latest equipment, for that was all this was.

Things were looking up. Soon I would be weaned off the antidepressants. It was now I thought of Emily with her long blonde hair blowing, not in the here and now but in her father's own wartime English Channel breeze. It was now I thought of Nick Drake's song and how he had died of an overdose of Tryptophan back in 1974. I had not found Princess Diana anywhere, though we had met a friend of her mother's, and I somebody who had met her. I had not found Prince Charles's dog though in a variety of locations I had felt it was there, including Paradise, or a nation where for a brief period there were signs pointing to it everywhere, and I had found Emily. How lucky I was to have met her. She was my Princess of the Sands.

Back at the house Emily was sleeping off her cold and Eryngo was exploring his new territory. Poor Eryngo was in for a shock though.

A few nights later we were in bed when I heard Eryngo miaowing outside the window. I let him in and instead of going to his usual place on top of Emily's suitcase in the cupboard he jumped on the bed where we were and looked at us. It was obvious he was badly hurt and must have had a fight. He was walking on three legs and was covered in a foul smelling liquid. I took him for a warm shower to clean him up. Poor Eryngo's rear offside leg was badly swollen at the knee and I deduced he must have encroached on a very aggressive local cat's territory. But what was this liquid he had on him? It looked like he had been fired at with a paintball gun full of liquid chicken shit and I actually found myself believing this. Not only did it seem that there were dark forces playing with me but also that they were not averse to having a go at Eryngo. That night I dreamt of a Forces' court-martial at which somebody was brought to book for firing at Eryngo. Next day we took poor Eryngo to the vet's where he was prescribed some cat painkillers. He would recover after a few weeks and eventually got back the use of his leg, which, amusingly, had a patch of grey fur on it, which I called his filler cap.

Now *I* went down with the cold and found I had terrible sinusitis and a bad headache but I ran it off in long jogs all the way to Lydd and back across the Romney Marsh and along the edge of the military firing range. One day I was running, completely carefree, along the Marsh road, when I noticed the red flags were flying to indicate firing on the range. I noticed a model aircraft flying along the coast and, remembering how I had once designed some equipment to be flown under such a drone when I was a student at the Imperial College of Science and Technology, I wondered if it was flying any of my equipment.

A few miles away, over the county border in Kent, I saw the deep plume of a tornado reaching to the ground. There were some birdwatchers looking at a great northern diver on the mere and I pointed out the tornado to them. Another plume appeared and I memorised the scene. Upon my return I drew a picture of what I had seen and sent it to the meteorological station in Stornoway, not so much for a laugh, but as an antidote to the psychiatric treatment I had been given in Bedford. Basically it made me feel better. I was getting ill again.

On another day I was jogging across the Marsh when I reached the high-voltage overhead cables, which stretched down to Dungeness Nuclear Power Station. I felt the urge to slow my run and then speed up at the exact moment I ran under the cables. My behaviour would not go unnoticed by the Special Forces, with a very good quiet Royal Jack Russell, hiding unseen in the reeds of the Marsh only a few feet away, HQ observing using all means available, including of course MTRUTH. A year later I would be watching a television programme about a gang of men whose job it was to paint the pylons on which these cables hung. I had never heard of such a thing. It was just the SAS trying (successfully of course) to entertain me.

We both recovered from our colds enabling Emily to continue her house hunting. I would cook, one night discovering, through pure experiment and the fact that we had not been to the supermarket for a few days, that you can cook chicken coated in marmalade and it is rather delicious. Emily enjoyed my cooking.

Each night we would go for a walk down the sands over the spectacularly high sand dunes, which reminded me of my times in the Sahara desert. Then we would go, with the dogs, into the pub. The dogs were lovely and everywhere we went people would come up and make a fuss of them, which they loved.

I thought the landlord was an Austrian as he had a Tyrolean-style cap hanging at the back of the bar. I was to discover a little adverse camber in his Camber pub. It was Emily's time-of-the-month and she was seriously uptight. I put my beer down on the mantelpiece whereupon it just slid off and smashed on the floor. The landlord said I should not have put it there and did not even give me another pint. No apology. We only went in there once more, on the following night actually, and I noticed that his hat had disappeared. I had written to the police about this incident so they knew all about it and had decided to confiscate his prized hat as punishment.

I continued writing to the police and also to the Editor, at HQ. So far, I had only told my story to the wind and rain in the northwest Highlands of Scotland and to the sheep on Romney Marsh. How much did the SAS really know about me? I wondered. Probably a lot more than I imagined – I thought. Meanwhile Emily had noticed I was writing down the number plates of cars driven badly and as she correctly suspected, I was reporting them to the police, whilst invariably receiving self-made-up messages from their number plates.

The post box in Camber was a rare type with a flap to stop the weather getting in and, in this case, the sand. Fearful of the very posting of my letters to the police, and the SAS, appealing for political and psychiatric asylum in Sussex, my thoughts turned to the fine legalities of posting a letter.

I visualised a Chinook helicopter hovering at several thousand feet and out of earshot a little like the one from which I had imagined the pub cat being winched down to the tree back in Barnes back in '94. I decided to not fully post my letters to the SAS, but instead leave them hanging out of the box. In the morning they had gone, collected I imagined by the SAS postman again, winched down silently from the hovering helicopter. Laughing to myself maniacally, I pictured this postman, dangling from a wire at the post box, being seen from a passing car: Bizarre and schizophrenic.

One evening at the supermarket in Hastings, whilst Emily was doing the shopping, I overheard a remark being made on a public telephone and felt sure it had been aimed at me. Sure enough down the road, whilst I was still fuming from whatever it was, I saw a parked police car ready to pounce. I could hardly now say I did not believe it had all been a dirty trick to try and get me arrested. This was because I had forgotten, if I ever knew, it was no longer 28 days you had to escape for. Now it was the full six months of the section due to a change to the law in 1995. But I was thinking the police could not arrest me now the 28 days had passed without me demonstrating I was a danger to either myself or others so, I thought, they were trying to give me an opportunity to do so: An utter delusion.

Extremely angry with this I called 999 from another box down the road to give the operator a piece of my deluded mind. But I thought better of it and hung up before receiving a reply. I imagined finding another box and calling 999 again, on receiving an answer it becoming apparent that I was listening to a *Woodentop's* soundtrack, perhaps an episode I was known to have actually seen.

Another attempt would be greeted by an MI5 tape recording of a conversation, apparently in a restaurant, between the former Chief of Defence Staff, Air Chief Marshal Sir Peter Harding, and his glamorous girlfriend, Lady Bienvenida Buck (he resigned over their affair in 1994).

Realising the potential danger of being arrested I managed to regain my composure to rejoin Emily without her having any idea of what I had just done. I had certainly been ill when I made the call because there was no emergency – but the replies I imagined receiving were so ridiculous it shook me into thinking there was no set-up after all. They weren't trying to arrest me.

The dividing line between good mental health and bad is extremely fine; much finer than those professionals present at psychiatric hospital ward-rounds might sometimes think applied to themselves. And once you are stuck in the system you need to be a wily fox to get out. This is why you hear stories of people with schizophrenia being extremely cunning and wanting to play games. One or two members of the Special Forces had learnt this lesson on some very shadowy manoeuvres. But I was thinking about myself. I was a member of the Special Forces under such deep cover nobody knew I was there. Like me, many others in the psychiatric system were up for full military honours too. VC? I was about to experience something worth about a thousand VCs per second. To think that for some 40 years poor patients had been given criminally murderous and despicable drugs like Chlorpromazine; this could only mean thousands of posthumous awards.

Not having much to exercise my mind on except this lunatic situation, I was now well enough to think about getting back to work. Lunatic situations require lunatic measures perhaps, and I thought back to my pint of Guinness in The Phoenix pub and the classic film *The Flight of the Phoenix*. In it they butcher parts of a crashed aircraft in the desert and fly victoriously across the desert to safety. I would like to do the same, and fly over those bloody hospitals, or take off in a crank start helicopter to get away from the foxes like Rupert Bear once did.

More than anything I needed something to concentrate my mind on, instead of writing all those mad letters, and getting wound up by the messages I was receiving, or making up for myself, from people's number plates. The difference between intuitively based actions and those born of a full logical breakdown of the situation was crucial to my staying free.

One day shortly before we left Camber for the last time a Coastguard helicopter came flying in low over the house. I don't recall if I thought it was spying on us but I hid a message for them behind the gatepost.

We moved into a caravan at the Coghurst Hall caravan village. It was by a lake and had its own garden, which was ideal for Eryngo who made many friends in the local cat community. The village, with several hundred caravans, was a magical place, surrounded on one side by attractive woods where, in the carpet of bluebells, I buried an angry letter full of racial abuse to the psychiatric consultant back at Bedford. He was a nice bloke and did not deserve such witchcraft. but I felt persecuted by him and his medications from which I had to escape – after all, he was wrong to diagnose me as having the delusion I had a job.

We spent our evenings at the caravan village bar, which was in the Great Hall of this ancient country house, Coghurst Hall. Old weapons and implements adorned the high brick walls, and stuffed deer heads looked down on us as we drank our beers with the dogs – neither of which minded a lap or two as well. The caravans seemed to be principally the property of well-to-do working class types who came down from London for the weekend. One or two of the men, it has to be said, displayed hairy chests and medallions on chains. Our caravan, number 69b, was cramped but pleasant and I did the cooking more often than not, which I enjoyed.

Our time there became perfused by the sound of a free CD which came with a copy of *The Big Issue* I had bought Emily – in particular the exquisitely beautiful Liz Fraser and Craig Armstrong song, *This Love*. It was magic and I am only too happy to be reminded of that time.

But my life was again about to take a turn for the worse, one that would violate my happy memories of this place in the most horrible of ways. But this was not before I found a pound coin in the King George VI car park in a village near the hall. I sent it to the District Judge, claiming to be the IRA, with the instructions that the old railway line into Bexhill Terminus Road Station was to be reopened. I had noticed how the wonderful old station building was so well maintained compared to the still operating central Bexhill Station, which did not look like it'd had a lick of paint since I got sunburn on the beach in 1967. It seemed a crime had been committed in closing down the branch and turning the station into offices – but at least the new owners had looked after the building. I did not notice if The Rother Arms, a pub inside the old station where I had once drunk with my great-uncle, was still open. In fact, it wasn't, though had reopened nearby. And anyway, I should have been talking to him about the Bedford to Sandy line.

Part XIX

I Clash With a Law Lord

Chapter Forty-Nine

Song for Ireland

A s I had now completely recovered from the depression it was time to get back to work, and I did what I had decided to do following my conversation with Joe, registering with a doctor in Lydd. From here, in H.G. Wells's *The First Men in the Moon*, the voyagers had taken off on their journey into space. I do not believe my desire to return to work was in any way a positive effect of the Clopixol – but it might have been. I tend to feel I'd had enough time out: I'd just had a two year schizophrenic holiday to research this story and I was refreshed.

So on 22nd April 2000 Emily drove me to the doctor's. Just as we were parking in the surgery car park an RAF Tornado flew over at a couple of hundred feet. I could see the pilot. What more proof did the mind of a schizophrenic who had been bombarding the Services with communications need to convince him that he was part of the bigger picture? As in Newquay, I had suspected my mail was being intercepted at source by a specialist intelligence unit in case I accidentally said something they did not want me to, and thought of my message to Stornoway Meteorological Office about the weather on the marsh a couple of weeks earlier. Emily hardly seemed to notice – though the ground itself was shaking. Walking into the surgery I thought back to my time at the DOAE. The chap sitting near me had been writing mission-planning software for the RAF. I wondered if it had been in action here.

In the waiting room we had an argument about whether she was going to come in with me or not. My name was called and I went in alone. I told the doctor that I had just overcome depression, which was true. I had learnt not to try and tell doctors and psychiatrists long and involved stories about where Prince Charles's dog really was, Princess Diana not being dead and the fact that either I was hallucinating or receiving strange messages from anything from a blade of grass to a car number plate. If I did they would only prescribe me more medication. So I was hardly likely to tell the doctor about the night six years earlier when, high on drugs, I had crashed my car. Nor would I say how I had heard, for example, that voice in my head saying "Classic! Classic!" over and over, or how when I saw a classic car I often thought it had been put there under the auspices of Prince Charles.

Instead I concentrated on the more immediate fact that I wanted a note, Form Med 3, saying I was fit to go back to work. This he duly gave me. Whilst I had recovered from the depression the Clopixol gave me one does not know what difference the Chinese cure made – and it did not stop me from behaving a little bizarrely during my time on the run. On the other hand it had not stopped the depression from going.

With the filled-in note still lying on the table the doctor asked why I kept getting depressed and, unwisely, I told him it was because they kept giving me medication against my will. At this point it was clear he thought things were not quite what they seemed and I saw him looking at the doctor's note still lying on the table wondering if he should take it back. But he didn't.

Little did I know that there was also drama going on just outside his door. Emily was listening to everything I said, and the surgery receptionist had gone up to her and said "Is everything alright?" Emily, hilariously, shooed her away, a mere annoying intrusion; at least that is what Emily told me. Having been told this, I visualised Emily crouched there using specialist eavesdropping equipment, it being obvious to the practice manager at her counter that it was just another MI5 operation against the British National Health Service. What with the RAF jet and all this, the situation was truly weird and this was not the end of it. I picked up the doctor's note which, as Joe had told me, was all I needed to return to work, this being something the consultant could not give me.

Having spent so much time off work I was in no mood to take any more, and so was determined to return to work the very next day. Emily and I celebrated my success in the car park. She gave me a big hug and told me she had heard everything I had said and that she was proud of me. I had read about the Ladies of the Marsh (a local women's group) in some free booklet – they were actually a specialist military unit, which Emily had joined covertly without telling me. I was proud of her. We drove off together to Coghurst Hall for the last time, at least for a horrible while, discussing how I was going to get into work the next day. Eventually we decided she would go to her mother's in the New Forest and drop me at the station to get the train from Southampton into work at Hook.

Little did I realise that our drink together that night would be the last for some weeks. All the happiness and stability I had built-up over the previous months at Telscombe, Camber and now Coghurst Hall was about to be cruelly snatched from me just when I had nearly made it. On the other hand, one does not know what might have happened if it wasn't "cruelly snatched" from me.

Up we got early and headed off along the south coast in Emily's new Rover. She kissed me goodbye at the station and I made my way into work. But when I arrived things did not go exactly as I had planned. I reported to reception giving my real name. The receptionist, a temp, asked for my ID which I gave her and she checked on the company database and told me I had not been in the company's employ since July the previous year, three months after my pay had stopped. But I had not resigned then; so the only explanation for this was that, whilst I had not had a company appraisal since 1992, there had also been another mistake. I knew I still had a job because not only had Emily been to company HQ to find out if I did but we had gone together only a few weeks earlier. One of the company's corporate hands did not know what the other was doing.

I sat down whilst the temp sorted things out. I insisted I still worked there and she said she would contact security. I did speak to one of the people under my named manager and he told me the manager was not there and I would have to get a taxi home and come back on Monday. But at least he seemed to know of me. I was hardly going to pay for a taxi all the way back to Coghurst Hall, the plan having been to meet up with Emily again in the evening. So I sat my ground and armed with my doctor's certificate (which I knew gave me the right to go to work) I asked for a desk and a telephone to work from.

I waited for some time without anything happening and without any sign of my office and desk becoming available. Now I saw a police van pulling into the car park! My immediate reaction was that it was nothing to do with me. So there was no need to make any escape attempt. What had I done wrong after all? There was nothing to fear.

The policeman came into the foyer where I was sitting and went over to the receptionist. Then he came over to me and asked me if I was Clive Travis. I said "Yes I am." Without my permission he searched my bag. Then he went over to use the telephone. After a while he came back and said he was arresting me for absconding from a psychiatric hospital. I was mortified. I had not realised that some bastard Law Lord had changed the law and not told me the previous 28 days was now six months. I had only been sectioned for not turning up to court to start with and I was hardly dangerous. I felt trapped and persecuted as I climbed into the back of the van. There was a half-smoked Hamlet on the floor, which I picked up and smoked to console myself. It had been put there on the instructions of Sir Stephen Lander, the then Director of MI5.

Was what was now happening right? All I know is that the law now says that an absconded patient *may* be returned to hospital within the duration of the six months. The previous 28 days had seemed quite fair, a bit like the count to 60 at the start of a game of hide and seek. But fairness did not really come into this. MI5, or somebody, thought that if they just screwed me again and again and again, maybe I would eventually do something useful in response. In reality I was just being punished – punished for nothing. At least that was how I felt. But then there were the letters, and a couple of debts, which no doubt the Masons would come after me for later on, if they weren't already, one to Drummonds at Admiralty Arch[132].

At the police station (in Aldershot, the home of the British Army) I stood at the charge-desk. The arresting officer told the Charge-Desk Officer that I was "an absconded patient who had turned up at a company claiming he worked there and saying he was a doctor." I later discovered that the officer who arrested me bore the name Hook, the name of the place he arrested me in, and the coincidence would seem too great. I imagined it was not his real name.

I realised then there was nothing I could do to get out of this situation, and I just resigned myself to what was to come. Surely I was not the only one to be congratulated in creating this situation. I felt a lump in my throat and felt utterly wronged. What had I done to deserve this? It was nearly May and it had taken all these months to recover from the drug-induced depression and now, I knew, the summer was ruined. *I was absolutely terrified: perhaps this time I would succumb to the drugs.*

The police called Emily for me and told her what had happened. She told them she thought I was alright but it was no use. My fate was sealed. Emily cried and returned home that evening alone. It was hardly as if she had been phoning the police non-stop, begging them to put me back in the loony bin.

I waited in the cell showing precisely no sign of mental illness for the next 24 hours. There was video surveillance; so at one point I made an arching gesture with my right arm pointing at my coffee cup. I wanted it to look like a moment in the *Monty Python* Ministry of Silly Walks sketch. "There," I said, "I have just, of my own free will, made a strangely schizophrenic gesture with my right arm to point at the coffee cup. That does not mean I am a paranoid schizophrenic though." It was a bit like the situation Paul Merton once described when talking about his spell in the loony bin. He said he told a member of staff his father was the Duke of Edinburgh, with the result that they kept him in another month!

At some point I heard a rumour on the police intelligence network (the custody officer bringing me another coffee) that my brother in the police was coming to get me. That did not happen.

The next afternoon at about one o'clock, three psychiatric nurses arrived keen to get some weekend overtime by coming to collect me. One of them was Bill, one of the nurses who had overseen me at Weller Wing before I absconded. There he had told me he could not see anything the matter with me. The Charge-Desk Officer agreed with him. Later, following my complaint, the police force sent me the custody notes. These indicated precisely no sign of mental illness though I don't suppose they would have conducted a careful video analysis to observe I had the presence of mind to make a legal representation of and on behalf of John Cleese.

It was a warm spring day, 24th April 1999, and Bill told me I was being taken to Fairfield Hospital, the Victorian asylum, again. Patients were taken there for punishment; I had seen them threatened with it at Weller Wing on a number of occasions – now it was my turn. He said I was going to be completely reassessed as he persuaded himself he had not just come to get me for the money. There seemed no clinical need for this other than to continue this murderous assault on me by the NHS. Horror of horrors – again! This meant I had to hold myself together until I got to Weller Wing and then until I got out. It could be months. Maybe I would not even be out of hospital before the end of the summer. Maybe this time I would not only succumb but also finish it.

That afternoon I was one of the very last, but tragically as it turned out, not *the* last patient ever to be admitted to this gruesome asylum before it closed down. Happily they did not inject me on arrival and a few days later, after showing no signs of mental illness whatsoever, Emily visited me there. It was my birthday, 3rd May 2000 and it was a beautiful day, just like the day I had been born on. Emily could see I was well and in good spirits, but that was not to last long.

For whatever reason they did it, the next day I was called into the treatment room where I was told I was to be given a drug I had not had before, Depixol. Little did even I imagine what horrors were ahead. After six years of this so-called treatment and minded to join the Irish Republican Army, I asked them "Why are you doing this to me?"

The Mauritian psychiatric nurse replied "I have complied with all the legal requirements necessary to allow me to do this." What other requirements might there be, I asked myself, like medical ones to start with. I had not taken this drug before but feared the worst. My fears were well-founded.

I lay down, not for the first time like a lamb to the slaughter, knowing that others had been in exactly the same situation in this exact room and had sought to defend themselves, in the process being marked down as dangerous animals. I remembered one person, the Scouser I had played pool with on my previous visit over three years earlier, who was no longer with us. I could well imagine why he'd had enough. I had noticed the tear in the pool table baize and suspected he had been the one responsible. Whether deliberate or not, it seemed like a last and sorry message from him. I called the police and said I had just been assaulted with a needle and a noxious substance. Within a matter of minutes I was before 'justice' Tommy Trinder who admonished me for calling 999 – but I hadn't. I wondered if I should have done and really he was admonishing me for that. There was no escape from this horrible avenue.

Soon after I'd had the injection I was allowed out into the garden where the weather was still good. Whereas the previous day I had been able to sit down relaxed under the perimeter wall enjoying the early summer sun, now all I could do was walk around and around the perimeter in a frenzied bout of the most horrendous restlessness looking like a laboratory rat on ecstasy, except this was not pleasant. Soon I tried, in desperation, going anticlockwise instead, but this provided no relief.

Naturally I took to smoking endless roll-ups. These I had hardly touched since the strange experience with the Ford Zephyr in Wavendon when I believed the Special Forces had challenged me to stop smoking.

Soon I found myself going into the worst of depressions. Emily phoned every day and I was a streaming wreck of tears down the phone to her. I was almost completely incoherent I was so low. It was way, way beyond awful. I could not grin and I could not bear it. But somehow I just had to hold myself together for the next four weeks and hopefully I would then be out. If I didn't already know what had happened to other people I knew now. *But I could not decide what the braver thing to do was: commit suicide or carry on.* There seemed no doubt that others faced with the beastly effects of this drug, and having no more obvious means of ending it, would have simply bitten into their wrist in silence, the release of death coming in minutes. I now knew, as if I didn't already, that all over this island are buried those who committed suicide not because of paranoid schizophrenia, but the drugs for it. Then there would be the ones who had no grave.

I recalled the occasion, a few months after I had previously been incarcerated here, when I did the last thing any one would expect – catching a bus and returning to Fairfield voluntarily to say hello to the nurses. The intention had been to remind myself how little I wanted to come here again against my will. But here I was again and right now a war was going on in my head. I had to just hold on. I must never come here ever again except of my own free will, I thought. Why they did not give me some Lorazepam I have no idea. Except I do. They expected me to carry on taking this shit but did not want me to be addicted to Lorazepam.

When I had been in the hospital a few days, having had the injection, a West Indian patient was admitted. He was obviously very ill and was helped in by one of the nurses who walked him down to the lounge. He was holding his hands out in front of himself like a blind man, and I thought to myself that here was somebody who really needed to be here. Up in the dormitory he was obviously very frightened and paranoid – unless he was from the Special Intelligence Service and was acting. One of the patients (who seemed like me in a way, in that he had a brother in the police) comforted him and said to him "Don't worry – there's nothing to fear here." He told me of one patient who would cut herself every time the full moon came around – a real lunatic.

Next day I found it hard to get up and nigh on impossible to make my bed but had no choice in the matter. I did it on some sort of automatic pilot – or as though I had a gun to my head and I *only just* did not want to die from a hole in my head. Downstairs, I had no appetite. Somehow, the food did not seem to be edible: it simply looked like objects on a plate, which were indeed of inedible substance. I pictured the sleeve of the German edition of an old Siouxsie and the Banshees single entitled *Mittageisen*.[133] The sleeve depicted the Daliesque scene of some people dining on bicycle chains and other metal objects. This food looked about as edible. I was losing weight fast and could feel the bones in my bum sticking out.

That day the newly admitted West Indian seemed much better and was drawing people. He was obviously an extremely talented and natural artist, and he drew me. I could hardly keep still, but he only took 10 minutes.

Unlike on my previous visit, we were allowed into the courtyard every day at least once. One of the other patients, another West Indian called Delroy, sang all the time, and would walk around the courtyard singing so loud he was on the point of shouting. I felt sorry for him. He had obviously had an unfortunate life. He was likeable despite his severe problems. He had the habit of walking around and asking, not towards anyone in particular, "Who 'm' a dealing with?" It was a good question to put and I was beginning to ask myself the same question. He would also sing aloud, and with great hope, "Django music music music is the key, is the key, Django music music music is the key." Perhaps he was referring to Django Reinhardt, the virtuoso jazz guitarist. Or perhaps he was referring to Lieutenant Colonel Bill Django of the New Earth Army, later played by Jeff Bridges in *The Men Who Stare at Goats*[134].

There was an Irish lady on the ward by the name of Geraldine. She told me she went to school with Thomas McElwee, the ninth IRA hunger striker. She told me stories of their childhood together and I felt very privileged to meet this lady. It seemed certain she had been sent to meet me, either by MI5 or the IRA. I was an important figure in the peace process and the world was a small place in which I had now met two persons who were friends with IRA hunger strikers. I felt I had to do something about it but short of continuing my symbolic search for Prince Charles's dog had no idea what. I did however summon the willpower to put pen to paper and ask him to arrange a homeopathic depot injection, possibly of the very drug I was on, or perhaps cyanide.

Of course, I gave consideration to escaping but I was in no condition to do so it seemed. The effects of the injection were so debilitating that I could almost see myself banging on the door to be allowed back in if I escaped. Can you believe that? I am not sure I can. From experience I hoped I would be out of this factory in four weeks if I just held myself together. I now knew why somebody, and in particular 10 Irishmen, would starve themselves to death.

Despite my hope to be out soon all my instincts led me to give full and proper consideration to the escape option. Whilst the courtyard was surrounded by a high wall made, like the building, from the no longer produced Arlesey brick, in one corner it was not quite so high as on the other sides.

I believed I could climb the wall unaided at that point. The other option was to somehow hide in the courtyard when we were called in and once the coast was clear, mount the wall by moving the table next to it. The other option was to seek the help of Delroy to help me scale the wall, and make a run for it. But what then? The hospital was deep in the countryside and I would have to run across the fields like the clappers. But the police, no doubt, would be called. If I could escape in the twilight, then my chances of getting away would be much improved but they might bring the dogs or helicopter (with infra-red camera) in to look for me.

As the hospital was about to close (and be turned into luxury flats) within a matter of days and we had already been told about the move to the new hospital, there seemed no damage could be done to future patients' escape opportunities if I bet one of the nurses I could climb the wall. My bet was accepted and as I had been allowed, escorted, down to the shop to buy tobacco, it was believed I would not double bluff them and make a run for it.

So I took a running jump at the wall and, pulling myself up, I was indeed able to surmount it. I climbed down again, we ascended the rusting old spiral iron staircase, which had a cage over it, and I claimed my carton of Ribena.

My drug-induced restlessness was total torture, and the days and weeks crept by at an agonisingly slow rate. Still I could not face my food and I was losing weight even faster. I could not sit still at the table at mealtimes and used any excuse possible to stand up and walk around. I got up and walked pathetically over to nurse Tommy and said "Please help me." He just told me to go and sit down. But I had been able to walk around for a few seconds. I was back on the fixed seat – and could feel the bones in my arse beginning to protrude still further.

There was another West Indian whose name I forget, who wore an unusual orange jumpsuit. Because of akathisia we would both walk up and down the ward, passing each other exactly every 53 seconds or something for hours per day. As he passed me his eyes were completely white due to the eyeballs facing vertically (an alarming sight) because of ocular gyric crisis. This was all so miserable. Yet despite the abject misery of the time I spent on this ward there is one memory I have which is a good one. When we both steeled ourselves for a break from the marching and took seats in the living room, he would lie on the settee. The room was full of sunlight all day and somehow, instead of being where he was, he seemed to be lying in a hammock on a Caribbean beach one evening with *Summer Breeze* by the Isley Brothers playing. There was magic about him. At dinner he told me how he had come from Northwick Park Hospital in London. I asked him if it was "fucked up" there and, suddenly brightening up and amused, he confirmed "Yeah, it was fucked up man!" It was a rare good vibe from this time.

One of the female patients was friendly to me (though she had a bit of an angry streak in her) and would give me massages, or rather healing therapy to my head and shoulders, which she barely touched in doing so. This helped a few of the intolerable minutes go by, so I was truly grateful to her. I returned the compliment.

One day an ex-patient with whom I once had a scuffle during my previous time there visited. He would be dead from an overdose within a year, using a syringe he had stolen from this hospital.

My parents visited but I refused to see them, and was aggressive towards them. But as I, or the latest sociological barrier between me and some sort of normality was battered into submission by the Depixol, I telephoned my father to find out what had happened to my flat. I am sure a psychiatrist would say this was a positive effect of the Depixol on my insight into personal well-being. It was the only one. He told me he had sold it at a considerable profit even allowing for the mortgage arrears and had bought me £20,000 of premium bonds with the rest of the money in my bank account. Well that was fine, but what did that do? It meant I would have to go and live with my parents again at nearly 40 – not very healthy really. It also lost me some £100,000 from the then forthcoming property boom[135]. Within days of the sale of the flat the best part of a year's back pay had gone into my account. But looking on the bright side it would save me having to get my flat exorcised and I could win £1 million on a premium bond – hardly a sociologically dysfunctional event. But it was not long before I began to imagine that British Intelligence would treat the possibility of winning the jackpot in the same way as the possibility of a nuclear explosion in the Mall. Losing my most valuable possession was a great blow.

I told one of the patients about how I came to be in hospital because of a change in the law. He told me to write to the Lord Chancellor. This I did and got a letter back referring me to an obscure section in the Department of Trade and Industry, LGD 34 in fact, because of my employment situation and the fact I had taken my employer to the Employment Tribunal. I also wrote to Lord Hailsham. I asked him why the 28-day rule in the Mental Health Act had not been changed to 107 days, 12 hours, 15 minutes and 27 seconds (roughly the exact time after the section started at which I was arrested) to ridicule its being changed to six months. I got a reply from his secretary saying he was ill, and I imagined him dying laughing.

Then at last, after four weeks, came the news I had been waiting for. Nurse Harry came up to me, exactly as he had done four years earlier, and told me excitedly that I was being transferred back to Weller Wing, the open wing of Bedford Hospital. He knew how much this meant to me, and happily shared my pleasure at this news. We were all just stuck in this terrible situation – with little option but to just press on.

So the next morning I was indeed taken back to Bedford Hospital where I continued to pace the ward knowing that it was only a matter of time to my release. Unfortunately I was now given another injection of this truly beastly drug Depixol. I knew other people could take it without undue side effects but this did not help me and I saw the summer ahead for what it was: a complete nightmare of restlessness and never-ending roll-ups. It really is true to say that absolutely nothing more mattered than getting this rubbish poison out of my blood stream – whatever the consequences.

Interestingly, there was a savant on the ward. You could give him a date either long in the past or future and he would say what day of the week it was. So I asked him what day of the week it was on my birthday in the year 401,234,921BC or something (during the Devonian period) and he duly obliged telling me it was early closing in Halifax! Of course I was unable to check this so I tried him again having found a calendar for 1998 and he was correct.

The community psychiatric nurse visited me in the Occupational Therapy Department and he could see I was not pleased to see him. I was angry at what was being done and I had good reason to be. Anyone could see I was in a terrible state. He too was from Mauritius, the country where the T-shirt I had stolen in Scotland four years earlier had been made. I made the delusional connection and imagined, when it later disappeared, that he had taken it. He could have stopped my flat being sold but hadn't.

After a week or so I was allowed out. I thought of running away but the section was nearly finished and it was unlikely they would extend it as I had been behaving well.

I was allowed to go down to Coghurst Hall for the weekend to see Emily. The train journey was a nightmare and it was all I could do just to sit still and not fling myself through the slam door. It was the rush hour and the train was full. It was truly unbearable. But if I bided my time it should not be too long before I could get off this rubbish – the only problem being that the injection was slow release and it would be another four weeks at least before it cleared my system. Hell on earth! I thought, nobody could conceive feeling this bad. I realised there must be worse still and in that condition, inferior to mine, lay the miserable little secrets of suicide which maybe even the coroner does not know or understand. Then again, maybe there was no worse. Perhaps I was now experiencing the worst psychiatric drug side-effect symptoms ever experienced by man. It was just that I was extremely resilient and somehow, only just, able to cope with them. Decide for yourself. In order not to throw myself from the train I had to be extremely hard. But then how hard did I have to be *to* throw myself from it? It seemed that whatever I did I was the hardest man who ever lived! There had, in fact, been no harder. This was why I had to believe I was in the Special Boat Service. It was a state of mind.

I could hardly stay in the caravan for more than a few minutes and had to keep getting up to pace up and down the garden smoking, smoking and smoking. Emily complained that I had been alright before I went in – there being a certain truth in her statement.

At the end of the weekend I had to return to the hospital to continue the torture. On the train it was only too easy to imagine why Scouser, and another acquaintance Kate Simpson, had jumped out to their deaths from trains.

This pattern continued for the next four weeks, and the time was coming when the second four-week hyper-nightmare injection would run out. Again I went down to Emily's for the weekend but of course I could not make love to her because of the injection.

The next day she was going down to her mother's, so I stayed to look after Eryngo and the dogs – who were always glad to see me and jumped up excitedly to greet me every time I arrived. Before she went, we went for a walk in the woods. I dug up the letter to my psychiatrist, written some weeks previously and buried there. Battered into submission, I admitted how ill I had been; though really there had been little harm in this. Emily told me not to worry and set off to get her train.

Leaving me alone or staying with me hardly would have made any difference to what now happened. Whereas previously I had been happy in the caravan now it was all just torture. So I took the dogs for a long walk, as I could not keep still. After the walk I went up and down on the verge of panic. I was badly in need of tranquillisers but had none – just some Procyclidine, but it had little effect. In my desperation, I telephoned a local doctor who spoke to me sympathetically and suggested I watch an old film. I very much doubt if he really knew how I felt. I could hardly watch *any* television my concentration was so poor. Everything was a nightmare. It hardly made any difference to me that any schizophrenia I previously had, had gone – but I did notice how quiet my imagination was.

There was nothing for it, but to walk to the hospital for help. When I got there of course there was a queue. It was a hot summer's day. I walked around and around in circles in the far reaches of the hospital unable to sit still. After perhaps one-and-a-half hours of this nightmare I got to see a doctor who gave me a Diazepam tablet. I walked back to the Hall. Still, I could not keep still. I told myself: try to stay calm, Emily should be back soon.

I went into the bar and drank a pint of lager: Carlsberg Export, then another – a serious mistake I believed. Maybe it would have been worse if I hadn't! Eventually Emily arrived back and it was just about all I could do to heat up the dinner, which I ate, even though I was not at all hungry. We went to the bar and had another drink and back to the caravan to bed. The only comfort was to see how happy Eryngo was here, and of course there was no danger to him from any traffic on the site.

In bed I was insanely restless and could not sleep. Also I was having strange hallucinations because of the interaction between the alcohol and the Diazepam. I got up and went to sleep on the floor but still could not sleep properly. In the early hours I got back into bed with Emily but was still tossing and turning. Emily agreed I had to go back to the local hospital; so we got up early, and she drove me down there.

When we got there we had to wait for some time before I saw the crisis counsellor. It all seemed a bit pointless on one hand and quite vital on the other. How could I get out of this? I was told I had to go back to Bedford Hospital and that Emily should drive me there. I had given up. It was a hot day and I felt terrible. Halfway there, we stopped at the services to water the thirsty dogs. The sunlight reflected from the cars and seemed very bright, as it had five summers earlier.

We arrived at the hospital where I was due to have another injection. My section still had not finished; so I could not refuse it. This time they changed the injection seeing what problems I was having. The nurse said he was giving me Piportil and told me it was a "nice drug" which they had been discouraged from prescribing because it was so expensive. Nothing could be worse than the Depixol, I thought. But I was to discover the Piportil was no better: A complete waste of money. The Nigerian psychiatric nurse, who had a therapeutic accent, came up to me after I'd had the injection and encouraged me to drop my appeal against the section under which they could forcibly give me this horrible medication. Very unseemly I would have thought in legal terms: a bit like receiving an opponent at your house in breach of a court order. I ignored him. It had nearly finished anyway. They tried to persuade me to stay in hospital. I looked a nervous wreck and was physically ill: as the doctor confirmed.

We got back to the house where my father just happened to be arriving. Mother was in bed and very ill as she had just had a hip transplant. I was terribly restless and depressed. Father and Emily had an almighty argument, which was not fair on Emily. She had tried to help me. The argument was, in effect, a direct result of my having been hospitalised. But what it was caused by was the hospital leaking Emily's confidential letters to the hospital to my father – and her helping me to abscond. I tried to keep them apart. As Emily drove off she and my father were shouting at each other. Once again it was most unseemly. I felt really terrible. Somehow I had to carry on. Emily was now banned from the house.

I managed to book a bed and breakfast in Reading for Emily and myself so we could attend the Royal Regatta at Henley. I went down and met her. I was just as restless, depressed and uncomfortable on the Piportil as I had been on the Depixol and also the Clopixol come to think of it. Let alone the Melleril, Chlorpromazine, Thioridazine and Droperidol all of which had turned me into a suicidal rag doll.

The only good thing I discovered with the Piportil was that I could drink a few pints without ill effect – the positive side effect being that I got more drunk than normal. But I did not enjoy Henley one bit whatsoever. The way somebody seemed to have deliberately smeared the door handle to the gents in The Red Lion Hotel with snot did not help either. The recollection of the strange incident with the policeman's helmet at a previous year's regatta did not even cheer me up. It was all too much of an effort and even just being with Emily seemed difficult. I wanted to be alone. *I wanted to get old and die as soon as possible – that was the only way out.*

I returned to Bedford and was able to go to the pub each evening. It was the only form of relaxation I had from spending the day pacing unendingly around the house. Still, now I was off the section; so they could not give me another injection without my permission. But I had to wait four horrible weeks of life hardly worth living until the drug cleared my system. Unspeakable. Then, horror of horrors, I imagined they might renew the section, as they did with others. The possibility of suicide was so tangible I could almost see the coroner looking at my dead body. I decided to write to him to tell him if I committed suicide it would not be the illness but the drugs' side effects. I noticed the coroner in Reading was Mr Bedford so it seemed a sensible ruse to send the letter to him, and not the coroner in Bedford. I visited Emily's mother's in the New Forest with her and barely enjoyed a second of it. I paced up and down her mother's garden wearing a path in the grass. We slept separately.

The four weeks came up and it was the date of my appointment at the hospital. I saw a new psychiatrist, Dr. Carmacciu. He told me he wanted me to take yet another new drug, Seroquel, and told me he knew I had been getting bad side effects but that many people took Seroquel, and claimed not to know they were taking anything. I'll believe it when I see it, I thought.

However, he warned me "But if you do not take this I can assure you it is 100 per cent certain that you will end up back in here." What he did not tell me was that prolonged exposure to this drug would cause me fever, extreme abdominal pain, diarrhoea and vomiting. Nor did he tell me that even after I had stopped taking it I would be unable to speak properly for months as a small muscle in my upper lip had become paralysed: it gave me a stiff upper lip! But I would only find that out beyond the end of this story.[136]

The day of the solar eclipse was coming and, with great difficulty, because of the depression, I booked accommodation for Emily and myself down in the West Country. The effects of the Piportil were beginning to wear off and I was not quite so restless. But now I had another problem. I'd had a fungal infection in my toenails for years and they were discoloured; so I was taking an oral medication for it, Lamisil. I wanted to cure my toenails once and for all, like some people were trying to do with my head. I was terribly sick with nausea and had not yet realised it was the Lamisil causing it. Everywhere we went I was being sick and life was pitifully miserable, what with the psychiatric drug side effects as well. Still, we got to see the eclipse. When the moment of totality came it was dark and cold and I went up to give Emily a kiss and big hug for all her support. The edge of the shadow raced past faster than the RAF – probably about four times at fast.

As well as the horror of the drugs' side effects they also eradicated the efficacy of my thoughts about the Special Forces and the omnipresence of Prince Charles's dog. In fact they eradicated my imagination completely and nor did I have any dreams. Basically I was not half the person I had been before, and I was nearly none, as you know from my Newquay story. I could however coldly state to myself that I might as well be a member of the Special Forces for what I'd had to put up with – without killing myself. I could even get myself a Jack Russell: how could I be sure exactly where it came from?

We took the train home to Bedford, and met a botanist who knew what Eryngo Eryngium, after which our cat was named, was. Quite ridiculously after what she had done for me, Emily had to book into a bed and breakfast. I had already told her back at Frogmore in Devon, that I had made the decision to come off the Seroquel. After all that had happened I still had the optimistic belief that I could stay well without medication, and I intended to prove that. I just felt I did not need it – or at least that I could get by drug-free without being arrested. I was wrong. Or at least I was wrong if I drank.

Come the autumn of 1999 I believed I had done it. Back on 22nd April I had known the summer was ruined, but I also knew I could get through it. I felt reborn, almost as though now was spring, not autumn. That is an important lesson for anyone to learn who encounters schizophrenia. I was fully recovered in more ways than one and I was taking no medication. But how long would I stay well? And what is being well anyway?

Part XX

Back to Work

Chapter Fifty

Never Come Down Again

November came and after two further months in which my employer kept me at home I was finally, after over two years away, back at work in Milton Keynes. But my employer was in a rather severe breach of contract: I had not had a company appraisal since 1992, when they took over my former employer, a specialist defence contractor. Nor had they given me any training since 1993. On the other hand in a major corporation there would always be somebody in the position I was. It just happened to be me.

I was happy to be back but how long would I stay this time? Life was about to present me with another major psychiatric challenge. On the way into work I decided I should pick some things up and look under them so I could say I had made some demonstrable attempts of a more usual style to look for Prince Charles's dog! Otherwise I did not really face too much of a problem going back to work. I telephoned Emily to tell her I was there and she was really pleased, proud and even amazed.

I spent my lunch hour drinking coffee in the Irish pub in Milton Keynes town centre. I got down to some good work and at Christmas I really had something to celebrate, the joy comparing well to that I had sometimes got on the street. By now though I had temporarily split with Emily. I had taken her to my doctor to see if we could have a baby. Amongst the questions he asked her was "Have you had any mental illness in your family?" My life has been a predominantly happy experience and I felt he had no business in asking this question, which smacked of eugenics, even Nazism, and upset me. If I did not think my life worth living I would not consider bringing somebody new into the world. Either way, it was no go. Emily and I had an argument during which I felt terribly sorry for her when she said, tearfully, "Now I'm all muddled." We split, but I was to see her again.

Even at this late stage in the story I had not really got to grips with the fact that I was a paranoid schizophrenic who would (in my case at least) get ill if I took no medication. To believe that was out of the question, as it meant having to cope with side effects as despicable as I have described – and that was naturally out of the question as it meant suicide. I was protecting myself by not acknowledging I actually was a paranoid schizophrenic. But just for a moment I considered insightfully that I was. And if I was why was I? I saw an article in a paper somebody had left behind at the table: "Do cats cause schizophrenia?" If cats, or a parasite in them, could cause schizophrenia I started thinking maybe dogs could do the same trick. My thoughts got a bit far flung by this notion to the point where the entire course of my illness (or whatever it was) since 1994 was down to none other than Prince Charles's dog itself, and not even some parasite it was carrying. Unless that is it did have a parasite: I mentioned before the possibility that it had MTRUTH. I could bring an action for damages against the dog posthumously under the Dangerous Dogs Act 1991. It might not even be posthumous: where was the proof it was dead, or even that it ever existed at all? What on earth had Prince Charles's dog done to me? It had a lot to answer for. Dead or alive it seemed the dog was well "out of control in a public place" and if Prince Charles was convicted he could go down for two years. But I loved the dog beyond compare.

It was around this time that I noticed how Bill, the landlord of The Ship in Bedford, would say, when calling time at the end of the evening, "Do your talking walking." This meant British Intelligence could hear everything I said via my MTRUTH. I even suspected Bill might be an MTRU himself. As for me I found myself given to asking, not for a Hamlet but an "amulet". When I did this and Bill handed me the opened tin so I could take one, a Saudi prince would appear in my mind's eye treasuring just such a piece of jewellery. This he would give me virtually as a charm to ward off evil. I did enjoy asking for my amulets.

In December I opened the newspaper to find that Melanie Jones, who had befriended me the previous January in Weller Wing, had thrown herself to her death from the top of the multi-storey car park. She had taken ecstasy the previous night. What a tragedy for someone so young! After the funeral I went home to see if the conker I had planted in a pot had germinated. It had done by the spring. It is her tree and is planted in a wood north of Bedford. I was disturbed to discover I was not, in fact, the last person to have been admitted to Fairfield Hospital. She took my place there when I went back to Weller Wing on the way out. Somebody in Club Rich UK told me they had seen her in Fairfield and, feeling shocked at this, I replied "What did you say?" For a moment I slipped back into my Comic Relief/MI5 disbelief conspiracy syndrome – a huge delusory penny dropping at that moment. She became one of the Comic Relief undead because I still wanted to believe Princess Diana was alive. Unfortunately the truth is that the last patient admitted to Fairfield Hospital in the 140 years it was open took her own life. At its peak the hospital held a thousand patients and yet when it closed there were only about 20.

At the funeral I looked at her family and wondered as to the reasons for her death. How could I know I would survive the illness and not become a victim like her, if not because of the illness, because of the treatment? As we sung *All things bright and beautiful* a 20-foot high gravestone appeared before me in the church into which I could see the stonemason carving

Sons and Daughters Terrorised
by Side Effects of Drugs for Schizophrenia

1952-

(1952 being the year the first drug for schizophrenia was introduced, the beast of a drug they had given me back at Fairmile and which I knew had driven many to suicide since). It was my father in the pulpit giving the reading saying, as the stonemason carved his words:

My son was first sectioned in 1994 after damaging some property, and was

placed in a Victorian "lunatic" asylum, which has since closed. Here he was given the diagnosis of paranoid schizophrenia. I visited him and was appalled by the primitive accommodation and the treatment he was receiving. The staff did not appear to be trained in dealing with psychiatric illness and the consultant seemed to lack all understanding of the extreme anguish and suffering my son was evidently enduring. All I could do was to ask if he could be transferred to the hospital in his hometown, so that his family could visit him more easily.

Four weeks after admission he was permitted to leave of his own accord and he came home and admitted himself to the local psychiatric ward. But once again I had little faith in the staff and their training. The greatest and most unfortunate difficulty was the failure to find a drug that as well as helping his condition, would not make it worse in other ways such as was the case with the Chlorpromazine he was being given.

Later he would be given injections and I often wept at the brutal treatment meted out to my son by male nurses forcing him to have these drugs which he soon learnt would give him suicidal clinical depression and other extremely unpleasant side effects. Can we imagine how terrifying this was for him?

From my subsequent reading, it seemed that treatment of schizophrenia was very uncertain as to the choice of drugs, and whilst new ones were appearing regularly which promised better results he was also unable to tolerate these. At no time was I offered any professional guidance in helping my son.

In despair, he absconded and even escaped from hospital and went missing for long periods in order to save himself from the unhelpful regime and find some happiness in his life as best he could. On one occasion he disappeared for over a year, and we were uncertain if he was still alive. Eventually he returned voluntarily, though he found himself back in the "revolving door" for a number of years.

In the early hours of June 21st 2004, tortured by anxiety, depression and akathisia, my son got up and went downstairs to the kitchen where he made himself a drink and had a roll-up. We'll probably never know exactly what happened next and we can only imagine what thoughts passed through his mind. We think he had a few more roll-ups and then, sometime around dawn that morning, midsummer's day, he must have gone back upstairs.

When we came in early that morning there was a sort of eerie silence in the house, punctuated only by the sound of the record he had played still going round in the run out groove. It was the side of his New Order album with Your Silent Face on it. I went upstairs and found him lying there motionless in bed. He still hadn't bloody got up by the afternoon.

RIP

On the shortest day of the year, I heard that Desmond Llewelyn, who played the gadget man "Q" in almost all the James Bond films, had been killed in a car crash on the main road near to Telscombe. His death did not prey on my mind: nor did it seem mysterious like the distant police car had done all those months ago as I walked to Rodmell. Nor was the body of Bernard Lee, who played M, lying outside my house when I got home from the pub that night. Not so much

MTRUTH, Q, but the truth about M!

In the New Year my firm moved me back to Wavendon. I was to work in the new part of the wing of the old country house I had been in over two years earlier – before my latest tour of Britain. Then, it had been full of old documents from mothballed projects. I supposed they had all now gone up in smoke, just as I had pictured in one of my previously more florid mental trips when I thought the place was no different to Waco.

Not long after I started work in this building I began to have some strange thoughts when I bought a packet of biscuits from the village shop and placed them next to my machine. They were McVitie's Digestives. Again I thought I might have some aggressive cookies on my machine and, given what I imagined about my having an MTRUTH, that there was significance in placing this packet next to my machine. In my latest descent I said to myself "Little does anyone here know how important I am, and little do they know what I do." Very, very few even knew of such a thing as an MTRUTH, an MTRU, or EAI, and as for whether I had actually got such a sensitive military status as these afforded, even less knew that.

I had read in *The Times* how GCHQ had been advertising for new recruits by hiding pieces of code in their website for prospective candidates to find. I believed I was one such candidate. This was true at least when I was in the building. It had that magical and mystical air about it that I sense whenever either that wonderful and alluring side of schizophrenia descends, or deluded yet inspirational intuition tells me Special Forces are in play.

I was deep in thought as to the legal consequences of my ruminations. At the same time I could not possibly tell anyone what I was experiencing. If I did they would not believe me and, it seemed, just saying what I was thinking might have been a breach of the Official Secrets Act. I gave further consideration to the possibility that my machine was being monitored. Again I wondered if I were an MTRU rather than a plain ordinary human being with a good visual imagination. Somebody monitoring closely, perhaps an electronic warfare expert, could tell which parts of my prose I was more interested in, not only by the movement of the scroll bar at the side of my computer screen, but also the mouse. I knew this was physically possible but, in addition, I actually thought it might be happening.

I could have a conversation with someone at an adjacent machine about whether or not there was some tiny difference between the information displayed on each of our screens. Because of the cameras in my eyes, or at least the motion sensors in them, as soon as I looked towards another screen, and away from my own, I could not be sure the other screen had not changed. My controller, outflanking me electronically, could have spotted the movement of my gaze changing what was on the other screen as a result.

If somebody really was there, monitoring my PC, then the natural urge was to pretend I had not noticed and press on – so I did. If they were doing it from an Army Land Rover in the lane, they would drive off before I got to see them. I eventually found the situation extremely disturbing. I even experienced feelings of mortifying embarrassment at what was nothing more than my own imagination. I was getting slower and slower. I began to observe effects which made me mindful of the possibility that my machine did indeed have dual controls. My belief that I might have not only a whole array of lodestone microchips inside my limbs, but also, for example, some kind of heart monitor, was still there. This would have been fitted on a free trial basis on the instructions of the Special Intelligence Service by the Royal Army Medical Corps or, more laughably, by the Royal Army Veterinary Corps Pedigree Chum Dog Display Team. It could be used to detect if I was lying. It seemed like I was one of the software components of the Borg Cube – the ultimate in MTRUTH and EAI! The only alternative to walking out and never coming back was to go on the attack at my keyboard. I chose to go on the attack because I had walked out before and ended up nearly being killed in Newquay.

I was trying, unsuccessfully, to import a file into my database. This was not particularly unusual as there were various reasons why I had not been able to do this in the past which appeared quite plausible. I now sensed the psychically pungent aroma of an invisible mouse, rather larger than mine and connected to my machine's copy. I thought it might be on the other side of the office screen, on board HMS Conqueror, in the Army Land Rover in the lane, or more likely at GCHQ, the machine's operator having Prince Charles's dog with him as the prince was out of the country and he was looking after it. I decided I was in the wrong job and others should be doing what I was. I wondered if they practically were. Then something worked when I did not expect it to; not an unusual event for a programmer. GCHQ had altered the state of my PC using their dual controls. But I would be lying if I said I totally believed that to the extent I would put money on it. It's just that, once again, the idea was too alluring not to go along with. Since I knew this was not impossible my mind would not let me rule it out. It had become rather dangerous to think things because somebody knew what I was thinking.

I went to have a look at the file that would not import. I was disoriented whereas on previous occasions doing the same job, I'd had no problem. When I looked at the file, on the screen, I had a peculiar feeling based on various other events, which had already taken place. One of these was my success in enabling the file to import by assuming some information was there, even though it did not appear to be, and going through the motion of deleting it. This, again, is a not uncommon situation in programming, having something there you cannot see and yet can remove. On a number of occasions I found myself thinking: did I just see that word change into another before my very eyes on the screen? My head would move back and forth, shake itself and start refocusing on the script, which even seemed to be going in and out of focus itself, and then I discovered the contrast knob did not seem to work properly. Having seen the article in *The Times* about hidden information on the GCHQ website, I was now wondering what the invisible information had been on my PC. Again it seemed like somebody was playing games with me.

Next I noticed that waves were travelling along the lines of my text, and also going up and down the screen. I was certainly not imagining this. I was sure it had not happened the previous day and was reminded of my strange print outs back in Brighton a few years earlier. I wondered if somebody was interfering with the earth's own magnetic field in the near vicinity of the building, say from that Army Land Rover which I had imagined, parked out of sight behind the trees. It looked a bit like some sort of remote degaussing process was underway. British Intelligence wanted to run a clinical trial of the effectiveness of Her Majesty's armed forces and magnetic radiation in the treatment of mental illness.

So I deliberately did something apparently nonsensical. Since I had not been shot at Wilton, that bank holiday weekend six years of madness earlier, I now recognised the opportunity to do what I felt was the legal equivalent – and started typing in messages for those I imagined were monitoring my machine. All the war gaming I had been involved in for the Ministry of Defence had now boiled down to an electronic war with GCHQ. This war was one which, at the highest level of security classification, one not previously confirmed to exist outside of this story – Absolute Secret – would be named with the codewords "LIVRE" (Learning Intelligence Vehicle Reality Engine) and "GLOVEBOX". The scope of these imaginary projects, only the former of which it seems got off the ground, included a contribution to the peace process in Great Britain and Ireland and, when later I lost my job, the possibility I would get a new one in exchange for receipt, by the Security Services, of intelligence. I was *The Man Who Thought He Knew Too Much*:

The Man Who Thought He Knew Too Much[137]

Some highly sensitive information has come to my attention –
But you didn't hear it from me, alright?
If they ask, you haven't seen me
And if they don't, you've got to ask yourself why.

He was the man who thought he knew too much.

In the apartment opposite a curtain twitches,
A phone rings and then it goes dead,
Something cold and snake-like crawls up inside my spine –
they're getting closer,
And these voices; I can't get them out of my head.

I'm only telling you this for your own protection;
You're not safe here,
Now erase this message.

He was the man who thought he knew too much.

You probably won't hear from me again,
And if you don't, then you'll know every word of this was true.
We are but specks of dust on the rag which cleans this mighty machine,
And whatever happens next, don't say I didn't warn you.

He was the man who thought he knew too much.
He was the man who thought he knew too much.

Somehow my PC seemed to have made me ill. There is a crossover point between the schizophrenic state and the state of hypnosis in which supposedly normal people can be seen to behave rather peculiarly. I was playing a game in my own mind in which I imagined that what I typed into these files was being reacted to elsewhere. Easily did I visualise a group of electronic warfare experts monitoring my every move.

Obviously the line had to be drawn somewhere though. It was decided, somewhere in GCHQ, if not simply my own imagination – an outstation of an unpublicised GCHQ Schizophrenics Support Group – to prevent my file from importing. The reason for this effectively being that the security gate to Her Majesty's Land Forces HQ Wilton had been closed, forever, after I had gone through it six years earlier. I was reminded of how the gates to Traquiar House in Peeblesshire are said not to have been opened since Bonnie Prince Charlie went through them. So I typed in a poem I knew called *The Gate*[138] by a war poet. Now the file read in satisfactorily. This reminded me of how I had driven back and forth in trepidation along the road outside the gate that day. A line from that poem was "Deep night laps in the water starry." I was "Deep Knight", a new pal for the dog Turbo in *The One That Got Away* – a canine MTRU – Deep Knight being his code name in the GCHQ Schizophrenics Support Group. Over my MTRUTH I received an honour on my chest where in reality, there was only a "Moss Bros for Horse and Rider" badge on my jacket. Next to the honour I pictured a counterfeit gold *Blue Peter* badge, still not having got back my own genuine standard sew-on one. My thoughts were florid and delirious, even more so than I have described, like those of somebody tossing back and forth in bed with 'flu and a heavy fever. I needed to get some fresh air.

In many ways I did feel I was back at the gate at Wilton and, to my mind, where in witchcraft terms the whole story went back to – the witch doctor in Ouagadougou market in 1984. But I would not actually be going back to the gate. I had conquered schizophrenia, for now – all I had to do was get away from the machine.

And whatever the real explanation for my presence at Her Majesty's Land Forces HQ Wilton that bank holiday weekend back in 1994 there now seemed no better explanation, apart from schizophrenia, than the witch doctor having imbued its very gate with magical powers. As I had realised in Newquay, if there really was a Comic Relief MI6 agent he was it. The symbolism of my original thoughts in driving through that gate now made complete sense. As for whether these years of madness were the price I paid for calling Robert Hubert a "complete lunatic" on that boat party invite who knows? I have often thought I brought it all upon myself with that faux pas. Perhaps more likely it was all caused by my modest drinking problem. God only knows.

The whole of my African trip went flashing before my eyes, stopping abruptly in the middle of the Sahara desert, entirely alone under the stars – so far from the hustle-bustle of work, and my sad goodbye to Amanda at St. Pancras that day all those years earlier:

> *Myriads of self-same commuters*
> *End their life-constricted journeys here each day;*
> *Where one bright winter's day,*
> *For the enormous sky of Africa*
> *I forsook our habitude and tryst-place.*
> *You'd seen my little-noticed tears.*
> *In the driest desert of love*
> *Tears later fell on sand*

My arms and legs outstretched, encompassed
Solid-angled time-vaulted stars and space,
Images of you and other peoples' legends.
I deal in truth,
Yet again I succumb to subjectivity.

Time had flown by and the office was empty. I started thinking I must be either very tired and hallucinating, or just becoming schizophrenic again. I actually thought that. I was watching an MoD film unit video supra-subliminally on my MTRUTH, shot *Blue Velvet*-style[139] from a cupboard in the small room in Shakespeare Road, Bedford, where Danny Ferguson had been murdered. It was overlaying the form I was working on. A Royal Mail postman had entered the room and was hacking with a large machete at the dummy body lying in bed, theatrical blood flying out and making splatters on the wall. When he had finished he put a letter on the bed. The postman now left and the cameraman emerged from his hiding place; went over, and focused on the letter, which was in a Buckingham Palace envelope.

The screen saver kicked-in, warp factor five. I left the building disturbed, and almost feverish, at what I had been thinking, imagining or seeing on my MTRUTH. I remembered the ghost tour of Bedford I had been on a couple of years earlier. Outside the house where Danny had been killed was said to appear a beautiful lady with a sweet fragrance.

I got down to the village pub. It was seven o'clock and I ordered a beer and let my body shudder to release these strange, involved and chaotic thoughts, which had just usurped my normal thinking processes. I could hear conversation in the other bar with occasional laughter. When there was laughter it seemed like the laughter was aimed at me, and even what I was thinking at that moment. I had to concentrate by saying to myself "Now I know nobody in here, nobody knows me and I am not famous; so nobody could possibly be laughing at me, particularly anything I am thinking. It is just my mind playing tricks. It is mild schizophrenia." I had mastered the technique of Cognitive Behavioural Therapy. It was not going to stop me being arrested again though.

Having thought it through logically, as before, the feelings evaporated. But then I reasoned that it would be possible to receive information via my MTRUTH whilst, on a signal, either through their MTRUTHs or some other way, a British Intelligence unit in the other bar laughed as they were interested in electronically-waged psychological warfare. They also knew I was always up for a laugh, being well seasoned in this condition. I had no doubt what the condition was: it was no more than one in which the words "schizophrenia" and "schizophrenic" can be observed to be used more frequently than in a control group. I imagined a classified operation having made this observation as an initial result of the investigation.

"Well Sir, the investigation, carried out along with the Special Investigations Branch, has been going on for six years now. Our initial assessment of the situation is that within a radius of one mile of The Ship public house the words schizophrenia and schizophrenic seem to being used more frequently in a well-defined group of people than in the control. Our investigations are continuing."

"Let me get this straight. Do you mean to tell me you have found a well-defined group of people amongst whom those words are used rather more than usual?"

"Yes, Sir, that's correct."

"Have you a code word for this condition?"

"Yes Sir, we've decided to call the condition X300907 and our investigations into its nature, along with SIB, are continuing as we speak."

"Have you discovered anything else of use?"

"Yes Sir. We believe there may have been other groups of people exhibiting X300907 since around 1912. Before that date there was no schizophrenia – just lunacy."

"Thank you, keep me informed and let Porton Down know immediately – it could be infectious, and if it is, I want to know. It could be useful to Counter Revolutionary Warfare."

On the train back to Bedford I had something akin to an epileptic fit. You'd have noticed if you were sat opposite. I did not go unconscious or, if I did, it was only momentary. I found my legs twitching uncontrollably for a couple of seconds. I decided it was caused by the St. John's Wort I had been prescribed by a Homeopathic/Herbalist Doctor, in my eagerness to stay well, along with a homeopathic remedy. When I stopped taking it the twitching disappeared. The doctor had told me that St. John's Wort is similar to the antidepressant Imipramine, which had played a large part when I crashed my car in a frenzied mania back in 1994. Perhaps I was high on St. John's Wort during the above episodes when my file did not import and I thought GCHQ was at my machine. When I stopped taking it I no longer had these strange thoughts either. But I was not out of trouble yet by any means. Just because I could not see definitive evidence GCHQ were active here, that did not mean they were not. So to rule out the presence of an Army Land Rover involved in the X300907 experiment, parked unseen in the lane, might be a mistake, it seemed.

The next day, free from these side effects, the germ of an idea crystallised in my head. I had, on occasions been haunted on this train journey down the little-used branch line from Bletchley to Bedford by the Irish navvies who built it, in 1846. The haunting came in the form of imagining that one or two of the few passengers on the train were actually IRA footsoldiers. I would think they had been told to travel on the train sitting near me to gather intelligence for the Republican movement as part of the peace process. It was easy to see the sectarian divide being imported onto this train – a sort of intelligence dance taking place on military lines: "At Lidlington, Grid Reference 989392, leave the train and walk up the hill. At the top turn right. A hundred yards along is The Green Man, Grid Reference 989388. Buy a pint of Guinness and a packet of salt and vinegar crisps. Ask the landlord when the next train is. He will reply '45 minutes – if you're lucky'. You reply 'Time for another pint then'. When you get back to the station the guard will call out, prior to the train's departure, 'All stations for Bedford and Cambridge.' Say to him 'I may be from County Derry but I do know that no train has run to Cambridge on this line since 31st December 1969.' He will reply 'Only joking Paddy – we'll be lucky to get to Bedford!' The chap who gets on at Millbrook will sit two rows away from you and is a former member of the UVF testing in-car MTRUTH systems for General Motors. On no account speak to him... here're your travel documents... Good luck Diarmuid."

Still on the train, I saw a man open his briefcase. From now on nobody would speak to each other but instead would put printed or other material in a briefcase, and then pass it around. On the signal, possibly through the BBC World Service, the cases would all be opened. One ought to be careful what one put in the briefcase because it might be in one's hands when the signal was given to "open briefcases". It was a bit like the IRA pass the parcel joke. Then I thought of the role of language in schizophrenia and how the illness might be changed using the briefcase method. I awoke from my dream and the train pulled into Bedford.

I went down to The Ship as usual. Little did I know I was to now find myself addressing a problem some would have said was unsolvable. I had been set one in mathematics once by Professor Dainty. He wanted to know if there was what is known as an "analytic Fourier Transform" of a circle with a slice taken off. To my knowledge there was only what is known as a "numerical" solution to the problem or in other words you need a computer or a lens to solve the problem and you could not just write it down. This reminded me there are different kinds of solutions to problems.

Somehow the other drinkers, including the landlord, but not his Irish wife, did not make me feel as at home as they might normally have done.

A chap asked me about my mental health troubles. This was the occasion I said I'd had schizophrenia and that was used to question if I ever really had. Like most of the general population, despite the fact that one in three people experiences some form of mental illness in their life, he believed there are ordinary people on one hand and paranoid schizophrenics on the other. Most people think there is nothing in between and once you have had schizophrenia, there is no way out of it. You find yourself trapped in a post-schizophrenia socio-pathological organism, call it X300907 if you will, which will not let you go. If you have had schizophrenia you can claim to suffer a disability even if you have not got it anymore. The diagnosis is an integral part of the illness. Somebody exhibiting a similar degree of mental health is treated as sane only because they do not have the diagnosis. They might even have caused the condition themselves. Sometimes I wonder if I would ever have got the diagnosis if I had never taken the drugs, which, I believe, caused me to damage cars.

This chap now told me he had been in the Merchant Navy and that at sea once his captain had ordered him to let off a fire extinguisher. He now said "What is the point of testing a fire extinguisher if, once it has been tested, you cannot use it anymore?" I pointed out that if the fire extinguisher was tested and it did not work then something useful would have been proven, that is the fire extinguisher was useless. He did not seem to accept my point and asked somebody else the same question.

The conversation now became quite heated as the topic arose of quality control at the factory where they make the canisters which propel the foam from the fire extinguishers.

Another chap now suggested that the manufacture of each and every canister was completely independent of any other adjacent canister. I pointed out that the manufacture of each canister was correlated with the adjacent canisters. He simply refused to accept there was any truth in what I was saying and got quite angry. Now he started tossing a coin and landing it, from his hand, on the bar. Angrily he lectured me on how each toss of the coin was completely independent. He was right there, but wrong with the canisters. Anybody who worked on the canister production line would understand that. All it needed was for the machine to run out of cans and a whole series of cans would consist of nothing but what was supposed to be inside them. He refused to see my point.

Next day, on the train to work I began writing a letter to the landlord. I worked on the letter for several days. It turned out rather well and, as the name of the pub was The Ship, instead of addressing it more usually to Bill, the landlord, I addressed it to "The Captain". It related the story of a fictitious chap by the name of Dick Richardson[140] who was taken by the SAS to work on the production line where they make these canisters. The empty canisters were stacked on pallets under an apple tree in fruit and nobody had remembered to pull the tarpaulin over them. The SAS knew one of the canisters was faulty because it had "The Beatles' own apple core" in it and he had to wager his home on it working.

So, as well as sending the letter to "The Captain", I also sent it to the other chaps invoking this fictitious character Dick Richardson who, in the letter was made to look a fool instead of anyone at the bar – including me I hope. But when I sent it I was not satisfied with just that. A couple of days later, before sending the letter, I met a chap in my own imagination, who said he worked at the DISC and who said he had seen the letter. He pointed out that I had resolved a dispute between two small groups of people and if that was possible it should also be possible between two large groups of people. He minded me to send the letter to the parties in the Anglo-Irish peace process – which I now did. When the letter was nearing completion something strange happened, leading me to wonder if my PC was being monitored again. Late one afternoon, I added the Chief of Staff, the Irish Republican Army to the list of circulants. Rather than just being an imaginary ship's manifest it seemed to me I had created a conceptual legal device. On the way home, after a trip to the town centre office and having emailed the letter to a friend, I found myself on the platform at Bletchley. From the platform I noticed the odd sight of a daylight firework display in Bletchley Park. So the firework display truly remained an enigma which I could not separate from what I would later realise was The Ship's manifest. Reaching Bedford the alarm was going off on the British Telecom building. I could hear it a mile away and believed it was in response to my email. It must have been the loudest alarm on the market.

I also sent the letter to the other various parties in the peace process. These included, for example, the Chief of Defence Staff, the Special Forces, David Trimble, Bernadette Sands (the sister of Bobby) and De Danann, with quite a few others besides. Some of the crew were dead so, whilst they were on this conceptual legal device, The Ship, and were on its manifest, I did not actually post them the letter.

A few nights later I went into the pub and the effect was remarkable. I had proved my point without offending anybody and now the atmosphere had changed. I seemed to have now become respected. I had won. One chap asked me where I worked and I told him, quite baldly, I was the youngest ever head of MI5. He swallowed and looked like he believed me. More likely he thought I was totally mad – or joking. Little did he know, I found myself thinking, that "head" could also mean "MTRU". He knew nothing of MTRUTHs and EAIs. It was all in my head, if you'll excuse the pun. Which reminds me. A man wanted to win a radio competition for the best pun. To give himself a better chance of winning he submitted ten puns – but "no pun in ten did"!

That night I had an especially vivid dream. I was standing in the front room listening to some particularly pertinent music when a black London taxi (the favoured means of transport of Irish Republicans in the six counties of North Ireland) pulled up outside the house. Three not very tall men got out. One came and knocked on my front door without ringing the bell, leaving as soon as he had done, to walk down the street, the taxi and the others following. I went to the door and called out after him to ask what they wanted. Back came the reply, as our eyes met, and in a heavy Dungiven accent, "Nothing to worry about, just a courtesy call, Irish Republican Army." Now a brand new green Bentley Continental R Turbo like Prince Charles drove, pulled up and parked outside the front door. It had the actual number plates I had ordered six years earlier, DOG 1. As I went in, a cyclist I did not recognise stopped right outside the front door and lit a cigarette. The atmosphere was eerie. As when I was down at Newquay, it seemed he wished to convey a message to me – a warm one. The driver of DOG 1 came over and gave me the keys.

I woke up, remembering my contribution to the peace process – my dream in which central Newquay became part of Ireland. The Newquay Chamber of Commerce would be grateful to me! But so, it now seemed, were the Special Intelligence Service and the Irish Republican Army: it had been an *MTRUTH* dream!

By June I was unemployed and received a £13,000 redundancy payment. I put £1,000 cash in an envelope and addressing it to Sinn Féin, c/o the Irish Removals Company, London and personally delivered it to a house in north London near that company. The number plate of the car outside the house had OUR in it. The number plate of the car next door had SLR, the type of rifle used by British Forces. This was the height of insanity because if I really wanted to give Sinn Féin the money I should have sent a cheque to their office in Belfast. I destroyed the letter to the Captain later in the summer in a schizophrenic and Gogolesque[141] fit of pique imagining it was as dangerous as a tactical nuclear warhead. I even wrote to those on *The Ship* enclosing a document destruction programme – feeling this to be rather allusive. A pity. It would have looked good here. But I imagine MI5 have a copy if you want to see it.

My imaginary ship was to make an interesting voyage, the story of which is beyond this book, or even this period of history. But it certainly led me into some rough waters (like getting me sectioned again). Nevertheless I loved my ship and could see it and its famous crew cutting powerfully through the raging sea in the psychic-ether! I felt like a ship's husband. I wonder where it's sailing now. I was to decide the ship was in fact the Clipper Maid of the Seas, the ship after which the Lockerbie plane was named; so I put Jo Hudson on it too as well as Kevin Lynch, handing the landlord a framed copy of a poem by R.P.Crowther (aged 9) which I found in the school magazine, *The Eagle*, from 1969:

The Ship

I look at the ship on the ha'penny.
And wonder what is its name.
Did it sail on the Indian Ocean
Or maybe the Spanish Main?

I think it might be the Mayflower.
Other names don't come to mind.
But I do have a faint recollection.
That it might be the Golden Hind.

It seemed appropriate since The Ship was said to have been built from the timbers of another one that had been broken up. Furthermore, in Irish mythology, the early settlers, the Tuatha De Danann, had come to Ireland in flying ships. Now their modern representatives, the folk band De Danann, were playing on this flying ship with the parties in the peace process drinking at the bar in my MTRUTH – in lego-military hyperspace! I would have my boat party without a hitch after all!

Then I remembered that every night I had been to The Ship over some 20 years, I had walked past the World Headquarters of the Panacea Society, a few yards from the pub. The Panaceans are the custodians of a box[142] left by their founder, Joanna Southcott, which contains prophecies destined to save mankind from the apocalypse. The Society, over two hundred years old, is extremely secretive, their history involving a putative virgin birth, a miracle cure and the building of Utopia in Bedford, which they believe is the Garden of Eden. They believe the actual centre of the Garden of Eden is the beautiful secret garden in the grounds of their HQ, in Albany Road, Bedford. So there was the answer to *The Question*, right on my doorstep! Jerusalem had been built, not amongst those dark satanic mills, but in the green and pleasant land of Bedfordshire – and the centre of the Garden of Eden was just around the corner from The Ship pub! Prince Charles's dog was barking away as hard as it possibly could in the Garden; I was one of the chosen few to see this. But even I had not access to the centre; I just had to make do with the sight of its ghost, or MTRUTH vision, through the garden wall. Also just around the corner from the pub, which as you know I *had* been lucky enough to have access to, the Panaceans have a house called *The Ark* all ready for the Messiah to live in.

They fully believed the Lord was to come to Bedford in 2000. Perhaps in all those times I had walked past their HQ, some of their beliefs had been unconsciously absorbed by me, though my beliefs for the same year about Princess Diana and her dramatic reappearance were a little more prosaic but no less revelatory. For me Diana was the woman clothed in sun in the Book of Revelation. I wondered if Bobby Sands, Kevin Lynch, John Peel, David Trimble, Lord Guthrie, Princess Diana, The Beatles and company would have been grateful to see an ark, The Ship, in which they were named as crew, appear in Bedford in 2000. For this was what the Panaceans had predicted, meaning all the crew were immortal. I recalled the light from the distant ship, which had saved my life in Newquay – and now it seemed to be *this* ship. The delusional symbolism of my Irish trips seemed complete when I remembered that a few miles south of Bedford there is a hamlet called Ireland. Kim Philby? Well he probably was just a traitor – but a patriotic one! And he loved listening to Test Match Special.

On midsummer's day I was outside The Embankment Hotel where the Morris Men were playing. They left in the twilight to march off playing down to the next pub. Something made me watch them as they gradually disappeared with their music into the distance – it was Eryngo on his hind legs at the back of the troupe playing his penny whistle – and I imagined they would go all the way to Belfast.

With Henley Royal Regatta 2000 coming around I decided to take a walk in the country. I walked to the edge of town north of Bedford, up Cleat Hill and along Graze Hill, where I had run on the morning of the announcement of Diana's death. Along the road, with Twinwoods in sight, an Army Land Rover pulled up. Out got the Major. "Your presence is required at Military High Command, Dr Travis," he said, directing me through into a field, where I heard the unmistakeable sound of a Chinook helicopter approaching. Soon it had landed. In I got and off we flew into the sunset. "Corporal Robert Hollis, Special Air Service Regiment Sir!" said the soldier inside, "And this is Prince Charles's dog" – except he didn't – this was just my imagination.

Part XXI

Addendum

Universal

It is with both pride and relief that I got here to announce the end of my story. Though Emily and I are no longer together I will always love her and treasure the memory of our times together. The same holds for Amanda even though I have not seen her for the worst part of two decades. It felt like she was mine, got killed in the Troubles and I was still grieving the loss. I still think of them both each day. Oh, and I did not tell you what happened after the point where I was hanging off the bridge in 1994.

Well I decided not to jump. I had to speak to Dr. Black. I climbed back over the balustrade and walked off back towards Barnes. The dog was still barking in Mortlake Cemetery, though a little less urgently. You know what happened after that: the next day was the day I was sectioned for the first of five times during this story, when I crashed my car. The rest, as they say, is history. Except I felt a bit of a wimp for not jumping and went back there again a year later and this time actually jumped in, aged 33 and a third, just to prove to myself I would have survived. But this time I made sure I was near the middle where, hopefully, the water was deep enough. Crucially I had not been in the middle when I nearly jumped back in 1994.

I had never fallen so far in my life and the tide was very low. I made a groan of fear, hit the water with a whoosh and my feet actually touched the bottom of the Thames itself. Surfacing, I swam off downstream towards the brewery. It was a beautiful moonlit night and the water was warm and clean.

As I reached the bank by the Stag brewery, I could have sworn that I felt my right leg being tugged on, but only very gently, so that the person who did it could not be certain I had noticed. Sometimes I still like to think it just could have been the Special Boat Service after all but it was probably just the local sub aqua club. Either way I hope that, by having written this book, there is no longer any shame attached to having this illness. I certainly feel none, have forgotten some of the shame I felt and actually I feel quite proud to have had this amazing ailment and come through it the other side – which many have not – despite some of the treatment I have received. Sometimes you know, I even forget the connection between the disappearance of Prince Charles's dog, the Vale of Glamorgan by-election result and a dog called Tatters.

Concerning the loss of my Harris tweed cap, I am still hoping someone, somewhere, will find and return it. Almost finally, and for the avoidance of doubt, our cat Eryngo is sadly no longer with us. He died in a road traffic accident. Eryngo was not driving, and was not to blame. And just to dispel any rumours to the contrary, Eryngo is sadly extremely dead and not pretending. I know, because I buried him myself. The reality is that I was as upset at losing him as; no doubt, Prince Charles was at losing his dog, Pooh. I buried Eryngo with a stick held in his paw as in the song *Erin-go-bragh*. I had my suspicions about his death, finding it difficult to accept he had died in a straightforward RTA. I imagined he had died in a total reality replacement exercise, being himself a Royal Army Veterinary Corps MTRU. He thought he was in the kitchen and was trying to jump onto his place on the cupboards when, in reality, he was by the road and about to be run over. He died to influence a hardened cat-loving criminal who MI5 wanted to recruit by making him feel responsible for the Eryngo's death. I felt angry.

Jumping off the bridge? Well you might think I was mad to do so. But my friend Edge, who appeared earlier in this story, told me he was planning to *dive* off all the bridges from Tower to Kew, as in Rudyard Kipling's poem, *The River's Tale*:

> *Seventeen bridges, from Tower to Kew*
> *Wanted to know what the river knew*
> *But the bridges were young*
> *And the Thames was old*
> *And this is the tale*
> *That the river told...*

Sadly, Edge died of lung cancer whilst I wrote this story, even though he never smoked. I'm not sure if he ever got to do the diving but the river, for sure, could tell of the night I jumped in and that to dive in it was only safe at high tide.

Oh, and before I go, about that concrete at the foot of my grandmother's garden. I don't suppose you believed it had the bodies of KGB/CIA double agents buried there with the Nazi gold and treasures secreted out of Germany during the last days of the War. Nor, do I hope, did you really believe that Prince Charles was an MI6/Soviet double agent – or that I had any sophisticated military electronics in my head other than those I had inherited in my genes. You see all along it was just me rationalising some of my more schizophrenic experiences. The Absolute Secret files? There were none – I just made them up as a vehicle for my MTRUTH theories. So no Sumo Rabbit 37 I'm afraid. And I suggest my thoughts about the 1926 meeting were more to do with the continuity of British Intelligence than any long term plan, conspiratorial or otherwise. But if you think I made this story up then why did the advertisement appear in The Aberdeen *Press and Journal*?[143]

I suppose you might agree, however, were you to look at the bottom of my grandmother's garden, it is a little odd. Especially if you are a British Intelligence agent looking through a family photo album of one of my grandmother's renowned parties held there and, by one of the photos, you notice my father has written: "N.B. KGB photographer in window of house opposite." Perhaps it would be safe to say, you just can't be sure. If anybody really is buried there, let sleeping dogs lie I say. But as for the treasure, well! And Comic Relief never got their £10 million to my knowledge. The sum was more a reflection of the boundless possibility the excitement of my illness engendered. But a proportion of the profits from this book are going to them, with the rest also going to charity as listed at the end of this book.

As for whether anyone will ever actually have an MTRUTH fitted without their knowledge, that is a good question. Perhaps it will be the chap at the MoD, just posted there from the Special Forces, who has to read this story to see if there are any security breaches. That could be quite amusing – the procedure simply being a military exercise.

Well this has been my tale, and I hope you enjoyed reading it. For much of the story I felt I was on a mission. That frame of mind was a self-fulfilling one – *I was* on a mission, a mission to write this story. Whether you have been a sufferer of schizophrenia or not, I wish you well. Good luck. As for me, well, the next time I see a car number plate with LBD in it. I will say to myself "Ah, I know what that is. It's not a car parked there especially by MI5 to make me think it is a reference to General Lebed, the gallant former Chief of Staff of the Russian armed forces. It's just me remembering what it was like to be in a paranoid schizophrenic state: when they did." As for Prince Charles's dog, well, I never *actually* found it. Or did I? Perhaps it is up to you to decide. Either way I did find myself – by writing this story.

Part XXII

Postface

Over the Side ₁₄₄

ollowing the end of this story I was sectioned a further four times, four more cycles of murderous treatment. These spells really just engendered more suicidal misery, during which I quite rightly felt extremely sorry for myself (at least when I forgot about Prince Charles's dog). But one of the visits was of note. I was given a drug, Seroquel, which did not make me suicidal, at least for several weeks. The problem was it then gave me irritable bowel syndrome, a known side effect of the drug. I ended up writhing about on the ward's shiny floor, my alimentary canal evacuating from both ends alternately in a one-minute cycle, the pain in my gut impossible to bear. It was quite terrifying and went after I secretly spat out the drug for a couple of days. Can you imagine how frightening it is being locked up and having to do that? When I confronted the psychiatrist with the facts she said "It could not be irritable bowel syndrome; you have to have that for six months." So I replied "What would it be after five months, 30 days, 23 hours, 59 minutes and 59 seconds: a teddy bear's picnic?"

In March 2004, towards the end of my fourth spell of incarceration after this story, I found myself talking to a newly admitted patient in the bed next to me. He had never been in hospital before. I asked him what he was taking for his cannabis-induced psychosis and he told me, saying he was getting no side effects.

It did not need a genius to see that without medication I would almost certainly have been sectioned again before the year was out. So in May 2004, following my release by the hospital managers and another cycle of drug-induced misery (on Risperdal Consta), I bit the bullet and visited my GP. There was really only one drug left I had not tried, the one the other patient had been on: Olanzapine. I asked my GP to put me on a dosage of 5mg. After 10 years of criminal, murderous and terrifying experiments I had finally found a drug I could take which did not cause me side-effects or make me suicidal. In the same year I finally won my case for unfair dismissal and disability discrimination and received compensation.

Cast of Voices I Heard[145]
(usually helpful) in order of frequency

1. His Royal Highness Prince Charles (always saying "Truly grateful").
2. Diana, Princess of Wales (usually saying "Oh yes, he must go to such and such a place and buy such and such an item").
3. Sgt. H.B.Travis (my policeman brother saying "He's topped out.")
4. Unidentified August male member of the Special Intelligence Service.
5. Unidentified retired male Army officer.
6. Unidentified SAS rookie (always saying "Shit-hot powers of observation".).
7. Amanda. (acting like an old friend)
8. Unidentified female member of the Special Intelligence Service (said "James Longhurst,…" for a few months.
9. John Squire (from the Stone Roses – always laughing).
10. Irish Republican Maze prisoner: very cross.
11. Unidentified male Rastafarian member of Black MI5 unit.
12. Her Majesty the Queen (always saying "Clive Travis, you have no idea what you have just done!" and "Getting warmer, every day.").

The Charities

All royalties from this project will be donated to the following charities:

The Prince of Wales International Centre for SANE Research
The Prince's Trust
The Diana Princess of Wales Memorial Fund
Catholic Aid for Overseas Development (CAFOD)
The Salvation Army
Build Africa
Médecins Sans Frontières
Comic Relief
The Speedwell Trust
The Dog's Trust
Look – Charity for Blind and Partially Sighted Children
Talking 2 Minds
UNICEF

I will disburse the money received to the charities yearly and the accounts will be published on my website www.paranoidschizophrenia.co.uk.

Appendix

Notes

[1] In *Schizophrenia: The Positive Perspective*, Chapter 4, "Hospital Life Whilst Psychotic", Peter K. Chadwick describes the very same non-existent organisation completely independently of me as "The Organisation". In *Autobiography of a Schizophrenic Girl* Marguerite Sechehaye refers to it as "The System". See also see footnote [7]. The Hitchcock film *The 39 Steps* is named after an organization of spies with that name.

[2] I imagined that persons in the Special Intelligence Service believed I would never succumb to such tactics. Instead they thought I would fight back, by for example writing this book. Hence I imagined them actively devising and carrying out attempts to drive me to kill myself.

[3] Professor Thomas Barnes disputes this figure but instead cites Jobe & Harrow (2005): "between 21 per cent and 57 per cent show good outcome". In his view the patients who are the source of that statistic are not "prospectively identifiable" in other words not all of the patients who went into the system have been covered.

[4] Holding strange beliefs, or promulgating rather contrary views or conspiracy theories about matters, is not, it seems, confined to sufferers of schizophrenia. Here are the top ten examples of such conspiracy theories: (10) The moon landings were hoaxed by NASA (10,700 websites); (9) Marilyn Monroe was murdered (one theory being that a barbiturate enema killed her); (8) Our airspace has been repeatedly invaded by UFOs; (7) Elvis is alive; (6) The Royal Family are German impostors or alien reptile shape-shifters; (5) Diana was murdered (200,000 websites); (4) Hitler lived; (3) People have been abducted by aliens (and had implants fitted by them); (2) Lee Harvey Oswald did not shoot John F. Kennedy – 61 other different people having been claimed to have shot him; (1) People are subjected to mind control including by implants (500,000 websites – but none mentioning MTRUTH at the time of writing).

[5](i) About a quarter of sufferers of schizophrenia will commit suicide (Source: *A Beautiful Mind* by Sylvia Nasar).

(ii) Forty per cent of individuals with schizophrenia will attempt suicide and ten per cent succeed (Source: *The Doctors' Guide*, www.pslgroup.com/dg).

[6] Of which I had a somewhat benign view, especially in the light of the much later Litvinenko polonium episode.

[7] In his autobiography, *My Silent War*, the British spy Kim Philby himself imagines the existence of such a body. "It seemed that somewhere, lurking in deep shadow, there must be another service, really secret and really powerful, capable of backstage machination on such a scale as to justify perennial suspicions."

[8] Murderous: "extremely arduous or unpleasant" – *Concise Oxford Dictionary*; "extremely difficult or unpleasant", "dangerous" – *Penguin English Dictionary*.

[9] *No Love Lost* (Joy Division)), published by Universal Music Publishing copyright control. Lyrics by Ian Curtis. Reproduction permission applied for.

[10] For the technophiles amongst you read about the head-related transfer function (HRTF) e.g. on Wikipedia.

[11] That is if the bombing was not carried out in response to the Americans shooting down Iran Air flight 655: a plane carrying 290 Iranian pilgrims on their way to Mecca. It was shot down by the *USS Vincennes* when the captain believed it was a hostile Iranian jet fighter.

[12] I imagined it would be rather more accomplished than the operation of that title in an edition of *Dad's Army*.

[13] A campaign of sabotage is being waged in a multimillion pound "board war" between rival estate agents. "Estate agency sabotages rivals as board wars turn dirty" (Source: *The Times* 14th June 2003).

[14] Free will – you only think you have it. *New Scientist*, 6th May 2006. Underneath the uncertainty of quantum mechanics could lie a deeper reality in which, shockingly, all our actions are predetermined.

[15] www.bathcaninesociety.co.uk/about.asp

[16] Lizzie Dripping – a character in a '70s BBC children's television programme by that name. She is a young girl who is friends with a witch (who only she and the audience can see) in the church graveyard. Lizzie is dreaming and daring at the same time and turns things upside down and inside out wherever she goes and whatever she does. Lizzie Dripping is a provincial term in the Nottingham area for a plucky girl who has difficulty in telling the difference between fact and fiction. (Sources: www.televisionheaven.co.uk, www.readingmatters.co.uk).

[17] See for example: *Catastrophe Theory* by V.I.Arnold, chapter 3, figure 6, page 8. In mathematics a catastrophe does not have to be a bad thing. It can be the exact opposite.

[18] *The Swimmer* – Burt Lancaster stars as a middle-aged man who decides to swim home across suburban Connecticut via the pools of all his friends. Fascinating evocation of schizophrenia, and a thoughtful performance from Burt Lancaster as he encounters increasing hostility on the way. The film is a real one-off and location filming in Connecticut perfectly recaptures the mood of the interesting John Cheever short story on which the film is based (Source: www.skymovies.com).

[19] Conrad's *Heart of Darkness* is a profound exploration into the human subconscious twinned with a terrifying portrayal of the dangers of imperialism. Trader Marlow tells of his journey to the heart of the Belgian Congo in search of the elusive Mr Kurtz. Away from civilisation as he knows it, he comes to reassess not only his own values, but also those of nature and of society. For in this heart of darkness, it is the terrifying face of human savagery that becomes most visible (Source: www.amazon.co.uk).

[20] One way of looking at this book is that it is me climbing out of a deep hole – my success depending on how many people know I've tried.

[21] The K Foundation is Bill Drummond and Jimmy Cauty. They made a million from their ventures in pop music, firstly as the Justified Ancients of Mu Mu (the JAMs), then as the Timelords, and latterly as one of the most successful British bands of the late '80s and early '90s, the KLF. After disbanding the KLF in 1992 Drummond and Cauty set up the K Foundation (Source: www.ellipsis.com).

[22] *The K Foundation Burn A Million Quid* – a book by Chris Brook and Gimpo (Alan Goodrick), published by Ellipsis. A year after the event Cauty (see [16]) and Drummond returned to Jura to show the people of the island the film *Watch the K Foundation Burn a Million Quid*. They also inaugurated a series of screenings and discussions held in various locations, all in an attempt to understand just what the K Foundation had done. Was it art? What was the morality of the burning? Was it a publicity stunt? What should they do next? (Source: www.ellipsis.com).

[23] The BMW M5, for example, now indeed has a head-up display.

[24] The Lazy House was one of the bands I would have liked to have had on my record label. They were wonderful.

[25] The process of "Morphic Resonance" has been proposed by Dr Rupert Sheldrake. See e.g. *New Science of Life: The Hypothesis of Morphic Resonance*.

[26] Full Press – strictly a full court press. In a full court press the team with the ball is marked man-to-man by the opposing team. In a half court press this occurs in the defending team's half of the pitch.

[27] The Strawberry Fair has been running since 1973 and has grown from humble beginnings to be the largest volunteer-run free event in the region. It takes place every year in the first week of June and is set in the heart of Cambridge on Midsummer Common.

[28] In chapter 4, "The (Live) Radio" of *Out of It: An Autobiography on the Experience of Schizophrenia*, published by an anonymous author, the very same phenomenon of personalized live radio broadcasts is described, with the Beatles fronted by an undead John Lennon playing.

[29] This is part of a poem, *Peace*, written by my father, Sqdn Ldr Edward Travis (ret) taken from *Evensong and Other Poems* available c/o the publisher.

[30] King John is said to have made an ill-judged crossing of the Wash in 1216, when he lost all his baggage and treasure including the Crown Jewels to the rapidly rising tide. Gloomily, he then made his way to the Abbey of Cistercians at Swineshead, there consumed an excess of peaches and new cider, was very ill the next day and was carried on a litter to Sleaford castle. The following day, he was taken to Newark castle, where he died.

[31] It died of heat exhaustion in space.

[32] K stands for degrees Kelvin and 0K equals -273.16C.

[33] *The Incredible Shrinking Man* – a pulp science fiction film classic about a man who starts to shrink after

being enveloped by a strange atomic cloud when on holiday. Notable for its relatively intelligent script (adapted from his own novel by Richard Matheson), for some imaginatively amusing effects, and for an existential streak which finally leaves the (tiny) hero pondering the meaning of existence (Source: *The 7th Virgin Film Guide*).

[34] In *The Forbidden Planet* huge impenetrable shutters come down to protect Dr. Morbius from the Monster of the Id – the monsters of his own mind.

[35] *Rogue Male* – a novel by Geoffrey Household. A lone operator, having attempted to assassinate a tyrant, is relentlessly tracked down by foreign agents and goes to ground in a Devon country lane where he is trapped but finally escapes with the unwitting help of his cat, Asmodeus. The tyrant is often said to have been Adolf Hitler though, at the time of publication, he chose not to reveal this.

[36] *The Secret Ways* – an Alistair MacLean novel. Britain's top agent is given the impossible assignment of entering Communist Hungary and returning a brilliant but traitorous British scientist. The drugging of Reynolds, the agent, by the Hungarian Secret Police (the AVO), seems rather salubrious and tame compared to what I was to endure at the hands of the NHS, both later in this story and during the writing of this book.

[37] Except the Ardbeg "Supernova".

[38] Hypoparanoia is a very rare psychiatric condition in which everyone can easily see somebody is being followed by the security services or is at the centre of a criminal conspiracy but they themselves cannot or are unable to see it. However hard the psychiatrist tries to reason the facts with them they are unable to see the truth. Without education there can be stigma and prejudice associated with the condition.

[39] For the soothsayer the other cards I got were The Son of Cups, The Empress, The Son of Wands, The Eight of Swords, The Ace of Stones, The Emperor and the Three of Wands.

[40] A comic trip through hell in Ireland, as told by a murderer, *The Third Policeman* is another inspired bit of confusing and comic lunacy from the warped imagination and lovably demented pen of Flann O'Brien. *The Third Policeman's Bicycle* is the play version (Source: www.constantreader.com).

[41] *The Prisoner* – set in Portmeirion. A cult '60s television series in which the star is followed by a balloon gathering intelligence on him. The ex-secret agent having been captured and brainwashed finds himself in a curious Shangri La civilisation from which he finds he cannot escape. Instead he is trapped forever in a mysterious security village (Source: *Halliwell's Television Guide*).

[42] Beyond this story I had a consultant called Dr Zaman. We would refer to him as Dr Zamania.

[43] *The Tenant* – Polanski-directed psychological horror film starring himself as an office clerk in Paris. He becomes increasingly obsessed with uncovering the mystery of what happened to the previous occupant of the flat he moves into and becomes possessed by her. The circular film is extremely, scarily effective (Source: www.tvguide.com/movies).

[44] "Selective erasure of human memory a certainty within decade", "Rewriting your past", *New Scientist*, 3rd December 2005.

[45] *The News Letter* is in fact a Unionist newspaper published in Belfast for the last 270 years. It is the oldest English language publication still in existence in the world. I believed this banner was only above the newsagent I was looking at or, if not, I was famous over here, probably the latter. But if so it was a secret fame I felt, which though perhaps more terrifying that the usual sort I nevertheless preferred.

[46] Knights of Old – a Northamptonshire haulage company – nothing to do with mediaeval chivalry and knighthoods for paranoid schizophrenics.

[47] Edie Sedgwick – a friend of Andy Warhol about whom Bob Dylan wrote the song *She Belongs To Me*.

[48] Bolt Thrower and their ilk were given to very short works, so I thought it would be nice to choose one of their longer pieces for this brief chapter.

[49] Mother Teresa of Calcutta's death so soon after Princess Diana's in 1997, would nag at my mind, their deaths seeming connected. After her death the following notes, in her own handwriting, were found on the wall of her room by her bed:

- People are often unreasonable, illogical or self-centred. Forgive them anyway.
- If you are successful, you will be sure to make some false friends and some true enemies. Be successful anyway.
- If you are honest and frank people may cheat you. Be honest and frank anyway.
- What you spend years building, someone could destroy overnight. Build anyway.
- If you find serenity and happiness others may be jealous. Be happy anyway.

- The good you do to people today will often be forgotten tomorrow. Be good anyway.
- Give the world the best you have and it may never be good enough. Give the world the best you've got anyway.
- You see, in the final analysis, it is between you and God. It was never between you and them anyway.

[50] Months later, suspicious of what had happened, I would visit the library and look up the drug Imipramine. Violent, aggressive and impulsive behaviour was listed as a side effect. See for example *ABPI Compendium of Data Sheets and Summaries of Product Characteristics*. Much later it would be explained to me that here I had been suffering from what is known in psychiatry as depersonalisation

[51] *The Atrocity Exhibition* (Joy Division)

[52] In reality I suspect such a weapon would be a little too unwieldy for an individual to carry.

[53] Yes there was one, and not just a pool one, in this asylum.

[54] Ballardesque – *The Atrocity Exhibition* is Ballard's pageant of sex and death, a collection of some of the most influential science fiction short stories of the period, one of which was later developed in *Crash* (1973) (Source: www.polybiblio.com). Lent its name to a track on Joy Divisions' classic album *Closer*.

[55] Fairmile Hospital closed in 2002 after 132 years. In 1977 it had 613 beds so work out for yourself the number of man-years of pain it had seen.

[56] King Edward VII is said to have said that no gentleman should score a break of more than 25. I had little trouble in obeying this matter of etiquette. I am reminded of some Major cigarettes and deliberately losing a game of pool in Galway earlier in that summer.

[57] I also posted a letter to Amanda wishing her luck in her marriage. I regretted not putting the p.s. "Think of me when you hear *Your Silent Face*."

[58] Criminal: "deplorable", "scandalous" – *Concise Oxford Dictionary*, "Disgraceful", "deplorable" – *Penguin English Dictionary*. Many of the drugs available to be prescribed for schizophrenia, particularly but not only the older ones, can cause clinical depression and akathisia as a side effect. A cigarette packet-style health warning in block red letters should be printed on the patient information leaflet. "Schizophrenia is a cruel disease: its treatments are too often toxic", *Schizophrenia Association of Great Britain Newsletter No.38*, summer 2004.

[59] The Elephant Man – Joseph Merrick – a tremendously deformed man in Victorian Times, spent part of his life in freak shows and was given a room high in the old Charing Cross hospital.

[60] In view of the statistic (see Foreword) that some patients recover to the point of requiring no antipsychotic medication it seems certain there are quite a number taking medication they no longer need.

[61] David Icke – the former BBC sports reporter who went right round the bend, started dressing in robes, and going around expostulating conspiracy theories more laughable than mine. He believes the Royal family are alien reptilian shape-shifters.

[62] The 1993 Turner Prize winner. She famously made a concrete cast of the interior of a 19th century terraced house in the East End of London, *"House"*, the ultimate monumental sculpture.

[63] Synaesthesia is an extremely rare medical condition where visual stimuli also produce a sense of smell and/or taste.

[64] On Caroline's first Warner Brothers' album *Spirit* she placed my name in the list of those she thanked, meaning my name was juxtaposed with Peter Gabriel, Nigel Kennedy and other exalted persons. I am very proud of that.

[65] The saloon version of which car I had passed my driving test in. Only 475 pickups were made and only a handful survive.

[66] The Great Lock-Out of 1913 is a well known event in Irish history.

[67] Heavy water contains deuterium which is a naturally occurring and stable heavy isotope of hydrogen. In nature about 1 in every 6,900 hydrogen atoms is deuterium. When combined with oxygen it produces heavy water, D_2O as opposed to H_2O, the difference being simply an extra neutron in each hydrogen atom. Heavy water is 10 per cent heavier than ordinary water. If it had been heavy water it would not have harmed me. However mouse studies have shown that drinking only heavy water along with normal feed eventually causes degeneration of tissues that need to replenish themselves frequently, and leads to cumulative damage from injuries that don't heal as quickly (Source: the Straight Dope Science Advisory Board). Heavy water can be

purchased in shops e.g. from www.exclusivecosmetics.co.uk at £14.95 per bottle as a skin care treatment. This is probably not pure though as the current world price is about $250-300 per kg.

[68] Bifurcation — see, for example, *Catastrophe Theory* by V.I.Arnold, chapters 1 and 5. Bifurcation means fork. Think of it as a fork in the road.

[69] Hieronymus Bosch – early Dutch painter famous for his depictions of hell.

[70] A book: *The Man Who Mistook His Wife For A Hat* by Dr Oliver Sacks. Consists of short stories relating patient 'oddities', including the said man, that the author has treated in his long career as a neurologist.

[71] *The Fly* – in this 1956 film a scientist experimenting in matter transportation accidentally finds his head, and parts of his body, have been replaced by those of a fly which managed, unnoticed, to get into the transportation chamber. Horrendously, he finds his own head shrunk to fly-size and instead of being on his own body it is on that of the fly.

[72] The longest escape from Broadmoor Psychiatric Hospital was one of 39 years by the Liverpool wife murderer James Kelly, who got away on 28th January, 1888, using a pass key made from a corset spring. After an adventurous life in Paris, New York, and at sea, he returned in April 1927, to ask for readmission. After some difficulties this was arranged. He died in 1930 (Source: *Guinness Book Of Records*).

[73] Look is one of the charities the royalties from this book go to..

[74] Did you know there is a sect of 'orthodox' anti-Zionist Jews in the United States? It's true. See e.g www.jewsnotzionists.org.

[75] I might have been closer if I had imagined a Union flag without the diagonal red stripes (the cross of St Patrick) since, prior to the Act of Union of England, Wales and Scotland with Ireland on January 1st 1801 the flag did not have them. See the white ensign and graphics on the cover of this book.

[76] Apparently this was not the case elsewhere.

[77] The cat had been killed by his attacker.

[78] Another poem by my father. Taken from *Evensong and Other Poems* by Edward Travis, available c/o the publisher.

[79] The spiders were probably Salticus Scenicus (Jumping Spider) though four species of jumping spider live in Britain, two of which are rare. Their behaviour is strongly influenced by their acute vision. They are able to focus on anything around them, including the rear, and jump on their prey in any direction from a range of several inches. They have the greatest acuity of any arthropod. You could say they have MTRUTH-type abilities.

[80] Bun fight – once a year there is an actual bun fight (a fight with buns, as opposed to a bun-fight) in a pub in East London. See, for example, *Discover Unexpected London*, author Andrew Lawson, published by Elsevier-Phaidon, 1977.

[81] All children of the '60s and '70s will remember Dick Dastardly and Muttley, Professor Pat Pending, Penelope Pit-Stop and the Anthill Mob. *The Wacky Races* were inspired by such movies as *Monte Carlo or Bust* and *The Great Race*. Those "way out Wacky Racers" battled it out over all manner of terrain to secure that elusive win on some of the world's most dangerous tracks in this classic Hanna Barbara series (Source: www.dfcom.freeserve.co.uk).

[82] It seems no coincidence that in Brent's cover painting for this story my cap looks rather more of a Donegal and not Harris tweed one.

[83] I do recall one person, over the years covered by this story, saying they did remember but cannot recall who they were.

[84] Later made famous by Keane in their song of that name about it.

[85] Sunny Jim – the rag doll wearing a peruke used to promote the breakfast cereal "Force". "High o'er the fence leaps Sunny Jim, Force is the food that raises him."

[86] Catch 22 – a dilemma or circumstance from which there is no escape because of mutually conflicting or dependant conditions (title of a novel by Joseph Heller (1961) featuring a dilemma of this kind) – *The Concise Oxford Dictionary*.

[87] This was a *Monty Python* takeoff of the *Superman* story. In it the world was populated by ordinary people doing ordinary things except they were all dressed up as Superman. Instead the hero was Bicycle Repairman who, when a bicycle breakdown occurred, would change from his Superman outfit to his bicycle repairman outfit, which included a brown coat. Onlooking Supermen and women would call, astonished: "Look! It's Bicycle Repairman!"

[88] Floccinaucinihilipilification – the longest word in the OED. It means "the act of estimating something as worthless".

[89] A conditioned response is an action carried out without any thought – for example the drooling of Pavlov's dog when it heard the bell announcing meal time.

[90] Tommy Trinder, along with Vera Lynn, Gracie Fields and Max Miller, was one of Britain's foremost entertainers in World War Two. He was a stand-up comedian.

[91] Horrendously there must have been those who preferred this to their illness but decided they wanted neither and chose to improve their life quality by bringing it to an end. Some would have done so in protest there then being a link between them and the IRA/INLA hunger strikers of the summer of 1981.

[92] *No Way Out But To Forward Go* – live album by Killing Joke recorded at Lorely, USA, 1985 – a sentiment to help you keep going if you feel like I did. We all die one day.

[93] From the 1971 film of that title. Army doctor Robert Neville (Charlton Heston) struggles to create a cure for the plague that wiped out most of the human race (Source IMDb).

[94] They're not actually. It's claimed they are "Ah, matter, much later". I don't think being told this would have cured me though.

[95] Peggy Guggenheim – was among the most intriguing cultural figures of her day – as intriguing as the vast collection of modern art she amassed over her lifetime.

[96] For the conspiracy theorist, people living near the Chernobyl nuclear reactor reported a strange tingling sensation on their faces in the hours after the explosion there in 1986.

[97] With MTRUTH one can potentially smell things remotely – see "Sony patent" in the glossary.

[98] There is such a thing as a phase-conjgate mirror but you would see practically nothing in it since it reflects light back exactly where it came from. Since not much light leaves the retina and exits the eye to the mirror you are looking at almost nothing would be seen.

[99] On occasions I also saw thousands of pixels in front of me each with the same image, the person in them being meant to indicate they were jealous.

[100] A golden retriever that bounded into the sea kept swimming until rescue crews finally retrieved him, five miles out into the Solent. Marie Palmer, 56, thought her dog, Solomon, would soon swim back. "But he seemed to be on a mission" she said. The lifeboatman said "It must have seen a cat on the Isle of Wight" (Source: "Dogged mission" *The Times* June 7th 2003).

[101] In *Schizophrenia: The Positive Perspective* by Peter K. Chadwick, there are numerous references to instances of so-called paranormal and psychokinetic events. The best example of the latter in the book you are reading, apart from this, is in chapter 27.

[102] Matt was one of my most favourite people and was a wonderful chap. He died in 2002. RIP Matt!

[103] Professor Sir Roger Penrose – Rouse Ball Professor of Mathematics at the University of Oxford and author of *The Emperor's New Mind: Concerning Computers, Minds and The Laws of Physics* and *Shadows of the Mind: A Search for the Missing Science of Consciousness*.

[104] Windows which emit sound are now available. The system, known as "Whispering Windows" is manufactured by a company called Media Zest.

[105] Jeremy Bentham – founder of the Utilitarian movement and the doctrine of utilitarianism – the doctrine that the greatest happiness of the greatest number should be the guiding principal of conduct.

[106] *If...* – 1968 British film. A surreal take on the darker side of British public school life, which involves a band of self-styled 'Crusaders' rebelling against the brutality of their institution. Launched Malcolm McDowell to stardom (Source: www.channel4.com).

[107] Cray Twin – a powerful supercomputer able to handle, sort and distribute vast quantities of data. Not to be confused with the East End gangsters – the Kray Twins.

[108] www.cornwallpictures.co.uk/html_1/86.htm. Porth Joke is known locally as Polly Joke.

[109] Fuck-off – the modern definition of this adjective is "the absolute best", for example "a fuck-off piece of music", meaning an extremely good piece of music. Whilst I have heard this usage I have not found it included in any dictionary.

[110] I thought what I said was being monitored on my MTRUTH and MI5 had swiped my bag and the Urban Hymns CD.

[111] A bank has admitted a cashpoint blunder gave customers double their money. Queues formed at Barclay's bank in Wooler, Northumberland, when word spread the ATM was dishing out £20 notes instead of £10 notes. In a similar incident, scores of customers swooped on a Halifax Bank dispenser in Urmston, Manchester after

it began giving out an extra £20 with each transaction. It is thought up to £65,000 may have been emptied from the machine in 12 hours during the cash bonanza (Source: *The Daily Telegraph*, April 2004).

[112] © Pimlico poet. I have not been able to trace the poet and have decided he would probably want me to go ahead.

[113] Ian McEwan – (1948 –) Booker Prize winner 2001, and author of *Black Dogs* (1992).

[114] Charles Bukowski – (1920 – 1994) German-born cult American beat-poet and author. His work included: *Love is a Dog from Hell: Poems 1974 – 77*. "Nothing can be taken from us but our lives" – Charles Bukowski.

[115] The actual definition should have no commas, the joke revolving around the placing of commas after "eats" and "shoots", as I have done in the text. There is a book: *Eats, Shoots & Leaves: The Zero Tolerance Approach to Punctuation*, by Lynne Truss, which addresses this sort of thing.

[116] Not for a few years later anyway when they were reintroduced.

[117] Leander Club – an elite rowing club with membership by invitation only, providing many members of the British National Rowing Squad.

[118] Range Rover Overfinch – a customised high-performance Ranger Rover, produced in very small numbers by the Overfinch Company for a premium price.

[119] In Soho there is a women's hostel, the House of St Barnabas at 1 Greek Street, which has a tube leading from the railings in the street to the basement appealing for coins to be placed in it.

[120] Costa Rica is the light of democracy in what for years was an otherwise dictatorial Central America and is the world's greenest country.

[121] For Corrs experts *Runaway* was not on the CD of this album but was on the cassette edition I bought her..

[122] Actually *Strange Meeting II* but I wanted this to be the title of this chapter.

[123] I was wrong and at the time of this book going to publication, miraculously I had been taking it for seven years.

[124] Section 17 leave – this refers to section 17 of the Mental Health Act and allows patients held against their will in psychiatric hospitals to go out, either on their own, or accompanied, provided they return to the hospital by an agreed time.

[125] Forced medication in the community will therefore put thousands onto the street – all destitute psychiatric patients hiding from the NHS and its murderous treatments.

[126] I have observed that some dogs can be taken near the road without being on a lead and do not cause a traffic hazard – these dogs are road dogs.

[127] Owl-light – the light by which owls go abroad. (*Webster's English dictionary*).

[128] The Barmy Army – the good-natured band of supporters of the England cricket team who follow the team wherever they play, often engaging in zany behaviour.

[129] In 1941 Virginia Woolf loaded her pockets with stones and walked into the River Ouse near her Sussex home in Charleston and drowned.

[130] At the time I thought he lived in Telscombe for some reason. It was the thought that counted: he comes from one of England's leading Roman Catholic families.

[131] One theory about the source of this name is that "Lilli" is a familiar form of William, and that bullero comes from the Irish "Buaill Léir ó", which gives: "William (of Orange) defeated all that remained". It is said the song sung King James II out of 3 kingdoms. If I had known this at the time I might have wondered what somebody was trying to tell me. Either way going to a Church of England faith school didn't stop me from becoming an atheist.

[132] In fact by the time I offered to pay them back they refused to accept it.

[133] *Mittageisen* – literal translation "midday iron", or lunch of iron, though the British version was called *Metal Postcard*.

[134] In real life the commanding officer of this experimental US Army unit of psychic warriors was Lieutenant Colonel Jim Channon.

[135] This was the fault of the various mental health teams and social workers whose caseload I was part of as well as my employers' human resources department. One of the key responsibilities of the professional carers for those with mental illnesses is to secure their properties and to arrange care for their (children and) pets. I had a company benefit of insurance sick pay to the value of 90% of my salary if I became long term sick, the rest made up by incapacity benefit. When my statutory sick pay stopped up in Edinburgh there should have been calls made between my mental health workers or social workers and employers' human resources department to get the appropriate form and have it signed by my psychiatrist or GP in order to get my insurance

pay claim in. No such call was made partly because I had no advance directive (otherwise known as a living will) prepared saying this was to happen if I became ill. I should have done as I'd had several cycles of illness. The knowledge that the flat had tripled in price in the years following its sale is most unpleasant. It took that time to eventually recover as you will see. Of course most people don't have sickness insurance pay but you will recall at the time I was in Edinburgh I had a tenant in the flat who unfortunately then moved out meaning his rental of around £1,000 per month was not there to cover the mortgage of around £400 per month. The Jobcentre may even have paid the mortgage interest for me. The people I don't blame for the selling of my flat are my father and me. My father because he got no support from the psychiatric team or social workers and me because I was very ill and had delusions about my flat like for example that it did not really belong to me and was an MI5 safehouse. The psychiatric team were too busy driving me to suicide to worry about issues like this and poor old MI5 were on the end of the usual accusations of a psychiatric patient! It is also true to say that a side effect of my illness was collateral damage to my credit rating potentially making it harder to get a mortgage and back on the ladder. The immediate outcome was the worst possible, bar my suicide.

[136] For the sake of objectivity, I also discovered Seroquel did not make me depressed which seems to give the lie to reports that I ever suffered post psychotic depression as an illness in its own right.

[137] This song title is a play on the 1934 Hitchcock spy thriller *The Man Who Knew Too Much*. His 1956 remake is an exciting event in its own right, with several justifiably famous sequences. James Stewart and Doris Day play American tourists who discover more than they wanted to know about an assassination plot. When their son is kidnapped to keep them quiet, they are caught between concern for him and the terrible secret they hold (Source: amazon.com).

[138] *The Gate*, *The Tomorrow Where Nobody Cares* and *Peace* as well as other poems by my father are taken from *Evensong and Other Poems* by Edward Travis, available c/o the publisher.

[139] *Blue Velvet* – It's a strange world. An innocent young man discovers that a dark underworld exists beneath the surface of his seemingly quiet hometown. One famous scene is eerily shot from inside a cupboard (Source: www.imdb.com).

[140] There *was* a Dick Richardson actually, but I didn't know this. He played in 1 Test Match for the England cricket team. He scored 33 runs and took no wickets. There was also a boxer with that name. In 48 fights he won 31 with 24 knockouts, lost 15 and drew 2.

[141] Gogolesque – Nikolai Vasilevich Gogol, author of *Diary of a Madman*, was told to destroy his writings by a spiritual leader as they were sinful. He burnt the second part of his greatest masterpiece, *Dead Souls*, just as I destroyed most of my letters to the Captain.

[142] A 1970 edition of *Monty Python's Flying Circus* featured the finish of a mile-and-a-half race between various items of furniture, a wc pedestal and Joanna Southcott's box, on a horse race track. The commentary on the race was interspersed with a scene where Michael Palin, dressed as a bishop, with others, was calling for the opening of the box. The opening of the box, in the presence of 24 bishops, is said to be the key to unlock the troubles of the world.

[143] (see page xiv)

[144] This postface was written after Professor Liddle wrote his foreword.

[145] It is common and normal to hear voices whilst going to sleep. These are known as hypnogogic voices whilst the same during waking are known as hypnopompic voices. and normal to hear voices whilst going to sleep. These are known as hypnogogic voices whilst the same during waking are known as hypnopompic voices.

Chapter titles

All the chapter titles are song titles. The artists are listed below after each title:

Introduction: It's All Too Much (The Beatles); Chapter One: Seashell (The Flashapjacks); Chapter Two: Part of the Fire (Caroline Lavelle); Chapter Three: Solsbury Hill (Peter Gabriel); Chapter Four: I'll Find My Way Home (Jon and Vangelis); Chapter Five: Mana Mani (Salif Keita and the Ambassadeurs); Chapter Six: Highlanders (Zexie Manatsa and the Green Arrows); Chapter Seven: Blow (2nd Skin); Chapter Eight: Alioune Sissòko (Super Biton de Segou); Chapter Nine: Cheduke Chose (The Fish and Chip Song) (The Bhundu Boys); Chapter Ten: Don't Worship Me (Pele); Chapter Eleven: Mystery (The Indigo Girls); Chapter Twelve: Colour-blind (Ringo); Chapter Thirteen: My Suitor (Berntholer); Chapter Fourteen: Lonely Rainbows (Vanessa Paradis); Chapter Fifteen: Standing On My Head (The Seahorses); Chapter Sixteen: The March of the King of Laois (Paul Dooley); Chapter Seventeen: We Are the Diddy Men (Ken Dodd); Chapter Eighteen: London Loves... (Blur); Chapter Nineteen: My Best Friend Paranoia (William Orbit); Chapter Twenty: I Still Haven't Found What I'm Looking For (U2); Chapter Twenty-One: Revolution (The Pretenders); Chapter Twenty-Two: Psychological Warfare (Bolt Thrower); Chapter Twenty-Three: Complete Control (The Clash); Chapter

Twenty-Four: Confide in Me (Kylie Minogue); Chapter Twenty-Five: Sun Bursts In (Eyeless in Gaza); Chapter Twenty-Six: Turn To Red (Killing Joke); Chapter Twenty-Seven: Dead Man's Hill (The Indigo Girls); Chapter Twenty-Eight: Wilderness (Joy Division); Chapter Twenty-Nine: Love Cats (The Cure); Chapter Thirty: Here Comes the Flood (Peter Gabriel); Chapter Thirty-One: She's So High (Blur); Chapter Thirty-Two: We Wait And We Wonder (Phil Collins); Chapter Thirty-Three: Ten Storey Love Song (The Stone Roses); Chapter Thirty-Four: Step into My World (Hurricane #1); Chapter Thirty-Five: Tremble (Crystal Trip); Chapter Thirty-Six: Hope Springs Eternal (The Sandkings); Chapter Thirty-Seven: The Heat in the Room (Bill Nelson); Chapter Thirty-Eight: Stairway to Heaven (Led Zeppelin); Chapter Thirty-Nine: The Omega Man (The Basement Five); Chapter Forty: Roll With It (Oasis); Chapter Forty-One: Waves (Slowdive); Chapter Forty-Two: The Headlight Song (Ringo); Chapter Forty-Three: Boats (Brian Jeffels Band); Chapter Forty-Four: Come On (The Verve); Chapter Forty Five: Forever Young (Rod Stewart); Chapter Forty-Six: Somewhere (Crystal Trip); Chapter Forty-Seven: Runaway (The Corrs); Chapter Forty-Eight: Princess of the Sands (actually a line from Strange Meeting II by Nick Drake); Chapter Forty-Nine: Song for Ireland (Dick Gaughan); Chapter Fifty: Never Come Down Again (The Milltown Brothers); Addendum: Universal (Caroline Lavelle) Postface: Over the Side (The Departure Lounge)

Copyright information

About The Author

D r. Clive Hathaway Travis was born in Buckinghamshire and schooled at Bedford Modern School where he was an Able-Bodied Seaman in the school Combined Cadet Force. He graduated from University College London with an honours degree in physics in 1983. After six months travelling in Africa in 1984 he obtained a masters degree in Applied Optics in 1985. In 1989 he gained a doctorate, sponsored by the Royal Aircraft Establishment, in the physics department of Surrey University. From 1990 to 2000 he worked for a defence company. In 1990 he began a record company, Seagull Records, and released two CDs. His interests include reducing the number of suicides caused by the side effects of drugs for schizophrenia, third world poverty and the peace process in Northern Ireland. The author supports children in Uganda and Kenya through the charity Build Africa.

Lightning Source UK Ltd.
Milton Keynes UK
UKOW07f0751171214

243277UK00004B/132/P